THE MIND OF SOUTH AFRICA

"COMPELLING."
The Washington Post Book World

"[This] authoritative work reduces previous histories to the status of antiques."

Time

"[A] magisterial new book... An instant classic."

Chicago Sun-Times

"Sparks' empathetic approach, his exquisitely limpid writing style, and above all his remarkable delvings into the psychological and historical whys and wherefores of all sides in South Africa combine to make [this] a brilliant book on a country deeply embedded in our own psyches."

The Cleveland Plain Dealer

"Nobody is better equipped to write a definitive, insightful book than Sparks... [His] greatest strength is his ability to see the centuries-old rift from all perspectives.... This is a book any informed citizen ought to read."

St. Louis Post-Dispatch

"*The Mind of South Africa* is audacious in its sweep and breathtaking in its prose."

Newsday

"Searingly documents the history of white cruelty and pig-headedness, and his people's stark, fanatical racism."

The Kansas City Star

"Fascinating... Understanding history is one of demythologising: and this is what he achieves with a depth of knowledge, a brilliant political intelligence, a vast research—all briskly expounded in fine and vivid prose."

The London Observer

"Writing as personal witness, political analyst, and historian, an eminent liberal Johannesburg journalist looks at his country from the earliest times when blacks first came there through the present seething confrontation between the 'neo-apartheid' government and the forces of resistance. Sparks synthesizes individual experience and global politics, past and present, in a gripping narrative that focuses... on daily life and the popular imagination."

Booklist

THE MIND OF SOUTH AFRICA

THE MIND OF SOUTH AFRICA

Allister Sparks

BALLANTINE BOOKS
NEW YORK

Published in the United States by Ballantine Books, a division of Random House, Inc., New York, and simultaneously in Canada by Random House of Canada Limited, Toronto. This edition published by arrangement with Alfred A. Knopf, Inc.

Grateful acknowledgement is made to the following for permission to reprint previously published material: HEINEMANN PUBLISHERS LTD.: Excerpt from "A Roadgang's Cry" by Oswald Mtshali from *Poets to the People,* edited by B. Feinberg; Heinemann Publishers Ltd., 1980. Reprinted by permission. INTERNATIONAL DEFENCE & AID FUND: Excerpts from *South Africa: The Struggle for a Birthright* by Mary Benson; International Defence & Aid Fund, London, 1985. Reprinted by permission. A. A. BALKEMA: Excerpts from *The Record—Or a Series of Official Papers Relative to the Condition and Treatment of the Native Tribes of South Africa,* edited by Donald Moodie, 1960, 672 pp., A. A. Balkema, P.O. Box 1675, Rotterdam, Netherlands/A. A. Balkema, Old Post Road, Brookfield, VT 05036. Reprinted by permission. OXFORD UNIVERSITY PRESS: Excerpts from "Safeguarding the Nations of South Africa" by S. Peinaar from *South Africa: Two Views of Separate Development* by S. Peinaar and Anthony Sampson, Oxford University Press, Oxford, England, 1960. Reprinted by permission. THE UNIVERSITY OF CALIFORNIA PRESS: Excerpts from *The Rise of Afrikanerdom: Power, Apartheid, and the Afrikaner Civil Religion* by T. Dunbar Moodie, The University of California Press. Reprinted by permission.

Library of Congress Catalog Card Number: 90-93515

ISBN: 0-345-37119-4

Cover design by William G. Geller

Manufactured in the United States of America

First Ballantine Books Edition: May 1991

10 9 8 7 6 5 4 3 2 1

TO SUE

My wife, companion, and fellow witness

dié land van herinnering
dié land van geen-geskiedenis-meer
dié land van die dooies
my land jou land ons land
dié land vra water en hy kry bloed
dié land wat die vuur in hom dra

eli lizwe lenkumbulo
eli lizwe elingasenamilando
eli lizwe labafi
ilizwe lam ilizwe lakho ilizwe lethu
eli lizwe linxanelw' amanzi lize linikw' igazi
eli lizwe elinomlilo walo

this land of remembrance
this land of no-more-history
this land of the dead
my land your land our land
this land craves water and is given blood
this land with fire in itself

BREYTEN BREYTENBACH
[translations by Mbulelo Mzamane
and Allister Sparks]

Contents

Acknowledgments xi
Author's Note xiii
Prologue xv

1 In the Beginning 3
2 A Fateful Wind 22
3 The Third Man 45
4 God's Stepchildren 72
5 The Great Dispersal 91
6 The Great Trek Inward 119
7 The Rise of Apartheid 147
8 Triomf 183
9 Of Contrasts and Blindness 214
10 A Spray of Doom 233
11 Of Violence and Restraint 245
12 A Theological Civil War 278
13 The Crisis of Apartheid 298
14 The Revolt of the Eighties 329
15 The Transition 362

Epilogue 398
Bibliography 405
Index 413

Acknowledgments

Many people over many years have contributed to the thoughts and insights that make up this book. Beginning with the Xhosa people among whom I grew up on the banks of the Swart Kei River in the eastern Cape Province, who taught me their language before any other and also, above all, a respect for cultures other than my own. This Xhosa education continued through my schooldays, some of which were before the Nationalists decreed that English and Afrikaner children should be educated separately. But I have learned the most during my thirty-nine years as a journalist, which experience put me in touch with everyone and every viewpoint and enabled me also to see with my own eyes.

Out of that great crowd of influences a few stand out whom I must acknowledge especially. First among them is Laurence Gandar, editor of the Rand Daily Mail in the 1960s, who took over a mediocre newspaper and turned it into a great one and in the process influenced a whole generation of young journalists. His incisive analytical mind saw far beyond his time and he gave me new eyes with which to view my country. There have been a string of other insightful colleagues over the years as well: Anthony Delius, Stanley Uys, Ameen Akhalwaya, Donald Woods, Zwelakhe Sisulu; an array of academic friends who have helped give my observations some shape: Andre du Toit, David Welsh, Hermann Giliomee, Mike Savage, Mark Swilling; black people who have shown me the view from the far side of the hedge: Desmond Tutu, Simeon Nkoane, Winnie Mandela, "Ma" Sisulu, Popo Molefe, Patrick

Lekota, and nameless young activists who have escorted me into the teeth of the storm that is buffeting their communities; remarkable Afrikaners who have had the rare courage to look deep into their own minds and those of their people and share what they found there with a journalist trying to understand his country: Beyers Naudé, Breyten Breytenbach, André Brink, Hennie Serfontein, Riaan de Villiers. One could go on forever. I pick out these few only to illustrate the many. I am grateful to them all for what they have taught me.

More particularly, I must thank the individuals and institutions who made the writing of this book possible: The Carnegie Foundation and Duke University for providing me with a grant and the opportunity to teach, study, and write for three semesters in the charming environment of North Carolina; and to my newspapers, the Washington *Post*, the *Observer* of London, and the *NRC Handelsblad* of Rotterdam, for giving me leave to teach and so readily taking me back afterwards. Above all, thanks to Avery Russell of Carnegie and Bruce Payne of Duke, who had the generosity of spirit to think it a good idea and the drive to put it all together.

My thanks to those who read chapters, corrected errors, and offered critical advice: Heribert Adam, of Simon Fraser University in Vancouver; Frederik Van Zyl Slabbert, the former Opposition leader who now heads an institute for promoting interracial dialogue; Nico Smith, former Dutch Reformed Church seminarian and Broederbonder; Sheena Duncan of the Black Sash, who is the most knowledgeable person in South Africa on the practicalities of oppression; Professors Bill Peck and David Newbury of the University of North Carolina. And above all to that marvellous editor, Elisabeth Sifton, for her warm encouragement and sensitive hand.

A special debt of gratitude to Benjamin Formigo, the foreign editor of Portugal's leading newspaper, *Expresso*, for sharing some recollections of events in his country that shaped those in mine. My appreciation to three classes of Duke students, who were stimulating associates and did more research for me than they realized; to my research assistant, James Harrison; to Helene Baumann of Duke's Perkins Library, who helped compile the bibliography; and to my sons, Michael and Andrew, who checked material for me at the University of Cape Town while I was in the United States. Finally, to my wife, Sue, my strongest supporter and sternest critic through the long gestation and labour pains of whatever it is I have given birth to here, thanks for such caring midwifery.

A.S.

Author's Note

Ever since reading W. J. Cash's *The Mind of the South* while I was a Nieman Fellow at Harvard University in 1962, I have wanted to write a book that might give the same kind of insights into South Africa that it gave me into the psyche of the American South. But Cash wrote only about white Southerners. To get at the true human drama of South Africa, one has to encompass all those involved.

This is an awesome task. No single book that I know of has attempted to cover the full complexity of South Africa's long racial conflict, looking into the forces of history and culture and circumstances that have moulded the major players, that determine the way they interact one upon the other, telling the whole story in its full historical panorama, from earliest beginnings to an analysis of the present, and trying to gaze into the future. It is a story of history's relevance to the present and the future, which follows Cash's superb analogy that searching out the mind of a people is like visiting one of those churches one sees in England: the facade and towers, the windows and clerestory, the exterior and superstructure may be later Gothic of one sort or another, but look into its nave, its aisles, and its choir and you find the old mighty Norman arches of the twelfth century, and if you look into its crypt, you may even find stones cut by Saxons, bricks made by Roman hands. Time changes us, but the imprint of our past is upon us all. And sometimes, as has happened with the white South Africans, a people can get caught up in the vortex of their own history.

That is what I have attempted here: to look into South Africa. I have tried also to bridge the gap between the mountain of academic literature and the mine-dump of popular journalism on South Africa; to strike a balance between the opaque and the superficial, between the unreadable and the uninformed. But in the end this remains a journalist's book, written with a journalist's eye and a journalist's pen. It is also a subjective book, as all journalism inevitably is. I have tried to explain the people of my country as I have come to understand them after thirty-nine years of reporting their conflicts, but I do so from my own vantage point as one of them, as a fifth-generation white South African and a journalist for the opposition English press. I cannot pretend a detachment I do not have.

But journalists do get to see things from all sides, and I hope that by taking readers through my own exposure over a long career to all sides this book may help my fellow South Africans, who live in such a uniquely compartmentalized society, to understand one another, and themselves, a little better. I hope especially that it may convey to that large audience abroad—an audience that knows of South Africa as a symbol of racism but knows little of what made it so—something of the tragic, beautiful power of the place, something of its endless agony and enduring hopefulness, something of the fire that it carries in itself which burns into the soul of everyone who ever goes there and which will not let them alone again, which burned itself into my soul the day I was born on its blazing veld and has driven me to attempt the impossible with the telling of its story.

Durham, North Carolina
February 1989

Prologue: A Hedge of Bitter Almonds

ON A STILL spring day in Cape Town's Kirstenbosch Botanic Garden the air is heavy with the scent of blossom. Here against the eastern slopes of Table Mountain, where three amber-coloured streams cascade down from the gray-green crenellation of Castle Rock and flow together to form the Liesbeeck River, is some of the rarest flora in all the world: a botanist's paradise of proteas and cycads and fine, heather-like plants of infinite delicacy called *fynbos* that are found nowhere else. It is a quiet, exquisite, aromatic place with a herb garden and a fragrance garden of indigenous plants whose leaves, rubbed together, release exotic perfumes. Here, too, among the *fynbos*, is a line of short, scraggly trees whose ancient limbs are twisted together into an untidy tangle. A metal plate pinned to one of the trees states that it is *Brabejum Stellatifolium*, or the Wild Almond. They have a long, blueish leaf and the nut, encased in a furry shell, is dry and bitter.

The trees are the remains of a hedge, planted here in 1660 by Jan van Riebeeck, leader of the first Dutch settlers to land at the Cape of Good Hope, to keep out the Khoikhoi cattle herders who inhabited this southernmost tip of the African continent. Van Riebeeck's orders when he landed were explicit: he was to barter cattle from the Khoikhoi to get fresh meat, but apart from that he and his small band of settlers were not to interact with them at all. The Dutch East India Company, for which they worked, was interested in the Cape only as a victualling station for its ships sailing to the rich spicelands of the Indies, and it did not want to incur the unnecessary expenses involved in a colonizing operation. So Van Riebeeck planted his hedge to seal off his little community from the indigenous inhabitants of Africa. The hedge started from this spot at the source of the Liesbeeck River and curved along the side of Wynberg Hill, where another fragment still grows beside Klaassens Road and the houses have names like Almondsberg and Amandel, down through what are now Cape Town's southern suburbs to the junction of the sweet Liesbeeck and the Salt River, where a pole fence ran the rest of the way to Table Bay. With the mountain barrier behind, the hedge cut off Van Riebeeck's little white community from the great African continent stretching away to the north, creating their own little enclave of Europe six thousand miles from home.

In fact the hedge was the second-best option. Initially a commissioner from the company, one Rijkloff van Goens, arrived from Amsterdam and surveyed the possibility of digging a canal from Table Bay to False Bay, a spectacular gesture of detachment that would have turned the Cape Peninsula into a European island literally cut off from Africa. He pronounced the project feasible and ordered Van Riebeeck to go ahead with it, but Van Riebeeck decided he did not have the manpower and quietly planted the hedge instead. The symbolic effect was the same.

Today, three-and-a-half centuries later, Europe still survives in this southern part of Africa in defiance of the rest of the world. Drive through the leafy suburb of Bishopscourt where the hedge used to grow, along its winding roads with their gracious old buildings and great oak trees, and you might be in some part of England, with a touch of Dutch antiquity. Africa, with its stirring millions, is kept at a distance, out of sight in rural reserves and urban ghettos. The bitter-almond hedge lives on, institutionalized in a thousand laws to exclude the dark-skinned indigenous people and preserve the illusion that South Africa is really a "white" country.

Stand there beside that strip of hedge in the Kirstenbosch Garden and look north, out over the Liesbeeck Valley with the Cape Flats beyond, with the haze-blue of the Hottentots' Holland mountains in the distance and the valleys of the Boland where the vineyards planted by the French Huguenots are, and the Cape-Dutch homesteads that are as old and gracious as the Virginia estates along the James River, and you get the feeling that on a clear day you could see all the way up Africa, all the way to Cairo. In the middle distance are the twin cooling towers of Athlone power station, like surveyor's beacons marking the dividing line that runs through this land. To the left and west of that line lie the white suburbs of Claremont, Kenilworth, Rondebosch, Newlands, Mowbray, Wynberg, and Pinelands. Out on the sandy flats to the right and east of it lie the "coloured" townships where the mixed-race people live—Athlone, Hazendal, Bonteheuvel, Heideveld, Belville, Elsies River, Lavender Hills, and Mitchell's Plain—and, beyond them, in a descending order of social status, the black townships and squatter camps of Langa, Nyanga, Guguletu, Crossroads, and Khayelitsha. There before you lies apartheid in all its obscenity, to be gazed upon from one of the most beautiful vistas on God's earth.

There is more to the bitter-almond hedge than what you see from where it grows. The world is familiar with the apartheid division that runs through South African society, separating its white and black living areas, its schools, its social amenities, its political institutions, its trains, buses, taxis, ambulances, hospitals, its cemeteries even. But what is deeper than any of these is the division that runs through the psyche of the nation. From here on the Cape Peninsula all the way to Kipling's great grey-green greasy Limpopo in the far north it runs like a San Andreas fault through the mind of South Africa. Two minds, two worlds, one country: the kind of country H. G. Wells might have invented, or that Jonathan Swift might have sent Gulliver to, where people occupy the same space but live in different time frames so that they do not see each other and perceive different realities. Though only a few miles separate their living areas, though they spend much of their working days together, the black South African world is as distant from the white world as Outer Mongolia; its mind a closed book to all but a handful of whites who keep contact with it. Probably no more than five percent of white Johannesburg has ever been to Soweto, its black dormitory suburb that is one of Africa's most populous cities in its own right. Most could not even tell you how to get there.

White South Africans are not evil, as much of the world believes. But they are blind—blinded by the illusion they have created for themselves that they live in a white country in Africa, that it belongs to them by right and to no others, and by the self-centredness this has induced. From the beginning they have regarded the people of Africa as "aliens," foreigners from beyond the hedge or beyond the frontier or beyond the city limits, people whose real home was somewhere else, in a "homeland" far away, out of sight. The notion of a border behind which white civilization must protect itself against the coming of the black barbarians is fundamental to the white South African psyche.

On the other side of the hedge, the blacks know more about the white world than the whites know of theirs, for most spend their working days in it and some even live there as domestic servants in white homes. They speak the whites' languages whereas few whites speak theirs. Yet many of them are blinded, too, by their overwhelming sense of injustice, so that their understanding of the white mind, with its complexities of guilt and innocence, arrogance and insecurity, gregariousness and isolationism, aggression and fear, is often simplistic. Hedges do not make for mutual acquaintance and understanding.

Some of this is now changing. Right here in Bishopscourt a black man has crossed the hedge to live in, of all places, Van Riebeeck's old home, Bosheuvel. It is called Bishopscourt today, which is where the suburb gets it name, and it is the official residence of the Metropolitan of the Church of the Province of South Africa, otherwise known as the Anglican Church, and since 1986 His Grace has been a black man, Desmond Mpilo Tutu. In terms of a law called the Group Areas Act, Archbishop Tutu lives in Van Riebeeck's home illegally, a fact to which the government grudgingly turns a blind eye. One thousand miles to the north, a white clergyman, the Reverend Nico Smith, crossed the hedge the other way to live among his black parishioners in the Pretoria township of Mamelodi. He decided to do it the legal way, which took two years as he hacked his way through a tangle of seven hundred laws and regulations before getting permission. Such is the density of this tough old hedge.

But slowly it is giving way, as those two symbolic breaches show, and this gives to South Africa a sense that something big is about to happen, as though a great dyke is about to burst, sweeping away the past and leaving behind a new landscape of human relationships; something on the scale of the abolition of slavery or the collapse of an empire that is going to change a way of life that has evolved over centuries. The awesomeness of that adds to the complexities of mind on both sides of the hedge.

THE MIND OF SOUTH AFRICA

CHAPTER ONE

In the Beginning

People
Are people
Through other people
XHOSA PROVERB

ANCIENT AFRICA, like Gaul, was divided into three parts.

The northern sector, above the great desert, has the oldest of all recorded history, going back five thousand years to the first of the thirty-one dynasties of ancient Egypt. It has always been more a part of the Mediterranean world than of Africa, with historical contacts with the Phoenicians, the Greeks, the Romans, and Islam. It was here that the first sparks of Western civilization were struck.

South of that lay the real Africa, the black man's Africa, which though ancient in itself, with its own vital civilizations that flourished and faded with the passing of the centuries, was a closed book to most of the rest of the world until recent times; much of its history is only now being written. It was the last of the earth's great land masses to be penetrated by outsiders. Sealed off by the Sahara Desert in the north, dense tropical forests around its west coast, and the Skeleton Coast, the Namib, and the Kalahari deserts farther south, it was a huge natural fortress.

It had few natural harbours and, apart from the Nile and the Gambia, no rivers navigable from the sea. It consisted for the most part of a high central plateau that dropped steeply down escarpments to the coastal lowlands, which meant its rivers cascaded to the sea in a series of white-water rapids and waterfalls that no vessel could traverse.

Within the fortress walls there was a second line of defence—patrolling squadrons of mosquitoes and tsetse flies—which meant that until the advent of modern medicine any traveller intrepid enough to penetrate to the interior was struck down with malaria, yellow fever, or sleeping sickness. Strangers arriving on the tropical coasts once died at rates as high as 50 percent in their first year of residence because they lacked immunity to these African diseases.[1] Internally, too, contact among different sectors of the continent was restricted by the tsetse fly, which is fatal to domestic animals, creating wide belts where animal-drawn transport could not go. So in many areas the wheel was not developed: without animal power it is of little use. Even colonial officials had to abandon wheeled transport and use human porters in many parts of Africa until the tsetse fly was brought under control in the twentieth century.

The fortress itself was further divided in two, cut horizontally by another great natural barrier, the equatorial rain forest. The upper half, a kind of outer barbican, had some flashes of contact with the outside world. Early Arab traders penetrated to it across long and perilous desert trails to reach the great African kingdoms of Ghana and Mali in the west, while in the east the Nile provided a broader pathway of two-way cross-cultural contact. Archeological remains make it clear that an industrious kingdom flourished around Meroë in the area of the middle Nile (south of where Khartoum lies today) from the sixth century B.C., conquering Egypt itself and ruling it for seven hundred years. It is possible that Meroë served as one of the diffusion points for early iron-working and smelting technology in other areas of Africa.

The southern sector, beyond the equatorial forest, was the most isolated of all, the innermost keep of Africa's ancient secrets. Slavers came from the Persian Gulf to raid and trade along the east coast. Further back in the mists of time, by some miracle of early navigation, more remote figures must have crossed the Indian Ocean in Kon-Tiki rafts from Indonesia, bringing with them the coconut palm, the banana, and the yam, and leaving their genetic imprint on the people of Madagascar. Roman coins and fragments of Ming Dynasty pottery have been found along the coast of Kenya, and passages in Claudius Ptolemy's *Geography* indicate that Alexandrian traders knew of Mount Kilimanjaro. But for the most part the early history of southern Africa is a fascinating mystery that the combined work of archeologists, anthropologists, linguists, musicologists, biologists, and African historians is only now beginning to piece together.

This remoteness has led to a popular notion of ancient Africa as a backward place, a dark continent of primitive savagery until the white

1. Paul Bohannan and Philip Curtin, *Africa and Africans* (Prospect Heights, Ill., 1988), p. 35.

man came to bring some small flashes of enlightenment to its mysterious jungles. In fact its backwardness was only partial. It lagged in technological and economic development as a direct result of its isolation. Technical advancement is a function of man's cross-cultural contacts: the knowledge of gunpowder introduced to Europe transformed that continent (and the world); horses from Spanish conquistadores transformed the North American Plains; motor transport restructured the map of India, as medical technology did that of Africa.

Socially and politically, however, Africa lagged not at all. Traditional African societies were sophisticated organisms, finely tuned to the exigencies of climate and environment in a harsh continent. In their communal relationships and elaborate links of mutual responsibility, with their generic love of children and respect for the aged, they cultivated a respect for human values and human worth far in advance of the materialistic West.

Political systems were interwoven with the social order, with chieftaincies based on extensions of family and lineage relationships. Whites, given their own history of autocratic monarchies, mistook the tribal chiefs for dictators and dealt with them accordingly. In fact, the chiefs' powers were heavily circumscribed and the systems they presided over incorporated a considerable degree of grass-roots democracy. At the time that the first Portuguese navigators made their voyages of discovery around the Cape of Good Hope, it is arguable that Darkest Africa was a more democratic place than the medieval Europe from which they had sailed.

Even the technological backwardness is relatively recent. Through all the long millennia of the Old Stone Age, Africa led the world, and carbon dating tests show that it entered the Iron Age at much the same time as Europe. Only after the fifteenth century, when the exchange of technological know-how became increasingly important, did Africa fall behind other parts of the world that were less sealed off from cross-cultural contact.

Geologists and archeologists believe that Africa is in fact the oldest continent in the world, that it was once the high central feature of a single great megacontinent which then, in a series of massive geological upheavals, split up, and that it was probably here that man made his earliest evolutionary appearance.[2]

The first pointer to this appeared in 1924 when Dr. Raymond Dart, of Johannesburg's Witwatersrand University, found the complete fossilized skull of one of man's extinct apelike ancestors in a limeworks

2. See Stanlake Samkange, *African Saga: A Brief Introduction to African History* (Harare, 1971), pp. 19–22.

not far from a railway station called Taungs on the fringes of the Kalahari Desert. It was the skull of a child aged five or six, and Dart called it *Australopithecus africanus*, or the South African Ape.

There was another breakthrough thirty-five years later when Dr. Louis Leakey and his wife, Mary, found two skulls in northern Tanzania. The first was of a heavy-jawed ape-man they called *Proconsul*, who used his teeth instead of making tools with his hands and so failed the test to be rated human; he was more of a "missing link." But the second, which Mary Leakey found in the bed of a gorge in the Serengeti Plain, was indeed a toolmaker of sorts: he split and shaped pebbles, which he used to scratch the earth and crack nuts. *Zinjanthropus*, as the Leakeys named the remains, therefore qualified to be called human—by far the oldest known at that time. The discovery transformed the time scale by which scientists thought of human evolution; since then the time scale has been nearly doubled again (by finds made by the Leakey's son, Richard, among others), confirming the claims of Africa as the cradle of humanity.

Dozens of related fossil specimens have since been found in South Africa and more than six hundred in East Africa, leading scientists to believe that it was in this general area that Man first became distinguished from the other primates. As the wet Miocene era gave way to the dry Pliocene about five million years ago, the forests began to recede and Desmond Morris's naked ape came down from the trees to run upright across the expanding prairies of southern Africa and begin a grubbing existence in the riversides with his simple pebble tools.

With the infinite slowness of the evolutionary process, early man gradually improved his tools and his weapons. He cast aside his pebbles and made a larger, all-purpose tool, the hand ax, with which he could dig in the ground, skin animals, and chop meat. He invented fire, and with that moved indoors into caves and simple huts where he could warm himself and cook his food.

From then on man's progress was marked by a ceaseless quest for an easier life. He began to develop his tastes and seek new comforts. Some moved into the forests, others farther out onto the plains, and yet others followed herds of game toward more northern regions as the icecap receded. Thus the evolving human species spread out across the globe. Thus, too, different racial groups began to appear as over millions of years they adapted to their different environments, with those in cool, cloudy climates becoming blond and fair-skinned, those exposed to the brighter sunlight of the semitropical regions becoming darker-haired and olive- or brown-complexioned, and those in the hottest regions of Africa becoming darkest of all.

Then, after tools and fire, came the third great revolution in human history—agriculture. Man learned to grow things and to domesticate animals. From being a hunter and a gatherer, he became a farmer. With that he settled down and built communities. And, his food supplies assured, he began to multiply wondrously.

This revolution, too, came early to Africa. Archeologists are fairly certain that it began in the Middle East, probably in the Jordan Valley around Jericho, whence it crossed the Isthmus of Suez into Africa. Once there it spread swiftly through the savannah belt between the desert and the equatorial forest, the barbican area of our African fortress, between the second and third millennium B.C. But it did not cross the forest into southern Africa. By a quirk of botanical distribution, not one of the world's great tropical food crops is indigenous to southern Africa. So the southward march of the great agricultural revolution had to wait another two or three thousand years until the arrival of the banana, the coconut, and the yam from southeast Asia. Then it surged through.

Until that time southern Africa appears to have been inhabited largely, perhaps exclusively, by Hottentot cattle herders and Bushmen hunter-gatherers, both yellow-skinned Stone Age people now more properly known as Khoikhoi and San. There were no black Africans. They came only when the food revolution broke through the equatorial-forest barrier. Just when and how this happened is still unclear, but the combined testimony of linguists and anthropologists suggests that the advent of cultivation in the northern sector of black Africa caused a population explosion there, and that some groups migrated along the waterways from the northern to the southern fringes of the equatorial forest, where they encountered the food plants brought by those mysterious early traders from southeast Asia, and flourished. As they multiplied they moved still farther south, bringing with them the Iron Age culture—the hoe and the spear—which by then had diffused widely throughout much of sub-Saharan Africa, and which enabled them to dominate the indigenous Khoi and San people, who were gradually absorbed except for a few who withdrew into the deepest recesses of the Congo forest, the deserts of the southwest, and the distant valleys of Africa's southernmost corner.

THIS SLOWLY EXPANDING population drifted into what is now South Africa in two main linguistic streams: the Nguni, who, though they spurned the eating of fish, followed the narrow coastal belt along the Indian Ocean seaboard where they found good water and grazing for the herds of cattle they idolized; and the Sotho and Tswana, who kept to the high central plateau and away from a tsetse belt that curved around the mountains of the escarpment.

South African government propaganda, seizing upon the fact of these infinitely slow population drifts, tried for a time to disseminate the myth that white and black settlers entered an empty country from opposite ends at much the same time, so that both have an equal historical claim to it. The premise is absurd. The archeological evidence shows tht iron-working and cattle husbandry in the northern Transvaale date back to at least 300–800 A.D., while shipwrecked Portuguese sailors reported meeting the Nguni along the coast 150 years before Jan van Riebeeck arrived with his first party of Dutch settlers in 1652.

What is true is that the black people had not yet reached the southernmost sector where this first settlement took place, so that Van Riebeeck found only the Khoi when he dropped anchor at the Cape of Good Hope. But his meticulously kept journal shows that he was aware of the black Africans farther up the coast.

The black migration was slow, moving at the pace of generational change. As a son reached manhood he would marry and leave his father's home to establish a *kraal*, or household, of his own, which would be an extension of the clan. When the old man died his kraal would be shut up and his children forbidden to go there. In this way tensions were eased and conflicts avoided. There were seasonal movements, too, as the tribes drove their herds between the sour grasses near the coast and the sweeter grasses farther inland. They would graze their cattle in the uplands during the summer, then leave the delicate sweet grasses to recover while they wintered in the warmer Suurveld (as the Afrikaners later named the coastal pasturage).

Thus the black tribes drifted southward in a slow, undulating rhythm that knew neither time nor boundaries. Though each chiefdom had its own residential base, usually on a water source, their grazing lands crisscrossed each other and one man might move through another's territory with complete freedom. It was an easygoing society with a low level of tension, but its serenity depended on an abundance of land and space that defused competitiveness.

There were wars, but these tended to be rather ritualistic and not very bloody affairs. The Nguni in particular cultivated a warrior tradition with a strong emphasis on physical courage and martial pride. Every young man learned how to fight with sticks and spears, and when a young chief and his agemates left the circumcision school they often tried to mark their coming of age with a daring exploit. But these were seldom more serious than a cattle raid on a neighbour's herd.

Such raids were frequent. Full-scale wars were rare and occurred only after exhaustive efforts to talk things over first. Senior councillors and relatives, even chiefs' wives, would be sent back and forth with messages trying to reach settlements through compromise or compensation. An unfortunate incident could usually be smoothed over with an exchange of presents. Only when an insult was deliberate would it lead to war. Even then certain courtesies were observed: there would always be a formal declaration of war followed by a period of preparation, allowing people on both sides time to muster and be informed of the causes of the dispute.

The armies would line up to *giya*, as it was called in the Nguni languages, which meant to prance before one another and exchange taunts and gestures of bravado. Women and children would turn out to cheer on their men. The long throwing spears would be hurled, but they were neither very accurate nor very lethal. Occasionally—but this was rare—the order "*Pakathi!*" ("Get inside!") would be given, at which the warriors would break off the shaft of a spear so that it could be used as a stabbing assegai and would charge the ranks of the enemy. Then the casualties would be higher. But usually the skirmish was more peripheral than that and ended when one army turned and fled. Then the victor would drive off the enemy's cattle and capture his women and children. Some homes might be set on fire, but the defeated tribe was neither killed nor expelled and its productive resources were not destroyed. As an eighteenth-century German explorer, Henry Lichtenstein, noted, it was even customary for the victorious tribe to return some of the captured cattle in accordance with the principle that "we must not let even our enemies die with hunger."[3]

The women and children captured in war were never killed. Even during the bloody frontier wars of the nineteenth century, when black warriors plundered the white settlement areas and killed many settlers, they meticulously avoided killing women and children; and even when they were driven to extremes in these struggles no white missionary or trader living among them was ever harmed. It was a remarkably selective form of warfare that targetted only those perceived as military activists among the enemy. During the battle of Grahamstown in 1819, when the warriors of a Xhosa leader named Makanda stormed the garrison town and the issue trembled in the balance for a while as the defenders ran low on ammunition, Elizabeth Salt, the wife of a British soldier, is said to have carried a keg of gunpowder, wrapped up as if it were an infant, through the ranks of the black warriors who allowed her to pass.[4]

3. Henry Lichtenstein, *Travels in Southern Africa*, vol. 1 (Cape Town, 1928), p. 343.

4. Guy Butler (Ed.), *The 1820 Settlers: An Illustrated Commentary* (Cape Town, 1974), p. 50.

White South Africa's propaganda has suggested that Africa was a violent and strife-torn place and that only the arrival of the white man and the order he brought saved the black tribes from decimating each other. The imputation, of course, is that if white rule were to end, this savage self-destruction would resume. The truth is that it was the arrival of the white man and his closing of the frontier which led to the one instance of real savagery that did occur. As the settlers gulped up the land they not only stopped the slow southward drift of the tribes but threw them back upon one another. The age-old rhythm of the tribes was disrupted. The pressure of space was upon them. Tensions arose as retreating tribes moved in on those behind them, as more and more people competed for less and less land and as the land itself became overstocked and impoverished. Rippling back like a shock wave through the layers of Nguni tribes, the tensions encouraged the emergence of a militant figure to exploit the situation of denied expectations and hardening lines of political identities. One such militant figure was Shaka, the black Napoleon who marshalled the Zulu tribe into a ruthless fighting nation that ravaged the subcontinent in the early part of the nineteenth century.

But in the beginning, before any of this happened, South Africa was a tranquil place. Even the retreat of the Khoi and San before the black advance seems to have been a relatively peaceful business. The influence of the Khoi and San languages with their repertoire of clicking sounds on those of the Nguni, especially the southernmost Xhosa, who were in closest contact with them, is evidence of long interaction.

Occasionally the Xhosa would mount reprisal raids against the San when the little huntsmen shot their cattle. But for the most part they coexisted. The *abaTwa*, the Xhosa called them. I remember as a child exploring a gorge called the Twa-Twa in what was once the heart of Xhosaland and marvelling at the rock paintings that these little hunters had left there. The San lived in caves and decorated the walls with wondrous pictures of the creatures they hunted but also respected as fellow inhabitants of the bush that was their home. There were antelopes and elephants, pythons and giraffes, and always, in a place of prominence in every cave, the stately eland, an animal of special spiritual significance to them.

They must have been remarkable people, these little Bushmen hunters: wonderful hunters who could track a wounded animal for days until it faltered and fell from the effects of their poisoned arrowheads; resourceful chemists who mixed their own deadly poisons and incredibly durable paints from the vegetable and animal substances of the bush country in which they lived; a wonderfully spiritual and artistic people who worshipped sky-gods and regarded the praying mantis as sacred, who loved to paint and to dance at moonrise in circular clearings outside their caves.

They are gone now. Extinct. Victims of one of history's successful acts of genocide. Pretoria's propagandists, in their tit-for-tat way, like to point fingers at their accusers and say that white South Africans never killed the indigenous people the way the American settlers did the Indians and the Australians the Aborigines. But they did. They hunted the little Bushmen hunters and shot them down like so much vermin. Thomas Pringle, South Africa's first journalist, who arrived with the British settlers in 1820, has left a vivid account of one of these hunting parties based on an interview with a Boer farmer who took part in it.

The commando force had ridden out to exterminate a San community in the neighbourhood. They took the hapless little tribe by surprise, opened fire and killed most of them.

> When the firing ceased [Pringle quotes the farmer as saying], five women were still found living. The lives of these, after a long discussion, it was resolved to spare, because one farmer wanted a servant for this purpose, and another for that. The unfortunate wretches were ordered to march in front of the commando; but it was soon found that they impeded our progress—not being able to proceed fast enough. They were, therefore, ordered to be shot. . . . The helpless victims, perceiving what was intended, sprung to us, and clung so firmly to some of the party, that it was for some time impossible to shoot them without hazarding the lives of those they held fast. Four of them were at length despatched; but the fifth could by no means be torn from one of our comrades, whom she had grasped in her agony; and his entreaties to be allowed to take this woman home were at last complied with.[5]

The butchery went on and on. Pringle tells of a commando force that stopped by his farm one day on their way back from a raid in which they had killed eighty San, and of an army commander who casually shot an old San woman as she slept. The commander was returning to base with his raiding party when he saw a figure wrapped in a caross lying beside the pathway. "Without uttering a word or asking a question," Pringle recounts, the commander "levelled his musket and fired. The caross heaved up—and an aged female, in the agonies of death, rolled out of it. And the party rode on, without considering the matter worthy even of a passing remark!"[6]

Soon they were eliminated. Not one San survives in South Africa

5. Thomas Pringle, *Narrative of a Residence in South Africa* (Cape Town, 1966), p. 226.

6. Ibid., p. 230.

today. A few still cling to existence on the fringes of the Kalahari Desert of Namibia and Botswana, where land dispossession, unemployment, and liquor are rapidly destroying the last vestiges of their traditional life and turning them into an endangered species.

The Khoikhoi too, are extinct. They were not butchered as the San were, but they died as a result of the white arrival all the same. They were dispossessed of their grazing lands, and when that happened their clans crumbled. The white man's diseases, which first arrived with smallpox in the mid-eighteenth century, did the rest. What remnants remained of these original inhabitants of southern Africa were absorbed into the polyglot community of freed slaves and mixed-race people that the ethnic categorists of apartheid have called "coloureds."

The black tribes varied a good deal in their social and political structure. Some were tightly organized hierarchical kingdoms; others were vaguely linked village communities with hardly any formal political structure at all. The Sotho and Tswana were craftsmen who produced metal and leather goods and congregated in large communities—towns really—of between two thousand and twenty thousand people. The Nguni, though they also smelted iron and made hoes and spears, were engrossed with their cattle, which held a mystical significance for them and to facilitate the herding of which they lived in scattered family units. In the far north was the small Venda tribe, goldsmiths and stone-builders who are thought to be related to the Karanga of Great Zimbabwe and the legendary kingdom of Monamatapa, whose supposed gold wealth fascinated white explorers for centuries; while in the east there were the Tsonga, another coastal people who, unlike the Nguni, loved fish, which they caught in elaborate communal traps.

Despite their differences the tribal communities all over Africa had many common features, for all had adapted to the same exigencies of climate and environment. Africa is a harsh continent; it has none of the temperate softness of Europe. Its sunlight is sharp and brittle, its nights sudden and dark. It alternates between long, parched droughts that bake the earth hard and sudden electric storms that split the air and send floodwater tearing at the soil and carrying it away in tumbling brown torrents.

Life as a subsistence farmer in such an environment was filled with uncertainty. Sometimes there was plenty, sometimes there was great scarcity, and sometimes there was complete disaster. African societies cushioned themselves against these capricious changes of fortune by building elaborate systems of mutual support. If disaster struck one person he could turn to another for help, and the same went for whole communities. The social systems were based on units of the extended family, in which ties of kinship, age group, and other associations were woven together into a web of relationships that extended over a wide area with many villages and stretched far back into the past to include family and tribal ancestors, who provided an intercessionary link with the supernatural and the divine. Thus was created a social security system of reciprocal obligations that supported and protected the individual and at the same time demanded certain commitments from him in return, and which was all intimately connected with religious observance.

A typical Nguni tribe would consist of perhaps twenty thousand people divided into subchiefdoms, each of which would consist of four or five extended-family households. These kraals were usually built on ridges, with a number of round mud-daub huts arranged in a semicircle with a cattle enclosure in front. The arrangement of the huts was important, for the placement of each denoted the status of the householder and thus his prescribed relationship with other members of the family and, beyond that, with members of other households making up the tribe.

Polygamy was the ideal, because it extended the family's lineage relationships and thus its social security network, but it was not always practiced. A man had to make a gift of cattle, called *lobola*, for a wife, so that a poor man might be able to afford only one wife. A chief might have half a dozen, the most important being his Great Wife, who would be chosen and paid for by the tribe as a whole, usually from the royal family of another tribe with which it wished to forge closer relations. She would be known as "the mother of the nation" and her eldest son would be the heir apparent to the chiefdom. She would occupy a central hut in the arc, while each of the junior wives and the wives of other men in the family would occupy a separate hut situated around the semicircle in order of rank.

A young chief would probably have taken a first wife of his own choosing by the time a Great Wife was acquired for him. This "right-hand wife" had a special status. She would set up her own household, often some distance from the chief's, and when her eldest son grew up he had the right to assemble his own following and move away to establish a separate independence. This was another way in which blood-letting rivalries were defused and in which the gradual southward drift of the tribes took place.

Jeffrey Peires, in an illuminating history of the Xhosa, has described the intricate rules that governed relationships between members of these households.[7] There were rules of avoidance in speech and behaviour between male and female relatives. A younger brother showed deference

7. J. B. Peires, *The House of Phalo: A History of the Xhosa People in the Days of Their Independence* (Berkeley, Cal., 1982), p. 4.

to an elder brother, a younger sister to her elder sister. The children of junior wives deferred to the children of senior wives. There was a division of labour according to sex and age: men tended the cattle and built the homes, women worked in the fields and did the cooking and housework.

There was not much room for individualism in the Western sense, for the emphasis was on the group and the individual was assigned his role within it. Yet the result was not oppressive or even stifling. In fact these traditional African societies placed a high value on human worth, but it was a humanism that found its expression in a communal context rather than in the individualism of the West. There is a word for it in the Nguni languages, *ubuntu*, that captures the essence of this particular kind of participatory humanism, which has survived the urbanization of South Africa's industrial revolution and is visible today in the communal spirit of the ghetto townships. It is a subtle and not easily translatable concept which means broadly that each individual's humanity is ideally expressed through his relationship with others and theirs in turn through a recognition of his humanity. "*Ubuntu ungamntu ngabanye abantu,*" goes the Xhosa proverb—"People are people through other people." It is a saying that Archbishop Desmond Tutu likes to quote, and it never fails to bring sighs and nods of understanding from his black audiences.

Buntu Mfenyana, a Johannesburg sociolinguist, says that to understand the full meaning of the word *ubuntu* one must first separate the prefix *ubu*-from the root *-ntu*:

> *Ntu* is an ancestor who got human society going. He gave us our way of life as human beings. It is a communal way of life which says that society must be run for the sake of all. This requires cooperation, sharing and charity. There should be no widows or orphans left alone—they all belong to someone. If a man does not have a cow, then give him a cow to milk. There should be no *ohlelekileyo*, or deprived person.
>
> *Ubu* refers to the abstract. So *ubuntu* is the quality of being human. It is the quality, or the behaviour, of *ntu* society, that is, sharing, charitableness, cooperation. It is this quality which distinguishes a human creature from an animal or a spirit. When you do something that is not humane then you are being like an animal.[8]

Though they did not know the word, this spirit of *ubuntu* caught the attention of early explorers, missionaries, and others who spent time with the tribes and who commented on the close bonds among their

8. *Sash* magazine, February 1986, p. 2.

members—the way they shared things and the warmth of their hospitality. Survivors of the Dutch ship *Stavenisse*, which was wrecked off the Natal coast in 1686, who spent three years living among the Xhosa, said of them after their rescue:

> It would be impossible to buy any slaves there, for they would not part with their children, or any of their connexions for anything in the world, loving one another with a most remarkable strength of affection. . . . In their intercourse with each other, they are very civil, polite and talkative, saluting each other, whether male or female, young or old, whenever they meet; asking whence they come, and whither they are going, what is their news. . . . One may travel two hundred or three hundred *mylen* through the country, without any fear from men. . . . Neither need one be in any apprehension about meat and drink, as they have in every village or kraal a house of entertainment for travellers, where these are not only lodged, but fed also.[9]

Lichtenstein, who travelled through the same region a century later, also referred to this special accommodation for passersby as well as to the general spirit of sharing. "Whenever anyone kills an ox he must invite all his neighbours to take part, and they remain his guests until the whole is eaten," he wrote in 1803.[10] Children were brought up by the whole community and old people particularly were cared for with love and kindness. "All persons advanced in years have particular respect shewn them, their advice is always listened to, and if they become sick and helpless, every one is eager to afford them assistance," Lichtenstein wrote. "Poor relations are not less kindly treated, and if any one is sick, and has not cattle sufficient to pay for being disenchanted, his nearest relations do not hesitate a moment to furnish what is necessary for his restoration."[11]

These early visitors were impressed, too, with the amount of democratic debate that took place within the tribal systems, with the high degree of freedom to criticize the chiefs that was permitted, and with the application of the rule of law through a sophisticated court system presided over by the chiefs but in which the chiefs themselves were beneath the law and could be tried and fined by their own councillors.

The position of a chief was an extension of that of the father of each family household within his tribe. He was, in essence, the father of the

9. Donald Moodie, *The Record* (Cape Town, 1960), p. 431.

10. Ibid., p. 335.

11. Ibid., p. 328.

tribe. Just as the father organized the economic activities of his family, settled its domestic disputes, and communicated with its ancestors, so did the chief do the same with the tribe as a whole.

He did so in consultation with a council of five or six tribal elders. He would consult with other chiefs as well: most tribes were subdivided under subordinate chiefs who acknowledged the superiority of a paramount chief, but the paramount chief could not make a decision binding on his juniors unless he had discussed the matter with them. It was in these open discussions that visitors were amazed at the degree of criticism that was permitted. "The king is absolute sovereign," Lichtenstein wrote. "Yet there is a power to balance his in the people; he governs only as long as they choose to obey."[12] The reason was that the chiefs feared a loss of support if they behaved tyrannically. Families would simply pack up and leave, emigrating to another chiefdom where they would be assured of a welcome since they would add to its wealth and prestige. This was the public's ultimate sanction against the abuse of power, and by all accounts it was an effective one. The Dutch-born missionary Dr. Johannes van der Kemp reported in 1799 that he twice saw the Xhosa chief Ngqika withdraw unpopular decrees when sections of the tribe began marching toward the borders of the chiefdom.[13]

Although the expression of dissent was permitted and even encouraged, the object was to reach agreement and avoid division. In this compromise and consensus one again sees the pervasive influence of the subsistence economy and the need to avoid divisiveness in order to survive its uncertainties. The concept of a majority vote prevailing over a dissenting minority was totally alien to traditional African societies and remains so in some measure to this day. With time never a consideration in these unhurried communities, they were prepared to continue the discussion for as long as it took to iron out the last point of disagreement and bring the last dissenter into a consensus agreement.

The court systems, too, were aimed more at reconciling disputes than enforcing a penal code, although punishments, including the death penalty, were exacted. The judicial systems were extraordinarily sophisticated, involving not only the right of each party to present its case but also a system of appeals to higher courts presided over by more senior and experienced chiefs.

It was not all idyllic, of course. Tribal society had its ugly side, too. Early visitors were horrified by what, to them, was a pagan belief in witchcraft and sorcery, with the smelling out of evil spirits and some

12. Ibid., p. 352.

13. See Ibid., p. 353.

acts of extreme cruelty, including torture, that accompanied them. They gave bloodcurdling accounts of people being buried alive, or left bound on the waterfront to be slowly drowned by the rising tide, or staked to the ground in the blazing sun with pounded chili peppers stuffed up their nostrils and into their eyes.

Lichtenstein gives his own account of a scene in which a witch doctor is summoned to diagnose the cause of a man's illness. He describes how, after laying some cow-dung pellets on the sick man's belly, the witch doctor made various incantations, produced in turn a snake, a tortoise, and a lizard, and finally pronounced the patient to be bewitched. Lichtenstein then recounts the process of exorcism that followed, presenting it as typical of general practice:

> For this purpose the whole horde must be collected together: the enchantress then shuts herself up alone in a hut, where she says she must sleep in order to see the malefactor in a dream. The people without, in the mean time, dance and sing for awhile, till at length the men go into the hut, and beg the enchantress to come forward. At first she hesitates, then they carry her a number of hassagais as a present, when she comes forth with the weapons in her hand; her eyelid, her arm, and thigh, on the left side whitened, but on the right dyed black: she is half naked, being only covered about the middle, but is soon clothed with mantles from all sides. She is then required to name the enchanter: she still hesitates, but soon throws the mantles aside, and rushes amidst the people with her hassagais, striking with one of them the person whom she means to point out as the aggressor. He is then seized, but before any punishment is inflicted, the enchantress must declare where he has concealed the instrument by which the enchantment was performed. She names the place; it is searched, and a skull, or some other part of the human body, is found. The punishment to which, according to her pronouncement, he is commonly sentenced, is either to be buried under an ant heap, there to be stung by these animals, or to be laid upon the ground and covered with hot stones.[14]

The horrors of witchcraft more than anything else shocked Westerners and evoked images of primitive barbarism. Yet it was an integral and comprehensible feature of society. Africans were a profoundly spiritual people, and the capriciousness of Fate in their erratic environment encouraged a belief in the intervention of powerful spirits. Like all prescientific people, they had no way of understanding unnatural events—the failure of the rains to come on time, the stillborn child, the sickness that refused to respond to traditional remedies—and so they could only

14. Ibid., pp. 315–16.

fall back on magical explanations and spiritual means to try to control or influence them.

Nor was the Western world without its cruelties in this regard. Witches were tortured in Europe and Scotland and the medieval church burnt heretics at the stake. Massachusetts was plagued with incidents of witchcraft throughout the second half of the seventeenth century, culminating in the grisly Salem witch trials and executions of 1692 in which nineteen people were hanged and one, Giles Cory, was slowly crushed to death by heavy weights piled progressively on his body. More than a thousand people were hanged for witchcraft in England under Elizabeth and James I, the last in 1685—one year before the *Stavenisse* survivors encountered the Xhosa.

It is tempting to make these points of comparison as another example of Western hypocrisy in judging Africa so adversely, but there is more to it than that. The witchcraft that these early travellers saw in Africa appalled them because it resonated in their minds in terms of what witchcraft meant in their own Judeo-Christian cultures. In this as in everything else, they viewed Africa through a Western prism instead of judging it in its own cultural context. Had they been less ethnocentric, they might have realized that African witchcraft arises from an entirely different psychosocial basis than Western witchcraft, with none of the emotionally and theologically disturbing implications attendant on the notion of a satanically inspired conspiracy. By comparison, though it was capable of great cruelty, as these travellers saw, African witchcraft is an altogether simpler and less traumatic phenomenon. Indeed, a brief look into these differences offers some insights not only into this particular dimension of misunderstanding but also into some aspects of mind that have caused white and black South Africans to view themselves and their relationship with the world around them somewhat differently.

The notion of evil spirits taking on subtle guises to deceive and possess us is probably common to all forms of witchcraft, but what characterized Western witchcraft is the idea that Satan himself is the ultimate power behind all such conspiracies—not just little devils or malevolent spirits, but the great Antichrist. It is powerful imagery, and just as powerful is the imagery of the traitor within who is Satan's agent: Judas Iscariot, one of the Twelve, one of the inner circle who turns out to be Judas the betrayer. These images are lodged deep in the psyche, and although, with the exception of a few isolated and aberrant cases, the practice of witchcraft has long since died out in the West, the psychology that gave rise to it has not. There is still a recrudescent impulse, especially in times of social stress, to blame the crisis on subversion from outside and betrayal within, and instead of attending to the underlying causes to seek out these imagined conspirators. Thus the witch hunt. As Arthur Miller so vividly conveyed in his 1953 play *The Crucible*, written as a parable about McCarthyism, it is in a direct line of descent from the witch-hunting frenzy that gripped Salem Village three centuries ago.

It is, of course, an impulse that carries with it a deep sense of guilt, for it is in fundamental conflict with the Christian faith and with Western ideals about justice and due process. These things were deeply worrying to the clergy of Massachusetts in 1692, even to the Rev. Samuel Parris, the tormented Puritan minister who was at the centre of the frenzy in Salem Village, and to the members of the Special Court of Oyer and Terminer that conducted the witchcraft trials.[15] They are troubling to the Christian conscience still, for they cast a long shadow ahead of them.

Not so with African witchcraft. Properly viewed in its own cultural context, this is less of a religious aberration than a psychosocial control mechanism. It is, in a sense, the obverse of the collectivist *ubuntu* support system and thus also its corollary. Just as individuality is subsumed into the interests of the whole and mutuality becomes everything, so anyone who is deemed a spiritual threat to the whole is expunged from it. And just as the inclusiveness is warm, caring, and patiently supportive, so the expunging is, as Hobbes might have put it, nasty, brutish, and short.

The process might have appeared arbitrary to outside observers, yet such societies are by their very nature hypersensitive to currents of mood and tension, to the individual idiosyncrasies that make up their organic wholeness. The witch doctor or *sangoma* (or "enchantress," to use Lichtenstein's term) was a person whose function in the tribe was to keep tabs on such nuances. It is unlikely that his or her selections were as arbitrary as they seemed—although of course they were wide open to political manipulation and abuse. But for the most part the witch doctor was a social therapist as well as a specialist in herbal medicines, and in both functions played a role very different from either the frenzied young "afflicted" girls of Salem, the Rev. Parris, or the Special Court of Oyer and Terminer.

There was, moreover, none of the lingering guilt that accompanied Western witchcraft trials. It was not an aberration. It was not in conflict with the basic social ethic but an integral part of it. Everything was in balance. The disturbing spiritual element would have been expunged

15. For an illuminating social analysis of the events surrounding the Salem witchcraft outbreak, see Paul Boyer and Stephen Nissenbaum, *Salem Possessed* (Cambridge, Mass., 1974).

with no more shock to the social body than a bowel movement would cause, and everyone would have been back at their routines the next day. Only the Western observer would have remained horrified, viewing it as he did within his own frame of reference.

There were other aspects of African life, too, which provided grounds for white misunderstanding and condemnation. The psychology of the subsistence economy has shaped the mind of black Africa over eons of time, since long before the Protestant work ethic became the driving force in Western culture. Subsistence thinking was not an energizing influence. It inclined to a fatalist outlook, which Europeans mistook for fecklessness and laziness. If the future is both uncertain and uncontrollable, it does not do to think or worry too much about it. Better to live for the moment, to eat heartily when there is plenty and to starve stoically when there is nothing.

There is no spirit of acquisitiveness in a subsistence economy, no deep-seated sense of work being intrinsically good apart from what it can produce, or of idleness being shameful; nor any great pressure to plan and save for the future when there is no snowbound winter. Time is of little consequence when it is related only to the rising and the setting of the sun and the slow-changing seasons, when there is nowhere to go and there are no deadlines to keep.

One thing the subsistence economy does produce is an intense, lifelong passion for land. For land means security—not only those patches that are actually under cultivation or providing pasturage for livestock but also the surrounding bushveld, which in the worst of times, when all the crops have failed and all the cattle have died, will still yield a few edible leaves and roots and grubs and so sustain the life of the tribe. Land and community became inseparable, woven together in the matrix of tribal society. The land was revered in ritual, it held the bodies of the tribal ancestors, it was the concretion of the tribe itself, the thing that gave it life and substance and security and identity. It could not be owned individually. It was held by the tribe collectively and vested in the chief, who could allocate its use but not its title.

This, too, the Europeans failed to understand as they advanced in their settlement, pressing the tribes back and dispossessing them of their land with little idea of the social disruption and psychological trauma they were causing.

From the beginning, whites saw only those surface manifestations of African culture and the African mind that conflicted with their own concepts of approved social behaviour. What they failed to see, because they were not disposed to get close enough to do so, was the complexity and subtle texture of traditional African social organization, the restraints on the exercise of chiefly power, the elements of grass-roots democracy, the balance between communal, family, and individual rights, and the pervasive spirit of mutual obligation and respect, the spirit of *ubuntu*.

The black people of South Africa have undergone a transition more dramatic in its compression of human experience into a short space of time than any other community in history. In little more than two centuries of interaction with the whites who came to settle here, they were catapulted from the Iron Age into the Scientific Age, wrenched out of their subsistence economy into the continent's only full-blown industrial revolution, dispossessed of their land, and deprived of their pastoral heritage. This has changed them dramatically. Yet, as with all the other players in our unfolding drama, the imprint of their past is still upon them.

The tradition of communal loyalty and social obligation survives, mutated but still recognizable, in the pullulating townships and squatter camps around the industrial cities. There has been a terrible rending of the whole fabric of African society by a political system that separates even nuclear families, as well as extended ones; yet one still finds a spirit of community, of shared grief and shared joy, in these otherwise soulless surroundings. There is still a collectivist style of decision making in the political movements and trade unions and the hundreds of civic associations that exist in the townships.

This is not a culture with a built-in attraction to individualist democracy and free-enterprise capitalism. Africans may eventually be won over by the perceived advantages of such systems, but in the meantime Westerners should not be surprised that many of them show a more historic affinity for the concept of communalism.

CHAPTER TWO

A Fateful Wind

For thou art an holy people unto the Lord thy God, and the Lord hath chosen thee to be a peculiar people unto himself, above all the nations that are upon the earth.

DEUTERONOMY 14:2

WHEN THE southeaster blows in Cape Town, waves of inky clouds billow over the summit ridge of Table Mountain and roll like lava down its slopes toward the city below. The wind, howling in from the roaring forties just six degrees farther south, flagellates the city, hurling litter through its streets and setting tall concrete lampposts swaying like sailboat masts. Out at sea the great Cape rollers, built up by the convergence of conflicting currents flowing along the two oceans that wash Africa's east and west coasts and meet at Cape Point, are whipped into mountains that can overwhelm a small craft. When the wind is at its worst, when the dark clouds are so thick they shut out the sun and the lashing takes place in a forbidding gloom, it is called the black southeaster. It is like no other wind. The southeaster has shaped the entire history of South Africa and the fortunes of half the continent beyond.

When it is not blowing and when the sun is shining on one of those still, crystal days that make the air tingle like champagne, the whole ambience of the Cape peninsula, with its gray-green slopes of mountain granite plunging steeply into a turquoise sea, is so translucently Mediterranean that it seems incredible it should have been bypassed by the southern Latins who were the first to land there and left instead to Protestant northerners from the lowlands of Holland. The mind's eye can easily picture the scene: white villas with flat, red-tiled roofs set against the mountain slopes; broad, tree-lined *avenidas* with pavement cafés and white-uniformed policemen directing the traffic; guitars and fado, olive skins and olive oil and the ubiquitous smell of dark tobacco.

But the fierce southeaster lashed the little caravels of the early Portuguese navigators, Bartolomeu Dias and Vasco da Gama, and so alarmed them that they sailed on to establish their bases on the little coral island of Mozambique and at Sofala, farther up the east African coast, from where they sailed on the monsoon across the Indian Ocean to Goa. So the history of South Africa literally turned in the wind. Had the Portuguese settled there, the Afrikaner people—and the ideology of apartheid that they fashioned—would never have existed. A mineral-rich Republica de Boa Esperance might have evolved as another Brazil perhaps, a society noted for its degree of racial integration rather than as a world symbol of segregation.

This is not to say that the Dutch were unique in having attitudes of racial superiority toward people of colour at that time. Such feelings were common to all European colonizers and to all those engaged in the slave trade, the Portuguese included. Yet there were differences of nuance and degree between Catholic and Protestant colonial powers that left a lasting imprint on the societies they touched. Grim though the historical record is of Portuguese and Spanish slavery, nowhere in Latin America did it leave a legacy of segregation and entrenched racism like that of the American South; no Ku Klux Klan crosses were burnt in Mexico or Brazil; nor, from Africa to the Indies, did either the British or the Dutch ever consider emulating the French and Portuguese colonial policies of accepting educated native *evolués* or *assimilados* into their metropolitan cultures. "Our ancestors, the Gauls" little black children were taught in Senegalese schools, to the chagrin of the Negritude philosophers. The idea of teaching black kids anywhere to consider themselves Englishmen was unthinkable.

Some social scientists think it was John Calvin's doctrine of predestination that gave the Protestant northerners their particular propensity for master-race notions, by inducing a belief that they were the Elect of the Lord. Others have suggested it was because the Latins were swarthy and had a long history of associating with the Moors in Europe that they found it easier to mix with dark-skinned people. Whatever the reason, it is agreed that the Portuguese were less bigoted in their racial attitudes than either the Dutch or the British to whom fate, and the wind, eventually assigned this heteromorphic piece of real estate at the southern tip of Africa.

Why were they headed that way anyhow, these intrepid seamen in their cockleshells? It was a question of pepper. In 1453 the Turkish conquest of Constantinople closed Europe's overland trade route to the spicelands of the East. It is difficult for us in these days of modern refrigeration to appreciate just how important spices were in an age when even in the most salubrious of homes meat came putrid to the table. The closing of the spice route posed a crisis for Europe comparable to a cutting off today of oil supplies from the Persian Gulf. The urgent need to get pepper to Europe by sea sent exploring navigators south and west seeking a way around the Turkish obstruction. In 1497 da Gama found the route around the Cape; the next year Christopher Columbus stumbled on South America and imagined he had got there too.

Yet it was left to the Dutch a century and a half later as they, too, plied their trade to these rich sources of epicurean deception to settle at the Cape, bringing with them a particular intellectual set and psychology that would be critical in shaping the mind of the Afrikaner *volk* in this alien environment.

The world they left behind them was one astir with new energies and new ideas. Europe had recently burst its way out of the somnolent Middle Ages and was in the throes of a revolutionary transformation, with changes in man's environment and an expansion of his intellectual horizons such as its people had not seen before. Gutenberg had just invented the printing press, opening the way to popular education. It was an age of brilliant artists and philosophers, of the birth of science and the rise of capitalism, with new wealth flowing to the merchants and a new self-confidence to the individual.

Above all it was an age of theological upheaval, with the ancient monolith of the Church being challenged and broken and new ideas about man's relationship to God and his role on earth being expressed by powerful preachers and moulding the minds of whole communities.

Holland was in the forefront of these events. Fired by Calvinist republicanism and led by their beloved William, Prince of Orange, the Dutch had just emerged from eighty years of bitter struggle to win their political and religious independence from the tyrannous domination of Hapsburg Spain. Now, as a confederation of seven autonomous provinces run by a States-General, they were surging forward as the world's leading trading nation, whose ships could bring goods from all parts of the world for transshipment up the Rhine to the heartland of Europe. As Simon Schama puts it in his colourful history of the period, they were "third-leg baton carrier[s] in the race that took capitalism from medieval merchant ventures through Renaissance banking to the Dutch international staple economy and onwards at a sprint to the finishing line of British industrialisation."[1] This was the Golden Age of Dutch civilization. Its trading stations ranged from Archangel to Recife and from New Am-

1. Simon Schama, *The Embarrassment of Riches* (New York, 1987), p. 6.

sterdam to Nagasaki; its society was the most literate in Europe; its cities were full of art, literature, and philosophy; it was home to Rembrandt and Frans Hals, Vermeer, Jan Steen, Spinoza, Descartes, and, for a time, John Locke. As Jan van Riebeeck readied himself to sail for the Cape in the spring of 1652 to establish a victualling station there, Amsterdam was the greatest commercial centre in the world and the Vereenigde Oostindische Compagnie (VOC)—the United East India Company—for which he worked was the world's biggest commercial enterprise.

But to understand the shape of the cultural bricks and stones that Van Riebeeck took with him to lay in the crypt of the new society he was to build there, one must look back a little at the events that had brought Holland to this point. The long war with Spain, which ended only in 1648, was the national epic that evoked the spirit of Dutch nationalism and profoundly influenced the generic mind. It was a war of appalling brutality, fought against heavy odds and frightful tyranny as Philip II imported the Spanish Inquisition and carried out wholesale massacres in pursuit of a vow either to bring the Netherlands back to Rome or "so waste the land that neither the native could live there nor thereafter desire the place for habitation." And because it was a war for religious as well as national independence, when the Dutch finally triumphed, their victory merged with the amphibious geography of their homeland to form a national myth of a reenacted Exodus. Spain was seen as the Antichrist from whom William of Orange had delivered his people by leading them through ordeal and exodus to a national rebirth in their promised land, 150,000 of them fleeing across the Zuider Zee from persecution in the southern provinces of Flanders and Brabant while the Pharaoh's fleet, led by Philip's tyrannous envoy, the Duke of Alba, was defeated at the battle of Bergen op Zoom and the Spanish sailors were flung bodily into the water.

The scriptural imagery gained power from the fact that the war coincided with a severe phase in Holland's age-old struggle against the sea, with a series of catastrophic floods inundating large parts of the country. "The Dutch regarded themselves as ordained and blessed survivors of the flood," writes Schama. And as they fought the Spanish and simultaneously launched into an energetic period of land reclamation, it was as though they were giving shape to their fatherland physically as well as politically.[2] It became doubly blessed.

The ultimate in this Biblical symbolism of water and redemption came with the relief of the besieged city of Leiden, when Prince William opened the Ijsseldijk and other river defences to flood the countryside,

2. Ibid., p. 35.

paralyzing Spanish troop movements and enabling a rebel flotilla to sail almost to the city walls as a relieving force. This, says Schama, was the national epic par excellence, after which William was portrayed as Moses in Dutch paintings and referred to as "Ons Moyses" in pamphlets.[3]

For years this Hebraic self-image was amplified and elaborated in Dutch art and literature, in the theatre and in popular folklore. It appears in a painting by Ferdinand Bol, *Moses with the Tablets of the Law*, in the Royal Palace in Amsterdam. It became pan-denominational, taken up by Catholic as well as Calvinist patriots. Holland's most celebrated poet of the seventeenth century, Joost van den Vondel, who was a Catholic, ended an epic poem with a specific comparison between the redemption of the children of Israel and the liberation of the Netherlands:

> O wondrous fate that joins Moses and Orange
> The one fights for the law, the other beats the drum
> And with his own arm, frees the Evangelium
> The one leads the Hebrews through the Red Sea flood
> The other guides his people through a sea . . . of tears and blood.[4]

The identification with the Hebrews became the explanation for Holland's seemingly blessed good fortune in commerce and for its ability to withstand the onslaughts of more powerful competitors. As Jacobus Lydius, a Calvinist, wrote after a Dutch victory over the English in 1688: "When men ask how the Netherlanders, with such little power, could overcome their enemies on land and destroy them at sea and on so many occasions snatch victory from the jaws of defeat . . . then we can only say that this could only have come about through the eternal covenant made between God and his children below [*nederkinderen*]."[5] And again, in the same anthology of verse and prose: "Above all else I thank Him / Who made Holland Jerusalem."

Of course Calvinist writers in other societies also invoked the Exodus analogy in their literature to suggest a special covenant with the Lord, but Schama suggests that it was precisely because the theme was taken up pan-denominationally in Holland that it became more of a national than a sectarian idiom there and imprinted the self-image of the Dutch as a chosen people more deeply on the national mind.

The imprint was further deepened by the ferocious religious disputes

3. Ibid., pp. 36, 110–13.

4. Quoted ibid., p. 113.

5. Quoted ibid., p. 45.

that broke out within Holland during the first decades of the seventeenth century. These raged around the doctrine of predestination, the most characteristic feature of Calvinist dogma, between the strict Gomarists, who were in the forefront of the struggle against Spanish Catholicism, and the more liberal followers of Jacobus Arminius, a theologian at the newly founded University of Leiden. The Gomarists won: Holland's leading statesman of the day, Johan van Oldenbarnevelt, was executed; the great jurist Hugo Grotius was imprisoned; and the Arminians were outlawed. The Dutch church summoned its ministers, elders, academics, and other important personages to the great cathedral at Dordrecht where in 1618 the Synod of Dort laid down as official dogma a sternly conservative interpretation of the predestination doctrine, which holds that God has foreordained some of mankind for grace and salvation and others for eternal damnation.

As Erich Fromm and other psychologists have suggested, this doctrine can form the basis of a "chosen people" outlook. Implicit in it is the principle of the basic inequality of men. It means there are two kinds of people, those who, regardless of any good or bad they may do in their lives, are predestined to be saved and those who are damned. By holding that God himself has divided all mankind into two categories, the chosen and the damned, Fromm contends, Calvinism induces a sense of individual powerlessness combined with a compensating psychological need to allay torturing inner doubts by becoming ever more convinced that members of one's own religious community must surely represent that part of mankind that God has chosen. The more conservative the interpretation of the predestination doctrine, the more fundamentalist the overall faith, the more pronounced will be this psychological need.[6]

Just how aware the men who accompanied Van Riebeeck to the Cape were of these weighty theological debates is a matter of conjecture. Certainly they were not intellectuals, except for Van Riebeeck himself, a medical doctor whose parents were folk of some substance and who was brought up in the home of his grandfather, mayor of Culembourg, which would have been the centre of the social and political life of the community.

The rest were drawn from the so-called *grauw*, or rabble, of Dutch society: a mixture of day-labourers, vagrants and local unemployed,[7] some of whom had drifted into the big commercial city in search of work from the nearby lowlands of Germany. The VOC had an insatiable

6. Erich Fromm, *The Fear of Freedom* (London, 1961), pp. 72–9.

7. C. R. Boxer, *The Dutch Seaborne Empire* (London, 1965), p. 61.

need for labour and sometimes commissioned *zielverkopers* (soul merchants) to raid the flophouses and bawdy *musicos* of back-street Amsterdam for layabouts who could be press-ganged into service at sea. Except for the two-hundred-odd French Huguenots who followed thirty-six years later, these first white settlers in South Africa were not religious zealots, like the New England Puritans, making their way purposefully to a new world to establish the ideal society there that they could not create at home. They were social and economic dropouts who, as Leonard Thompson points out, had failed to make it in the competitive society of seventeenth-century Holland.[8] Louis Leipoldt says of them that they were "a mixture of diverse nationalities, adventurers who had volunteered their services in the hope of more certain reward than could be obtained elsewhere, men coarsened by the conditions under which they had lived ashore and on the sea, with their vices redeemed by the one great virtue they had, physical courage."[9] When fourteen of them presented Van Riebeeck with a petition of protest five years after their arrival at the Cape, only half could sign their names.

Still, even people such as these were probably aware of at least the fundamentals of the great theological debate that dominated the times. Even the lowliest of folk feared for their immortal souls in those pious days and went to church or joined great open-air congregations on Sundays, where they would have heard the fire-and-brimstone sermons that cascaded from every pulpit and were meant to strike fear and obedience into their hearts. It would have been a simplified explanation that they were given, stripped of its more abstruse theological nuances, but, yes, they would have had a basic understanding of what Dort was about and they would have taken this with them to South Africa, where it acquired a new and sharper meaning when they found themselves among seemingly primitive heathens; the presence of these strangers must have been reassuring to people whose low station back home would have heightened their anxiety about which half of God's great divide they belonged to.

That most thorough of South African academics, André du Toit, has seriously questioned the assumption of many historians that the first Afrikaners regarded themselves as a "chosen people"; his exhaustive search of the primary literature has revealed no evidence that they described themselves as such before the late nineteenth century, by which time, he suggests, Nationalist political myth makers were at work re-

8. Leonard M. Thompson, "The South African Dilemma," in Louis M. Hartz, *The Founding of New Societies* (New York, 1964), p. 182.

9. C. Louis Leipoldt, *Jan van Riebeeck* (London, 1936), p. 113.

writing folk history to provide evidence of a deep-rooted national ethos.[10] No doubt this is so. There is little to suggest that they even regarded themselves as a "people" in any nationalistic sense at that early stage; they were too simple and too scattered to have sustained any inspirational spirit of collective mission as the New England Puritans did. There were no John Winthrops or John Cottons among them, indeed few clergymen of any description; no one was capable of dealing with intellectual and theological issues as did the 130 university graduates among the pre-1640 New Englanders. Except for the Huguenots, who were people of some erudition, these were sailors and mercenary soldiers of the rank and file. It was more than a century and a half before Afrikaner society at the Cape developed anything approximating an intellectual elite.

This is not to say that they brought no national folklore with them from Holland or that the social environment they found themselves in did not induce them to believe in their membership in the divine elect, and to view the Khoikhoi heathens around them as the Biblical descendants of Ham. We know that the Dutch held such views in Batavia,[11] and they seem to have had an even more contemptuous attitude toward the indigenous inhabitants of Africa from the day they landed. "Although descended from our father Adam," wrote one Wouter Schouten in 1665, "[the Khoikhoi] yet show so little of humanity that truly they more resemble the unreasonable beasts than reasonable man . . . having no knowledge of God nor of what leads to their Salvation. Miserable folk, how lamentable is your pitiful condition! And Oh Christians, how blessed is ours!"[12]

Even before he was based there, Van Riebeeck warned the VOC in a memo that on a previous visit to the Cape he had found the Khoikhoi to be dangerous savages. "They are by no means to be trusted, being a brutal people living without conscience," he wrote.[13] In subsequent entries in his meticulously kept diary he referred to them as "dull, stupid

10. See André du Toit, "No Chosen People: The Myth of the Calvinist Origins of Afrikaner Nationalism and Racial Ideology"; "Puritans in Africa? Afrikaner 'Calvinism' and Kuyperian Neo-Calvinism in Late Nineteenth Century South Africa"; and "Captive of the Nationalist Paradigm: Prof. F. A. van Jaarsveld and the Historical Evidence for the Afrikaner's Ideas and His Calling and Mission."

11. Boyer, op. cit., p. 231. The contempt was reciprocated. Boxer reports that the Malay and Indonesian Muslims of Batavia called the Dutch *kaffirs*, the Islamic word of contempt for unbelievers, which Afrikaners and other white South Africans adopted as a pejorative appellation for black Africans.

12. Quoted by Richard Elphick, *Khoikhoi and the Founding of White South Africa* (Johannesburg, 1985), p. 195.

13. Leipoldt, op. cit., p. 90.

and odorous" and as "black stinking dogs." He established no personal contact with them except through a series of troublesome interpreters, and in his ten years at the Cape made no attempt to learn their language or anything about their culture, as he had done with great enthusiasm during briefer spells of service in Tonkin and Japan.[14] Instead Van Riebeeck kept begging the Company to send "industrious" Chinese workers and slaves to do the dirty work his settlers didn't wish to do, and in that act of striking symbolism, which leaps at us across the centuries, he planted the bitter-almond hedge to fence his little white community off from the continent's indigenous inhabitants.

The early Afrikaners carried these attitudes with them as in time they drifted inland and up the east coast, and it is clear that by the early nineteenth century a fierce sense of racial superiority over the indigenous inhabitants had become embedded in their minds. As a magistrate at Uitenhage noted in his report to the Batavian government in 1805:

> It is difficult and often impossible to get the colonists to understand that the Hottentots ought to be protected by the laws no less than themselves, and that the judge may make no distinction between them and the Hottentots. According to the unfortunate notion prevalent here, a heathen is not actually human, but at the same time he cannot really be classified among the animals. He is therefore a sort of creature not known elsewhere. His word can in no wise be believed, and only by violent measures can he be brought to do good and shun evil.[15]

The notion of being a chosen people was perhaps not the sort of thing that would have been much spoken about or considered appropriate for the written record; the community would have regarded such views as axiomatic and its members wrote very little anyway. As Max Weber notes, the important thing about the social effect of religious doctrine is not so much its public expression as its subconscious influence on practical conduct.[16] All the circumstantial evidence suggests that this is something the early Afrikaners brought with them from Holland, and that it was reinforced when they found themselves among people they considered dark, sinister, heathen, shiftless, and unclean—thus conspicuously lacking in the outward signs of grace—and which was evoked

14. Ibid., p. 67.

15. Quoted by T. Dunbar Moodie, *The Rise of Afrikanerdom: Power, Apartheid, and the Afrikaner Civil Religion* (Berkeley, Cal., 1975), pp. 28–9.

16. Max Weber, *The Protestant Ethic and the Spirit of Capitalism* (New York, 1958), pp. 97–8.

easily and powerfully later on when the myth makers got to work. In this initial stage it was not nationalistic, but when it blossomed forth as such in another two centuries, the nationalism emerged in a particularly fervent form: the sacral nationalism of a chosen people in their promised land, imbued with a sense of divine mission and equipped with a utopian ideology for reordering society that amounted to a civil religion. As Daniel Malan expressed it on coming to power as the prophet of this new doctrine of apartheid in 1948:

> Our history is the greatest masterpiece of the centuries. We hold this nationhood as our due for it was given us by the Architect of the universe. [His] aim was the formation of a new nation among the nations of the world. . . . The last hundred years have witnessed a miracle behind which must lie a divine plan. Indeed, the history of the Afrikaner reveals a will and a determination which makes one feel that Afrikanerdom is not the work of men but the creation of God.[17]

It is this which makes South Africa's race problem so much more intractable than those of other multiethnic societies in Africa or elsewhere around the globe. It is not simply a matter of race prejudice to be overcome by a judicious blend of enlightenment, reassurance, and the discovery of economic self-interest. Prejudice is there, to be sure: it has saturated South African society for three and a half centuries. But that is only part of it. The other part is a power struggle for control of a country, between a racial minority long imbued with the belief that its divinely ordained national existence depends on retaining control of the nation-state, and a disinherited majority demanding restitution of its rights, which would make that impossible.[18]

It would be wrong, of course, to suggest that apartheid has but one single taproot reaching back to the earliest Afrikaner settlement at the

17. Quoted in Moodie, op. cit., p. 1.

18. See Hermann Giliomee and Lawrence Schlemmer, *Negotiating South Africa's Future* (Johannesburg, 1989) and *From Apartheid to Nation-Building* (Cape Town, 1989). These academic authors characterized the South African struggle as a "bicommunal conflict," which they liken to the struggles in Israel and Northern Ireland, where two conflicting nationalisms lay claim to the same territory as their rightful homeland. The authors suggest that the conflict should be resolved by a power-sharing contract between the two nationalisms. While the characterization is deceptively appealing, it is flawed in that the nature of African nationalism in South Africa is inclusivist and does not seek to exclude the whites. Its most important policy declaration, the Freedom Charter, states explicitly that "South Africa belongs to all its people, black and white alike." That distinguishes the situation fundamentally from the Irish and Israeli conflicts, and, as another academic specialist on South Africa, Heribert Adam, has warned, it makes the power-sharing proposal both inappropriate and potentially dangerous.

Cape. It was fed by many lateral roots along the way, not all of them of Afrikaner provenance, and academic historians have become involved in a chicken-and-egg argument about where it all began, with Marxists downplaying the importance of the early years and emphasizing the importance of industrial capitalism from the late nineteenth century.[19] The Dutch planted another seed right at the beginning when they classified different status groups by law—with company servants at the top of the scale, white "free burghers" second, and Khoikhoi, free blacks, and slaves at the bottom—setting a pattern of legal discrimination that continues to this day.[20] Apartheid's exploitative roots are to be found in the early nineteenth century, when Britain's occupation of the Cape drew it into the world economy and created a need for cheap labor to step up wine and grain exports.[21] The administrative ground was laid by Sir Theophilus Shepstone, a British commissioner in Natal, who imposed a comprehensive system of segregation on the colony between 1845 and 1876.[22]

But in terms of mind, no one who has spent any considerable time around the political hustings of white South Africa listening to the great virtuosos of Afrikaner Nationalist oratory, to what touches the heart and moves the crowd, who has felt the pulse-beat of platteland electioneering and heard the primal scream of the atavistic far right, or who has monitored the seminal role of the Dutch Reformed Church in both initiating and sanctifying the apartheid system, can be in any doubt about the centrality of the civil religion. For the Afrikaner it was a theology of liberation whose emotional appeal was pervasive. Though it has lost some of its animating force in recent years, it remains at the core of the South African dilemma: the inability to allow the possibility of ever being subordinate again, of not being a nation in control of its own national territory, of having to survive and find a way to be an ethnic minority in a country run by others. That is the survival imperative. That is what Afrikaner Nationalists mean when they equate black majority rule with national suicide. It is the death of the chosen people, no less.

19. See Martin Legassik, "The Frontier Tradition in South African Society" (a published paper).

20. Richard Elphick, "The Origins and Entrenchment of European Dominance at the Cape" (a paper delivered at a conference at Yale, November 1987).

21. D. van Arkel, G. C. Quispel, and R. J. Ross, *De Wijngaard des Heeren? Een ondersoek naar de wortels van "die blanke baasskap" in Zuid-Afrika* (Leiden, 1983), amplified by personal interview.

22. David Welsh, *The Roots of Segregation: Native Policy in Colonial Natal, 1845–1910* (London, 1971).

In seeking to demonstrate that the "chosen people" myth does not go all the way back to the early Afrikaners but is a relatively recent political innovation, André du Toit expresses the hope that it may prove to be correspondingly less significant and durable than has been supposed—"a relatively late, and in all probability transient phase in Afrikaner history."[23] Perhaps, but I doubt it. Whatever its true provenance, the notion has so powerfully gripped the Afrikaner mind for at least the past half century that it will not easily disappear. Those who wish to see South Africa move toward a democratic future would do well not to underestimate it.

A NOTION OF their own racial superiority as the Elect of God was not all that Van Riebeeck's settlers brought with them from Holland. They came, too, with a curious moral ambivalence that was uniquely the product of the Dutch Golden Age. This underwent a mutation on the South African veld and became one of the most enduringly puzzling characteristics of Afrikaner nationalism.

It was the peculiar dilemma of the Dutch that their self-image as the New Israel conflicted with their growing affluence as Europe's most commercially successful society. On the one hand their value system led them to see wealth as a presumptive sign of membership in the Elect, and on the other hand as corrupting and morally dangerous. So they lived in a state of tension, trapped between godliness and gain, between the Protestant work ethic and its commercial results. The wealthier they became the more their preachers thundered at them about the sins of money making and its portents of moral enfeeblement and collapse. The analogy of Israel was invoked again, this time to warn how the corruption of Baal had been the herald of disaster and to raise again the Hebraic imagery of chastisement by flood, always significant in the Netherlands. The fear of *overvloed* became the keynote of this moral discomfort, the word itself embodying the double meaning of both overabundance and of flood. If there were not greater restraint, if wealth were not tempered with greater humbleness, enjoyment of the good life with more asceticism, then the punishing flood would surely be sent, even as in Noah's time, as chastisement for the overabundance that was swamping the land.[24]

The tension was by definition unresolvable because the moral value

23. André du Toit, "Captive of the Nationalist Paradigm," p. 79.

24. See Schama, op. cit., especially pp. 188 and 289–371, for a vivid exposition of this moral dichotomy.

system drove the Dutch in both directions at once. They had no choice but to live with it, containing their discomfort within a code that became dichotomous. If it was easier for a rich man to pass through the eye of a needle than to enter into the kingdom of heaven, then all that the pious merchants of Amsterdam could do was keep up appearances of a sober and austere lifestyle. But the temptations of the flesh kept bubbling out, revealing themselves in the richly paradoxical culture of the age, in Pieter Breugel's swarming genre canvasses redolent of conviviality and those of other Dutch masters, which blended an outward soberness with the discreet contemporary sex symbolism of long-stemmed pipes and empty wineglasses waiting to be filled; in the elaborate ornamentation and scrollwork of the architecture and the furniture; in the velvet and gold tapestries and the rich embroidery; and in a sartorial dash of brocaded coats and cockaded hats that is nicely preserved in the figure of Van Riebeeck on its pedestal at the bottom of Cape Town's Adderley Street.

Above all the Dutch acquired a reputation as great eaters and drinkers. Banquet tables groaned while the preachers called for frugality, and as they thundered against the evils of smoking and alcohol the Dutch became the world's first connoisseurs of tobacco and gin. Home brewing became an avocation, with an array of recipes using fruit and herbs, hops and barley.[25]

All this had an echo one day in the fall of 1983 when some three hundred Afrikaner families gathered on an arid cattle ranch in the Groot Marico district of the western Transvaal to celebrate the art of making a fiery home brew called *mampoer*, handed down to them from their Voortrekker ancestors, who had trekked in ox wagons into these lonely parts in the early nineteenth century. The pioneers had boiled their mampoer out of fermented peaches, apricots, wild berries, the fruit of the prickly pear cactus, or whatever was at hand. It was a tough liquor for a tough frontier people, and as time passed and the country modernized, its strait-laced legislators sought to outlaw it. But in 1983 there came a partial reprieve: the law was changed to allow the few remaining licences held by old pioneer families to be handed down from father to son once again. And so it came to pass that people were gathering on the farm of Oom Apie van Staden, a rotund 74-year-old father of ten and the holder of one of the licences, to celebrate the reprieve.

Burly men arrived in baggy shorts and open-necked shirts, followed by women with bouffant hairdos and high-heeled shoes, who tottered over the rough ground to Oom Apie's big iron shed where the ceremony was held. There, laid out on long trestle-tables, was the mampoer: green,

25. Ibid., p. 203.

red, yellow, and brown bottles containing spirits distilled from every fruit imaginable. Some had been sweetened and flavoured to make them into liqueurs: orange, banana, honey, apple, coffee, and aniseed. Beside the shed Oom Apie's own big copper still boiled away, a colourless liquid dripping from a pipe at the bottom of an old 44-gallon oil drum filled with water. When the liquor ignited at the touch of a match and poured in a flaming stream to the ground, Oom Apie pronounced it ready to drink.

But before the proceedings could begin they had first to be solemnized with a reading from the Bible and a prayer. Dominee Daniel Jakobs of the Nederduitsch Hervormde Kerk, sternest of South Africa's three Dutch Reformed Churches, quoted from Genesis to warn the celebrants of the evils of liquor. Then he noted that the Bible is also abundant in its approval of the preservation of a people's cultural heritage—and mampoer was, after all, a piece of Afrikaner culture. So he pronounced it admissible, said a grave Amen, and the great booze-up began.

The moral ambivalence revealed on this innocent occasion is as recurrent a part of the Afrikaner mind as the notion of racial superiority. It is the stuff of ethnic humour. "I don't mind you getting down on your knees," says Van der Merwe, the generic Afrikaner of these jokes, to the black man scrubbing the floor in the segregated church, "but don't let me catch you praying." As the sacral nationalism took hold and evolved its doctrine of racial singularity it pulled against the broader Christian injunction to love one's neighbour. Once again a moral value system drove these descendants of the Dutch in two opposite directions at once. Once again the result has been a dichotomous code that fills the South African system and its public debate with contradictions. Piety coexists with cruelty, prayerfulness with an aggressive militarism, a yearning to be understood and to be loved with a national bellicosity and an impulse to tell the rest of the world to go to hell.

The paradoxes crowd in thickly. The everyday enjoyment of multiracial South Africa has been heavily circumscribed by the asceticism of the politically influential Dutch Reformed Church. For years organized sport on Sunday was prohibited by law in the province of Transvaal, women were not allowed in bars, and television, thought to be a particularly corrupting influence until its power as a propaganda tool was discovered, was barred until 1972. There were laws forbidding interracial marriages and sex across the colour line. Films and books are strictly censored for salacious material. All forms of gambling are prohibited, and in the 1960s a morals commission of the Dutch Reformed Church inveighed against the children's game of snakes-and-ladders because it is a game of chance that uses dice.

Yet again: as apartheid has evolved the concept of nominally independent tribal "homelands" as a formula for solving South Africa's race problem while preserving the sovereignty of the Afrikaner nation, those responsible for implementing the programme have found that the only way to finance these undeveloped ministates is with the help of casino-hotels. Since the "homelands" are legally not part of South Africa, they do not have to abide by its blue-stocking laws, so that with independence they have each acquired a set of gambling tables and blue-movie theatres along with the flags, anthems, parliaments, and other trappings of ersatz nationhood. Sun City, Thaba N'chu, Bisho, Wild Coast, Thohoyandou—each one a Las Vegas in the bush, a fleshpot of monied indulgence in the midst of grinding poverty. The "casino-states" they are jestingly called, and starved white South Africans flock to them by the thousand for their thrills and kicks and weekends of sensual permissiveness. Thus the chosen people are to be saved and their sacred mission fulfilled with the blessed assistance of the roulette wheel and blackjack, porn movies, nude stage shows, and the opportunity for cross-colour dalliance.

The South African government's penchant for euphemism is part of the same syndrome. When the so-called open universities were compelled to close their doors to blacks in 1959 and separate tribal colleges were built instead, the enforcing law was called the Extension of University Education Act. The pass-law system restricting the freedom of movement of blacks was codified and extended by the Abolition of Passes and Coordination of Documents Act. The vast government department that rules over black South Africans like an internal colonial office has progressed from being called the Department of Native Affairs to the Department of Bantu Administration and Development, to the Department of Plural Relations, to the Department of Cooperation and Development. Apartheid itself has undergone name changes: it has been called separate development, separate freedoms, and, currently, multinational democracy. Foreign observers usually see such euphemisms as a clumsy attempt to improve the country's image abroad. That is true, but only in part. A major purpose is self-deception. Such gestures at legitimizing the system are necessary to ease the inner tension; there must be enough at least to activate the process of rationalization.

This is why, for all the continuity of the South African system, there is so much soul-searching in the Afrikaans press and the Afrikaans churches. It is why, for all the brutality of its regime, South Africa has never become completely totalitarian. As Heribert Adam has noted, it is ruled by a small racial oligarchy that cannot afford disunity, and whose leaders know that if they use power too cynically without any attempt to make their actions appear justified, there is enough tension in the

Afrikaner value system to risk alienating some important elements.[26] So the gestures are made. Certain restraints operate. Some democratic institutions and processes are permitted. Thus a token parliamentary opposition is allowed, a partially free press, a judiciary that is independent to judge a lopsided body of law.

Most puzzling of all to outsiders is the paradox of an administration that violates the rule of law with impunity yet still in some measure adheres to the process of law. An authoritarian president with the power to issue a decree without reference to Parliament may suddenly find his decree nullified by a court. He can change the law and issue it again, so that nothing is achieved except a brief embarrassment, but a token process has been maintained. South Africa has some of the world's most fearsome security laws, which bypass the courts completely. Its political police can detain anyone they like without warning or warrant or any reasons given, and hold him indefinitely, incommunicado and in solitary confinement. They can refuse to let the prisoner see his lawyer or his doctor. They can interrogate him for as long as they like in any manner they like. Though publicly denied, torture is condoned. Yet, after all this concealment and remoteness from the protection of the law, if anyone should die in this brutal and secret process, as many have, an inquest is held in open court where often the most horrifying details become public. In the end the police are always exonerated by the state-employed magistrates who preside over these inquests, but the disclosures are hugely embarrassing nonetheless. Thus a brutal authoritarianism presents periodic glimpses into its own gulag. That is the paradox par excellence.

IT WAS A MATTER of singular importance in the shaping of the Afrikaner mind that the Cape was settled not by the Dutch government but by a commercial company. The VOC had the power to make laws and to conduct its own military operations, but its impelling motivation was profit, not patriotism. It had no interest in establishing a colony in South Africa, only in operating a service utility that would provision its scurvy-stricken ships plying the trade route to the East with fresh meat and vegetables. The outpost was to consist of a fort and a garden, no more, which the Company wanted to be as small and as economical as possible. It was not interested in developing the place or in exploiting its resources. The Cape was simply a base that was to have a minimum of involvement with the locality and its inhabitants.

26. Heribert Adam and Hermann Giliomee, *Ethnic Power Mobilized* (New Haven, 1979), p. 29.

When Van Riebeeck led his tiny fleet of three ships, the *Goede Hoop*, *Reyger*, and *Dromedaris*, into Table Bay on April 6, 1652, his instructions were specific. He was to keep his distance from the indigenous inhabitants. He was to trade with them, exchanging trinkets for cattle to supply the ships with meat, but he was not to conquer them, seek to colonize them, or employ them. Such interaction, the Company knew from experience, would inevitably involve it in unnecessary trouble and expenditure, and it was the bottom line that counted. The station commander was told bluntly to stick to his cabbage patch.

Thus was established a settlement whose identification with Africa was minimal. From day one it was an outpost of Europe set apart from the continent in which it was located and from the people among whom it had to live. This was the premise on which the bitter-almond hedge was planted, and on which Commissioner Van Goens dreamed up his scheme for turning the Cape peninsula into an island. An island of Europe, separated from the continent of Africa. It was in keeping with this vision that in drafting its legal definitions for the new settlement, the VOC classified the Khoikhoi as "aliens": foreigners in their native continent, which had become a piece of Europe.

Yet these people who came without intending to settle stayed to become the most permanent and ineradicable settlers in all of Africa. They cut their ties with Europe, called themselves Afrikaners, and evolved a new language called Afrikaans, yet they continued to set themselves apart from Africa and its people.

The economic imperative of the VOC had other consequences, too. Preoccupation with costs meant that Van Riebeeck was under constant pressure to reduce staff. He reckoned he needed 163 men to run the settlement and man the fort; the Company told him to cut back to 100. The answer was to lay off some of the men and compensate them with land where they could grow produce and sell it to the Company. So four years after Van Riebeeck's arrival the first nine "free burghers" left the payroll and were settled on twenty-eight-acre farms along the fertile banks of the Liesbeeck River in what are today Cape Town's affluent white southern suburbs.

This suited everyone except the unfortunate Khoikhoi, whose traditional grazing lands these were. Any thought that the land might belong to the Khoikhoi, that their age-old usage gave them a prior right to it or at least the right to be consulted about its expropriation, simply never occurred to the settlers. Van Riebeeck's instructions were not to become involved in disputes with the Khoikhoi, yet he commandeered their land for the "free burghers" and was astonished and aggrieved when they took exception to this and rose up to fight black South Africa's first war of resistance. When the brief conflict was over Van Riebeeck lamely claimed title to the land by right of conquest. As he wrote in an official dispatch to the Company directors, the Heeren XVII, or Lords Seventeen, in Amsterdam:

> The reason advanced by them for making war upon us . . . [was] that they think they had cause for revenge . . . upon people who had come to take and to occupy the land which had been their own in all ages, turning with the plough and cultivating permanently all the best land, and keeping them off the ground upon which they had been accustomed to depasture their cattle, so that they must consequently now seek their subsistence by depasturing the land of other people, from which nothing could arise but disputes with their neighbours; insisting so strenuously upon the point of restoring to them their own land, that we were at length compelled to say that they had entirely forfeited that right, through the war which they had waged against us, and that we were not inclined to restore it, as it had now become the property of the Company by the sword and the laws of war.[27]

Thus was established the right of conquest and a tradition that the land was the white South Africans' for the taking. It was the first act in a long process of land dispossession that combined with slavery and cheap labour to create the institutions and the habits of the apartheid society.

These "free burghers" were the first white South Africans, cast loose in a vast continent that had no proper government or civil administration. The Company issued regulations restricting their activities, but, chafing at these, the "free burghers" began moving inland beyond its reach, gobbling up the land they now believed they were freely entitled to, and the VOC was not disposed to incur the expense of trying to pursue and police them except in the most token way. And so, as their numbers slowly grew, there took place at the southern tip of Africa one of the most remarkable settlements in the history of colonialism. A small and scattered community of white men drifted beyond the effective reach of any law or administrative arm and lost themselves like so many Robinson Crusoes in the vastness of Africa for a century and a half.

For almost the length of time that separates us today from Napoleon they lived on their own, out of touch with the world, four months' sailing time from Europe and another one or two by ox wagon from where the ships called in, without roads, railways, newspapers, telephones, radio, or even a postal service. The only communication was through the occasional itinerant trader or ivory hunter who might bring

27. Donald Moodie, op. cit., p. 206.

some snippets of news from Cape Town. There was little immigration to bring a transfusion of new blood and ideas. To the extent that their numbers increased, it was by the fruitfulness of their own seed.

There were no books and no schools among these solitary Trekboers, only the great States Bible that had been commissioned by the Synod of Dort, which each family carried with it and which was read with solemn ceremony and increasing difficulty as literacy dwindled. One pictures the bearded patriarchs gathering their families about them in their little mud-walled cottages each evening and, with fingers tracing the line of Gothic print in the flickering candlelight, laboriously intoning the difficult High Dutch phrases in which the Word of God was written. It is easy to imagine that in such a harsh and lonely environment those sonorous words took on a direct and personal meaning. This was the God of Abraham talking directly to his people of their circumstances.

Moreover, what was contained in those pages was the sum total of all knowledge. There was no other source, no other education. Here was the only truth and the only authority, none of it to be questioned. There were few ministers and fewer churches around, so that the patriarchal family head became his own theologian, interpreting the difficult texts as best he could and applying them with the literal mind of elemental man to the personal world in which he lived.

But it would be an exaggeration to portray all the early Afrikaners in this same form. Many lingered closer to Cape Town and thus to the one thin line of communication with the outside world that there was. They settled in the lush valleys of the Boland where, instructed by the Huguenots, with their Latin understanding of a Mediterranean climate, they grew wheat and made wine and established a plantation society of some pretension, with grand gabled homes and carriages on fine estates with plenty of slaves. Though they never claimed the aristocratic ancestry that the Virginians did, the Afrikaners of the western Cape did acquire just a touch of that same lifestyle of leisured grace and easy hospitality that set them apart from their rougher-hewn brethren out east. It was a distinction that was to become a permanent dichotomy in the Afrikaner *volk*.

Always it was the most intransigent and disputatious spirits who trekked farthest, drawing ever deeper into isolation as they went. The isolation sank into their souls, feeding their pride and intensifying their obduracy. Each man became king on his own estate, unwilling to tolerate any challenge to his authority or questioning of his judgment. It made them a schismatic people who never acquired the habit of settling disputes through negotiation and compromise. Instead they would turn their backs on any disagreement, pull up stakes, and trek on to new ground where their authority would once again be unchallenged. Thus, as the result of a kind of Darwinian process of selective migration, the farther north you go in South Africa today the more virulent the brand of Afrikaner nationalism you will encounter.

As befits its location in the Southern Hemisphere, South Africa has inverted the geography of American racism and developed a "Deep North" problem of white extremism, with the rural fastnesses of the northern Transvaal its equivalent of Mississippi and Louisiana. That is where Dr. Andries Treurnicht's far rightist Conservative party and the neo-Nazi Afrikaner Resistance Movement have their strongholds, while a gentler, if not exactly liberal, outlook has been the tradition of the Cape Afrikaners, especially those of Cape Town itself and its environs.

As you drive north along the straight ribbon of road that stretches across the flat plains beyond Pretoria, you will come after about 150 miles upon a sign in the Dutch of pioneer days that says *De Nyl Zyn Oog*—The Eye of the Nile. The little dirt road it points to leads to a farm of that name where there is a reedy swamp with bubbling springs whose waters turn into a stream called the Magalakwena River, a modest tributary of the Limpopo, which drains these wide plains and forms South Africa's northern border with Zimbabwe.

Here the most extreme of all the Afrikaner trekker groups arrived in the middle of the nineteenth century, inspired by the apocalyptic imagination of a political and religious fundamentalist named Johan Adam Enslin. Calling themselves the *Jerusalemgangers*, they were following what they took to be the travel instructions in Enslin's big States Bible in a fantastic attempt to trek all the way up Africa to Jerusalem and the Promised Land. When they reached the Magalakwena after heavy rains and saw the stream flowing northward, they believed they had reached the headwaters of the Nile. Scouts were sent ahead and, espying a conical-shaped hill nearby that local black tribesmen told them was a resting place of spirits, reported back excitedly that the pyramids were just a few miles ahead.

As it turned out, what the Jerusalemgangers had reached was the edge of the tsetse fly belt. With their cattle decimated, further trek was impossible. They settled where they were, establishing the town of Nylstroom, or Nilestream. The river flowing through it is still called the Nile. Nylstroom is today the main town in Treurnicht's personal constituency of Waterberg, which is the most solidly far-rightist polling region in all of South Africa.

By contrast, Treurnicht's party has made little headway in Cape Province, which instead has become the scene of left-wing dissent in Afrikaner ranks. While Treurnicht scored an important breakthrough in the Deep North during the white election of 1987, a reformist revolt in the gracious old winelands around Cape Town came close to unseating the powerful provincial leader of the ruling National party.

BUT I AM LEAPING ahead too fast, and skimming too easily over the major role that Cape Afrikaners played in the forging of Afrikaner nationalism and its ideology of apartheid. It is enough at this stage to point to the different strains of attitudes that evolved between those who trekked and those who did not. Strike the average between them and you will have the core around which the mind of the Afrikaner was shaped during the six generations they were lost in Africa: a people who missed the momentous developments of eighteenth-century Europe, the age of reason in which liberalism and democracy were born and which had its climax in the great revolution of the French bourgeoisie; a people who spent that time instead in a deep solitude which, if anything, took them back to an even more elementary existence than the seventeenth-century Europe their forebears had left; a people who became, surely, the simplest and most backward fragment of Western civilization in modern times.

As C. W. de Kiewiet puts it, it was in the long quietude of the eighteenth century that the Boer race was formed. Their isolation froze them in time, causing their imagination to lie fallow and their intellects to become inert. It bred in them "a tenacity of purpose, a power of silent endurance and the keenest self-respect."[28] Above all it bred a fierce individualism. The early Afrikaners developed, in their way, perhaps the most boundless individualism that has existed anywhere. They built few villages and felt cramped if they lived within sight of a neighbour's chimney smoke. They had almost no institutions. Each man was absolute master of his own affairs, self-reliant, unencumbered, free. Here was the very opposite of *ubuntu* and the communal black African to whom "people are people through other people." Here was the ultimate loner who needed to take no one else into account. The Afrikaners would come together briefly in times of danger, but otherwise each would be on his own, doing his own thing. So he became inward-looking, concerned only with himself and his immediate family, unaccustomed to relating to others or to considering the views and feelings of outsiders. It made him proud and self-assertive, but it also made him stubborn and intolerant. So the Afrikaners became a disputatious and schismatic peo-

28. C. W. de Kiewiet, *A History of South Africa: Social and Economic* (London, 1941), p. 17.

ple, with groups constantly splitting and moving away from perceived interference toward greater autonomy.

This individualism and schismatic trend has been repressed in the latter-day phase of Afrikaner nationalism, during which a strict conformity has been imposed to discipline and contain it within the family, as it were, with public disagreement regarded as a danger to the *volk* and an act of ethnic disloyalty. But it remains part of the national character still, a constant source of inner tension that is breaking out into the open once again as apartheid runs into its crisis of impracticability and the civil religion begins to decline as a bonding force. The self-centredness has remained, however, intensified by a history of struggle and suffering and a sense of persecution into a national narcissism, a massive preoccupation with the group self—with the exigencies of Afrikaner identity and self-determination and survival—which has become oblivious to the pain of others, blind to its own cruelty, devoid of empathy, and heedless of the self-threatening enmity it is creating all around it.

In other respects the early Afrikaners came more and more to resemble the indigenous Africans. Out on the eastern frontier, as the Trekboers drifted farther and farther from what little commerce there was and adapted to conditions that favoured pastoralism above agriculture, they became seminomadic, subsistence-economy cattle herders little different from the black tribesmen into whose territory they were moving. They settled the land haphazardly, living in tented wagons or simple mud-walled cottages like those of the blacks. To the extent that they had a social structure at all, it consisted of large families extensively intermarried and headed by patriarchal figures of chiefly authority.

In all that they became a white tribe of Africa, adapting to their environment and, like the black tribes, living in partnership with it rather than trying to tame and exploit it. But they continued to refuse any identification with those black tribes. They had little that was superior in either skills or education, but they possessed guns and a religious faith that established both a physical and an imagined superiority that set them apart absolutely.

From their earliest settlement, slavery had induced in the frontiersmen a belief that hard physical toil was the task of the black people. Slaves were black or coloured; so were the indigenous inhabitants. Manual labour was their work, "kaffirs' " work, the predestined function of a servile race, the children of Ham, the hewers of wood and drawers of water. So Afrikaner society developed in a peculiarly stunted way: lacking both an intellectual and an entrepreneurial class, it failed also to develop a working or an artisan class. What evolved was a semiliterate peasantry with the social status of a landed gentry.

Their antipathy to physical toil did not mean they were idle, these early Afrikaners. They lived hard lives, hunting their meat and herding their flocks in the hardest of continents. They had the courage and tenacity and innovative genius of people who could plunge into the unknown and survive alone. But they did not do "kaffirs' " work. Nor did they mix with "kaffirs" except as master and servant and sometimes, in dark and guilt-ridden encounters, for sex. A certain paternalism arose in some of the work relationships, but overall their attitude engendered a deep-rooted and pervasive racial prejudice.

Twenty-five years after Van Riebeeck established his settlement a man named Hendrik Bidault shouted *"Ik ben een Africaander!"* when Company officials came to arrest him for disorderly conduct. Afrikaners have sanctified this cry as their first declaration of identity, but from the moment Bidault uttered it he and his descendants in fact denied their Africanness and set themselves apart, behind bitter hedges of physical and mental separation.

CHAPTER THREE

The Third Man

> I contend that we are the finest race in the world, and that the more of the world we inhabit, the better it is for the human race. Just fancy, those parts that are at present inhabited by the most despicable specimens of human beings, what an alteration there would be if they were brought under Anglo-Saxon influence.
>
> CECIL JOHN RHODES

THE MIND OF South Africa, shaped from the beginning by irony and paradox, had no more seminally perplexing experience than the juxtaposition of opposites that began with the British annexation of the Dutch Cape Colony in 1795. Having been lost in Africa for a century and a half and become the most backward fragment of European civilization on earth, the Afrikaners were suddenly confronted on their arcadian frontier by the world's most modern society, which at that moment was leading the way into the age of industrialization. The black tribes, having encountered one kind of expansionist white intruder, who engaged them aggressively but had limited destructive power, now encountered another, who spoke softly of Christian values and humanitarian ideals but introduced the concepts of total war and territorial conquest. This social variation on the theme of the eternal triangle inflamed group passions and created the conflicting nationalisms that have brought South Africa to its present impasse.

It is strange that the British took so long in coming. English ships had been sailing around the Cape, plying their own lucrative spice trade with the East, ever since Sir Francis Drake called there in 1580 on his voyage of circumnavigation and proclaimed it to be "the fairest Cape we saw in the whole circumference of the earth," yet no thought was given to wresting it from the flimsy hold of the Dutch VOC. But now, with Britain engaged with France in a final sprint of the last leg of capitalism's relay race, the Cape suddenly took on a new strategic importance. It commanded the route to India, Britain's most important overseas possession and the source of its spice trade; and with Napoleon ranging Europe and the Levant Britain decided to occupy the Cape to protect this vital sea link. She came gently at first, at the request of the Prince of Orange when French troops invaded Holland, but this brief interlude ended with the Peace of Amiens in 1803. She came back in force three years later as the struggle with France intensified. The Union Jack that was hoisted then was not lowered again until South Africa declared herself a republic in 1961, after 155 years of ambivalent step-parentage. And even after the flag was gone the English-speaking South Africans remained to continue the equivocal relationship and play their curious role as the third man in a drama cast for two.

The impact on the Afrikaners of the British arrival was enormous. Having missed the eighteenth century, they had the nineteenth burst in on them. Having lived as free men with almost no administrative restraints, the rule of law and pervasive orderliness of a major imperial power arrived to entangle them. The intrusion at first irked then angered the Afrikaners, and over time it produced a legacy of grievance that fired their nationalism and turned a community of undisciplined individualists into a cohesive national unit that baffled the world with its obduracy.

The impact on the blacks was no less profound. By the time the black tribes encountered the Trekboers on the eastern frontier, the latter had adopted a lifestyle not much different from their own. Only with the arrival of the British did they feel the destabilizing force of the modern world on their ancient institutions. Though the Afrikaners acquired the notoriety, it was the British who first broke black power, crushing the tribes in war, annexing their territory, and eroding their institutions with Christianization, education, and finally industrialization and urbanization.

In truth the British created modern South Africa. Whereas the Afrikaners left Europe behind them, the English brought it with them. They opened up the country economically where the Afrikaners had merely penetrated it physically, bringing with them the spirit of a new age. They turned a subsistence-farming economy into a *Wirtschaftswunder*, discovering the world's most fabulous deposits of diamonds and gold and using these to launch the continent's only full-blown industrial revolution and build its most powerful economy.

The British dominated the Afrikaners economically and defeated them militarily, but they lost out to them politically, and the English-speaking South Africans are now a curiously helpless and rather pathetic community who do not identify with either side in the conflict of nationalisms they helped to create and cannot define a role for themselves in between. They remain apart from and slightly aloof toward the Afrikaner Nationalists whose political extremism jars them, but they shrink from the numbers and perceived radicalism of the Black Nationalists. Faced with a choice between two unattractive alternatives they have opted out, withdrawing into a private world of business and home and sunlit leisure. Politically they have atrophied. They arrived in Africa as dynamic entrepreneurs and imperial visionaries, but they have become politically powerless in the country they dominate economically, and they have no vision of South Africa's future or their role in it.

In part this is a matter of numbers. The English-speaking South Africans number 1,720,000 out of a total white population of 4,900,000, so that at an early stage it became an unwritten convention that the leader of any political party that appealed to both language groups in the whites-only electorate would have to be an Afrikaner. Since the civil service was also dominated by Afrikaners, the English-speakers felt shut out of all key positions in the political system and resorted instead to trying to play a game of indirect rule through Afrikaner surrogates. With the growth of Afrikaner nationalism that, too, became increasingly difficult until in the end the English simply left politics to the Afrikaners while they concentrated on the economic sector. They comforted themselves with the notion that politics was in any event a dirty game—particularly in a situation that required the constant subjugation and control of the large black population—best left to people with fewer qualms about doing what had to be done.

It is also a matter of identity. The English-speaking community does not burn with a sense of grievance or sense of mission. It has no positive, purposeful creed. It lacks cohesion: it is an amorphous community with little sense of any collective identity. They do not even have a proper name: "English-speaking South Africans" is an appellation so vague as to make them almost anonymous. They define themselves more by what they are not than by what they are—and, above all, they are not Afrikaners. As Alan Paton put it:

> The white English-speaking people of South Africa have only one thing in common and that is their language. They consist of many groups. There are those who are attracted by any South African who holds the same ideals as they do. There are those whose whole life appears to be bound up in business. There are the rich, whose children go to schools for the rich. Many of them support the Progressive Federal Party and the New Republic Party, the successor to the United Party. Some support the National Party, and if they achieve prominence thereby, they are regarded as having done something rather reprehensible. And there are a great many English-speaking people who just don't want to know, and

> don't want their children to know either. While Smuts was alive they could leave it all to him. We are a mixed bunch, and we don't have the bonds that bind so many Afrikaners together; we never had a Karoo, we never trekked, we never developed a new language, we never were defeated in war, we never had to pick ourselves up out of the dust.[1]

The British settlers never cut ties with their country of origin the way the Afrikaners did, nor is their commitment to South Africa so total and irrevocable. However long an English-speaker or his forebears may have been in South Africa, he remains also a member of a larger international community which he knows that, in extremis, he can always join. It lessens his commitment to South Africa as it broadens his sense of cultural identity. He is not engaged in the politics of survival that the Afrikaner is. It makes him more relaxed. This means that the Afrikaners view the English-speaking South Africans as second-class citizens and lukewarm patriots, which cripples them politically.

Above all, the English-speaking South Africans have been paralyzed politically by their own historic conservatism. Their tradition of justice and pragmatism, a broad live-and-let-live philosophy, has meant that they cannot outdo the Afrikaner Nationalists at their game of racial domination. But—and here we are talking of the majority, the average—they have also inherited from their Victorian forebears of the Pax Britannica an ingrained conservatism and a sense of racial superiority that has made them unable to face up to apartheid's radical alternative. They have dithered ineffectually in the middle. They have failed where the vast majority of white people in Africa have failed—in not recognizing that the best hope for white and black alike lies in a shared society.

Margaret Ballinger, a doughty white liberal who was a special representative for blacks in the South African Parliament in the days before apartheid abolished such leftover tokens of imperial paternalism, once suggested to me in conversation that if Prime Minister Jan Smuts's United party had narrowly won the 1948 general election instead of narrowly losing it to Daniel Malan's National party, Afrikaner nationalism might never have come to power.[2] Her theory was that Smuts, jolted out of his complacency, would have thrown open South Africa's doors to the wave of assisted postwar emigration from Europe that boosted the populations of Australia, Canada, and other parts of the

1. Alan Paton, *The Afrikaners and the English* (Optima, Sept. 1981), p.96.

2. In a shock general-election result not unlike Winston Churchill's postwar defeat, South Africa's internationally acclaimed wartime leader, Field Marshal J. C. Smuts, was ousted by a hairsbreadth eight seats: the National party and its allies won 79 seats, to 71 of the United party and its associates.

Commonwealth. As it was, sixty thousand immigrants entered South Africa in the year before the election, a number that could easily have been doubled had Smuts not been sensitive to Afrikaner accusations that he was trying to plough them under numerically. Mrs. Ballinger, who knew Smuts well, believed that is exactly what he would have done if he had been spurred by an election fright. Under Commonwealth rules, new immigrants from Britain could become naturalized in two years. In the five years before the next general election Smuts could have offset the Afrikaner Nationalists' electoral majority and ensured that his United Party won in 1953 and remained in power thereafter. Afrikaner nationalism, thwarted at the post, would have lost its fervour and withered on the vine. As things turned out, Malan's narrow victory allowed him to stop the immigration programme, remove mixed-race "coloureds" from the voters' rolls, begin gerrymandering electoral constituencies, and ensure that the National party remained in power thereafter.

The intriguing question is, how different would South Africa have been if Mrs. Ballinger's scenario had worked out? Afrikaner nationalism would have dwindled, and its ideology of apartheid would never have been implemented as national policy. English-speaking South Africa would have ruled instead, albeit with the help of Afrikaner moderates, pursuing a more pragmatic course that would have tried to maintain its Commonwealth membership and its good relations with the Western world. But as decolonization swept the world, along with demands for majority rule and an end to segregation, how would such an Anglicized South Africa have responded?

The short answer is simply to look north to Rhodesia. Here, essentially, was a model of English-speaking South Africa, established as a kind of extra colony by that quintessential English-speaking South African of the nineteenth century, Cecil John Rhodes, in an attempt to bypass the obstruction to his imperial dreams posed by the Afrikaners in their Voortrekker republics. Its spirit was that of the English-speaking South Africans: most of its white population came from South Africa, speaking English with the same clipped accent and flattened vowels, adopting the same attitude of contemptuous superiority toward the Afrikaners to the south of them and the same blend of paternalistic benevolence and social distance to blacks. The Rhodesians never pursued a policy of apartheid, which they considered crude and distasteful; they talked of "partnership" rather than domination, and of maintaining "standards" rather than racial identity, but the system they imposed was segregationist and discriminatory and designed to keep the white minority in overall control. It was less dogmatic, less severe, less overt, and more hypocritical. In the end it proved no less inflexible or more capable of averting its own revolutionary overthrow. The revolutionary war it provoked resulted in 35,000 deaths; if apartheid South Africa, three times larger in population, suffers 100,000 deaths through its transitional upheavals, it will have done no worse.

But perhaps, because racial extremism never rose as high in Rhodesia as it has in South Africa, the polarization between black and white there was less extreme as well. Zimbabwe, as the country is now called, is conspicuously relaxed in its race relations today. In part this is because most of its hard-line white racists left for South Africa rather than endure the unendurable when black rule came in 1980. In part, too, it is because of the exemplary gestures of reconciliation made by Zimbabwe's black leader, Robert Mugabe. Perhaps there is an element of postwar catharsis. But perhaps, too, the milder nature of English-led white rule, for all its paternalism and perfidy, and the absence of an ideology as declamatory and as excoriating as apartheid, left an atmosphere in which it was easier for black and white to set aside the past than is likely to be the case in South Africa.

That may not seem much of a political legacy for a proud people to leave their country, but there is another side to the picture. Of those white South Africans who have had the moral courage to recognize and accept the logical alternative to apartheid, the great majority have been English-speakers. From the moment the first substantial number of British settlers landed at the Cape in 1820, there was among them a minority of enlightened and concerned people who brought with them the habits of free expression and the ideals of democracy. They had been struggling for these principles in Britain and they continued their struggle in South Africa. They campaigned for the abolition of slavery and cried out against injustices inflicted on the Khoikhoi and the frontier tribes. They lobbied for more equitable laws. They fought for a free press. In sum, they established a liberal tradition that has endured through six generations and today constitutes the core of a dissenting element in the white population. Though small, it is vocal, brave, and energetic and has managed through all the dark years of apartheid to reach through the tangled growth of the bitter-almond hedge and maintain an empathetic contact with black South Africans. Some of these white dissenters have been jailed for what they have done. A few have died. Some have been driven into exile and some have left the country in despair. Others soldier on in the face of daunting odds. They are hated by the other whites but acknowledged by the blacks. They are a unique element that did not exist to the same degree in any other African country facing the prospect of transition to black rule, and to some extent they are a counterinfluence to the polarizing effects of apartheid.

In sum, it is not so much what the English did as what they did to others that has been their major influence on events in South Africa. Politically powerless themselves, their actions have spawned political movements, provoked political attitudes, and implanted political ideas that have given shape to the whole conflict.

It began with their arrival. The first British settlers who landed in South Africa in 1820 came in all innocence to establish farms on the eastern Cape frontier. Nobody told them that the real purpose of their settlement was military rather than agricultural, and that the reason they were being packed close together on small, uneconomic allotments was to close a disputed border rather than to grow produce on allegedly fertile land for sale on a market that did not yet exist. Not surprisingly the project was an economic disaster, but its indirect effects in other spheres still reverberate.

Because the agricultural settlement failed, the desperate settlers moved into other occupations, starting towns and businesses and embarking on the economic revolution that was to create modern South Africa. By closing the frontier the British settlers triggered thirty years of war, flight, misery, and adventure: the greatest social upheaval in the history of Africa, with thousands of people, black and white, trekking in crisscross patterns across the subcontinent, bumping bloodily into one another as they went. When finally the turmoil subsided the Afrikaners had penetrated a thousand miles to the north, and the black Africans had been dispossessed of 90 percent of their land.

Thus, at a stroke, the English-speaking South Africans created both a legacy of Afrikaner grievance and the basis of an industrial economy with a landless black peasantry that provided the captive labour force to service it. Though they were never the main actors, they produced the conditions out of which both Afrikaner and Black African nationalism emerged. Like the straight man in the comedy turn, they were the foil, never the star—but without them there could be no show.

THE BRITAIN THAT the first settlers left was turbulent, too, as it made its rough passage out of the old world into the modern one. Here was the world's first industrial revolution, ushering in an altogether new society, a new age, for which none of the institutions and ideas of the previous centuries would suffice. The nineteenth century was a time of transition, dynamic and disrupting and filled with ambiguities—ambiguities which the first British settlers took with them to the Cape and made part of the founding culture of the English-speaking South Africans. As the Cambridge historian G. Kitson Clark has put it, it was a time when there was a "strange compromise between what claimed to be liberal and democratic and what was certainly authoritarian, supported uneasily by what was traditional."[3]

Five years before the settlers embarked for South Africa, the Duke of Wellington had finally crushed Napoleon at Waterloo. That had established Britain as the world's undisputed leading power. Nearly a century of peace lay ahead during which Britain could develop her industrial energies virtually unhindered, spreading her imperial net around the globe to obtain raw materials and establish new markets for her goods. Her industries burgeoned spectacularly. The number of powerlooms increased from 14,000 in 1820 to 100,000 in 1833; raw cotton imports rocketed from 82 million tons in 1815 to 1 billion in 1860; iron output went from 150,000 tons in 1800 to nearly 1,400,000 tons in 1840. This created a huge appetite for coal to feed the new machines, which in turn demanded increased production of steam pumps, hauling engines, safety lamps, and wood props—all of which required the swift expansion of canals, railways, and steamships, which again cried out for more coal. So coal production more than trebled between 1800 and 1845.[4]

This economic leap ahead brought unprecedented wealth to the nation—the value of British exports trebled in the first two decades of the century—but unprecedented misery also. Teeming industrial cities erupted in what had been the quiet countryside of Merrie England, and in them the once contented handcraftsmen became an ill-fed and overworked proletariat. Britain's golden age was also the Dickensian dark age of *Oliver Twist* and *Nicholas Nickleby, Hard Times* and *Dombey and Son.* The grim conditions and the greedy exploitation marked the start of the class conflict.

> The new conditions tended to a weakening of sympathy between the classes. Hitherto the landed aristocracy had understood the villagers, their immemorial neighbours, and some part of them had been in alliance with the traders of the towns. Now things were different. . . . Few among the gentry, few among the rich middle class, understood the feelings of the grimy slum-dwellers. Understanding little and therefore fearing much, the ruling class regarded the poor almost as a subject race whose poverty and ignorance might prompt, as in France, to violence.[5]

The tensions became enormous. The old aristocratic class still ruled under an anachronistic system based on privilege and patronage, while

3. G. Kitson Clark, *The Making of Victorian England* (Cambridge, 1962), p. 51.

4. J. R. M. Butler, *A History of England 1815–1918* (London, 1928), p. 31.

5. Ibid., pp. 15–16.

the rising common man clamoured for democracy. The popular cry was for political reform, but the government stuck stubbornly to the status quo. A wave of libertarian ideology swept the country. This was the age that gave birth to Jeremy Bentham's Utilitarianism, Robert Owen's Utopian Socialism, Samuel Taylor Coleridge's harrowing poetry, and William Cobbett's flaming journalism. Popular organizations arose alongside the literary works: the shoemaker Thomas Hardy's London Corresponding Society, a series of "friendly societies" that were really the forerunners of trade unions, and a network of mammoth political unions organized by a London tailor named Francis Place.

Riots and strikes broke out all over the country. There was frame-breaking in the lace districts for which twelve men were executed. An attempt was made on the life of the Prince Regent. The unrest culminated in the Peterloo Massacre of 1819, when a platoon of cavalry charged a crowd of demonstrators on a field in Manchester, killing nine and injuring scores. There was a surge of popular fury. The government responded with repression. A session of what became known as the "Savage Parliament" passed six laws permitting arbitrary arrest and drastically curtailing freedom of the press, freedom of speech, and the right to hold public meetings.

It was a classic prerevolutionary situation, a reenactment of events in France a mere thirty years before. Yet no revolution occurred. Alone in all Europe during this period of tumultuous transition, Britain made its way into the age of popular democracy by a process of evolution. Three reform acts, passed in 1832, 1867, and 1884, left the working class fully enfranchised by the end of the century. It was a rare example of a ruling elite relinquishing power by a process of evolutionary reform rather than being forced from power.

How did it happen? Élie Halevy, a distinguished French historian who was fascinated by this question, has suggested that the primary reason was the quietistic influence of the great religious revival initiated by John Wesley and George Whitefield, which peaked among the working and lower-middle classes at this time. "We shall explain by this movement," Halevy wrote, "the extraordinary stability which English society was destined to enjoy throughout the period of revolution and crisis."[6] He reckoned social, political, and economic conditions were such that Britain would almost certainly have plunged into revolution had the workers found militant leaders among the middle class. Instead, "the elite of the working class, the hard-working and capable bourgeois,

6. Élie Halevy, *England in 1815: A History of the English People in the Nineteenth Century*, vol. 1, trans. E. I. Watkin and D. A. Barker (New York, 1949), p. 387.

had been imbued by the evangelical movement with a spirit from which the established order had nothing to fear."[7]

This evangelical movement, which began with Wesley's Methodism, then widened to include Presbyterians, Baptists, and independents in a broad Nonconformist condemnation of the established Anglican Church, was essentially a movement of and for the new underclass of the industrial revolution. Wesley, initiating Calvinism's last great surge, broke its taboo of the predestined elect and reached out to "Christ's poor" with the dramatically simple message that all could be saved if they would give themselves to the Lord.

> Outcasts of men, to you I call,
> Harlots, and publicans, and thieves!
> He spreads his arms to embrace you all;
> Sinners alone His grace receives:
> No need for him the righteous have;
> He came the lost to seek and save.
>
> Come, O my guilty brethren, come,
> Groaning beneath your load of sin!
> His bleeding heart shall make you room,
> His open side shall take you in;
> He calls you now, invites you home:
> Come, O my guilty brethren, come.[8]

The groaning outcasts responded enthusiastically to this opportunity for eternal salvation. It offered them not only the consolation of knowing that they were likely to be compensated for their present sufferings and grievances but also a satisfying feeling of revenge against their oppressors by imagining their torments to come.[9] Thus the evangelical movement mobilized the working class, but effectively neutralized their anger and militancy with its promise of redemption. Unlike the revolutionary Puritans of the seventeenth century, Wesley's Methodists were under no injunction to establish God's ideal society on earth. Instead they were enjoined to suffer this life's hardships with fortitude in the knowledge that there would be compensation in the life hereafter. It was the basis of Marx's gibe about religion being the "opium of the people."

Even at the time of the American War of Independence, when he

7. Ibid., pp. 424–5.

8. Quoted by E. P. Thompson, *The Making of the English Working Class* (New York, 1966), p. 37.

9. Ibid., p. 34.

published two pamphlets urging loyalty on the colonists and the British public, Wesley was on the side of conservatism, but it was the French Revolution that really brought this to the fore. The Jacobins radiated a spirit of irreligion that repelled these born-again Christians, while the bloody excesses of the Place de Grève and the grim war of survival against Napoleon created a climate of opinion in England that was hostile to all that had happened across the channel. At the height of the French Terror the Wesleyan body issued statutes demanding that their members show loyalty and obedience to the king of England and his government. "None of us," the statutes proclaimed, "shall either in writing or declaration speak lightly or irreverently of the Government. We are to observe that the oracles of God command us to be subject to the higher powers; and that honour to the King is therefore connected with the fear of God."

So the revolutionary spirit was contained and became law-abiding, respectable. The religious revival also gave shape to a ponderous middle-class morality, with the Victorian emphasis on thrift, temperance, and solid family virtues. Yet the clamour for democracy also continued, and the new spirit of Christian charity ushered in a more humanitarian age, with campaigns for the abolition of slavery and child labour and for penal and prison reform, all done within orderly and respectable bounds.

The great paradox, of course, as in seventeenth-century Holland, was that this upsurge of Christian piety and moral rectitude coincided with the rapacious thrust of imperialism. Once again one finds a society where contrapuntal themes crowd in with the density of a Bach fugue, prayerful yet avaricious, abstemious yet materialistic, liberal yet overweening, humanitarian yet militaristic, democratic yet authoritarian, abolishing slavery even as it sent its armies around the globe subjecting whole peoples to colonial bondage. These contradictions found their synthesis in the paternalistic liberalism which was the hallmark of Victorian England. As Britain's empire spread around the world and she became the self-appointed guardian to millions of the earth's inhabitants, Englishmen took on an air of smug superiority and came to believe that what they were doing was for the inestimable good of the less fortunate souls they were dominating. Thus the spirit of imperialism and democracy, of exploitation and Christian charity were reconciled in the notion of the White Man's Burden. "Surely of all 'rights of man,' " wrote Thomas Carlyle in 1839, "this right of the ignorant man to be guided by the wiser, to be, gently or forcibly, held in the true course by him, is the indisputablest."[10]

The settlers who went to South Africa in 1820 contained all these

10. Thomas Carlyle, *Chartism*, in *Works*, vol. 8, (New York, 1869), p. 73.

elements that characterized British society at that time. They were far more representative than Van Riebeeck's *grauw* were of Holland. With Britain in such a state of turbulence, with the bleakness and uncertainty of life in the industrial cities aggravated by a serious recession, which followed Waterloo and the repression after Peterloo, there was a scramble to emigrate to the newly acquired colonies. Englishmen hoped to find new opportunities and a freer society in the new world. When advertisements were posted offering free passage to South Africa and free land to farm there, an astonishing ninety thousand people applied for five thousand berths. The government, anxious to demonstrate an even-handed concern about the serious state of unemployment, chose the emigrants from all parts of the kingdom and all social classes except the aristocracy. It was a representative cross section of early nineteenth-century Britain: essentially conservative, respectable, God-fearing, and antirevolutionary, but including also a number who were filled with the humanistic and philanthropic concerns of the age.

Thus both the rampant materialism of the industrial revolution and the moral crusade of William Wilberforce's abolitionist movement and other campaigns to protect the aborigines of the new colonies went to South Africa, there to affect conflicting attitudes toward the blacks and, in their different ways, perplex the Afrikaners. The British settlers brought their energies and their skills and their ideals. They established towns and shops and banks and factories. They also established their little Nonconformist chapels, dotted about the countryside of the eastern Cape Province where they first settled and where some established a Methodist community called Salem.

A more radical element was added to these first English-speaking South Africans with the diamond rush to Kimberley in the 1870s and the gold rush to the Witwatersrand that followed it. These were adventurers and individual fortune-seekers, more irreverent and less puritanical than the 1820 Settlers. They injected a more dynamic entrepreneurial spirit into the small-town respectability of the established community. By then the great European revolution had passed another milestone, with the appearance of Marx and the socialist response to the growth of capitalism, so that a small strand of left-wing radicalism found its way into English-speaking South Africa along with the bankers and financiers as the country's own industrial revolution got under way. Later still came Jewish fugitives, first from Russia and Eastern Europe and then from Germany, to add both to these strands and to the intellectual life of the country, in which they played a part out of all proportion to their numbers.

But the core culture of the English-speaking South Africans remained essentially unchanged, essentially conservative, antirevolutionary, middle class. That is what it was when they first arrived in 1820, and that is what it is today.

THE DIVERSE COLLECTION of British families who were lowered into longboats and rowed through the surf to the desolate shores of Algoa Bay on the Cape Colony's east coast between April and July 1820 had one thing in common. They had been conned. Seldom can any group of migrants to a new country have been so grievously misled about the place they were going to or the true purpose of the scheme that was taking them there.

The place where they were to be settled "resembles a succession of parks," Lord Charles Somerset, the governor, had enthused in a report to the colonial office, "in which upon the most verdant carpet, Nature has planted an endless variety; the soil well adapted to cultivation is peculiarly fitted for cattle and pasturage." And in a later dispatch: "Here is indeed a very fine country upon which to employ and maintain a multitude of settlers. . . . This tract of country, particularly healthy for every description of cattle and sheep, well wooded, and having very fine springs in it, is very nearly uninhabited."[11]

It was a lie. The Suurveld, as the place's Afrikaans name indicates, is a sour-grass coastal plain suitable for winter pasturage and peculiarly unfitted for cultivation. The rainfall is erratic and the water sources, when they are flowing at all, are deep down in almost inaccessible gorges. Cattle can make out there, but the settlers were specifically discouraged from keeping them. They were to be market gardeners on hundred-acre allotments, growing vegetables on land more suitable for ranching (and where the Trekboers were running herds on six-thousand-acre tracts), and with no conceivable market closer than Cape Town—five hundred miles, or a month by ox wagon, to the west.

As for being "nearly uninhabited," the Suurveld was in fact hotly disputed territory between the eastward-moving Trekboers and the westward-moving black tribes. Five frontier wars had already been fought between them as they rustled one another's cattle and competed for the diminishing amount of land that had once seemed in such limitless supply but which they had gulped up in their two-way continental drift until now they were eyeball to eyeball among the aloes and euphorbias of the eastern Cape. Indeed this is why the British settlers were being placed there. The idea was to separate the Boers and the blacks with a closely settled community of agriculturalists who had no cattle to tempt

11. John Benyon, in *The 1820 Settlers, An Illustrated Commentary*, ed. Guy Butler (Cape Town, 1974), pp. 46–7.

the inveterate rustlers. It was to be a cheap way of closing and stabilizing the frontier without having to maintain a strong military and police presence.

The only trouble was, nobody told the settlers. True, Somerset did include a paragraph in his fanciful report to the effect that there might be some problems from "restless neighbours," but this was omitted when the project was debated in the House of Commons and it certainly got no mention in the official advertisements for the settlement scheme. Had it done so, a different type might have volunteered—more cavalier spirits in search of adventure, who might have been better prepared for the kind of challenges that lay ahead of them. They might have taken some guns with them and perhaps made some defensive arrangements in the design and positioning of their dwellings as they settled down on what turned out to be a battlefield.

As it was, the innocent carpenters, blacksmiths, shopkeepers, and labourers who straggled ashore at Algoa Bay with their wives and families had no idea that the real purpose behind the scheme that had brought them there was military rather than agricultural. They were lured by the offer of a free land allocation of 100 acres for every male adult—a perfectly adequate size for a farm in England—with seed and implements at special low prices to get them started. It was an opportunity to escape the grim times in Britain and to be elevated to the social status of landed gentry in what *The Times* blandly assured them would soon become "another England."[12] They had no idea that the scheme itself was an agricultural absurdity in the South African environment. No official with any experience of farming had ever been to the Suurveld to study its feasibility; the only on-the-spot survey of any kind had been done by an army officer whose interest was confined to the security advantages of having a dense settlement there. So in all their diversity, they came like lambs to the hardship and slaughter of the eastern frontier. They were to be involved in four devastating wars with the black tribes over the next thirty-three years in which more than 120 of them lost their lives.[13]

Disillusionment came quickly. Even as the longboats pitched through the surf the settlers regarded the "barren and unpromising" coastline with dismay. "The hearts of many sank within them," the Rev. William Shaw, the spiritual leader of a large party of Methodists, wrote in his diary, "and the inquiry was often reiterated—'Can this be the fine country, "the land of promise," to which we have been lured

12. *The Times*, London, June 18, 1819. Quoted in Guy Butler, op. cit., p. 65.

13. H. E. Hockly, *The Story of the 1820 Settlers* (Cape Town, 1957), p. 70.

by highly coloured descriptions, and by pictures drawn in our imaginations?' We are deceived and ruined, was the hasty conclusion of many."[14]

They were an extraordinarily mixed bag of people. Pringle the journalist, who arrived with the settlers and left a wad of illuminating reports on these first English-speaking South Africans, walked through their temporary tent camp on the beach the morning after his own party landed. They were, he said, "a motley and rather unprepossessing collection of people." He identified three broad groups: higher-class people who had picked the most pleasant spot on the beach among some evergreen bushes and with a nice view of the bay, who had pitched tents and had a few handsome carriages standing around. The people in this part of the camp were elegantly dressed. Some were sitting in the tents reading books, others were rambling among the shrubbery admiring the view. "I could not view this class of emigrants, with their elegant arrangements and appliances, without some melancholy misgivings as to their future fate," Pringle observed, "for they appeared utterly unfitted by former habits, especially the females, for roughing it (to use the expressive phraseology of the camp) through the first trying period of the settlement."

Nearby were what Pringle called the middling and lower classes, "respectable tradesmen and jolly farmers, with every appearance of substance and snug English comfort about them. There were watermen, fishermen, and sailors from the Thames and English sea-ports, with the reckless and weather-beaten look usual in persons of their perilous and precarious professions." There were "pale-visaged artisans and operative manufacturers, from London and other large towns, of whom doubtless a certain proportion were persons of highly reputable character and steady habits, but a far larger proportion were squalid in their aspect, slovenly in their attire and domestic arrangements, and discontented and discourteous in their demeanour." Finally there were pauper agricultural labourers, "healthier perhaps than the class just mentioned, but not apparently happier in mind."

Viewed overall, Pringle reckoned about a third were people of "real respectability of character" and some wordly substance. The rest were "persons who had hung loose upon society—low in morals or desperate in circumstances."[15]

The settlers' initial disillusionment deepened as they moved inland from the camp to the Suurveld. Boer farmers, commissioned by the

14. Quoted in Guy Butler, op. cit. p. 97.

15. Thomas Pringle, *Narrative of a Residence in South Africa*, op. cit., pp. 12–13.

government, drove them there in ox wagons, a journey that took a week over rough terrain with no roads. It was a strange, untamed land full of wild animals, scary insects, inverted seasons, and unfamiliar vegetation, and as they travelled their Boer guides shook their heads and sucked their pipes and told them dark tales about the savagery of the tribes and how difficult it would be to make out on a hundred acres in dry ranching country.

To disillusionment was added culture shock. The countryside was strange and the people they encountered were even stranger: brown-skinned Khoikhoi and black tribesmen dressed in skins and feathers or sometimes nothing at all. "Can you imagine," says Guy Butler, a settler descendant who still lives in the area, "what a shock it was to these Victorians, who dressed themselves from head to toe, to see people walking around naked?" One young girl was so horrified at the sight that she recorded the fact in her diary in code. Thus fear and prejudice were stimulated in minds that were already disposed to regard the English as a superior race whose position of dominance in the world was surely no historical accident. But still greater ravaging of race attitudes was to come.

The Suurveld—later to be called Albany—was precisely chosen as the settlement area. Eight years before, in the fourth of the frontier wars, the black tribes had been driven across the Great Fish River and now the colonial government was determined to establish that as a fixed frontier. The river, a sluggish brown stream that is reduced to a trickle for much of the year, makes a bend in its southeasterly course and for fifty miles flows northeast before turning southeast again to the sea. This bend formed a salient jutting into the black man's territory. The salient was the Suurveld—exposed, vulnerable, and bitterly disputed. The government wanted the settlers there.

In effect, it was a re-creation of Van Riebeeck's bitter-almond hedge. Once again a line was drawn between settler citizens and native aliens. Once again an attempt was made to establish an outpost of Europe and fence it off from the continent of Africa. Once again interaction was prohibited. The British settlers were forbidden, just as Van Riebeeck's had been, to employ the indigenous people on the other side of the barrier or to trade with them. And once again the hedge failed in everything except the mental attitudes it instilled. It made it impossible for whites to regard blacks as fellow South Africans.

For the settlers, the prohibition on interaction made life on their minifarms doubly impossible. Denied both slaves and hired hands there was no way they could make their enterprises viable. They could not hope to compete with the established Afrikaner farmers close to the Cape Town market, who had large farms and were allowed slaves. The only solution to their economic plight would have been to trade with the indigenous people across the border, but the distant authorities in the colonial capital said no. The purpose of the settlement was to separate the races, and interaction would defeat that purpose.

Interaction went ahead nonetheless, just as it had done before and just as it would do again in the age of apartheid. Economic necessity tends to override such political obstructions. This was as true for the blacks as it was for the settlers—indeed, more so, since the very notion of a fixed boundary was alien to them and in conflict with a lifestyle established over millennia. So when it came about that the boundary that the white authorities had so arbitrarily proclaimed cut the Xhosa tribespeople off from a major deposit of a red clay called *imbola*, an important cosmetic used in tribal ritual and for decorative purposes, the Xhosas kept right on coming across the Fish River to the clay pits as they had been doing for centuries.

For the settler families of John Stubbs and Thomas Mahoney, whose land adjoined the clay pits, it was a short-lived boon. They found the black folk eager to trade, and Stubbs and Mahoney were soon doing brisk business exchanging metal implements, beads, and trinkets for ivory, cattle, hides, and mimosa gum. Both sides were happy with the arrangement, but as word reached the colonial authorities they stepped in and stopped it. The blacks were forbidden to come to the pits for their imbola and a fort was built to stop them. Soon afterward, in a clash between a patrol from the fort and a group of blacks, Stubbs was killed. It was a classic example of the kind of mindless official interference with human relationships that has dogged South Africa, fouling up natural interaction and turning it into racial conflict.

To the wicked misrepresentation and blundering amateurishness of the settlement scheme was added disastrous bad luck. First blight, then rust, then locusts decimated the settlers' crops for three successive years. Scorching drought was followed by floods that washed away the flimsy wattle-and-daub dwellings the settlers had erected and carried their provisions and implements and few bits of furniture into the sea. By the end of 1823 the settlement was in ruins. The families, destitute and demoralized, abandoned their hopeless little allotments and trekked like so many refugees to such towns and villages as there were in the colony. Only a third remained on the land.

In that ignominious failure lay the seeds of South Africa's early development. The failed farmers turned in their desperation to the means of livelihood they had pursued back in industrial Britain. Former carpenters and wheelwrights went to Grahamstown and began making wagons; builders made bricks and opened contracting businesses; traders opened shops, or bought wagons from the carpenters and became travelling traders among the Trekboers, or moved into the black man's country to barter there and bring back goods that could be sold in the colony. Commerce flourished and the towns grew. Municipalities were established, councils were elected, and public affairs began. Thus as the urban and commercial development of South Africa got under way, the English-speaking South African established himself as a townsman and a businessman, increasingly in command of the economy, while the Afrikaner remained on the land. When, fifty years later, diamonds were discovered at Kimberley, some of these early settlers and their descendants were able to move in ahead of the rush with their expertise and accumulated resources, then leapfrog onto the goldfields of the Witwatersrand in the 1880s.

The departure of these future townsfolk gave breathing space to those who remained in the Suurveld. They took over the abandoned plots, enlarging their holdings to a more viable size and enabling them to start ranching cattle. Some moved onto sweet-grass pasturage a little farther inland where they found that sheep did well, and a flourishing new export industry was established. So the agricultural settlement was abandoned and the frontier farmers became pastoralists.

That changed everything. The one thing the colonial authorities had understood correctly is that cattle would mean rustling, and rustling would mean war. So the conflict that the settlers had been interposed to prevent now resumed because of them, and with greater intensity than before. The Xhosa were a people infatuated with cattle for whom the animals held an almost mystical importance. Young men in particular needed cattle for bride price, and a daring cattle raid was also a traditional way of proving one's manhood. The settlers, in breeding larger, sleeker cattle just across an unrecognized and unprotected frontier, presented the tribesmen with an irresistible temptation. The Xhosas stole the cattle and the settlers struck back with reprisal raids that eventually turned into plundering expeditions. Four times between 1834 and 1878 the conflict exploded into war, involving the people on both sides in total war, with homes destroyed and families shattered.[16] This brutalizing experience soured the milk of human kindness and poisoned the racial attitudes of those settlers who remained on the frontier, deepening the ambivalences they had brought with them from "home" between a belief in democracy and an innate sense of racial superiority, between the humanitarianism of the evangelical movement and the exigencies of survival on a disputed frontier, between a tradition of chivalry and a brutality born of fear and contempt.

The trauma began one sunny spring morning in 1821 when fifteen-

16. There were five frontier wars with the Xhosa before the arrival of the 1820 settlers.

year-old Benjamin Anderson went out to herd the cattle of a neighbouring farmer. He took some schoolbooks with him to work at his sums while the cattle grazed, a small example of how the settlers hoped to transplant the values of Victorian England to this wild frontier. When evening came and young Benjamin had not returned, a search party set out and found his body lying in a riverbed. He had been stabbed to death and the brass buttons had been cut from his coat—buttons by now were an established currency in the barter trade with the tribes. Some of the cattle were gone. "It is time to put away our books and take up our guns," the boy's anguished father wrote in his diary, capturing in a phrase the end of the time of innocence in the lives of the settlers.

From then on the conflict and the bitterness and the hardening of attitudes increased. Atrocities became commonplace as settler volunteers and frontier regulars rode out on their reprisal raids. Black women and children were killed indiscriminately. Prisoners were shot and the wounded and infirm were left to the hyenas. "It is a lamentable truth," wrote Thomas Pringle after an incident in which an emissary from a Xhosa chief was seized and threatened with death unless he disclosed the chief's whereabouts, "that in our treatment generally of savage nations, all respect for common honesty, justice, or humanity, appears to be often utterly forgotten; even by men otherwise generous, kind, and sensitively honourable."[17]

Peires tells the story of how Hintsa, king of the Xhosas, was persuaded to come to the British camp for peace negotiations at the height of the Sixth Frontier War in 1835. He was given an assurance of his personal safety by the governor, Sir Benjamin D'Urban, but no sooner had the chief entered the camp than he was held as a hostage against the payment of a ransom of 25,000 cattle and 500 horses as compensation for the settlers. When the ransom was not forthcoming, an armed posse led by Colonel Harry Smith—who was himself later to become a governor of the Cape—rode out with the king to round up some of the cattle:

> As the column marched along above the Nqabara River, Hintsa made a dash for freedom. He was pulled off his horse, shot through the back and through the leg. Desperately he scrambled down the river bank and collapsed into a water-course. A scout named George Southey, coming up fast behind him, blew off the top of his head. Then some soldiers cut off his ears as keepsakes to show around the military camps. Others tried to dig out his teeth with bayonets. Thus died Hintsa, king of the Xhosa, for trusting the honour of a British Governor.[18]

17. Pringle, op. cit., p. 275.

18. J. B. Peires, *The House of Phalo*, p. 111.

The conventional wisdom, taught in all South African schools, is that the settlers were the victims of an arrogant and incompetent colonial administration which bungled its dealings with the blacks and then left the frontiersmen to face the consequences. In part this is true, but it is by no means the whole story. What is downplayed is the dynamic expansionism that was generated by the settler community. As Peires notes, the settlers were products of the age of mercantile capitalism, and once they recovered from their initial setbacks the spirit of accumulation naturally began to assert itself more and more.[19] In this they were qualitatively different from the Afrikaner Trekboers. Although the Boers hungered for land, the force that drove them ever onward was the need for individual space and freedom and the right of every son in their enormous families to become a king upon his own estate. What drove the British settler was the profit motive. Where the Boer farmer operated on a subsistence basis, producing what he needed and exchanging the surplus for what he could not produce, the English-speaking South African from the moment he found his feet was intent on investment and expansion, and regarded the land as a capital asset rather than just a natural resource to sustain the necessities of life.

As the settlement on the Suurveld thinned out, the departing farmers found they could get a good price for land they had obtained for next to nothing. This generated a rapacious demand for more grants in new settlement areas. The wool industry grew rapidly and increased the demand for more sweet-grass pasturage. Greedily the settlers eyed what they regarded as the underutilized tribal land across the Fish River. "The days when our plains were covered with tens of thousands of springboks; they are gone now, and who regrets it?" cried one of the leading settler figures, John Mitford Bowker. "Their place is occupied with tens of thousands of merino. . . . I begin to think that he too [the Xhosa] must give place, and why not? Is it just that a few thousands of ruthless worthless savages are to sit like a nightmare upon a land that would support millions of civilized men happily?"[20]

The shift from defensive frontier skirmishing to expansionist warmongering was subtle and barely noticeable. The colonial authorities allowed frontier farmers to follow the spoor of stolen cattle across the border and retrieve them. If the animals could not be found, equivalent compensation could be claimed from the tribe arbitrarily held responsible for the theft. The system was wide open to abuse and it was exploited ruthlessly. On the smallest of pretexts volunteer commandos

19. Ibid., pp. 121–7.

20. Ibid., p. 123.

rode across the frontier to claim and drive off huge herds of cattle. It had been done by the Boers before the British arrived. Now the settlers joined in and intensified the practice. It became not merely a way of supplementing their herds but also of provoking war, which allowed for the conquest of new territory for colonial settlement.

By this means the Nguni tribes had been steadily driven back upon themselves ever since their first encounter with the eastward-moving whites. In 1771 the VOC had declared the boundary to be at the Gamtoos River, fifty miles west of Algoa Bay. Through a succession of frontier wars it was driven back a hundred miles to the Bushman's River, then another thirty-five miles to the Fish. Now the settlers clamoured for further appropriations. It was a vicious cycle: the more the blacks were pressed back upon themselves the more they were driven to pillaging and the whites to reprisals. War erupted in 1835 and again in 1846. In the second of these the colonial forces waged a scorched-earth campaign aimed at wasting the tribal territory and making it untenable for the Xhosa. They were urged on by the settlers and their newly established press:

> Let war be made against Kafir huts and gardens. Let all these be burned down and destroyed. Let there be no ploughing, sowing or reaping. Or, if you cannot conveniently, or without bloodshed prevent the cultivation of the ground, take care to destroy the enemy's crops before they are ripe, and shoot all who resist. Shoot their cattle too wherever you see any. Tell them that the time has come for the white man to show his mastery over them.[21]

It was more than just an angry cry for retribution against the inveterate cattle rustlers. It was a campaign for more land. And when the war was over the land beyond the Fish was indeed appropriated for white settlement and the frontier was pushed back another twenty-five miles to the Keiskamma River. Soon afterward another large chunk of territory was placed under British administration and the boundary was set at the Kei River, seventy-five miles east of the Keiskamma. Thus in sixty years was more than thirty thousand square miles of prime land taken from the frontier tribes.

With this expansion, and as the colonial economy was drawn into the dynamic new imperialism of free trade, the demand for labour expanded, too. Consumer goods were flowing into the country, creating a need for foreign exchange. That meant stepping up wine, wheat, and wool exports. Labour was needed to do this, and it had to be cheap labour

21. *Grahamstown Journal*, April 10, 1847.

if South Africa was to compete from such a distance on the world market. Yet Britain had just ordered the abolition of slavery.

The answer, quite simply, was to move from slavery to serfdom. The prohibition on the employment of indigenous blacks was first bent, then scrapped. With thousands of blacks left destitute and landless after the wars of dispossession, they had no choice but to enter the colony in search of work for whatever pittance wages they could get. Many squatted on the land that until recently had been theirs, offering their services to the white settler farmers in exchange for the right to stay and keep a few cattle of their own. A Master-Servants Act made it a crime for a black man to quit his job, and a vagrancy law forbade him to be in the colony without work. It was the start of the migrant labour system.

From then on, and for their first time in the immemorial history of the black tribes, a working class emerged among them that grew in response to the labour needs of the developing white economy until eventually it was to encompass the entire black population. The policy of trying to preserve racial peace through total segregation was at an end, and the attempt began to force more and more blacks onto the labour market while still keeping them socially and politically apart. It was the end of black independence and the beginning of black servility and exploitation.

Meanwhile, four hundred miles to the northeast, in the new colony of Natal, an administrator named Theophilus Shepstone was instituting a system of black tribal reserves and of indirect rule through the chieftaincy, with the white lieutenant-governor holding the position of Supreme Chief, that in time provided a model for the administration of black people throughout South Africa.

And so it came to pass that the English-speaking South Africans, though never the creators of the ideology of apartheid, laid the basis for its political and administrative framework and for its exploitative labour system. They did so even as, in 1834, in the name of humanitarianism, they abolished slavery and issued Colonial Ordinance No. 50, or the "Hottentots' Magna Carta," which gave the Khoikhoi equal legal status with whites and meant an abused Khoi servant could take his white master to court and have him fined for ill treatment.

TWO MORE THINGS need to be said about the founding fathers of English-speaking South Africa. They concern the work of the missionaries and of a liberal governor, Sir George Grey, who performed the counterpoint in South Africa's contrapuntal themes, and in a different way contributed to the breaking of black power and to setting the Afrikaners on their long march to nationalism.

English missionaries throughout the British Empire brought with them the humanitarian concerns and proselytizing spirit of the evangelical revival. As they carried the Word of God to the heathen multitudes of the earth, their bearers trailing behind them through jungles and across desert plains, they became as much a symbol of the imperial age as the district commissioner in his white pith helmet. The first to arrive in South Africa in 1799 were John Phillip and Jan van der Kemp of the London Missionary Society. They were followed by Robert Moffat, who established a mission station at Dithakong among the Tswana and whose work was later taken up by his son-in-law, David Livingstone. They championed the cause of the black South Africans, challenged the excesses of the settlers, and pressured the colonial authorities to restrain them. These were the crusading days of emancipation, and Dr. Phillip especially had a close relationship with the abolitionist William Wilberforce in London, which made the Colonial Office receptive to his petitioning.

The settlers resented the missionaries. In particular the Boers despised them, regarding them as arrogant and meddlesome nigger-lovers who epitomized all they resented most about the new interference with their traditional way of life that had begun with the British occupation. Above all the Boers feared and resented the missionaries' influence and their successes in striving for emancipation and racial equality. *Gelykstelling*, it was called, or equalization, and to the Boers, brought up as they were to believe in their fundamental rights over inferior beings of colour, it was an abomination. The very word "missionary" became a curse, and the legacy of it lingers still in Pretoria's hostility toward meddlesome priests who interfere with the administration of apartheid, preach a theology of liberation, and petition the outside world to impose sanctions and other punishments on South Africa.

The black tribes, on the other hand, welcomed the missionaries, took them in and never harmed one of them through all the racial violence that disrupted the frontier. They saw them as friends and protectors; in the process of being converted by them, many were weakened. For Christianizing eroded the very basis of the blacks' tribal institutions, and thus their resistance, almost as effectively as the settlers' frontal assault. With his taste for the piquant, Archbishop Tutu likes to tell a joke that has an edge of bitter truth to it. "When the white man first came here," Tutu says, "he had the Bible and we had the land. Then the white man said to us, Come let us kneel and pray together. So we knelt and closed our eyes and prayed, and when we opened our eyes again, lo!—we had the Bible and he had the land."

In the certitude of their faith the missionaries gave no thought to the social function of the tribal institutions, or the reasons for the delicate matrix of tribal culture, or the destabilizing effect their destruction might have. They proselytized in the absolute conviction that Western Christian norms were the only way. Savages had to be civilized, and that was that. So they attacked polygamy and *lobola* (bride price), and they tried to stamp out the worship of tribal gods, the intercession of the ancestors, and above all the power of the medicine men. They taught that work was good and idleness evil, and in all these matters they upset the rhythm and habits of tribal life and undermined its stability.

Education did the same. The missionaries started schools and so did Sir George Grey. Lovedale, Healdtown, and the University College of Fort Hare became the first major educational institutions for blacks in Africa. Grey had become convinced while working among the Maoris in New Zealand of the benefits of letting indigenous people learn by example from white settlers, so he broke up the fixed demarcation that he found on the frontier and settled black farmers beside whites in a checkerboard pattern that was to be a headache to the apartheid geographers a century later as they tried to construct a coherent tribal "homeland" in the area.

All this hastened the process of Westernization in the eastern Cape. In the long run it was to make the region the birthplace of African nationalism and a stronghold of the movement resisting apartheid, but in those early days the Westernization created a cleavage between tribal traditionalists and Westernized elements—or "red" and "school," as they were called in the vernacular, the former because of the red *imbola* clay the tribesfolk used—that is still there today. Whereas now the modern, urbanized, politicized elite spearhead the resistance, while the traditionalists are co-opted to administer the apartheid system, it was the other way around in the heroic age of the frontier, when the chiefs led the wars of resistance, and the educated Christians represented the soft underbelly of ambivalent loyalty.

Two tales, separated by nearly a century and a half, illuminate the high points of these two types of resistance. One concerns a speech made on behalf of a war-prophet named Makanda as he was being taken to prison on Robben Island in 1819, the other a speech by Nelson Mandela, leader of the African National Congress, before he too went to Robben Island in 1964. Their words fuse together across six generations of oppression.

Makanda consulted the spirits before he led nine thousand inspired warriors in a daylight attack on Grahamstown in the Fifth Frontier War. The defending garrison reeled under the onslaught and Makanda might have won, had he not observed the Xhosa war code and allowed Elizabeth Salt to walk through his ranks carrying her hidden keg of gunpowder; in the end, his attack was beaten off. Three days later, as commandos searched the Suurveld for him, Makanda calmly walked into the garrison town unattended. "People say that I have occasioned the war," he announced. "Let me see whether delivering myself up to the conquerors will restore peace to my country." Such an inspired gesture deserved reciprocation, but instead the British authorities arrested Makanda and bundled him off to the prison island. A few days later a group of his councillors appeared in the place where he had surrendered and addressed themselves to his captors:

> The war, British chiefs, is an unjust one; for you are striving to extirpate a people whom you forced to take up arms. When our fathers, and the fathers of the Boers, first settled in the Suurveld, they dwelt together in peace. Their flocks grazed on the same hills; their herdsmen smoked together out of the same pipes; they were brothers—until the herds of the Amaxhosa increased so as to make the hearts of the Boers sore. What those covetous men could not get from our fathers for old buttons, they took by force. Our fathers were *men*; they loved their cattle; their wives and children lived upon milk; they fought for their property. They began to hate the colonists, who coveted their all, and aimed at their destruction.
>
> Now, their kraals and our fathers' kraals were separate. The Boers made commandos on our fathers. Our fathers drove them out of the Suurveld; and we dwelt there, because we had conquered it. There we were circumcised; there we married wives; and there our children were born. The white men hated us, but could not drive us away. . . . You came at last like locusts. We stood: we could do no more. You said, "Go over the Fish River—that is all that we want.". . .
>
> We quarrelled with Gaika about grass—no business of yours. You sent a commando—you took our last cow—you left only a few calves, which died for want, along with our children. You gave half the spoil to Gaika; half you kept for yourselves. Without milk—our corn destroyed—we saw our wives and children perish—we saw that we must ourselves perish; we followed, therefore, the tracks of our cattle into the colony. We plundered, and we fought for our lives. We found you weak; we destroyed your soldiers. We saw that we were strong; we attacked your headquarters:—and if we had succeeded, our right was good, for you began the war. We failed—and you are here.[22]

Not long afterward Makanda and some fellow prisoners overpowered the crew of a small boat and tried to escape from Robben Island, but the boat capsized in heavy seas. It is said that Makanda clung to a rock for a while and his deep, sonorous voice could be heard shouting encouragement to his comrades before he was swept under the waves.

22. Pringle, op. cit., pp. 285–6.

Mandela also has a deep, sonorous voice and the courtroom in Pretoria was quite still as he came to the end of his final speech in the trial that was to send him to Robben Island for life, a sentence levied after his conviction on charges of forming a military arm of the ANC to wage a guerrilla struggle against white domination:

> This, then, is what the ANC is fighting for. Their struggle is a truly national one. It is a struggle of the African people, inspired by their own suffering and their own experience. It is a struggle for the right to live.
>
> During my lifetime I have dedicated myself to this struggle of the African people. I have fought against white domination, and I have fought against black domination. I have cherished the ideal of a democratic and free society in which all persons live together in harmony and with equal opportunities. It is an ideal which I hope to live for and to achieve. But if needs be it is an ideal for which I am prepared to die.[23]

Two men, opposites in personal terms, doing the same thing in the same cause in their different times. And both equally unheard by the whites who drove them to it.

"THEY MUST GRIN and bear their political impotence in the country they dominate economically. They are the largest, richest, most influential non–self-governing community in the world." That is how a perceptive foreign correspondent in South Africa described the English-speaking community twenty years ago.[24] Their continued insentience since then has endorsed the description. It is a conundrum to most of the world: to the Marxists who believe that all political truth stems from the economy and the dynamics of capitalist exploitation; and to the Americans who are accustomed to big business having political clout and cannot conceive of a system where this may not be the case. Yet it is a fact: the English-speaking South Africans dominate their country's economy but are outsiders when it comes to the politically dominant Afrikaner Nationalist movement forged in opposition to them. The prince of South African businessmen, Harry Oppenheimer, the nearest thing they have had to a leader since Cecil John Rhodes at the turn of the century, could not sit down and talk with any South African prime minister about the state of the nation until 1981 when he was already over seventy years old.

23. Mary Benson, *Nelson Mandela: The Man and the Movement* (New York, 1986), p. 159.

24. Douglas Brown, *Against the World* (New York, 1968), p. 97.

Does this really mean they are politically impotent? "What we say to the government bounces off them like a ping-pong ball," says Anthony Bloom, one of the few genuine liberals in the business community, whom frustration drove into exile. Critics think this is a spurious cop-out for people who do nothing to end a system that business knows is evil but that guarantees a continuous supply of cheap, captive labour. The truth lies between. Business is not powerless, but its influence is indirect and limited compared with what it might be in other capitalist countries where the political system is not ethnically based, and this limit offers an excuse for doing nothing. There are at least as many negatives as plusses in maintaining a primitive exploitative system as the economy becomes more sophisticated and the international climate more hostile, but the thought of black majority rule is scary and it requires courage to confront the authorities. Courage of this sort is something the English-speaking South Africans do not have. They are deferential, reluctant to confront authority. Unlike their cousins the Australians, with their irreverent convict background, English-speaking South Africans have always been establishment-oriented. Their forebears in Britain were a curiously "deferential" electorate, as Walter Bagehot noted in his chronicles of nineteenth-century political behaviour,[25] and as Thomas Pringle found when he clashed with authority at the Cape and sought in vain for friends who would stand by him.

Pringle and an associate, John Fairbairn, had started a newspaper in Cape Town called the *South African Commercial Advertiser* but closed it in 1824 when the authoritarian governor, Lord Charles Somerset, censored them for publishing critical material. Casting about for something new to do, Pringle and Fairbairn decided to launch a Literary and Scientific Society. They got most of the leading citizens of Cape Town, including the chief justice, to sign up as members, but when the governor made his disapproval known in a conversation with one of these signatories, the word got around and within a few weeks nearly all the names were withdrawn. An educational academy the two men were running likewise withered and died as parents removed their children from the influence of men disapproved of by the establishment. "Many illustrations, at once ludicrous and humiliating, of the pusillanimous prostration of the public mind at this crisis, remained vividly in my mind," a disgusted Pringle observed.[26]

So it has been with the English-speaking South Africans ever since.

25. Clark, op. cit., p. 51.

26. Ibid., p. 198.

CHAPTER FOUR

God's Stepchildren

"We are all God's children," the Rev. Andrew Flood said.

"But is God Himself not white?" asked Cachas.

And, as the Rev. Andrew Flood hesitated for a reply, she made a suggestion:

"Perhaps we brown people are His stepchildren," she said.

SARAH GERTRUDE MILLIN

IT SEEMS APPROPRIATE to the founding of a perverse society that it should have imported slaves *to* Africa. Such contrariness was, of course, the corollary of the bitter-almond hedge. Having established his outpost of Europe and fenced it off from the continent and people of Africa, Van Riebeeck found he needed labour and so he sent for slaves. The slaves came, from other parts of the Dutch seaborne empire and from other parts of Africa, from Indonesia, Malaya, Indo-China, Ceylon, India, Madagascar, and Mozambique, and for the next 182 years South Africa was a slave state—an experience that established the pattern of its labour relations, and in the manner of its abolition sowed the seeds of a bitter resentment that over time grew and was compounded into the fateful phenomenon of Afrikaner nationalism.

The slaves toiled by day and, in the manner of all slave societies, they were abused by night. Few company officials took their wives to the Cape, and with thousands of sailors and soldiers coming ashore each year, the women in the company's slave lodge became the objects of large-scale sexual exploitation. Out on the lonely farms, free burghers and their sons likewise beat a path to the backyard slave quarters on dark and guilt-ridden nights, while the slaves intermixed, too, with the Khoikhoi, as those hapless hunter-herder clans disintegrated under the impact of settler expansionism. So was procreated a new community of mixed blood on the already heterogeneous landscape of South Africa. The so-called "coloured" people. God's stepchildren. The people in the middle, whose mixed ancestry leaves them nowhere in a country obsessed with racial identity, who are trapped between white and black nationalisms, between privilege and oppression, between today's and tomorrow's power.

The almond-hedge mentality brought in another community as well. At the new colony of Natal, which Britain annexed in 1844 and where Theophilus Shepstone was herding black tribes into segregated reserves, the white settlers of that subtropical region on the Indian Ocean coast found they could get no one to work their new sugar plantations. By now slavery had been abolished, and the Zulus, driven back into their tribal ways by Shepstone's policy, were not forthcoming as employees: to the Zulu men, cultivation was women's work. So the colonial authorities sent to India for indentured labourers. Between 1860 and the end of the nineteenth century more than one hundred thousand Indians arrived in South Africa on five-year work contracts, followed by a train of free traders who set up shops and started produce gardens to supply the new market. They came and they stayed and they multiplied until today they outnumber the whites of Natal and have spread as an enterprising minority into other provinces as well.

There are fewer than a million Indians in a total population of 30 million in South Africa, yet their impact has been disproportionately great. Through Mohandas Karamchand Gandhi, who founded his Indian Congress movement and formulated his strategic philosophy of *satyagraha*, or power of truth, during the twenty-one years he spent in South Africa at the turn of the twentieth century, the Indian community gave dark-skinned South Africans their first organized political resistance movement and began their long fight for racial justice and equality. Gandhi's influence in awakening political consciousness among the blacks was enormous. His Congress movement inspired the early formation of the African National Congress in 1912, the first black liberation movement in Africa, and influenced the ANC's long commitment to the principle of nonviolent resistance, which was finally abandoned only with reluctance in 1961 and still exerts considerable restraint.

The Indian influence on white attitudes has been negative, however. From the beginning their political articulateness and business acumen made the whites feel threatened and resentful. Combined with the effects of Shepstone's segregationist philosophy, this produced a naked racism among the English-speaking whites of Natal which is palpably different from that of their more benign brethren in other parts of South Africa.

The effect of the "coloured" people has been less overt, more diffuse, but in the end perhaps more profound. They have exercised a nagging influence on the conscience of the Cape Afrikaners, tugging at ties of language, faith, and an unconfessed kinship, and straining on the solidarity of the Afrikaner Nationalist movement. Here are South Africa's equivalent of black Americans—not a people culturally alien to those in power, seeking to replace them through a struggle for national repossession (which is what black South Africans are) but an acculturated adjunct of those in power. They are "brown Afrikaners," just as blacks in the United States are essentially Americans in accent and culture and faith, whose historical struggle has been to gain acceptance as such and to be admitted into the system, not to take it over.

The vast majority of "coloureds" speak Afrikaans as their mother tongue: indeed they were primarily responsible for its creation as a simplified form of Dutch that emerged from communication between the early Boer settlers and their slaves. They have Afrikaans names, Afrikaans poets, Afrikaans folksongs, and most of them are devout members of the Dutch Reformed Church. All they ever wanted was to be accepted by the whites, to be admitted to their father's house, as it were. But the whites rejected them, and the pain of it was terrible. For years they hesitated to identify with black Africans, because that would have meant stepping below their station and forfeiting their half-status and half-privileges. In any case they were none too sure that the blacks would accept them any more fully than the whites did. So they were caught in the middle without power and without certainty, unsure whether apartheid was an evil that kept them separated from the whites or a blessing that kept them separated from the blacks. In this state of confusion they were pulled every which way by conflicting emotions. Light-skinned "coloureds" were contemptuous of dark-skinned "coloureds," the darker ones were resentful of those who were fair, and God knows how many shades of prejudice were in between.

But all this is changing now. There is a limit to the endurance of pain. There comes a point at which anguish hardens into bitterness and disappointment into resolution. This has happened to the "coloured" people. Suddenly they are not pleading and petitioning any more. They have become angry. They no longer want to be part of the white community. Years of rejection have at last produced a counterrejection. In the 1960s Steven Biko started his Black Consciousness movement, urging blacks to take pride in their blackness, to cast off the psychology of inferiority and lift themselves up by their own bootstraps. The movement has run its course now, giving way to a resurgence of the African National Congress, which sees things in terms of a class rather than a colour struggle. But its impact among the "coloureds" was enormous and lasting. Gone is the shame at the dark side of their parentage. Gone, too, is the fawning desire to be patronized by whites. Instead there is a positive, almost vehement, rejection of the white community and a growing identification with the black cause. This change is partly emotional and partly a matter of simple political judgment. "Coloureds" can see which way the political wind is blowing in South Africa.

"When I was a child," says the Rev. Allan Boesak, until recently chaplain at the "coloured" University of the Western Cape and a leading political activist, "everybody wanted to be accepted by the whites. Other children were not allowed to play with us because we were too dark-skinned. And I remember my mother, who was very fair, being approached and told that if she would give us out for adoption it could be arranged for her to be reclassified white. But today I doubt whether ten percent of the 'coloured' community would see their future as being with the whites. People are not inclined to join a sinking ship."

They are turning away from the Dutch Reformed Church, too. Boesak, a DRC theologian who was trained in Holland, says that when he first went to the university only a dozen or so students turned up for services. Only his own radicalism won them back, after which he regularly got congregations of three hundred. They are even turning away from Afrikaans, preferring to struggle in inadequate English on public occasions. Many young people are learning Xhosa, the predominant black African language in the Cape Town area where most "coloureds" live. Young couples are avoiding Afrikaans names for their children, giving them English, Xhosa, or even Spanish or French names.

Adam Small, a leading "coloured" poet and playwright, has come to the painful conclusion that he must stop writing in the language that has brought him fame. "Every time I sit down to write something I have this tussle," he told me in a soul-baring conversation. "On the one hand [I] share the language with P. W. Botha and his crowd; on the other I cannot accept that it is the language of the oppressor because it is the language my mother taught me. To have that kind of love-hate relationship with your language must be one of the most difficult cultural experiences it is possible to have. It is too painful. I shall probably write in English in future."

But nothing so vividly illustrates the depth of this alienation as the mass rejection of the government's reform constitution of 1984, which granted political concessions to the "coloureds" and Indians while continuing to exclude the black majority. This belated gesture, which offered precisely what the "coloureds" had yearned for over so many generations, not only failed but backfired, being perceived as an attempt to co-opt the dark-skinned minorities as allies of the whites against the blacks. It triggered the 1984 uprising and plunged white South Africa into its current crisis.

. . .

A MYTH HAS BEEN propagated that South Africa's system of slavery was more benign than those of other slave states. This is not true. It was as vicious as any. The Dutch, hardened by the cruel experiences of their seventeenth-century war against Spain and the imported Inquisition, adopted a penal system both at home and in their colonies that placed retaliation and deterrence ahead of Christian forbearance. They were inured to a system that regarded beheading and strangulation as merciful punishments, and in which to be burned alive was the usual ecclesiastical sentence for heretics and schismatics. So they found nothing strange about prescribing such brutality in their own law. The use of torture in investigations and cruel forms of execution were common practice in early seventeenth-century Holland and set the pattern for the punishment of slaves in the Dutch colonies, some of which became notorious for their sadism.[1]

The small white community at the Cape was a fearful one, moreover, and the product of its fear was severity. Almost from the beginning the settlers were outnumbered by slaves, which, given the smallness of their numbers and the fact that they were living in a huge continent full of strange, dark people, gave them a pervasive sense of insecurity that sank into the white South African mind and became part of its survivalist reflex. Inadequate policing and the mountainous terrain of the Cape peninsula meant that slave escapes were frequent, and these always caused a wave of anxiety to sweep through the white community, intensifying the demand for brutal punishments to serve as a deterrent.

Recaptured escapees were whipped and branded. A first offender was branded on one cheek, a second offender on the other cheek, and a third offender had his nose and ears cut off. James Armstrong has told us that by 1727 there were so many mutilated and disfigured slaves in Cape Town that the law was changed out of consideration for the feelings of whites—particularly pregnant women—who encountered them. Thereafter escaped slaves were branded on the back.[2]

Punishments for insubordination and other more serious offences were horrendous. Slaves convicted of theft were likely to be hanged. Those who murdered other slaves or Khoikhoi were broken on a wheel with the coup de grâce. Killing a white meant being broken on a wheel without the coup de grâce. In particularly violent cases the slave would first have eight pieces of flesh torn from his body with red-hot pincers.

1. C. R. Boxer, *The Dutch Seaborne Empire, 1600–1800*, pp. 232–41. According to Boxer, the treatment of slaves was particularly bad in Surinam, where "man's inhumanity to man just about reached its limits."

2. James C. Armstrong, "The Slaves, 1652–1795," in *The Shaping of South African Society 1652–1820* (Cape Town 1979), p 90.

When the victim was the slave's own master, the condemned man would be impaled on a stake driven up his anus and left to die—which might take two or three days.[3]

Anders Sparrman, a Swedish explorer and travel writer, was shocked at the evidence he found of this brutality when he visited the Cape in 1772. He saw three gallows in Cape Town itself, then still little more than a village with a resident population of about seven thousand. One of them, "the largest I ever saw," had been erected in a "place of honour" on what is now Cape Town's Grand Parade and had "racks and other horrid instruments of torture" attached to it—grim evidence, wrote Sparrman, that "the well-known hardness of heart of the Dutch settled in the Indies has shewn itself here."[4]

Nor was there immediate improvement after the British occupation in 1795. Despite the success of Wilberforce and his abolitionists in stirring up public feeling against slavery and getting the slave trade ended in 1807, the law in the new colony at the Cape remained little changed for more than two decades after that. Just eight years before slavery was finally abolished in 1834, a full bench of the Court of Justice at Cape Town delivered a verdict in a case in which slaves had risen in revolt on a farm in the Cold Bokkeveld district that would have done justice to the Duke of Alba and his Inquisition. "The 1st, 2nd and 4th prisoners, Galant, Abel and Thys," the eight judges ruled, are "to be hanged by the necks until they are dead; the heads of Galant and Abel to be struck off from their bodies and thereupon stuck upon iron spikes affixed to separate poles to be erected in the most conspicuous places in the Bokkeveld, there to remain until consumed by time and the birds of the air."[5]

Individual slave-owners had the legal right to punish their slaves for laziness or failing to obey orders. It was called "domestic correction" and there were supposed to be limits to the amount of violence used. A slave could complain of maltreatment to an official called the *fiscaal*, who was a kind of public prosecutor and police chief combined, and if the slave-owner was widely known to treat his slaves brutally there might be some small chance of redress. But mostly these complaints were not taken seriously and the slaves were returned to the power of

3. Robert Ross, *Cape of Torments: Slavery and Resistance in South Africa* (London, 1983), p. 2.

4. Anders Sparrman, *A Voyage to the Cape of Good Hope Towards the Antarctic Polar Circle and Round the World*, vol. 1 (Cape Town, 1975), p. 49.

5. The incident is the basis for André Brink's searing novel *A Chain of Voices* (London, 1982), in which Brink appends the full verdict of the court, pp. 500–12.

their masters, who as likely as not would take retribution for their insolence in making such complaints.

Out on the expanding frontier even this small safeguard blurred into a mirage of distance and isolation. The Trekboers treated their slaves as they pleased in their own ad hoc way, and the slave's value as a capital asset became his only safeguard against disablement and death. The common form of punishment was to tie a slave to a wagon wheel and flog him with a *sjambok*, a thick whip made from rhinoceros hide. And so a tradition was established of controlling labour by means of institutionalized coercion and physical violence that has survived long after the abolition of slavery itself and, though changed and modernized, is still the core feature of today's apartheid economy.

To a degree the concept of employees as property survives also, especially on farms in some of the remoter regions. "My boys" is how white farmers commonly refer to their black labourers, revealing a residual attitude of proprietorial paternalism. In the mind at least, the black worker still belongs to the farmer, and to whip him into shape if he is insolent comes close to being regarded as a basic civil right. Afrikaner folk humour is full of this. "What's freedom coming to," asks Van der Merwe after being fined by the local magistrate for assaulting a black worker, "if you can't hit your own kaffir on your own farm with your own *sjambok*?"

For the slaves, the choice between resistance and submission was more theoretical than real. The violence on the farms drove some to greater acts of insubordination, and there were pockets of insurrection that turned into brief moments of guerrilla resistance. One such involved a slave named Slamath, who with other runaways formed a robber band that survived for eight years in the Boland before they were finally captured and Slamath was executed by impalement.[6] A few found refuge for a time in the crevices and caves of the mountains behind Cape Town, from where they vengefully set fire to the mountain slopes, menacing the town and forcing a change in its architectural complexion by inducing householders to abandon the gracious thatched roofing so characteristic of the surrounding countryside in favour of flat roofs made of a fireproof compound of clinker and lime.[7] But for the most part the slaves were too isolated and too lacking in cohesion to mount any serious threat of resistance; and though there were many escapes only a handful made it to the land of the Xhosa beyond the shifting eastern frontier, where they could find freedom and acceptance into the easygoing life

6. Ross, op. cit., pp. 36–7.

7. James Walton, *Homesteads and Villages of South Africa* (Pretoria, 1952), p. 17.

of the tribes. In the end most knuckled under, accepting their state of bondage as best they could and gradually being absorbed into the culture, though never the society, of their white masters. The safest course was not to buck the system. Sometimes years of faithful service could lead to manumission. It bred an attitude of obsequiousness, tinged sometimes with a sarcastic wit and the craftiness of the survivalist, but likely to turn quickly to pleading and grovelling when faced with any threat.

The slaves had come from many lands and for the most part they came singly or in small groups, rather than in shiploads, so that there were few ties between them. Once in South Africa they were scattered thinly about the countryside, only a few to each farm, which meant they did not get to know one another and developed no common bonds. There were no family ties even: slaves were bought individually, there were four times as many men as women, and such relationships as developed were often transient and charged with the violence of sexual competition. So although slaves outnumbered settlers, they were an atomized community with no common culture and no cohesion.

They did not even have a common language. They brought with them a multitude of Asian languages, mostly Indonesian, and the languages of the East African coast, together with a smattering of creolized Portuguese which was the lingua franca of the trade routes. At the Cape they could not even communicate among themselves, let alone with their Dutch, German, and French masters and the tongue-twisting Khoikhoi who increasingly came to work alongside them. Out of this linguistic confusion there emerged a patois, a pidgin Dutch of simplified articles and pronouns, stripped of its complex Teutonic gender forms and verb conjugations and compensating with an onomatopoeic inventiveness for its lack of vocabulary.

How ironic that this wonderfully expressive and cosmopolitan new language, which the slaves invented out of their necessity for communication and then passed on from black nanny to white child while the sophistication of High Dutch wilted on the dry and distant veld, should have become the talisman of a narrow racist nationalism dedicated to the oppression of its real creators. A monument to the Afrikaans language stands on a hillside above the wineland town of Paarl with a series of spires reaching toward the sky and a quotation from the Nationalist poet C. J. Langenhoven exulting in its soaring growth. But then, almost as a footnote amidst all this phallic symbolism of the chauvinist ideal, there is also a plaque bearing a quotation from a more thoughtful Afrikaner poet, N. P. van Wyk Louw. In words of haunting simplicity it states the challenge that the language truly symbolizes but that so far white South Africa has been unable to face:

> Afrikaans is the language that binds Western Europe and Africa together. . . . It is a bridge between the great lucid West and the magical Africa . . . and what greatness may spring from their union—that perhaps is what lies ahead for Afrikaans to discover.

There was one exception to this lack of cohesion. Some of the slaves from Bengal, the Malabar coast, and the Indonesian archipelago managed to cling to their Muslim faith and through that build a degree of cultural solidarity that prevented them from being absorbed into the white culture quite so much as the others. Some of these were skilled craftsmen, in demand at the Cape as stonemasons, carpenters, plasterers, tailors, seamstresses, and handymen. These Malayan and Javanese slaves sculpted the graceful curvilinear gables of the Cape Dutch and Flemish homesteads that are such a magnificent feature of the Western Province landscape. Their special value ensured them better treatment, and they lived under generally less oppressive conditions, so that they could remain more intact within themselves and hold on to more of their own heritage. Many were also able to earn commissions for their work and so save up enough to buy their manumission and become *vryezwarten*, "free blacks."

They moved, these "free blacks," into the Bo-Kaap, a small enclave of terraced houses and cobbled streets poised steeply at the top end of Cape Town on the slopes of Signal Hill. Here they built their mosques and established a Muslim burial ground and nurtured their Islamic faith. Inadvertently, the Dutch helped them. First the VOC began using the Cape as a penal colony, sending political prisoners there from their East Indian colonies. Most of these rebels were Muslims. They were also men of learning, some of whom had made the pilgrimage to Mecca, and they became the first imams among the small Islamic community at the Cape, providing it with an intellectual as well as a religious leadership.

The first of these was Sheikh Yussuf of Macassar, a Bantamese resistance leader, who arrived at the Cape with a retinue of forty-nine Muslims in 1694 and was placed on a farm thirty-six miles outside Cape Town. Others followed, the most famous being a prince from Tidore, a sultanate in the Moluccas, named Imam Abdullah Kadi Abdus Salaam, or Tuan Guru, who was imprisoned for a time on Robben Island, where he is said to have handwritten a copy of the Koran from memory.

By a stunning irony, these early literati among the Cape Muslims were the first to write in Afrikaans. The first book ever published in that language (which is such an emblem of the white nationalist movement) appeared in 1856—in Arabic script!—a book on the Islamic faith written by Cape "coloured" Muslims who used Arabic lettering to convey Afrikaans sounds. (The first Afrikaans book in Roman type did not appear until six years later.) In 1873 another Afrikaans book was published in Arabic script, this time on Islamic jurisprudence. It was written by a Turkish Muslim named Abu Bakr Effendi, who had come to South Africa to found a theological school; it was printed as a gift by the Ottoman Empire to the Cape Muslim community.[8]

The second unwitting Dutch boost for Islam came with an eighteenth-century decree prohibiting the sale of baptized Christian slaves. It was an expression of the Dutch Reformed Church's ambiguity on the issue of slavery: it was acceptable for those of God's flock who were regarded as heathen "savages," but it caused unease when it came to those who had been persuaded by the church's own missionaries to embrace the Christian faith. The token prohibition was enough to make the colonists fear that a Christianized slave would lose his value, so they discouraged baptism. By the turn of the century, the benches in Cape Town's Groote Kerk traditionally reserved for slaves were empty.[9] Many of the slaves turned to Islam instead, particularly since the imams continued to perform the marriages and funerals they could not obtain in the Christian churches.

Even so, only about one-tenth of the "coloured" community in South Africa is Muslim today. The majority are members of the racially segmented Dutch Reformed Church. But the Cape Muslims have played roles out of proportion to their numbers, as an exotic element in an already colourful community, as a skilled artisan class, and as an early intellectual elite. For the most part they have been industrious and conservative, building carefully on the small privileges they won for themselves at the beginning. But once in a while there has been a flash of rebelliousness stemming from that small degree of cohesiveness that has always characterized them within an otherwise fractured community.

This first revealed itself in 1886, when the Cape authorities, alarmed by a smallpox epidemic then sweeping the colony, closed the Muslim cemetery in the Bo-Kaap on the grounds that it was a health hazard. Outraged at this affront to their faith, the Cape Muslims defied the law and rioted. It was the first instance of spontaneous civil disobedience by South Africa's powerless people of colour. A century later I witnessed a recrudescence of this spirit in the "coloured" township of Athlone, outside Cape Town. On October 15, 1985, an orange-coloured truck with three wooden crates on the back drove down Thornton Road, a moderately affluent road in an otherwise run-down ghetto with a high percentage of Muslims living in it. It was at the height of the great wave

8. Achmat Davids, *The Mosques of Bo-Kaap* (Cape Town, 1980), pp. xvii–xxiv.

9. Ibid., p. 42.

of racial unrest that had begun to sweep South Africa a year before, and as the truck rolled along, a group of chanting, jeering youngsters threw rocks at what they assumed was some kind of official vehicle. That was exactly what the security forces had anticipated. As television cameras filmed the scene, a dozen armed riot police leapt up from inside the crates and opened fire. Three of the kids fell dead—Michael Miranda, eleven, Shaun Magmoed, sixteen, and Jonathan Claassens, twenty-one. They were Muslims.

Two days later, as outrage swept the world over what became known as the "Trojan truck massacre," an angry crowd thronged Thornton Road. The police had refused to hand over the bodies for quick burial before sunset, as required by the Muslim faith; intent on preventing yet another mass political funeral—there were many in 1985—they were demanding that the parents first sign a pledge that no more than fifty people would attend the burials. Infuriated at such sacrilege added to injury, the Muslims of Cape Town poured into Thornton Road, many of them dressed in their religious robes, to yell defiance at the authorities and cry revenge. *"Allahu-Akbar!"* yelled some. "God is great!" And the call for a *jihad*, or holy war, was heard. That night, as a protest rally was held in a nearby mosque, a shot rang out from behind a minaret and a riot policeman on standby alert outside fell to the ground with a bullet in his stomach.

Shades of Teheran. The Cape Muslims are Sunni, but as militancy grips the "coloured" community, the spirit of Shiite fundamentalism is striking a resonant chord among some of the youth. It is a new thing of still unquantifiable significance.

FROM THE MOMENT Van Riebeeck drove the Khoikhoi from the banks of the Liesbeeck River to provide pasturage for his first free burghers, the hunter-herder clans began to disintegrate. They did so with astonishing speed. They were small nomadic clans with little institutional strength to help them withstand the impact of a superior culture, and they could not unite for long against a common enemy. Their grazing lands were easily appropriated because they had no fixed claim to them, and, once these were gone, the pattern of their lives was disrupted. As they had told Van Riebeeck, losing their land meant they would have to depasture the land of others, and that could only lead to trouble. Intertribal conflicts became endemic.

Worst of all was the shrinking of the cattle herds. Hunting and herding were the Khoikhoi's only means of subsistence and cattle their only form of wealth, their only insurance for the future. As white-settler farming expanded, the game herds diminished; and as the whites took over the best pastures, the Khoikhoi were left with insufficient land for their herds. Most devastating of all, the herds were depleted by the Cape victualling station's voracious appetite for meat.

The VOC directors had told Van Riebeeck to count on delivering eight cattle and eight sheep to each ship, and to expect about thirty ships a year. This was a hopeless underestimate. The number of ships increased rapidly, averaging about sixty-five by the mid-1690s and more than eighty-five in the early 1720s, while the number of stock slaughtered per ship rose even more steeply. After seventeen years the station had consumed 4,656 head of cattle and 18,683 sheep.[10] Apart from a few breeding rams, the VOC brought in no livestock of its own so that one way or another all these animals were obtained in the first instance from the Khoikhoi. It was a rate of consumption that far exceeded the natural increase, so that the pool of Khoikhoi livestock was seriously diminished.

The animals were bartered for copper wire, beads, and tobacco, raising the painful question of whether the Khoikhoi did not sell their birthright for a few worthless trinkets. As the herds began to run dangerously low and the Khoikhoi became more reluctant to trade, the Dutch resorted to raiding, driving off thousands of cattle and sheep. At the same time trading expeditions were sent to the distant Guriqua and Namaqua tribes in the north, so extending the depredation to the outer fringes of Khoikhoi society.

Their land gone and their herds depleted, the Khoikhoi clans collapsed. They had no choice but to turn to the white farmers who occupied their grazing lands and offer themselves for service. The labour-hungry farmers snapped them up, since they were skilled herdsmen, and often paid them no more in wages than a basic food ration and the right to run a few cattle of their own on the farm. And so the Khoikhoi population became a permanent labouring class.

As they flocked onto the labour market, the British colonial government compiled South Africa's first labour regulations for people of colour. Whites became nervous at the growing numbers of Khoikhoi wandering about the countryside, so the regulations made it illegal for any of them to be unemployed and compelled all to carry passes. So began South Africa's notorious pass-law system. A Khoikhoi worker had to enter into a labour contract with his employer, and when this was completed he had either to renew it or to engage himself on a new contract with another employer. That placed him in a state of permanent bondage. Missionary pressure brought some small measures of legal protection for the Khoikhoi, culminating in a proclamation in the 1828

10. Richard Elphick, *Khoikhoi*, pp. 152–53.

Ordinance 50, which freed them from the need to carry passes, but their basic position remained unchanged.

They were not slaves, because both VOC and British law prohibited the enslavement of Khoikhoi, but they were treated like slaves. Indeed, as Thomas Pringle observed, they were often treated worse because of their lack of monetary value. "A miserable abject race of people" is how he described them, "generally living in the service of the Boers, who had so many of them that they were thought of little value as servants, and were treated more like brute beasts than human beings."[11] The Khoikhoi labourers were accommodated in the *slavenhuys*, where they lived with the slaves and ate with the slaves, and by day they worked with the slaves. In all but name they became a subdivision of the slave force, and in that capacity were a part of the transition of South Africa's labour system from slavery to the contractual serfdom that has continued in only slightly amended forms until the present time.

As Robert Ross has noted, just as the Khoikhoi were treated like slaves before abolition, so were the freed slaves treated like Khoikhoi after abolition. An alternative system for the impressment of "coloured" labour was already in operation.[12] What had already been done with the Khoikhoi could now be done with the slaves—and in due course, when the blacks were similarly dispossessed and compelled to offer themselves as labourers to the whites who had taken their land, it was done with them as well. The road from slavery to apartheid was across the broken backs of the Khoikhoi.

They died soon afterward. A series of smallpox epidemics ravaged the scattered and demoralized remnants of these most indigenous of all South Africans. They had as little resistance physically as they had culturally to the white world and its noxious appurtenances that had come among them. They died by the thousands. Those who survived became intermixed with the freed slaves to the point where they lost any separate identity. Only their genes live on: in the eastern Cape especially, where they survived a little longer, one will occasionally see a small, wrinkled, gnomelike face like a snapshot from the past. But of their language and culture there is no trace.

They and the slaves and the occasional descendants of the San and the other bit-players who don't fit neatly into any of the more precisely definable race groups in South Africa's labelled and compartmentalized society have all been lumped together into this hold-all category called the "coloureds." It is a sort of "miscellaneous" category of the ethnically

11. Thomas Pringle, *Narrative of a Residence in South Africa*, p. 237.

12. Ross, op. cit., p. 52.

undefinable, a penumbral group in apartheid's stark world of light and shade.

The racial categorists have done their best. The Population Registration Act, which is really the cornerstone of the whole apartheid structure, defines the "coloureds" with an impressive attention to ethnic detail. According to the Act there are seven subgroups: (1) the Cape Coloured group; (2) the Malay group; (3) the Griqua group (descendants of racial mixing between whites and outlying tribes on the northern fringes of the Khoikhoi area); (4) the Chinese group ("Persons," the Act explains, "who are generally accepted as members of a race or tribe whose national home is in China"); (5) the Indian group; (6) the Other Asiatic Group (consisting of Zanzibari Arabs and anyone originating from anywhere in Asia other than China, India, or Pakistan); and (7) the Other Coloured Group (which means anyone who is not in any of the above groups and who is neither white nor African).

BUT IT WOULD BE wrong to suggest that the abolition of slavery meant nothing to either slave or slave-owner. It freed the slaves but did not liberate them, and a system of institutionalized segregation and forced vassalage quickly replaced it; but even so, as in the other South, it was a traumatic event in South Africa. It was the end of an institution that had been entrenched for 182 years—longer than the time that separates us today from abolition. The whites bitterly resented it, and for the Afrikaners it began a century of grievance that culminated in a terrible war and became the burning fuel of their nationalism; the so-called "coloureds" were both exhilarated and thrown into confusion by it. Combined with the lifting of the pass laws by Ordinance 50, it meant that the former slaves and serfs were at least free to move. And move they did. A series of mass migrations from the countryside to the city eventually turned the "coloured" people into a predominantly urban proletariat. Today fewer than 15 percent of them are still on the farms.

The farmers tried desperately to stop this hemorrhage of cheap labour, and liquor was their main means of doing so. Quite simply, they tried to keep the labour hooked. The western Cape is wine country, and at an early stage the wine farmers introduced what became known as the "tot" system: paying part of their "coloured" workers' wages in daily rations of cheap wine. Not only was it economical, it also ensnared the work force. The result is that alcoholism became and has remained an endemic problem. Drive into the Boland, as the wine valleys beyond Cape Town are called, on a Friday afternoon and you will see "coloured" folk reeling about the roadsides in a state of mass drunkenness that is astonishing. Douglas Laurie, a missionary at Franschhoek in the heart of the wineland, says it is not that they drink so much but that they drink to get drunk. "It's escapism," he says. "I've seen a man get drunk on half a bottle of table wine."

With drunkenness goes brawling. Men beat up their wives and one another. The domestic carnage at weekends is frightful, and children grow up in an environment saturated with violence. "When you're a kid in that situation you can go one of two ways," says Boesak. "Either you start drinking yourself or you vow never to touch the stuff."

Drunkenness, violence, improvidence, illegitimacy—these are the indexes of the massive social and psychological damage that has been done to the "coloured" people. Yet there is a cheerfulness with it all—a sharp-tongued wit and a raciness of conversation that has a Cockney flavour to it. "I resist generalizations," says Laurie, "but there are a lot of Andy Capps around."

The survivalist spirit is even stronger in the city. The migratory waves headed for an area just off-centre of Cape Town, called District Six, which spilled in a jumble of tenement shacks down the lower slopes of Table Mountain. The late writer Richard Rive, who grew up there, warned against the temptation to romanticize about slum life. "I endured a harrowing childhood in District Six," he said, "where drunkenness, debauchery, and police raids were the order of the day."

Yet for all its squalour the teeming life of the District had cohesion. People knew people—sometimes too intimately, it is true, as married couples shared rooms with other married couples in the appalling overcrowding. But it was not a world of strangers. A roaming child would be spotted by someone who knew him and be sent home. Newcomers from the countryside would have a relative they could move in with until they found rooms of their own. It was a Dickensian world of petty traders, pimps, musicians and shoemakers, tinkers, tailors, magicians and drug-pushers, pickpockets, bag-snatchers, hustlers and craftsmen; a place of jazz music and bare-chested street fights, of noise and smells; a place into which the white world seldom ventured but which to the "coloured" people was the nucleus of their existence.

In 1966 a death warrant was signed on District Six. With everyone in the country classified according to race, apartheid's next task was to separate them into ethnic compartments. Being so close to the downtown area, District Six was classified as a "white area" and the "coloureds" who had been there for five generations were told to go. The bulldozers moved in, on the orders of the man who was then minister of coloured affairs, P. W. Botha.

At its height, District Six was home to some sixty thousand people. Today it is a wasteland of broken bricks and rubble with only a few churches and mosques left standing—monuments to the religious fastidiousness of a ruthless regime. The whites of Cape Town, who have a reputation for liberalism, have protested admirably by refusing to live there, so that after twenty years its dilapidated vacancy remains as an unsightly admonition in the heart of the Mother City. It is like a vast bomb site, overgrown with weeds and strewn with the debris of demolished homes and abandoned utensils. An old stove, a child's feeding cup, bits of broken crockery, the remnants of uprooted lives. "Ahmed was here," runs a line of faded graffiti on a jagged piece of wall, while beyond it like a label over the white man's shiny city of steel and glass a cigarette advertiser's billboard on a skyscraper proclaims that LIFE IS GREAT!

District Six's sixty thousand people were scattered along a ribbon of new townships on the sandy Cape Flats, ten, twenty, forty miles from Cape Town, the fine-spun web of their communal life rent apart. The housing in the new townships is better than it was in District Six, and the shopping complexes are more modern. But they are soulless places, frightened and frightening. There is no throbbing street life here. People scuttle into the safety of their houses, for the new townships are ruled by gangs, of which there are dozens. They go by flashy names: the Cape Town Scorpions, the Born Free Kids, the Vultures, the Mongrels, the Total Killers, the Never Minds, the Pretty Boys, the Sicilian Kids, and many more. At night you can see a gang on nearly every block, clusters of young men looking bored and dangerous in the unlit gloom of the deserted streets. They are heavily into drugs and live by robbing, running protection rackets, and acting as fences for stolen goods. The crime rate in these townships on the Cape Flats is the highest in the world.

There were other evictions, too, in cities and towns all over South Africa—a total of 860,400 "coloureds" and Indians have been uprooted over the past twenty years.[13] As the apartheid programme got under way, "coloureds" were kicked out of jobs as well as homes; they were shoved to the back of buses and trains, and zealous bureaucrats pried into their ancestry, examined the whites of their eyes and ran pencils through their hair to test the degree of its wiriness, as the state set about the massive task of classifying everyone according to race. And before they were done the apartheidists inflicted on the "coloured" people the ultimate in human insults. They passed a law called the Immorality Act, outlawing sex across the colour line. It was a statutory declaration that the "coloured" people should never have existed, that their procreation was a sin and a crime which should have been prevented.

13. Laurine Platzky and Cherryl Walker, *The Surplus People: Forced Removals in South Africa* (Johannesburg, 1985), p. 35.

It has been a story of cruel and willful rejection, which does not even have the one mitigating argument that white South Africa uses to justify apartheid—that the whites, particularly the Afrikaners, would be swamped and lose their national identity if they allowed integration. The "coloureds" are a minority who represent no numerical threat to anyone. Nor, as "brown Afrikaners," are they any kind of cultural threat. Yet they have been treated abominably and have been greatly damaged. But today a new spirit of commitment rises from the ashes of this psychologically ravaged community, a passionate concern amid the social disintegration, as the "coloureds" discover a cause and even an identity in the idea that they will be black rather than white. A political revival has taken place, catalyzed by the attempt that was made too late to co-opt them as acolytes of the whites and that succeeded only in adding insult to three and a half centuries of injury.

IT WAS BEING thrown off a train in South Africa that started Gandhi on his lifelong crusade.

He had arrived in South Africa from India, a British-trained barrister aged twenty-three, to represent an Indian trading firm in a legal action that was to be heard in the Pretoria Supreme Court. His ship docked in Durban and the shy young barrister, dressed in the frock coat and patent leather shoes that were the uniform of Chancery Lane in 1893, bought a first-class ticket and boarded the train for Pretoria.

Sitting in a first-class compartment befitted his profession, and there was no thought in young Gandhi's mind of making a demonstration, but to the white conductor on the segregated train he was just another Indian, and people of colour were not allowed to travel in first-class compartments. He ordered Gandhi out, and when the lawyer refused there was an argument. It was quickly settled. When the train made its first stop at Pietermaritzburg, the conductor had the impertinent Indian thrown off, frock coat and all. As Gandhi wrote later:

> I was on the horns of a dilemma. Two courses were open to me. I might either free myself from the contract with Messrs Dada Abdulla on the ground that circumstances had come to my knowledge which had not been disclosed to me before, and run back to India. Or I might bear all hardships and fulfill my engagement. I was pushed out of the train by a police constable at Maritzburg, and the train having left, was sitting in the waiting room, shivering in the bitter cold. I did not know where my luggage was, nor did I dare to inquire of anybody, lest I might be insulted and assaulted once again. Sleep was out of the question. Doubt took possession of my mind. Late at night, I came to the conclusion that to

> run back to India would be cowardly. I must accomplish what I had undertaken. I must reach Pretoria, without minding insults and even assaults. Pretoria was my goal. The case was being fought there. I made up my mind to take some steps, if that was possible, side by side with my work. This resolution somewhat pacified and strengthened me but I did not get any sleep.[14]

By such small twists of fate is history made. The decision taken in the waiting room of the Pietermaritzburg train station that winter's night not only affected the course of events in South Africa but led to the founding of a strategic philosophy which began the great groundswell of postwar decolonization that may be seen in retrospect to have been the most important event of the twentieth century, which inspired the American civil rights movement, and which still permeates nationalist, dissident, and humanist movements three-quarters of a century later.

Gandhi had resolved to take "some steps." The first, like Neil Armstrong's on the moon, was small but in its own way a giant leap. Gandhi appeared in the Pretoria court wearing a turban and was ordered to remove it. He immediately petitioned for recognition of his right as an Indian to wear a symbol of his homeland in a foreign court—and won. It was the first time any person of colour had challenged authority in South Africa. There was a long, long road ahead and there is still no end in sight ninety-six years later, but this was the moment when resistance to white rule began.

It developed rapidly. Gandhi's court case ended and he prepared to leave, but before he could do so the Natal colonial administration published a bill to disenfranchise the local Indians. By then the young lawyer had made a number of public speeches on the subject of racial injustice, and the local community begged him to stay to lead a campaign against the new bill. He delayed his departure by a month and organized a petition bearing ten thousand signatures to the colonial secretary, Lord Ripon, to disallow the Disenfranchising Bill. It was vetoed.

The month became twenty-one years. Gandhi formed first the Natal Indian Congress, then the Transvaal Indian Congress. Special-interest organizations were formed to administer community needs. As his ideas on social philosophy developed, he established a community centre at Phoenix Farm in Natal where men, women, and children lived in a communal setting based on mutual cooperation. Later, with the help of a wealthy white admirer, he established a similar refuge near Johannesburg, which he named Tolstoy Farm after his great friend and mentor,

14. M. K. Gandhi, *The Selected Works of Mahatma Gandhi*, vol. 3: *Satyagraha in South Africa* (Ahmedabad, 1968), p. 56.

Count Leo Tolstoy. He founded a newspaper called *Indian Opinion*. Hundreds of volunteer workers were drawn into these activities and the Indian community became highly politicized.

With his people mobilized, Gandhi launched campaign after campaign to protest laws that discriminated against Indians in both Natal and Transvaal. For the first time the world saw the potency of passive resistance as a weapon of protest. *Satyagraha*, Gandhi called it, or power of truth, a strategy that involved totally honest nonviolent noncompliance with the offending law, the enduring of suffering or imprisonment if necessary, while at all times showing respect to those who made the law or enforced it. When the Transvaal passed a law in 1906 requiring all Indians over the age of eight to carry passes bearing their fingerprints, 2,300 burnt their passes in a giant iron cauldron in Johannesburg and presented themselves for arrest and imprisonment. When a court ruled that all marriages not celebrated by Christian rites were invalid, Gandhi organized a protest march by five thousand men, women, and children across the Natal-Transvaal border without the permits required for Indians to cross provincial boundaries, which meant they again invited mass arrest and overflowed the jails. To ease the pressure on the prisons some were sentenced to work in the mines, but they refused, were rearrested, and sentenced again.

These campaigns brought Jan Smuts, later to become prime minister, into personal conflict with Gandhi on several occasions. Smuts became obsessed with the Indians. He looked to the northeast, beheld their huge numbers in the Indian subcontinent, and became convinced that they would head across the Indian Ocean to the comparatively empty land mass of Africa in search of *Lebensraum*. South Africa should get ready to withstand this invasion. *"My seun, pas op vir die Indier,"* he would warn young neophytes in his United party—"My son, watch out for the Indian." His obsession transmitted itself especially to his English-speaking followers in Natal and added to their already strong prejudices against the Indians.

But for black South Africans, Gandhi was an inspiration. Though he never campaigned on behalf of the black Africans, limiting himself to the cause of the Indian community, he was the trailblazer who started the resistance movement and gave it the techniques that it followed for half a century and that exert a profound influence still. In 1914, as war clouds gathered over Europe, Gandhi left South Africa to build his liberation movement in India. Two years earlier the African National Congress had been formed. He was in a sense its progenitor.

CHAPTER FIVE

The Great Dispersal

And I am come down to deliver them out of the hand of the Egyptians, and to bring them up out of that land unto a good land and a large, unto a land flowing with milk and honey.

EXODUS 3:8

Your land, strangers devour it in your presence, and it is desolate, as overthrown by strangers.

ISAIAH 1:7

BY THE SECOND DECADE of the nineteenth century the ethnic stage was set for the enactment of an epic drama. Four groups of people as different from one another as any on God's earth were cast together in a closed setting on the eastern frontier of South Africa. There were the world's most isolated whites, locked in their seventeenth-century time capsule, convinced of their God-given rights over the unelected pagans around them, and offended by the doctrine of black rights that was being foisted on them. There were the world's most advanced whites, bringing with them the spirit of a new age but sowing confusion as they did so with their ambiguous blend of racial superiority and philanthropy, of exploitation and humanism. There were the black tribes, proud and secure in their own immemorial culture but bewildered by the strangers now blocking their path and the turmoil that was beginning to build up in their rear. And there were the Khoikhoi and the slaves, stripped of land and cultural heritage and merging together into a new racially defined category of servile workers.

The economy of the region, static since the beginning of time, was beginning to stir and add new elements of conflict to this explosive heteromorphism. Britain was drawing her new colony into the dynamic stream of free trade. Consumer goods were flowing in, creating a need for foreign exchange, which in turn was creating a need for cheap labour just as the pressures to abolish slavery were beginning to mount. Discriminatory labour laws accompanied progress toward emancipation, perplexing black and white alike. Class conflict was being added to race conflict. The first dim outlines of the future pattern of racial capitalism were beginning to appear.

For a century and a half the main players had been in the wings as it were, eyeing one another from a distance, making only peripheral contact. The land was still large enough and the populations were still small enough for them to keep out of one another's way. But now their numbers had grown and the land between them had shrunk until they were face to face on the coastal strip, competing for the same grazing and water sources that were crucial to their survival and way of life. And now the Third Man in the cast had arrived on stage to establish his own settlement and close the frontier. The age of separate freedoms was at an end. The age of interaction had begun, an age that commenced with the drama of attempted escape and a blood-spattered dispersal before the players came together again into an ongoing relationship of rejection and attraction, of mutual antipathy and dependency. It is a relationship not unlike that of Arthur Schopenhauer's porcupines on a freezing night, who bunch together for warmth only to prick each other and move apart, causing them to freeze again and move closer once more. That is the story of modern South Africa.

One may liken the closing of the South African frontier to the damming of two streams flowing languidly in opposite directions. The slow drift forward stopped and the pressures increased as the waters backed up on both sides, the effects of the stoppage moving ever farther upstream into the hinterland of each. The seminomadic Trekboers, accustomed to a freedom verging on lawlessness, chafed under new regulations that pinned them down and interfered with their lives, while the crowding of tribal land disturbed the pattern of Nguni life deep into Natal among clans who had never encountered the white race far to the south of them. Tensions on both sides rose until they burst, and two great floods of humanity poured into the swirling interior.

With the stage thus set, two men living 450 miles apart each set in motion a train of events that culminated in the eruption. In April 1813 Freek Bezuidenhout, a headstrong Trekboer living on the banks of the Baviaans River on the eastern frontier, refused to release a Khoikhoi labourer named Booy when his work contract expired and held back his pay and the few cattle he had been allowed to run on the farm. Soon after this, far up the coastal plain on the banks of the White Umfolozi

River in Natal, about 100 miles north of where Durban is today, Chief Dingiswayo of the Mtetwa took note that an elderly chieftain of a small clan within his suzerainty had died, and he dispatched a promising young protégé named Shaka to take his place. Small events both of them, but with large consequences.

Bezuidenhout's withholding of Booy's pay and livestock was not uncommon practice on the frontier in those days. It was just one more way of exploiting the captive work force. But it was illegal under the labour regulations which the British had introduced in 1812 and Booy, as it turned out, was not the typically abject Khoikhoi worker described by Pringle. He was a man of some spirit who decided to fight for his rights, so he walked thirty-five miles from Baas Freek's farm to a new frontier post called Cradock where he laid a complaint at the *landdrost's* office. For two years Bezuidenhout refused to respond to the *landdrost's* summonses to appear in the local court. To him and to the Boer community as a whole it was intolerable that a white man should be haled before court to answer a Khoikhoi servant's complaints. The labourer was his "boy," to deal with as he pleased. For the British to interfere with this natural order of things was "a presumptuous innovation upon his rights and an intolerable usurpation of tyrannical authority."[1] So when the Circuit Court came to the area in 1815 Freek Bezuidenhout again refused to heed the summons, whereupon the judges sentenced him to a month's imprisonment for contempt of court.

On a hot October morning in the southern spring an undersheriff, supported by a military detachment of two white officers and sixteen "coloured" soldiers, arrived at Freek Bezuidenhout's farm to arrest him and take him to jail. But the determined Trekboer was ready for them. He had stashed food and ammunition in a cave on a hillside, and as the undersheriff's party arrived he withdrew into this fortress with an illegitimate "coloured" son and opened fire on them with a long-barrelled elephant gun. For several hours the battle raged until Bezuidenhout, craning forward to get a better aim, was hit by a shot from one of the "coloured" soldiers and killed.

Outrage swept the Boer community, and a few days later a group of them gathered on a nearby farm to swear vengeance against those who had caused Bezuidenhout's death and to plot rebellion against the British

1. Thomas Pringle, *Narrative of a Residence in South Africa*, pp. 66–75. Although the incident occurred before Pringle's arrival at the Cape, he settled in the Baviaans River area and, good reporter that he was, gathered the information from the official report and interviews with neighbours.

regime. To achieve their objective the conspirators sought the help of the Xhosa chief Ngqika and sent a messenger to put the proposition to him, promising to restore the Suurveld to his people if the rebellion succeeded. But Ngqika was sceptical of such an alliance with the people he regarded as his most hostile enemies, and as the plot stalled news of it leaked out to the British authorities. A force of dragoons was sent after the conspirators, and it caught up with them on a mountain pass known as Slagtersnek.[2] After some hours of parleying most of the rebels surrendered, but Freek Bezuidenhout's brother Hans and members of his family took off into the mountains with several followers. The dragoons gave chase and overtook the little group eleven days later. The followers gave themselves up, but Hans Bezuidenhout, emulating his brother's desperate courage, opened fire on the soldiers. He had seven muskets with him, and as his wife Martha and their twelve-year-old son reloaded them, he kept up a barrage until eventually he was gunned down and Martha and the boy were badly wounded.

Forty-seven of the rebels duly stood trial before the Circuit Court. Thirty-three received sentences ranging from banishment to short terms of imprisonment and fines, but five were sentenced to death by public hanging. By the standards of the day the sentences were not exceptional, but a gruesome bungling followed.

The government in Cape Town sent instructions to the hangman, but in doing so gave the impression there was only one prisoner to be executed. So the hangman set out with only one rope. Not until he reached the town of Uitenhage in the eastern Cape did he discover that there were in fact five condemned men. He obtained four more ropes but these were rotten, with the result that when he pulled the lever to spring the trapdoor only one man fell to his death. The other ropes broke and four live men fell to the ground. Amid scenes of anguish and hysteria they jumped to their feet and ran to the *landdrost* pleading for mercy, but that hapless official insisted he had no power to pardon them. So the men were hanged again, one by one, from the sound rope, in the presence of distraught friends and relatives, who believed the intervening hand of the Almighty had been defied.

The repercussions of this appalling episode were not felt immediately. Indeed it faded into obscurity for a time in a frontier community that lacked the cohesion and political consciousness to sustain a sense of collective grievance. But it marked the imposition of British rule on the frontier Boers—"the first bloodstained beacon which marks the

2. See Leonard Thompson, *The Political Mythology of Apartheid* (New Haven, 1985), p. 114.

boundary between Boer and Briton in South Africa" is how it was later described by the mythologizers of the awakening nationalism[3]—and the start of a chain of conflicts that was to culminate twenty years later in the mass exodus of Boers from the Cape Colony in 1835–37. Eventually some fourteen thousand of these Voortrekkers joined the Great Trek to the north, changing the geopolitical map of South Africa and providing Afrikanerdom with the sacred saga of a reenacted Exodus, a pilgrimage of ordeal and faith and deliverance that was to become the centrepiece of its sacral nationalism.

But thunderous as it was, the Great Trek was not the only or even the greatest mass migration to take place at that time. As the ropes broke at Slagtersnek on that grim day in March 1816, the tall young commander of Chief Dingiswayo's *iziCwe* regiment was on his way to the White Umfolozi River to take over the chieftainship of the small Zulu clan on the outer fringes of the Mtetwa paramountcy. The Nguni heartland was filling with people behind the closed frontier, and as this disrupted the ancient pattern of movement among the clans, competition between them increased for the overstocked grazing lands and for the water sources. Warfare was becoming incessant and Dingiswayo, the most astute of the Nguni chieftains, was trying to stabilize the situation by extending the hegemony of his Mtetwa tribe over its weaker neighbours so that each could be pinned in place and regulated. His young military commander, Shaka, was a key figure in this process. Now Dingiswayo was sending him to take over the clan of his birth, which he had left as a child. Shaka was just twenty-nine, a magnificent physical specimen and a budding military genius. During the next twelve years he, too, was to change the geopolitical map of South Africa, as he turned the Zulus into the most aggressive military power black Africa has ever seen and ravaged the subcontinent.

Millions of people fled before Shaka's plundering regiments. Splintered groups scrambled out of the coastal plain over the jagged jaws of the Drakensberg—the mountains of the dragons running down the eastern escarpment—onto the highveld and the flat plains of the Transvaal, where in their frenzied desperation they put yet other clans to flight, causing waves of disruption to radiate outward across the interior as far north as Lake Tanganyika and to the Kalahari Desert in the west. Every community throughout one-fifth of the African continent was pro-

3. F. W. Reitz, *A Century of Wrong* (London, 1900), p. 6. This book, a catalogue of Boer grievances against the British, was issued by Reitz in his capacity as state secretary of the South African Republic at the outbreak of the Boer War. It is said to have been written by Jan Smuts and Jacob de Roos.

foundly affected.[4] Ancient chiefdoms disintegrated and disappeared, new ones came into existence, and then they vanished too, while fragments of the shattered tribes found refuge in broken and hilly country and on the fringes of the desert. It was a time of devastation and death that the Tswana and Sotho clans of the highveld called the *Difaqane*, or the "forced migration."

As the Voortrekkers, making their way into the interior, came upon this scene of confusion they in turn clashed with the wandering tribes. The two eruptions from the closed frontier merged, as it were, into a single convulsion that shook South Africa for three decades. It changed the distribution of the population. It also changed the balance of economic power. For when things finally settled down and the straggling tribal fragments reemerged from their sanctuaries, they found the Boers had taken over the land. Many became squatters on the huge white farms that had once been their land, exchanging their labour for the right to stay and run a few cattle. From that moment onward black South Africans have been a dispossessed peasantry left only with those small "reserves" where they took refuge, forced en masse into the role of a captive working class.

IT IS HARD TO SAY whether things might have turned out differently had there been no Shaka. Did the circumstances create the man or he them? Such tantalizing questions litter the pages of history and have no answers.

Certainly Dingiswayo responded militarily to the mounting pressures within the crowded Nguni heartland, but his motives were more benign than expansionist. He built a standing conscript army, which he used to conquer clans and draw them into a broad confederacy where relations among them could be regulated and kept peaceful. By seeking to strengthen these bonds with a series of dynastic marriages, he tried to stabilize an increasingly turbulent situation.[5] Perhaps it was only a matter of time before such enlightened militarism inevitably turned rapacious. If Shaka had not done it, probably someone else would have. But there is no doubt that Shaka's unique talents and tormented personality added to the fury of the Zulu eruption.

4. Leonard Thompson, in *The Oxford History of South Africa*, vol. 1, ed. Monica Wilson and Leonard Thompson (New York, 1969), p. 345.

5. Thompson (ibid., p. 341) quotes Henry Francis Fynn, one of the earliest white settlers in Natal, as stating that Dingiswayo gave as his reason for his conquests "that he wished to do away with the incessant quarrels that occurred amongst the tribes, because no supreme head was over them to say who was right or who was wrong."

There is ambivalence in black South African minds today about Shaka. On the one hand there is pride in his achievements, in the triumphs of a Napoleonic era when for a glorious moment a black nation stood as a mighty power in its own right, able to challenge the white intruder with his superior technology and, a full fifty years after Shaka's own death and after his realm had begun to decline, still inflict on the British army the most grievous defeat that modern troops have ever suffered at the hands of aborigines.[6] The knowledge of that glorious past is important to people who have been humiliated racially and crushed into servitude.

But there is also resentment that it was Shaka's actions that smashed the other tribes and lost them their ancestral lands; so that when Zulu power was finally crushed and their last capital burned at Ulundi in 1879 there was no black resistance left anywhere and only servitude lay ahead for them all. Half a century later a white author was able to note the irony that those leaping warriors with their fearsome assegais and waving battle plumes now made the best house servants in white suburbia and had sunk "to the cooking of food, the polishing of floors and even the tending of babies."[7]

This ambivalence extends to the present-day role of the Zulus under Chief Mangosutho Buthelezi in their KwaZulu "homeland." Buthelezi, who traces his lineage from one of the first clans to be incorporated into Shaka's kingdom and whose royal ancestors were the king's chief councillors, embodies the pride of his people's history, which he has sought to reclaim by building his capital on the ashes at Ulundi and bringing back the ceremonies and symbols of the golden age. The warrior *impis*, or regiments, march again at the mass rallies of his Inkatha movement, waving their shields and assegais and shouting their war cries. The name of Shaka is invoked. Cheers ring out. The blood stirs. But KwaZulu is a part of apartheid's "homeland" system and the revival of tribalism is a part of the white regime's divide-and-rule strategy, both of which are anathema to South Africa's modern black nationalists, including many young Zulus, so that Buthelezi is increasingly accused of being a tool of the oppressors and of prolonging black servitude. The conflict has become as bitter now, and in parts of Natal almost as bloody, as it was a century and a half ago.

But let us return to Shaka himself and the dark side of his character

6. The Battle of Isandhlwana, in which the Zulu army overran a British military camp and wiped out eighteen hundred men, including six full companies of the Second Warwickshire Regiment, on January 22, 1878. For a vivid account of the battle see Donald R. Morris, *The Washing of the Spears* (London, 1973), pp. 355–90.

7. Sarah Gertrude Millin, *The South Africans* (New York, 1927), p. 34.

that drove him to such fanatical conquests and such a radical break with the ancient Nguni traditions of democratic chieftaincy and limited warfare.

The story begins with the rarity in African society of an unhappy childhood: around 1787 Senzangakona, chief of the small Zulu clan, had an affair with a beautiful, spirited girl called Nandi, the orphaned daughter of the recently deceased chief of the neighbouring Langeni clan. Marriage was against the rules of exogamy, since Senzangakona's mother came from the Langeni, but tribal custom did not frown on a dalliance that included a form of limited intercourse which the Nguni called *ukuHlobonga*. Pregnancy was another matter, however, so that there was a sense of scandal when a few months later the Langeni elders arrived at Senzangakona's kraal to tell him Nandi was with child.

With the whole clan facing humiliation, the Zulu elders tried to duck responsibility, replying that the girl could not possibly be pregnant and that it must be the work of *iShaka*, a supposed intestinal beetle that was sometimes blamed for menstrual irregularities. But there could be no further denial when in due time the Langeni elders called again and requested that Senzangakona send for Nandi and her *iShaka*.[8]

Nandi was installed as Senzangakona's third wife, but the marriage was clouded with shame and mother and child lived amid sniggers and jeers. It was clouded, too, by constant quarrels, as the strong-willed Nandi protested at the slights she suffered and demanded an enhanced status in the royal compound. After several stormy separations Senzangakona finally sent her back to the Langeni with Shaka and an infant daughter.

That compounded the shame. Nandi had disgraced her tribe by her affair with Senzangakona; now she humiliated them further by being returned as an unsatisfactory wife, forcing the tribe to refund her bride price. Her abrasive manner did not make things any easier, so that life among the Langeni became even more unpleasant than it had been among the Zulus. What added to little Shaka's misery, according to Donald Morris, is that he apparently had undersized genitals, and since small children ran around the kraals with no clothing this made him the butt of constant cruel gibes.[9] He grew up lonely and embittered, with only his mother to turn to as together they faced a hostile world.

When Shaka was fifteen a great drought struck the area and the Langeni, running short of food, evicted the troublesome Nandi and her family. She went to live first with a man called Gendeyana, who had

8. Morris, op. cit., p. 44. I have relied heavily on Morris's research into Shaka's early life and training.

9. Ibid., p. 45.

shown her kindness before, and then with an aunt who married into the Dletsheni clan, which was part of the Mtetwa confederacy. It was there that Shaka's military career began. With the onset of puberty he quickly shook off his previous puniness and began to develop a fine physique, at the same time showing qualities of assertiveness that made him the natural leader of his *ntanga*, or youth group. By the time he was twenty-three he measured six feet three inches with a powerfully muscled body to match. He caught the eye of Chief Dingiswayo and was drafted into one of the Mtetwa's best regiments, the *iziCwe*.

For Shaka it was the start of a time of happiness and fulfillment, but the scars of his childhood were still upon him. It seems clear from his later behaviour that he had developed an Oedipus fixation of excessive adoration for his mother and hatred of his father. Most historians think he was impotent and maybe a latent homosexual, who sublimated his sexual urges in intense military activity and discipline which, once he was chief of the Zulus, he imposed on the whole nation. He took to bathing daily in public, showing off his magnificent physique to the tribe in an apparent attempt to wipe out the repressed pain of those childhood gibes.

From the start Shaka was fascinated by military strategy. He spent hours pondering new tactics of attack, the design of new weaponry and new techniques of infighting. He regarded the throwing spear as a hopelessly inefficient weapon and devised a new stabbing assegai with a shortened haft and broadened blade which he called the *iKlwa* in onomatopoeic imitation of the sucking sound it made when withdrawn from the body of a slain victim. He lengthened his rawhide shield so that it covered his whole body and he could advance behind it through the shower of thrown spears to engage the enemy in hand-to-hand combat. At close quarters he would hook the left edge of his shield over the right edge of an opponent's, and with a powerful outward sweep spin the opponent's body off balance to its right. This would also drag the opponent's shield and left arm across his body, exposing the left armpit to Shaka who would sink in his *iKlwa* with a blow that was a natural continuation of the shield-hooking movement. *"Ngadla!"* he would shout. "I have eaten!" It became the blood-chilling battlecry of the Zulu *impis*.

He threw away his rawhide sandals to give himself greater speed and surer footing. The countryside was filled with thorns, but Shaka hardened his feet to make them impervious. He trained until he could run effortlessly all day across the trackless veld. As a warrior he was brilliant, innovative, and obsessed. Dingiswayo soon made him commander of the *iziCwe*. He also drew him into the Mtetwa council where political policy was discussed. He was grooming the young man for leadership.

It soon became apparent, however, that Shaka was not in full accord with the chief's attitude to warfare. To Dingiswayo war was an unfortunate necessity to bring clans into his confederacy and stabilize the relations among them. He was therefore always ready to make peace at the first sign of an enemy's willingness to submit and he would reinstate the vanquished chieftaincy under his own paramountcy. But Shaka had seen too often how a defeated enemy that had not been crushed might rise again and have to be fought a second time. He believed in annihilating them totally the first time and incorporating the remnants into his own ranks. Nor did he hesitate to massacre women and children in achieving this total defeat.

Shaka rejected other aspects of the Nguni code of limited war as well. He was impatient with the ritualistic exchanges that preceded a battle, preferring the effectiveness of a surprise attack; and he was particularly contemptuous of the tradition of *giya*, in which individual warriors would run forward to yell taunts and put on a display of bravado before the real fighting began. Morris recounts how, in the war against the Buthelezi clan in 1816, when a warrior came forward to *giya*, Shaka dashed out of the ranks of the *iziCwe* and killed him with a single blow before charging the stunned Buthelezi alone.[10] Thus the concept of total war made its appearance for the first time in the long history of the black South African people, and over the next two decades spread throughout the region like a consuming plague.

The Zulus, meanwhile, came under Mtetwa suzerainty as well, and when Senzangakona died in 1816 Dingiswayo sent Shaka to take over the chieftaincy. It was the year of the Slagtersnek executions.

Shaka arrived with an escort from the *iziCwe*. He marched silently into the assembled ranks of the clan that had evicted him as a child and immediately ordered the execution of those who had been hostile to his mother, including the elders who had sent the insulting message to the Langeni about her pregnancy. That done, his reign began. When it ended twelve years later, the Zulus had grown from an insignificant clan numbering fifteen hundred people and occupying perhaps one hundred square miles into the mightiest kingdom black Africa has known with more than two million subjects inhabiting hundreds of thousands of square miles.

Shaka immediately set about reorganizing the Zulus in accordance with the ideas he had developed while leading the *iziCwe* and sitting in Dingiswayo's council. First he abandoned his father's kraal, where he had suffered so much misery, and built a new one to which he gave the ominous name of Bulawayo, or "the place of the one who kills."

10. Ibid., p. 47.

Then he set about building an army, calling up all the able-bodied men and forming them into regiments equipped with their own distinctive uniforms and colour-coded shields. These he trained in the rigorous techniques he had developed, equipping them with stabbing assegais and long shields and forcing them to harden their feet and to jog in formation until they could cover fifty miles in a day. He organized teenage herdboys into logistical support units trained to run behind the regiments carrying supplies of food, cooking pots, sleeping mats, and spare assegais. Suddenly the range and speed of attack of the Zulu army was extended far beyond anything Africa had known before.

All this was done under the fiercest discipline. The warriors were drilled to the point of exhaustion. Between campaigns they were forced to live in celibacy in military kraals. Young girls were organized into guilds, and occasionally Shaka would give the regiments permission to engage in *ukuHlobonga* with these female guilds. But apart from that the celibacy rule was strictly enforced until the warriors were in their forties, when Shaka would give batches of them permission to marry. He himself never married, and although he established a seraglio of more than a thousand captured maidens, among whom he spent much time, he never produced an heir. He explained this by saying he did not want a son who would one day oppose him, but historians attribute it to his presumed impotence.

Politically, too, Shaka centralized power in himself. The unrestrained power of the chief had always existed in theory but never before had it been so fully exercised. All checks and balances of the consensus system melted away under the force of his personality and the fear he instilled in those around him. It became a military dictatorship, something utterly alien to the traditions of black South Africa.

As his restructuring took shape Shaka began to look beyond the little clan he commanded. He turned his attention first to the neighbouring Langeni, sending an *impi* to surround their kraal at night. He ordered the entire male population to assemble before him, singled out those who had made his life miserable as a child, and had them impaled on the sharpened stakes of their own kraal fences.[11] He then incorporated the surviving Langeni into the Zulu clan.

So the process of expansion began. While Dingiswayo lived, Shaka continued to acknowledge his paramountcy and confined his expansionism to the small clans in his immediate neighbourhood. But after Dingiswayo's death in 1818 he saw no further need for such restraint and rapidly absorbed the entire Mtetwa confederacy into his unitary domain. Then he began looking even farther afield. He had built a great

11. Ibid., p. 53.

nation, but it was a nation built only for war, and as the army swelled with the new conquests it had to be kept constantly occupied.

As the Zulu *impis* ranged across the crowded coastal plain between the Drakensberg mountains to the northwest and the Indian Ocean to the southeast, they sent shattered fragments of desperate humanity fleeing in all directions. Some fled down the coast to the southwest and hurled themselves into the turbulent frontier scene where they became known as the Mfengu, or beggar people. Others scrambled over the Drakensberg onto the highveld, where they put the unsuspecting Sotho clans to flight. The *Difaqane* had begun.

It became a deadly chain reaction. Even before Shaka's rise to power, Dingiswayo and a neighbouring chief named Zwide had launched successive attacks on a clan called the Ngwane, sending them fleeing into the foothills of the Drakensberg, where they displaced another clan called the Hlubi, who became the first to escape over the mountains to the Transvaal highveld. In 1822 Shaka attacked both the Ngwane, led by Chief Matiwane, and Zwide's Ndwandwe. Matiwane, too, scrambled onto the high central plateau, where he clashed again with the Hlubi; in their wandering desperation without land or food or cattle, both clans resorted to pillaging. One of the first Sotho tribes they disrupted was the Batlokwa, led by a formidable woman called Mantatisi, whose fugitive horde rolled across the highveld crushing all before it and drawing refugee remnants along in its train until by 1823 it had swelled into an unstoppable mass of more than fifty thousand starving men, women, and children. "Clan upon clan perished beneath Mantatisi's advance," writes the Basotho historian Peter Becker. "Thousands of people, on learning of her approach, fled into the highlands. . . . Waves of refugees rolled forward like animals before a band of hunters. Sotho groups that for many generations lived side by side in comparative harmony became bitter enemies. A general scramble for cattle took place. Bands of brigands zigzagged across the Caledon Valley in search of unharvested fields to strip and granaries to raid."[12]

Zwide was crushed in the attack on him, but two of his warriors, Shoshangane and Zwangendaba, escaped Shaka's clutches with small bands of followers, which they also managed to enlarge as they drove forward like hunters over the terrified little clans in their path. Shoshangane made his way into present-day Mozambique, where he overwhelmed the local Tsonga people and established what is now the Shangane tribe. Zwangendaba struck out northward, crossed the Limpopo and the Zambezi, and established the Nguni kingdom along the

12. Peter Becker, *Hill of Destiny: The Life and Times of Moshesh, Founder of the Basotho* (London, 1969), p. 41.

western shores of Lake Malawi, from where it spread as far north as Lake Tanganyika, two thousand miles from his starting point.

Another of Zwide's warriors, Mzilikazi, was captured by Shaka, who made him a regimental commander. It was a fateful appointment. When a few years later Shaka sent the young commander on a cattle raid into Sotho country, Mzilikazi absconded with both the cattle he had rustled and the two regiments entrusted to him. He, too, headed for the interior, swallowing up Sotho clans as he went and building a mighty new nation of his own modelled on the Zulu. Mzilikazi's Ndebele became the dominant military power in the Transvaal, on the high central plateau beyond the Drakensberg, with some five thousand warriors trained in Shaka's total-war tactics. For two decades they ravaged the interior from the mountains to the desert to the far northern Transvaal until eventually a Voortrekker commando drove them across the Limpopo where today they form the Ndebele people of southwestern Zimbabwe.

These four groups—the Hlubi, the Ngwane, the Ndebele, and the Batlokwa—became the main agents of the disruption on the highveld. They in turn dislodged scores of secondary agents until some two or three million people were stumbling back and forth across the land, plundering and being plundered, killing and being killed. Not a clan was left untouched, and across the length and breadth of the central plateau not a single permanent kraal remained. Cultivation ceased and as food ran out many people crazed by famine turned to cannibalism, something totally alien and repugnant to black South African culture. A Hlubi survivor captured something of the atmosphere with a description of his wanderings during these grim times:

> I was wandering on a path. I saw a man who called to me to stop. He came to me and told me to sit down. He caught hold of my skin mantle. I left it in his hand and ran as fast as I could. He was a cannibal, and wished to kill me. Afterwards I met two children. . . . One was dead. The living one was eating the flesh of the dead one. I passed on. Next I saw a company of people digging plants. I was afraid of them and hid myself. When I was still going I saw a long stone wall, not very high. There were people sitting there cooking. I saw human heads on the ground. I took another way and escaped from these cannibals.[13]

It was a time of desperation during which man was reduced to bestiality and the spirit of *ubuntu* disappeared from the land. Those who survived did so by taking refuge in mountain and desert country. Sobhuza, an Nguni chief of the Dlamini clan, retreated into mountains

13. Quoted by Thompson, op. cit., p. 395.

north of the Pongola River, created an army on Zulu lines, and laid the foundations of what later became the kingdom of Swaziland, named after his son, Mswazi, who took over the chieftaincy when Sobhuza died in 1840. The Venda melted into the Soutpansberg Mountains of the north, the Tswana into the fringes of the Kalahari Desert in the west.

Farther south a young chieftain named Moshoeshoe gathered about him the remnants of the shattered Sotho clans and in 1824 led them into the Maluti Mountains at the southern end of the Drakensberg range. There he installed them atop a remarkable flat-topped mountain he called Thaba Bosiu, or the "Mountain of the Night," because they reached it after dark at the end of a terrible march during which Moshoeshoe's uncle, Peete, was captured by cannibals.[14] The mountain rises some 350 feet on all sides and is topped by a sheer cliff through which there are only a few narrow passes to the summit. On top Moshoeshoe found two square miles of lush pasturage with an abundance of spring water. It was an impregnable natural fortress, and from there he proceeded to gather in refugees and build the Basotho nation which in time came to rival that of the Zulus in fame. But whereas Shaka's fame was martial, Moshoeshoe's was diplomatic. He was shrewd, subtle, generous, and humanitarian and he saved the soul of black South Africa from its age of darkness.

IT WAS INTO this maelstrom that the Voortrekkers plunged.

By 1836 the dam had burst on the other side of the closed frontier too. The waters of grievance and confinement had backed up to the point where the low level of Boer tolerance was overflowing. "Don't fence me in," runs an old Gene Autry cowboy song. The Boers felt that way too. They hated boundaries. They had grown up with a sense of spaciousness that was part of their concept of freedom, and they hated being enclosed and restricted in their ability to move on and appropriate a new farm for each newly grown man. Above all they hated being interfered with in the regulating of their own affairs on their own farms. That was a kind of sacrilege. The long years of VOC neglect had left them with a sense of total autonomy on their own domains, to intrude on which was to violate a free man's fundamental rights.

When the Dutch government had tentatively tried to introduce some small degree of administrative control toward the end of the eighteenth century, the Trekboers had rebelled and declared two independent republics in the outlying districts of Swellendam and Graaff-Reinet. Now

14. Becker, *Hill of Destiny*, op. cit., p. 51.

this rebelliousness surged up again as the British drew their boundaries and imposed their regulations. Like the children of Israel they murmured against the alien rulers who afflicted them with these burdens. And the *trekgees*—the trek spirit—was upon them: the old urge if one was dissatisfied with anything to take one's wagons and one's span of oxen and one's horses and servants and households goods and go; to trek on under the clear blue skies in this endless land to some new ground where one's authority and independence would once again be unchallenged.

There were some genuine grievances, particularly over the abolition of slavery, and much has been made of them. The British offered compensation, a pro rata share of £20 million that was being divided among nineteen slave colonies, but it had to be collected in London. London! How was a Boer to get to London? There were agents offering to do the collecting but they had to be paid a commission. In the end very little compensation was received. Some Boers were too incensed to accept anything at all.

But the worst bitterness was over the imperial government's piecemeal granting of rights to people of colour. There was the right of a Khoikhoi servant to lodge a complaint against his master and take him to court, which had so enraged Freek Bezuidenhout. In 1828 Ordinance 50 ended the pass system for Khoikhoi and manumitted slaves and gave them equal legal status with whites. Six years later slavery itself was abolished. The cumulative effect represented the threat of *gelykstelling*, or equalizing, which the Boers considered an affront to their inherited principles.

"The shameful and unjust proceedings with reference to the freedom of the slaves," cited Anna Steenkamp, niece of Trek leader Piet Retief, in a famous exposition of the grievances that caused the Boers to leave their homes. "And yet it is not so much their freedom which drove us to such lengths as their being placed on an equal footing with Christians, contrary to the laws of God and the natural distinction of race and religion, so that it was intolerable for any decent Christian to bow down beneath such a yoke; wherefore we rather withdrew in order thus to preserve our doctrines in purity."[15]

Those were the overt reasons for the Great Trek. But as De Kiewiet has noted, there was an instinctive strategic reason as well. The black people on the coastal strip stood in the way of a continuation of the movement of white expansion that had been going on for a century, so the trekkers simply changed direction to outflank the obstruction. They headed inland and around the Nguni heartland to continue their expan-

15. Quoted in Gustav S. Preller, *Voortrekkermense*, vol. 2 (Cape Town, 1920), pp. 30–1.

sion as before.[16] And as they did so they entered upon a land that was largely abandoned as its original occupants fled the ravages of the *Difaqane*. Hungrily they ate it up in ten-thousand-acre gulps.

As they headed into the new territory they also headed into the maelstrom of unrest. Standing in their way were the two black military powers that had arisen there and were putting the smaller tribes to flight, the Ndebele on the highveld and the Zulus on the Natal coastal plain, and although the Voortrekkers overcame both they paid a heavy price in blood and suffering. But they endured their disasters and hardened their resolve, forging themselves as they went into a people of formidable resilience.

Within nine years some fourteen thousand Boers had sprung free of British rule and spread themselves thinly across most of the South African hinterland.[17] The area of contact with the blacks was massively increased, but it was a contact that produced neither greater understanding nor sympathy. As the Boers' view of Africa was enlarged they saw it at its darkest moment, which reinforced all their worst notions of native savagery and internecine belligerency. These blacks were surely the descendants of Ham, warlike and cruel, who had migrated southward from Arabia and should be compelled to work for the whites.

And so the Boers took over the land, confined the blacks to an arc of shrunken territory that curved around the central plateau, and drew thousands who were displaced and landless into servitude. They regarded it as their country, and since they had broken away from the unholy liberalism of the British with its threat of *gelykstelling*, they could now establish "proper" relationships with the blacks throughout the whole of it. For the rest of the century that was entrenched as the standard pattern of race relations in what later became the dominant region of South Africa.

The Boers' pioneering movement opened up the interior of South Africa, but it did not develop it. Unlike the pioneers who opened up the Australian interior or the American West, the Voortrekkers were not fortune seekers in search of new opportunities. They were not driven by the impulses of the industrial age to conquer the wilderness and wring new wealth from it. They were fugitives from that age, not the bearers of its ethos. In escaping the British they were essentially seeking to escape the nineteenth century and rediscover the arcadian simplicity of the seventeenth as they had known it before the British arrived. They went into the interior and, as they had done in the Cape before, they

16. De Kiewiet, *A History of South Africa, Social and Economic*, pp.53–4.

17. Eric A. Walker, *The Great Trek* (London, 1960), p. 6.

languished there with their imaginations lying fallow and their minds inert once more. "For two generations more," wrote De Kiewiet, "the children and grandchildren of the Voortrekkers continued to receive the education of the farm, the veld and the Boer home," carrying their nonliterary and nonindustrial attitudes and habits of mind right through to the end of the nineteenth century.[18]

They took along their almond-hedge mentality as well. Though the Voortrekkers were venturing into the African interior, it was to establish their own brand of European civilization there and keep Africa itself at arm's length. They had no intention of doing without servants, so the Great Trek had as many "coloured" retainers and "apprenticed" ex-slaves as it had Boers in the groaning ox wagons that set out from the Cape Colony.[19] But the country the Boers occupied was theirs alone. The republics they established recognized only whites as citizens. The blacks were there but they were ignored, essential but invisible appendages.

It meant that the Boer republics acquired a curious kind of equalitarianism-within-the-family. Since whites owned all the land and blacks did all the manual labour, no white person had to work for another white. All were equal in their racial aristocracy. All were fierce individualists with their own individual estates, so that none dared try to interfere with another's affairs or order him about. And since it was government that they had escaped from in the Cape Colony, they saw to it that government was kept to a minimum in their republics. Taxation was frowned on and the collection of it nearly impossible, which meant such government as they had was weak and ineffectual from want of revenue. Nothing could be done except by general consent of the equal and opinionated individualists who made up the nation. It was highly democratic, probably as close to the practical functioning of Jean Jacques Rousseau's general will as the world has ever seen. But it totally excluded all people of colour. In these first independent African republics, Africans were aliens.

For the blacks, it was the start of their long subjugation. Until then they had confronted the whites as equals, albeit mostly as enemies, each in his own territory and secure in his own culture. Now they had lost most of their territory and were compelled to enter into the service of the whites. The relationship was no longer between equals but between master and servant, in a situation the master believed to be the natural

18. De Kiewiet, op. cit., p. 56.

19. To cushion the effects of abolition, the British government ruled that slaves should be "apprenticed" to their masters for four years before they were freed.

and divinely ordained order of things and in which the servant worked under compulsion and the constant threat of violence.

Black power was broken. With the eventual defeat of the Ndebele and the Zulus, there was nothing left. Only the stubborn Xhosas on the eastern frontier remained unconquered. They fought nine frontier wars between 1778 and 1878 and were frequently defeated, but they were never conquered. In the end they broke themselves. Frustrated by their inability to ward off the encroaching whites who kept driving them back as their own overcrowding increased, they eventually turned in desperation to their ancestors for help. A young girl named Nongqawuse, niece of a powerful medicine man, had an apocalyptic vision one day while walking beside a river. As recounted by her uncle, a councillor to the Xhosa Chief Sarili, the tribe's ancestors bade her tell the Xhosas to kill all their cattle and burn all their grain. Then on a given day the sun would rise as usual in the east, reach its zenith, turn and set again in the east. At this sign all the graves would open and yield up the great warriors of the past, fat cattle would fill the kraal enclosures, the grain pits would overflow, wagonloads of guns and ammunition would appear and a great wind would arise to help the warriors drive the white people into the sea.

It was a last, desperate act of resistance. The result was a national disaster. Tens of thousands of Xhosas died. Thousands more left their scorched land to stumble, starving, across the frontier to the white farms looking for work. Xhosa power was broken at last and another migration into servitude took place.

Only in a few small retreats were there any elements of independence and resistance left: the Venda and the Pedi, who held out for a time against the Transvaal Boers; Moshoeshoe on his mountaintop, who continued to resist Boer expansionism in the Orange Free State until eventually, in extremis, he sought the protection of British subject statutes; and the Swazis and Tswanas, who did the same.

The psychological impact on the blacks was enormous—the successive blows of military defeat, then of dispossession, then of servitude. As they lost their land so, too, did their institutions begin to collapse, for the land was the most important foundation on which social life was built. Without land there was no room for the cattle, which were of such importance to the tribal way of life. The chiefs lost authority, and it was further eroded with the appointment of white magistrates who became the new focal points of power. And as the power of the chiefs faded so did the strength of traditional religious belief and ritual in which they played such an important part.

The disintegration of these social institutions removed the sheet anchor of black self-confidence. Thrust as they were into conditions of servitude and racial denigration on the white farms, blacks began to develop a sense of inferiority and an attitude of submissiveness. As the whites looked down on them, they began to look up to whites. It was a syndrome that was to have no positive counter until the advent of Steve Biko and his Black Consciousness movement six generations later, by which time subservience had become an ingrained part of black South African culture.

HISTORY IS IN the eye of the beholder. To the blacks the Great Trek was a time of defeat and dispossession. "The northward march of the Voortrekkers was a gigantic plundering raid," declared Dr. Abdul Abdurahman, a black political figure of the early twentieth century. "They swept like a desolating pestilence through the land, blasting everything in their path and pitilessly laughing at ravages from which the native races have not yet recovered."[20]

To Afrikaners it was a sacred saga, a thunderous reenactment of the story of Exodus during which God made known his will to his chosen people and brought them out from under the burdens of the British through trial and tribulation into their promised land. It was a "pilgrimage of martyrdom" they had to undertake to escape persecution "until every portion of that unhappy country had been painted red with blood, not so much of men capable of resistance as with that of our murdered and defenceless women and children." And as they went they were followed by the British army, like that of Pharaoh, and were beset everywhere by the unbelieving black "Canaanites."[21]

Thus the prisms of perspective on either side of the bitter-almond hedge.

There is little evidence that Piet Retief and the other Voortrekkers saw it in such apocalyptic terms as they went their way. They were simple folk, fed up with the interfering British and their *kaffirboetie* ("nigger-loving") ideas, and they were intent on moving on to where they could be on their own to deal with the blacks as they pleased. They were strongly religious, and they believed themselves to be part of God's Elect among the black pagans around them, but as yet they had no

20. Dr. Abdurahman was president of the African People's Organisation, a pioneer black political movement that later merged with the African National Congress. His description of the Great Trek was given at a congress of the organization on September 29, 1913, and is quoted by Sol T. Plaatje, the first black chronicler of these times, in *Native Life in South Africa* (London, 1916), p. 136.

21. See T. Dunbar Moodie, *The Rise of Afrikanerdom*. pp. 2–5, and F. W. Reitz, *A Century of Wrong*, pp. 92–3.

collective sense of nationalism, of being a special people or nation. They were still too individualist for that.

It took another forty years of British pursuit and harassment for that nationalism to blossom, and another fifty years after that for it to acquire its sacral overtones, to become what Dunbar Moodie has called the "Afrikaner civil religion." And when that happened the story of the Great Trek was revivified and sanctified and mythologized into the national epic of a divinely ordained people with a God-given mission to establish themselves as a nation in South Africa.

In 1938, one hundred years after the central event of the Voortrekkers swearing a Covenant with God and going on to defeat the Zulu army at the Battle of Blood River, the priests of this new sacral nationalism built a monument to the Trek on a hill outside Pretoria. It is a great gray granite structure, 135 feet high and 133 feet square, with a cornice on top and a semicircular, gauzelike panel in front that makes it look curiously like an old-fashioned radio. The symmetry of the design, so the visitors' brochure informs one, is meant to symbolize the order and civilization which the Voortrekkers brought to the interior; just as the head of a black wildebeest above the entrance represents the defeated Zulu warriors and "the barbarism that yielded to civilization." A small oil lamp burns in a niche in the crypt—the "Light of Civilization," the visitor is informed, that the Voortrekkers supposedly brought into this dark interior. The monument is surrounded by a *laager* or circle, of sixty-four granite wagons. Inside, a bas-relief frieze tells the story of the Trek with the themes of suffering and death and faith and retribution etched into the walls. There is nothing else in the cavernous interior except for an empty marble tomb set at a lower level with the words ONS VIR JOU SUID-AFRIKA inscribed on it. "We are for you, South Africa."[22] At noon on December 16 each year—the Day of the Vow—a ray of sunlight shines through an opening in the monument's upper dome and picks out this inscription. Here is the Ark of the Afrikaner Covenant set in the shrine of the civil religion.

But let us return to the event itself, before any of this consecration took place. It was, to be sure, an escape from the British, an attempt to move outside the British Empire's sphere of influence and authority. And while to begin with the British seemed happy to let such fractious people go off into the wild and useless interior, it is also true that when these tracts turned out to be rather more valuable than they at first imagined, the British edged closer and by various ploys and strategems for which perfidious Albion was famous sought to incorporate them into

22. The words are taken from the national anthem, "Die Stem van Suid-Africa" ("The Call of South Africa"), written by the Afrikaner Nationalist poet C. J. Langenhoven.

the imperial dominions. That provided the harassment, the catalogue of grievances, the century of wrong, that in the end produced Afrikaner nationalism. Whatever South Africa may represent today as the world's ultimate symbol of racial injustice, of whites repressing blacks, it is a syndrome that had its origins in a conflict between whites. It was the British who prompted Afrikaner nationalism into existence—and that sacral nationalism in turn evolved the theologized ideology of apartheid.

Some four thousand trekkers left British-controlled territory in the first two years. From the beginning their contentiousness revealed itself and they split into a number of factions, quarrelling about which direction to take. Eventually they took two divergent routes, some heading due north into the Transvaal to get as far away from the British as possible, others curving around to the east across the Drakensberg and into Natal in order to establish a seaport so that they would not be dependent on the British colony for their few essential imports of coffee, sugar, and gunpowder. Both ran head-on into the two main black military powers of the day—the Ndebele on the highveld and the Zulus in Natal.

Mzilikazi's Ndebele warriors fell upon the northbound trekkers, led by a tall, peppery man named Hendrik Potgieter, at a place called Vegkop—Battle Hill—in the northern Orange Free State in October 1836. For the first of many times the Boers circled their wagons into the famed defensive *laager* that became the symbol of their military strategy and ultimately of their mentality as well. While the women primed the old muzzle-loaders, the men fired from this makeshift fortress and, with a sharpshooting skill honed by generations of hunting and surviving in the wild, cut down the charging *impis* with their stabbing assegais. At the end of the day the Ndebele drove off thousands of Boer cattle, but the trekkers survived, and in due course they mounted a punishing reprisal attack and drove Mzilikazi and his people out of the country. In the latter-day mythology this was the first sign of God standing by his people and helping them to beat off their enemies.

It was to be thunderously repeated soon afterward in Natal. As the eastward-bound trekkers crossed the Drakensberg, Piet Retief, the oldest and most sophisticated of the Trek leaders, decided to seek a negotiated land deal with the Zulus. Shaka was dead by that time, assassinated by his half-brothers Dingane and Mhlangana, and Dingane had taken over as chief. He was a man of unstable temperament, lacking Shaka's intelligence and self-confidence and fearful of the confusing new forces swirling around him. Shaka had met some early white traders who had settled in Natal and had displayed an attitude of friendly curiosity toward them and the formidable technological culture they represented. There was no hint of animosity. But Dingane was nervous at the news of the trekker arrival, sensing that some threatening new power was invading his territory. He had heard how the Voortrekkers had smashed Mzilikazi and he decided on a preemptive action to stop them from settling in his vicinity.

Dingane purported to agree to Retief's land request and put his mark to a treaty. It was a trick. After inviting Retief and his party to a celebration, Dingane had his warriors seize and kill them. He then dispatched his *impis* to the main Boer encampment at a place now called Weenen—the place of weeping—where they attacked the unsuspecting trekker families, slaughtering 281 white men, women, and children and some two hundred "coloured" servants.

It is then that the Vow of the Covenant was sworn. The surviving Voortrekkers, reinforced by newcomers from the Cape Colony, mustered a powerful commando against the Zulus. Led by Andries Pretorius it trekked into the heart of Zululand and formed a laager beside the Ncome River. There the Boers held prayer meetings and sang psalms. On the Sunday before the great battle, a trekker named Sarel Cilliers, who had been a church elder back in the Cape Colony, is said to have mounted a gun-carriage and led the gathering in the swearing of a vow. The exact circumstances of this ceremony are the subject of some doubt, but the official version that is now the Te Deum in the liturgy of the civil religion is as follows:

> My brethren and fellow countrymen, at this moment we stand before the holy God of heaven and earth, to make a promise, if He will be with us and protect us and deliver the enemy into our hands so that we may triumph over him, that we shall observe the day and the date as an anniversary in each year and a day of thanksgiving like the Sabbath, in His honour; and that we shall enjoin our children that they must take part with us in this, for a remembrance even of our posterity; and if anyone sees a difficulty in this, let him return from this place. For the honour of His name shall be joyfully exalted, and to Him the fame and the honour of the victory must be given.[23]

The Lord did indeed deliver the enemy into their hands. The Zulu army, numbering perhaps ten thousand warriors, attacked on the morning of Sunday, December 16, 1838. Wave after wave of them charged the laager, to be shot down by the 530 Boer marksmen inside the circled wagons until the adjacent river ran red with their blood. As the plumed warriors began to waver, the Boers moved a wagon aside and a mounted commando rode out to pursue and cut them to pieces. More than three

23. Voortrekker Monument brochure, p. 4.

thousand Zulus fell at what became known as the Battle of Blood River. Three Boers were slightly wounded.

Here was the ultimate revelation of God's special favour, and so it is recorded in the sacred history. But again the men on the spot were somewhat less fervent in their civil faith than the gospel writers who came after them. The victory won, they promptly forgot their vow for the next thirty years. Only when the British prodded Afrikaner nationalism to life in the 1870s was it suddenly remembered and turned into the annual thanksgiving ceremony and celebration of the *volksgees*—the national spirit—that it is now.

After the battle the victory commando found Retief's body with Dingane's treaty in a coat pocket. Claiming the land, they settled down to found their Republic of Natalia. But if Table Bay was strategically important in the eyes of mariners and merchants so was Durban Bay, and the British had no intention of letting it fall into the hands of such antagonistic aliens. So in 1842 they sent a force to annex it. Bitterly the Boers trudged back over the Drakensberg onto the highveld. Doggedly the British followed them and annexed their Free State Republic too, proclaiming it to be the Orange River Sovereignty under British imperial control.

The repeal of the Corn Laws brought a time of economic stringency and a change of outlook in London. Britain decided to reduce her imperial responsibilities and so in 1852 and 1854 agreed to recognize the independence of the two Boer republics, the Free State and the Transvaal (the latter was called the South African Republic). But it was a short-lived respite. The discovery of diamonds on the banks of the Vaal River in 1870 ignited British interest once more. Both the Free State and the Transvaal claimed the land was theirs, and there can be little doubt that it was indeed Free State territory, but Britain, proclaiming a doctrine of paramountcy over the whole southern African region, appointed a commission under the lieutenant governor of Natal, Robert Keate, to decide the issue. Keate awarded the land to a mixed-race chief of Khoikhoi extraction named Nicholaas Waterboer, who promptly requested and was granted British citizenship. Thus the diamond fields became part of Britain's Cape Colony.

The Orange Free Staters, meanwhile, with the Boers' insatiable hunger for more land, were extending their territory eastward through a series of wars against Moshoeshoe in his mountain kingdom. The desperate Basotho king, on the verge of total collapse, sought British protectorate status—and in 1868 the British, fearing that if he did indeed collapse thousands of refugees would pour forth in a repeat of the *Difaqane* and disrupt the eastern Cape frontier, obliged. The Free State, furious at having the fruits of victory plucked from them by the British *kaffirboeties*, chalked up another grievance.

By now the spirit of nationalism was burning brightly in the Free State. But not yet in the Transvaal. That remote republic, with its go-as-you-please, undisciplined trekker citizens, existed in a state of near anarchy. Individuality reigned supreme. Everyone went his own way. Egos were big, tempers short, and the spirit of negotiation and compromise totally absent. The Transvaal trekkers established five separate republics and rose up against one another ten times in the first twenty years of their settlement. Even their church split into three separate factions of the Dutch Reformed Church.

It was a ramshackle administration. There was no police force and no standing army. Officials and the government itself were largely ignored. Taxes were not paid, and appeals for the mobilization of commandos went largely unheeded, especially when it was ploughing time on the farms. Sometimes in the midst of a campaign, when it looked like rain or the farmers felt they had been away long enough, the phrase "*huis-toe!*" (home time) would pass through the ranks and the troops would turn for home, leaving their disconcerted commanders with no choice but to follow.

It was a life of stark simplicity, austere and isolated. The utter loneliness of it generated a warmth and hospitality toward the few visitors who happened to call, and turned shopping visits to the little country towns and the monthly evening services of the Dutch Reformed Church into major social occasions. But there was little sense of community, and even less of nationhood, in the Transvaal until one day in April 1877 when a contingent of British police marched in and annexed it. The galvanizing effect of the annexation was stunning. Overnight the lack of cohesion vanished and the ramshackle republic came together in a spirit of angry common purpose.

At first the Transvaalers adopted a strategy of passive resistance, refusing to cooperate with their new British overlords. Then as fury mounted, the national leaders, among whom a big-game hunter named Paul Kruger was a rising star, decided the time had come for the situation to be discussed at a general meeting of the people. Some five thousand of these outback farmers gathered at a place called Paardekraal. And they decided to go to war against the most powerful empire the world had ever known.

The war was as remarkable as the sudden national awakening. Britain was quite unprepared for such a presumptuous action and had only small garrisons of troops in the little country towns, which the Boer commandos quickly overran. Then, as the British troops retreated toward Natal, their commander, General Sir G. Pommeroy Colley, resolved to make a stand on a conical peak called Majuba Hill on the Drakensberg escarpment. On February 27, 1881, he took seven hundred redcoats up to the rocky summit, where he thought he would have a commanding position, but as a posse of seventy-eight Boers crept up the steep slopes to attack him the British soldiers found they had difficulty seeing them from the top; and as they raised their heads above the summit rocks the Boer sharpshooters picked them off with lethal accuracy. When the attackers eventually stormed the ridge, many redcoats fell to their death trying to scramble down the rock face. The final toll was eighty-six British soldiers killed, including General Colley, 134 wounded, and fifty-nine taken prisoner, for the loss of only one Boer killed and five wounded. Once again the God of their fathers had intervened to give the Boers victory against the odds. "God's hand has become noticeable in the history of our nation as never before since the days of Israel," avowed their Commandant-General, Piet Joubert.[24]

In the shock of this debacle Britain returned the Transvaal to the Boers in a face-saving deal that placed it under nominal British "suzerainty."

But nationalism had been born.

YET IT WAS still only a Transvaal nationalism, just as it was an Orange Free State nationalism in the republic farther south. There was still no broad ethnic nationalism embracing all Afrikaners across the whole of South Africa. To Kruger, elected president of the Transvaal after Majuba, Afrikaners were still largely confined to "the old people of the country" who had been led out of the Cape Colony. And the keynote speech at the inauguration of a new government building in the Free State in 1875 invoked the notion of an essentially parochial national unity with the words: "May there no longer be talk of German or Englishmen, or Hollander or Afrikaner, but may they all be Free Staters, with one interest and one aim, all one people and one aim."[25]

Outrage at the annexation and the stirring events of the brief war had changed some of this, eliciting sympathy and fellow-feeling throughout the Free State. But it was really the Cape Afrikaners who brought this nascent ethnic nationalism to its full flowering.

It is another of the riveting ironies of the South African story that by importing their modern influences to this backward land the British

24. F. A. van Jaarsveld, *The Awakening of Afrikaner Nationalism* (Cape Town, 1961), p. 172.

25. Ibid., p. 94.

brought about their own eventual undoing. For it was they who transformed the Cape Afrikaners, exposing them to these modern influences and turning some of them into an intellectual elite that was then able to articulate and polemicize the grievances of the *volk* at large. And it was this which ignited the veld fire of Afrikaner nationalism.

While the emigrant Afrikaners trekked back into the past and another half-century of cultural and intellectual stagnation, the Cape Afrikaners went to school. Between 1806 and 1880 the number of children in Cape schools rose from eight hundred to thirty thousand, while in the republics there were hardly any at all. Some Cape Afrikaners went on to universities in Europe and returned to practice law, enter the church, or become politicians as the colony acquired responsible government with its own parliament. For the first time in its entire history Afrikanerdom acquired an intellectual elite, and it played a crucial role in the formation of Afrikaner nationalism. It was the headstrong rustics who went forth and experienced the grievances, but it was their milder cousins who stayed home and got educated who articulated these grievances and gave them ideological shape.

On the whole the Cape Afrikaners were not unhappy with their lot. British occupation brought with it a number of material advantages. Culturally the community began to advance. Cape Town grew into a fair-sized city with shops and libraries and schools and the governor's garden parties, and out in the adjoining winelands a society of some baronial pretension developed. The growing volume of world trade brought more and more ships past this tavern of the seas and gave it something of a cosmopolitan air. In the swiftly changing mental climate the Cape Afrikaners began to shed some of their rough edges and become more urbane, and more liberal. Some went even further in their adoption of British ways and a class of polished Anglo-Afrikaners emerged, *plus royalistes que la reine*, to become objects of scorn to their blood relatives in later years.

But the Anglicizing process also produced a reaction. In 1840 Dutch was prohibited as a medium of instruction in the schools, and English was made a compulsory qualification for a job in the civil service. It was the language used in commercial life and it became the sole language used in Parliament. Scottish Calvinists were imported to serve as ministers in the Dutch Reformed Church and they soon dominated its Cape synod. The Cape Afrikaners faced the threat of cultural absorption and some members of the newly emergent intellectual elite began to react against this. By the end of the 1870s a national self-consciousness began to develop among them. There was a sense that if their language was submerged in the sea of English washing about them, their identity as Afrikaners would be lost.

The central figure in this movement was an intense young minister of the Dutch Reformed Church, the Rev. S. J. du Toit. He and his friends formed what they called the Genootskap van Regte Afrikaners, the Society of True Afrikaners. In 1876 it began publishing a magazine, *Die Patriot,* in Afrikaans. A year later the British annexed the Transvaal. Where this galvanized the Transvaalers and stirred the Free Staters, it electrified their True Afrikaner friends in the Cape. It crystallized their feelings of ethnic solidarity and collective grievance. In their indignation their thoughts turned from language to history—to the aggrieved sense of a historical as well as a cultural imperialism in which the English always wrote the history from their own perspective, distorting the wrongs the poor Afrikaners had suffered and painting themselves in a favourable light. They determined to rectify this. With Du Toit doing most of the work, the True Afrikaners produced a history of their own, written in Afrikaans, which they called *Die Geskiedenis van ons Land in die Taal van ons Volk* (The history of our country in the language of our people).

It was a powerfully emotional and unashamedly polemical document. Its declared aim, the foreword announced, was "to make our children familiar from an early age with what their forefathers had to go through and what they suffered in this land where strangers now want to trample us underfoot."[26] It traced the history of the Afrikaners back to Van Riebeeck, stressing that they were all members of one nation of Dutch, Huguenot, and German extraction, a nation with a just cause that had suffered a long list of injustices at the hands of the British—starting with Slagtersnek. For the first time in sixty-one years the grisly events of that abortive rebellion and the bungled execution were recalled. An emotional passage in the book laid the basis of a historical legend that was to become part of the national myth.

> Weep Afrikaners!
> —Here lies your flesh and blood!
> —martyred in the most brutal fashion.
> Wrong it was to rise up against their government:
> yet they did it not without reason!
> Wrong it was to take up weapons;
> only because they were too weak!
> They were guilty, says the earthly judge;
> but what will the Heavenly Judge have to say?
> . . . But come! It grows darker!
> —If we sit here too long we shall be regarded as conspirators!

26. Ibid., p. 119.

—come, another day will dawn,
—then we shall perhaps see the grave in another light!
—come, let us go home with a quiet sigh!

The impact of the book was enormous. It was read throughout South Africa and letters poured in to *Die Patriot* expressing the new sense of nationalism it had awakened. It provided the catalyst that brought the nascent feelings of ethnic self-consciousness in the colonial South and the republican North together into a single pan-Afrikaner blood-brotherhood, into a sense that all were members of a single nation that had been historically wronged.

And in this redressing of the historical record there was also a sanctifying process. The people so wronged were God's people, their history a sacred history. As Van Jaarsveld puts it:

> According to the Rev. S. J. du Toit God had "brought together" members of various nationalities in South Africa and "given" them a language. The "pious" Huguenots had been specially "sent" to preserve the raw elements from neglect. God's hand had, in the view of the Afrikaner leaders, particularly in the Transvaal, become clearly "visible" in the history of the nation. They were descendants of "religious refugees." The idea that they had been chosen, made its appearance strongly in the nation's nationalism. They had been called, like Israel from Egypt, had lived in the desert, and were entering the land of Canaan. The Afrikaans-speaking people had a "task," "mission," or "calling." It was presented as the opening up of the interior for civilization and Christianity and the propagation of the Gospel among the heathen. It was stated that it was God's will that the Afrikaner people would once and for all live free from British authority under one flag in South Africa.[27]

So began one of the most powerful myth-making processes in modern times.

27. Ibid., p. 223.

CHAPTER SIX

The Great Trek Inward

Alas, this trek does not lead from the straits into the open spaces. This is a trek from a condition of freedom and abundance to one of poverty and want. This is a journey from Canaan to Egypt.

D. F. MALAN

THE DISCOVERY first of diamonds then of gold was the watershed event in South African history. Overnight it turned a pastoral country into an industrial one, sucking country folk into the city and changing their lives. Overnight it reversed the trend of the great trek outward, the great escape from the closed frontier, of Boer from Briton and white from black and Sotho from Zulu, and turned it into a great trek inward—toward the city—and turned the city itself into a new frontier.

No more was South Africa a refuge from the modern age, locked away in a fortress continent at the other end of the earth. Overnight it became a Mecca for fortune hunters and empire builders. No more was there a fleeing from the tyranny of the British or from one's neighbour's smoke to establish a private domain on ten thousand acres of land. No more was it a slow, meditative life of kraal and stoep, of ancestors in their graves and the Bible in the parlour, with the dignity and security of advancing years surrounded by a large extended family. Now it was a new life in a city slum surrounded by strangers where there was no security and even less dignity. South Africa had escaped the roar of the shuttling loom only to be overtaken by that of the battery stamp. The nineteenth century had caught up with the seventeenth—with a vengeance.

What made the impact greater was the bewildering speed with which it came. A visitor named Schalk van Niekerk saw a group of children playing a game of *klip-klip* (five stones) with shiny pebbles on Daniel Jacobs's farm near the junction of the Orange and Vaal Rivers one day in 1866, and only twenty years later George Walker went for a stroll on the widow Oosthuizen's farm below a ridge called the Witwatersrand and stubbed his foot against a rock that gave off a dull glint: the world's greatest diamond rush, followed by the world's greatest gold rush, occurred in only two decades. It was not an old-style gold rush with bearded prospectors with pans and handmade sluice boxes. The gold-bearing ore, low-grade and deep underground, could be mined only by a sophisticated process that required massive investment and a complex business and financial backup system. A huge and startlingly modern industry sprang up on the veld, to the bewilderment of the slow-moving, preindustrial people whose country it was.

It all began in as unprepossessing a spot as it is possible to imagine: a flat, featureless plain near the geographical centre of the country where the muddy Vaal and Orange rivers flow sluggishly together; a kind of no-man's-land not clearly part of any established territory lying between the Great Karoo to the south, the undulating grasslands to the northeast, and the Kalahari Desert to the northwest. It was the kind of place where one could ride for days across the gray, stony veld without seeing a soul, for there were only a few mixed-race people of Khoikhoi ancestry, called Griquas, living here along with a handful of white farmers who had trekked up from the Cape Colony to settle along the river banks.

Mining began in 1870 with river diggings for alluvial diamonds, then moved to dry diggings on two nearby farms called *Bultfontein* and *Dutoitspan*—and, a year later, on one called *Vooruitzicht* belonging to an Afrikaner named Johannes Nicolaas de Beer. It was on a small hillock on De Beer's farm in April 1871 that a surveyor's wife, Sarah Ortlepp, picked up a diamond while picnicking with her family and started what became known as the New Rush, for she had stumbled on the world's richest deposit of blue diamond-bearing kimberlite. By August there were 5,000 people digging frenziedly on the hillock, which was rapidly converted into a hole that looked like a block of gorgonzola with spoonfuls of cheese gouged out of it. A town, Kimberley, sprang up. Behind the diggers came the speculators. Poor De Beer, unable to cope with the rush, sold his farm to one of them, Alfred Ebden, who formed a syndicate. Thus was born De Beers Consolidated Mines, the giant corporation that today controls two-thirds of the world's diamond industry. An extraordinary cast of characters soon emerged from the ruck to take control and dominate the mining scene. There was ferocious, bullying J. B. Robinson, descended from one of the eastern frontier settler families; wily Alfred Beit, a Sephardic Jew from Hamburg; Julius Wehner, a former cavalry officer who was Beit's friend and partner; flamboyant Barnett Isaacs, a Cockney Jew who earned a living as a street hustler, prizefighter, juggler, and circus clown before he changed his name to Barney Barnato and went to South Africa to make his fortune; and tall, thin, anaemic Cecil John Rhodes, a vicar's son from Bishop's Stortford in England, who was sent to South Africa because of his weak chest (the doctors said he had consumption, but it was probably an atrial septal defect, or hole in the heart) and there became its richest man, prime minister of the Cape and the British Empire's most ambitious visionary.

When gold was discovered on the Witwatersrand in 1886, it was largely these same aggressive entrepreneurs who leapfrogged from Kimberley to Johannesburg with their established wealth and know-how to dominate the gold-mining industry as well. There was one newcomer of note: Ernest Oppenheimer, who arrived at Kimberley in 1902. With the help of American financier Herbert Hoover and the finance house J. Pierpoint Morgan & Co., Oppenheimer founded the Anglo American Corporation in 1917, which gained control of De Beers and, after the death of the first-generation magnates, most of the gold-mining interests as well and which today controls 49.6 percent of the market capitalization of the Johannesburg Stock Exchange.

The industrial revolution came slower to the older countries, and even then caused massive social trauma that shuddered through a century of literature and reshaped the politics of Europe. But in South Africa technology could be imported overnight, and the black and white tribesfolk of Africa, unlike settlers in America and Australia and other parts of the new world (including the English-speaking South Africans), were even less prepared for it than the guildsmen and villagers of Merrie England. Black and white poured into the cities, all the faster because of the crisis on the land: subdivision among sons on Boer farms had reduced them to uneconomic units, while at the same time farming had been hit by a great cattle plague, a locust plague, and the worst drought the country had known. Neither the Afrikaner nor the black tribesman was equipped to cope with life in the city—the alien city where the Englishman was *baas*—and as they surged there in their economic plight they came into explosive contact and competition.

The impact on both was immense. It hardened and changed the whole focus of Afrikaner nationalism, switching its reference point from conflict with the English to conflict with the blacks. And it ripped apart the fabric of black tribal life, turning a landless peasantry into an urban proletariat, and awakening a political consciousness that eventually demanded its own national liberation from white mastery just as Afrikaners had demanded theirs from the British.

As the great trek inward began, the first to register its impressions and implications was the Victorian writer Anthony Trollope. Like Pringle, here was another trained observer and professional communicator who was able to cut through the clutter of the day and find a way between the sightlessness of those involved and the opaqueness of the academic historians to bring us a clear picture of what things looked like and what struck him as significant. The author of *Barchester Towers* was sixty-two when he sailed to Cape Town and bought a horse and Cape cart to tour South Africa and write about it. He was no equalitarian. As his Palliser novels showed, he admired the lifestyle and ideals of the Victorian gentry, but he was a man who had travelled, who had toured and written about America, Australia, New Zealand, and the West Indies, and he had the eye of a good reporter. He rode into Kimberley on a summer's day in 1877, and he found it hot and odious. "It is foul with dust and flies," he wrote. "It reeks with bad brandy; it is fed upon potted meats; it has not a tree near it."[1] But he was riveted by the huge open-cast mine, Kimberley's Big Hole, which is still the biggest man-made cavity on the African continent. In a vivid passage he described the scene at the place where South Africa's industrial revolution began:

> It is as though you were looking into a vast bowl, the sides of which are as smooth as should be the sides of a bowl, while round the bottom are various marvellous incrustations among which ants are working with all the usual energy of the ant-tribe. . . .
>
> The stuff is raised on aerial tramways. . . . As this is going on round the entire circle it follows that there are wires starting everywhere from the rim and converging to a centre at the bottom, on which the buckets are always scudding through the air. . . .
>
> When the world below is busy there are about 3,000 Kafirs at work. . . . Their task is to pick up the earth and shovel it into the buckets and iron receptacles. . . . You look down and see the swarm of black ants busy at every hole and corner with their picks moving and shovelling the loose blue soil.
>
> But the most peculiar phase of the mine, as you gaze into its one large pit, is the subdivision into claims and portions. Could a person see the sight without having heard any word of explanation it would be impossible, I think, to conceive the meaning of all those straight cut narrow dikes, of those mud walls all at right angles to each other, of those square separate pits, and again of those square upstanding blocks, looking like houses without doors or windows. You can see that nothing on earth was ever less level than the bottom of the bowl—and that the black ants in traversing it, as they are always doing, go up and down almost at every step, jumping here on to a narrow wall and skipping there across a deep dividing channel as though some diabolically ingenious architect had contrived a house with 500 rooms, not one of which should be on the same floor, and to and from none of which there should

1. Anthony Trollope, *Old Man's Love* (London, 1984), p. 68.

be a pair of stairs or a door or a window. In addition to this it must be imagined that the architect had omitted the roof in order that the wires of the harp above described might be brought into every chamber."[2]

Looking down upon these black worker-ants skipping about in the pit of the white man's mine, Trollope saw into the heart of the future South Africa. "Though we abuse the Kafir we want his service," he noted, "and we want more than our share of his land." And as he crossed the Bay of Biscay on the voyage back to England, this conservative but farsighted Victorian who had scorned the Aborigines of Australia and the Indians of America penned his final conclusion. "South Africa," he wrote, "is a country of black men—and not of white men. It has been so; it is so; and it will continue to be so."[3] Blacks were "the people" of South Africa, and ultimately the future of the country would be determined by their interests.

What was true of the diamond fields was doubly so of the gold fields. The stream to the city became a flood. They poured in from the countryside and they poured in from abroad, Boer and black and British and fortune-seeking foreigners. They came as workers and they came as entrepreneurs and they came as adventurers. They set up their tents and corrugated iron shacks in a seething squatter settlement called Ferreira's Camp that Kruger's government demarcated in a desperate effort to control the influx. So Johannesburg was born. In less than forty years it was the biggest city in South Africa, with a population of more than 300,000.

It was a rip-roaring honky-tonk Zane Grey of a place, the ultimate gold-rush town. Life there was hectic and dissipated. The atmosphere was that of a casino, of gamblers on a spree. There was horse racing and prizefighting, dog fighting and cock fighting, billiards and cards and dice, with betting on the outcome of everything. There was drinking and whoring. Grogshops abounded and a survey in 1895 disclosed that there were ninety-seven brothels in a town of 25,000 white men. "Monte Carlo superimposed on Sodom and Gomorrah" was how one visitor described it.[4]

But there was another side to it, too, the side of Big Money and the handful of powerful mining magnates who owned and controlled the city. They had the social pretensions of the nouveaux riches and

2. Anthony Trollope, *South Africa*, reprint of the 1878 edition (Cape Town, 1973), pp. 361–2.

3. Ibid., p. 16.

4. Quoted in Geoffrey Wheatcroft, *The Randlords* (New York, 1985), pp. 2–4.

the haughtiness of successful empire builders and they established themselves as an aristocracy among the English-speaking South Africans. They built grand homes a sanitary distance from the hurly-burly of Ferreira's Camp, and an English gentlemen's club, all leather and silence, where they could gather alone without blacks and Boers and Jews, and where Rhodes's boyish face still stares down from the walls, and where as you pass along the fusty corridors with their creaking wooden floors you can see, and even touch, a bronze replica of his right hand. The Randlords, they were called, and their lifestyle and social values set the standard by which Johannesburg still lives.

As he sat on his little trellised stoep in Pretoria drinking coffee and sucking his pipe and spitting from time to time, President Kruger contemplated these developments with grave dismay. It was an extraordinary twist of fate, cruel in its perversity, that had produced this irruption in the midst of the most distant and isolationist of the Voortrekker exiles. After all those years of trekking to escape from the modern world with its corrosive influences into an Arcadia of piety and simple living, here it was in its most vulgar form bursting in on them again. Having suffered so much in their epic struggle through the wilderness to reach their promised land, here were the Egyptians swarming in on them to build their temples within the walls of the New Jerusalem.

Kruger was a simple man, as different from the Randlords and the rollicking gamblers of Ferreira's Camp as it is possible to imagine. He was a boy of ten during the Great Trek, then became a big-game hunter. The thumb of his left hand was blown off when his ancient muzzleloader exploded as he fired at a rhinoceros, and he walked with a limp from another hunting accident. He was married to a dutiful wife who bore him sixteen children. He never spent a day in school; his only education had been to read the Bible. He was a man of deep piety and stubborn principle, the archetypal Boer, who believed emphatically that the earth was flat and that the "old people" of the Trek were indeed the Elect of God who had been led out of bondage to the Transvaal. His world was the world of the Old Testament, and he cut a Biblical figure with his stolid features and bearded face. He was an Abraham to his people, and as he watched the teeming gold-reef city rise just thirty-five miles from his capital he trembled for them. On the one hand the gold was welcome, for the Transvaal lived on the edge of bankruptcy, but Kruger knew it was a gift from Satan that would bring corruption in its wake. He trembled because of the foreigners who were flocking in, the Englishmen, Americans, Australians, Germans, Frenchmen, Italians, Greeks, and Lithuanian Jews. The *uitlanders*, he called them, the outsiders, who soon threatened to outnumber the Boers. If he let them become insiders they would take over the land from the chosen few to whom God had given it.

But he trembled most of all because he knew that the gold would bring back the British. They had itched before when the Transvaal was nothing, and now that it had acquired wealth beyond imagination Kruger knew there was no way they would continue to hold back and let a handful of backwoodsmen prevent them from adding such a jewel to the imperial crown. Rhodes the empire builder, with his vision of an unbroken stretch of British territory from the Cape to Cairo, was by 1890 prime minister of the Cape Colony; he had established himself in Rhodesia to the north and in Bechuanaland to the west, and now through his mining interests he effectively controlled the Transvaal economy as well. Kruger felt himself to be surrounded and infiltrated. It could only be a matter of time.

And so the great trek inward led first of all to war. It was the greatest war the African continent had ever known, but it was fought between whites. The blacks were largely spectators, yet in the end it was they who were the most profoundly affected. The Boers lost the war, but in a wave of reparative sentiment for the perceived injustice done to a small nation by a powerful one they won the peace. And in that victory their exclusionist credo—the notion that the land was theirs by divine right and that the indigenous blacks were aliens in it, whose role was to serve but not participate—was extended from the two Boer republics over the whole of South Africa. It triumphed over the more inclusionist liberalism that had been established in the two British colonies and became national policy in a new independent country created out of a union of all four territories.

The Trekboers had carried Van Riebeeck's bitter-almond hedge with them from the Cape peninsula to the eastern frontier to the republics of the north, and now it returned to flourish over the entire land.

THE BOER WAR of 1899–1902 and Lord Milner's reconstruction programme represented an attempt by Britain to destroy Afrikaner nationalism in its nascent state. And after the Peace of Vereeniging in 1902 it seemed to have succeeded. The Boer republics were defeated, the land was reduced to desolation, and the egregious Milner, Britain's viceroy in the conquered land, was setting up his elite corps of bright young Balliol blues—his "kindergarten," it was dubbed—to restructure the old republics on British lines and Anglicize the new generation of Afrikaners in the schools.

But the victory was an illusion. Though the war had smashed the

Afrikaner world, it had left its mind and will intact, indeed strengthened. Like the American Southerners and other proud people who have fought and lost defensive wars, the Afrikaners were enormously strengthened in their national pride by the knowledge that they had fought against the odds and given a good account of themselves, yielding in the end only to irresistible force. An army of backward farmers had measured themselves against the regiments of the world's mightiest military power and emerged with the knowledge that they were as good and better. Out of the war came new heroes to worship, new martyrs to mourn, and new grievances to nurture. As Dunbar Moodie has noted, it was another national epic of suffering and death, and it has been woven together with the Great Trek into the sacred history of the Afrikaner *volk*, the basis of their apocalyptic vision of themselves as a chosen people with a special mission to fulfill.[5]

Nobody expected them to do so well. "As the wounded antelope awaits the coming of the lion, the jackal, and the vulture, so do our poor people all over South Africa contemplate the coming of the foe," Smuts wrote bitterly as the Boers braced themselves for the assault:

> Every sea in the world is being furrowed by the ships which are conveying British troops from every corner of the globe in order to smash this little handful of people. Even Xerxes, with his millions against little Greece, does not afford a stranger spectacle to the wonder and astonishment of mankind than this gentle and kind-hearted Mother of Nations, as, wrapped in all the panoply of might, riches, and exalted traditions, she approaches the little child grovelling in the dust with a sharpened knife in her hand. This is no War—it is an attempt at Infanticide.[6]

In the event, the little child in the dust gave the Mother of Nations her longest, costliest, and bloodiest war since Napoleon. When the war began in October 1899, the British expected it to be over by Christmas. But it took two years and cost 22,000 lives and half a billion dollars to subdue the brat, and even then the victory was a humiliating one as opinion at home and abroad swung in favour of the heroic infant. It was an early lesson, later to be bloodily relearned by the Americans in Vietnam and the Russians in Afghanistan, in how difficult it can be for a major power to take on a small but determined people in a distant place.

The sense of national awareness of this small people was greatly increased. If the republics the Boers had cheered had seemed a little nebulous, they were not so any longer. Now they seemed the most real

5. T. Dunbar Moodie, op. cit., p. 12.

6. Quoted in Reitz, op. cit. pp. 95–6.

of things. The Boer people, man, woman and child, fought and suffered and died to preserve the independence of these republics, and the feeling grew more sharply that their heritage, their identity, everything they held to be their own—their *eie*—was wrapped up in that independence and dependent on it. Without their own land they could not be their own people; there could be no Afrikaner *volk*, or nation, with its own culture and language and *eie* identity. No one remembered any longer that they had gone out to die for the Transvaal or the Free State. Now they were all one, all Afrikaners together.

They learned to love the land itself with a keener love than before. They rode across it from end to end, they knew every river and every forest and every rocky outcrop where a man might take shelter from the Lee-Enfield rifle; they knew every farmhouse and every man and woman who might offer help, and they came to love it all with the intensity of personal involvement and shared suffering. More than ever they felt it was *their* country. *Ons vir jou Suid-Afrika.*

A new unity. They came together out of the four quarters of the country and for two years the war moulded them to a common purpose. The rugged individualism of the frontier was suppressed in the interests of a coordinated effort. No more was it a question of "*huis-toe*" when they had had enough, for now the house was on fire and the children were gone. Military discipline did its work here as everywhere. It inculcated the habits of following and of obeying. In those two years there grew up an acceptance of the right of generals to ordain and to command, and in the generals in turn an imperious conviction of their right, indeed their duty, to tell the *volk* what to think and do.

For all their individualism, the Boers had always tended to be a patriarchal society: they had given fierce loyalty to their leaders during the Great Trek; within each family the father was a law unto himself and a total autocrat over his domain. Now, with the war, this personality cult was reinforced. Just as the heroic past became sanctified, so did the heroes become deified. This made Afrikaner nationalist politics at once intensely personal and authoritarian. Followings developed more because of the personalities involved than the ideas and philosophies they advocated, and leaders acquired an aura of infallibility. This also entrenched the Afrikaners' already deep conservatism by making it impossible to deviate from what a previous leader had said. To do so was apostasy. It established a kind of infallibility in matters of doctrine and ideology in which any change had to be sanctioned by some reference to a dead predecessor. Thus President Botha in introducing his reformist innovations in the 1980s felt the need to quote from Daniel Malan's speeches of 1948 to preserve the impression of doctrinal continuity.

Of course one of the problems about personality-cult politics is its proneness to schism, and this is something that has haunted Afrikanerdom throughout its history: schisms between the Trek leaders, between Botha and Hertzog, Smuts and Hertzog, Hertzog and Malan, and between Botha and Treurnicht. And because of this tendency to schism, as the Afrikaner Nationalist revolution got under way and grew in intensity, the pressures for total conformity were massively increased.

But of all the consequences of the Boer War, none was more lasting than the deepened sense of Afrikaner grievance. It was a total war, as the Civil War in America was a total war. Gone were the days when opposing armies faced each other across a battlefield like teams of gladiators while their followers awaited the outcome from a distance. Now wars were fought for territory and for the capture of towns and capitals, and as the armies ranged across the countryside, whole populations were caught up in their destructiveness. As Lord Kitchener's British army invaded the Free State and Transvaal, overrunning farms and taking over land, the Boer commandos struck back with lightning hit-and-run raids. As these guerrillas made their forays behind British lines they used the farmsteads as their supply depots and bases of refuge and information. The British retaliated by burning down the farmsteads and removing all livestock and food that the raiders might use to sustain themselves. "To strike at an enemy's sources of supply is and must be one of the principal aims of a belligerent," wrote *The Times* in its history of the war.[7] Thousands of Boer families were left homeless and destitute, and the British high command ordered that they be accommodated in camps.

Thus the British introduced to history the dread phrase "concentration camp." The intention was humane, but under the conditions of a difficult war in a hard continent, intention and outcome do not always coincide. Epidemic diseases broke out in the overcrowded camps and there was a hopeless shortage of doctors, nurses, and medicines. Enteric fever raged, and dysentery, typhoid, whooping cough, diphtheria, and measles. The Boer refugees died in catastrophic numbers, varying in estimates between 20,000 and 26,000, of whom more than three-quarters were children.[8] Then, as the Boer commandos returned after the war to their stricken families and devastated farms, there was Milner and his "kindergarten" trying to turn those children who had survived into little Englishmen, prohibiting Afrikaans in the schools and forcing them to use the language of the conqueror. It was the culmination of the Century of Wrong.

The grievances sank into the soul and became part of the new Af-

7. Quoted in A. C. Martin, *The Concentration Camps 1900–1902* (Cape Town, 1957), p. 6.

8. Ibid., p. 31.

rikaner nationalism—a bitter, resentful, self-pitying nationalism. "A poor, weak, downtrodden, suppressed and wronged people," Piet Joubert had declared in 1881 just before Paardekraal. As the war added to it and as the myth makers worked on it, lovingly nurturing and embellishing it, the litany of grievance and self-pity turned into a massive preoccupation with the self, a national narcissism that has blinded it to the injustices it is now inflicting on others. The black struggle for independence today, the blacks' own deep sense of grievance and injustice and of being made aliens in their own land, is in many respects a repeat of the Afrikaners' struggle against the British through the Century of Wrong. Yet such is the scale of Afrikanerdom's absorption with itself that it is quite unable to see this, to see that it is doing unto others as was done unto it. It has lost all capacity for empathy to a self-destructive degree. That is the irony of it. For Afrikaners should know better than anyone the power and consequences of a resentful nationalism. As they pile grievance upon grievance they should know that they are building up a legacy of hatred against themselves that could sweep away the very thing they seek to preserve; that, as their leading poet Breyten Breytenbach has warned them, their commitment to survival through repression will carry them inexorably "from murder to suicide";[9] that, like Narcissus, one can die from self-absorption.

But at the time the grievances were real and the sympathy was more than self-generated. For a time during and after the war, these international pariahs of today possessed the sympathy of the world. Their cause was a popular one among the liberals and humanitarians they despise so deeply now. An Englishwoman of great humanitarian compassion named Emily Hobhouse sailed out to South Africa to minister to the suffering women and children in the concentration camps and send flaming protests back to Britain. She was the equivalent of the women of today's Black Sash civil-rights movement who would risk being banned under the security laws, but she holds a place of honour in the sacred history, and her figure is included in a group sculpture that stands outside the Women's Monument in Bloemfontein.

Support groups were formed in Germany, Holland, France, and Belgium to collect money and send it to the suffering Boers in South Africa. Foreign brigades were formed, as in the Spanish Civil War, to fight on the Boer side against the forces of English oppression and capitalist imperialism. They included Irishmen and Americans, Hollanders and Frenchmen and some 250 Russians. One of the Russians, Eugeny Maximov, became a general in the Boer forces. Another, Alexander Guchkov,

9. Breytenbach's speech in the State Opera House, Pretoria, on receiving the Rapport Literary Award, June 12, 1986.

was wounded and taken prisoner by the British. He recovered in a London hospital and fifteen years later, as president of the Duma, was the man who accepted Tsar Nicholas II's abdication. The Boer cause was a popular one among the embryonic Communist movement in Russia and the song "Transvaal My Country" was a hit in Moscow at the turn of the century.[10]

Sympathy swept Britain, too, as the war drew to a close, and when the Liberal party came to power in the general election of 1905 the new government of Sir Henry Campbell-Bannerman decided on a policy of reconciliation with the defeated Boers. Sir Henry had met with Emily Hobhouse and been shocked by what she told him about the concentration camps. "When is a war not a war?" he asked in a celebrated phrase. "When it is carried on by methods of barbarism in South Africa."[11] Reparation was called for. Four years later Campbell-Bannerman gave the defeated republics back their independence in a union with the two British colonies. It was an act of unprecedented generosity to a defeated enemy.

It was also an act of unprecedented betrayal of the black South Africans. For it was the first and only time an imperial power has given sovereign independence to a racial minority.

WHATEVER THE WAR may have done to change the shape of men's minds and the trend of politics in a fateful way, it did nothing whatever to change the economic trend. As the war raged and farmsteads blazed, a mile below the ground men went on digging out the gold that was fuelling South Africa's industrial revolution. When finally the guns fell silent, the land was devastated but the mining camp was growing into a metropolis. Thousands of Boers, facing ruin as they returned to their scorched farms, turned in desperation toward its beckoning lights.

It was an experience even more searing than the war. The city was an alien place to these rural Afrikaners whose ethos was bound up with the land. It was the citadel of Anglo-Saxon culture and English-Jewish money power where the Afrikaner felt out of place and afraid. It was the place of the oppressor who looked down on him and scorned his ideals, of the exploiter who was out to get him. The language of the city and even of the small country towns was overwhelmingly English, so that the Afrikaner was hesitant to speak his own tongue in the shops

10. I am indebted for this information to Professor Apollon Davidson, head of the Africa Department of the Institute of General History of the Soviet Academy of Sciences.

11. T. R. H. Davenport, *South Africa: A Modern History* (Toronto, 1987), p. 217.

and business establishments. Culturally and linguistically, he felt like a foreigner among aliens.

Worst of all, he could not cope. Without money and without skills he found there was no natural place for him in the urban economy. He was not trained in a trade and he had an inbred aversion to manual labour; that was *kaffirwerk*, "nigger's work," that no white man could be expected to do. And wherever he went in search of a job, there was the black man beside him, a competitor, equally unskilled and equally alien, but offering as much for less. It was *gelykstelling* at its worst.

And they kept coming, these desperate Afrikaners, as the crisis on the land worsened. It went something like this. A young man returned home from the war to find his parents dead, the livestock gone, and a lawyer from the nearby town telling him the family farm was to be divided between himself and his four brothers. He was a sturdy young man who had ridden with General Koos de la Rey's commando, and now here he was, all proven and proud and patriotic, ready to become a farmer in his own right. So he betook himself a wife, cleared a bit of land and built a raw-brick house of two rooms below a ridge on his thousand-acre portion. That is a small farm, little more than a small-holding, on the arid and unproductive Transvaal *platteland*, but if things went well he might make out.

With his meagre inheritance he bought a few sheep and cattle and a plough. The first year he tilled a small patch and planted some maize, but the rain never came and the stalks shrivelled and died under the hot Transvaal sun. He tried again the next year but the locusts came and took the crop. The drought went on and on, turning the veld to dust, and many of his cattle died. He still had his sheep, which seemed to thrive in the dryness, but the price of wool went down to four pence a pound. That gave him just twenty pounds on which to live until the next shearing. He squatted on his haunches, scratched some figures in the dust, and reckoned it was not enough for a man who now had a wife and four children to feed. So he went to see his eldest brother Willem, who had inherited the best piece of land and was doing somewhat better, and after a long conversation full of sighs and silences Willem agreed to take over his thousand acres of dust bowl in exchange for a wagon and a span of oxen.

With a wagon and oxen a man might make a living as a transport driver in this country, hauling goods to the merchants in the towns. It was a hard life, but the money was good, and he could call at the farm every so often to see his wife and children, whom Willem had allowed to stay on in the little raw-brick house. But then the railway system was extended and the merchants needed him no longer. So he sold his wagon and his oxen and bought a horse and Cape cart. With that he could drive to the train station in Johannesburg and pick up passengers who would pay him a few pence to take them to an inn or one of the mine compounds. But then an electric tramway was installed and there were not enough passengers to pay for the horse's fodder. What might a farmer do now in this growing city of gold? Make bricks, perhaps. He had made his own bricks to build the little house back on the farm and surely there was a need for them with all this construction going on. But when he asked about it he learned that English financiers had started big brick-making companies now, and there was no room left for the small-time Afrikaner operators who had made a living that way.

About this time, too, a letter arrived from Willem telling him things had gotten worse on the farm and he was having to sell out to Oom Piet Bezuidenhout from over at Rietfontein. Oom Piet had been understanding, kind. Said he could stay on as a sharecropper in the little house under the ridge, so yes, well, sorry, brother, but could you please take the wife and kids away. You'd better take them with you to Johannesburg.

Dear God, where could one stay with a wife and four children in Johannesburg? From door to door he shuffled in his rough rawhide shoes and his baggy khaki pants, searching, begging, pleading. Try Ismael Mohammed who runs the fruit shop, someone suggested. A *Koelie*! God no, how could he do that? He belonged to a people who prided themselves on their dignity and self-respect. But there was nowhere else, so he and his wife and four children moved into a room above the fruit shop in Fordsburg. From there he went out each day to join the queues at the mine compounds and the factory gates. Each time the conversation was the same.

"What can you do?"

"Garden work, fencing, anything like that?"

"Sorry, nothing today."

And then one day he returned to the squalid little room above the fruit shop to find his wife sobbing. There was no more food, she told him, and in her desperation she had gone to see the Indian, who had said he could pay her three pounds a month to help in the fruit shop. Her words fell like a thunderclap between them. To work for the Indian! That was the ultimate humiliation.

They came in their thousands and trod this same dismal path until they constituted the world's worst poor-white problem. At the height of the Great Depression, Gwendolen Carter estimates that perhaps 60 percent of the Afrikaner population was reduced to this status.[12] The

12. Gwendolen M. Carter, *The Politics of Inequality* (New York, 1958), p. 25.

impact on the collective Afrikaner mind is impossible to exaggerate. It was not just the poverty and the hardship: for the first time in their history these proud, free men of the veld tasted the bitter juice of humiliation. To be poor was bad enough; to be deprived of their dignity as individuals violated their whole tradition. They had been bred to the notion that every white man was a king upon his own estate and the equal of any other. Now to have to beg for a job, to be stood over by a taskmaster with a stopwatch, to be checked on each time one went to the toilet or stopped for a smoke, and to have to stand there sometimes and take a dressing-down like a "kaffir" for not working hard enough —for such a people this was intolerable beyond words.

In the city, more than in the war, the Afrikaners lost their independence and were reduced to a state of *knegskap*, or servitude, and of squalour. For ever after, they were to nurse the dream of one day returning to the land. Some would keep a sheep or a goat in a suburban yard as a symbol of this forlorn hope. They idealized the land and farming, and though the urbanization process was to keep on sucking them in until nearly 90 percent of them are now city dwellers, the platteland has remained the conservatory of Afrikaner ideals.

The pain of the Afrikaner loss deepened their sense of grievance and hardened their nationalism. And it bred in them an abiding hostility toward the original agents of their misery, the gold-mining industry and the financial power of the English and Jewish groups who controlled it. These sentiments were encapsulated in a cartoon character called Hoggenheimer, who appeared in Afrikaans newspapers, a bloated Uriah Heep, odious, avaricious, and obviously Semitic, who devoted his manipulative skills to despoiling the Afrikaner *volk*.

But most of all the experience of poor-whiteism hardened Afrikaner attitudes on race. Gone was the security of the master-servant relationship back on the farm where the Boer's authority was unquestioned and he might even show a certain benevolent paternalism toward *his* "boys"; where a young Afrikaner would grow up in a certain intimacy with blacks, with a black nanny and black playmates and an old black sage who called him *kleinbaas*, young master, and filled his days with earthy wisdom. Now, in the harshness of the city, the poor white found himself on an equal footing with the black person, both members of competing proletariats, and all the Afrikaner had to assert his superiority was his white skin, his racial status symbol. It made his whiteness the most supremely important thing, all that prevented him from sinking to the very bottom, and the maintenance of racial distinctions a compelling necessity. More than that, he now felt a need to demonstrate his superiority. It was no longer automatic, and especially if the black person was a little educated, a little uppity, the Afrikaner felt threatened and had to show the cheeky bastard who was *baas*. So a new level of violence and the violent use of racist language entered into the relationship.

All this was aggravated by the fact that they came into a new closeness in the cities. In the swarming slums around the fringes of the city, natural master and natural servant lived cheek by jowl and the distinction was not so apparent anymore. And here, surely, lay the gravest threat of all to the preservation of the *volk*, to the national identity. For in that intimacy what mixing might take place, what loss of race consciousness by the Afrikaner, and, worst of all, what loss of respect by the black person for the white?

So compulsory segregation began. The colour bar became the hallmark of the South African way of life. For the poor whites in the cities, demoralized and alienated as they were, had one thing that the poor blacks did not have; they had the vote. And since Afrikaners were the majority of the electorate, and since Afrikaners ran the government of what was now a sovereign, independent country, that meant they had political power. Things began to happen to reinforce their position, to protect them from competition, to uplift them culturally, educationally, and economically. And everything that happened was to the disadvantage of the blacks.

In the first instance the government tried to deal with the problem by keeping more whites on the land. That meant squeezing off more blacks to create the space for more white *bywoners*, or squatters. It meant aiding and subsidizing the struggling farmers, which established forevermore a featherbedded and inefficient agricultural industry.

But even more vigorously it meant supporting and protecting the poor whites in the cities. The industrial colour bar was established. A strike in 1907 saw large numbers of Afrikaners enter the mining industry as "scab" labour and from then on successive governments were intent on creating a protected area for them there, with job-reservation laws prohibiting blacks from doing skilled work in the mines. State corporations were established to provide jobs for unemployed whites: nationalized steel and electrical power industries and the railways, which became the biggest single refuge for poor whites. In this way South Africa eventually acquired the largest amount of nationalized industry of any country outside the Communist bloc.

Thus Afrikaner nationalism took on socialist overtones. Within four years of Union, the growing chauvinism and militancy of the nationalist movement produced a split, with General Barry Hertzog breaking from the party of reconciliation led by his former comrades-in-arms, Generals Botha and Smuts, and forming the National party, which rules South

Africa today. Its cause was that of Afrikaner upliftment, of both the crushed nation and the indigent individual, and its method was that of state intervention. "Socialist nationalism," the writer Bill de Klerk calls it, a phrase that was soon to undergo a sinister inversion as some of the young Turks in Hertzog's party became infatuated with a new political philosophy that arose in Europe. But for the moment it was simply socialism intermixed with nationalism. "No largely Afrikaner government coming to power at this time could be anything but socialist and nationalist," De Klerk notes with a certitude that makes one wonder why white South Africans should think it could be any different for a black nationalist party today.[13]

So, in perhaps the greatest of all South African ironies, the National party first came to power in a coalition with the Labour party and with the support of Communists, who raised the stunning slogan "Workers of the world unite for a white South Africa!" Afrikaner members of the Mine Workers' Union mounted a workers' revolt in 1922 that set the Witwatersrand ablaze and led to martial law, and when four of the strike leaders were sentenced to death they went to the gallows singing "The Red Flag." Socialist nationalism, but its purpose was the protection of a white proletariat from the competitive claims of a black one. It was a racist socialism.

The protection took many forms, but the underlying theme was to keep blacks out of skilled work and, as far as possible, out of the city. The idea evolved that the towns were not the proper place for blacks. That was where a "good kaffir" got "spoiled." They belonged more naturally in rural areas. "It should be understood," a Native Affairs commission reported in 1921, "that the town is a European area in which there is no place for the redundant Native, who neither works nor serves his or her people but forms the class from which the professional agitators, the slum landlords, the liquor sellers, the prostitutes and the undesirable classes spring."[14]

It was a notion that conflicted with the industrial revolution's insatiable demand for labour—cheap labour, moreover, not artificially inflated white labour. It conflicted, too, with the fact that more and more land was being taken from the blacks in rural areas to create space for poor whites and to force more of them into the labour pool. It was the recurring contradiction that Trollope had noted at Kimberley fifty

13. W. A. de Klerk, *The Puritans in Africa: A Story of Afrikanerdom* (London, 1975), p. 108.

14. David Welsh, *Oxford History of South Africa*, vol. 2, p. 187.

years before. White South Africans wanted the black man's service but not his presence; and they expected him to stay on the land though they had taken too much of his land from him.

And so inexorably South Africa moved toward the fantasy of apartheid, the delusion of the temporary urban black worker with a mythical rural "homeland" where he could "develop along his own lines" and not impinge on the white person's world or lay claim to a share of the prosperity he was helping to create. It was all to be done with mirrors.

BLACKS HOPED THAT with the defeat of the Boers, the more liberal policies of the Cape, where they had enjoyed a limited franchise since 1854, would be extended over the whole of South Africa. Instead the reverse happened. With independence under a white electorate dominated by Afrikaners, the policies of the Boer republics were soon extended to the two former British colonies. The brief hope of an integrationist future disappeared.

The long march to national exclusion and apartheid began dramatically, within three years of Union. Three little years, or ere those hopes were cold, a Land Act was passed by the new sovereign Parliament prohibiting blacks from buying land outside designated "reserve" areas that constituted less than 10 percent of the total country. The new law made it a crime for any but servants to live on white farms and ordered the eviction of those who were "squatting" there.

At a stroke the indigenous black population became aliens in South Africa, a country that now belonged only to whites. As the black writer Sol Plaatje put it at the time: "South Africa has by law ceased to be the home of any of her native children whose skins are dyed with a pigment that does not conform with the regulation hue."[15]

It was the triumph of the bitter-almond hedge. The stunning oxymoron "foreign native" found its way into South Africa's political vocabulary and over the next sixty years the concept was to grow and fructify into an attempt to turn all blacks into de jure as well as de facto foreigners by denationalizing them and making them citizens of independent "homelands." "The goal," declared Cornelius Mulder, cabinet

15. Sol T. Plaatje, *Native Life in South Africa*, p. 83. Despite his Dutch name, Solomon Tshekisho Plaatje was a Tswana-speaking African of the Baralong tribe who was born in the Orange Free State in 1876. This remarkable man, though he received only a primary-school education, mastered six African languages as well as English, Dutch, and German; he was the first in a long line of fine black South African writers, and his *Native Life*, first published in 1916, was the first book of its kind.

minister in charge of black affairs in 1976, "is that eventually there will be no black South Africans."

The immediate result was to uproot nearly a million so-called squatters and send them wandering about the countryside, homeless and starving. Some were absorbed on white farms as labourers, some found a parking spot in the already overcrowded "reserves," a few found refuge in neighbouring Basutoland and Bechuanaland, but most eventually drifted into the towns—the towns where they could stay only if they were going to serve the white man's needs, which constituted that "European area in which there is no place for the redundant Native." Here indeed was a second trek for the black South Africans as well, a second *Difaqane*, a trek into their own Egypt of alien status.

Plaatje, who met some of these refugees on the banks of the Vaal River in the winter of 1913, gives a harrowing account of their tribulations; of how white farmers extorted their livestock from them, offering black tenants and sharecroppers the choice of a job—and thus the legal right to stay on the farm—on condition they handed over their animals, or immediate eviction. Those who refused to hand over their livestock found themselves out on the road with their cattle and sheep and children and few pathetic possessions, with nowhere to go and no right to stay where they were. All they could do was keep moving on the public road, and even then they were in danger of being arrested as vagrants. And as they wandered without grazing for their animals in the bitterest winter the highveld had known for years, the animals weakened and died and some of the children too.[16]

Plaatje met a man named Kgobadi, who had lived as a sharecropper on a white farm, giving half his harvest to the farmer but still making more than a hundred pounds a year. After the Land Act the *baas* told him he could stay if he handed over his oxen and if he and his wife would work as servants for a joint wage of thirty shillings a month, or eighteen pounds a year. When Kgobadi said no, the farmer handed him a note ordering him to "betake himself from the farm of the undersigned, by sunset of the same day."

Kgobadi's goats were beginning to kid as he hit the road, and his wife sat in the back of their jolting ox wagon with a sick baby. The goat kids died as fast as they were born. Two days out the baby died. They didn't know where to bury the little corpse because the law meant they had no right to be on any of the land through which they were passing: they had to stick to the public road. So the family crept over a fence that night to dig a grave under cover of darkness and bury their baby in a

16. Ibid., pp. 78–90.

secret spot that they hoped the landowner wouldn't find. For blacks, Plaatje noted, even the dead had no right to their six feet of ground in their ancestral home.

At Thaba Nchu, which is not far from Vegkop in the eastern Free State, Plaatje met thousands of blacks driving their stock toward the Basutoland border, hoping to leave them there and return to search for a place to stay. He learned of one family who had been ambushed and shot by Afrikaner farmers who drove off their cattle. Bitterly Plaatje reflected on the events following the Battle of Vegkop, when tribesmen of Thaba Nchu came to Hendrik Potgieter's aid after Ndebele raiders had driven off the Voortrekkers' cattle and left them stranded. The local chief, Moroka, took a collection among his tribe and presented the Boers with draught oxen, milk cows, sheep, goats, and even rawhide shoes and clothing to help them on their way. What price the white man's gratitude now!

Plaatje did not live to see it, but when at last the white authorities did attempt to show their gratitude sixty years later the result was even more ironic. When the black "homeland" of BophuthaTswana was granted nominal "independence" in 1977, Moroka's Tswana descendants living at Thaba Nchu were included as a far-flung addition to the main fragments of tribal land in the western Transvaal. That was their historical reward. The snag, apart from the fact that it stripped the Thaba Nchu Tswanas of their South African citizenship and made them statutory foreigners, is that there were many people of Sotho tribal origin living among them who in terms of apartheid's concept of ethnic compartmentalization did not belong in the Tswana "homeland." So they were moved out of it and settled on land three miles away which the Department of Black Administration bought from a white farmer. There, today, live 700,000 souls in the biggest dumping ground in all South Africa—people who are surplus to the white man's needs in the city and who have been driven off the farms by mechanization and new "squatter" laws to wander, homeless and bewildered as in Plaatje's time, until they turned up here, the only place they could find where it was legal for them to stay.

It is called Botshabelo. As you speed along the highway toward the provincial capital at Bloemfontein, you can see rows of neat, freshly painted houses and a shiny industrial park fronting the road. It looks like a prosperous settlement, a fitting monument to the white man's appreciation of black generosity long ago. But it is an illusion. Botshabelo is not just a Potemkin village. It is a Potemkin city. Turn off the highway and drive over the low ridge where the nice houses are and you will see before you a sprawl of tin shanties and mud hovels stretching to the horizon. It is a massive, desperate rural slum, three-quarters of whose inhabitants are unemployed. And if you go into the factories you will find industrialists paying their workers between six and seventeen dollars for a fifty-hour week.[17] That is the true monument—and the culmination of what Sol Plaatje saw beginning to happen after the 1913 Land Act.

Why? What was the purpose behind such massive disruption and the inflicting of so much misery? The answer is, to provide labour—labour for the farms and labour for the mines.

There was a secondary reason, too, which was to make space on the land for the poor whites who were streaming into the city. General Hertzog, minister of native affairs, toured the country appealing to farmers to get rid of the black sharecroppers and rent-paying tenants on their land and take in white *bywoners* instead, but the farmers were not keen because they reaped easy profits from the blacks while the *bywoners* paid no rent and, being unwilling to do manual labour, cultivated few crops to be shared. So the government forced the evictions.

But labour was the chief reason. South Africa's gold was deep down and the ore was low grade. Similar ore in the United States or Canada or Australia would probably have stayed in the ground. Only the plentiful presence of cheap labour—dirt cheap because it was black—in South Africa made the founding of the world's most bountiful mining industry possible. In 1910 black miners on the Witwatersrand were paid two shillings a day, compared with a white miner's twenty shillings, and when after a decade they asked for a three-shilling raise the Chamber of Mines replied that to grant that would close down the whole industry.[18] That is how marginal it was. As costs rose and new competitors for labour appeared on the scene, the supply had to be kept plentiful and it had to be kept cheap. And as the mines gulped up the labour the farmers squealed because it was being drawn away from them.

From the two prime users, therefore, the Afrikaner farmers and the English mining companies, the government came under pressure to increase the supply of labour. The white political adversaries found a common purpose when it came to the blacks. And the action they demanded was to stop the growth of an independent black peasantry so as to force them all to become migrant workers.

For a curious thing had been happening on the land. After their massive dispossession following the *Difaqane*, blacks had been making something of a comeback, gradually working their way back onto the land as tenants and sharecroppers. In the absence of commercial agri-

17. These wages were verified by the author during a visit to Botshabelo in May 1987.

18. Frederick Johnstone, *Class, Race and Gold* (London, 1976), p. 182.

culture, many white farmers found they could not make use of all their land and that it was more profitable to lease some of it to black tenants. Sometimes these tenants paid a cash rental and sometimes they paid the farmer by working 90 or 180 days a year on his farm, and sometimes, especially in the Free State, they stayed on a sharecropping basis, or "farming on the half," growing their own crops and running their own livestock on the white person's farm and sharing the profits equally with him. In this way, as Colin Bundy has shown, a whole new peasant class began to emerge toward the end of the nineteenth century and reestablish a degree of independence.[19]

The conviction exists in white South African minds today that blacks are inefficient farmers, primitive, improvident, and lazy, working just enough to provide for their barest needs and then idling away the rest of their time. These white folks look at the scrub cattle and scrawny crops as they drive through the overcrowded and leached black "reserves" and they are confirmed in this view. But the historical evidence is otherwise. The black peasants who emerged in the late nineteenth century showed themselves to be hard-working and productive, which is why the farmers preferred having them to white *bywoners*. As one visitor to a black farming community remarked: "Man for man the Kafirs of these parts are better farmers than the Europeans, more careful of their stock, cultivating a larger area of land, and working themselves more assiduously."[20]

So the reemergent black peasants prospered. By 1875 black produce in the Cape Colony was estimated to be worth £750,000.[21] And as they prospered they occupied more and more of the white people's land. They began leasing whole blocks of farms from whites who were happy to sit back and live comfortably off the rent, and they began buying land of their own. One tribe in the Transvaal leased twenty-two farms for grazing, another eighteen, and by the end of the century a quarter of a million acres of Transvaal land had been bought by blacks.[22]

This posed a multiple threat to whites. It meant the blacks were establishing a foothold of independence once more; it meant they were posing a commercial challenge to the white farmers and a social chal-

19. Colin Bundy, *The Emergence and Decline of a South African Peasantry* (Oxford, 1972), pp. 369–88.

20. V. Sampson, "A Letter on Frontier and Natal Travelling," quoted in Bundy, op. cit., p. 377.

21. Ibid., pp. 376–7.

22. Ibid., p. 182.

lenge, too, as some of them became richer than the poor whites; and it meant the cheap labour pool was drying up.

Hence the Land Act. At a stroke it prohibited the further purchase of land by blacks, put a stop to the tenant and sharecropping systems, removed the foothold of independence, and poured nearly a million blacks back into the captive labour pool. It was the start of the most comprehensive system of labour coercion on a racial basis that has been devised since slavery. And it was introduced in the face of a dire warning by one of the most perceptive minds of the day about where such an exploitative course would lead. With astonishing foresight the writer Olive Schreiner wrote on the eve of Union:

> If, blinded by the gain of the moment, we see nothing in our dark man but a vast engine of labour; if to us he is not man, but only a tool; if dispossessed entirely of the land for which he now shows that large aptitude for peasant proprietorship for the lack of which among their masses many great nations are decaying; if we force him permanently in his millions into the locations and compounds and slums of our cities . . . ; if, uninstructed in the highest forms of labour, without the rights of citizenship, his own social organisation broken up, without our having aided him to participate in our own; if . . . we reduce this vast mass to the condition of a great, seething, ignorant proletariat—then I would rather draw a veil over the future of this land.[23]

In fact the forced march into the labour pool had already begun when Schreiner wrote that. Blacks, too, had been driven off the land by the cattle plague, the locusts, and the drought. A new pass law required blacks on the Witwatersrand to display badges showing they were employed. Labour and hut taxes were imposed in the Cape to penalize black men who were not wage earners. In Rhodes's words these "removed the Natives from that life of sloth and laziness, teaching them the dignity of labour, and made them contribute to the prosperity of the state, and made them give some return for our wise and good government."[24]

But the Land Act was the big one. It sent them to the city in their thousands, tribal men and women, chiefs and commoners, herdboys and

23. Olive Schreiner, *Closer Union* (Cape Town, 1960), p. 29. Schreiner's treatise on the pending National Convention was first published as a series of letters to the *Transvaal Leader* in 1908.

24. Quoted in Eddie Webster, "Background to the Supply and Control of Labour in the Gold Mines," in *Essays in Southern African Labour History*, ed. Eddie Webster (Johannesburg, 1978), p. 10.

witch doctors and cattlemen, and pitched them into a fantastic new world of gold mines and factories, of skips and hoists and dynamite explosions, of arc-welding lamps and screaming machinery, of garden "boys," kitchen "boys," messenger "boys," and boss "boys," of service and subservience.

The shock of their arrival in the city can only be imagined. The cultural distance from kraal to mine compound, from the slow life of the tribe to the teeming slum, from the extended family to no family at all in a single-sex barrack room with rows of concrete bunks like slabs in a mortuary, is so immense as to stagger the mind. One could see them arrive at the train station in Johannesburg, in groups with heavy tin trunks on their heads and fear in their eyes as they stared at the tall buildings and flashing lights and thundering traffic. As they alighted from the train they stepped from the Iron Age into the Industrial Age, having travelled a greater distance in less time than any other people in the history of the world. Starting from further back they underwent in fifty years a transformation that took several centuries to complete in Europe. For, as Charles van Onselen points out, South Africa's industrial revolution was really compressed into the period between the discovery of diamonds and the outbreak of the First World War, by which time the foundations of a modern capitalist state had been firmly laid.[25]

The transformation was cruel not only in its swiftness but also in its malevolence. Where the poor-white Afrikaner felt alienation in the city, the poor black felt enmity. He was despised and abused and, often enough, beaten up. When blacks first began arriving in Johannesburg a Transvaal *Volksraad* law prohibited them from walking on the pavements and required them to doff their hats to white women on the street. That fell away, but the attitude behind it remained—the belief that the black person should know his place, that he did not really belong in the city and was there only to serve the white person's needs, that every black person was potentially available to do the white's bidding. "Hey John, come here and help me lift this thing. . . ."

Worst of all were the low wages. Everything flowed from the mines' low profit margin. The system devised to keep black labour cheap for the mines kept it cheap for all other employers as well. It amounted to the prohibition of a free labour market. Blacks were forced to work but prevented from selling their labour to the highest bidder—first by ensuring a heavy oversupply so that there was no bidding, then by constructing a legal framework that bound them to a single employer and

25. Charles van Onselen, *Studies in the Social and Economic History of the Witwatersrand*, p. 74.

allowed no security of tenure in the city except in his service, and finally by preventing them from acquiring skills with a market value. So the wage level remained low, for most below the minimum subsistence level as living costs rose, and in the struggle to survive many were forced into prostitution and crime.

The shebeen, a speakeasy, arose and became an institution in the black ghettos, a social meeting place as well as a source of illicit liquor in days when there was prohibition for blacks. And big crime gangs arose, the Americans, the Berliners, and the Msomi gang, Chicago-style gangs with larger-than-life leaders who affected what they imagined was an American lifestyle. America, the land of Jesse Owens and Joe Louis, was perceived as the place where the black man was free, or at least where he was a man of the city, of the Big Time—a man of flashy suits with a fedora hat pulled low over the eyes, big American cars with extra chrome attachments, and racy speech. *Tsotsitaal*, a ghetto slang of English, Afrikaans, and vernacular spoken with a colourful use of Runyonesque idiom. The Big Time, man, and robbing whites was not really crime, it was equalization, a kind of rough justice in this Sherwood Jungle of gold and squalour.

But if the gang leader became a role model so did the church leader, the *umfundisi*. As the ways of the tribe broke down in the city, as the black people left the places where there was intercession with the ancestors and as they were scattered about this wide country, they turned for solace and social cohesion to the Church, to the *umfundisi* with the Bible that said the Christian God was the God of the poor and that the rich could never get to heaven. To these deeply spiritual people there was comfort in that, and there was comfort in the big stone church on a hill in Sophiatown, in the middle of the slum, where one could go and meet one's friends and sing with them in one's own language and look at coloured windows with their pictures of saints who were the Christian ancestors. And there was comfort in the smaller groups that sprang up, in the little group from one's own home area who had formed their own church with their own bishop and who would put on white robes and sing and pray and baptize in the river and be possessed by the spirit all together in a frenzy of fellowship on Sunday afternoons.

Thus the black person's city. Tough, violent, strange, and a terrible wrench from the old way of life; a place where survival is the ceaseless purpose of existence for everyone; a place where you go to be exploited and where the dice are loaded heavily against you; but for all that a place of remarkable warmth and vitality, where the shattered fragments of close-knit societies have brought with them their sense of community, of *ubuntu*, and in their togetherness are able to maintain great courage and cheerfulness in the face of adversity.

If the Land Act was the start of systematic exploitation, it was also the start of organized resistance. A year before it was passed its appalling implications galvanized South Africa's small black intellectual elite into trying to prevent it from becoming law. A young lawyer named Pixley Seme, who had graduated from Oxford and Columbia before returning to open a practice in Johannesburg, called together three colleagues and together they decided to convene a national conference of chiefs and other black leaders.

So it came about that on January 8, 1912, the African National Congress was formed in the old Boer republican capital of Bloemfontein. Though blacks had no vote it was South Africa's first national opposition party, formed a full two years before Hertzog's National party, and the first black political movement of its kind on the continent. It was formed as the voice of the black majority then and it unquestionably is still so today.

The delegates came from all parts of the country and from the neighbouring territories of Bechuanaland, Basutoland and Swaziland, a mixture of chiefs and tribesmen from the "reserves" and the emerging middle class of lawyers, teachers, and ministers of religion. Mary Benson gives a colourful description of the scene as they assembled in the community hall of Bloemfontein's black quarter. "The platform was filled with eminent formally dressed Africans," she writes, "some in frock-coats with top hats, carrying furled umbrellas. A Sergeant-at-Arms in a tunic with sergeant's stripes, breeches and gaiters, and carrying a hide shield, knobkerrie and axe, kept order."[26]

The proceedings began with a prayer and the singing of the beautiful Xhosa hymn *"Nkosi Sikelel' i-Afrika"*—"God Bless Africa"—which has become the ANC anthem and that of at least three independent countries in East and Central Africa. Then Seme explained the purpose of the convention:

> Chiefs of royal blood and gentlemen of our race, we have gathered here to consider and discuss a scheme which my colleagues and I have decided to place before you. We have discovered that in the land of their birth, Africans are treated as hewers of wood and drawers of water. The white people of this country have formed what is known as the Union of South Africa—a union in which we have no voice in the making of laws and no part in the administration. We have called you, therefore, to this conference so that together we can find ways and means of forming *our*

26. Mary Benson, *South Africa: The Struggle for a Birthright*, p. 25. (A knobkerrie is a heavy club with a knob on the end.)

> national union for the purpose of creating national unity and defending our rights and privileges.[27]

The Congress—called the South African Native Congress at that stage—sent a delegation to London to protest the Land Act, but there they were politely reminded that South Africa was an independent country now and that they should return and work patiently through the South African political system to achieve their objectives—a system from which they were excluded by law.

But the politics of resistance had started. Seme hurried back from London to form the African Farmers Association and buy up as much land as possible before the bill became law, thereby establishing a number of "black spots" in "white" South Africa that the zealots of apartheid are still trying to erase with their removal schemes. In the same year Seme launched the first national newspaper for blacks called *Abantu-Batho*, or People.

There was a strike by thirteen thousand black mine workers in 1913 and in Bloemfontein a number of women, angry at the introduction of a pass system for them, marched to the municipal offices and dumped a bagful of passes at the deputy mayor's feet.

The First World War and its aftermath brought a surge in prices while black wages remained static. Discontent spread in the mines. There were more strikes and a consumer boycott of goods in one of the mine-compound stores. Encouraged by Woodrow Wilson's statement that now was the time for everyone to claim their rights as free men, Congress sent a delegation to the Peace Conference at Versailles to plead the cause of the black South Africans.

In Johannesburg black municipal workers went on strike, refusing to empty the city's night-soil buckets. Militancy and political consciousness were on the rise and the Congress organized a passive resistance campaign against the pass laws. "We came to the conclusion that passes prevent money," the ANC leaders declared in a circular.[28] Mass meetings were held. As they were to do in the decades that followed, the authorities reacted with force. Troops were called out to break the strikes and police arrested the campaign organizers. As crowds marched to the police station to protest the arrests, unrest broke out and tramcars and automobiles were stoned in Johannesburg.

In 1919 a dynamic clerk from Nyasaland, Clemens Kadalie, formed

27. Quoted ibid., p. 25.

28. Quoted in Johnstone, op. cit., p. 178.

the Industrial and Commercial Workers Union, which also joined the antipass campaign. Kadalie toured the country recruiting members with the promise to win higher wages and better conditions for black workers. It was South Africa's first black trade union and it burgeoned into a nationwide movement with more than fifty thousand members before it split and went into decline a decade later.

Looking back, two things stand out. The first is how quickly blacks adapted to the twin shocks of rapid industrialization and urbanization. In less than two generations they were coping with the city, the mine, and the factory; they were organizing themselves politically and industrially, forming parties and unions, mounting protest campaigns, petitioning the government, and lobbying abroad to gain international support for their cause.

The second striking thing is the manner of this rapid adjustment. The experience for the blacks was harsher in every way than it was for the Afrikaners; the cultural shock was greater, the alienation greater, the exploitation greater, and the struggle for survival infinitely greater. The black South Africans have suffered more than a Century of Wrong—they have suffered much greater wrongs, their grievances are much deeper. Yet they have not responded by turning in upon themselves with the same aggrieved self-obsession as the Afrikaners. Their experience has produced a black nationalism, just as the Afrikaner sense of grievance produced Afrikaner nationalism. But it is not a narrow, narcissistic, exclusivist nationalism intent on preserving its own little *volk* and isolating itself in its self-centred anxiety from the rest of mankind. Black nationalism embraces mankind. It does not shrink from humanity, it wants to be part of humanity. "People are people through other people. . . ." It is an open, inclusivist, integrationist nationalism. "South Africa belongs to all who live in it, black and white," says the Freedom Charter adopted at an ANC-sponsored Congress of the People in 1955.

It is a vision of a future without hedges.

CHAPTER SEVEN

The Rise of Apartheid

The Boer nation wishes to ensure a fatherland for the white man in South Africa that for ages to come can serve as a home for posterity.

GEOFF CRONJÉ

The great danger of idealism lies in the fact that it turns men into fools. . . . Through the extravagant, everyday invocation of the highest ideals, reality may perish.

MOELLER VAN DEN BRUCK

IF THE TREK to the city was a devastating experience for the Afrikaner, it was also his time of rebirth. The city crushed the Afrikaner worker and violated the tradition of Afrikanerdom, but even as it did so it brought into existence a new Afrikaner intelligentsia. As happened in the Cape during the nineteenth century, when the supposed bane of British colonialism brought the benefits of education and contact with a wider world, producing Afrikanerdom's first intellectual elite, which set a match to the powder of nationalist sentiment, so with urbanization and industrialization in the twentieth century came schools and universities, and as the rustic Afrikaner came to town he got educated. Out of the ashes of war and defeat and the Depression and poor-whiteism a new political intelligentsia arose that was not only able to articulate the grievances of the century of injustice, as the Rev. S. J. du Toit had done, but this time to formulate an ideology, a political eschatology for the redemption of the *volk*. Their goal was radically to restructure South African society in order to ensure, in the words of one of the earliest prophets of this millennial idea, that the white Afrikaner nation would have a home for posterity, even unto the remotest future in this continent of swelling black numbers.

The massive buildup of the black proletariat in the cities prompted this new ideologizing. As the numbers rose the focus of Afrikaner anxiety switched from the fear of being Anglicized to the fear of being swamped by blacks. To the ancient fear of *gelykstelling* was now added the even more emotive one of *uitbastering*, or the destruction of national identity through "bastardization." The mixed-race ghettos were the worry. "This mishmash cohabitation carries the germs of blood-mixing," railed Geoff Cronjé,[1] professor of sociology at Pretoria University and one of the leading lights of the new intelligentsia. This evil, if allowed to continue, would contaminate the blood-purity of Afrikanerdom's posterity, destroying its national identity and submerging it in a single, unidentifiable "mishmash" race. So if the long-term survival of the *volk* was to be ensured, there would have to be not only a home for posterity but safeguards for its racial purity as well. That meant its home would have to be separated from that of the blacks. The "mishmash cohabitation" would have to cease. Segregation was essential for national survival. There could be no common South African society.[2]

The young Afrikaner intellectuals were as much influenced by the general spirit of the times as they were by the social crisis in the cities. The 1930s was the age of fascist dictators in Europe and of a reborn, crude nationalism. Hitler was on the rise, trumpeting the glories of *Volk* and *Reich* and leading a resurgent Germany back from the humiliations of defeat and depression to a triumphant rebirth of national pride. Afrikaners had always had an emotional bond with Germany, ties of ancestry and a related language, and now many of the new generation of Afrikaner graduates headed there for doctoral studies at the universities of Berlin and Munich and Cologne and Leipzig. From the humdrum remoteness of the South African veld they were pitched into the dazzling power and excitement of great rallies and great orations, of a New Idea on the rise that was maybe going to sweep the world and that was echoing the very themes they felt deep in their own bosoms—the apocalyptic themes of national death and redemption and a glorious new Reich that was going to last a thousand years.

It was heady wine, and so, too, was their discovery of the German romantic philosophers and of Oswald Spengler's *Decline of the West*, whose work was drawn on by the political choreographers of the National Socialist revolution to provide a veneer of intellectualism for their racist demogoguery. It was gratifying to these country folk to find their bucolic prejudices endorsed by a rising superpower, one of the most

1. Geoff Cronjé, *'n Tuiste vir die Nageslag—Die Blywende Oplossing van Suid-Afrika se Rassevraagstuk* (Johannesburg, 1945), p. 65. Cronjé's emotive use of language is particularly strong in the original Afrikaans of this quotation: "Die mengelmoes-samelewing dra die kieme van bloedvermenging."

2. Ibid., pp. 42–90.

sophisticated nations in Europe. Now they could face up, man to man, to their supercilious English critics. It was gratifying, too, that Germany was a traditional adversary of Britain, and that the two were even now moving toward a new confrontation which might provide a satisfying sense of vicarious revenge and, who knows, perhaps even give the Afrikaner his republic back minus the accursed trappings of British crown and flag and anthem.

They returned to South Africa, these young Ph.D.s, to form a new Afrikaner political intelligentsia imbued with a new messianic idealism and also to take over the faculties of politics and philosophy and sociology and psychology at the new Afrikaans universities in the burgeoning cities. There they merged with young theologians of the Dutch Reformed Church, who had likewise returned from Europe with new ideas about the divine right of each nation to a separate existence and who had taken over the church's theological seminaries. What they had absorbed, they taught. They helped restructure the education system according to the Christian National ideas they now evolved, so that in time a new generation of urbanized, educated Afrikaners arose steeped in the values of the new nationalism and the new politics.

The two streams, political and theological, flowed together and were synthesized into a new *wêreld-en-lewensbeskouing*, a philosophy of life, based on the fundamental concept of the nation as the supreme expression of human fulfillment. The old ideas of a chosen people with a special "calling" took on a new meaning and a new impetus. The Afrikaner *volk* became a special nation with a special mission, which was to restructure South Africa in such a way as to preserve not only its own national identity but that of all other *volkere*, or ethnic nations, as well. "The Afrikaner believes," wrote Cronjé, "that it is the will of God that there should be a diversity of races and nations and that obedience to the will of God therefore requires the acknowledgment and maintenance of that diversity."[3]

Thus the new concept of apartheid, or the comprehensive separation of all the *volkere* of South Africa into their own national units, became not only politically necessary for the survival of the Afrikaner *volk* and its posterity but theologically necessary as well. It was not just an Afrikaner tradition, it was God's will.

This was more, much more, than the traditional system of segregation that had been practiced for generations in South Africa, which was familiar, too, throughout the colonial world and in the United States. This was not a matter of mere separate entrances and separate lunch counters. This was the radical, programmatic restructuring of a

3. Ibid., p. 10.

country, of a socially intermixed society becoming daily more integrated economically, dividing it into separate living areas, separate towns, separate economies, separate "nations." Total separation, Geoff Cronjé called it.

To implement this revolutionary idea for their own survival and in fulfillment of the divine will became the special "calling" of the Afrikaner people, for which the National party began to mobilize them.

BUT BEFORE PLUNGING deeper into the story of this ideologizing and the new nationalism it produced, I must first deal with the strange demise of the old one. In a sense Afrikaner nationalism has undergone two overlapping revolutions, the first inspired by its conflict with Britain, the second by its confrontation with the rising force of black nationalism. It was in the city that the overlap occurred, and as it did so it was like the firing of a booster rocket that put the Afrikaner revolution into a higher and steeper arc, just as the first phase was reaching its Thermidor.

For James Barry Munnik Hertzog, who had founded the Afrikaner National party in 1914 and led it to power in the 1920s, it was a perplexing and painful disillusionment. He had launched the Afrikaner Nationalist revolution, insisting, like Steve Biko and his Black Consciousness movement half a century later, that his people needed to be uplifted psychologically and economically before there could be any talk of joining hands with their erstwhile conquerors and oppressors. The Afrikaner had to do his own thing first, haul himself up, fight for his rights, demand reparation and affirmative action. He had to be rehabilitated in his national pride, and only when that was done and the Afrikaner could hold his head high and face the Englishman on a basis of equality could he treat with him as a friend and merge with him into a larger South Africanism.

For two decades Hertzog fought for that, and when after nine years as prime minister he felt he had achieved it, that all the rights he had claimed for Afrikanerdom were now secured and that the time had arrived for its act of reconciliation, the booster fired and Hertzog fell away like the spent shell of a launching rocket while Afrikaner nationalism soared away on its new course.

In a sense he suffered the fate of all moderates in revolutionary times. As Crane Brinton notes, it is the great haters, the single-minded men of heroic emotion, who ride revolutions to their successful conclusion,[4]

4. Crane Brinton, *The Anatomy of Revolution* (New York, 1962), p. 153.

and Barry Hertzog was not a great hater. He was essentially a decent, logical, pragmatic man who was filled with enough passion to want to uplift his defeated people but who was not imbued with a great messianic idea, and he had no conceptualized, rationalized programme to follow.

In particular, he had no vision of the black challenge ahead. He belonged to an era when blacks were part of the South African landscape, like the animals and the thorn trees, and had no political significance except in so far as they could provide labour and be of service to the white person's needs. Hertzog believed in segregation as part of the natural order of things, and during his premiership he moved vigorously to eradicate some of the residual traces of British liberalism still in the South African constitution. But of the rising black proletariat in the cities as the primary threat to the future survival of the Afrikaner nation he had no concept at all. To him, the totality of the Afrikaner struggle lay in its conflict with the English, and he thought that was over.

But the real importance of the Afrikaners' rejection of Hertzog is that the manner of his going created the circumstances for the "purification" of the National party into a new and more truly revolutionary movement, cleansed of the old compromisers and led by the new intelligentsia with their messianic zeal and new millennial ideas. When the National party next came to power it was they who took over the country, ready to implement their radical doctrine of apartheid.

In 1933, in the depths of financial crisis and with the Depression causing rumblings of discontent in the white electorate, Hertzog made his reconciliatory move. To stabilize the country and ward off a challenge from an Afrikaner judge named Tielman Roos who quit the bench to form a new political party, Hertzog proposed the formation of a coalition government to his old adversary, Smuts. The time had come, he said, for Brit and Boer to join hands as fellow South Africans. Smuts accepted, coalition led to fusion, and a new United party ruled the country with a huge majority under Hertzog as prime minister and Smuts as deputy prime minister. There was rejoicing in the land. A new national unity seemed to have been born out of the generations of strife between the two white groups.

But the Jacobins of the Nationalist movement would have none of it. A year after Fusion they broke away to form the Gesuiwerde Nasionale party, or Purified National party, under the leadership of Dr. Daniel Malan, a former minister of the Dutch Reformed Church who had done his graduate study at Utrecht in Holland and then become founding editor of the first major Afrikaans daily newspaper in South Africa, *Die Burger*. Lean years followed for the Purified party, with only 19 members in a Parliament of 150, but they were a dedicated few who knew themselves to be the custodians of the Afrikaner *volksgees*, the keepers of the Holy Grail. Here were Brinton's hard-eyed, steely-minded extremists, fanatically devoted to their cause and endowed with the effective blindness that keeps successful revolutionaries undistracted in their rise to power.

The 1930s rolled on in a kind of blissful calm before the storm. Hertzog's "civilized labour" policy gave job preference to "civilized" whites instead of "uncivilized" blacks, absorbed large numbers of poor whites in the enlarged public sector, especially the railways, and the economy moved slowly out of the doldrums. Life returned to normal and white South Africa was infused with a new spirit of unity and optimism.

But if anyone had eavesdropped on the earnest discussions taking place every morning in the *koffiehuis* across the road from Parliament between the little groups of intense young men and the older, round-faced *doktor* with his thick-lensed spectacles; or if they had listened to Malan's oratorical expositions of the new theologized ideology, or to the coloratura performances of the young political preachers fresh out of the Dutch Reformed Church seminaries, they would have realized that something powerful was astir beneath the complacent surface.

It broke surface with the outbreak of World War II in September 1939. The leitmotif of Hertzog's premiership had been that South Africa should establish its complete sovereign independence from Britain, in spirit as well as in the letter of constitutional law. He had striven for that with a didactic persistence, and it became an article of faith for him now that South Africa should demonstrate that independence by not following Britain automatically into its war with Germany. Constitutionalism aside, Hertzog knew, too, that it would be an unpopular war with many Afrikaners who felt an emotional bond with Germany and a historical antagonism toward Britain. And so he was for neutrality in what he saw as "England's war."

To Smuts, on the other hand, neutrality was unthinkable. He did not share Hertzog's narrow, nationalistic view of things. His was a philosophy of holism that saw the reconciliation between Boer and Briton as an opportunity for South Africa to participate in a larger community of nations. He had served in the British war cabinet during World War I, had helped structure the League of Nations, and saw Hitler's racial theories and aggressive expansionism as a dire threat to the world which South Africa was duty bound to help oppose.

The lobbying over the weekend after Hitler marched into Poland was intense, and when the vote was taken in the South African House of Assembly on Monday, September 4, 1939, Smuts won by eighty votes to sixty-seven. With a majority of thirteen, South Africa declared war on the German Reich.

It was the end of Fusion. Hertzog resigned and crossed the floor with nearly forty followers to join Malan and his Gesuiwerdes in opposition, while Smuts took over as prime minister.

Overnight the Purified party was more than doubled in strength. This windfall was not without its problems for the dedicated band of Jacobins, who wanted no moderate dilution of the purity of their ideals; but in the months and years ahead they applied their fanatical energy to a ruthless campaign of securing their own control of the party and eliminating all other claimants to the role of being the political voice of Afrikaner nationalism. When Malan offered Hertzog the leadership, the cry of "Principles before people" was raised and the party congress turned him down.

Rejected and disillusioned, Hertzog withdrew to his farm in the Orange Free State where occasionally he could be seen, a lonely and reflective figure, standing among the thorn trees. One night in November 1942 he arrived alone at a Pretoria hospital and asked to be admitted. He gave his occupation as "farmer," and the receptionist taking down his details failed to recognize him. He died soon afterward, the Comte de Mirabeau, if not the Kerensky, of the Afrikaner revolution.

"THE NATIONAL PARTY at prayer" is how South Africans sometimes refer to the Dutch Reformed Church. It is a jest that speaks not only of the fact that the vast majority of the party's supporters belong to the church, but even more of the extent to which the church has been involved in the formulation of party policy. It was a coauthor of apartheid, some would say its initiator. It helped devise the policy and continues to this day to support it.

While the state has implemented the political philosophy, the church has supplied the theological justification for it. Thus has Afrikanerdom been largely relieved of what Leon Festinger would call the "cognitive dissonance" of a devoutly religious people imposing a discriminatory, oppressive and manifestly unjust system on others of God's children.[5] More than that, the church's endorsement gave great impetus to the apartheid idea. It replaced the sense of guilt with a sense of mission, teaching not only that apartheid is not sinful but that it is in accordance with the laws of God. To implement it is therefore a sacred task which the Afrikaner people have been specially "called" to perform.

This was a powerful addition to the older notion of the Afrikaners

5. Leon Festinger, *A Theory of Cognitive Dissonance* (New York, 1957). Festinger's theory holds that where there is such dissonance between belief and behaviour, a psychological need to reduce the tension will bring about an attitude change.

as a "chosen people." In the new eschatology they became a *volk* with a divine right to exist as a separate nation in their promised land, a nation with a special, ordained mission to separate all the other *volkere*, or races, of South Africa so that each might develop its own nationhood according to its own cultural norms in its own apportioned sector of the country.

The role of the church in this, like that of the secular elite, was largely a latter-day phenomenon. The church had long sanctioned segregation, but it was only with the pressures of the city environment and the emergence of a new generation of nationalist-minded clergy that it became politicized.

Back in 1838 the Cape synod of the Nederduitse Gereformeerde Kerk, the main Dutch Reformed Church,[6] had officially dissociated itself from the Great Trek. It regarded the trekkers as disloyal to their lawful government and urged them to remain or return. Its attitude on race was pragmatic in the political context of the day. Through the nineteenth century it practiced a sporadic segregation without ever being doctrinaire about it. In 1829 it had pronounced upon the unity of the body of Christ, declaring that "persons of colour . . . must be served in the communion service on an equal basis with born Christians."[7] There were, of course, few "coloured" members of the church in those days, since there were scarcely enough ministers to keep the church going among the Trekboers, let alone engage in missionary work among the Khoikhoi, the slaves, and the black tribes. But as the century advanced and more converts joined "out of heathendom," the pressure for segregation increased.

Conflict between the church's basic teaching about all Christians being one in the body of Christ and the Trekboers' passionate hostility to the idea of *gelykstelling* reached an emotional climax in the wake of the mass Afrikaner exodus from the eastern Cape. An incident on that troubled frontier brought the issue before the synod in 1857, and an uneasy compromise was reached in which the church declared that while the Scriptures required all converts to be accepted into the church

6. There are two smaller Dutch Reformed churches, the Gereformeerde Kerk and the Nederduitsch Hervormde Kerk van Afrika. The NGK, to which 40 percent of South Africa's white voters belong, is the one commonly known as the Dutch Reformed Church and has exercized the major influence on Afrikaner cultural and political affairs.

7. Acta Synoda 1829, p. 79. Quoted in F. E. O'Brien Geldenhuys, *The Dilemma of the Dutch Reformed Church in South Africa* (Optima, Sept 1983), p. 151. It should be noted, however, that at this time church decisions were influenced by the presence of British colonial officials in the synod, a legacy of VOC days when the NGK was virtually a state church at the Cape. This presence ceased soon after the 1929 synod.

whenever possible, if, "on account of the weakness of some" the cause of the kingdom of God might suffer, then Christians from different races might be allowed to have separate communion services and be organized into separate congregations as circumstances might require.[8]

That perfidious concession soon became the rule and led to the formation of a separate church for "coloureds" in 1881. The basis for church segregation, and thus for the eventual theological justification of apartheid, had been laid. But it was still pragmatic, not yet ideological. The change came in the greenhouse environment of the industrial city in the late 1920s and 1930s, when so many seeds from Afrikanerdom's past began to germinate.

As the defeated and demoralized Afrikaners flocked to the city and ran into their crisis of poverty and disorientation, the church became their anchor and rallying point. It involved itself at every level with their plight, becoming a major institution of social assistance. Wherever there were Afrikaner families in distress, there was the DRC *predikant* doing what he could to encourage and help them. He became a central figure in the life of a demoralized people. The church took the lead in organizing a *volkskongres*, or people's conference, to devise ways to combat the poor-white problem. It started feeding schemes for the poor, created job opportunities for them, and started Afrikaans schools in the vestries of its churches to establish what it called "Christian-National education." And it began focussing attention on the threat to Afrikanerdom presented by the burgeoning black proletariat.

Through the intensity of this involvement with the material plight of the Afrikaner people in the cities, the DRC came to be regarded as the *volkskerk*, or people's church. From the days of the Rev. S. J. du Toit and his language movement, DRC ministers had been the driving force in the upsurge of Afrikaner culture and national self-awareness. Now the identification became even closer and more visceral, the church's leadership role more politically pointed. The volkskerk became literally an organ of the people, the theological arm of the emerging *volksbeweging*, or people's movement, which was soon to start mobilizing the Afrikaner people politically for the realization of their nationhood and fulfillment of their calling.

Then in 1928 there occurred an event that gave a sharper doctrinal edge to this. A bitter dispute arose between the church and one of its senior teachers at the seminary at Stellenbosch University, Johannes du Plessis. The point at issue was an abstruse theological one to do with different interpretations of the relationship between Christ's deity and His humanity, but the essence of it was that Professor Du Plessis's

8. J. C. Adonis, *Die Afgebreekte Skeidsmuur Weer Opgebou* (Amsterdam, 1982), p. 56.

theology was undergoing what the church considered to be a liberal drift. It tried him for heresy and found him guilty. Although Professor Du Plessis was able to get the verdict overturned on appeal to the Cape Supreme Court, it cost him his job at the seminary and led to a watershed decision by the church's governing council.

Professor Du Plessis had strong links with the University of Utrecht in Holland, to which most young ministers of the DRC had gone for their graduate studies up till then. Now the church council blamed the liberal influence of this institution for Du Plessis's deviationism and decided to discourage its young ministers from going there. Instead, it advised them to go to the Free University of Amsterdam.

This brought them under the influence of the theological ideas of the Free University's founder, Abraham Kuyper, which were to play an important part in the development of the new ideological thinking back in South Africa. It was not long before these returning Kuyperians came to dominate the teaching faculties of the DRC seminaries at Stellenbosch and Pretoria universities. These ideas were also strongly implanted through the small Gereformeerde Kerk's seminary at Potchefstroom University, which had a formal tie with Kuyper's church in Holland and, through that, with the Free University.[9]

Kuyper was a politician as well as a theologian, and in 1901 he became prime minister of the Netherlands. He was a minister of Holland's Hervormde Kerk, but when that church refused to concede to his demands for doctrinal reform in accordance with his ideas, he resigned and joined the Gereformeerde Kerken Onder het Kruis (Reformed Churches Beneath the Cross). It then became the ecclesiastical base for his political platform.

Education policy was the main theme of Dutch politics at that time, and Kuyper's platform was to win the right to teach religious doctrine in schools. The government refused, insisting that public education should remain neutral on religious matters, and in the political struggle that followed Kuyper developed a theological rationale to strengthen his case.

The kernel of this was the concept of *sowereiniteit in eigen kring*, or sovereignty in one's own sphere. According to Kuyper, the sovereignty

9. For varying analyses of the influence of Abraham Kuyper's theology on Afrikaner nationalism and apartheid see T. Dunbar Moodie, *The Rise of Afrikanerdom*, pp. 52–72; W. A. de Klerk, *The Puritans in Africa*, pp. 204, 257–8; and Gerrit J. Schutte, "The Netherlands, Cradle of Apartheid?" in *Ethnic and Racial Studies*, vol. 10, no. 4, 1987, pp. 392–411. My readings on the subject were supplemented by interviews with Dr. Nico Smith, former head of the Department of Missiology of the NGK seminary at Stellenbosch University, and various theologians and church historians at the Free University, Leiden, Utrecht, and Kampen in the Netherlands.

of God, as it descends upon man, separates itself into two spheres—the *mechanical* sphere of state authority and the *organic* sphere of various "social circles": the personal, the corporate (universities, guilds, associations, and so forth), the domestic (family and married life) and the communal (cities and villages). Each of these organic spheres has its own authority—"that is to say, it has above itself nothing but God." The government therefore has no right to interfere in the spheres of social life.[10]

Explaining the difference between these spheres, Kuyper goes back to creation. Since God created man, all the human race is from one blood. This would have resulted in its developing into a single world empire but for man's falling into sin. Man's sinful degeneracy changed everything as God intervened to prevent his contumelious building of the tower of Babel and divide humanity into separate nations and states.

This disintregration would have led to chaos without laws and some ruling authority to control it, "so we have received from God the institution of the State with its magistrates as an indispensable means of preservation."[11] The magistrate is thus God's instrument to preserve his work of creation from destruction, and citizens are therefore bound to obey the government. But the instrument is "mechanical": it has no inherent authority over man, only that which is vested in it by God:

> It is not a natural head, which organically grew from the body of the people, but a *mechanical* head, which from without has been placed upon the trunk of the nation. A mere remedy, therefore, for a wrong condition supervening. A stick placed beside the plant to hold it up, since without it, by reason of its inherent weakness, it would fall to the ground.[12]

On the other hand the spheres of social life are not mechanical but originate directly from creation. They are part of what Kuyper calls the "ordinances of creation," original, natural, "organic," part of God's will when he created the universe and therefore immutable. They developed *organically* like "the stem and branches of a plant" or the birth of children through the innate power of reproduction.[13]

The government therefore has no right to impose its laws on the four social spheres, which do not owe their existence to it but directly to

10. Abraham Kuyper, *Calvinism* (Grand Rapids, Mich., 1931), p. 143.

11. Ibid., p. 130.

12. Ibid., p. 146.

13. Ibid., p. 144.

God. They have a divine sovereignty. "God rules in these spheres," writes Kuyper, "just as supremely and sovereignly through His chosen virtuosi, as He exercises dominion in the sphere of the State itself through His chosen magistrates."[14]

This doctrine of "sovereignty in one's own sphere" provided Kuyper with his justification for opposing the Dutch government's interference in religious education, a matter which he contended belonged to the sovereign "social sphere" of the family. Ironically, in light of the way South Africa's apartheidists have used it to justify a system of massive state regulation of social life, it was also a powerful doctrine of anti-authoritarianism and individual liberty. "Calvinism places our entire human life immediately before God," Kuyper wrote. "It follows that all men or women, rich or poor, weak or strong, dull or talented, as creatures of God, and as lost sinners, have no claim whatsoever to lord over one another, and that we stand as equals before God, and consequently equal as man to man."[15]

But the point the young Afrikaner theologians fastened onto, that they selectively adopted and adapted to their new nationalist thinking, was Kuyper's assertion that "nations," too, were part of the "ordinances of creation." It lay in that interpretation of the story of Babel, so fundamental to his dual-sovereignty thesis and so often quoted by DRC theologians themselves in support of their idea of a sacral nationalism. "For God created the nations," Kuyper declared. "They exist for Him. They are His own. And therefore all these nations, and in them all humanity, must exist for His glory and consequently after His ordinances."[16]

It is easy to see how this fed into the formulation of the new ideology. The *volk*, the Afrikaner nation, itself becomes a separate "social sphere" rooted in the "ordinances of creation" with a divine right to sovereignty in its own sphere. It is part of God's will that it should exist, and that it should exist separately from the other *volkere* in South Africa, the black and "coloured" races, each of which must exercise its own sovereignty in its own sphere. As one of these Afrikaner Kuyperians, Professor H. G. Stoker of Potchefstroom, put it:

> God willed the diversity of peoples. Thus far he has preserved the identity of our people. Such preservation was not for naught, for God allows nothing to happen for naught. He might have allowed our people to be

14. Ibid., p. 151.

15. Ibid., pp. 52–3.

16. Ibid., p. 130.

> bastardized with the native tribes as happened with other Europeans. He did not allow it. He might have allowed us to be anglicized, like for example, the Dutch in America. . . . He did not allow that either. He maintained the identity of our people. He has a future task for us, a calling laid away. On this I base my fullest conviction that our people will again win back their freedom as a people. The lesson of our history must always be kept before our eyes.[17]

The new ideological thinking revealed itself first of all within the DRC itself as the young politicized theologians who were now in control moved to apply it to the relationship between the church's own *volkere*—its white Afrikaner members and its "coloured" and black members, who had been drawn into the body of the *kerk* by its missionary effort over the years.

As Hannes Adonis, a leading figure in the "coloured" branch of the church, has shown in a doctoral thesis on this subject, these theologians drew further justification for their separatist ideas from several missionary sources that championed the idea of establishing indigenous churches rooted in the native culture of colonized communities.[18] Foremost among them were German missionaries who declared that the ultimate aim of their Lutheran mission was to found an indigenous *Volkskirche*, or national church, in which the national character and social relations of the indigenous people would be preserved.

Taking his cue from the injunction of the risen Christ to "Go ye therefore and teach all nations" (Matthew 28:19), Gustav Warneck, one of these German Lutherans, set as his goal the idea of *volkskerstening*, or the conversion of whole peoples instead of individuals. The entire community should join the church as a body to preserve its national unity and folk customs, but Warneck was against any early independence for the newly baptized *Volkskirchen*. Its members were still just "children beginning to be taught by Jesus."[19] Warneck believed that people of colour particularly started with the handicap of all but ineradicable racial weaknesses and so should be led by whites, especially Germans with their emphasis on good order and discipline.[20]

Bruno Gutmann, another Lutheran who worked among the Chagga tribe at the foot of Mount Kilimanjaro in what was then German East

17. Quoted in T. Dunbar Moodie, op. cit., p. 67.

18. Adonis, op. cit., pp. 58–71.

19. Peter Beyerhaus and Henry Lefever, *The Responsible Church and the Foreign Mission* (London 1964), p. 46.

20. Ibid., p. 54.

Africa, was likewise concerned with the preservation of what he called the "organic folk unit." Gutmann wrote rapturously of the pristine importance of the *urtümliche bindungen*, or primordial ties of blood relationship, neighbourhood and age group, which he regarded as "nationally organic."[21] There are echoes here of Johann Herder's concept of the *Volksgeist*, the quintessential folk-spirit of a nation derived from its indigenous culture, which the Nazis appropriated and made a central theme of their National Socialist philosophy. To Gutmann the *urtümliche bindungen* were rooted in the "ordinances of creation" and were therefore an expression of God's will.

The concept of *volk* as an organic entity derived from the creation also featured strongly in the writings of Christian Keysser, another German missionary whose work influenced the DRC theologians. During the Third Reich, Keysser became part of a movement through which the Lutheran Church adopted an *Ordnungstheologie*, or theology of ordination, that elevated the concepts of *volk*, fatherland, blood, and race to the level of organic life-spheres rooted in creation.

From all these sources, then, the DRC theologians drew support for their exegesis in claiming a Biblical basis for a policy of church segregation. A commission was appointed to draft the policy, which provided for a white "mother" church and separate "daughter" churches for "coloured" and black congregants. An Indian church was added later.

The policy declaration, written by G. E. B. Gerdener, then professor of mission history at the DRC seminary at Stellenbosch, was a thunderous exposition of the civil religion and provided a solid theological undergirding for the political programme to come. As it proclaimed in its preamble:

> The Church is deeply convinced of the fact that God, in His wise Counsel, so ordained it that the first European inhabitants of this Southern corner of Darkest Africa should have been men and women of firm religious convictions, so that they and their posterity could become the bearers of the light of the Gospel to the heathen races of this continent, and therefore considers it the special privilege of the Dutch Reformed Church of South Africa—in particular—to proclaim the Gospel to the heathen of this country.[22]

21. Ibid., pp. 68–9. See also Ernst Jaschke, "Bruno Gutmann's Legacy," *Occasional Bulletin of Missionary Research*, vol. 4, no. 4 (October 1980), pp. 165–9.

22. This and the following quotes from the policy statement are taken from the text published as Appendix A in G. B. A. Gerdener, *Recent Developments in the South African Mission Field* (London, 1958), pp. 269–75.

While acknowledging that God "made of one blood all nations of men for to dwell on the face of the earth" (Acts 17:26), and that all are equal in the eyes of God, the policy declaration went on to present the church's rationale for dividing the congregants into separate "national" churches. "It must not be forgotten," it said, "that evangelization does not presuppose denationalization. Christianity must not deprive the Native of his language and culture, but must eventually permeate and purify his entire nationalism."

The statement proclaimed the church to be in favour of "co-equal" education for "coloureds" and blacks "in their own sphere," and declared that "they must develop their own economic solidarity as far as possible apart from the European." It then went to the heart of what was to become the apartheid vision:

> The traditional fear of the Afrikaner of *gelykstelling* between black and white has its origin in his antipathy to the idea of racial fusion. The church declares itself unequivocally opposed to this fusion and to all that would give rise to it, but, on the other hand, as little begrudges the Native and Coloured a social status, as honourable as he can reach. Every nation has the right to be itself and to endeavour to develop and elevate itself. While the church thus declares itself opposed to social equality in the sense of ignoring differences of race and colour between black and white in daily life, it favours the encouragement and development of social differentiation and intellectual or cultural segregation, to the advantage of both sections.
>
> The policy of trusteeship, as exercised at present, must gradually develop into a policy of complete independence and self-determination for the Coloured and Native in his own community, school and church. The DR Church considers all differential treatment as a means of enhancing life and independence.

This "mission policy" was officially adopted by the Dutch Reformed Church in 1935. And so twelve years before the ideology of apartheid was fully developed and adopted by the National party as its political programme, the church laid down the theological justification for it and introduced the essence of it in its own racial relationships. The effect of this on a deeply religious people was enormous.

THE EXTENT to which Afrikaner nationalism was influenced by the ideas and political ethos of Nazi Germany during these formative years of the apartheid ideology is something that has been heavily downplayed since the collapse and exposure of the Third Reich. As in Germany itself, it has become difficult to find anyone in South Africa today who will confess to having been an admirer of Hitler. Fifteen years of vicarious intoxication and opportunistic expectation have been quietly swept under the carpet.

You will hear Afrikaner Nationalists repeat Hertzog's theme that they opposed the war not out of sympathy for Hitler but only because it was "England's war" and they wanted to assert South Africa's independence. But anyone who lived through those times knows well enough that there was much ardent support for the Nazi cause, and as late as January 1945, just four months before Germany's capitulation, Eric Louw, soon to become foreign minister in the Nationalist government, was still reassuring readers of his column in the official party newspaper, *Die Kruithoring*, that Allied reports of German military setbacks were exaggerated. Hitler's Ardennes offensive just before Christmas had greatly upset the Allied festivities and might well have become a second and greater Dunkirk, he wrote, while Field Marshal Albert Kesselring's retreats on the Italian front showed him to be "a master in the art of strategic withdrawal."[23]

You will also hear these apologists cite the National party's sometimes bitter clashes with two openly pro-Nazi organizations of those years, the Ossewa-Brandwag, or Ox-Wagon Sentinels, and Oswald Pirow's New Order movement. But again this fratricidal struggle had more to do with the National party's determination to establish its own paramountcy as the sole authentic voice of Afrikaner nationalism than with any serious policy differences with these rival groups. As Malan acknowledged at the time, the National party was 85 percent in accord with Oswald Pirow's New Order programme, which was explicitly and unreservedly National Socialist.[24]

The fact is that the influence of Nazi Germany on the minds of those who fashioned apartheid was very great, especially among key members of the Broederbond secret society, the inner body of Afrikanerdom's new political intelligentsia where the actual ideological groundwork was laid. This is not to say that the two are the same thing. To equate apartheid with Nazism is an overstatement that invites incredulity: its evil is in a different category from the calculated genocide of the death camps. But they are of the same genre. Apartheid and National Socialism both

23. *Die Kruithoring*, January 17, 1945. Louw's column, "Daar Oorkant die Water" (There across the seas), consistently took a pro-Axis, anti-Allied line in its commentaries on the progress of the war.

24. Michael Roberts and A. E. G. Trollip, *The South African Opposition 1939–45* (London, 1947), p. 97.

arose from the same witches' cauldron of national grievance and economic depression. Driven by the same sense of cultural despair, the same group hatreds and personal resentments, and feeling much in common with their Germanic kin, the Afrikaner ideologists responded to the national revival that Hitler kindled. They responded to the vision he conjured up of a conservative revolution that would recapture an idealized past in an imaginary future in which the old ideas and values and institutions and folk-spirit of the preindustrial period would once again command universal allegiance. A revolution that seemed capable of achieving spectacular results in an incredibly short time. And, moreover, a revolution that pushed so many of Afrikanerdom's own emotional buttons—that was nationalist and anticapitalist, that hated communism and liberalism and sickly humanism, that understood the meaning of the word *volk* and the importance of "blood" and "race," which exhorted its people to "think with your blood" and expounded the creed of *Blut und Boden*, blood and soil.

It was a spiritual as well as an ethnic kinship. And as Franco's Falangists took over in Spain, and with Mussolini in power in Italy and Antonio Salazar in Portugal and a whole crop of similar movements appearing in other Continental countries, a new age seemed to be dawning. This was the new politics, the new nationalism in Europe, and the new Nationalists in South Africa felt themselves to be in tune with it. As they began their ideologizing they borrowed much from it and tapped into many of the same intellectual sources that it was drawing on.

Ernst Malherbe, a leading educationist who was Smuts's director of military intelligence during World War II, has claimed that Hitler sent a spy to South Africa in 1934, a professor named Graf von Duerckheim Montmartin, to assess the extent of pro-German sympathies, spread cultural propaganda, and encourage Afrikaner students to go to German universities. He claims, too, that pro-Nazi elements in the Broederbond arranged for selected Afrikaner students to go to Germany to study and report on the methods used there in the education of the nation's youth.[25]

Whatever the truth of these allegations, the fact is that a number of Afrikanerdom's brightest and likeliest did find their way to German campuses in the 1930s. They included Nico Diederichs, Piet Meyer, Geoff Cronjé, and Hendrik Verwoerd, probably the most influential foursome in the development of the apartheid concept. It was Diederichs

25. Ernst G. Malherbe, *Education in South Africa*, vol. 11: 1923–75 (Cape Town, 1977), pp. 27–8. According to Malherbe a copy of Montmartin's report to Hitler was found among papers seized at the headquarters of the German diplomatic representative in South West Africa when South African forces moved into that territory in 1940.

who first laid the philosophical basis for it, Cronjé who first conceptualized it, Meyer who was its key backroom strategist, and Verwoerd who finally implemented it in its most absolute form. That they were all influenced by their German experience there can be no doubt. Just how much may be evidenced by the fact that Meyer named his son Izan, which is Nazi spelled backward, although since the war the family has claimed the spelling is coincidental and that the name is derived from a different source.

While the DRC theologians were absorbing and adapting their Kuyperian ideas in Amsterdam, these young secular students were tapping into the German Romantic philosophers at the universities of Berlin, Hamburg, Leipzig, Munich, and Cologne. They turned particularly, as the National Socialists were doing and in the same selective way, to the works of Johann Fichte, Johann Herder, Friedrich Schleiermacher, the brothers Friedrich and August Wilhelm von Schlegel, and others, to find intellectual justification for their ideas on *volk* and race and nation. Writing at a time when Germany was still fragmented in a number of weak and discordant states in the late eighteenth and early nineteenth centuries, these Romanticists had evolved a philosophy of nationalism that the ideologists of the new politics found congenial to their cause.

German culture had stagnated, and so the Romanticists emphasized the importance of the national *Kultur* and *Literatur*. The German language had fallen into neglect as the upper classes engaged French tutors and governesses for their children and German became, in Voltaire's words, the language "for servants and for horses," and so the national language, the *Muttersprache*, was consecrated as the quintessence of the national soul. History had been downgraded by the rationalists of the Enlightenment, and in reaction to this the Romanticists glorified it, seeking their ideals for the future in a magnificent past that had been corrupted by a moral decline and a spiritual malaise.

Above all, the Romanticists shared a conviction, through all their despair at the wretchedness of the national condition, in the future greatness of Germany. Theirs was a redemptive philosophy. The past had been great and there would be a regeneration of that greatness through a spiritual awakening of the nation.

The writings of these philosophers was a veritable treasure house of material for the National Socialist and Afrikaner Nationalist ideologists to adapt to their themes. Fichte, in a series of lectures following Napoleon's conquest of Prussia in 1806, had exhorted the German people to rediscover their national and racial pride. "It is only by the common characteristic of being German," he declared, "that we can avert the downfall of our nation, which is theatened by its fusion with foreign peoples, and win back again an individuality that is self-supporting and quite incapable of any dependence upon others."[26] Fichte inveighed against liberalism, rationalism, individualism, and materialism—all the core features of the modern, democratic, capitalist culture that Europe's new conservative revolutionaries claimed were afflicting Western civilization and sending it into decline. On his own the individual was nothing, rootless and sterile. Only within the group could the individual realize himself. And so the nation became the supreme expression of individual fulfillment.

That was the basis of the Romanticists' philosophy of nationality. As Herder saw it, nationality was an organic entity rooted in natural law. To picture a world without definite divisions into nationality was to misinterpret the whole meaning of creation. As with Kuyper, nations were therefore part of God's will. To Herder, writes Robert Ergang in a comprehensive analysis of the philosopher's work, "nationality was a part of the divine plan in history. In the development of each nationality he saw the unfolding of the divine will. Into the order established by the divine will, Herder said in effect, the individual must fit himself if he desires the highest self-development, for otherwise he is destined to sterility."[27] Developing this theme further, Schleiermacher wrote: "Every nationality is destined through its peculiar organisation and its place in the world to represent a certain side of the divine image. . . . For it is God alone who directly assigns to each nationality its definite task on earth and inspires it with a definite spirit in order to glorify himself through each one in a pecular manner."[28]

And Fichte, in language that Verwoerd might have used in one of his expositions of the apartheid vision: "Only when each people, left to itself, develops and forms itself in accordance with its own peculiar quality, and only when in every people each individual develops himself in accordance with that quality—then, and then only, does the manifestation of divinity appear in its true mirror as it ought to be." This, Fichte declared, was in accordance with the rule of law and the divine order. "Only in the invisible qualities of nations," he went on, ". . . is to be found the guarantee of their present and future worth, virtue and merit. If these qualities are dulled by admixture and worn away by friction, the flatness that results will bring about a separation from

26. Johann Gottlieb Fichte, *Addresses to the German Nation* (London, 1922), p. 4.

27. Robert Reinhold Ergang, *Herder and the Foundations of German Nationalism* (New York, 1931), p. 250.

28. Quoted ibid., p. 250.

spiritual nature, and this in turn will cause all men to be fused together in their uniform and conjunct destruction."[29]

Nation, *volk*, and language. Language, declared both Fichte and Herder, was the outstanding mark of nationality, the medium for the communication of ideas within a community and from generation to generation so that it shaped and transported the culture and so defined the nation, forming the people who used the language far more than they formed it. One can hear echoes of the Rev. S. J. du Toit and his Afrikaans language movement of the 1870s in Herder's evocative identification of language and nationality. "Has a nationality anything more precious than the language of its fathers?" he wrote in his *Humanitatsbriefe*. "In this language dwell its whole world of tradition, history, religion and principles of life, its whole heart and soul. To rob a nationality of its language or to degrade it, is to deprive it of its most precious possession."[30]

Out of this reverence for language and culture as the expression of nationhood came a concept that the Nazis were to usurp and turn into one of the most emotive tools of their demagoguery—the concept of the *Volksgeist*, or the folk-spirit of a people. It is difficult to translate the word into English without losing the emotive power it has in the Teutonic languages, and that in itself is part of its peculiar potency as something with a special meaning understood only by members of an ethnic club. To Herder who first used it, a nation's *Volksgeist* was the product of all the various phenomena of its indigenous cultural development as expressed through its art and literature, its folk songs and folk tales and folk poems. This constituted the soul or spirit of the nation. Any undue alien influence, Herder warned, would weaken that spirit and so threaten the nation's creative potential. Adapted to the Nazi cause, this reinforced the Third Reich's obsession with what it called *Rassenkunde*—racial science—and the purity of the Aryan race.

It was a travesty, of course. For Herder the concept of *Volksgeist* did not imply the superiority of any nation to any other. Instead he preached the equality and value of all cultures. The foundation of his nationalism was human brotherhood, not *Deutschland über Alles*. But in the business of ideologizing, such niceties are overlooked. The readings of the Romanticists were selective, the adaptations tendentious. So it was in South Africa as well as in the Third Reich.

The Afrikaner graduate students gulped all this up with the eagerness of intellectual starvelings as they watched the grand parades and listened

29. Fichte, op. cit., p. 232.

30. Herder, op. cit., p. 258.

to the blood-stirring oratory of the new *Reich* taking shape around them. It was enough to turn any young ethnic nationalist's head. The most comprehensive rendering of what they absorbed came from Nico Diederichs, who returned to South Africa to become a professor of political philosophy at the Grey University College of the Free State and, a few years later, chairman of the pivotally important Broederbond. Shortly after his return, in 1935, Diederichs published a pamphlet entitled *"Nasionalisme as Lewensbeskouing en sy Verhouding tot Internationalisme"* (Nationalism as a philosophy of life and its relation to internationalism). What it amounted to was an Afrikaner *Weltanschauung,* the first comprehensive statement of political philosophy ever presented by an Afrikaner, and it formed the basis for much of the theorizing and ideologizing that followed.

The essence of Diederichs's *lewensbeskouing* was a Fichtean view of the supreme importance of the nation. Individual man was as nothing. Only within a group could he develop as a spiritual being, and the supreme group, the most sublime, was the nation. Man was therefore called upon to fulfill himself through his membership in a national community.

> Man is not only called upon to be a member of a community, but also and especially to be a member of a *nation.* Without the uplifting, ennobling and enriching influence of this highest all-embracing unity that we call nation, man can never reach the fullest heights of his human existence. Only through his dedication to, his love for and his service to the nation can man realize the rounded and harmonious development of his full personality. Only in the nation as the most total, most all-embracing human community can man realize himself fully. The nation is the fulfilment of the individual life.[31]

Like Fichte, whom he acknowledged in the foreword to his booklet, and the other German Romanticists, Diederichs considered nations to be rooted in creation. They were established not by man but by God, and were therefore instruments of the divine will.

> God willed that there should be nations to enhance the richness and beauty of His creation. Just as He destined that there should be no deadening uniformity in nature but that it should present a rich diversity of plants and animals, sounds and colours, forms and figures, so, too, He willed that at the human level there should be a multiplicity and diversity

31. Nico Diederichs, *"Nasionalisme as Lewensbeskouing en sy Verhouding tot Internationalisme"* (Cape Town, 1935), pp. 17–18.

> of nations, languages and cultures. . . . And just as it would be a violation of God's natural law to try to reduce all colours to one colour and all sounds to one sound, everything in nature to one dull monotony, so is it just as much of a desecration of His law to want to destroy the multiplicity of nations in the world for the sake of a monochromatic, monotonous and monolithic humanity.[32]

By the invocation of such high-sounding ideals was the ground laid for a programme that would uproot millions of people, split families, demolish homes, shatter whole communities, and ravage people's lives in an incredible attempt to reverse the integrating forces of South Africa's industrial revolution and divide its people of various races, colours, and tribes into separate "nations"—according to "God's natural law." Thus did reality begin to perish in South Africa and its inhumanity get under way behind a cloak of righteousness.

Not only were separate nations part of God's will, Diederichs went on, they were also instruments for implementing the divine purpose. God entrusted each—the smallest as well as the greatest—with a special mission to be fulfilled as part of his overall plan for the whole of creation. Thus did the new ideology blend in with and build upon the older concept of a chosen people and a civil faith. Thus did it become theologized.

Piet Meyer's writings, more opaque in their metaphysical complexity, echoed the same theologized National Socialist themes. In 1942, he declared:

> To Afrikanerdom belong only those who by virtue of blood, soil, culture, tradition, belief, calling form an organic unitary society. This nation is by nature an organic wearer of authority with the patriarchal leader as chief bearer of authority of the nation, and with the members of the nation as active and cooperative workers. The national Afrikaner state of the future is therefore the political embodiment and ordering of the whole of Afrikanerdom as an organic articulation of authority, and is in this sense also a medium of Afrikanerdom to protect and promote its own fulfilment of calling.[33]

BUT IT WAS the style of National Socialism as much as its ideas that caught the imagination of Afrikanerdom's new Nationalists. They were impressed by Hitler's spectacular success in mobilizing the German

32. Ibid., pp. 22–3.

33. Quoted in De Klerk, op. cit., p. 214.

people and fascinated by the leadership techniques that achieved this —the stirring of ethnic emotions through the powerful use of symbolism and of historical and political myths. The political style of the new Nationalists soon started to reflect this. It became more evocative and demonstrative. There was increased emphasis on the themes of the sacred history, and the *stryddag*—a party rally featuring flags, patriotic folk songs, and fiery speeches—became the centrepiece of political campaigning.

The high point of this new symbolic politics was reached with a ritual reenactment of the Great Trek to mark the centenary of that national epic in 1938, an event that stirred Afrikaner emotions in the most extraordinary way and gave huge impetus to the spirit and thought of the new nationalism. The idea for the symbolic trek originated with a man who in many ways epitomized the new, urbanized Afrikaner. Though not one of the emerging intellectual elite, he was a product of the painful transition from *platteland* to city. Henning Klopper had left the parental farm at the age of fifteen in the bleak years of Afrikaner discontent during World War I and, clutching a Bible given him by his mother, gone to Johannesburg to join that haven of poor-whiteism, the railways. There a burning Afrikaner patriotism and a way with words soon propelled him into the company of the new political intelligentsia. While still a teenager he became a founder of the Broederbond secret society and, some years later, of an organization called the Afrikaans Language and Cultural Union of the South African Railways and Harbours, or ATKV, which represented the cultural interests of some eighteen thousand Afrikaner railway workers. He also became an admirer of National Socialism and of Hitler's dazzling style of stage-managed political drama.

It was through the ATKV that Klopper proposed his idea of celebrating the centenary of the Great Trek and the Vow of the Covenant by means of an ox-wagon procession that would retrace the footsteps of the old Voortrekkers across what he called "the whole path of South Africa." It was to be the ultimate symbolic pilgrimage, starting from the foot of Van Riebeeck's statue in Cape Town, calling at all the sacred sites along the way, and culminating in a great rally of the people on a hill outside Pretoria where a monument was to be erected that would be Afrikanerdom's most sacred shrine. The ATKV accepted Klopper's suggestion, other sponsors joined in, and the planning began.

Nine wagons were built for this five-month reenactment of the sacred history. They were named after hero figures and revered symbols of the national saga: Piet Retief, the martyr; Andries Pretorius, the victor of Blood River; Sarel Cilliers, the originator of the Covenant Vow; Louis Trichardt, the first trekker; Hendrik Potgieter, the early Transvaal leader; Dirkie Uys, a fourteen-year-old boy who died alongside his wounded father rather than flee from the Zulus; Johanna van der Merwe and Margrieta Prinsloo, two little girls who survived the Weenen massacre when their mothers hid them under their own bodies; and Vrouen-Moeder (Wife-and-Mother, in honour of the heroic women of the Great Trek.) The wagons set out on nine separate routes, calling at towns and villages across the country. The Dutch Reformed Church minister in each town was asked to appoint a committee to receive the wagons, arrange local commemoration activities, and obtain fresh teams of oxen from local farmers to haul the wagons on to the next town. Thus thousands of people became involved in the drawn-out pilgrimage.

Passionate enthusiasm seized Afrikaners throughout the country as the wagons groaned their way northward. Entire populations of the little *dorps* turned out to meet them and join in the campfire ceremonies of folk singing, folk dancing, and sonorous sermons drawn from the sacred saga. Men grew beards, women dressed in Voortrekker costumes, babies were baptized beside the wagons (many with the contrived name of "Eeufesia," from the Afrikaans word for centenary), and in town after town streets and public buildings were renamed after heroes of the Trek.

As the wagons rolled into Johannesburg, South Africa's most perceptive journalist of the time, T. C. Robertson, captured the scene with some vivid reporting:

> Modern Voortrekkers, Afrikaners whose pulses beat to the rhythm of the wheels of industry, heard the rumble of wagon wheels among the skyscrapers of Johannesburg yesterday. Grandchildren of the men whose flocks once grazed on the hills of the Witwatersrand stood among the cheering thousands in the city of gold, the gold the old Voortrekkers feared. Girls in Voortrekker *kappies* leaned out of the windows of factories in Fordsburg, where the relentless assembly belts stopped moving as the wagons passed. . . . Miners came up from underground and raced off to watch the procession.[34]

In Pretoria the slow buildup of patriotic fervour reached fever pitch, ignited by a spectacular torch marathon by members of an Afrikaner scout movement. Two torches symbolizing the light of freedom and of "white civilization" were carried by relays of young runners along the "path of South Africa." They had set out from Cape Town fourteen days before, scheduling their arrival at the monument site outside Pretoria together with the wagons on the eve of the Day of the Covenant, December 16.

34. *Sunday Times*, December 1938.

As the runners arrived in the darkness on a hill near the monument site, they were met by three thousand other young scouts each with a torch of his own. Together, wrote Robertson,

> they marched down towards the camp like a winding river of fire more than a mile long. There a crowd of more than 60,000 stood waiting in silent amazement. Then, as the chain of light wound past them, they started cheering—more lustily and enthusiastically than I have ever heard a South African crowd cheer. Women rushed forward and burned the corners of their handkerchiefs and *kappies* in the flame of the two torches, to keep as mementoes of the great event.[35]

A huge bonfire had been lit and as each young torchbearer marched past it he hurled his torch into the flames. The blaze leaped skyward, a signal for other bonfires to be lit on other hilltops around Pretoria so that the capital should stand encircled by the light of freedom and "white civilization."

> The hill is on fire; on fire with Afrikaner fire; on fire with the enthusiasm of Young South Africa! You are nothing—your People is all. One light in the dusk is puny and small. But three thousand flames. Three thousand! And more! There's hope for your future, South Africa!

So wrote Ingrid Jonker, aged sixteen, a future Afrikaans poet and author who was one of those three thousand flame-bearing scouts.[36]

It was pure Nuremburg, and there was more to come at the foundation-stone ceremony two days later when 200,000 gathered on Monument-hill for the biggest, most elaborate, and most emotive folk rally in the history of the Afrikaner people.

With the outbreak of war the following year and the spectacular triumphs of the German armies in its opening phases, pro-Nazi sentiment in South Africa really surged to the surface. As Norway, Holland, Belgium, and France capitulated in quick succession, a wave of excitement swept Afrikanerdom at the prospect of the early overthrow of Britain followed by the disintegration of the Empire and the Commonwealth, out of which Afrikaner Nationalism might be able to negotiate with the victorious Germans to take over the country and establish a Christian National republic based not on what was called "British-

35. *Rand Daily Mail*, December 14, 1938.

36. Quoted in Moodie, op. cit., pp. 183–4. Jonker wrote these words in an entry for an essay competition on the ox-wagon trek run by *Die Burger*.

Jewish democracy" but on the traditional principles of the old Boer republics.

The breakup of Fusion and the Gesuiwerdes's rejection of Hertzog as leader created a new fluidity in Afrikaner politics, and in this situation a crop of new, explicitly National Socialist movements sprang up. A totalitarian extremist and virulent anti-Semite named Louis Weichardt formed the South African Christian National-Socialistic movement, later called the Greyshirts, which advocated the exclusion of Jews and other "unassimilable" elements and the institution of a Hitlerian dictatorship. Oswald Pirow, who as Hertzog's defence minister had travelled to Europe the year before and met with Franco, Salazar, and Hitler, publicly identified himself with National Socialist doctrines and formed a New Order group within the National party. Most formidable of all was the Ossewa-Brandwag, the Ox-Wagon Sentinels, a paramilitary movement that grew directly out of the commemorative trek of 1938 and swiftly gained massive grass-roots support.

The OB, as it was called, attracted some of the most influential members of the new political intelligentsia and formed an elite inner unit called the *Stormjaers*, or Storm Troopers, which adopted terrorist tactics to disrupt the South African war effort. The administrator—or governor—of the Orange Free State province, Hans van Rensburg, resigned his office to take over the leadership with the title of commandant-general. A bright young lawyer, John Vorster, later to become prime minister, was assistant-chief commandant. Hendrik van den Bergh, who became Vorster's security chief and founder of South Africa's CIA, the Bureau of State Security (BOSS), held the rank of general. Scores of other key Afrikaners became members, including Piet Meyer and Geoff Cronjé. Meyer, who later became chairman of the South African Broadcasting Corporation and controlled the state radio and television services for nearly twenty years, was its information director.

The OB was openly pro-Nazi. Its members wore storm trooper–type uniforms and gave stiff-arm Nazi salutes. Many, including Vorster and Van den Bergh, were interned under wartime security laws. Van Rensburg confessed his acceptance of National Socialism without reservation or dilution. In September 1941 Radio Zeesen, Goebbels's propaganda station, broadcast a eulogy of him as the destined saviour of oppressed Afrikanerdom. In the same month the *Munchener Illustrierte Zeitung* carried a photograph of him with a long caption describing his career in terms of high praise.[37]

The OB grew by leaps and bounds as it capitalized on the spirit of renaissance that the Trek had awakened. Afrikaners of every shade of

37. Ibid., p. 112.

opinion flocked to its banner. "The OB had the proud consciousness that they had fired the imagination of the Afrikaner youth," wrote the two primary historians of this period, Michael Roberts and A. E. G. Trollip. "They knew that they had brought the Nationalist cause home to the people—from the *bywoner* to the banker, from the university student to the railway ganger—as it had not been brought home these forty years."[38]

Pirow's New Order was less populist and so posed less of a direct political threat to the National party's paramountcy in the Afrikaner community, although Pirow himself was a man of prestige who had been freely spoken of during the thirties as a possible future prime minister. Its mission was to inculcate National Socialist ideas in South Africa. It differed from the OB only in that its preoccupations were more exclusively ideological while those of the OB were "activist."

Meanwhile the rump of Hertzog's following, led first by himself and them by his younger lieutuenant, Klasie Havenga, formed themselves into the small Afrikaner party. Afrikaner nationalism was thus divided into five different parties and movements as the war got under way. Popular sentiment was for unity, *volkseenheid*, in preparation for national deliverance through a German victory, but behind public posturing in support of the idea a bitter struggle was fought out for inheritance of this ascendant constituency that held the key to future political power.

It was a struggle that Malan eventually won. His campaign against *groepsvorming*, or group forming, was relentless and skilfull. Roberts and Trollip have chronicled the details of the complex infighting that took place in their meticulous history of the South African Opposition during the war years, and what they reveal essentially is Malan's single-minded determination to ensure, without ever giving the impression of being opposed to Afrikaner unity, that the National party emerged as the sole authentic voice of Afrikaner nationalism. When a German victory seemed imminent in 1940 Malan yielded to popular pressure for unity by forming an agreement with the OB in terms of which he was named overall *volksleier* of the Afrikaner people. The agreement divided the spheres of activity between the two organizations: the National party would take care of the political side of things while the OB would look after Afrikanerdom's nonpolitical and cultural interests. But it was not long before Malan accused the OB of trespassing on party territory and called on party members to resign from the "cultural" organization.

When Russia seemed on the point of collapse in September 1941, Malan again responded to the clamour for Afrikaner unity. He proposed

38. Roberts and Trollip, op. cit., pp. 121–2.

the formation of a National Committee, a kind of shadow cabinet of fifteen to twenty members, that could present a united Opposition front to the victorious Germans. But Malan took care to ensure that all members of the National Committee would be selected by himself and then approved by a *volksvergadering*, or people's assembly. Not surprisingly, the OB rejected the proposal, which amounted to subordinating itself to the National party.[39] Gradually, subtly, the more experienced Malan outmanoeuvred his rivals and piled up the points in the close infighting.

But it was a party-political, not a doctrinal struggle. The National party could live with many of Pirow's and Van Rensburg's ideas, but not with the political rivalry they represented. The ideological overlap was considerable. Though in a more muted way, the National party expressed much of the anti-Semitism that was outspoken in the New Order and the OB. Tirades on the "Jewish question" and praise of Hitler's handling of it filled the columns of the party newspaper, *Die Kruithoring*. As Jewish refugees from the Nazi persecutions began arriving in South Africa, Eric Louw, the future foreign minister, moved a private bill in Parliament to halt the immigration and prohibit Jews from entering certain occupations. At its Transvaal congress in December 1940, presided over by two future prime ministers, Hans Strijdom and Herdrik Verwoerd, the provincial division of the party voted to deny membership to Jews.

This is not to say there were no policy differences between Malan and the OB and New Order. The OB and New Order were both opposed in principle to the parliamentary system and thus to political parties, which Malan thought threatened the role and very existence of his organization, but he did not go along with their totalitarianism or their acceptance of the *Führerprinzip*. But even here the differences were more pragmatic than ideological, related more to the practicalities of the Afrikaner power struggle than to any deep-felt issues of democratic principle. That Malan was not inherently uncomfortable with the National Socialist philosophy of his rivals is evidenced by the fact the he had no difficulty absorbing the ultraextremist Greyshirts, who were small in number. What made him uncomfortable about the others is precisely the fact that they were rivals. Once they ceased to be that he had no difficulty absorbing them either.

Let me take care, though, not to give the impression that all or even most Afrikaners were pro-Nazi. Many thousands supported Smuts, whose popularity rose as Allied fortunes in the war improved and he became an international star, a member of the British War Cabinet and a friend and confidant of Churchill and Roosevelt. Growing numbers of

39. Ibid., pp. 117–20.

Afrikaners joined Smuts's volunteer army in North Africa and Italy: an Afrikaner, Group Captain "Sailor" Malan, flew with "the Few" in the Battle of Britain and became one of the most highly decorated heroes of that decisive conflict.

But at the beginning especially, and until the tide turned in North Africa at the battle of El Alamein in 1942, a considerable number of Afrikaners identified with Nazism and hoped with varying degrees of passion for a German victory. The important thing is that this element was dominant in the crucial institutions where the apartheid ideology was formulated, in the church and in the universities, in the new political intelligentsia generally, and, most important of all, in the Broederbond.

It is important, too, that while the National party never specifically embraced National Socialism, it never specifically opposed it in its fundamental aspects of ethnic chauvinism and racial nationalism. Because of this implicit accord, the ideological ideas of these institutional think tanks, coloured as they were with Nazi influence, were easily accepted. As the war ended, with Germany in defeat and Nazism in disgrace, the OB disintegrated and the New Order died, and their remnants were absorbed into the National party. The overt identification fell away, but many of the ideas were carried into the heart of what was soon to become the government of South Africa.

FINALLY, IT WAS in the Broederbond where all these ideas and influences were synthesized into the ideology of apartheid. In that inner circle of Afrikanerdom's new political intelligentsia all the strands of the new thinking were drawn together—theological and political, practical and metaphysical—and fashioned into a radical programme of action for tearing South Africa apart socially and restructuring it as a diversity of separate racial "nations" in which white Afrikanerdom would be assured of the permanent existence of its own separate nationhood with its own distinctive culture.

The Broederbond is a remarkable organization, perhaps unequalled in the world for its pervasive back-room power wielded over nearly every aspect of national life. It has been the nucleus of the Afrikaner Nationalist movement, exercising its influence over both church and state and establishing a wide network of social, cultural, and economic institutions to help uplift the Afrikaner people, weld them together, and mobilize them politically. It started modestly enough with a meeting in 1918 of six young men who were concerned about the condition of the Afrikaner in those bleak years of his urban disorientation and decided to form an organization to uplift and restore him to his rightful place in South Africa. Henning Klopper was one of the six. So, by a strange twist of fate, was a Dutch Reformed minister named Johannes Naudé, father of Afrikanerdom's most courageous present-day dissident, the Rev. C. F. Beyers Naudé.

From there the organization evolved into a ubiquitous political Mafia, with a presence in every community and institution in South Africa. It has changed somewhat in recent years as Afrikaner nationalism enters its crisis phase, but at its peak in the 1970s the Broederbond was reputed to have a total membership of twelve thousand carefully selected people who took a vow of secrecy and swore to serve the cause of Afrikanerdom in a semireligious initiation ceremony conducted in darkened rooms. Its members, drawn from the committed elite of Afrikaner society—lawyers, doctors, academics, theologians, teachers, journalists, businessmen, and senior civil servants—were organized into some eight hundred cells around the country.[40]

Over the years the Broederbond sought to control Afrikaner cultural life through the Federation of Afrikaner Cultural Unions, which brought scores of small cultural bodies all over the country under its umbrella. It formed the Voortrekkers, the scout movement that performed the torch marathon at Monument-hill in 1938; the Studentebond; the Ruiterwag, a junior Broederbond; the Rapportryers, an Afrikaner equivalent of the Rotary Club; and the South African Bureau for Racial Affairs, a think tank on race policy. It formed Afrikaner trade unions and was responsible for the founding of two universities and a teachers' training college. It even established a burial society.

Most striking of all was its drive to give the Afrikaners a foothold in South Africa's English-dominated economy. To this end Nico Diederichs gave up his professorship in 1938 to start the Reddingsdaadbond—literally, the Rescue-Deed League—begun with a fund financed by subscriptions of sixpence (a dime) a month. Half the capital raised was used to launch an Afrikaner investment company called Federale Volksbeleggings, 20 percent was invested in two insurance companies called Santam and Sanlam, and the rest went in loans to small retailers and to help Afrikaners study trades and business.

The results over time have been remarkable. The Reddingsdaadbond helped launch some ten thousand Afrikaner businesses between 1939 and 1949.[41] One of these, the Rembrandt Tobacco Corporation, has grown into a huge multinational enterprise. Volkskas, started in a pri-

40. For a well-informed and up-to-date analysis of the Broederbond's structure and workings, see Ivor Wilkins and Hans Strydom, *The Super-Afrikaners* (Johannesburg, 1980).

41. Ibid., p. 424.

vate home in Pretoria, is now the third largest bank in South Africa. Two building societies, Saambou and Nasionaal, have merged to produce another giant. Sanlam is a major conglomerate with investments reaching into all sectors of the South African economy. Federale Volksbeleggings has become a major finance house, out of which emerged Federale Mynbou, which gained control of General Mining in 1965, which in turn took over Union Corporation to establish Gencor, one of South Africa's five biggest mining houses.

But it is in politics that the Broederbond exercized its most profound influence. For more than half a century no major new idea in Afrikaner politics was expressed in public without first being pondered, analyzed, and intensely debated by this dedicated "band of brothers." The government used it as both a think tank and a sounding board. No Nationalist prime minister would dream of taking a major policy step without first checking it out with the Broederbond, both for its opinions and for its crucial assistance in ensuring institutional support.

So it was the Broeders who were the real authors of apartheid, which is why the influences on these select few are of such disproportionate importance—men such as Professor J. C. van Rooy, a Kuyperian theologian at Potchefstroom University, chairman of the Broederbond from 1932 to 1938 and again from 1942 to 1952; Diederichs, chairman from 1938 to 1942; Piet Meyer, who ran it from 1960 until 1972, when Andries Treurnicht, another political theologian who is now leader of the far-rightist Conservative party, took over. During the formative years in the 1930s and 1940s, men like Meyer, Verwoerd, Geoff Cronjé, Henning Klopper, and the authors of the Dutch Reformed Church's separatist policy declaration were all dominant figures. It was through the Broederbond, too, that the OB as the carrier of Nationalist Socialist ideas exercised its most lasting influence. Many leading OB members were Broeders during these crucial years—Van Rooy, Meyer, Cronjé, L. J. du Plessis, Klopper, and more.

These were the men who in intense discussion sessions, held mostly at night, from 1935 until the end of the war, painstakingly worked out their positions on every aspect until finally they had drafted a total policy concept. By 1945 they were nearly ready, and an outline of what they had been discussing appeared in a book by one of their leading members, Geoff Cronjé, who had returned from his doctoral studies in Germany to take the chair in sociology at Pretoria University. Cronjé's book, *'n Tuiste vir die Nageslag—A Home for Posterity*—was the first comprehensive draft of the apartheid ideology, and with remarkable completeness it spelled out the details of the coming system.

The primary aim of the political policy, Cronjé wrote, should be to guarantee a national home for the Afrikaner nation and its posterity.

But in doing this it should also ensure that the blacks and "coloureds" had "their separate homes where through their own strength they can develop their own nationhood along their own lines and create their own culture and make their own contribution."[42]

And that, he contended, could only be done through complete racial partition. Traditional segregation was not enough, because it would leave the black races within the white sociopolitical structure where they could never develop their own culture and nationhood properly. It had to be complete, radical partition. Only thus could the racial and cultural diversity of South Africa be preserved in accordance with the will of God.

Cronjé professed a great concern to act with justice toward the black communities, and his book reverberates with protestations of good intentions and honesty of purpose.[43] It was only right and moral, he contended, that Afrikaners should give to blacks what they demanded for themselves. More than that, the Afrikaner had an obligation to help salvage the black man's racial and cultural identity, to save him from himself and from the "unscrupulous imperialist-capitalist system," because the Afrikaner had had his own culture and nationhood trampled on and so had a special understanding of the importance of these things. And hadn't he lived with the black man for three hundred years, grown up with him on the farms, and didn't he therefore know him better than anyone else? He was historically bound to be the protector of the black man. The new policy should therefore be introduced in a spirit of "responsible guardianship." "It is the duty of the Afrikaner," Cronjé declared, "to show the way in which the native must be led in his own interests and with a view to his own development."[44]

But beneath this veneer of high-sounding idealism a fundamental racism underlies the whole concept. In Cronjé's view, whites were clearly superior—not just culturally but biologically. Separation was therefore necessary to protect the white race from biological degeneration. Cronjé's assertions on this theme reveal the extent to which he and some of his Broederbond colleagues were influenced by the German *Rassenkunde* they had picked up during their years in the Third Reich. It was beyond question, he said, that blacks were physically, mentally,

42. Cronjé, op. cit., p. 25.

43. Cronjé expanded on this theme in a second book, *Regverdige Rasse-Apartheid* (Righteous Racial-Apartheid) coauthored with two leading theologian-Broeders, William Nicol and Professor E. P. Groenewald, and published by the Dutch Reformed Church publishing house in 1947.

44. Cronjé, *'n Tuiste vir die Nageslag*, pp. 95–97.

spiritually, and morally inferior to whites. They lacked the intelligence, they had a higher crime rate, their health was poorer and they were more decadent in every way. It followed, therefore, that racial mixing would degrade the whites. It could also lead to "physical disharmonies," such as large native teeth in small European mouths, and tall Eurafrican men with small internal organs and deficient circulatory systems. These physical disharmonies in turn were liable to lead to "mental and moral disharmonies," such as "violent outbursts of temper, vanity and sexual instability."[45] For page after page Cronjé goes on in this vein about the dangers of *bloedvermenging* arising from the "mishmash cohabitation" in mixed-race ghettos, of the "infiltration" of black genes into the white genetic pool that could result in "throwbacks," and ultimately in the white race being "bastardized out" of its identity.[46]

What it meant was that the separation of the races was doubly necessary if the white nation was to be preserved for posterity. There would have to be separate living areas to end the "mishmash cohabitation," and there would have to be laws to prohibit interracial marriages and sex across the colour line.

The only realistic policy choice, Cronjé declared, lay between what he called "local segregation" and total separation—of which separation was "the most consistent with the Afrikaner idea of racial apartheid." Segregation could only be a temporary palliative. Total separation could solve the problem for all time. It should aim at dividing the country into separate racial nation-states with a large white zone that would have all the harbours—"for the sake of international trade"—and three or four ethnically grouped black areas that should include the territory of the then British protectorates of Swaziland, Basutoland, and Bechuanaland.

The "coloureds" should be developed as a separate community in their own living areas, with political representation in their own Coloured Council. A "coloured nation" with its own "coloured government" could thus be brought into being under the trusteeship of the whites. The Indians, meanwhile, should be repatriated to India. It had never been the intention that they should stay permanently.[47]

The separation would have to be complete throughout the society, Cronjé insisted, with separate educational systems for the blacks that would "concur with their culture and level of development" and with total economic separation as well. "Complete racial separation will re-

45. Ibid., p. 74.

46. Ibid., pp. 42–95.

47. Ibid., p. 39.

quire that the black labour force must be gradually excluded from our economic life. That can only happen if our economic structure undergoes a radical reorientation and reorganization—that is, if it is recreated according to the new circumstances that will arise."[48]

This would not be easy, Cronjé conceded. Whites would have to learn to do without black labour, to which they had grown accustomed. They would have to overcome their ancient antipathy toward doing "kaffir's work" and realize that anything performed in the service of the *volk* was honourable. "We will have to be prepared to make great sacrifices . . . which we must regard as an honour . . . and if we must give up much of our leisure that the presence of the native has afforded us, and put our own hand to the plough and the spade and the pickaxe and the broom, then there must arise in us a high sense of duty that it is all in the interest of creating a home for posterity."[49]

In a spirit of national-socialist solidarity it could be done. There would have to be a return to simple living. Cheap holiday resorts would have to be built for the hard-working whites. Some imaginative schemes would have to be launched to help the transition. Farmers could adopt cooperative schemes, helping each other in relays at sheepshearing- and harvest-time; and school vacations could be timed to coincide with labour requirements on the farms. Whites would have to take over the labouring jobs in the mines, where there were now 324,427 blacks and only 37,360 whites. Yes, the whites would have to be paid more, but then the mines could be nationalized so that the profit factor would matter less. And, yes, production might be affected, but in the end that was not the main consideration. "The main point is not the maintenance of gold production, it is over time to keep the white race's blood pure," Cronjé declared in a remarkable precursor to Prime Minister Verwoerd's famous statement in the 1960s that when confronted with a conflict between the requirements of the ideology and the economy, South Africa should choose "to be poor and white rather than rich and multiracial."

Cronjé recognized, though, that all this would take time. Perhaps a generation, he thought, to reconstruct the economy on separationist lines. In the meantime a policy of intensified social segregation should be implemented, but only as a transitional phase on the way to total separation.

This interim "emergency" programme should include immediate steps to enforce strict segregation of living areas, transport services, and all public amenities; to protect whites against job competition by re-

48. Ibid., p. 127.

49. Ibid., p. 128.

serving categories of work for them, prevent them from having to work in a direct relationship with blacks, and make sure that no white worker would ever be in a position subordinate to a black worker; to prohibit mixed marriages and interracial sex; to end all vestiges of political *gelykstelling* by removing the few "coloureds" who qualified as voters under a special concession in Cape Province, a hangover from the British colonial system, and place them on a separate roll; and vigorously to remove all "coloured" and black "spots" in regions of the country defined as being for white occupation only.

The inherent unreality of the programme that caused apartheid's crisis of impracticality in the 1970s should have been obvious from the beginning. Like Canute on the beach, what it amounted to was an attempt to halt and reverse the forces of a powerfully driven industrial revolution.

Had idealism not already taken leave of reality, the daunting nature of the odds might also have given the Broeders cause to hesitate. The policy had to succeed in its entirety or it would be no use at all. If the ultimate summit of total separation—including economic separation—were not attained, the whole incredible exercise would be politically worthless because, as Cronjé warned, segregation was not enough. The blacks would still be within the white socioeconomic and political system and they would not be satisfied with a permanently subordinate position there. They would be bound to continue fighting for *gelykstelling*, and the whites would be bound to continue resisting it because they knew that *gelykstelling* would end their supremacy and without that they would be overwhelmed numerically and doomed as a "nation," and so there would be continuous, irresolvable friction. There would be no secure home for posterity.

It was an all-or-nothing option in which the all was clearly unattainable from the beginning. Cronjé and his fellow Broeders were trying to thrust the genie of modern development, of urbanization and industrialization, back in its bottle, building an ideology based on their own romanticized vision of the past with nice, simple, unthreatening, preindustrial "natives" living contentedly and unchangingly in their traditional systems, frozen in time and untouched by the forces of the modern world bursting in on South Africa. They had an instinctive, morbid fear of black Africa, with its superior numbers, emerging as an equal, educated, urbanized, and acculturated competitor. And so in their minds they tried to deny its possibility. They constructed an ideology based on the belief that the old tribal system could remain static in the face of the industrial revolution. With their fantastic notion of economic separation they even imagined they could isolate the blacks from that revolution.

The irony of it is that they themselves, the new urbanized Afrikaner elite, were the living evidence of the impracticality of what they were proposing. What had happened and was continuing to happen to the Afrikaners in the city was happening to the black Africans also, making nonsense of the Afrikaners' ideas even as they formulated them.

Looking back, one can see two distinct strands of thought that were later to acquire a certain importance: the concept of separate nations, to save the Afrikaner "nation" from being swamped and to protect its members from black economic competition; and the more crudely racist belief in black genetic inferiority and the need to preserve the "blood purity" of the white race. When the crisis of the 1980s caused President Botha to start reshaping the system and giving it a new face, he showed himself prepared to drop features belonging to the latter category, which he described as "outdated and unnecessary," while retaining the bedrock essentials required for keeping whites in power in order to preserve the Afrikaner "nation" and its home for posterity.

But now, at the outset, it was the whole package that was adopted. It became the political programme of the National party, and, by mobilizing the ethnic emotions of the Afrikaner population, propelled it into power within three years of Cronjé's book appearing. It has kept it there for more than forty years, a world record in continuity of office in the face of the most universal condemnation that any government and people have ever known.

CHAPTER EIGHT

Triomf

> If our policy is taken to its full conclusion, there will not be one black man with South African citizenship. There will then no longer be a moral obligation on our Parliament to accommodate these people politically.
>
> CORNELIUS MULDER

"TODAY SOUTH AFRICA belongs to us once more," exulted Malan in his victory speech in May 1948. He had squeaked in by a hairsbreadth margin of eight seats in a result that took the whole country by surprise. Smuts stood at the height of his international reputation and everyone had expected him to win in a repeat of his 1943 landslide. Malan's triumph was like a bolt from the blue, to himself included. Once again as at Blood River and Majuba, the Boers saw the hand of Providence in the upset victory. For the new Nationalists it was an exhilarating moment of joy and anticipation. They had their country back and now they could make sure they never lost it again. It was theirs for posterity. It was theirs to begin reshaping according to their vision of the ideal society, a new land of many nations that they were called by God to create. A sublime moment.

But it was also the moment when South Africa parted company with the world. Afrikanerdom chose to intensify and codify the segregationist system and to articulate racism as a national philosophy at precisely the moment that the rest of the world began moving in the opposite direction.

Until World War II the kind of pragmatic segregation that was practised in South Africa was scarcely out of tune with racial practices throughout the Western world. More stringent perhaps, but not so much as to attract attention or criticism. It was still the age of imperialism and the assumption of white racial superiority that went with it. From Srinagar to Jakarta and from Saigon to Stanleyville, the white Western world took for granted its right to dominate the rest of mankind. Woodrow Wilson had made his declaration about the inalienable right of every nation to self-determination, but no one seriously considered that to be applicable to the nonwhite peoples of the earth. White Englishmen, Frenchmen, Belgians, Dutchmen, and Portuguese continued to lord it over their colonial subjects. In black and yellow countries around the world white *sahibs* and *bwanas* continued to live in big white homes in secluded white zones, waited on by deferential servants, sipping their sundowners in the cultural exclusivity of the Ikoyi Club and the Mombasa Club, while in America segregation was firmly entrenched in the South and the Supreme Court had pronounced it to be in accordance with the Constitution.

South Africa's wartime leader, Jan Smuts, had become an international star and the darling of the British Commonwealth, the one-time enemy who had accepted the hand of reconciliation and at considerable political risk to himself had taken his country to war at Britain's side. They had made him the chancellor of Cambridge University, he had been a member of the British war cabinet, a confidant of Churchill and Roosevelt, and as the war ended he was invited to participate in the founding of the United Nations and became a coauthor of the preamble to its Charter. The fact that he was a segregationist who believed emphatically in the preservation of white supremacy in South Africa seemed not to matter.

But the war itself changed all that. It was one of those great watersheds in human history when one era came to an end and another began. Future historians will say, I think, that the most remarkable event of the twentieth century, the one with the greatest effect on the shape of the world and the nature of human relationships, was the revolution in racial attitudes that occurred halfway through it, which caused the great imperial powers of the West to withdraw their hegemony over billions of coloured people around the globe, allowing nearly a hundred new nations to come into existence in the space of a single generation and replacing the old assumption of white superiority with a new concept of the equality and dignity of man.

It may not be universally honoured. Racism still lingers in many societies, revealing itself in indifference to the distress of America's largely black underclass or to the Australian Aborigines, to the West Indians in Britain or to the *Gastarbeiters* in Europe. Jesse Jackson is regarded as unelectable to the presidency of the United States, and there are not many black faces in the Reform Club in London. But then no moral norm has ever commanded total observance. The point is that despite the hangovers of old attitudes, nonracism *is* now a moral norm by which the postwar world judges the behaviour of individuals and nations. Whatever traces may still be apparent, no one will publicly proclaim himself to be a believer in the inherent inferiority of the black races and the superiority of whites. There may still be ghettos, but no one will proclaim himself to be a believer in segregation. Such views became morally objectionable in the postwar world. And South Africa put itself at odds with that world. As the world moved in one direction, South Africa moved in the opposite one.

It is possible that white South Africans still don't properly understand why or how this happened. I have heard President Botha fume at the perceived injustice of it, at the fact that there is a statue of Smuts in London's Parliament Square while he, Botha, is treated like a leper. Even among his white political opponents you will hear complaints of hypocrisy, of double standards. White South Africans are genuinely bewildered that they should be treated as an outcast nation when other countries, too, have racial skeletons in their cupboards, when many are more overtly dictatorial and at least a dozen are guilty of more tyrannical behaviour. They fail to understand that whatever other sins there may be in Old Adam's garden, on this one issue at least the postwar world reached a consensus: any public declaration of racism is morally objectionable. And at the very moment that consensus was reached, white South Africa declared just that, more emphatically and comprehensively than had ever been done before.

There is a strange chemistry by which the world from time to time reaches a consensus on some great moral issue such as this. Take the case of slavery. It was practised for millennia. None of the great religions or great philosophers of antiquity denounced it. To the ancient Greeks slaves stood outside the moral community and were not entitled to full human rights. When Odysseus returned from the Trojan wars, so the legend goes, he hanged a dozen of his household slave girls all from one rope, because he suspected them of misbehaving while he was away. There was no question of ethics involved. They were his property to dispose of as he pleased. And so it remained for the next three thousand years. Neither Christ nor Muhammad spoke out against it, nor Saint Augustine nor Saint Thomas Aquinas nor the great reformers Luther and Calvin. Then all of a sudden toward the end of the eighteenth century a groundswell of moral concern began to rise in Europe. Slaveowners protested at the time that the system was in accordance with natural law, with God's law. They claimed, sometimes with justification, that there were greater evils in the world at that time; that the slaves would be worse off if they no longer had the security of their bondage but were turned loose to fend for themselves in a harsh world where they would be exploited and abused. To no avail. Slavery's time was over, and though in many societies it was soon replaced by something very like it in the combination of segregation and exploitation, the thing itself was declared morally unacceptable and anyone who upheld it was considered a reprobate.

Thus by periodic spasms of concurrence have people gradually expanded their concept of our moral community, the groups of human beings whom it regards as worthy of equal respect and toward whom one is obligated to behave ethically. It reached such a consensus again on ending child labour, and is in the process of reaching it on the rights of women.

It was, of course, the excesses of National Socialism in Germany that catalyzed the new groundswell of opinion against racism in any publicly proclaimed or institutionalized form. To be sure, there was some movement in European colonies between the world wars, a new restlessness brought on by education and by the steady development and unwitting implantation of the West's own ideas of freedom, democracy, and the fundamental rights of man; Gandhi and his Indian Congress pointed the way to the great revolution ahead. But World War II brought it to a head, as the white Western world stood horrified at the evidence of the Holocaust and saw in Germany's crime a grotesque caricature of itself, the ultimate implications of its own inherent master-race ideas.

Thereafter the liberation movements in the colonies found themselves pushing against more or less open doors. They were stimulated by the knowledge that the imperial powers had been weakened by the war and, in the case of France, Holland, and Belgium, badly humiliated by it. The Japanese tidal wave that swept over Southeast Asia after the bombing of Pearl Harbour in 1941 had given the lie to notions of white Western superiority, and when eventually the Japanese withdrew and the French and Dutch imperialists came limping back with their prestige in tatters, the colonists were not disposed to welcome them as liberators or natural overlords. In Indonesia and Indochina, India, Pakistan, Ceylon, the Philippines, Jordan, Syria, Lebanon, Libya, Morocco, Tunisia, and Egypt the groundswell began. Within five years of the war's end ten new nations had become independent. Within a generation the membership of the United Nations had more than tripled from its original fifty-one; by 1954, in the United States the Supreme Court's *Brown v. Board of Education* decision swept aside the constitutionality of segregation and opened the way for the civil rights movement.

All the while South Africa was moving dramatically and publicly in the opposite direction. What was happening in the rest of the world made no impression on Afrikanerdom's new nationalists in the outpouring of their revolutionary zeal. It is doubtful whether any of it ever penetrated to those earnest, ongoing *koffiehuis* and Broederbond discussions. In part this was because of South Africa's historic isolation: Afrikanerdom had always been cut off from the main currents of world opinion and it was not in the habit of taking them into consideration. But it was also an expression of the incipient self-obsession that became such a consuming feature of Afrikaner nationalism. "South Africa First," is the National party's motto, but it is more than just a patriotic slogan; it reflects an insularity of mind that views the world through the most parochial of prisms, that sees South Africa as the centre of the universe around which everything else revolves. You see this in the way the newspapers report world affairs, as though South Africa were the central issue in every international debate and of every British and American election campaign. The "outside world," as it is called, is not a reference point. The gaze is overwhelmingly, obsessively inward. And so South Africa stepped out of line with the world and seemed neither to notice nor care.

TAKE BREE STREET out of central Johannesburg heading west, and you will come in time to one of the city's more colourless suburbs, little stucco-plastered houses on eighth-acre plots surrounded by prefab walls, many in wagon-wheel designs, and with concrete gnomes in the garden. A glimpse through the windows will reveal living rooms furnished with cheap modern furniture, plastic doilies, kitschy copper ornaments, and sentimental Tretchikoff prints, while the driveways, likely as not, will contain more than the usual number of powerful motorcycles and supercharged Volkswagens. This is lower-middle-class white suburbia, clean, conformist, macho, and dull.

The only remarkable thing you may notice about the place is the big church on a hilltop overlooking the suburb, a lovely red-brick basilica with a bell tower and a row of arched clerestory windows. A notice on the gate tells you it is the Pinkster Protestantse Kerk, one of the modern pentecostal sects that has gained some popularity in the Afrikaner community in recent years, and you may wonder how such a new and still relatively minor denomination came by such a splendid old building.

The other thing to notice about the suburb is its name, Triomf. As you may deduce from that, this otherwise unremarkable suburb is in fact a triumphant symbol of Afrikaner racial domination. Because here briefly in the 1930s, 1940s, and early 1950s flourished South Africa's closest approximation to a free black society, a vital, vibrant community, a living example of what a free South Africa might have been and may yet be. But for precisely that reason it cut across what the apartheid visionaries had in mind and so they eliminated it and built Triomf in its place.

Sophiatown, it was called. In the early mining-camp days a speculator named Tobiansky had bought a stretch of land here with the intention of establishing a white residential suburb. He named it after his wife, Sophia, but after pegging out the plots and streets he ran into problems with the upstart Town Council's newfangled regulations about sewage disposal. Finding himself unable to sell the plots to whites, Tobiansky sold them to blacks instead. That was well before the Land Act of 1913 made such transactions impossible, and so a black freehold area arose to the west of Johannesburg and as the city expanded, white suburbia grew around it. It became what is known in the apartheid nomenclature as a "black spot" in a white area.

The freehold rights are what gave Sophiatown its special quality, for with them came those elements of security and independence, variety and self-expression that are so essential for the flowering of the human spirit. By any conventional standards, Sophiatown was a slum. Its rutted streets and shanty dwellings and the tumultuous density of its population violated our modern concepts of orderly urbanization. But it was a living community, a place with soul, where hardship and violence and tragedy were shot through with so much laughter and vitality that everyone who ever went there was struck by the wonder of it. It was here that Alan Paton's Kumalo came in search of his son Absalom. And it was in Sophiatown that Trevor Huddleston, a charismatic Anglican priest who became a legend to the black community, lived and preached for twelve years in the big Church of Christ the King on the hill. Archbishop Desmond Tutu grew up here and still recalls an indelible moment from his childhood when the tall white priest walked past the Tutus' home in Sophiatown and raised his hat to Tutu's mother, a washerwoman. He had never seen a white man do anything like that before.

Here lived a new kind of black African, second- and third-generation city people, detribalized, modern, working-class people, aspirant artists, politicians, writers, musicians, prostitutes, pimps, con men, shebeen queens, and gangsters; people discovering and creating a new world, suffering under its burdens but hugely stimulated by the adventure of it. It was an exciting place and it attracted some whites of a liberal and artistic disposition to move in too. The playwright Athol Fugard was among those who lived in Sophiatown for a time. By the mid-1950s it was offering a glimpse of what the new industrialized South Africa might become.

But to the Afrikaner zealots who had just come to power it was an abomination, the epitome of all the evils of "mishmash cohabitation" that Geoff Cronjé had railed against, septic with the germs of *bloedvermenging*. And so in 1954 the bulldozers moved in and Sophiatown was flattened, and government trucks transported its sixty thousand inhabitants a sanitary distance out of town to a new "home" in a sprawling conglomerate of dormitory units known simply as the South Western Townships—later to go by the acronym Soweto. The rubble of Sophiatown was cleared and the area fumigated. A new suburb was laid out and white families moved in. It was apartheid's first big achievement. Triomf!

Since then more than three million people have been uprooted in this way, living communities shattered and bundled off to strange new soulless places where they are dumped, atomized, and left to begin again as best they may. This social devastation on an appalling scale is wrought in pursuit of the theoretical objective that South Africa is not one country but many, and that therefore no melting pot can be allowed and no black roots may be put down in the white man's sector. Blacks may be needed as workers, but a sense of impermanence should be preserved and a social and physical distance maintained. It was not enough simply to segregate living areas: a law of 1954 required that there should be a buffer strip at least five hundred yards wide between any black quarter and the town it served. Five hundred yards of bare, windblown veld littered with trash to mark the boundary between the "nations," between civilization and barbarism, between Van Riebeeck's white descendants and the black people of Africa. The modern version of the bitter-almond hedge.

The bulldozing of Sophiatown set the tone for the apartheid revolution, but it was only one act among a bewildering number as the new Nationalists went to their task with the zeal of men who have a vision of Utopia. A torrent of legislation poured forth from the Parliament in Cape Town. "Never in history have so few legislated so programmatically, thoroughly and religiously in such a short time for so many," is how one author described it.[1] The laws set specific limits to racial contact in almost every aspect of life—in housing, education, employment, entertainment, sport, public amenities, and personal relations. They gave legal force to apartheid on park benches, in buses, taxis, and railway waiting rooms, in theatres and concert halls and even in the ocean. They excluded blacks from the established universities and tried to exclude them from white church services. They passed a Population Registration Act requiring every citizen to be registered according to his race group, which, if it was in doubt, was determined by a special Race Classification Board that took testimony from family and friends and employed special investigators who sometimes examined a questionable person's cuticles and eyeballs for traces of pigmentation. Most lurid of all, in a replication

1. W. A. de Klerk, *Puritans in Africa*, p. 241.

of Hitler's Nuremburg Laws they prohibited mixed marriages and made sexual relations between consenting adults of different skin colours a criminal offence.

Yet what strikes one today, looking back, is that much of the legislation covered what was already social practise. Segregation of the races had long been the convention in all these spheres of South African life. Every town had its separate black quarter of makeshift shacks known simply as a "location," as if to emphasize the black man's anonymity, and at night a curfew bell would ring and the blacks would disappear to the "location" from the white homes and businesses where they worked as housemaids and nursemaids, garden "boys" and labourers. Buses and trains were segregated. There were separate sections for blacks at the post office and the bank, at the hospital and at the doctor's surgery, and even at some of the shops. Blacks went to separate schools, did separate work, and were buried in separate cemeteries.

Except in employment, little of this segregation was enforced by law. It just happened, more or less automatically. Black and white lived separate lives in separate worlds and never met except in the relationship of master and servant. Though no law prohibited mixed marriages, they were exceedingly rare. In the Cape Province "coloured" men were allowed to vote on a qualified franchise, but no one doubted that they were still a subject race and that white civilization was not for them. It was not so much a system as a way of life, and because it was a pragmatic rather than ideological matter occasional exceptions like Sophiatown were permitted that gave life just a little flexibility and held open the possibility of evolutionary progress.

This is what changed when Malan and his Gesuiwerdes came to power. They substituted enforcement for convention. What had happened automatically before was now codified in law and intensified wherever possible. On the face of it the change was one more of degree than of substance, but it ended the flexibility, and the cumulative effect of all the new laws gave it huge declaratory impact. Segregation was now a national principle and not just a social practise, and that made it substantive. Until then what had been done in race policy was a matter of economic exploitation or just plain prejudice. Now it became a matter of doctrine, of ideology, of theologized faith infused with a special fanaticism, a religious zeal.

Ideology also produces abstraction. Ideologists deal not with flesh-and-blood human beings but with ideals and concepts and principles, bloodless factors that are immune to pain and tears and feel nothing when the bulldozers thunder in and demolish Mrs. Tshabalala's home over her head. They do not know Mrs. Tshabalala. She is merely a statistical unit in a problem attended to in a systematic, programmatic way. If she and other statistical units must suffer, well, that is unfortunate, but it is all in the interests of a larger good from which everyone will eventually benefit. This is tough work requiring an iron will, and only the Afrikaner has the strength of will to do it. That is his divine mission.

So ideology abstracted the action and the civil religion validated it. Since the goals of apartheid were in accordance with the will of God, it followed that any action taken to implement them was justified. By the same token opposition to apartheid was invested with an aura of evil, justifying ruthless measures to deal with it. And because apartheid was in accordance with the laws of God, sanctified by the church, it was expected of all Afrikaners that they should support it. Any who did not were regarded as ethnic traitors, to be expelled and ostracized as *volksverraiers*. Thus did the descendants of those rugged old individualists of the frontier become a nation of conformists.

All of this presented problems for the English-speaking South Africans. Though they had gone along with the old-style segregation and regarded it as part of the natural order of things, the crassness of putting it all into law and proclaiming it to the world offended their traditional pragmatism and sense of decency. It was so graceless, so boorish! There was in this attitude, of course, a good deal of prejudice and hypocrisy: it was motivated less by a concern for the blacks than by a resurgence of the Englishman's old contempt for the Boer and sense of superiority to his crude country cousin who now ruled over him with such arrogance.

Nor did the English, the captains of South Africa's industry, challenge any of the economic essentials of the system. The Land Act had created a landless peasantry and forced it to become a captive labour force; a complex set of pass laws had prohibited blacks from moving about the country to sell their labour on a free market and classified those who were unemployed as vagrants; the Master and Servants Act had made the breach of a labour contract a criminal offence; and the Mines and Works Act prevented blacks from doing skilled work in the mines. Together this body of laws had set up the framework for a system of exploitative racial capitalism, much of it put in place by previous administrations which the English had supported.

The result was a further expansion of that ambiguity that paralysed the English-speaking South Africans politically. They proclaimed themselves to be anti-apartheid but continued to believe in white supremacy. Apart from the few liberals and radicals among them, who played a role far greater than their numbers, English opposition crumbled as Afrikaner nationalism mobilized its ethnic power base and carried the apartheid revolution unimpeded to its climax.

. . .

THAT CLIMAX CAME with the rise to power of Hendrik Frensch Verwoerd in September 1958. Until then the emphasis had been on the purely segregationist aspects of apartheid, that part of the concept that Cronjé had prescribed as an interim phase that should lead to the more dramatic and permanent solution of total racial separation. As the apartheid revolution entered its second decade under a new leader, this climactic phase began.

Whether it did so out of a conscious adherence to Cronjé's prescription is doubtful, however. It was more a matter of personalities. Both Malan and his successor as prime minister, Hans Strijdom, for all their acceptance of the ideological principles involved, had little practical enthusiasm for the kind of grand design that Cronjé had propounded. Thoroughgoing segregation and the entrenchment of Afrikaner power were what topped their agendas. Malan was nearly eighty when he came to office, a man mellowed by age and moulded by long practical experience who was also leader of the more moderate Cape branch of the National party. He lacked the ideological fervour of the younger firebrands. Strijdom was different. He was the leader of the Transvaal extremists, a firebrand who had become known as "The Lion of the North," a man of limited intellectual capacity and a certain blunt honesty. He was little interested in fancy theories. To him apartheid was about keeping the white man, meaning the Afrikaner, on top. *Wit baasskap*, he called it. White mastery.

Verwoerd was altogether different, a consummate ideologue—intelligent, obsessive, and doctrinaire. Malan had made him minister of Native Affairs and during his years in that huge department he had been steadily refining his ideas, expanding on the ideological base set out by Cronjé and seeking to give it practical shape. If Cronjé was apartheid's Marx, then Verwoerd was its Lenin, the man who added to it conceptually and then sought to put it into practise in its total-separation form.

But even he might not have gone as far as he did had it not been for the pressure of events, which persuaded him to try to come to terms with the changing world. A year before he became prime minister, Ghana became an independent nation—the first African colony of a European power to take this step—starting what Harold Macmillan was to call "the wind of change" blowing through the continent when he visited South Africa as Verwoerd's guest. The age of empire was at an end, the cry was going up everywhere for the liberation of the world's dark-skinned people, and South Africa's intensified system of white supremacy was looking more and more unacceptable. Resolutions condemning apartheid were passed at the United Nations, and the United States had stopped abstaining from them. Early in 1959, in what became known as his "new vision" speech, Verwoerd announced that the black tribal reserves, which he called Bantustans, could advance toward self-government and ultimately even full independence. "We cannot govern without taking into account the tendencies in the world and in Africa," he told Parliament.[2] Thus, in an attempt to present a new image of apartheid as a form of decolonization within South Africa, Verwoerd launched into the grand design of Cronjé's second phase. His determined effort to put this incredible sociopolitical theory into practise brought the apartheid revolution to its climax.

It was perhaps significant, too, that Verwoerd was not born an Afrikaner. The feeling of constantly having to prove one's commitment to a community, of never being able to wear one's nationalism lightly, often causes an adopted outsider to acquire his people's prejudices in distilled form. *Plus royaliste que la reine.* It was no mere coincidence that Napoleon was born a Corsican, Hitler an Austrian, Stalin a Georgian. Or Verwoerd a Hollander.

He came to South Africa at the age of two, the son of a building contractor who wanted to be a missionary and saw an opportunity to do so among the "coloured" people of the Cape. The family settled in Cape Town's predominantly English suburb of Wynberg, where the young Verwoerd went to an English boys' school. Later Wilhelm Verwoerd, his father, received a calling from the Dutch Reformed Church in Rhodesia to do missionary work there, so the family moved north to that British colony and again Hendrik, by then a teenager, had to go to an English school and endure the anti-Afrikaner gibes of his schoolmates. He was brought up as an Afrikaner but not until he was sixteen and the family returned to South Africa, to a small country town in the Orange Free State, did Hendrik Verwoerd actually live in a predominantly Afrikaner environment. That seems to have intensified his need to identify with Afrikanerdom. "When it came to Afrikaner nationalism Verwoerd was a fanatic," recalls a fellow student who knew him at Stellenbosch University.

At Stellenbosch, like so many other figures in the Afrikaner Nationalist movement, Verwoerd studied theology. After graduating he switched to psychology, got his Ph.D., then became one of those impressionable young Afrikaner intellectuals who went to Germany—to the universities of Hamburg, Leipzig, and Berlin—just as National Socialism was beginning to breathe its noxious fire into the air. He returned to accept the chair of applied psychology at his alma mater.

But the backwaters of academia were not for this energetic and am-

2. House of Assembly Debates, 1959, col. 62.

bitious New Nationalist. When an offer came to be founding editor of a new Afrikaans daily in Johannesburg, which would be the mouthpiece of the party in the Transvaal, Verwoerd jumped at it. He edited *Die Transvaler* through the war years, revealing a clear pro-Nazi bias and a consistent anti-Semitism in which he called for restrictions on Jewish immigration and denounced "British-Jewish sham democracy."[3] After the war came the National party victory and his job as minister of Native Affairs.

Verwoerd formed a close relationship with the ministry's secretary, Werner Eiselen, the son of a German missionary who had been a faculty colleague at Stellenbosch. Eiselen was an anthropologist with strong ideas about the need to protect black tribal culture from the deleterious effects of "Westernization." The aim of government policy, he had written, should be to prevent blacks from becoming part of the general South African environment and to "encourage them to form an existence of their own." It should be pointed out to the black intelligentsia that "their first duty is not to become black Europeans but to raise their people to a higher Bantu culture."[4]

These ideas fitted in with Verwoerd's exactly. Together the two men set out to restrict the flow of blacks to the cities, restore the tribal system, and undercut the emerging black intellectual elite. Verwoerd's Native Laws Amendment Act of 1952 limited blacks with a right to live permanently in the urban areas to those who had been born there, those who had lived there continuously for fifteen years, and those who had worked for the same employer for ten years. Everyone else was supposed to return to his allotted tribal Bantustan, whence he could come to the city only as a migrant labourer on a six-month or one-year work contract obtained through a labour bureau in the Bantustan. If a person lost his job before completing his ten- or fifteen-year residence requirement he had seventy-two hours to get another; otherwise he lost his right to be in the city and had to return to what was considered his rural "home" and join the migrant queue. The new law applied these requirements also to women, thereby splitting families, for a man might qualify for urban residence and his wife not. These details had to be stamped in a pass book which black people were required to carry with them at all times in the cities on pain of instant arrest. Within a few years of the law's enactment, pass-law arrests were averaging two thousand a day.

3. In a celebrated court action, Verwoerd sued the Johannesburg *Star* for accusing him of falsifying the news in support of Nazi propaganda. He lost the case, the judge holding that the accusation was true.

4. Quoted in Henry Kenney, *Architect of Apartheid* (Johannesburg, 1980), p. 88.

As a corollary to this clampdown on urban rights, Verwoerd sought to bolster traditional institutions in the Bantustans by giving limited powers of local administration to a network of Bantu Authorities based on the old and rapidly disintegrating tribal chieftaincies. At the same time he abolished a body called the Native Representative Council which had been set up by the previous administration to advise on policy matters affecting blacks. The council—consisting of leading black intellectuals, mostly members of the African National Congress—represented an early attempt to shape black political development along Western lines. But Verwoerd wanted to channel black political development back into the tribal system while cutting out the new political intelligentsia, the "black Englishmen," as he described them, whom he regarded as "agitators" and not true representatives of the black population. The Bantu Authorities system amounted to an elaboration of the old British colonial technique of indirect rule that had been developed by Lord Lugard in Nigeria; its additional divide-and-rule advantages enabled the government to break down the black majority into separate tribal entities—or "nations" in the making—instead of facing it as a united body, which Western-style political development would have led to.

It also had the considerable advantage of obviating any need for an electoral testing of black political preferences, which might—almost certainly would—have gone against the government's nominees. Elections could be dismissed as Western innovations, alien to the black tradition, while the tribal structures represented the "the natural Native democracy." It was like using a judo throw against Verwoerd's liberal critics, flooring them with the weight of their own respect for black Africans and their culture.

It was of course highly convenient in practise. Not only was it relatively easy to find compliant chiefs ready to be co-opted into the new system—they, too, felt threatened by the modernizing process that eroded their institutions and by the new middle class that threatened their authority—but the law, which also instated the constitutional head of state as the supreme chief of all black tribes, allowed the minister of Native Affairs, Verwoerd himself, to exercise a chief's authority. He could appoint, dismiss, promote, or demote any chief in any region and in this way ensure that "the natural Native democracy" presented him with willing acolytes to work through.

Next came a drive to bring black education in line with the new policy and get it out of the hands of the missions that were producing the despised and dangerous "black Englishmen." A special Native Education Commission headed by Eiselen recommended that all black education be brought under the control of the Department of Native

Affairs. That meant the government would take over all the mission schools as well as the University of Fort Hare, founded by Scottish missionaries in 1916 as the first university for blacks in all Africa. Later a law was enacted—called, with savage irony, the Extension of University Education Act—that prohibited blacks from attending the major English universities of the Witwatersrand, Cape Town, and Natal.

Separate and "different" was the principle on which the new Bantu Education Act was based. Verwoerd explained it in Parliament during the debate on the new bill. Education for blacks should not clash with government policy, he said, and should "not create wrong expectations on the part of the Native himself." Then he went on:

> Racial relations cannot improve if the wrong type of education is given to Natives. They cannot improve if the result of Native education is the creation of frustrated people who, as a result of the education they received, have expectations in life which circumstances in South Africa do not allow to be fulfilled immediately, when it creates people trained for professions not open to them, when there are people who have received a form of cultural training which strengthens their desire for the white collar occupations to such an extent that there are more such people than openings available.[5]

Blacks inevitably saw this as education for inferiority, and their view was substantiated by the disparity in state expenditure on schooling for the different races. In 1953, the year of the Bantu Education Act, the government spent $180 on each white child in school compared with $25 on each black child.[6] Many of the best black teachers quit rather than participate in an educational system designed, as they saw it, to condition young members of their race for an inferior station in life, and this contributed still further to the decline of black education. This perception of calculated inferiority, indeed of bending young minds to an acceptance of inferiority, made education one of the most explosive grievances in the black community, and it provided the spark for both the 1976 student uprising in Soweto and, to a somewhat lesser degree, the great national convulsion that shook South Africa in the 1980s.

But it was as prime minister from 1958 to 1966 that Verwoerd made his indelible mark on South Africa, imposing an ideological cast of mind on Afrikaner nationalism that still keeps it in thrall, holding his successors captive long after the ideology itself has been revealed as manifestly unworkable. Whatever else may be said of the man and his works,

5. House of Assembly Debates, 1953, col. 3576.

6. Kenney, op. cit., p. 119.

that was a formidable achievement. As his biographer, Henry Kenney, notes, he dominated his time more completely than any other South African leader since World War II.[7]

Yet for many of us who watched and reported him during those years, this dominance was always something of a mystery. That he was a man of formidable intelligence there was no doubt, but he had none of the charismatic appeal that is normally associated with political success. He was quite a good-looking man in a benign and grandfatherly way, but his style was professorial and pedantic. He was no orator. His speeches were tedious, seldom less than two hours, delivered in a high-pitched voice with the points emphasized by a chopping action of his left hand, unbroken by either humour or moments of passion. He droned on while in the Parliamentary Press Gallery we fought against drowsiness.

Yet his audiences listened to him with rapt attention. The serried ranks of National party MPs would lean forward on their benches, hanging on every word of his long perorations. He seemed to mesmerize them with the sheer strength of his convictions and the authority of his personality. You could hear a pin drop as they stared at their leader with expressions of utmost respect and admiration. The merest hint of an interjection from the Opposition would bring howls of rage, as though someone had uttered a blasphemy in church.

They were listening, it seemed, not just to a political leader but to the bearer of a message, a prophet of his people who was leading them into the paths of righteousness and salvation. Verwoerd brought the civil religion to its apotheosis, and, as with all religions, this assured Afrikaners of a purpose in life and gave them a sense of control over their destiny at a time when they were being subjected to intense criticism at home and abroad. He gave them a sense of moral reassurance as well, for Verwoerd coated the crude slogans of apartheid with a certain intellectualism and respectability. Under his grand design it was no longer just *wit baasskap*. It became a vision of justice in which the blacks were given their rightful share, their own homelands where they could develop their own nationhood just as the whites were doing. They were no longer regarded as inferior, only different. That made the policy seem more modern, more sophisticated, and helped Afrikaners to believe they were not the primitive racists their critics made them out to be. Verwoerd even stopped using the word apartheid and began calling the policy "separate development," sometimes "separate freedoms."

Never mind that the Bantustans into which the regime forced the blacks were hopelessly small, fragmented, and economically inade-

7. Ibid., p. 9.

quate—just 13 percent of South Africa's land for 75 percent of the people. The idea could be presented in grand visionary terms with fine phrases about nationhood and culture and freedom. Few whites went anywhere near the dusty little patches of leached soil and overstocked veld to see how little this related to reality. It was the fiction that counted, not the reality. And that fiction not only offered Afrikaners a justification for denying political rights to the blacks in their midst, but also promised them that the blacks would return to an earlier and less threatening way of life—tribal and not urban, submissive and not challenging, separate from the cities and from them.

Verwoerd actively fostered the aura of a man divinely chosen to reveal a redemptive faith to his people. "In accordance with His will it was determined who should assume the leadership of the Government in this new period of the life of the people of South Africa," he declared in his inaugural speech.[8] It became a recurring theme for which the English newspapers mocked him: for years the *Cape Times*'s cartoonist, David Marais, drew him with a hot-line to God sitting on a cloud near the top of the picture. But to Afrikaners the imagery was no joke, and it took on powerful new meaning when in 1960 Verwoerd miraculously survived two small-calibre bullets fired into his head at point-blank range by a mentally unbalanced white farmer. Here surely was a man divinely protected for the salvation of the *volk*. The scenes that greeted him on his return to the House of Assembly after that verged on the reverential.

Yet when in 1966 he was finally assassinated, stabbed to death spectacularly in the prime minister's seat of the Assembly by a deranged parliamentary messenger, Verwoerd was dismissed, if not forgotten, with surprising speed. There was no worshipping at his shrine. Perhaps this was because, for all the awe in which he was held, he was not loved. He was not a lovable man. Perhaps it was because his successors needed to escape from the shadow of so dominant a figure. Perhaps, too, it was because by the time he died it was already becoming apparent that the elaborate programme he had outlined in such detail and pursued with such rigour was not working out in practise and perhaps could not.

But his ideology still casts its shadow over the country. It provided white South Africans with an elaborate system of make-believe that has become a habit of mind and continues to delay their inevitable confrontation with reality. Fictional though it may be, Verwoerd's concept of grand apartheid also has an institutional impetus that keeps it going

8. A. N. Pelzer (Ed.), *Verwoerd Speaks* (Johannesburg, 1966), p. 161.

and its bedrock fundamentals still provide the framework for government policy decisions.

Worst of all, although the Bantustans existed more in the political imagination than on the ground, the government made a determined and hugely disruptive effort to give them substance. Development boards were established, capitals built, parliaments established, presidents inaugurated, flags designed, national anthems composed and, above all, mechanisms of control and compulsion introduced to try to bring about the required relocation of the population. That, too, is still ongoing.

Central to this whole idea was the requirement that the millions of black people living in what was officially classified as "white" South Africa must return to their little rural "homelands," where they could exercise their full citizenship rights and develop their own national independence. As the attraction of this "separate freedom" lured them away, the argument went, the black townships—the huge concentrations like Soweto with up to two million inhabitants—would gradually wither away somewhat in the manner of the nation-state in classical Marxist theory and about as realistically. Their only remaining occupants would be migrants working in the cities for brief contract periods, "temporary sojourners" whom Verwoerd likened to Italian *Gastarbeiters* working in Germany, with political rights not there but only in their home country. These migrant workers would no longer be South Africans at all but citizens of their tribal "homelands," which were about to become foreign countries; and so they should not be allowed to put down any roots in the townships.

Avoiding permanency became the salient feature of the government's urban black policy. The Native Laws Amendment Act already limited the number of blacks who could qualify for permanent urban rights, and it was clear that Verwoerd had wanted eventually to phase out these categories too. The Land Act prohibited freehold outside the reserves, so urban blacks could not own the homes they lived in; they could only rent them from the white administration. To this Verwoerd added a prohibition on normal business development in the townships. Whites were not allowed to trade in the townships and regulations were proclaimed limiting the number of trading licences issued to blacks to a few who would provide only "daily essential domestic necessities"—wood and coal merchants, milk-sellers, small greengrocers, and the like. There could be no banks, clothing stores, or supermarkets, for these would give the townships an aura of permanency. Moreover the trading licences had to be renewed every year, and township administrators were instructed to make sure that no black business grew too large. "When a Bantu trader in a location [township] has sufficient capital," the regulations stipulated, "he must move his business to his Bantu area where the necessary facilities exist, among them the establishment of Bantu towns. Another Bantu trader must then replace him."[9]

"You might as well try to sweep the ocean back with a broom," Smuts had warned years before,[10] but the New Nationalists were imbued with a faith that through sheer force of will even the most stubborn economic laws could be made malleable. For some arbitrary reason he never explained, Verwoerd named 1978 as the year when the tidal influx would turn and the ebb of black people back to the "homelands" begin. It was a date that acquired the status of an oracle's prediction.

The pursuit of this chimera had large consequences. It massively disrupted the black population and grotesquely distorted urban and rural development. The reserve areas, supposedly havens of traditional African life based on subsistence farming, became overpopulated dust bowls disfigured by large "resettlement camps" where hundreds of thousands of uprooted people were dumped. Outside South Africa's cities huge complexes arose where hundreds of thousands of other blacks lived—with no business centres, no downtowns, no highrises, just endless sprawls of little gray, drab, uniform, matchbox houses; these were not so much townships as gigantic barracks to accommodate an army of workers.

By pegging the amount of new housing built to ideological projections, the apartheid administration also ensured hopeless overcrowding with up to twenty people to a house, and the proliferation of squatter settlements as economic necessity sought its own solutions. Since there was no "homeland" for the people of mixed race, Verwoerd declared the western half of the Cape Province to be a "coloured preference area" where no black worker might be hired unless the employer could prove there was no suitable "coloured" person to do the job; no new black housing was built in the area after that. The result was a weedlike growth of shantytowns around Cape Town, of which Crossroads became the most famous, as its resilient inhabitants returned again and again to rebuild their shanties each time the government bulldozers flattened them and government trucks hauled the people off to their distant "homelands."

It was another of those great South African ironies that Verwoerd's determined effort to bring about a total separation of the races came at a time when this was least capable of achievement. For it coincided with the take-off phase of South Africa's industrial revolution, the tran-

9. Quoted in David Welsh, *Oxford History of South Africa*, vol. 11, p. 195.

10. Ibid., p. 189.

sition from its primary stage of agriculture and mining, both extractive industries that needed large quantities of cheap, unskilled labour, to a more sophisticated manufacturing phase in which skills, and therefore training and permanency, became increasingly important.

World War II had begun this phase. As South Africans found themselves without many of the goods that had been imported from abroad before the war, local entrepreneurs responded to the demand and a manufacturing industry got under way. Now, in the 1960s, the country entered on a period of unprecedented growth. It was a self-generating process: as industry sucked more and more blacks into the city, they created an expanding market stimulating greater industrial output, which required ever more workers.

In vain Verwoerd tried to reverse the process. He warned business against starting labour-intensive industries in the cities and tried, through a combination of incentives and enforcement, to get them to move to areas bordering the Bantustans, so that blacks could live at "home" and commute to work across the supposed international borders. A Physical Planning Act compelled industrialists to apply for government permission to make any expansion that would require more black labour. A Job Reservation Act prohibited blacks from doing skilled jobs in the cities but did not apply to the "homelands" and border areas.

Still the flow to the cities continued. Industrialists showed little interest in setting up factories in the bush, far from markets and with little economic infrastructure. The only result was to burden business with irritation, inconvenience, and enforced inefficiency. It brought Verwoerd into conflict with the business community, but they never came out openly in revolt. Their innate conservatism and dependence on government contracts—and now increasingly on exemption permits to circumvent the new regulations—prevented that. When businessmen complained in their polite way that the controls were inhibiting economic growth, Verwoerd told them bluntly to get their priorities right. "If South Africa has to choose between being poor and white or rich and multiracial," he said, "then it must rather choose to be white."

That became one of the fundamental dictums of Verwoerd's philosophy. There could be no concessions to expediency. The integrity of principle was of supreme importance. Breach the line of principle anywhere and it would introduce illogicalities that would weaken the position. People imagined that you could ease the pressure by being more flexible and yielding a little here and there, but they were wrong. Making concessions gave an impression of weakness and so encouraged more demands, not less. "They [the blacks] will perhaps accept it and perhaps it will keep the wolf from the door for six months," Verwoerd said, "but then one has allowed one's feet to be knocked out from under one and one will have to make increasingly more concessions in the direction of integration at an ever-increasing pace."[11]

To the Dutch-born Verwoerd, principles were like dikes: a breach anywhere, in sport, on beaches, in hotel accommodation, would widen into a flood of uncontainable demands that would culminate in the dreaded swamping of one-person-one-vote. For a small, embattled nation like South Africa there was only one way to survive: never yield an inch. When New Zealand included a few Maoris in its national rugby team to tour South Africa in 1966, Verwoerd killed the tour and began South Africa's long sports isolation by refusing them visas. If the Maoris came, he explained, they would not only play with whites but would also stay in white hotels in white areas. Then local "coloured" folk would want to play on those fields and stay in those hotels, and on what grounds could white South Africa refuse them? The line of principle and logicality would have been breached. One thing would lead to another.

Verwoerd was right. One thing does lead to another. When, inevitably, apartheid ran into its crisis of implementation after 1978 and President Botha began making modifications to the system, these quickly set up a chain reaction of unintended consequences the end of which we have not yet seen.

CECIL MYERS is a genial man. By his lights he is also a benevolent one, for Myers's job is to place black people in jobs, and, heaven knows, in a place like the Ciskei where he works, there is certainly a great need for that.

To others, though, Cecil Myers may appear as an Orwellian figure operating the world's most sophisticated system of captive-labour exploitation. What he does is to run an institution called the Manpower Development Centre in the nominally independent black "homeland" of Ciskei, which functions as a kind of filter and pipeline that supplies "trouble-free" labour from a storage reservoir to wherever it is required in South Africa. In its way, Myers's centre represents the essence of the Verwoerdian dream.

The centre is in the township of Mdantsane at the southern end of the Ciskei, a wedge of land one-quarter the size of Wales situated on the old eastern Cape frontier where the settlers and the Xhosa tribes fought their wars. Supposedly the national home of the descendants of these old resistance fighters, it was granted its independence under the

11. Quoted in Pelzer, op. cit., p. 568.

separate development policy in 1981, but to a casual visitor unfamiliar with such ideological niceties it might be mistaken for a dumping ground of unemployed blacks. Nearly half a million people regarded as surplus to the economic needs of white farmers and the industrial cities, and who therefore have no legal right to be in "white" South Africa, have been deposited in this their putative "homeland" over the last twenty-five years. They live in crowded "resettlement camps" where the poverty is extreme and malnutrition diseases are endemic.[12]

There is no prospect of work. The Ciskei can provide wage-earning jobs for fewer than half as many people as there are pensioners. So Ciskeians have to try to get jobs as migrant labourers, and to do that they have to go through the Manpower Development Centre.

At the centre every work-seeker is registered on a computerized index. Employers phone up and place their orders, the appropriate records are called up from the data bank, and the selections are made. The workers go away on one-year contracts, at the end of which the employer is asked to report on new training given and "how the worker performed his duties." This report goes into the data bank. As the centre's brochure says, when workers are selected "preference will be given to those who have acquired experience and a clean work record." So if your boss reports that you are a "troublemaker" you may never get another job.

Membership in a trade union may also be a mark against you. The Ciskei government has outlawed unions in the "homeland," and though this does not apply in "white" South Africa, where the jobs are, it is a strong disincentive against joining. So ordering labour through the Manpower Development Centre is one way of ensuring that it will be union-free. When I interviewed Cecil Myers he denied that he would ever allow the centre to be used for strikebreaking, but even as we spoke his phone rang and the managing director of Dunlop Flooring in East London was on the line to ask for two hundred operators to be delivered the following week. Later I learned that there was a strike at Dunlop Flooring and five hundred strikers had just been fired.

The system of migrant labour colours the whole of life in South Africa's "homelands." You notice when you go into the resettlement camps that there are few young men around. They have nearly all gone away, leaving behind the old, the disabled, the women, and the children. Their departure casts a pall: the camps are quiet, heavy with apathy. Just a few low voices, little activity, and no laughter at all. Even the children are quiet, their vitality sapped by malnutrition.

In the camps you find that state pensioners are the main breadwinners, the only people with a regular income: $55 a month. If you are

12. Conference Associates, *The Quail Report* (Pretoria, 1980), pp. 30–1.

not old you may be lucky enough to be disabled: that also qualifies you for a pension. Unfortunately pensions are often cut off after removals, lost in the switchover from one authority to another. This can take months to sort out and no arrears are paid when it is.

I found Nowatcha Mehlo in that situation. I met her in the northern camp of Zweledinga ("the promised land") where she was living with her daughter, Nongaba, and four grandchildren. Nowatcha was sixty-five and qualified for an old-age pension, but her Ciskei papers had not come through and so she was not getting it. For more than a year the family had had no income at all. They begged from others in the camp who were almost destitute themselves. "When there is no food," Nowatcha said, "we just drink water. Sometimes we have been three days without food. The children get sick very easily."

A month before I saw her, Nongaba's husband, Simon, had at last got a job in the mines and gone off to the Witwatersrand, but he hadn't sent home any money yet. Perhaps he would; or perhaps he would *tschipa*, which is Xhosa slang derived from "cheap" and means to abandon your family to go your own way and live with city women. There is much *tschipa*-ing among the migrant workers.

Meanwhile little Xolani, aged eighteen months, had a bad cough and now Nowatcha was not well. Not only poor diet lowers resistance but the climatic extremes in northern Ciskei: snow and subzero temperatures in winter, heat up to 100 degrees Fahrenheit in summer, against which the mud-daub shacks and rusty corrugated-iron roofing provide little comfort. And there is no doctor in the whole of this northern region, which contains the worst of the camps: Zweledinga, Thornhill, Oxton, Inyembezi ("village of tears").

Perhaps the worst cases are among the people displaced from white farms. All their lives they had lived a feudal existence, enjoying paternal solicitude from their employers. They may not have been paid much, but at least they were secure—or so they thought. Now, as mechanization renders many redundant, they are being sent to the "homelands," often after decades of service. After a life of utter dependence they are unable to cope. And they don't understand.

Along the road near the resettlement camp of Dimbaza I came upon Kleinbooi Sam, riding with his two daughters on a wobbly wagon drawn by two cows. They had been into the mountains to fetch wood because there was no more fuel nearby. Kleinbooi told me he was born during the Boer War (1899–1902) and married during the eclipse of the sun (1940). He worked for forty years for a farmer named Danie du Plessis in the Cradock district. Then he became too old to work and Baas Danie told him it was time to go "home."

"Home" was the Ciskei, though Kleinbooi had never been there.

Baas Danie was good enough to bring Kleinbooi and his family along in his truck and drop them off near Dimbaza. They moved into a camp called Madakeni and built a one-room wattle-and-mud shack. Kleinbooi, his daughters Maggie and Elsie, two sons, and eight grandchildren were living in the one room, thirteen of them, on Kleinbooi's pension of $35 paid every two months.[13] Two years before, Kleinbooi's wife had deserted him, adding to his bewilderment. Perhaps, he mused, the eclipse had been a bad omen.

At Kammaskraal camp I met families who had been moved from a chicory farm at Alexandria, south of Grahamstown. Nokwenwa Totye and her friend Emily Mcube told me their story. The farmer died and a new "master" took over, who said he had no place for them. They were offered piecework picking chicory at five cents a bag, but couldn't live on that so they sent a deputation to see the Ciskei representative in Port Elizabeth. He promised to look into their problem. His solution came three weeks later: a convoy of trucks arrived and they were loaded up and brought to Kammaskraal where there was no work at all. Life may have been hard at Alexandria, said Emily, but at least they had some livestock which gave them a little milk and meat. "Do you not get meat here?" I asked. "Hau!" they exclaimed together, slapping their hands to their faces. "He asks if we get meat here. Have you ever heard of such a thing?"

Meanwhile, fifty miles away a new capital for the new independent Republic of Ciskei has arisen on the dun veld. It is called Bisho and it cost $100 million to build. It has a House of Parliament and an Independence Stadium and government offices and a palace with a marble staircase for the president, Chief Lennox Sebe. And, of course, a casino where the whites come to gamble.

WHEN THE KNOCK came at 3:00 a.m. on Isaac More's door and flashlights shone through the windows, he thought he was about to be attacked by a robber gang. "Open up," shouted voices outside, but More was not disposed to let gangsters have their way that easily. He might be eighty-six-years old, widowed and living alone, but he was a man of pride, an elder of his tribe, and he objected to such impertinence. He reached under his bed for the ax he kept there.

Moments later a window was smashed open and in stepped a white policeman, followed by others. Why had he not let them in, they demanded, and what was he doing with that dangerous weapon. "You're a *skelm*, eh?" said one, using the Afrikaans word for a rascal.

13. Old-age pensions were later increased to $55 a month.

This was the start of the forced removal of the small Bakwena tribe from their farming village of Magopa, 150 miles west of Johannesburg, to a resettlement camp called Pachsdraai in the black "homeland" of BophuthaTswana, another 150 miles away to the northwest. As More and six hundred other villagers stumbled out into the early morning darkness, they saw scores of police and officials milling about, some holding revolvers. The village had been cordoned off during the night and declared an "operational area" to prevent reporters and other interfering elements from entering. A convoy of trucks drew up and the people were ordered to load up their belongings and climb aboard. By noon they were gone. A few days later bulldozers came and demolished their little cut-stone houses. Magopa was no more.

The Bakwena had lived at Magopa for seventy-two years. Their grandfathers had bought the farm before the Land Act was passed, and so they had legal title to it, but now in terms of the apartheid laws it was classified as a "black spot" in a designated "white area," and they were supposed to move to their apportioned "homeland," which, since the Bakwena were a clan of the larger Tswana tribe, was deemed to be BophuthaTswana. A new area had been prepared for them there, its grid of streets already laid out with plot numbers, water taps, a school building and row upon row of shiny metal lavatories glinting in the harsh Transvaal sunlight. You can always tell when a removal is going to take place in South Africa by the forest of lavatories that suddenly springs up on some patch of bare veld. Then you know that in a few months the trucks will come bringing the people, by which time temporary metal huts for them to live in will also have been provided. But always it is the lavatories that come first, harbingers of the purgative action that is about to take place.

Some of the Magopa villagers accepted the government's inducements to move, but the majority did not. They clung to their land and the rare right of ownership and security it offered. Here the Bakwena could produce enough to feed themselves; their families could live together and their children go to the school they had built on the farm; and the young men, if they wished, could get jobs in Johannesburg and come home at weekends. It was as near to personal freedom as black South Africans could get.

This was 1983 and the government of P. W. Botha was in power. He had proclaimed himself a reformist who wanted to move away from apartheid, and the administration had said there would be no more forced removals, people would be moved only "voluntarily," yet somehow the words did not match the deeds and things kept happening that suggested there was a momentum about the apartheid process that no one could stop. In the months before the eviction the authorities sent bulldozers to knock down the village's two churches and the schoolhouse in what seemed to be an attempt to encourage the Bakwena to "volunteer" to leave. But still they resisted. Civil-rights organizations rallied to their cause. Churchmen came and held a candlelight vigil. Activists camped under the trees. Reporters and television crews arrived to tell the story.

The Bakwena appeared to win a stay of execution when, in the midst of these demonstrations, the deputy minister of information, Louis Nel, stumbled into an existential experience of their distress and momentarily seemed affected by it. A feature of the apartheid system is that the ideologists who devise the policies seldom come face to face with the people on the receiving end of them. They can remain in their make-believe world of theory and ideals while the dirty work is done by lesser cadres, by the police and officials of the Department of Black Administration who have become inured to it, their sensitivities buried beneath a carapace of indifference, and who in any case can disclaim personal responsibility on the grounds that they are merely doing their duty, obeying orders. *Bevel ist bevel.* But on this occasion the carefully maintained distance between cause and effect, between rationalization and reality, was inadvertently crossed. Nel, still new in his job, decided to take a group of foreign correspondents on a helicopter tour of the condemned village to show them, as he put it, "the other side" of a story he contended was getting distorted coverage. Instead it was he who saw another side of apartheid from the depersonalized theories he usually dealt with.

As the deputy minister's helicopter clattered down beside a spreading shade tree just outside Magopa, it turned out there was a protest meeting of about 250 villagers in progress under the tree. Nel hesitated for a moment as he saw what was happening, then he plunged in among them uttering words of greeting. The emotionally charged villagers swarmed about him, reaching out toward him with their hands, pressing him with pleas for a reprieve, begging him not to "throw us into the street." They began singing a lament in their Tswana language with the words, "Jesus saw me and I was crying."

Caught unprepared, Nel seemed moved by their distress. He clambered onto a chair and tried to assure them of the government's good intentions. No one was going to be thrown into the streets, he insisted. Oppression was not the intention. "The government's attitude is that we must help the people to have a better life in this beautiful country." With that the deputy minister beat a retreat to his helicopter with the agitated crowd still milling around him, and the air force pilot started the rotors to put a windy end to the embarrassing encounter.

It was ten weeks after that when the knock came on Isaac More's door and the forced removal began. Nel by then was a thousand miles away in Cape Town, attending to the business of government ideology. He did not see their faces or their agitation again.

I did. I met the people of Magopa three months later, bewildered and demoralized and reduced to poverty, in a squatter camp called Bethanie. The sight of them and the tales they told took one back to Plaatje's refugees in the winter of 1913. They had lost nearly everything. Unharvested crops had been left behind. In the confusion of the forced removal many had lost their livestock along the road. Others had sold their cattle to the first white farmer they came across, getting $65 for animals worth $350. When they arrived at the resettlement camp they hated it and most refused to stay, paying white farmers with trucks to transport their belongings to this spot at Bethanie where they knew the tribal chief and hoped he would let them stay. They had put up temporary shanties, but things were going badly with the chief, there was no work in the area, and the future looked uncertain.[14]

I met John Ramatoto, eighty-two and grizzled, who told me there was no way at his age that he could build a house like the neat stone cottage he had put up at Magopa back in 1930, and the compensation he was paid by the government was not enough to hire a builder. "Now I'll die in this thing," he said, gesturing at the tin shanty neighbours had helped him rig up with roofing sheets salvaged from his cottage.

I listened to George Rampou, a village councillor, make a little speech whose flat, metronomic delivery in imprecise English seemed to capture the mood of contained bitterness:

> They did not discuss with us. They just come. They come in the middle of the night all armed with revolvers. They come and surround your house as though you killed somebody. Then they force you to leave your house without you knowing why, how you must go. They decide how much to pay you without talking to you about it. But you must accept because they already break your house. They tell you you must go to Pachsdraai although you tell them you would rather go to Bethanie. They tell you if you want to go to Bethanie you must fetch your own transport. They must be great cowards to come and surround people when they are all fast asleep to do these things.

AT THE HEIGHT of the Verwoerd era, Afrikanerdom's most elegant journalist, Schalk Pienaar, wrote an essay in a little booklet published

14. Protracted representations by civil-rights lawyers have elicited an undertaking by the government to relocate the people of Magopa on new land of their own, but no site has yet been allocated. In the meantime they have been moved to a temporary site near the western Transvaal town of Onderstepoort. Isaac More died there in February 1989.

in Britain which contained the most sophisticated defence of apartheid that I have seen. Essentially it was an exculpatory plea based on the Afrikaner nation's right to life:

> History so decided that of all countries in Africa and Asia colonized from Europe there was to be one and one only that cradled a new nation with a new language and a distinct culture, allied to but at the same time different from its countries of origin. A little nation, it is true, but with as great a right as any other on God's earth to its place in the sun, as fiercely determined as any other in the last resort to fight for its existence with every weapon at its disposal.
>
> It also so happened that this new nation was moulded in the mills of a struggle for survival that has lasted for three centuries. It was but yesterday that the Afrikaners wrested from British imperial occupation the right to be a nation, to be independent in partnership with their countrymen of British stock. And today, with this battle that is all of Afrikaner history hardly fought, the demand comes that they submit to a new imperialism, not this time to the weapons of Europe, but to the numbers of Africa.
>
> The answer, not unnaturally, is no.
>
> Unlike the English in India and the Dutch in Indonesia, the Afrikaner has nowhere else to go. For him there is no Britain and no Holland to return to; for him no central shrine of national existence to survive the death of the outposts. On the soil of Africa he, and with him his history, culture and language, stay or perish.
>
> Individual English and Dutch chose to stay behind in India and Indonesia on Indian and Indonesian terms. That in no way affected the continued existence of a British and Dutch nation to maintain them as Englishmen and Dutch on foreign soil. But if the Afrikaners are to stay—and where can they go?—on Bantu terms, they cease to exist as a nation. They will be absorbed into something that, whatever it will be, will not be an Afrikaner nation. Three hundred years of history, a century and a half of national endeavour in face of fearful odds, a fleeting moment of victory, would have been wiped out as though it never existed.[15]

One cannot read those words without being moved by the authenticity of the Afrikaner dilemma. It is all very well for me, an English-speaking South African, to adopt a liberal stance, to be prepared to risk the leap of faith involved in committing oneself to the principle of majority rule when the majority is overwhelmingly of a race and cultural heritage different from one's own. I know that my own racial and cultural

15. S. Pienaar, "Safeguarding the Nations of South Africa," in a volume coauthored with Anthony Sampson, *South Africa: Two Views of Separate Development* (London, 1960), pp. 3–4.

heritage are not at stake, that whatever happens in a black-ruled South Africa an English-speaking world will always be there, and that, if necessary, in extremis, I can rejoin it, whether in Australia or Canada or New Zealand or the United States or England itself, and be culturally secure.

I may have other problems as an English-speaking South African—alienation from the land of my birth because it stands for things I abhor, no sense of pride when I hear my national anthem or see my national flag, or, though I sympathize with the black cause no full identification with it since I am not black and have not had the existential experience of their oppression; and a sense of being emotionally stateless and disoriented. But the one problem I do not have is that of cultural insecurity.

Not so the Afrikaner. He has the vulnerability of an endangered species, and the fact that his attempts to safeguard himself exacerbate rather than reduce his dangers does not make the psychology of it any less real. He is portrayed by the world as a racist monster, and much of what the apartheid system does is indeed monstrous, but would others have behaved very differently in his situation? Pienaar points to the trouble Britain has had absorbing a few thousand coloured immigrants and asks, "What would she do with 160 or 170 million of them?"[16] Such *tu quoque* repartee has become a cliché of South African diplomacy, but the point remains valid. As Heribert Adam reminds us, prejudice is not a demon that emerges in people simply because they are depraved; it is a product of situations.[17]

Yet when all this has been said, when every concession to the Afrikaner dilemma has been made, there remains the truth that no people have the right to build their nationhood on the deprivation of the rights of others. The Afrikaner nation may have a right to its place in the sun, but it has no right to bulldoze Isaac More into back-of-the-moon darkness to achieve it, or to programme an artificial and exploitative prosperity for itself into Cecil Myers's computers. A nation that has built itself on the moral foundations of 18 million pass-law arrests and 3.5 million forced removals has forfeited the right to speak of rights.

There is a duplicity in Pienaar's argument that lies at the bottom of this. He bases his case on the immutability of history and then ignores the greater part of it. Which is that history so decided, too, that the Afrikaner nation would arise in a country they would have to share with others; that South Africa was not theirs alone; that they would consti-

16. Ibid., p. 29.

17. Adam, op. cit., p. 20.

tute only one-tenth of its population; that in no part of it, in not one single district, would they constitute a majority. The injunction of history is surely that the Afrikaners must come to terms with this truth.

Yet they have defined their nationalism in exclusionist terms to deny this. To share means to die, to "cease to exist as a nation," to be "absorbed into something that, whatever it will be, will not be an Afrikaner nation." Compare that with Nelson Mandela's concept of nationalism given at his trial in 1961: "We were inspired by the idea of bringing into being a democratic republic where all South Africans will enjoy human rights without the slightest discrimination; where Africans and non-Africans would be able to live together in peace, sharing a common nationality and a common loyalty to this country, which is our homeland."[18]

Defined as it is, the existence of the Afrikaner nation becomes contingent on the exclusion or oppression of the other people with whom it shares the country. Ultimately that can only be done by physical and institutionalized force, at which point Afrikanerdom loses its claim to legitimacy. "The Afrikaner state is illegitimate," says that other elegant son of letters Breyten Breytenbach. "A minority regime which can only be maintained through violence has forfeited its right to exist, because it is unjust in conception and application."[19]

Afrikaner nationalism's reply, of course, is that the black South Africans are being given a share in the "homelands." "We will not deny the Bantu what we have claimed for ourselves," writes Pienaar, echoing Cronjé and Verwoerd, "and do not use against them the argument that was used against us, that they are a lesser breed incapable of achievement."[20]

But again the claim is duplicitous. The deceit begins with the lopsided apportionment: 13 percent of the land for 75 percent of the population means that each white person gets twenty times more land than each black person, with a huge disparity in resources besides. That is the black man's portion, his one-twentieth share of a common heritage with which he must be satisfied so that the Afrikaner nation can have its place in the sun. Isaac More and John Ramatoto and Kleinbooi Sam are beneficiaries of this bountiful share, as are Nokwenwa Totye and her friend Emily Mcube, who have forgotten what meat tastes like, and Nongoba Mehlo and little Xolani with the nasty cough and old No-

18. Quoted in *Centre Against Apartheid*, p. 14.

19. Breytenbach speech in the State Opera House, op cit.

20. Pienaar, op. cit., p. 11.

watcha who is probably dead by now. Homelanders all, citizens of BophuthaTswana and the Ciskei, which have both reached the pinnacle of this promise of separate freedoms—independence.

The deceit is compounded in the form of administration that apartheid has evolved. This is neither traditional government nor even self-government, but an elaborate system of manipulative control in which the white government in Pretoria pulls all the puppet strings. This was done by banning the major black political parties and, in the vacuum created, installing a political and administrative apparatus operated by approved chiefs and their acolytes, all beholden to Pretoria for their power and privileged positions. The government has the power to choose, manipulate, and depose, and it has budgetary control over the economically helpless "homelands." Reinforcing this is a pervasive control exercised by the South African Security Police and, in reserve behind them, the South African Defence Force, which has trained subsidiary units within the "homelands."[21]

This is not black self-determination. It is Afrikaner nationalism's determination of what the black man's future should be. No man is ordained to determine the fate of another, yet that is what has happened here. Afrikaner nationalism has taken the concept of its divine mission to mean that it has a God-given right not only to its own national existence but also to reorder the world around it according to its own vision, a right to define not only its own nationhood but the black man's as well. It has not sought the black man's opinion or consent in this, but claimed the right in the name of "trusteeship" and "responsible guardianship."

"It is the duty of the Afrikaner," wrote Geoff Cronjé, "to show the way in which the native must be led in his own interests and with a view to his own development."[22] The Afrikaner knows best what the black man needs, because the Afrikaner has suffered defeat and humiliation and then found himself again, and so he understands the meaning of nationhood and can show the black man the way.[23] He should try to persuade blacks that apartheid is in their own best interests, but if he cannot do this then he must press ahead with the policy anyway because the blacks must be saved from themselves and because they have always

21. The South African Defence Force intervened to reinstate President Lucas Mangope when he was overthrown in a coup in March 1988, and the Transkei's small South African–trained Defence Force overthrew the government of Mrs. Stella Sigcau and established a military regime following the ousting of President Kaiser Matanzima in that "homeland" in 1987.

22. Geoff Cronjé, *'n Tuiste vir die Nageslag*, p. 97.

23. Ibid., p. 25.

respected firmness. "The native has very little respect for the white man if he acts hesitantly or tentatively, whereas he respects the white man if he acts decisively, when it is clear what he wants and if he is convinced that the white man is determined to carry out his plan."[24]

Verwoerd put it less crudely but just as explicitly. In giving blacks the opportunity to manage their own affairs in their own areas, he said, the whites would act as guardians and for a time would have to maintain some unpopular control methods. "There is nothing strange about the fact that here in South Africa the guardian in his attempts to uplift the Bantu groups who have been entrusted to his care must in various ways exercise supervision over them during the initial stage," Verwoerd added.[25]

Entrusted to his care! By whom? By God, presumably. Once again there is the assumption of divine selection, a special people with a special mission.

There would be no Milnerism in apartheid, claimed Pienaar. The blacks would not be "denationalized" the way Lord Milner tried to denationalize the Afrikaners and turn them into Englishmen. They would be helped to develop their own Zulu and Xhosa and Sotho nationhood instead.[26] But in fact it is more Milnerist than anything the despised viceroy dreamt of, for Afrikanerdom has defined for the blacks what their nationhood should be and in forcing that upon them is not only denationalizing them but turning them into statutory foreigners in the land of their birth.

In the name of "trusteeship" and a divine ordination, Afrikaner nationalism has assumed the right to decide for the black South Africans how they should feel and think without any reference to their own self-selected political leadership, which has a vision of nationalism that is diametrically different. It requires them to view the world and themselves through the prism of Afrikaner nationalism's *wêreld en lewensbeskouing*. There can be nothing more jingoistic than that, nothing more certain to provoke exactly the kind of angry reaction that Milner provoked among the Afrikaners. By setting up a vicious cycle of resistance and repression it has come in the end to pose a dire threat to the very thing it was intended to secure—Afrikaner survival. The fate of Narcissus.

24. Ibid., p. 108.

25. Quoted in Pienaar, op. cit., p. 18.

26. Ibid., p. 11.

CHAPTER NINE

Of Contrasts and Blindness

For what is a man profited, if he shall gain the whole world, and lose his own soul?

MATTHEW 16:26

APARTHEID IS BOTH cause and effect. The ethnocentrism that gave rise to it flourishes within it, since in a compartmentalized society, people of different race and language groups have no real contact with one another or any sense of what is in the other's heart and mind.

White South Africans like to tell you that they know the black African, that they have lived with him for three and a half centuries and know his foibles, know his ways, know his mind. Yet they have never met him outside the master-servant relationship. Black South Africans, meanwhile, like oppressed people through all the ages, have developed defence mechanisms that conceal their innermost thoughts and present an image that they think the white *baas* expects and wants to see. Servitude produces habits of everyday resistance on the part of people who feel they are victims of an exploitative system they cannot fight or change, and who try therefore to work it to their minimum disadvantage. Foot dragging, evasiveness, negligence, desertion, false compliance, pilfering, feigned ignorance, carelessness, sabotage—these have been the weapons of the weak in the class struggle throughout history and their use in South Africa reinforces the stereotype. Geoff Cronjé, a professor of sociology supposedly disciplined to avoid such stereotyping, included among his arguments in favour of total racial separation the need to prevent the damage to property that black workers inflicted on the farms and in the homes of white South Africans. "They work with trucks, cars, farm equipment and household goods worth millions of pounds," he wrote, "and it is the general impression that the non-whites are much more destructive and careless with property than whites are." He concluded that they lacked an appreciation of mechanical things because of their lower level of development.[1] It is a view you still hear echoed by farmers and other whites all over South Africa—though it is blacks who operate most of the machinery, who drive the heavy trucks, who do most of the repair work on cars, who assemble them in the automobile factories.

To this stereotypical image of the black African—as stupid and feckless, mildly dishonest but generally good-natured, a child dependent on whites for guidance and who, given it, is basically content with his lot provided he can be shielded from the influence of "agitators" and the outside world—certain ethnological embellishments get added. Thus you will hear that the Zulu thinks this way, the Xhosa behaves that way, the Sotho is hard-working, the Tswana passive, and so forth. No visitor to South Africa will travel far without being subjected to some such lecture in amateur ethnology, a field in which every white South African fancies himself an expert.

Essentially, this stereotype derives from an idealized folk memory of life back on the farm when white kids and little black *klonkies* hunted birds, played *kleilatgooi*—a boys' game, slinging bits of clay with sticks—and swam bare-arsed together in the dam. Of the modern, politically aware, city-born African there is very little conception. White Johannesburgers do not visit Soweto, where he lives, though they travel by the thousands to London, Paris, and New York. The strip of bare veld that separates them from Soweto is more than just a physical barrier; it is a mental barrier, too, cutting them off from Africa like Van Riebeeck's bitter-almond hedge, isolating them psychologically from the people who live there.

As a reporter, shuttling between the black townships and the white suburb where I live, I have often felt as though I were crossing some invisible Berlin wall between different perceptions and different realities. One can spend the day witnessing events in one place and then cross the barrier into another only a few miles away but as distant as another planet.

It is September 4, 1984, and the townships of the Vaal Triangle, south of Johannesburg, are ablaze after a protest against rent increases has erupted into rioting. For two days the pent-up fury of an aggrieved community has raged here, and I have driven to Sharpeville, the best known of the Triangle townships, to report on the upheaval.

Now, as the second day draws to a close, the adrenalin has subsided and there is a lull. A crowd of about five thousand has gathered at the

1. Geoff Cronjé, *'n Tuiste vir die Nageslag*, pp. 177–9.

entrance to Sharpeville where Seiso Street, still strewn with the rubble of burning barricades and uprooted street signs, sweeps up from a shallow dip between the drab little dwellings. Facing them, drawn up in a double column five hundred yards away, are a dozen of the bulky, top-heavy armoured personnel carriers that the blacks call Hippos. Riot police, dressed incongruously in jungle camouflage uniforms, crouch inside them, repeater shotguns at the ready. For six hours they have waited thus while a meeting has taken place in the crowd. As the sun sinks low three figures step out of the crowd led by a tall, thin priest in a black cassock carrying a white flag on a stick. Slowly the three make their way across the stretch of no-man's-land toward the Hippos. The policemen tense, load their guns, and take up positions beside the big vehicles. Cautiously their officer advances a few paces and waits in the road. It is a moment of truce at the start of three years of violent confrontation between the apartheid authorities and the black populace—the most traumatic crisis in South Africa's history.

As I drive away from Sharpeville in the late afternoon, the acrid smell of tear gas still clinging to my clothes, the road takes me around a curve, over a small rise, past a row of tall blue-gum trees and onto a highway that leads to the town of Vereeniging three miles away. Sharpeville cannot be seen from the highway with its passing white traffic; it is hidden behind the trees and the rise. At the entrance to Vereeniging I pass a sports field where two teams of white cricketers are playing a game. Sharpeville, barely a rifle shot away, could be at the other end of the earth.

Different worlds in one country. And the whites live in their world oblivious of the others. The messenger at the office, the housemaid in the white family's home, are inhabitants of that other, remote world. They are James and Jane, not Mr. Kumalo and Mrs. Tshabalala, and the perceived part of their existence relates only to their working hours. They may have relatives and children somewhere, and hopes and anxieties, but these have no reality in the white world where they spend their days. Their presence is that of a utility, like the kitchen clock. And sometimes even that acquires a kind of invisibility, with discussions at white dinner tables ranging over the most intimate and confidential subjects without regard to the nonpersons hovering in the background.

This mind-set can have its uses for those of us in the reporting trade. When the *Rand Daily Mail* was investigating a chain of events in 1975 labelled the Muldergate scandal, we received word that a key figure in the affair, a certain Dr. Hubert Jussen, was about to leave the country. But confirming this proved difficult. Neither Dr. Jussen nor his wife would speak to our reporters, a security guard at the gate to their home prevented reporters from entering, and there was no response from Jussen's office. So we sent in a black reporter, who slipped unhindered by the tradesmen's entrance, went to the kitchen door and spoke to the household staff. An hour later he was back in the office with information on the Jussens' date of departure, the airline they were taking, their destination in Europe, and the name of the removal firm that was transporting their furniture.

It is June 16, 1985, the ninth anniversary of the great Soweto uprising, and there is a huge crowd at the Regina Mundi Cathedral in Soweto to commemorate the event. The police are outside in their Hippos, waiting. As the crowd spills out, some of the young radicals shout taunts at the police, a stone is thrown, shots ring out, all hell breaks loose. I dive for cover. Stones clatter about me as some of the radicals mistake me for a security force man. Then a "sneeze machine" passes close by and I am overcome by clouds of tear gas. Someone carries me into a nearby home where concerned black women revive me with cloths soaked in water and cooking oil. Some hours later, my face still burning from the gas, I am able to drive home. My wife is on the tennis court, hitting up with one of the children. She sees me and waves. "Hi, how'd it go?" she calls.

South Africa is covered by a grid of these barriers. The influence of apartheid has gone beyond the separation of white and black to create divisions in the white community as well. In separate English and Afrikaner schools the children play in separate sports leagues. Once, while addressing a group of three hundred pupils at an English-speaking high school in Johannesburg, I asked how many knew an Afrikaner child of roughly their own age whom they could even loosely describe as a friend. Five put up their hands. When I asked how many knew a black child outside the master-servant relationship, there were three hands.

This early estrangement in the white community continues into later life, as most go to separate universities and grow up reading separate newspapers, listening to separate radio channels and to a degree even living in separate suburban areas, working in separate businesses and belonging to separate clubs, churches, and cultural institutions. Even television is segregated into black and white channels and different time slots for English and Afrikaans programmes.

Blacks are separated not only from the whites but also from "coloureds," Indians, Chinese, and to a lesser extent even from one another according to their ethnic classifications. The whole country is a honeycomb of cellular group ghettos, full of ghetto attitudes of "us" and "them."

Worst of all is the whites' lack of insight about blacks. They have the power, but since they do not understand they do not react to the pain they cause, which is why every racial crisis catches them unawares. If you do not see the townships, how can you respond to what is happening in them? Six weeks before the Soweto riots broke out in June 1976, Manie Mulder, the white official in charge of the area, reported that the people of Soweto were peaceful and happy. "Apartheid has created a no-man's land between peoples where it is almost impossible for whites to recognise the political pain of others," says Hermann Giliomee. "Whites seem doomed to be perennially startled by the political responses of the subjugated."[2]

Breytenbach puts it more vividly:

> Apartheid works. It may not function administratively, its justification and claims are absurd. And it certainly has not succeeded in dehumanizing—entirely—the Africans, the coloureds or the Indians. But it has effectively managed to isolate the white man. He is becoming conditioned by his lack of contact with the people of the country, his lack of contact with the South African inside himself. . . . His windows are painted white to keep the night in.[3]

There lies the other half of it also. For apartheid has cast a darkness upon white as well as black. The world looks upon apartheid as a system that has brought whites nothing but profit, a unique system of racial oppression and economic exploitation that has given them power, privilege, and affluence. But it has cost them dearly in ways that perhaps neither the world nor they fully realize. As Hegel noted, the relationship between lordship and bondage holds both inextricably together.[4] Slavery debases master as well as slave; the warder becomes a prisoner in his own jail; he is never free from the business of oppression and confinement. In South Africa, white and black are bound together in a web of mutual destructiveness. Apartheid, brutalizing the whites as it destroys the self-esteem of the blacks, robs both of their humanity. As Allan Boesak puts it: "Whites will never be free as long as they have to kill our children in order to safeguard their own privileged position."[5]

The white South African, creating ghettos for the blacks, has turned South Africa itself into a ghetto, where he lives cut off from Africa and

2. Hermann Giliomee, "Changing Everything (Except the Way We Think)," in *Leadership SA*, vol. 3, no. 3, 1984, p. 125.

3. Quoted by Giliomee, ibid., p. 125.

4. See J. R. Baillie's translation of Hegel's *Phenomenology of Mind* (New York, 1931), pp. 228–67.

5. Allan Boesak, *If This Is Treason, I Am Guilty* (Grand Rapids, 1987), p. 22.

the world, unable even to identify properly with the country he loves. Denying the African within himself, he is himself denied, and isolated, and as his isolation increases and the international condemnation mounts, his self-obsession deepens into paranoia. Listen to the speeches of South Africa's political leaders, and in their indignant, fulminating rhetoric you hear the symptoms of a society afflicted with that neurotic condition that projects personal conflicts onto the supposed hostility of others, and leads to aggressive acts performed in the belief that they are necessary for self-defence. Aggression and guilt, guilt and anxiety, anxiety about survival and anxiety about guilt. This is a Christian society brought up on a strict Calvinist ethic and imbued with a high-minded image of itself as the covenanted agent of a divine mission. So the guilt and anxiety are repressed, displaced, and projected onto others in the form of yet more aggressiveness.

Repression cannot exist without violence. Pervasive, everyday, institutionalized violence, built into the polity and made part of the law, is the essential element by which a minority can hold power over a majority, and it is fundamental to the apartheid system. It is there in the compulsion and regulation, in the vagrancy laws and the squatter laws, in the forced removals and the police raids, in the daily confrontation between white authority and black subject. It is there in South Africa's overcrowded prisons (which hold a daily average of 110,000 people, the vast majority of them black, for a population of under 30 million). Television viewers around the world have seen glimpses of this violence on their screens, with police lashing out at fleeing demonstrators with what sometimes seems almost sadistic relish, an unleashed violence that goes far beyond what is required to maintain order, even by authoritarian standards. But though they may look as though they are enjoying it, they are not, for they are in the grip of powerful emotions, the violent release of displaced guilt and fear. I saw this for the first time as a teenage reporter in the early 1950s when I watched a police baton-charge on a crowd of black demonstrators outside a courthouse in the eastern Cape town of Queenstown during the Defiance Campaign. In the resulting stampede, an old woman fell to the ground. As she lay there, a helpless tangle of skirts and shawls, with a *doek* wrapped around her head like a Russian babushka, I saw one of the white policemen pause in his charge and lash out at her with his boot. He was a man I knew, and I knew he was not a vicious man. I called on him every day on my crime beat and always found him amiable and helpful, even kindly. But in that moment he was seized with a viciousness that was beyond himself.

I saw it again one day in Athlone township in 1986, when police opened fire with tear gas and shotguns to break up a crowd of demonstrators outside the Hewitson Training College. I had taken shelter behind a wall when the shooting started and from there I watched two young white policemen, their repeater shotguns at the ready, move down the road to clear it of stragglers. Ahead of them a young "coloured" student stood at the fence of one of the college residences. There was hate in his eyes and he had a stone in his hand. The policemen saw him and moved at him, their shotguns thrust forward. *"Kom boetie, gooi jong, gooi!"* they taunted him in Afrikaans—"Come on, chappie, throw! Go on, throw!" They were lusting to shoot, not ten yards from the student—and at that range their shotguns would have been lethal. At that moment a member of the college staff, a "coloured" man, raced out from the residence waving his arms and shouting at the policemen to hold their fire and at the student to drop his stone. This strange scene was not unusual: a member of the oppressed community, one of the supposed "agitators," intervening to restore the peace against the violence of the law enforcers.

What were they thinking, those two young policemen, as they lowered their guns and continued their patrol? Were they ashamed? angry? guilty? frustrated? Or did they feel nothing at all? Was it just another incident, quickly forgotten, in the holy war to protect the sacred nation against the Communist infidel who would otherwise destroy it? And what did the "coloured" student feel? Was he grateful that his life had been saved, or would he rather have had his moment of catharsis and bloody self-sacrifice? I could not read their expressions. Only the older staff man put his face in his hands and wept.

In the interrogation cells this mutually destructive violence of oppressor and oppressed reaches its apex. Apartheid, like all oppressive systems, survives behind an army of security agents and secret informants whose function is to police the frontiers of the mind, seeking out and stamping out attempts to organize dissension into active resistance. That is where oppressor and oppressed have their closest, most intimate, and most destructive encounter. It is an unequal joust because the interrogator has all the weapons while the prisoner has none, yet nowhere else is Hegel's bond more tangibly revealed.

Everyone who has been through it testifies to the strange syndrome of dependency and domination that develops between interrogator and detainee, in which each enters some way into the soul of the other and shares in his debasement. "What happens in bare rooms where all time has been twisted is not just dirty work," says Breytenbach, who has experienced his share of both interrogation and imprisonment, "it is the heart-rending flowering of evil which will profoundly alter all the actors." The interrogator's power is absolute. He has the power to hold, the power to torture, the power to kill even, and having the detainee know that is his most powerful weapon of all. "But ultimately it rots him utterly," says Breytenbach. The prisoner gets broken. He ends up confessing and sinks into an abyss of self-disgust. He has been raped. But the raping interrogator shares the humiliation and the violation of human dignity. "The two of you, violator and victim (collaborator! violin!), are linked, forever perhaps, by the obscenity of what has been revealed to you, by the sad knowledge of what people are capable of. We are all guilty."[6]

If the interrogation cell is the ultimate stage for this Sophoclean drama of interwoven fates, then the death of Steve Biko was the ultimate play. In a cell in Port Elizabeth's Sanlam Building where the security police have their regional headquarters, the leader of the Black Consciousness movement and a team of South Africa's most ruthless interrogators met. It is the purpose of the interrogators when they deal with black political prisoners to break down their reserves of self-confidence, to confront them again with the dilemma of the all-powerful white man until those reserves crumble and they revert to the submissive plea *"Ja baas, asseblief baas"* (Yes master, please master). Then the extraction can begin and, if the interrogator is really skilful, the political activist may even be turned around into a political informer. But what if those reserves don't crumble? What if the prisoner is the inspirational force behind a new philosophy of black racial pride and self-assertion, a man with a strength of personality and will and a dedication to match and exceed his interrogators?

Biko, a charismatic young man who had dropped out of medical school in the late 1960s to found the Black Consciousness Movement, was all of these things: the propounder of a new doctrine that said black liberation could be achieved only by the black people themselves and had to begin with them breaking free of the shackles of psychological inferiority. At the age of thirty, he was already a legend in the black community, especially in his own age group, and it was largely his influence that triggered the 1976 Soweto uprising. As the security police set about crushing that rebellion, they stopped his car at a roadblock near Port Elizabeth one night in August 1977 and took him to their interrogation cells.

Biko had been detained before and he had not broken. He liked to tell that once when an interrogator hit him he stood up and punched him back. One can only imagine what excesses his interrogators were eventually driven to, what an acceleration there was in the cyclic syndrome of fear and guilt turned into aggression. All we know is that he

6. Breyten Breytenbach, *The True Confessions of an Albino Terrorist* (Johannesburg, 1984), pp. 311–2.

ended up in a coma, his brain fatally damaged by a terrible blow to the head, and that his interrogators, in shock themselves, thought he was shamming and kept him for three days naked and shackled, lying on a mat in his cell that became soaked with the urine that dribbled out of him in his state of comatose incontinency. Government doctors examined him and kept silent about what they saw. And then the interrogators, guilt and anxiety stripping them of their last vestiges of humanity, loaded him in the back of a jeep, still unconscious, still naked and still shackled, and sent him on a seven-hundred mile journey through the night to a prison hospital in Pretoria with no medical records to accompany him. There he died the next day, unattended.

Thus did apartheid's holy war destroy the humanity of black and white alike with an indecent death and an obscene murder. At the inquest the magistrate found no one was to blame. Death was due to injuries inflicted by persons unknown. That is always the way of it. There have been more than fifty deaths in the interrogation cells and no one has ever been found to blame. How can there be? The dead are dead and the only witnesses are the interrogators themselves. Six years later the officer in charge of the interrogation, Colonel P. J. Goosen, was promoted to deputy commissioner of police.

It is the same with torture. Torture has become routine, a standard tool employed in the name of state security. Everybody knows this. Even the techniques are a matter of widespread public knowledge. There is the helicopter, when a handcuffed prisoner is hung from a stick thrust between the folds at his elbows and knees and lashed with *sjambok* whips as he is twirled around. There is the submarine, when his head is held under water until he nearly drowns; or, as a refinement, when he is suffocated by having a wet sack pulled over his head. There is the telephone, when electric wires are attached to his nipples or genitals and he is subjected to repeated shocks. Often, too, prisoners are made to stand for hours on end, even days, sometimes on bricks that are placed on edge, sometimes in squatting positions with their arms outstretched, sometimes naked and blindfolded with creeping things sent crawling over their bodies. They are hit and kicked, burned with cigarettes and hung out of windows. Hardly a political trial is held without there being a trial-within-the-trial to hear allegations of these tortures, but never are the complaints upheld. Again the only witnesses are the interrogators and the prisoners, and the prisoners, political "agitators," can produce no corroborating testimony.

The higher authorities know, of course. The doctors know because you cannot have systematic, ongoing torture in any country without the medical profession knowing. The lawyers know, big business knows, the public knows, but there is no concerted action to stop it. Like ripples in a disturbed pond, the waves of culpability radiate outward, corrupting the whole society.

Yet the fact that there are public inquests after each death in detention, and trials at which charges of torture can be made publicly, are encouraging signs. They may be fruitless and they may be window-dressing, but it is not without significance that a need is felt to put on a show of democracy and justice; it may be self-delusion, but it is noteworthy that the self needs to be deluded, that there is a conscience ill at ease and requiring appeasement. Most totalitarian states have no such problem. The full agony of the South African situation includes the truth that the whites who rule the country so oppressively are not brutes. They have within them deep traditions of democracy and justice. It shows in the paradoxical tokenism of the institutions and procedures they maintain: a parliament with Opposition parties, which they bypass with executive decrees and proclamations; independent newspapers that are then shackled with restrictions; courts with independent judges, but laws bypassing them and permitting detention and interrogation and torture without trial. And when someone dies while in the toils of this police-state process, they bring the matter back to court and reveal their own abuses, only to condone everything again and make a mockery of their own tokenism. It is absurd, but it is not without meaning and not without hopefulness. The traditions are still there, the desire to abide by them is not quite dead, though they have been corroded and vitiated by the effort to build a nation on the deprivation of the rights of so many of its people.

Triomf! Apartheid gave the Afrikaner back his country. It has given white South Africa power, privilege, and prosperity. But at what a cost in corruption of the self and of the civilized values they imagined they were bringing to Africa!

SUCH IS THE HAVOC that apartheid has wrought on the psyche and soul of white South Africa. But let me not give the impression that the harm done to whites is in any way comparable to that which blacks have suffered. Nor is it simply that apartheid inflicts great hardship on black people. It not only determines the kind of lives they lead, but also influences the kind of people they become. The psychological damage it has caused is probably incalculable. Helen Kivnick, a California psychologist who did field research into the subject a few years ago, concluded that it had exerted a "unique destructiveness" at every stage in the life-cycle development through which an individual moves from birth to death, stifling the proper growth of life's delicate balances between individual and society, between self-interest and self-restraint, between trust and mistrust and a sense of right and wrong. Yet she also found that black South Africans were, as she put it, "gracious and unexpected teachers of cultural wisdom and moral integrity."[7]

Traditional African culture has powerful resources that have enabled black South Africans to survive the ravages of apartheid. The still pervasive spirit of *ubuntu* provides unity in shared adversity. But the damage has been great nonetheless.

Consider the life cycle of a black South African. The black baby is born into a community where it is treasured, cosseted, and loved by all. It spends the first months of its life wrapped to its mother's body. In the "homelands," on the farms, and even in the cities black mothers walk about with their babies blanketed to their backs and their bundles balanced on their heads, the infants snuggled there like marsupials, the rhythms of the mother's body providing them with an infinity of closeness and trust. The sounds and the resonances of the words the mother utters, the songs she sings to herself and with others, give the baby a sense of the world around it that engenders trustfulness.

But when that baby comes down off the mother's back it enters a world that becomes increasingly unreliable, treacherous, and violent. The child will be awakened by pass raids in the night, with strangers bursting noisily and aggressively into the house. When he goes to school—if he goes to school—he will have to pass through streets harassed by *tsotsis*, the terrifying young township gangsters who live fast and high off violent street crime; and when the child comes home again as likely as not mother and father and older siblings will not be there. They may have been arrested in a pass raid, a political raid, or some other raid. Or they may be missing altogether, for reasons unknown. Or they may simply have been held up by the long queues, the crowded trains, the roadblocks, and the myriad other obstructions that pervade black life. At an early age the black child will find himself on his own, without the security of adult presence and adult supervision, more and more in the company of others his own age, moulded more by peer pressure and survival instincts than by parental influence.

At school, what does the child learn? The Bantu Education system is designed to stifle ambition and train a working class. Our young black boy or girl will be going to a school in a dilapidated building with filthy and inadequate toilet facilities, broken windows, too few desks, not enough books, and a hundred or more children to a class. The teacher,

7. Helen Kivnik, "Black Psychological Development Under Apartheid: A Theoretical Consideration," a paper delivered at an African Studies Association conference, Chicago, November 1988.

likely as not, will have no more than an elementary-school education and will be tired and uninspired by the hopeless task. The school may have police and soldiers on the premises to keep an eye on the students and spot "agitators." They may even be in the classrooms during classes, in their uniforms and with their guns, and in their strutting arrogance strip the headmaster and staff of any dignity or authority. There will be informers in the school, too, black kids desperate for food, security, and the little prestige that money can buy. And there will be political heavies out to get the informers, and political rivals to clash among themselves.

Our child will not be challenged to develop academic skills. He may, of course, develop other skills—street smarts and the art of surviving the white oppressor, which means hiding one's feelings, telling lies in order to survive his wrath. And since expertise in township crimes often seems to provide the only viable sources of income and prestige, that may lead our child to one of the *tsotsi* gangs. He may join for the thrills, or the fellowship, or, more likely, the protection, since the simplest way to survive gang harassment is to become a member of the toughest of them. Sooner or later a gang member will go to prison where he will meet adults with more highly developed skills than his own, become a member of a prison gang perhaps, and link up with them again when he comes out.

At home, meanwhile, insecurity is total. Mother or father or both may lose their jobs, capriciously, at any moment. The family may be evicted from its home, or be sent back to a "homeland" which they have never seen, where there are no jobs, and the only hope will be migrant labour.

Insecurity and humiliation. The worst kind of humiliation is to see one's own parents cringe before the wanton abuse of the police and fawn in their pleas for work, "*Ja baas, asseblief baas.*" How does one learn to feel pride in oneself, in one's race, in one's heritage, when one's earliest childhood memories are of such scenes?

And what of initiative? All parents want their children to do well, to do better than they did, but how does a black parent teach his child to show initiative when the system they live under stifles it? How do black parents encourage curiosity when they have no answers for the questions that are asked? How do they encourage enterprise when they know how limited the opportunities really are?

Helen Kivnick tells of a Soweto mother watching her small son playing at being an airline pilot. "What can I say to my son at such a time?" she asks. "Can I talk with him about his dream, and make him think it can become a reality? Must I tell him that he will never be allowed to become an airline pilot because he is black? Will he discover the limitation soon enough for himself? But will he then hate me for playing along with his fantasy? Today his eyes are shining. But soon I will have to watch that light go out."[8]

How does a black South African child learn about right and wrong? There is nothing in his life to suggest that "right" has anything to do with human goodness or obeying the law of the land, or that "wrong" has to do with breaking the laws. His whole experience demonstrates that "justice" is what serves the interests of the white authorities, that the courts enforce that, that the law is oppressive, and that the police are his most dreaded enemies.

How does he find privacy, the privacy that balances against interaction with one's community and offers reflective moments when one can find oneself, contemplate one's place and role in the cosmos? If he is lucky, he lives in a matchbox house in one of the townships, with perhaps four or five people sleeping in each room; if he is less fortunate, he lives in a shanty in a squatter camp, a makeshift structure of cardboard and corrugated iron and bits of old boxes, the roof held down by heavy stones, and which provides a single space maybe twelve feet square in which a dozen people may live. There, on a typical evening, schoolchildren are studying, younger children playing and whining, teenagers listening to transistor radios, granny lying sick on a blanket in a corner, aunt cooking dinner, uncle sleeping before going out to work a night shift, mother and father just back from work, friends dropping in to socialize, all in a room heated by kerosene, lit by candles, filled with noise and smoke. Our child cannot find privacy there, nor can he find it in the streets and alleyways outside, where violence stalks, and there are no parks and forests where he can walk alone.

How does our young adolescent prepare for adulthood in an environment like that? How does he learn about love and intimacy, faithfulness and mutual trust when he lives in such congestion, when his parents have so little opportunity for expressing tenderness? When the family ties may be almost nonexistent, with father away on a migrant job most of the year living in a single-sex hostel and finding an outlet for physical tenderness only in the company of prostitutes and casual relationships, or perhaps more permanently with another woman raising another, separate city family, and coming home only occasionally as a virtual stranger? Or when mother works as a domestic, living in a room in the backyard of the white "madam's" house where she is not allowed to have her husband or children with her, so that the child is sent to granny in the township, or in a distant "homeland," where he will live

8. Ibid., p. 26.

with a dozen others in a similar situation and be brought to see mother maybe once a month or year?

And how does our young adult develop a healthy balance between trust and scepticism in a world distorted by official strategies of control and manipulation? The government pays informers to report on the activities of people it regards as dangerous. It also offers financial inducements to black people willing to help run its administrative machinery in townships and "homelands." Apartheid is largely a system of indirect rule, directed by whites at the top but administered by blacks at the bottom. The blacks who perform these functions are viewed by other blacks as traitors who have sold out to the white government, collaborators who evoke feelings of contempt and anger. But black people are starving in South Africa, and a mother may agree to inform on a stranger in exchange for a payment that will enable her to feed her children for a few more days. Business opportunities are almost nonexistent for blacks, so in exchange for a trading licence to operate one of the rare supply stores in black areas a man may agree to serve on the township council or take a seat in a "homeland" parliament. Getting somewhere to live, having a secure job, and avoiding police harassment are perhaps the three most important considerations in a black person's life—and the simplest way to obtain all three is to join the police force. It means becoming part of the repressive arm of the apartheid system, of participating in the day-to-day subjugation of one's own people, but once one is part of it one will not be harassed by it. Fully half the manpower of the South African police force is black, making it, ironically, one of the most integrated institutions in the country.

How, then, does community life function? People know that treachery lurks in their midst, that at any moment the friend next door may turn out to be an informer, or that a relative, a colleague, a father even, may become a collaborator and be labelled an enemy of the people. They know, and at some level they even understand. In the little town of Brandfort, to which she was banished for more than a decade, Winnie Mandela, wife of the imprisoned African National Congress leader, Nelson Mandela, had policemen living on either side of her. It was clearly no accident. They had been placed there to watch and, to a degree, intimidate her. Yet she managed to build a fairly amiable, neighbourly relationship with them. When I asked her how she could do it, she gave a wry smile. "They are victims too, you know—and they have to be conscientized."

So much for the agony of growing up black, but what of the agony of the black parent? Without control over home, food, shelter, education, employment, or personal liberty, black parents cannot feel themselves to be truly their children's providers and protectors. Fathers who are gone for most of the year know that all they can offer their families is a remitted share of their meagre pay packets. They cannot offer regular guidance or love as the children grow, or experience the immense satisfaction of watching them emerge from the chrysalis of babyhood into young adulthood. But these are deep psychic needs, fundamental to the health and happiness of all God's creatures, and they are denied to millions of black South Africans.

Throughout the ages each generation has strained to enable the next to do better. Parents pass on to their children what they have learned, what they have achieved, hoping that the children can improve on it. But what can the black parent bequeath, proudly, to his progeny to complete that final obligation to posterity that was so important to Geoff Cronjé and his fellow Afrikaner idealists? Except in a few isolated cases, blacks cannot build up businesses or accumulate wealth or possessions or other things that white parents and grandparents are so proud to pass on. They have little chance to train them for better jobs with better pay and greater security. For the most part they know that they must leave them as they themselves were left—with nothing but the prospect of a lifetime of struggle. To the very end of the generational cycle they are deprived and demeaned.

And yet when one has considered all this adversity, all the violence and oppression and psychological damage, one comes back again and again to the wondrous truth that the black townships of South Africa are not places of despair. As Trevor Huddleston described them, so they are still today—full of vitality, life, and laughter, still exuding an enduring sense of survivability.

Helen Kivnick thinks the Africans' love of song has much to do with this, that this deep and pervasive cultural tradition serves "as an ongoing source of psychosocial strength contributing to essential health and resilience in the face of overall pressure towards psychosocial ruin."[9] It is certainly true that for the black people of South Africa—indeed of all Africa—singing is an integral part of life as it is not for any other society I know of. Mothers sing to their children and the children themselves sing when they are very young. People sing solo, in groups, and en masse. They sing in all sorts of situations—at work, at play, in church, in the fields, as they walk along the road or as they sit around the fire, at every political rally, every trade-union meeting, every funeral. It is a different kind of singing, too, not the unison of repeated stanzas as you will hear from a Western church congregation or a crowd at a football game, but a call-and-response style in which an individual calls out a song line of

9. Ibid., p. 54.

his own—perhaps a commentary on the day's events, or a statement of political protest—and the crowd takes the theme, repeats and harmonizes it, until a new line is called out by someone else, embellishing the first theme or starting a new one, all to the beat of spirited rhythms and interspersed with shrill ululations. In this spontaneous, creative social commentary everyone participates, and all are bound together in a spirit of unity and uplifted morale.

It is an activity that has a certain safety from the authorities, a private domain for black Africans, a cultural refuge, in a sense, where they can strengthen themselves and create beauty in the midst of ugliness. And humour. That satirical, taunting, mocking humour that has been the self-sustaining weapon of the oppressed through all the ages can be chanted out loud, as by Oswald Mtshali's roadgang lifting a heavy sewer pipe into a trench in a busy city street, under the very nose of the uncomprehending white foreman:

> It starts
> as a murmur
> from one mouth to another
> in a rhythm of ribaldry
> that rises to a crescendo
> "Abelungu ngo'dam—Whites are damned
> Basibiza ngo Jim—They call us Jim."[10]

SURVIVABILITY. I tell a story to illustrate this survivability. There is a resilience among black South Africans, a capacity to absorb blows, suffer grief and disruption and still come up smiling, that is a matter of astonishment to all who move among them. It stems in part from the ancient conditioning of a people who learned to withstand Nature's capricious blows in this unpredictable continent, but also, I think, from a deep inner knowledge that whatever the present may deliver, the future is theirs. They may have been wrenched out of their ancient ways, uprooted and exploited, but they have not been completely crushed and acculturated, as slave communities were. They are not a minority group seeking nondiscriminatory absorption into a dominant culture, but a majority group demanding its own democratic right to be their country's dominant influence. Above all they have the confidence of numbers: four-to-one today, five-to-one tomorrow, six-to-one the day after. They

10. Poem by Oswald Mtshali, "A Roadgang's Cry," in *Poets to the People*, edited by Barry Feinberg (London, 1980).

know—and they know that in their hearts the whites know—that they are going to win in the end, and that gives them courage and endurance, whatever the odds against them in the short term.

There are many tales one could tell of this survivability: Nelson Mandela's twenty-eight years in prison that have left him with no trace of bitterness or grievance; his wife, Winnie's, ebullience after thirty-three years of marriage during which she has spent a total of only five weeks with her husband in broken spells; aging Albertina Sisulu's rock-like strength, though her husband spent twenty-six years in jail, though she has two children in exile, another under restriction, a fourth in prison and she herself has spent most of her life under banning orders of one sort or another. But the story I choose to tell is that of Mamphela Ramphele, a young woman of gentle demeanour and steely resolve who not only survived but grew with the kind of adversity that few white Westerners her age can even imagine.

Ramphele and Steve Biko met while both were medical students at Natal University in the late 1960s, and they fell in love. It was a deep, special relationship that involved a harmony of political ideas as well as personal emotions. Biko's political activities led to his being suspended from the medical school, and while Ramphele went on to become a doctor, he founded and became leader of the Black Consciousness movement. As the movement burgeoned, the South African government, alarmed at the impact he was having, placed Biko under a banning order in 1973, restricting him to the country town of King William's Town in eastern Cape Province. Soon afterward Ramphele moved there to be near him, founding the *Zanempilo* community clinic as a project in line with Biko's philosophy of self-help as the key to liberating black people from the psychology of oppression.

Ramphele was pregnant with Biko's child when the security police banished her from King William's Town in 1977 to the remote tribal village of Lenyenye, a thousand miles away in the northern Transvaal tribal "homeland" of Lebowa, where she knew no one and had only a sketchy understanding of the local language. The banishment order prohibited her from leaving the area, from being in the company of more than one other person at a time, from making any public statement, from writing for or being quoted by any publication, and from engaging in political activities of any kind. It was a desolate experience for the young doctor, lonely, hot, isolated, and in an environment of extreme poverty and despair among mostly illiterate people, more and more of whom were being transported there because they were surplus to "white" South Africa's labour needs. She was traumatized by the experience and soon after her arrival in Lenyenye Ramphele was taken to hospital in a nearby town with a threatened miscarriage.

She was there when news reached her of Biko's death. "I didn't believe it at first," she told me in an interview a few years later. "I didn't think they would dare kill him. Then, when I could no longer deny it, I nearly disintegrated."

Suddenly the birth of the baby became desperately important to Ramphele. "I was frantic to keep the baby," she said, "to keep alive something of our relationship, and of course the more agitated I became the more the threat of a miscarriage increased." She nearly died, but eventually she recovered and after eight weeks in the hospital she was sent back to her village prison, where she spent the remaining five months of her pregnancy in bed. "I just lay there thinking about my misery, going through all kinds of destructive, nonproductive emotions," she recalled.

Then the baby arrived, a boy, "the spitting image of Steve." Ramphele named him Hlumelo, a word in Biko's Xhosa language that means "the shoot from a dead tree." "From that moment I decided to turn my anger into action," she said.

Appalled at the toll nutritional diseases were taking in this expanding and mostly unemployed community, and at the pervading apathy and defeatism, Ramphele decided to do something about it. She started a medical clinic in some rooms behind a church, then raised $80,000 from business and church organizations in Johannesburg to build a proper clinic, which she called Ithuseng. She was just twenty-nine-years old.

Over the next six years Ramphele transformed the lives of those among whom she had been dumped—a community that more than doubled, from twenty thousand to fifty thousand, during those six years. She did so by teaching people to help themselves, organizing groups that would then go out and organize others. People who helped finance her projects compared her efforts with those of Albert Schweitzer, the 1952 Nobel Peace Prize winner who ran a community hospital in the jungle of French Equatorial Africa.

The Ithuseng Clinic expanded until it had a full-time staff of twelve and was treating eighteen thousand patients a year. It became the nucleus of a range of other self-help projects: two branches of the clinic were established in neighbouring villages; a twice-weekly soup kitchen and milk project was started; five local groups were organized to teach home economics, hygiene, and health care; a play centre was started for the children of the lucky few mothers who had jobs; gardening clubs taught the villagers how to grow vegetables, and an adult literacy programme was operating in five neighbouring villages. Local women were organized into sewing and knitting clubs that sold their products. Ramphele raised enough money to build and stock a public library and to start a scholarship fund to send the brightest local children to college. She even started a communal brickyard to cut local building costs, and within a few years it employed sixteen people, had its own tractor, and was producing twenty thousand bricks a month.

"Sometimes I despair," Ramphele said, looking up from examining a sick and malnourished infant who died later on the day that I interviewed her in 1983. "What I am doing here is such a drop in the ocean. Sometimes I feel I am just wasting my time and energy. I wonder whether anyone realizes the magnitude of the crisis that is building up in these areas. Pretoria has shifted the responsibility for all these desperate people onto the tribal 'homeland' governments, which don't begin to have the ability or the insight to cope. I wonder whether even our black liberation movements understand the scale of the problem. If we had liberation tomorrow, I don't think they'd know how to handle it. It will take years. The psychological destruction that goes with oppression at this level is unbelievable." Then, brightening at the sight of a large and cheerful peasant woman bustling into the surgery, Ramphele added: "But just when you are feeling defeated you see somebody you have been able to help and it all seems worthwhile again."

Mamphela Ramphele's banishment order was lifted in 1983, but so involved had she become with her work there that she stayed on voluntarily for another year to make sure others were able to keep the clinic and the various community projects going. Only then did she leave her hot and dusty Siberia. Today she is attached to the University of Cape Town as a nationally recognized authority on the subject of rural poverty, and recently coauthored a major book on the subject.[11] Hlumelo Biko is eleven. He knows all about his father and how he died and is enormously proud of the name he bears. The two of them, mother and child, do not look back in anger, only forward in strength. Thus African survivability.

11. Francis Wilson and Mamphela Ramphele, *Uprooting Poverty: The South African Challenge* (Cape Town, 1989).

CHAPTER TEN

A Spray of Doom

in a flash
of the eye
of gun-fire
like spray flayed
they fled they fell
the air fouled
the minute fucked
and life fobbed

our heads bowed
our shame aflame
our faith shaken
we buried them for what they were
our fallen heroes and our history

SIPHO SEPAMLA

MICHAEL ZONDO is a taciturn, middle-aged, high school teacher. He is soft-spoken, courteous in an old-fashioned way, and conservative, an unremarkable man who just happened to be part of the crowd the day South Africa's still unfinished revolution began.

He remembers the day well. It was sunny and warm, with just one cloud about the size of a man's hand. It rained a little later on, just enough to soak some of the blood into the sand and clean the road. But at that stage, early on the morning of March 21, 1960, in Sharpeville township, it was bright and clear.

There had been some trouble over the weekend. The African National Congress and the Pan-Africanist Congress were organizing an anti–pass-law protest, and the police had come into the township arresting people. A neighbour said he had heard some shooting during the night. Zondo was worried about his students: they were inclined to get headstrong at times like this. So he took his bicycle and rode over to the school, but there was no one there. The place was closed. People were moving up Seiso Street toward the police station at the top end of the township.

Word was going around that the Congress leaders wanted everyone to go there and present themselves for arrest for not carrying their passes.

Zondo was not political but, well, everyone was heading that way so he went along too, pushing his bicycle in the thickening crowd. When he arrived at the police station a sizeable crowd was already gathered around the place, chanting and singing and pressing up against the high security fence that surrounded the squat red-brick building. A number of armed policemen were lined up inside the grounds and, just thirty yards from where Zondo was standing, were two Saracen armoured cars with machine guns mounted on their turrets.

The crowd thickened as the day wore on. Now word went around that someone from Pretoria, someone important, was coming to speak, perhaps to tell them that the pass laws had been abolished, that the campaign had been successful. Anticipation rose. More people arrived. The noise and the pressure on the fence increased. At 1:50 exactly, Zondo recalls, there was a commotion at the gate over to his right. He couldn't see just what was happening, but it seemed a fat woman had been bumped by a police car as it tried to drive through the gate. Suddenly, as he was looking at this, Zondo heard a chattering noise in front of him.

"Brains," he murmured, shaking his head in a vague way that conveyed a sense of disbelief still, after twenty-nine years. "I just saw brains. Skulls were bursting open in front of me."

He fell, spread-eagled over his bicycle. Bodies fell on top of him. He was facing the Saracen and he could see a tongue of flame turning into a white haze "like hailstones in a storm" coming from the barrel of its gun as it raked back and forth across the crowd. It stopped and there was silence for a moment, then it started again.

When it stopped a second time there was a great silence. Everything was still. Then a few people started to get up and Zondo heard some sobs and cries. "I woke up. I looked around. If you Doom flies, you see how they lie down," Zondo said, using the trade name of an insecticide spray. "It was something like that. I got up and started to walk away. I saw some kids from my class. They started shouting, '*Tichara othunswe! Tichara othunswe!*' which is Sisotho for 'Our teacher has been shot.'

"I was shocked," Zondo said. "I thought, am I dead? I remembered magazine stories I had read as a child, of King Arthur's soldiers in battle, who kept on running after they had been beheaded, and I wondered if that had happened to me."

The children, wide-eyed, pointed to his leg. He looked down and saw that his left calf muscle had been shot away. At the sight of it he collapsed.

Sixty-nine people were shot dead at Sharpeville that day and 180 were wounded. Michael Zondo spent three months in Soweto's Baragwanath Hospital recovering from his wound. When it had healed he was arrested and charged with incitement and public violence, along with seventy-four others. He was acquitted after a fifteen-month trial, but he never got promoted in the state-run education system and still holds a junior position at the age of fifty-seven.

THERE IS NO memorial to the Sharpeville Massacre as there is to the women and children who died in the Boer concentration camps, but it holds the same symbolic place in the pilgrimage of martyrdom of an oppressed people. Its powerful imagery of peaceful protest ending in violent death burned itself into the soul of the black resistance and changed its course of action in a fateful way.

Sharpeville was the turning point when black Nationalist politics was outlawed, when it went underground and switched from strategies of nonviolence to those of guerrilla struggle. When what had been a civil-rights campaign turned into a civil war of sorts. When the white government poured forth a torrent of security legislation as it had a torrent of apartheid legislation before, and South Africa started becoming a police state. When violence met violence in an escalating spiral. When, with the black opposition silenced, what little public debate there had been between black and white ceased and the possibility of a political solution to the race conflict was replaced by the certainty of confrontation.

For nearly fifty years black South Africans had pursued their struggle against oppression and exploitation with consummate patience. Politely, deferentially they had petitioned the white government for a better deal and been ignored. They had put their faith in a white change of heart, believing that one day the white man's professed commitment to Christian charity, democracy, and justice would bear fruit, but nothing ever came of it. For most of this time they were not even asking for equality, never mind claiming the right to run the country. All they asked for was a better deal under the system of white "trusteeship," but even this was ignored and the deal they got became steadily worse. When they faced dispossession by the Land Act in 1913 and the loss of their small but important voting rights in the Cape in 1936, they had gone to London to plead for intercession and been advised to go home again and work through the domestic political system in which they had no vote and no leverage. They had gone to Versailles and to the League of Nations to seek support from the international community and they had been ignored there. But they never lost patience and they never wavered in their commitment to nonviolent methods of conducting their campaigns.

The African National Congress had been founded under the strong influence of Gandhi's philosophy of nonviolence, and it had been further influenced by Booker T. Washington, the conservative black American leader who advocated black advancement within the framework of segregation rather than confrontation with the system. In particular the ANC leaders were influenced by the white missionaries in the schools and the white liberals in the South African Parliament who were their friends and mentors, who were in fact the reference group for the black intellectual elite with its bourgeois aspirations, and who counselled patience and moderation. Do not show impatience, they advised, and above all do not give the impression of militancy or radicalism, for that will seem like black unruliness, and it will provoke resistance within the white establishment and delay the change of heart without which there can be no hope of black advancement. Strikes and protest demonstrations occurred in the 1920s when the pressures of the Depression and Clemens Kadalie's unionism brought a brief surge of militancy, but for the most part the notion that blacks might force political change through their own self-assertion and through the mobilization of the masses had not yet occurred.

World War II brought a change in this as in so many other things. The demands of the wartime economy brought a surge of industrial growth and with it a rapid expansion of the urban black labour force. With so many white workers drawn into the armed forces, blacks advanced into more of the semiskilled occupations. And, as always happens with deprived communities, as their economic circumstances improved their aspirations and sense of frustration increased also. There was a revival of trade unionism, which had faded after the decline of Kadalie's Industrial and Commercial Union in the 1930s. Above all the war itself brought hope to blacks just as it had done to the Afrikaner Nationalists. While Afrikaners hoped that a German victory might give them back their longed-for republic, blacks hoped that their loyalty to the government and support for the war effort would be rewarded in the event of an Allied victory. Thousands of blacks had volunteered for military service, and although by a curious twist of the racist mind they were not allowed to bear arms—blacks should not shoot whites, even if they were the enemy—they served as drivers and stretcher bearers and died like the combat troops in the dust of the western desert and in the drive up Italy. And in those countries they tasted life without the colour bar for the first time and sensed what it might be like not to be treated as second-class citizens in their own country. From Cairo to

Tripoli to Naples and Pisa, they went into cafés and bars and bordellos and no "whites-only" signs stopped them. They had gone there, often enough, with buddies who were white—Cockneys and Kiwis and Yanks and sometimes even white South Africans, drinking and carousing as soldiers do in a mateship born of danger shared—and they had gone home again to tell of this new freedom that would surely come soon to liberate South Africa now that Hitler and racism had been defeated.

For it had been a war fought against racism, a war for freedom and liberty. Prime Minister Smuts had said so, time and again, in his addresses to the nation and to the troops "Up North." The Atlantic Charter endorsed national self-determination, and so did the newly founded United Nations with its Universal Declaration of Human Rights. Throughout the nonwhite world, all this lit a flame of expectation, and when decolonization began the flame burned brighter still.

When it all came to nothing, when after the war Smuts showed more interest in reconciling his white political rivals than in rewarding the blacks, there was bitter disillusionment. The intransigence of white South Africa was brought home with a vengeance within a year of the war's end. First the Smuts government, responding to pressure from conservative English voters in Natal, passed a "Ghetto Act" prohibiting Indians from owning property outside of certain designated areas. Outraged Indians launched a passive resistance campaign for the first time since the days of Gandhi, and two thousand of them went to prison.

Three months later Smuts ordered the crushing of a major black miners' strike. Postwar inflation was sending prices soaring, but the black miners' wages remained pegged at the paltry prewar level of £3 11s 6d a month. Poverty among the migrant workers' families in the reserves was extreme, and the infant mortality rate was rising rapidly, but the Chamber of Mines rejected a demand by the African Mine Workers' Union for a minimum wage of ten shillings a day. When the union asked for an interview to put its case the chamber did not even reply. And when the union called a strike, Smuts called out the police. In a week of ugly confrontations that shattered black illusions about a white change of heart, the police drove the miners back to work with batons and rifles, killing several and wounding more than a hundred. Two years later came Malan's election victory and the start of apartheid. It was the ultimate white rebuff.

Out of this disillusionment came a new militancy. Young blacks, catching the spirit of the times, formed a group within the ANC called the Youth League, which began pressing for a more assertive policy of civil disobedience. The group was led by a charismatic young intellectual named Anton Lembede, who developed a philosophy of "Africanism" based on the ideas of black racial pride, self-reliance, and self-assertion.

He rejected the old approach of appealing for a white change of heart and held that blacks would gain their rights only through militant and unrelenting struggle. Other members of the Youth League were Walter Sisulu, a self-educated washerwoman's son who had worked through a score of mine, factory, and domestic jobs picking up a fund of practical wisdom along the way, and two young lawyers, Oliver Tambo and Nelson Mandela.

The Youth League drew up a radical Programme of Action that called for civil disobedience, strikes, boycotts, and stay-at-homes. It thus committed the ANC to a new strategy based on mass action in defiance of the law. It also committed it to the goals of "national freedom" and "political independence." When the congress's old-guard leaders showed reluctance to adopt such confrontationist tactics, the young rebels organized their ouster, voting in a supporter of the Programme, Dr. James Moroka, as president and Sisulu as general secretary.

The Programme of Action was adopted and ushered in a new phase in the black resistance struggle. As the apartheid government poured forth its torrent of ideological legislation in the early 1950s, the ANC issued an ultimatum: unless six particularly unjust laws were repealed, a countrywide passive resistance campaign would be launched to defy them. So began the Defiance Campaign, a phase of the resistance struggle in South Africa that was roughly equivalent to the American civil-rights campaign with its marches and sit-ins and acts of civil disobedience, but that ended very differently.

For seven months blacks defied the apartheid laws, using whites-only entrances at railway stations, going into restricted areas without passes, defying curfew regulations and other laws. More than 8,500 people altogether went to jail. "Hey Malan," they chanted as they went, "open the jail doors, we want to enter, we volunteers. . . ." "*Senzenina*?" they sang, "What have we done, we the African people?" A new genre of freedom songs emerged as they did during the civil-rights campaign in America, but there was one key difference between the two experiences. In South Africa there was no Constitution guaranteeing the equality of all men and no Supreme Court to interpret that constitutional law. South African law prescribed inequality, so that is what its courts enforced. The defiers went to prison, and the more they defied the tougher the laws became and the longer their prison terms. A new Public Safety Act and a new Criminal Law Amendment Act made it a serious offence for anyone to defy any law or to "incite" anyone to do so. That made it a crime for newspapers even to report on the organization of something like the Defiance Campaign. The penalties were up to five years' imprisonment or a fine of £500, or both, with the possibility of ten lashes added. Moroka, Sisulu, Mandela, and others were tried under the Suppression of Communism Act for their leadership of the campaign, and fifty-two ANC leaders were served with banning orders prohibiting them from attending gatherings.

There were, too, several violent incidents during the course of the campaign despite its commitment to nonviolence and the fact that a code of discipline was put to every volunteer. Some activists claimed these were provoked by the authorities to discredit the campaign, but the facts are certain. As the activist Frantz Fanon put it, when tensions rise and the state tries to intimidate rebellious elements by bringing out guns and putting on displays of force, nerves get jangled, aggression prompts aggressiveness, and the guns start going off by themselves.[1] At a railway station near Port Elizabeth a white policeman opened fire on two blacks he suspected of having stolen a pot of paint. An enraged black crowd at the station rioted and eleven people were killed and twenty-seven injured. In East London, a government ban on meetings resulted in a prayer meeting being held instead. When police baton-charged the prayer meeting the crowd threw stones at them and the police opened fire in return, killing several blacks and wounding many. In a paroxysm of rage the crowd turned and killed the first whites they saw—a nun and an insurance agent who were coming to help the wounded. In Kimberley police opened fire on a black crowd, killing fourteen and wounding thirty-five, and elements in the crowd responded by attacking administration buildings in the neighbourhood.

So the Defiance Campaign ground to a halt without achieving its objectives, but it was not without significant consequences. It mobilized huge numbers of blacks who had been politically dormant and submissive, and by involving them in political activism made them newly aware of their situation and laid the foundations of a new political culture in the townships. The signed-up membership of the ANC soared from a few thousand to more than one hundred thousand and it became firmly established in the black mind as the movement of the people.

Other nonviolent campaigns followed. When the government ordered black women to carry passes too—they had been exempt before—women all over the country organized protest demonstrations, culminating in a massive march on Pretoria on August 9, 1956 when twenty thousand of them stood before the Union Buildings while their leaders knocked on the prime minister's door and presented their petitions of protest.

Most important of all, at a Congress of the People the so-called Freedom Charter was adopted as a vision of a future South Africa beyond apartheid, a democratic, nonracial South Africa in which black and white

1. Frantz Fanon, *The Wretched of the Earth* (New York, 1963), p. 71.

would live together in peace and harmony. Here was Martin Luther King's dream in a different setting, presented not in the grand theatre of a capital city with the Lincoln Memorial as backdrop but on a battered stretch of veld under some blue-gum trees at a place called Kliptown, in what is now Soweto.

It was June 1955. The ANC had formed an alliance with the Indian Congress, the Coloured People's Congress, a white organization called the Congress of Democrats, which contained many members of the outlawed Communist party, and the nonracial, left-wing South African Congress of Trade Unions. They all participated. The ANC invited others as well, the Liberal party and even Smut's old party, the United party, which was now the official Opposition in the white Parliament and growing steadily more conservative in its quest to win back voters from the National party. Though they did not come, the gesture of inviting them was significant. As Albert Luthuli, the new ANC president who had replaced James Moroka, envisaged it, the gathering was a practical demonstration of what the national convention of 1910 should have been.[2] More to the point, it served to demonstrate how the ANC envisaged a future national convention.

Three thousand delegates turned up under the blue-gum trees, two-thirds of them black and the rest more or less evenly divided between whites, "coloureds," and Indians. Mary Benson describes the scene:

> Along the roadside, stalls sold bright soft drinks and mixed confections. One visitor from England thought it more like a black Derby Day than a solemn conclave of revolutionaries, as the crowd rolled up singing, laughing, shouting, wearing gay clothes—men in vivid Basotho blankets and straw hats, women in brilliant saris or in congress blouses, with a variety of scarves and *doeks*. It was like South Africa in miniature—doctors and peasants, labourers and shopkeepers, ministers and domestic servants, students and city workers, teachers and housewives; and all the races in due proportion.[3]

Midway through, armed police arrived. The police commandant approached the chairman of the gathering, a white man, Piet Beyleveld, and they spoke briefly. Beyleveld announced to the crowd that the police wanted to remove all papers and documents and he appealed to them to cooperate, to keep calm and not make trouble. The police then moved through the crowd taking their papers and removing posters and banners.

2. Mary Benson, *The Struggle for a Birthright*, p. 174.

3. Ibid., p. 175.

> As Special Branch men crowded the platform and rifled the pockets and handbags of the speakers the addresses went on—whites speaking with a new emotional intensity; an Indian with high-strung truculence; but the Africans seemed joyful, almost triumphant. . . . To an outside observer it seemed that in the incongruous tension, the jeering policemen and the laughing Africans were teetering on the edge of violence. Once, the African band in its shabby uniforms with its battered instruments began banging out a compulsive rhythm—the crowd started to sway in a way that looked as if it could only have one climax. But the band changed its tune—the moment passed.[4]

Despite this provocation the gathering went ahead to draft and adopt its Freedom Charter, an inspired declaration that still stands today, thirty-five years later, as a monument to the remarkable spirit of reconciliation that somehow manages to survive under apartheid and that has acquired a kind of canonical status in the resistance movement. It is like a combination of King's dream and a political programme. It begins in sonorous language: "We, the People of South Africa, declare for all our country and the world to know: that South Africa belongs to all who live in it, black and white, and that no government can justly claim authority unless it is based on the will of all the people." It then goes on to set out its aims: the people shall govern; all national groups shall have equal rights; the people shall share in the country's wealth; the land shall be shared among those who work it; all shall be equal before the law; all shall enjoy equal human rights; there shall be work and security; the doors of learning and culture shall be opened; there shall be houses, security, and comfort; and there shall be peace and friendship.

In more specific terms the Charter pledges that all homes will be protected by law from arbitrary police raids, that people will be free to travel from countryside to town without restriction, that everyone will have the same right to work, that the aged, the disabled, and the sick will be cared for by the State, and, in its most explicit commitment to socialism, that "the mineral wealth beneath the soil, the banks and monopoly industry shall be transferred to the ownership of the people as a whole."

A year later there was a knocking on doors in the small hours of the morning all over South Africa as the authors of this document and the organizers of the Defiance Campaign were arrested and charged with treason. Eventually 156 leaders of the resistance movement, including a number of whites and nearly the entire national executive of the

4. Ibid., p. 178.

ANC—Luthuli, Mandela, Tambo, Sisulu, the organizers of the women's protests and the march on Pretoria—appeared in a special court in Pretoria to begin a trial that was to drag on for five years before the state case collapsed. By a fine twist of irony the chief prosecutor during the early years of the trial was Oswald Pirow, the old Nazi who had led the New Order movement during World War II and, by siding with his country's enemy while it was at war, might have been considered a prime candidate for a treason trial himself.

Pirow's case was that the accused were members of a conspiracy inspired by international communism to overthrow the South African state by violence. The Freedom Charter showed that the ultimate objective was the creation of a Communist state, and that it might also serve as a prelude to revolution.

So ended the decade of South Africa's civil-rights campaign. Though the accused were all acquitted, it was March 1961 before the final judgment was given, and by then the fateful turning point of Sharpeville had been passed.

Sharpeville was not the first massacre that had occurred in South Africa, nor even the worst. Thirty-nine years before, at a village in the eastern Cape called Bulhoek, Smuts had called out the police and the army to force a community of religious zealots to leave land on which they had settled in violation of antisquatting laws. The sect, known as the Israelites, were led by a charismatic prophet named Enoch Mgijima, who had gathered his flock there to await the end of the world. When they refused to leave, insisting that they could only obey orders from God communicated directly to Mgijima, five detachments of troops and police opened fire with rifles and machine guns, killing 183 of them. That was a casualty figure almost three times as high as Sharpeville, yet it aroused no international outcry and little sense of shock within South Africa. A judge at the trial of surviving Israelites concluded that they had used their religion as a cloak. They were bound together, he said, by "a crazy notion that the day was coming when the black man would have his freedom."[5]

Nothing more vividly illustrates the change that has taken place in the postwar world than the contrast in reaction to these two events. Sharpeville produced an outburst of international horror and condemnation the likes of which South Africa had not experienced before. The shock waves sent the Johannesburg stock market crashing, property prices plummeted as thousands of whites emigrated, and a new sense of rage swept through the black community.

5. A vivid account of the Bulhoek Massacre is contained in a booklet by Robert Edgar, *Because They Chose the Plan of God*, published by Ravan Press (Johannesburg, 1988).

"Sharpeville was decisive for me," says Neville Alexander, a "coloured" intellectual, who explains that the massacre prompted him to accept the principle of violent struggle for which he served eleven years in prison on Robben Island. "The day after Sharpeville I behaved in a very reckless fashion. I was so angry that I got very drunk that evening and started a terrible fracas, threatening to kill people with a tiny penknife. It had that effect. We were all pushed willy-nilly across this great divide. It marked a turning point to violence in a very systematic way." Countless others were radicalized in the same way.

The switch from nonviolence to violence was not immediate. For a time the ANC and the Pan-Africanist Congress, an offshoot movement which had broken away a year before, tried to continue as before but found it increasinglg difficult. A week after the massacre, wth mass protest marches and strikes occurring all over the country, the government declared a state of emergency and rounded up thousands of activist leaders. A fortnight later, on April 8, 1960, it declared both the ANC and PAC "unlawful organisations." That meant not only that the two main black political movements—all of black nationalism—were outlawed but that to further any of their aims was a criminal offence. They became unmentionable in the press and as factors in the South African public debate they ceased to exist—except as demonized images which the government could use to frighten white voters into supporting ever tougher security legislation.

Luthuli was banned and restricted to the remote district of Groutville in Natal. Robert Sobukwe, leader of the PAC, was imprisoned on Robben Island for three years for his part in organizing the pass-law protests—a sentence that stretched to nine years as year after year Parliament decided to extend it, after which Sobukwe was released to live under house arrest at his home in Kimberley until his death in 1978.

The ANC developed a New Plan, reorganizing itself to function underground. It sent Tambo abroad to lobby international support and made Mandela leader of a National Action Council whose job was to organize continuing protest activity. Working underground, Mandela issued a demand for a national convention to establish a new Union of *all* South Africans, warning the government that if it did not assent to this before declaring the country a republic under a new whites-only constitution on May 31, 1961, there would be a three-day stoppage of work nationwide.

The government responded by mobilizing the army and putting on a massive show of force. There were more detentions. The government warned that strikers would be fired from their jobs and endorsed out of the urban areas. The night before the stoppage was to begin troops encircled every major black township and helicopters flew over flashing searchlights on them. In the event many blacks did stay away from work, but not in sufficient numbers to make an impact. On the second day, conceding failure, Mandela called off the strike.

It was at that point that the ANC took the fateful decision to abandon nonviolence, reasoning that if naked force was to crush every peaceful demonstration it was futile to continue relying on nonviolent methods. So it was that in June 1961 Mandela and a handful of other ANC leaders who had managed to evade detention met secretly and decided to form a guerrilla arm called *Umkhonto we Sizwe*, or Spear of the Nation, which would sabotage selected installations and economic targets but endeavour to avoid harming human life.

Mandela slipped abroad to arrange training and the supply of weapons. He underwent a course in military training himself in Algeria before returning to South Africa, where he continued working underground until he was captured and imprisoned.

Umkhonto's first action took place on December 16, 1961—the day of Blood River and the Afrikaner Covenant—when saboteurs blew up electricity installations and government offices in Johannesburg and Port Elizabeth. A few days before, in Oslo, King Olaf of Sweden had presented Albert Luthuli with the Nobel Peace Prize.

CHAPTER ELEVEN

Of Violence and Restraint

> To be, or not to be—that is the question.
> Whether 'tis nobler in the mind to suffer
> The slings and arrows of outrageous fortune,
> Or to take arms against a sea of troubles
> And by opposing end them.
>
> WILLIAM SHAKESPEARE

VIOLENCE IS the Rubicon of revolution. It is the crossing point at which the civil disobedient, remaining within the political system and striving to reform it, becomes a revolutionary seeking to overthrow it. And, as Crane Brinton has shown, that process, once begun, has a dynamic within it that tends to ever greater extremism as the firebrands, the great haters, cannibalize the moderates.

Frantz Fanon, the Martiniquan psychiatrist who was a spokesman for the revolution that gave Algeria its independence from France in 1962 and whose writings have acquired an almost scriptural importance for some Third World revolutionaries, has offered a glimpse of where that process can lead. To Fanon the use of violence in achieving the revolutionary overthrow of an oppressor is not merely a means to an end, something to be reluctantly embarked upon, but itself an essential part of the liberatory process.[1] Fanon saw the mind of the oppressed as being set in what he called a Manichean mould in which everything about the colonizers is regarded as evil and everything about the oppressed as good.[2] To the oppressed native the colonizer never ceases to

1. See Frantz Fanon, *The Wretched of the Earth*, pp. 35–106.

2. Manicheanism, a religion founded by the Persian prophet Mani in the third century, spread to many parts of the world, including Europe, until the twelfth century—a combination of Gnostic Christianity, Buddhism, Zoroastrianism, and other elements; its basic doctrine concerned the conflict between light and darkness, with the light being good and the darkness evil.

be the enemy, the opponent, the foe that must be overthrown. It is a syndrome that produces a need for cathartic violence and revenge.

"The appearance of the settler," Fanon wrote, "has meant in the terms of syncretism the death of the aboriginal society, cultural lethargy, and the petrification of individuals. For the native, life can only spring up again out of the rotting corpse of the settler."[3] The oppressed masses have an intuition that they can achieve their liberation only through violence, for that is the only thing that can break the power of the oppressor and restore their own emotional health. "At the level of individuals, violence is a cleansing force. It frees the native from his inferiority complex and from his despair and inaction: it makes him fearless and restores his self-respect."[4]

The colonizer's world is a hostile world which spurns the native but of which the native is at the same time envious. So the native is filled with anger and an impulse to take the settler's place, to turn the tables on him. "He is in fact ready at a moment's notice to exchange the role of the quarry for that of the hunter. The native is an oppressed person whose permanent dream is to become the persecutor."[5] Fanon's revolutionaries despise compromise and reconciliation. Like Brinton's great haters, they have a single-minded objective, which is to kill and cast out their oppressors until "the last shall be first and the first last," whereafter, their sins and their abasement washed from them in blood, grace will be unto them, and peace—and the millennium of liberation.

More than a generation has passed since the black nationalist movements in South Africa crossed their Rubicon of violence, and although they have gone some way down the road to greater extremism, elements of reluctance and restraint are still evident. At the outset it briefly seemed that there might be a Fanonesque development when the PAC formed an armed wing called Poqo—meaning "pure" and "alone"—which adopted a crudely simple strategy of calling on the masses to kill and drive out the "white bosses" and take over their homes. In late 1962 a posse of men carrying axes, pangas, and various self-made weapons marched into the old wineland town of Paarl, near Cape Town, and managed to kill two whites and wound four others before the police overwhelmed them. There were a few other incidents, but Poqo was poorly organized and quickly crushed, and it disappeared. No other movement has sought to go that way since.

As for the ANC and its Umkhonto wing, although the South African

3. Ibid., p. 93.

4. Ibid., p. 94.

5. Ibid., p. 53.

government portrays them as bloodthirsty terrorists, they have never tried to polarize the struggle along Fanonesque lines, nor do they subscribe to Fanon's ideology of violence or his apocalyptic vision of retribution.

Inevitably the commitment to avoid harming human life has not been maintained. As militant black youths poured out of South Africa after the 1976 Soweto riots and the crisis of 1984–87, brutalized and radicalized by their encounters with the police and swelling the ranks of the exiled ANC from one thousand to fourteen thousand, the leadership came under pressure to intensify the struggle. First it decided to target security-force personnel as well as installations and economic targets; then to regard farmers in border areas as legitimate military targets because they are enlisted in the civil-defence units of the armed forces; then to condone civilian casualties that might be inflicted in the course of such actions. The pressure from some of the young radicals now is for a no-holds-barred campaign that would include attacks on "soft" civilian targets to maximize impact and break the barrier of insularity that seals whites off from the pain of the townships. The older leaders resist but have little control over what the Umkhonto cadres do once they are in the field.

The lines have become blurred. In May 1983 a car-bomb exploded in a crowded street in downtown Pretoria outside a building housing the headquarters of the South African air force, killing nineteen people and injuring nearly two hundred, many of them civilian shoppers and office workers. When the ANC began land-mining farm roads in the northern Transvaal in 1985, the blasts killed women and children as well as black farm workers. There have been bombings in a shopping centre in the seaside resort town of Amanzimtoti, in a Durban beachfront restaurant, in a fast-food Wimpy bar in downtown Johannesburg, outside a courthouse, and outside a rugby stadium.

Oliver Tambo, president of the ANC in exile, has made known his disapproval of guerrillas violating the guidelines. At a press conference in 1984 he publicly criticized a bombing in Durban that killed four civilians and wounded twenty-seven. "Somebody was inexcusably careless," he said. "This sort of thing has the effect of distorting our policy. The failure to take precautions and to avoid hitting people who are not intended to be hit has become intolerable." But the blurring has continued, and differences of opinion on the issue revealed themselves in a more recent statement by Umkhonto's new chief of staff, Chris Hani, whose views are closer to those of the young militants. He condoned bomb attacks like these. They were intended, he said, to shake the whites out of their complacency. "Their life is good. They go to their cinemas, they go to their *braaivleis* [barbecue parties], they go to their five-star hotels. That's why they are supporting the system. It guarantees a happy life for them, a sweet life. Part of our campaign is to prevent that sweet life."[6]

But although the violence has escalated and become more indiscriminate in its targetting, it is still remarkably low level for a conflict that has been going on for so long. Considering the violence of state repression, the degree of restraint is quite unusual in modern revolutionary movements. Although the ANC has been the target of several assassinations and assassination attempts, it has never sought to retaliate in this way. It has no hit squad and no hit list. No black person has ever made an attempt on the life of a white South African leader, and President De Klerk and members of his cabinet move about with less security protection than just about any other political leaders in the Western world.

Is there going to be a blood bath? People in Europe and America keep asking that question, in a way that suggests that they think such prolonged repression must surely have such a result. Technically it is possible, of course: as black orators sometimes point out in moments of anger, there are domestic servants in the homes of nearly every white family in South Africa who could quite easily perform some kind of *Kristallnacht* of mass retribution. But I don't think there will be. I believe this kind of Fanonesque impulse is alien to the black African mind; it is not part of the culture as it perhaps is among the North African people Fanon observed, and I do not believe it will manifest itself for any instinctive or inevitable reason. It has not happened elsewhere in sub-Saharan Africa. Everywhere in the continent white minorities have feared the worst and nowhere has the worst happened. They feared the worst in Kenya when Jomo Kenyatta took over in 1964, "a leader to darkness and death" as a British governor had called him, but they came to respect and put their faith in him after independence, the Mzee, the father of the nation, who stabilized the place and made whites feel secure and led Kenya into an era of unprecedented racial harmony. They feared the worst in the Congo, and in Ruanda and Burundi, and in Northern Rhodesia and Nyasaland and it did not happen. Whites fled in the thousands from these countries, and in the tens of thousands from Angola and Mozambique, planeloads and carloads and truckloads and even yachtloads, and when they arrived in Salisbury and Johannesburg and Durban they explained that they had to get out before their throats were cut, so adding to the fears and prejudices of those whites who lived farther south. But it was not true. Their throats were not going to be cut. Those who stayed have prospered, including a sprinkling of Afri-

6. Interview by John Battersby, *Weekly Mail*, October 16, 1988.

kaner farmers near Eldoret in the Kenya highlands and around Enkeldoorn and Chipinge in Zimbabwe.

Zimbabwe, of course, has been the most remarkable of all. A terrible war was fought, great suffering endured, to stave off this fate worse than death in what was Rhodesia. And when finally in 1980 it was over and the unthinkable happened and that extremist Robert Mugabe, the worst of them all, took over, he offered—reconciliation! Thirty-five thousand people died in the Zimbabwean war, black Africa's ugliest, with fearful atrocities committed on both sides, yet today, a handful of years later, black and white live together harmoniously and with no sign of vengeance or retribution. The tables have not been turned. The former prime minister, Ian Smith, who imprisoned Mugabe for ten years and refused even to let him attend his only child's funeral when the boy died tragically during that time, who inflamed the white resistance with his horror stories of what black rule would mean, lives unmolested in retirement on his farm and until recently had a seat in Parliament. Other white farmers, who were Smith's most ardent supporters, who financed his party, supported his repressive policies, and fought in his war are prospering today and thanking God that that good chap Mugabe is there to stabilize the country and keep the extremists in check.

No lust for vengeance, no apocalyptic retribution, despite the legacy of grievances. The past, as they like to say, is another country. Something in the African psyche, in that old collectivist spirit of *ubuntu*, the notion that people are people through other people, diffuses the individual ego and makes it less prone to the phenomena of repressed anger and displaced aggression that characterize other cultures and lead white Westerners to believe that a bloodbath *must* be the logical outcome of apartheid. Black Africa has had more than its share of internal strife since independence, of ethnic conflicts and coups and civil wars, but the one problem it has not had—anywhere—is a racial conflict of any seriousness between black and white.

This does not mean that black South Africans are not capable of great anger, hatred, and violence, even a ritual violence and perhaps an experience of a cleansing catharsis. I have seen all of that at various times. And there have been acts of spontaneous vengeance against whites, too, such as the killing of the nun and the insurance agent in East London in 1952, and of a social researcher, Melvyn Edelstein, who was caught in the middle of a riot in Soweto in 1976 and hacked to death. What I do not believe is that the black African masses have an intuitive yearning for vengeance and retribution. A yearning for justice, yes, and for release from poverty and oppression, but no dream of themselves becoming the persecutors, of turning the tables of apartheid on the white South Africans. For too long black South Africans have been the victims of racism and, like Jews, they abhor it. They do not want to invert it, they want to eradicate it.

No blacks I have ever met envisage a future South Africa without whites. Not since the days of Nongqause and the frontier wars have they dreamt of driving the whites into the sea. Although as I have said in no African country has the black majority sought to oust or turn the tables on its white settlers, it was at least possible for them to contemplate doing so, and during the anticolonialist campaigns it was expedient to speak of it, to cry "out with the whites," and rouse the masses with the slogan "Africa for the Africans." In Ghana, where Kwame Nkrumah began the process in the 1950s and became the symbol of a new spirit of pan-Africanism, there were never more than seven thousand whites; even in Kenya it was not unthinkable to envisage the ejection of thirty thousand white settlers. But 4.5 million whites is another matter. Moreover, during the span of three and a half centuries—the same length of time as the white settlement of North America—white culture, white religion, white cities, and white factories have woven themselves into the lives and minds of the black South Africans in a complex, frustrating, love-hate relationship which simply cannot be unravelled and which makes thoughts of antiwhiteism and black separatism far more drastic in South Africa than anywhere else on the continent.

Other blacks have some difficulty understanding this. In Accra, the Ghanaian capital where some of Nkrumah's Africanist spirit still lives on after him, I heard students and journalists ask hard questions of an ANC delegation that was having talks there with a group of Afrikaner dissidents that had flown out to meet them. What are you doing talking to these whites? they asked. Aren't they your enemies, your oppressors? Why aren't you killing them instead of talking to them? Patiently, labouriously and to the considerable confusion of the white Afrikaners who had been conditioned by years of propaganda to think of these people as antiwhite terrorists bent on the destruction of the *volk*, the ANC spokesmen explained their movement's commitment to nonracialism, to building a future South Africa that will belong to all its people, black and white, while their questioners listened and looked bemused. What kind of freedom fighters were these?

Part of this is the black South Africans' strong religious ethic. The Christian faith, when it was implanted in South Africa, found fertile soil and flourished wondrously—and in a particular way. While Afrikaners joined the segregationist Dutch Reformed Churches and developed their exclusionist civil religion, blacks joined the evangelical churches founded by English and Continental missionaries who preached the brotherhood of man and were at least nominally integrationist. Their Christian churches became something of a refuge from the psychological annihilation of white prejudice and helped to inculcate an inclusionist view that was the counterpoint to the DRC and Afrikaner nationalism.

From the earliest frontier days of Phillip, Van der Kemp, Moffat, and David Livingstone right through to the present there have also been white men of the Church who have identified with blacks and championed their cause. Their actions and the kind of Christianity they preached have deeply influenced the black population at large. Together with the mission-school teachers associated with them, they exercised a powerful influence on South Africa's emerging black political intelligentsia, contributing to both their inclusionist outlook and their distaste for strategies of violence even on the part of those who have now adopted them. Albert Luthuli, leader of the ANC through the Defiance Campaign until it was banned, was a Methodist lay preacher. Oliver Tambo, the leader in exile now and the man who has made the tough decisions on violence, had hoped to become an Anglican priest. Winnie Mandela, wife of the imprisoned Nelson Mandela, presumptive head of the ANC and the man who founded Umkhonto we Sizwe, is a devout Anglican, and when she was banished to Brandfort the bishop of Bloemfontein drove out regularly to conduct a communion service for her at her place of confinement. Barney Pityana, Steve Biko's closest associate in the Black Consciousness movement in the 1970s, has become a priest in exile. And then of course there are Archbishop Desmond Tutu, Dr. Allan Boesak, and the Rev. Frank Chikane, major theologians and major spokesmen for the cause of black liberation, the ultimate symbols of the way faith and rebellion are intertwined in South Africa, each influencing the other.

As with the Church, so with the white liberals and radicals who from Thomas Pringle's day have spoken out against the mainstream of white prejudice. They have done so in far greater numbers, with greater courage, greater consistency, and over a much longer period of time than any other group of whites elsewhere in Africa, and over the years their commitment to the ideal of nonracialism helped to blur the lines of racial division.

Black recognition of the role such whites have played found its most vivid expression in a mass turnout of black people at the funeral of a white civil-rights campaigner, Molly Blackburn, in Port Elizabeth in 1986. Molly Blackburn was not a radical: she represented the liberal Progressive Federal party in the Cape Provincial Council and was a member of the Black Sash, an energetic and effective women's civil-rights organization. Nor did she die a political martyr: she was killed in a road accident. But Molly Blackburn had acquired a personal reputation in the region for her courageous individual efforts to help detained prisoners and their families and expose abuses by the authorities, so that when she died twenty thousand black people from Port Elizabeth's townships and beyond turned up at her funeral service in a little church in a white suburb. It was at the height of the massive racial crisis then shaking South Africa, when one might have expected antiwhite feelings to be running high in the townships, but they came en masse, many carrying banners with political slogans and wearing the colours of the outlawed ANC, to honour a white anti-apartheid crusader who had died.

Not least has been the influence of white Communists. The South African Communist party, quickly recovering from its aberrant support for the white worker cause in 1922, turned at an early stage to offering practical assistance to the burgeoning black working class in the cities. The party ran night schools at which volunteer teachers gave adult education courses and instruction in trade unionism. Over the years a series of remarkable individuals committed themselves to the black cause with a dedication and selflessness that made a deep impression, beginning with a lawyer named S. F. Bunting, who defended blacks in court free of charge in the twenties, through Bram Fischer, a top barrister who defended them in the treason trial in the 1950s and then died in prison serving a life sentence for aiding the sabotage campaign, to Ruth First, who was assassinated by a letter-bomb in Maputo in 1982, and her husband, Joe Slovo, now general secretary of the Communist party and a member of the ANC's national executive in exile.

These white people won the trust of blacks by identifying with them and by building close personal friendships. Thirty years before any other white party, the South African Communist party dropped all colour barriers and welcomed blacks into its ranks. "We don't know communism," Luthuli once said, "all we know is that those men and women came to us to help us. I don't deny that some might have had ulterior motives; all I am concerned about is that they came to assist me fight racial oppression, and they have no trace of racialism or of being patronizing—just no trace of it at all."[7] Their influence spread well beyond the leadership level. Not long ago, while visiting a threatened "black spot" community in the western Transvaal, I was struck by the articulateness of one of the village councillors, an elder of the tribe now well into his seventies. On learning that he had never had any formal schooling, I asked where he had learnt to speak such excellent English. "At the Twentieth Century cinema," he replied, explaining that he had

7. Quoted in Mary Benson, *South Africa: The Struggle for a Birthright*, p. 201.

worked as a projectionist's assistant at Johannesburg's biggest movie house, absorbing the language and, somewhat in the manner of Ronald Reagan, a cinematic view of the world from years of movie watching. "I got my education there—and from the Communists," he added. It turned out he had attended one of the Communist night schools as a young man, and his recollections of the volunteers who taught there, who befriended him and took him into their homes, seemed as warm as of Carmen Miranda, the tutti-frutti dancer who had been his favourite star.

This relationship, spun out over so many years, has also influenced the nonracialist outlook of mainstream black nationalism. In addition to the personal bridges it has built, it has encouraged the ANC and other supporters of what is now called the Charterist movement—made up of supporters of the Freedom Charter—to apply a Marxist analysis to the South African conflict, to regard it more as a class struggle than a racial one, with the forces of capitalism making exploitative use of the race factor. Surprising as it may seem in a conflict whose global image is so starkly racial, this analysis is widely accepted in the black community and gives strong underpinning to the nonracialist outlook. Ironically the influences of communism and Christianity have in this sense both worked in the same direction.

There are more practical considerations, too, behind the commitment to nonracialism. Black nationalists in South Africa have seen the consequences of a mass white exodus from countries that gained their independence from European rule. They saw Mozambique and Angola particularly crash to ruin, their people plunged into starvation instead of being liberated, as white expertise and technical know-how withdrew overnight from an integrated economy. Even less drastic flights can cause a crisis of expectations for governments that have promised a new dawn and are faced with declining living standards instead. Black South Africans do not want that, and they know that a large-scale white departure from their country would be more catastrophic than anywhere.

This does not mean all blacks subscribe to the nonracial idea. There has long been an Africanist strain running through black South African politics, which at times has exercised a strong emotional appeal, both as a negative reaction to apartheid and as a positive identification with what was happening elsewhere in Africa and among black Americans. But each time it has subsided again and nonracialism has returned as the mainstream view.

The Africanist tendency first appeared in the early 1920s, at the time when Clemens Kadalie was leading the first black militants with his Industrial and Commercial Union and when echoes of Marcus Garvey's back-to-Africa movement reached South Africa from the United States.[8] Word went around that Garvey, who had formed his Black Star shipping line to transport black Americans back to Africa, was sending a fleet to liberate South Africa and establish a black republic. *AmaMelika ayeza*, the Americans are coming: it began as a rumour and became a slogan until the South African government, growing alarmed that the militant black American might arrive himself to put a match to the keg his ideas had primed, declared him a prohibited immigrant.

The movement deepened into something more serious when a black intellectual named James Thaele, who had become an ardent follower of Garvey's Universal Negro Improvement Association while doing graduate study in the United States, returned to South Africa to spread the association's message of "Africa for the Africans." Thaele settled in Cape Town and quickly moved the Western Cape Congress of the ANC in a Garveyist direction. Kadalie, then operating from Cape Town, became an admirer. The South African police described Thaele at the time as "intensely anti-white in sentiment." A special report said of him that he had "refused point blank to cooperate with European communists, stating quite openly that he does not trust or wish to associate with any white man."[9]

In the militant atmosphere of the day, with Afrikaner nationalism in power for the first time and the Great Depression looming ahead, Thaele's influence spread. The official organ of the Cape ANC was named *The African World*, to identify it with Garvey's *Negro World*, and adopted the slogan: "Africa for the Africans and Europe for the Europeans." When Garvey wrote his treatise on "African fundamentalism" from a prison cell in Atlanta in 1925, *The African World* translated it into Sotho and published it in full with a message to its readers stating that "this letter is a guideline of the principles of government that shall be ours."[10] A year later the Johannesburg ANC newspaper, *Abantu-Batho*, also published a major article on Garvey's philosophy and commended him for arousing black racial consciousness. But by the end of the decade the movement had disintegrated and the ANC returned to the moderate mode it had been in before, petitioning once more for a

8. For the most thorough study of this neglected phase of South African political history, see Robert A. Hill and Gregory A. Pirio, "Africa for the Africans: The Garvey Movement in South Africa, 1920–1940," in Shula Marks and Stanley Trapido (Eds.), *The Politics of Race, Class and Nationalism in Twentieth Century South Africa* (London, 1987), pp. 209–43.

9. Ibid., p. 232.

10. Ibid., p. 235.

change of heart and a better deal within the white-run system. "Africa for the Africans" faded from the scene.

Africanism returned with Anton Lembede and the Youth League in the 1940s. Lembede had lived for a time in the Orange Free State to improve his knowledge of the Afrikaans language, and while there, observing Afrikaners and reading Verwoerd's *Transvaler* regularly, he had been struck by the political discipline and single-mindedness which their ideology had given to the Afrikaners. He decided blacks needed this, too, and so started developing an ideology of "Africanism." Not surprisingly since it was a counterpoint to Afrikaner nationalism, it was racially assertive and exclusivist. The slogan "Africa for the Africans" came back. "Africa is the blackman's country," Lembede wrote in a newspaper article in 1946. "Africans are the natives of Africa and they have inhabited Africa, their Motherland, from times immemorial; Africa belongs to them."[11]

His intellectual observations aside, it may be that the personal experience of living in the Free State also influenced Lembede's views. As Gail Gerhardt has noted, a high percentage of the Africanists originated in the Orange Free State and Transvaal, those old Boer republics where race relations have always been most strained, and she suggests that this may have bred an ingrained mistrust of whites not found to the same degree among blacks who grew up in the Cape Province and Natal where the core of ANC leadership has tended to come from.[12]

Like Hertzog, Lembede decided the uplifting of the oppressed had to begin with overcoming their fundamental psychological handicaps. Blacks had to throw off their crippling complexes of inferiority and dependence and rediscover a pride in their own cultural identity, their own history, and above all in their own God-given blackness. Not only did this have touches of Afrikaner nationalism but, in Lembede's anti-whiteist rhetoric and in his assertions that this revivified black pride could be achieved only through freedom, which in turn could come about only through unrelenting struggle, there were touches of Fanon as well. It stirred the youth of the day and moved the ANC into a new phase of militancy, but as an ideology Africanism faded once again after Lembede's sudden death in 1947 at the age of thirty-three.

It is a matter of speculation today whether Lembede would have stuck with his Africanist ideology or whether, like fellow Youth Leaguers Mandela, Tambo, and Sisulu, he would have been drawn back

11. In Thomas Karis and Gwendolen M. Carter (Eds.), *From Protest to Challenge: A Documentary History of African Politics in South Africa 1882–1964*, vol. 2 (Stanford, 1973), p. 317.

12. Gail M. Gerhardt, *Black Power in South Africa* (Berkeley, Cal., 1978), p. 142.

to nonracialism once the ANC had adopted the Programme of Action. The pattern, whenever this Africanist sentiment has burgeoned, has tended to be of that kind of synthesis. Africanism has been borne, almost generationally, on waves of renewed militancy by young people impatient for change and critical of what they regard as the excessive caution and timidity of the older leadership, and as each wave has its impact the movement has shifted toward a more militant position and the youth group has been absorbed, shedding its racial extremism in the process. The result each time has been a more militant movement but still a nonracialist one. "Sometimes young people come out who are strongly anti-white," Tambo told me in an interview in Lusaka in 1986. "Then we discuss it with them and they soon get to learn what the struggle is all about. It doesn't take away from their resolve and their determination, but it makes them loyal to the policies and the principles that govern the ANC." But as we have seen, the influx of angry youth has also pushed the ANC toward greater and more indiscriminate use of violence.

Not all the Youth Leaguers were fully absorbed, however. Some, notably Ashley Mda, who had been one of Lembede's closest associates and succeeded him as president of the Youth League, cleaved to the ideas of their mentor and formed a distinct group within the ANC which in 1954 began publishing its own journal, *The Africanist*. So the tradition was kept alive.

The great African revolution that began with Ghana's independence in 1957 brought its next resurgence. Everywhere the cry of "Africa for the Africans" and "White man go home" was being raised as the black people of the continent demanded the withdrawal of the colonial powers and Kwame Nkrumah articulated his utopian vision of a United States of Africa stretching from the Cape to Cairo and from Morocco to Madagascar. Every black person in South Africa thrilled to these developments, but it was adrenalin particularly to the Africanists who identified most directly with Nkrumah's themes and felt the ANC leadership, with its emphasis on inclusiveness and nonracialism, was out of step with the times. As the conflict sharpened, it led to the worst split in the history of the black resistance movement, when the Africanist group broke away from the ANC in 1959 to form the Pan-Africanist Congress (PAC) under the leadership of Robert Sobukwe, a respected intellectual then teaching at the University of the Witwatersrand.

The PAC attacked the Freedom Charter for its assertion that South Africa belonged to all. It belonged primarily, they contended, to black Africans, to the indigenous "sons of the soil." Whites were immigrant foreigners, guests of the Africans, who would have to adjust themselves to the interests of Africa and Africans. The Africanists attacked the leadership of the ANC for allowing this true doctrine of "Africanism" as conceived by Lembede to be swamped by foreign ideologies. It had succumbed, they said, to the influence of its white and Indian sympathizers and been taken over by Communists for their own extra-African purposes.

The central theme of the PAC was that the struggle to liberate South Africa had to be planned and carried out by blacks on their own. No white could ever work wholeheartedly for the total dismantling of the social order; however sympathetic whites might profess to be, as members of a pampered and privileged minority they would inevitably seek, consciously or unconsciously, to control the liberation movement and guide it in directions that would not be too destructive of their interests.

Therefore, only blacks could formulate the policies and programmes of the liberation movement and decide on the methods of struggle to be employed, and because they were the most ruthlessly oppressed group, only blacks in the end could establish a genuine democracy in which all inequality would be erased. "We aim politically," said Sobukwe in his address to the PAC's inaugural convention in 1959, "at government of the Africans by the Africans, for the Africans."[13]

Yet it was still not totally exclusionist. Faced with the implications of a future South Africa without whites, even the Africanists drew back. Everyone who owed his only loyalty to Africa and was prepared to accept the democratic rule of an African majority, Sobukwe explained, would be regarded as an African. It was the same kind of ambiguity that Hertzog had used in defining an Afrikaner during the Fusion years in the 1930s. Like Hertzog, too, Sobukwe presented his exclusionism as a transition phase, a sort of two-stream policy in which blacks would be separatist only until they had uplifted themselves psychologically and "pigmentocracy" had been destroyed, at which point all races would come together again as equal citizens and a person's colour would become irrelevant.

So the means were different but the end was the same as the democratic nonracialism envisaged by the ANC, the Africanist argument being that the ANC would fail to achieve that goal in any authentic way because of the interference their white allies would run along the way. Yet pursuing the Afrikaner analogy further, one is bound to wonder whether Sobukwe would have been any more successful than Hertzog was in dismounting the racist tiger without more extreme elements thrusting him aside and taking it over, as Malan and the Gesuiwerdes

13. The text of Sobukwe's address is in Karis and Carter, *From Protest to Challenge: A Documentary History of African Politics in South Africa 1882–1964*, vol. 3, pp. 510–17.

did. There is something inherently implausible about the idea of mobilizing a revolution on a racialist basis to achieve a nonracial objective.

One paradoxical twist in the tale expresses the kind of splayed thinking that sometimes occurs, in Western minds as well as South African, when whites view African politics through the prism of their own ideological prejudices. At the time of the PAC split a number of white liberals sided with the pan-Africanists because of their perceived anticommunism, even though communism per se was not the main issue on which their differences with the ANC turned. The incongruous result was that these white liberals found themselves in bed with the most determinedly antiwhite elements in the black community, while the Africanists found themselves embraced by the very people they most wanted to thrust aside. The same kind of incongruity shows itself today as the United States, in its search for black "moderates" to support against the "extremists" in South Africa, continues to stand back because of a perceived taint of communism from the one movement that throughout its history has consistently taken the most moderate position on race.

In any event the PAC tripped over its own militancy. In its eagerness to outdo the ANC, and perhaps out of a misguided faith in its own propaganda that black South Africa was ready for a mass uprising, it sought a major confrontation with the government before it had the organizational strength to survive it. In 1960, just one year after the PAC was formed, Sobukwe called for the national campaign to defy the pass laws that led to Sharpeville. The ANC had called for a campaign of demonstrations against the pass laws to begin on March 31. To upstage it, Sobukwe announced a more militant PAC campaign to begin on March 21, calling on people to go in their thousands to the police stations and invite arrest.

It made confrontation a certainty. And when it came and the government launched its crackdown, banning both organizations and arresting leaders, the ANC was better able to survive. The Africanists had always been few in number—Gerhardt estimates that those who thought of themselves as orthodox Lembedists had never numbered more than a few dozen[14]—and with only a flimsy organizational infrastructure, the PAC had little to hold it together, while the ANC, with a long history to keep it alive in the minds of the black community and an organizational network that by now had managed to establish itself in exile, was in a much stronger position.

The PAC still exists today in terms of political recognition abroad, at the United Nations and the Organization of African Unity, but its

14. Gerhardt, op. cit., p. 212.

internal existence has dwindled to a fraction of its external profile. The Africanist tradition did not disappear however. A decade later it was reincarnated in the Black Consciousness movement and in that form reached its most advanced and intellectually sophisticated level, before again going into decline. It could surge back again should the ANC ever falter: the Africanist philosophy has an inherent appeal to the spirit of militancy.

Black politics, in effect, went into recess through the 1960s. With the major black parties outlawed, it fell to white liberal organizations to articulate black grievances and keep the politics of protest alive. Blacks joined some of these organizations, until another law called the Improper Interference Act prohibited that too. There were some whites who spoke out bravely: Helen Suzman, the Progressive party's lone parliamentary representative; the writer Alan Paton, who was leader of the Liberal party; several white newspaper editors; and the National Union of South African Students (known by its acronym, Nusas). Robert F. Kennedy visited South Africa as Nusas's guest during those years and made an impact with his compassionate oratory. It was the high point of white liberalism and of white surrogate spokesmanship for the suffering blacks, and it is now obvious that sooner or later there had to be a reaction against it.

That reaction came toward the end of the decade, once again among the young and the militant, among the new generation of black students being educated at segregated universities but working politically with whites in Nusas. The resentment had slowly built up and now it overflowed. Not only did black students resent the fact that whites dominated the organization, but they believed this imposed limits on its militancy. The whites protested orally, over and over again, almost ritually, but that was as far as they were prepared to go. To Steve Biko, a young medical student at the University of Natal, this epitomized liberalism. It was not, as he saw it, an inspirational force that could lead to constructive action but a sterile dogma that concealed an unconscious attachment to the status quo. White liberals could concern themselves just sufficiently with the black man's plight to appease their consciences, and then switch off. As Biko put it, the liberals' view of apartheid was "an eye sore spoiling an otherwise beautiful view," an eye sore they could "take their eyes off" whenever they wanted to.[15]

This was a return to Africanist criticism against political cooperation with whites. Because of their privileged position even the most sympathetic whites would always, albeit unconsciously, seek to control the resistance movement and guide it in directions that would not be too

15. Quoted in Aelred Stubbs, *Steve Biko—I Write What I Like* (New York, 1978), p. 22.

destructive of their interests. So in 1969 Biko and a group of black students broke away from Nusas and formed their own organization, the South African Students Organization, or Saso. Around this core the Black Consciousness movement flourished for the next eight years.

But this time the theme of white rejection was less chauvinistic and more intellectually developed. With university students shaping it, the new version of Africanism was less narrowly based than the old, taking in a wider range of philosophical views. The slogan this time was not "Africa for the Africans" but "Black man, you are on your own," emphasizing the theme of self-reliance rather than racial exclusivity.

By the end of the 1960s nearly all of Africa was independent, while in the United States the civil-rights campaign had run its course and its Black Power aftermath had begun. A substantial body of literature emerged from these experiences, so Biko and his fellow students could draw on the work of many black leaders, writers, and intellectuals to broaden and reinforce their own thinking. They delved into Cheikh Ante Diop, the Senegalese cultural historian who has sought to reestablish the authenticity and importance of African race and culture in a world that denied it recognition; they read Léopold Senghor's philosophy of *négritude,* Kenneth Kaunda's African humanism, Julius Nyerere's concepts of self-reliance and African socialism, and the polemical writings, poetry, and plays of black Americans like Eldridge Cleaver, Stokeley Carmichael, Charles Hamilton, Langston Hughes, and Amiri Baraka. Above all they read Frantz Fanon. Although they never adopted his ideas of vengeance and racial hatred, they were deeply interested in his psychological analysis of the mind of both oppressor and oppressed, in his rejection of gradualism, and in his belief in polarizing the conflict to bring it to a head.

While Biko and his associates were occupied with these themes, at the same time a considerable cultural renaissance was taking place in the black South African community, with a new crop of writers and other artists producing work that echoed similar Black Consciousness themes. Indeed the literary movement preceded the political development and did much to lay the ground for it. Through the silent decade of the 1960s when overt black political activity seemed impossible, almost the only black voices that were heard were the writers'. New novelists, short-story writers, and poets appeared almost every day, articulating the frustrations and aspirations of South Africa's rapidly developing black urban industrial society, a society that had all other doors of expression closed to it and that was grappling with the twinned threats of cultural domination and political oppression. A whole new genre of protest theatre emerged, with black actors and directors dramatizing situations of everyday township life in workshop presentations, sometimes performed spontaneously and scripted only later. Some of these stunning successes went on to be acclaimed in London and New York.

The poetry in particular became an instrument of protest and an expression of black rage—rage and the desperate need to reestablish black pride and cultural identity:

> On a canvas stretching from here
> to Dallas, Memphis, Belsen, Golgotha
> I'll daub a white devil.
> Let me teach black truth
> That dark clouds aren't a sin of doom,
> but hope. Rain. Life.

That poem was written by Stanley Motjuwadi, a gentle journalist who until the 1960s spent his life writing stories for photomagazines. Sometimes the themes glorified blackness, sometimes the earthiness of Mother Africa, and sometimes, as in this poem by Mongane Wally Serote, a spirit of global black unity united in its African heritage:

> I'm the seed of this earth
> ready with my roots to spread deep into reality
> I've been a looked after
> black seed; by black saints and prophets
> by Sobukwe Mandela Sisulu
> Fanon Malcolm X George Jackson
> I'm the tree of this earth
> the breeze of the night makes my leaves whistle
> sad tunes of my earth
> I weep dew in the morning my way of meditation
> I'm the fruit of this earth, this time
> when I become ripe my beloved,
> let me be food for the children,
> I've been restless like leaves
> blown by the winter wind,
> my heart has been dry, brown like a wind-bitten tree stem
> my blood has been frozen, like twigs of a dead tree,
> but now my beloved,
> the season of the horizon, the sun, the night
> has fallen upon my life,
> the dream-wish of my saints.

To an extent this cultural flowering was to black nationalism what the Afrikaans Language movement and the writings of C. J. Langenhoven and N. P. van Wyk Louw had been to Afrikaner nationalism. Popular sentiments were articulated in a powerfully emotive way and gave the movement a new intellectual status. And it meant that by the time Biko and his fellow students began forming their new organization and shaping its ideology, the intellectual elite of the black community was affected by this line of thinking.

Biko, with his medical training, was especially concerned about the psychological effects of oppression that had so worried Lembede. The primary necessity, he believed, was for blacks to emancipate themselves and reach a point where they could deal with whites on equal terms in their own minds: otherwise the inequality would continue, with whites calling the tune and the blacks following submissively. Integration on those terms, which the white liberals were advocating, would be a farce; the whites would still dominate. "The integration they talk about is . . . artificial," Biko wrote in the *Saso Newsletter* of August 1970, "[because] the people forming the integrated complex have been extracted from various segregated societies with their in-built complexes of superiority and inferiority, and these continue to manifest themselves even in the 'nonracial' setup of the integrated complex. As a result the integration so achieved is a one-way course, with the whites doing all the talking and the blacks all the listening."[16]

Black Consciousness rejected liberalism as an ideology, too. Biko argued that the liberals' idea of integration meant the assimilation of blacks into a set of norms and code of behaviour set up and maintained by whites. "I am against the fact that a settler minority should impose an entire system of values on an indigenous people," he wrote in the same article. "A country in Africa, in which the majority of the people are African, must inevitably exhibit African values and be truly African in style."[17]

But again there was never any vision of a future South Africa without whites. As Sobukwe had, Biko saw the black avoidance of white collaboration as no more than a necessary transitional tactic to eradicate the psychological attitudes of white superiority and black submissiveness, which made genuine integration impossible. "Once the various groups . . . have asserted themselves to the point that mutual respect has to be shown, then you have the ingredients for a true and meaningful integration . . . [and] a genuine fusion of the life style of the various groups."[18]

Black Consciousness burgeoned in the townships, especially among

16. Quoted in Gerhardt, *op. cit.*, p. 263.

17. Ibid., p. 265.

18. Ibid., pp. 265–6.

young people, to whom its stress on the need for psychological emancipation had a particular appeal. They had experienced the humiliation and thought control of the Bantu Education system and they responded enthusiastically to the call to break these mental chains. The movement spread from black universities to black high schools and from there to primary schools; in Soweto a Students Representative Council was formed that helped to launch what became a children's war in the townships.

In the end Black Consciousness suffered the same fate as the PAC, becoming involved in a major confrontation with the government and its security forces before it had the organizational strength to survive it. Unlike the PAC, it had decided on patience rather than heroics, recognizing that long-term development was necessary, but the 1976 uprising in Soweto burst upon it spontaneously and there was nothing for it but to pitch in. By the time it was over South Africa had been shaken to its foundations once again, the Black Consciousness organizations were banned, Steve Biko was dead, other leaders were in prison or exile, and another phase of Africanism was over.

As thousands of young adherents left the country to join the guerrillas or simply escape into exile, there was once again only one viable organization they could join—the ANC. And when in the 1980s the next wave of insurrection arose, it was the Charterist movement that mushroomed up to lead it in the shape of the United Democratic Front; many who had been leading figures in the Black Consciousness movement joined. Some remained apart, forming the Azanian People's Organization[19] and the National Forum, so keeping the Africanist tradition alive as a minority movement. But for the most part synthesis occurred once again, and there was a massive return to the nonracist ideal as the mainstream movement.

THE LITTLE wayside hamlet of Rayi, just off the highway that connects the old settler towns of King William's Town and Grahamstown in the eastern Cape Province, is a sleepy place: half a dozen mud-daub houses, a few cattle and goats, wisps of lazy smoke, a few wide-eyed children, and the ubiquitous scratch chickens that are to an African settlement what fleas are to a dog.

But on a Sunday afternoon in August 1985 there were ten thousand people in Rayi. A daughter of the village had died—killed, it was said,

19. Africanists have chosen Azania as the name they would give to a black-ruled South Africa. It is taken from the writings of the ancient Roman explorer Ptolemy, who, some historians believe, managed to circumnavigate the Cape.

by black vigilantes who had come to her home in a distant Durban township and gunned her down in front of her children. Her body had been brought back for burial in her native village, and it was going to be a political funeral, a great political rally: the dead woman, Victoria Mxenge, had been an important political activist, a civil-rights lawyer and a member of the United Democratic Front, and people were coming from all over the country to pay their respects and join in the rally for the cause of freedom for which she had died.

There was an explosive mixture of anger and grief in the air as the crowd gathered around a makeshift platform that had been erected in front of the little houses. This was not the first time such an atrocity had been committed. Only four years before, Victoria's husband, Griffiths, had been killed in similar fashion in Durban, hacked down with machetes and his body dumped on a soccer field. The name of Inkatha, the political movement that controls the Zulu "homeland" in Natal, was being mentioned, accused of complicity.[20] No one seemed to have any evidence, but bitter clashes were taking place around Durban between members of Inkatha and the UDF. In the mood of the day that was enough. Homelanders, collaborators, were the subject of dark murmurings in the crowd.

There was a sprinkling of whites in the big crowd—Molly Blackburn, soon to have her own funeral rally, among them. But the anger was not directed at them. They sat among the crowd, chatting with acquaintances, holding up newspapers to shade their pale faces from the African sun. It was "the system" that was under attack from the speakers on the platform, the white government with its armed forces and its black collaborators. "We are the authors of the present state of emergency in our country and we are committed to seeing that South Africa comes down to her knees," thundered the main speaker, Steve Tshwete, who was soon to slip into exile and join the ANC. "We want to bring them down. There is no apology for that." The crowd murmured its approval and its level of passion rose a little higher.

As the sun sank low and the speeches ended at last, the bearers raised the coffin and the crowd began following them across the highway to the little cemetery on the other side where a fresh grave had been dug

20. In October 1989 a former security policeman, Butana Almond Nofomela, who had been sentenced to death and was awaiting execution in Pretoria Central Prison, made a sworn statement to human rights lawyers claiming he had been part of a hit squad that killed Griffiths Mxenge on police instructions. Nofomela, who claimed he was paid R1,000 (about $385) for the assassination, said he was told he might be needed later to kill Victoria Mxenge as well but received no further instructions about that.

beside that of Griffiths Mxenge. They moved slowly, to the lilting, haunting melody of a song that is always sung at this moment when coffins are borne to the graveside at political funerals. Softly, sweetly they sang: "*Hamba kahle Umkhonto . . .*"—Go well, Umkhonto—a song of praise and encouragement to the guerrillas. May they return to avenge the dead.

They were crossing the road in their thousands when a little pickup truck happened along, a little truck with the registration plates of the Ciskei "homeland" government, and in it, two uniformed soldiers of the "homeland's" army. Collaborators! The singing stopped and an angry buzz rose from the crowd as from a swarm of bees. The crowd congealed—that is the only word for it—around the truck, forcing it to a stop. First one, then another, then a hail of stones began crashing against the cab. As the fury spread people began hurling rocks from far back, heedless of their aim so that many in the crowd were hit by them. The body of the truck began to crumple like tinfoil.

Seized by this moment of desperation the driver leapt out and raised his fist in the Black Power salute. "*Amandla!*" he cried. Power to the people! He might as well have thrown fuel on the flames of their anger. A roar went up and, sensing that fate was at his heels, the soldier turned and ran.

He came sprinting down the road, weaving through the crowd like a rugby three-quarter through a flatfooted defence. He ran past me and I saw his eyes, wide like a gazelle's, and heard the slap of his heavy army boots as they hit the tarred road. For a moment it looked as though he might run right through the surprised mob and get away, but then he spotted a group of a hundred or so young "comrades," the militant shock troops of the 1980s uprising, farther down the road. He swerved off the highway, ducked through a fence, and sped off across a stretch of open ground. The "comrades" saw him and gave chase.

Like hounds at a fox hunt, they raced across the dun veld, the gap between them and their quarry slowly closing until they caught him, pulled him down, and fell upon him with collective savagery. They stoned him to death, there on the veld beside the little village, and when he lay still someone produced a tyre and a can of gasoline. To chants of "Necklace! Necklace!" they pulled the tyre over the soldier's body, spread-eagled his legs and arms on either side of it, poured gasoline into the rubber casing, and set it alight.

By the time I reached the scene the branch of a dead tree had been thrown on the soldier's body to add to the blaze. Another white reporter was beside me. One of the youngsters who had done this deed came up to us. "Kentucky fried chicken!" he shrieked, dancing a little jig before us, his eyes wild and his arms akimbo. "We must kill them all!" But he showed no sign of wanting to harm us. Whatever it was that had driven him to do this, it was not a lust for revenge against whites.

As I stood there watching the blazing body it put me in mind of the burning of the great whore in Revelation who corrupted the earth with her fornication. Was that what this grisly scene was about? The ritual burning of the collaborator who corrupted the black people's cause by prostituting himself, selling his services to the oppressive white system. "The merchants of the earth are waxed rich through the abundance of her delicacies. . . . She hath glorified herself, and lived deliciously." And so she was burned and the smoke rose up for ever and ever.

Was this, then, the start of the Fanonesque apocalypse? Was this the buried impulse that made the great haters, that drove the revolutionary mind to burn, to cleanse, to end in a reign of terror and virtue?

Was there building up in these angry youths who spearheaded the revolt of the 1980s a blind hatred that would carry the black South African revolution toward the climax of death and catharsis that Fanon predicted and prescribed? Was this where we were headed after all the years of nonracialism and restraint?

The burning at Rayi was not an isolated incident. There were numerous "necklacings" and other grisly executions elsewhere in South Africa. In Sharpeville a group of rioting youths pulled Sam Dhlamini, deputy mayor of the Community Council, out of his house, hacked him to pieces on his doorstep, threw his body in his car and set it on fire. In Kwanobuhle "comrades" attacked the home of Benjamin Kinikini, a well-known and much hated collaborator, put a torch to it when he and his eighteen-year-old son Selumko barricaded themselves in, and danced on their ashes in front of television cameras recording the scene for all the world to see. In Duduza township, west of Johannesburg, they "necklaced" a young factory worker, Maki Skosana, who was suspected of being the girlfriend of a man suspected of having issued booby-trapped grenades to three "comrades" who blew themselves up when they tried to use them. No proof, just suspicions. They chased Maki across the veld at the funeral of the dead "comrades," caught her, stoned her, tore her clothes off, and set her on fire, and while she burned someone rammed a broken bottle into her vagina.

A culture of violence seemed to be emerging as the uprising of the 1980s intensified. In Alexandra township "comrades" established a "people's court" to hear charges of collaboration, and ominously hung two tyres on the wall in place of the scales of justice. "Kill a cop for Jesus," proclaimed a graffito on a wall in Athlone township. *"Jihad!"* yelled the young Muslim youths in Thornton Road, calling for a holy war. In Ilingelihle, outside Cradock in the turbulent eastern Cape, a fourteen-year-old boy named Lucas spoke to a reporter of his ambitions. "When I am 18," he said, "I will go to become a cadre in Lusaka. Then, instead of stones, I will have a bazooka."[21] In townships around the country children in their early teens began turning up at funeral rallies with wooden models of AK-47 automatic rifles to identify with the Umkhonto guerrillas.

> Look at my big black hands
> Shaking and itching to hold
> and pull your gullet out,
> to throw into the filth and dust
> your stomach, insides and all.

So Duncan Mathlo had written in a cry of rage as he went into exile to join the guerrillas after watching the slaughter of black children in the streets of Soweto during the riots of 1976.

During the crisis of the 1980s, I wrote about the possibility of a Khmer Rouge generation emerging, a generation of black youth so brutalized and desensitized by its violent encounter with white South Africa's repressive forces that it would lose all sense of life's value, a generation grown up in the institutionalized violence of apartheid and the endemic violence of the ghetto, that was having superimposed on that the violence of street rioting and of bloody clashes with the police and the army.

What happens to a ten-year-old who is put in jail, threatened, abused, beaten, tortured, tear gassed in the street, shot at; who sees his friends killed, learns to throw stones at an armoured car, set fire to a house, maybe kill a cop if he can? Paul Verryn, a Methodist minister who works for a counselling service that deals with black children who have been in detention, says the experience ages them in an instant. "And when you torture a ten-year-old," he adds, "and expect from him the psychological sophistication you might not expect of a forty-year-old, then you've begun a process that must be very difficult to undo and it will be almost impossible for parents to resume disciplinary control."

Saths Cooper, a clinical psychologist and former president of the Azanian People's Organization, believes the process of violent repression sets up a cycle of brutal behaviour. "When you traumatize a community through repression," he says, "when you brutalize children who simply objected to the education which is preparing them for a servile status in society, then there is a very small gap between being a victim of or witnessing brutalization and modelling that aggressive behaviour."

21. Interview by Alan Cowell, *New York Times Magazine*, April 14, 1985.

In what comes close to being a Fanonesque analysis, Cooper believes this can produce a need for cathartic violence. "When children see how their elders have been humiliated and denigrated, and have no hope or aspirations for their own future, then violence can be cathartic," he says. "The level of repugnance for the system is so great that very little is required to spark off a need for a cathartic expression to purge oneself and one's community."

Nico Smith, the dissident Afrikaner minister living in Mamelodi township, has won the trust of the "comrades" there and got closer to them than any other white person, agrees with Cooper and predicts a growth in cathartic violence. "They have lost their sensitivity to life," he says. "They don't care if they kill and they don't care if they die. They are quite capable of rushing straight into the guns."

This is a phenomenon that worries the ANC. Late one night, sitting in a Dar es Salaam hotel talking about the situation in South Africa, a congress official brought a sudden silence to the group: "I really fear a blood bath," he said. "They're making animals of some of our people there." This official was involved with a reorientation centre in Tanzania where most of the blacks who flee South Africa eventually wind up. After being interviewed, assessed, and sorted into different categories, some are sent for military training, others go to a school the ANC runs in Tanzania, and yet others go on to training institutions in Scandinavia, Holland, and Eastern Europe that offer scholarships to black South African refugees. The man in the hotel was saying that some of the young refugees he was seeing then, in 1986, were different from any he had seen before.

Yet they are still not antiwhite. There is still no sign of the cathartic violence turning into the kind of vengeful crusade Fanon spoke of, the yearning to turn the tables and become the hunter and persecutor. It may come to that, but it has not done so yet. The wild "comrades" of Mamelodi do not wreak revenge on Nico Smith, the white man who lives among them. The violence at Riya did not turn against whites. (There were several dozen whites there and at no time did it direct itself to them. The shrieking youth did not want to attack me.) I have attended scores of the great funeral rallies in the townships, as have other white reporters, and been in the midst of great emotion, but never have I felt a moment's anxiety or sensed the slightest hostility toward my whiteness. It is the same in riot situations, where white reporters have quite often been rescued by blacks and the security forces are those whom all fear most.

In part we are speaking of the well-known phenomenon of ghetto violence, of anger and frustration turning in upon itself. With black townships miles away from the city, some surrounded by army camps, the government has succeeded in restricting black fury to black neighbourhoods. But I do not think that's all there is to it. The anger is not racist because of the long education of the Charterist movement, because the dividing line has been blurred by so many white martyrs and so many black collaborators, and above all, I believe, because black Africans are not instinctively racist as so many whites are. They do not have an ingrained belief in their own inherent superiority that leads them into the complex syndrome of prejudice, guilt, and aggression.

THE DECISION to cross the Rubicon of violence remains controversial. Was it unavoidable, was it justifiable, was it the right tactical decision? Has it advanced or retarded the cause of black liberation?

By turning the South African struggle into a revolutionary one, did the black leaders put it on the slippery slope toward ever greater extremism, which can have only one end, the apocalyptic race war that will devastate the country and appall the world? Or would it have happened anyway, and by getting ahead of the game has the ANC been able to control the process and exercise a measure of discipline over more extreme elements?

Looking back on the events leading up to the decision, one can see why it was taken. Passive resistance can work only if there is a certain level of sensitivity within the ruling community that will recoil from the use of naked force against peaceful protestors; a current of political reaction makes it impossible for the government to carry on in the old way, so that it has to yield and start making concessions. But if isolationism in a cellular society has dulled that sensitivity, if people cannot span the no-man's-land that separates them, then the naked force will continue to be used with impunity, and something more explosive is needed to penetrate the sealed-off consciousness of the ruling group.

Other considerations weighed with South African blacks in the early 1960s. This was the high point of the great anticolonialist revolution, when a whiff of guerrilla action seemed all that was needed to roll back the forces of imperialism. There seemed an invincibility about it. From Indochina to Cuba to Algeria, the vision of the triumphant freedom fighter swimming like Mao's fish in a sea of popular support was at its most enticing. It is not difficult to see why a turn to guerrilla struggle seemed an attractive option at the time, but it involved a fateful choice. It meant abandoning domestic political activity and placing all the eggs of the black liberation movement in the revolutionary basket, as it were. No doubt it seemed the right choice then, given the stifling of political activity at home and the high rate of success of revolutionary movements elsewhere, but we now know (even the Russians, who arm South

Africa's black guerrillas and are supreme experts on revolution, know, as does the ANC itself) that it cannot succeed alone in the South African situation.

Guerrilla struggle works most effectively in a colony or against a foreign occupier, where the costs can be driven up to the point where they become unacceptable to the occupying power, which then withdraws. Thus the French withdrew from Indochina after their defeat in battle at Dien Bien Phu and thus they finally quit Algeria. The Americans got out of Vietnam; they were not defeated militarily—their overall military power was unbroken and remained overwhelming—but they were no longer prepared to pay the rising political, economic, and other costs. These results were hailed as victories for the new techniques of guerrilla struggle.

Giving enthusiastic support to this popular image of the modern guerrilla's effectiveness, Fanon ridiculed Friedrich Engels's theory of violence, in which Engels argued that "the arms manufacturer triumphs over the producer of primitive weapons" and that "the triumph of violence depends on the production of armaments, and this in turn depends on production in general, and thus . . . on economic strength, on the economy of the State, and in their last resort on the material means which that violence commands."[22] Fanon points to the triumphs of the weak, of the Spanish guerrillas over Napoleon's great army of 400,000 in the spring of 1810, of the American militia over the British in the Revolutionary War, of General Vo Nguyen Giap over the French in Vietnam. These triumphs, he argues, were the result of a changed situation in colonies, previously regarded simply as suppliers of raw materials but now as a market, where the colonial power did not want to have a garrison state inhibiting buying and selling. Thus while a victory like the one at Dien Bien Phu infuses the oppressed people with revolutionary zeal, it fills the colonial power with alarm. "The colonialists become aware of manifold Dien Bien Phus," Fanon writes. "This is why a veritable panic takes hold of the colonialist government. Their purpose is to capture the vanguard, to turn the movement of liberation toward the right, and to disarm the people: quick, quick, let's decolonize. Decolonize the Congo before it becomes another Algeria. Vote the constitutional framework for all Africa, create the French Community. They decolonize at such a rate that they impose independence on Houphouet-Boigny."[23]

22. Fanon, op. cit., p. 64.

23. Ibid., pp. 63–72. Felix Houphouet-Boigny, president of the Ivory Coast. After his country opted to remain part of the French Community, France offered him independence.

But in South Africa there is no colonial power to withdraw. There is no mother country to withdraw to. It becomes for the whites a war of survival that transcends the economic analysis or at least modifies it. Guerrilla warfare, economic sanctions, and the like may drive up the costs of apartheid in human and monetary terms, they may make life more painful, but they do not cause white South Africans to withdraw in order to maintain a market. Up to a point they will be prepared to pay the cost, and if they remain deluded that the alternative will be even more costly and more painful, they may continue to pay to a very high point: they are making a choice between unattractive alternatives in which perceptions are everything and the devil you know is better than the one you don't.

White South Africans will change only when the perceived consequences of changing seem less painful than the perceived consequences of continuing as they are. And that is a matter of perceptions rather than of reality.

Without that change they cannot be overthrown. And there cannot be a forceful overthrow of a powerful government by unarmed, or scantily armed, people without a defection of the armed forces. Oliver Tambo cannot ride into Pretoria on a Russian tank unless Umkhonto we Sizwe has first defeated the South African Defence Force and the South African Police Force, or unless significant elements of those have defected to join the ANC—both unlikely prospects, to be sure. At most the blacks' guerrilla struggle against the South African government can be only one factor among many, one pressure point in a multifaceted strategy that may in the end tip the pleasure-pain balance of white South Africa's perceptions. There must be reassurance as well as pressure, carrots as well as sticks. And there must be a certain compatibility among the different facets of the strategy—and guerrilla warfare, especially if it begins attacking "soft" civilian targets, is *not* compatible with a strategy to win sympathy and support among dissident whites and among the major Western powers, key factors in increasing economic pressure on Pretoria.

It is not just that a strategy of violence conflicts with a strategy of political and diplomatic advancement. Whether intended or not, the decision of June 1961 meant that for more than a decade black politics virtually ceased in South Africa. A silence fell over the black community more complete than at any time since before the formation of the ANC in 1912. It entered a period of deep demoralization and malaise as the Verwoerd government forged ahead with the implementation of its grand apartheid schemes and the only voices raised in protest were those of white liberals and the lone Zulu leader, Chief Mangosuthu Buthelezi. Not until the stirrings of the Black Consciousness movement at the end of the decade and of worker dissent in Natal in 1973 was there any significant revival of black political activity.

In this sense the decision let the South African government off the hook. It was reeling after Sharpeville. At no other time before or since did shock waves run so deeply through the white community. The stock market crashed, property values plummeted, thousands of whites left the country in the belief that it was doomed and black rule could not be more than five years away. But then the government was given time to recover—even to counterattack. The commitment to violence lent colour of fact to the charge that had long been made that the ANC was a bunch of treacherous, treasonous saboteurs. That the ANC had to turn to the Soviet Union and Eastern Europe for arms—the only countries that would supply them—strengthened this impression and gave apparent substance to the charge that they were Communists controlled from Moscow.

Thereafter they were fair game. The support Luthuli had begun to draw from the white community—several huge multiracial rallies were held just before he was banned—melted away. And when the entire ANC underground leadership was arrested before it had time to develop a sophisticated cell network, in a single raid on a farmhouse in the semirural suburb of Rivonia in July 1963, not only was the ANC's internal infrastructure smashed but both the legal pretext and the white public-opinion backup was there to sentence them all—including Mandela and Sisulu—to life imprisonment.

It provided the justification, too, for a massive crackdown on lesser figures and even minor sympathizers. Security police swept through the countryside, especially in the eastern Cape, rounding up thousands of ordinary members of the ANC and securing jail sentences of twelve years and more. The minister of justice, John Vorster, soon to succeed Verwoerd as prime minister, had no difficulty getting Parliament to pass a new General Laws Amendment Act with the support of the Opposition United party, under which anyone suspected of having information to give to the security police could be kept in solitary confinement for ninety days, repeatable thereafter, as Vorster put it, "until this side of eternity." Gratuitously, he later extended the detention period to a repeatable 180 days.

In one stroke black opposition was annihilated. Worse still—and this is still true, nearly thirty years later—it has been possible for the government to demonize the ANC. The congress's long commitment to nonviolence and nonracialism, its long record of moderation, its still conciliatory views about the future get brushed aside; for three decades it has been smeared as a Communist, terrorist organization to the point where today it occupies, in the average white South African mind, the place that the PLO does for Israelis. What this annihilation of the black opposition meant was that the government was able to bounce back from its position on the ropes and have a clear decade in which to establish the basic structures of the Grand Apartheid scheme with minimum resistance.

Several times I heard Verwoerd say during those years that he wanted to implement apartheid so thoroughly and deep-rootedly that no future regime might undo it. To some extent he succeeded. When one looks at South Africa today, one is struck by how appalling the problems are that await a future black government as it tries to dismantle the huge structural ziggurat of the cellular society. What will it do with Botshabelo, for example, with its 700,000 people, who may number 1 or 2 million by that time, and the scores of other resettlement camps in the "homelands" and elsewhere? It is inconceivable that there could be another mass removal programme. Can unrestricted urbanization be allowed? What chaos would result if it were? Yet how could a black government retain a system of pass laws or influx control?

Logically the restructuring should begin where apartheid began, with land reform, yet there are few African farmers left. The black peasantry was decimated three-quarters of a century ago and what you have now is a massive, artificially created lumpen proletariat, much of it living in rural areas but economically dependent on the cities. As Zimbabwe realized in time, a new black government must take care not to disrupt the established agricultural economy; food supplies at affordable prices must be maintained. A post-apartheid regime will face a massive crisis of expectations, which means giving blacks access to the economy, not destroying it.

What can a future black government do with Soweto? Bulldoze it? Obviously not; there are 2 million people living there who cannot easily be rehoused. A few middle-class *evolués* may be able to jump out of the ghetto, but the masses will not. White suburbia will become integrated, but what whites will move to Soweto? Racial segregation will become class segregation; and since residential segregation means school segregation, separate education will continue for most blacks, which means inequality will be perpetuated.

Then there are the "homelands," four of them nominally independent, with substantial bureaucratic structures of their own, all providing a constitutional and legal complexity that cannot be easy to unravel. The decade of silence also allowed other forms of black politics to develop around these "homelands," among those who decided to take what they could get within South Africa's system when overt opposition seemed impossible. Out of the politics of despair a new constituency arose, prepared to reach for the half loaf—or, more accurately calculated, the one-thirtieth loaf—as being better than no bread at all and led by the old tribal traditionalists whose declining status in the modern industrial society made them susceptible to official inducements of money and prestige. The policy of co-option began, and a pattern of future government strategy that combined repression and co-option.

It was in this decade of the silent 1960s, too, that Chief Mangosutho Gatsha Buthelezi and his Inkatha movement arose. He is a figure of major controversy today, with supporters and detractors dividing around him with an emotional ferocity that tears South Africa's black community apart and does much to destroy its effectiveness.

Chief Buthelezi arose, quite simply, to fill a void. I recall a conversation with him early in the decade, when he was agonizing about whether to seek office within the system as head of the KwaZulu "homeland" that the government planned to establish. I was one of those who encouraged him to do so. The void needed filling, I thought, and the position seemed to offer a platform from which a black politician might with relative impunity articulate the grievances of his people—indeed their rejection of the system itself—for the government could hardly gag someone installed under its own system. Had he not done so, the only black voices heard through that decade would have been those of the government's co-opted acolytes. Moreover, if the Zulu King Zwelithini Goodwill, the government's favourite for the job, had been installed instead of Buthelezi as political head of the KwaZulu "homeland," there can be little doubt that South Africa's biggest tribe would have been pitched, like the Xhosas, the Tswanas, and the Vendas into nominal independence and the massive disabilities of legal denationalization. Others would have followed, so that instead of being stopped in its tracks the separate development programme would have been fully implemented and we would not be seeing the retreat from it that is now beginning to take place.

Not only did Buthelezi resist the government's notions of spurious independence, but for more than a decade he provided the country's only internal black political resistance. Buthelezi saw Inkatha as an internal wing of the ANC, adopting its colours of black, green, and gold and literally keeping its flag flying. He became a rallying point for a demoralized people. His attacks on government policies and calls for intertribal unity drew wide publicity, and his popularity soared. I recall inviting him to lunch at the *Rand Daily Mail* in the early 1970s, and while he sat there talking with our senior staff thousands of black people gathered outside: messengers, cleaning women, tea "boys," canteen assistants, every black person in the city, it seemed. They thronged the streets and hung from office windows. When I accompanied Buthelezi to the front door after our lunch, I was amazed to discover that the

Traffic Department had closed off four city blocks around our building because of the size of the crowd that had gathered to catch a glimpse of the only black political leader then on the scene.

But not long after that, conflicts began. As the Black Consciousness movement gathered momentum, its reaction focussing on both the white liberals and black accommodationists who had been such a feature of the 1960s, Buthelezi came increasingly under attack. The mood of the new movement was militant and purist: it was not disposed to make distinctions, or too many exceptions, among those who held office in the despised government. Total rejection was required. For a credible politician like Buthelezi to operate within the system merely gave it a gratuitous credibility and confused the minds of the people, who needed to be mobilized into a state of total opposition. So Buthelezi found himself even more vigourously condemned than the real collaborators in other "homelands." The conflict came to a head at Robert Sobukwe's funeral in 1975, when Buthelezi, who had known Sobukwe as a fellow student at Fort Hare, was abused and physically threatened by militant youths who forced him to leave. As his bodyguards hustled him away from the ceremony, one was photographed drawing a pistol from under his jacket. The picture, blown up large, was splashed across the front page of a black newspaper under the damning caption, "Which side of the gun are you on?"

From that point on the conflict became two-way. The attacks and the criticisms, particularly the labelling of Buthelezi as a "stooge" and a "collaborator," which he manifestly is not, have aggravated the worst features of his hypersensitive personality and caused him to lash back with unrestrained ferocity. Taking umbrage at what he considers to be a slighting of his chiefly dignity, he has retreated more and more into the personal pride of his own royal status and the martial pride of the Zulu nation, turning Inkatha into a rampant ethnic movement that is increasingly at war with the nationalist movements, Black Consciousness and Charterist alike. From being once an ally and internal representative of the ANC, Buthelezi today has turned into one of its deadliest enemies and fiercest detractors.

The prime benefactor, of course, is the apartheid government, but the longer-term implications of such a deadly conflict are as ominous for the whites as for the blacks. The fearful consequences for stability of Moise Tshombe in the Congo, Odumegu Ojukwu in Nigeria and Jonas Savimbi in Angola should serve as a warning, but for the moment the politics of opportunism are too alluring for Pretoria to think in other terms. So Buthelezi's young *impis*, reincarnations of the Zulu regiments of old, and the United Democratic Front's young "comrades" do battle in the townships around Pietermaritzburg and Durban in what has become an endemic black civil war in which more than two thousand people have been killed and thirty thousand displaced while the police stand by and watch and let it happen.

The question remains: Should the ANC have tried to remain politically active through the crucial years when apartheid was entrenched and other forces arose, instead of abandoning the political field in favour of its revolutionary commitment? The Black Consciousness movement, the United Democratic Front, and particularly the black trade union movement showed that effective political action was still possible despite the restrictions. Indeed the ANC itself made a considerable political comeback in the 1980s, being remarkably effective from its various exile bases.

The record is not all negative. By establishing an external network and a guerrilla army, the ANC reaped a number of significant advantages. The bases abroad enabled the movement and a core of its leadership to survive the onslaught and to provide a continuity of principle. It was able to establish a central organization that has gathered about it new leaders who cleave to the principles of a colour-blind democracy. It runs a large network of institutions in many countries: refugee transit camps and assessment centres; farms and schools; scholarship programmes; medical clinics and social security services; military training camps; operational centres; diplomatic, information, and broadcasting services; and a political bureaucracy to coordinate all this. Over thirty years, these operations have given the ANC considerable range and depth of administrative experience.

In fact, it has become South Africa's government-in-exile, although it resists styling itself as such out of a reluctance to give the impression that it is not rooted in South Africa. It has established missions abroad—forty-four, compared to the South African government's twenty-five embassies and forty-six other missions—staffed by people who have studied at foreign universities, are familiar with world affairs, and are fluent in a wide range of languages. In my view, it has acquired a global view and a sophistication superior to that of the Pretoria government, and I am acquainted with both.

The ANC's commitment to guerrilla struggle, meanwhile, has given it an aura of militancy that, so far at least, has enabled it to ride the wave of mounting radicalism. Young black South African militants who go into exile, eager like young Lucas to get military training so that they can come back with a bazooka, find when they get abroad that there is only one organization with the support network, training facilities, and guerrilla army that they can join. So they join the ANC and are subject to its political influence and organizational discipline. This has kept the development of a counterracism under control. It has also prevented more extreme and indiscriminately violent organizations developing and capturing the constituency of the young and angry, which would seriously challenge the ANC and its doctrine of nonracism.

But it has also meant problems for the ANC. It has meant digesting what I have called the Khmer Rouge element, keeping it within the disciplined fold, and as we have seen this has not always been easy. Necklacings have occured, and the bombings of soft targets: The ANC does not approve, but what can it do? If it denounces its young radicals it risks driving them out into a more extreme organization, which in time would pose a deadly threat to everything it believes in. If it does not, it risks losing disciplinary control as well as credibility among the white sympathizers it is trying to cultivate inside South Africa and abroad. "We disapprove, though we understand what drove them to it," is Oliver Tambo's uneasy compromise.

How long can this centre hold? I do not know. All I know is that white South Africa does not even know it exists.

CHAPTER TWELVE

A Theological Civil War

Onward, Christian soldiers,
Marching as to war,
With the Cross of Jesus,
Going on before.

S. BARING-GOULD

I WELL REMEMBER my perplexity when, as a child during World War II, an older cousin showed me a German army belt he had brought back as a souvenir from the front. GOTT MIT UNS said the slogan on the buckle. But God, I thought, was supposed to be on our side.

That puzzle of my childhood has an echo in today's racial conflict in South Africa that outsiders find equally confusing. Both sides claim a divine imprimatur for their cause in a country that is as universally religious as it is socially divided. Just as the themes of faith and politics have been intertwined in the history of Afrikaner nationalism, so have they, too, in the struggle of the black South Africans. Both sides have their long lineages of political preachers and preacher politicians: from the Rev. S. J. du Toit to the *Gesuiwerde* theologians of the 1930s to Daniel Malan to Andries Treurnicht to Carel Boshoff; and from the early black mission-school graduates to Albert Luthuli to Desmond Tutu to Allan Boesak to Frank Chikane. The one has produced the apartheid civil religion with its claim that the Afrikaner nation has a divine right to its own separate existence; the other, no less fervently and potently, a black theology of liberation which claims that Christ's mission on earth was to identify with the poor and the oppressed. As the two nationalisms square up to each other, it is as much a theological civil war as a political and military one.

"The difference in colour," wrote Malan in 1954 to a group of Reformed Church clergymen in Grand Rapids, Michigan, who had asked him to explain the harsh apartheid laws then being enacted, "is merely the physical manifestation of the contrast between two irreconcilable ways of life, between barbarism and civilization, between heathendom and Christianity, and finally between overwhelming numerical odds on the one hand and insignificant numbers on the other." To survive in such a situation, to avoid being "submerged in the black heathendom of Africa," Malan said, the white minority had to throw an impenetrable armour around themselves—"the armour of racial purity and self-preservation." This they were doing in a Christian spirit. "Apartheid is based on what the Afrikaner believes to be his divine calling and his privilege—to convert the heathen to Christianity without obliterating his national identity."[1]

"I am in Congress precisely *because* I am a Christian," wrote Albert Luthuli in his autobiography not long afterward. "My Christian belief about society must find expression here and now, and Congress is the spearhead of the struggle."[2]

Thus was the battleground staked out for the theological civil war, which has now reached a climax with the black theologians getting the World Alliance of Reformed Churches to declare apartheid a heresy, resulting in the suspension from the alliance of the Dutch Reformed Churches, and the white state-president countering with a charge that the liberationists are false prophets with treasonous objectives.

In the course of time, as apartheid's protagonists learnt more about the ways of the modern world and became slicker in their public-relations techniques, they cleaned up Malan's explanation, introducing a new rhetoric that speaks of "a nation of minorities" instead of "overwhelming numerical odds," and which has dropped the crude references to "barbarism" and "heathendom" and substituted more acceptable synonyms such as "atheistic communism" and "Marxist terrorism." The bedrock essentials remain the same, however. They still construe it as a holy war in which white Western Christian civilization must remain in control and arm itself against the godless forces of darkness and death that are enfilading the very citadels of the faith.

Today the government accuses the protagonists of black liberation theology of being the agents of a satanic revolution bent on the destruction of the Christian state. To the South African Council of Churches, the main ecumenical body of non-Afrikaner churches where the liberation theologists have their stronghold, President Botha said, "You love and praise the ANC/SACP with its Marxist and atheistic ideology, land-

1. D. F. Malan, "Apartheid: A Divine Calling," in *The Anti-Apartheid Reader*, ed. David Mermelstein (New York, 1987), p. 95.

2. Albert Luthuli, *Let My People Go* (Johannesburg, 1962), p. 154.

mines, bombs and necklaces perpetrating the most horrendous atrocities imaginable; and you embrace and participate in their call for violence, hatred, sanctions, insurrection and revolution."[3] "The question must be posed," he wrote to Archbishop Tutu in March 1988, "whether you are acting on behalf of the kingdom of God, or the kingdom promised by the ANC and the SACP? If it is the latter, say so, but do not then hide behind the structures of the cloth and the Christian Church, because Christianity and Marxism are irreconcilable opposites."[4]

To which Tutu replied:

> My theological position derives from the Bible and from the Church. The Bible and the Church predate Marxism and the ANC by several centuries. . . . The Bible teaches that what invests each person with infinite value is not this or that arbitrarily chosen biological attribute, but the fact that each person is created in the image of God. Apartheid, the policy of your government, claims that what makes a person qualify for privilege and political power is that biological irrelevance, the colour of a person's skin and his ethnic antecedents. Apartheid says those are what make a person matter. That is clearly at variance with the teaching of the Bible and the teaching of our Lord and Saviour Jesus Christ. Hence the Church's criticism that your apartheid policies are not only unjust and oppressive. They are positively unbiblical, unchristian, immoral and evil.[5]

Of course, there has always been a certain ambiguity in the position of the Christian religion on the questions of obedience and resistance to state authority, indeed on the question of war itself. In its earliest phase, when Christians were being persecuted in Rome and the church had no relationship at all with the state, it was unquestioningly and militantly on the side of the subversive poor. But during the fourth century, when the Emperor Constantine found it expedient to negotiate with the church and was himself converted, this changed. Christianity virtually became a state religion, giving its support to the political authority and enjoining the faithful to civil obedience. The emphasis shifted from Christ the champion of the humble to Paul's admonition in Romans 13: "Let therefore every person be subject to the governing authorities. For there is no authority except from God, and those that exist have been instituted by God. Therefore he who resists the au-

3. In *Journal of Theology for Southern Africa*, no. 63, June 1988, p. 78.

4. Ibid., p. 73.

5. Ibid., pp. 82–3.

thorities resists what God has appointed, and those who resist will incur judgement."

In the centuries that followed, the church was transformed into a community of wealthy and powerful people who sided with the dominant rulers of each successive age. Even the Reformation did little to change this. Martin Luther especially came out strongly in support of authority against the rebellious German peasantry, establishing a deep-rooted Lutheran tradition against rebellion and legitimizing the use of violence to maintain law and order.

Yet the residual tradition of those early Christians has remained, and periodically it has revealed itself in times of moral crisis and extreme injustice. Out of that tradition the black theology of liberation has arisen. As Allan Boesak puts it, "It is the proclamation of the age-old gospel, now liberated from the deadly hold of the mighty and the powerful and made relevant to the situation of the oppressed and the poor."[6]

Other, similar theologies have arisen elsewhere, and the South African theologians have drawn on some of these. It is another of those stunning ironies which litter the South African story that one of these sources of inspiration should be none other than a German active during the Third Reich: Dietrich Bonhoeffer, a theologian of great courage and moral commitment who played a key role in resisting the Nazification of the German Evangelical Church in the 1930s, then went on to oppose German militarization, advocate conscientious objection at a time when this was tantamount to treason, help Jews escape the holocaust for which he was imprisoned by the Gestapo, and, finally, participate in the plot on Hitler's life, which led to his execution in Flossenbürg camp a week before it was liberated by Allied forces in 1945.

There is much in Bonhoeffer's life of struggle and witness against the tyranny of the Third Reich that has helped shape the thinking of the black Christians involved in mapping out a theology of resistance to apartheid. Not least is the fact that even before any of it began, while Bonhoeffer was still a student in New York, he attended a church in East Harlem, an experience that awakened in him an awareness of racial injustice and oppression as well as of a vibrant spirituality among black Americans. In the sense in which the phrase is used today, he became a "black theologian" way back then, learning, as his South African chronicler John de Gruchy puts it, "to do theology from the perspective of those who suffer on the lower side" of society.[7] It was a capacity that he took back to Germany with him, working among the poor and the

6. Allan Boesak, *Farewell to Innocence* (New York, 1984), p. 10.

7. John de Gruchy, *Bonhoeffer and South Africa* (Grand Rapids, Mich., 1984), p. 8.

unemployed in the working-class slums of Berlin during the Depression; and then, as the Nazi tyranny intensified, actively helping Jews to escape the country.

Allied to this was a theological activism, called *praxis*, that is fundamental to the theology of liberation. The idea, strongly advocated by Bonhoeffer, is that the church must not hide in a closet of ritual and piety but must involve itself in the realities of life of the poor and the oppressed. It must identify with them and champion their cause.

Important, too, for South African Christians faced with the dilemma of increasingly violent resistance to state oppression, was the fact that despite his respect for authority and a personal abhorrence of violence that led him to espouse pacifism, Bonhoeffer accepted that there were circumstances of tyranny and injustice that could require a Christian to resort to civil disobedience and even violence. Hence his participation in the plot to assassinate Hitler.

Indeed, the whole German church struggle during the Third Reich, the *Kirchenkampf*, in which Bonhoeffer was involved, has been an important paradigm for South African Christians involved in the struggle against apartheid. Its climactic moment came when pastors and laypeople of the Lutheran, Reformed, and United Churches gathered in the small town of Barmen in May 1934 to oppose the Nazification of their churches. They formed themselves into a "Confessing Synod" and issued the Barmen Declaration, a defiant assertion that the church belonged to Jesus Christ alone and rejected as "false doctrine" that its message and form in the world could be shaped by the Nazi *Weltanschauung*. This is what is known in theological language as a *status confessionis*, a moment when the church is faced with a challenge so great that it must declare its faith again, and it has become a major theme of the theologians of liberation that such a situation exists in South Africa.

The movement has drawn, too, on the Roman Catholic liberation theology of Latin America, although it is not solely an outgrowth of it, as popular opinion among white South Africans has it. Whereas the Latin American theology focusses more on economic suffering than political oppression, the South African version reverses that emphasis; and there is no Latin American counterpart to the central role of "blackness" in the South African theology, a concept that grows out of the apartheid experience, in which blackness becomes the defining characteristic of oppression, although it is not in itself colour-bound: all the world's oppressed share in this blackness, and all are redeemed as one people regardless of colour.

The greatest outside influence has, not surprisingly, been that of black theologians in the United States. The ties are so close that Tutu and James Cone, a leading black American cleric, have described the two as "soul mates." They are linked by their blackness, their common ties to Africa and their similar experiences of racism at the hands of whites. That shared experience convinced both that it was the white power structure that determined the reality of life for blacks, and that the only solution to that lay, in Boesak's words, "not in screaming to white people that they are devils, but in confronting their power with another kind of power."[8] So the concept of black power arose jointly in the United States and South Africa, with a black theology of liberation as a natural corollary.

Like so much else in the resistance movement, the move toward this alternative theology began with Sharpeville. That traumatic event caused the South African members of the World Council of Churches to convene a meeting in the Johannesburg suburb of Cottesloe in December 1960 to try to find a way to unite in Christian witness against racism. The Cottesloe Consultation, as it was called, began a chain reaction that has split the church in South Africa and culminated in the development of separate, diametric theologies.

The Cottesloe debates were the most intense and soul-searching that had ever been held in South Africa on the question of race at that time. They probed such sensitive issues as the prohibition of mixed marriages, the labour laws, the social effects of the migrant labour system, and the denial of political representation to people of colour. The delegates tried hard to maintain unity and, by discussion and compromise, succeeded in taking the Dutch Reformed Church representatives along with them in issuing a Consultation Statement afterward that went much further than their churches had gone before in criticizing core features of the apartheid system. Most important of all, it unequivocally rejected church apartheid as unchristian. "No one who believes in Jesus Christ may be excluded from any church on the grounds of his colour or race," they declared, adding that "the spiritual unity among all men who are in Christ must find visible expression in acts of common worship or witness, and in fellowship and consultation on matters of common concern." The Nederduitsch Hervormde Kerk delegates, whose church's constitution has a clause specifically excluding blacks from membership, refused to accept this; but the representatives of the main Dutch Reformed Church, the Nederduitse Gereformeerde Kerk, did so despite their own segregated structure and their church's historic role in formulating the Afrikaner civil religion and coauthoring the apartheid ideology.

Verwoerd was furious. It was vital to him that the major Afrikaner church continue to give its theological approval to the grand apartheid

8. Boesak, op. cit., p. 56.

vision he was then unfolding. So he leaned on it, and within days the Dutch Reformed Church leadership recanted, repudiating its Cottesloe delegates and reaffirming its theological justification for government policy. Soon afterward, both the NHK and the NGK resigned their membership in the World Council of Churches.

For the NGK's Cottesloe delegates, it was an acute moral crisis. Foremost among them was the Rev. C. F. Beyers Naudé, moderator of the Southern Transvaal Synod and a rising star in the Afrikaner nationalist establishment, who was being freely spoken of as a possible future *volksleier*, perhaps even prime minister. Naudé had impeccable credentials. The son of one of the six founders of the Broederbond, himself a senior Broederbonder, he bore the name of a famous Boer general and martyr, Christiaan Frederick Beyers, whom his father had served as pastor during the Boer War and until the general died in a rebellion of Afrikaner militants at the outbreak of World War I. And he was bright, personable, and charismatic besides. But Beyers Naudé was also a man of deep moral integrity, and for him Cottesloe was a moment of enlightenment on the road to Damascus, a road that has led him to be the most implacable foe of apartheid that Afrikanerdom has produced, and an important contributor to the theology of liberation.

Naudé had studied in Germany during the 1950s and become acquainted with the events of the *Kirchenkampf*, Bonhoeffer, and the Barmen Declaration. That and his own critical reexamination of the Biblical texts the Dutch Reformed Church relied on to justify apartheid brought him to the point where he began to doubt that the ideology could be squared with Christian principles. Cottesloe clinched it. He decided that a *status confessionis* had arisen in South Africa and that the time had come to start a confessing church movement similar to the one formed at Barmen. Naudé and several young Dutch Reformed Church admirers formed an ecumenical body called the Christian Institute that was intended as a spearhead for such a movement.

Two things modified his plans. One was the heavy counteraction of the church and state authorities; the other was the emergence of a specific black theology as part of Steve Biko's Black Consciousness movement in the 1970s.

The counteraction was swift and savage. Sensing danger at the very heart of the Afrikaner *wêreld en lewensbeskouing*, the Dutch Reformed Church ordered Naudé to choose between his ministry and his institute. He could not serve both, its leaders warned. They meant to intimidate him, but they had reckoned without Naudé's obstinacy and singleness of purpose, as much a part of his Afrikaner heritage as of their own. In a moving sermon to his packed congregation of fashionable and influential *nomenklatura* in Johannesburg, he told them he was bound by

Biblical injunction "to obey God rather than men" and so would be leaving them to pursue his God-given task of seeking racial reconciliation through the institute. From then on he was branded a racial and ethnic traitor and subjected to ostracism and harassment. The church defrocked him. The government outlawed the institute. Its spokesmen, even a commission of inquiry, strongly implied that he was a subversive agent. He was banned, house-arrested, and legally silenced for seven years. But he never stopped working for his new cause.

Naudé's encounter with black theology was more formative. Like the Black Consciousness movement itself, black theology began among students in what was called the University Christian Movement. In an effort to supplant white missionary religion, it was part of the thrust toward black emancipation and self-assertion, part of the rediscovery of black cultural authenticity. It drew on aspects of African tradition, stressing the ancient religious concept of *ubuntu*, the unity of humanity and God, and the oneness of the community.[9] The effect of this on questioning white theologians like Naudé was profound. They realized, as Bonhoeffer had years before, that it was not enough simply to disapprove of the status quo as a conscience-stricken member of the privileged class; one had to "do theology from the lower side," in other words to cross the bitter-almond hedge both physically and psychologically, to experience the reality of the black world and develop a perception of what apartheid meant from that vantage point. This Naudé and a handful of other white clergymen did. It completed their journey to Damascus. It also affected the black theologians they came to know, helping to bridge the racial gap so that the black theology of liberation did not become one of an inverted racism. As Allan Boesak has said, it was Beyers Naudé who prevented his anger from turning into antiwhiteism.

In every Christian denomination blacks form a majority of the total membership, some by as much as 80 percent, so that as the new theology developed its influence was felt more and more by the established churches. Eventually they began to take tougher positions on apartheid: the Catholic, Presbyterian, Lutheran, and United Congregational churches, as well as the South African Council of Churches as a whole, all issued statements denouncing apartheid as being in conflict with Christian principles. Then in 1981, a quantum leap was taken when Boesak, by then the most dynamic force within the new theological movement, took the lead in forming an Alliance of Black Reformed Christians under a charter that denounced apartheid as a sin and declared

9. See *African Theology en Route*, conference papers edited by Sergio Torres and Kofi Appiah Kubi (Maryknoll, N.Y., 1977), p. 184.

that "the moral and theological justification of it is a travesty of the Gospel, a betrayal of the Reformed tradition, and a heresy."[10] The major battle of the theological civil war had begun, with the medieval-sounding concept of heresy as the central issue. And though the losers did not stand to be burned at the stake, the outcome was likely to be no less lethal to a vital source of strength for their political belief system.

A year later Boesak took the heresy issue before a conference of the World Alliance of Reformed Churches in Ottawa. In a powerful speech to the conference in 1982, he declared, "The struggle in South Africa is not merely against an evil ideology; it is against a pseudoreligious ideology which was born in and is still being justified out of the bosom of the Reformed Churches." Racism was a sin, Boesak argued, because it denied the truth that all human beings were made in the image of God, because it was a form of idolatry in which a dominant group assumed for itself a status higher than the other, and because it denied Christ's reconciling, humanizing work. In South Africa this sin was accompanied by a theology to rationalize it. That theology, developed by the Dutch Reformed Churches, amounted to a "pseudo-gospel" that challenged the authority of the true Gospel. For that reason, and because it was also a denial of the Reformed tradition, apartheid should be declared a heresy.[11]

The world alliance accepted Boesak's indictment. "We declare with Black Reformed Christians of South Africa," it said, "that apartheid ('separate development') is a sin, and that the moral and theological justification of it is a travesty of the Gospel and, in its persistent disobedience to the Word of God, a theological heresy." It suspended the membership of the Nederduitse Gereformeerde Kerk and the Nederduitsch Hervormde Kerk, saying they could be readmitted when they rejected apartheid, began working to dismantle it, and gave concrete support to those who had suffered under it.[12] The world alliance went on to elect Boesak its president.

It was a thunderous victory for the black theologians, the implications of which are still being felt in South Africa. As at Cottesloe, the extremist Nederduitsch Hervormde Kerk stuck to its guns and resigned from the alliance, but the main Dutch Reformed Church responded more equivocally. It accused the WCC of being one-sided and of swallowing liberation theology, which, it countercharged, was itself in conflict with the Bible and Reformed tradition. It agreed racism was a sin but insisted

10. John de Gruchy and Charles Villa-Vicencio, *Apartheid Is a Heresy* (Grand Rapids, Mich., 1983), pp. 161–3.

11. Ibid., pp. 1–9.

12. Ibid., pp. 168–73.

that "race-consciousness and the love of one's own nation" were not. In the end it said it did not accept the suspension of its membership willingly and would stop paying its fees, but it did not resign.[13] Since then it has edged toward a marginally more liberal standpoint on race, with much foot dragging and deep divisions in its ranks.

The black theologians did not let up their pressure with the Ottawa victory. Later that year the Anglican Church, soon to be headed by Tutu, issued its own statement declaring apartheid a heresy. And in 1985, at the height of the great black uprising, 150 clergymen of all races and denominations drafted a theological commentary on the "situation of death" in South Africa. *Kairos* is a Greek word meaning "moment of truth," and the declaration about this *Kairos* in South Africa stands as the clearest and most comprehensive exposition of the new theology offered so far. Its language is forthright, its positions are bold. Of the god of the civil religion it says bluntly:

> This god is an idol. It is as mischievous, sinister and evil as any of the idols that the prophets of Israel had to contend with. Here we have a god who is historically on the side of the white settlers, who dispossesses black people of their land and who gives the major part of the land to his "chosen people."
>
> It is the god of superior weapons who conquered those who were armed with nothing but spears. It is the god of the Casspirs and Hippos, the god of teargas, rubber bullets, *sjamboks*, prison cells and death sentences. Here is a god who exalts the proud and humbles the poor—the very opposite of the God of the Bible who "scatters the proud of heart, pulls down the mighty from their thrones and exalts the humble." From a theological point of view the opposite of the God of the Bible is the devil, Satan. The god of the South African State is not merely an idol or a false god, it is the devil disguised as Almighty God—the antichrist.[14]

The declaration challenges the state's claim that it has a divine right (in terms of Romans 13) to use force to maintain law and order and that resistance to its authority is sinful. Those verses have been read grossly out of context, it contends, and in a way that is contrary to the Bible's central theme. The state does indeed have a right to maintain law and order, but it must be a just law and a right order. If it is not, then Christians have a right to rebel. God calls his people to resist injustice, regardless of its source: thus Moses defies Pharaoh, Paul resists Rome, and Jesus is executed as a political prisoner.

13. Ibid., pp. 182–4.

14. *The Kairos Document: Challenge to the Church: A Theological Comment on the Political Crisis in South Africa* (Braamfontein, Johannesburg, 1986), p. 7.

The church has an obligation to avoid collaborating with tyranny and lending legitimacy to a morally illegitimate regime. Therefore it may sometimes be necessary to engage in civil disobedience, and "a church that takes its responsibilities seriously in these circumstances will sometimes have to disobey the state in order to obey God."

In a carefully considered section, the liberation theologians offer a limited justification for the use of violence in resisting tyranny. While they condemn violence in general, they say it should, like all things, be considered in context. Can the force used by a rapist be equated with the struggle of his victim? "Is it legimitate to use the same word violence to cover the ruthless and repressive activities of the State and the desperate attempts of the people to defend themselves? How can acts of oppression, injustice and domination be equated with acts of resistance and self-defence?"

This does not mean, the *Kairos Document* adds, that "any use of force at any time by people who are oppressed is permissible simply because they are struggling for their liberation." It acknowledges that there have been killings and maimings in the South African struggle that no Christian can condone, but condemnation of these should be on the grounds that they are unjustifiable in themselves, "not because they fall under a blanket condemnation of any use of physical force in any circumstances."[15]

The document also chastises the lack of active opposition to apartheid on the part of the "English-speaking" churches. While these churches criticize apartheid, they do so in a limited, cautious way, and do not become involved. Their "Church theology," as the liberationists call it, regards reconciliation as the key to resolving the conflict, but, the *Kairos Document* warns, this is a problematic concept. Reconciliation cannot be an absolute principle. Some conflicts cannot be reconciled, where the one side is right and the other wrong. "Nowhere in the Bible or in Christian tradition has it ever been suggested that we ought to try to reconcile good and evil, God and the devil. We are supposed to do away with evil, injustice, oppression and sin—not come to terms with it. We are supposed to oppose, confront and reject the devil and not try to sup with the devil." Thus in South Africa it is unchristian to plead for reconciliation before the injustices have been removed. Christians must confront the forces of evil, and only when the apartheid regime shows signs of genuine repentance can there be talk of reconciliation and negotiation.[16]

15. Ibid., pp. 11–13.

16. Ibid., pp. 8–10.

Similarly, "Church theology" sees religion and spirituality as separate from the world and so makes a virtue of neutrality and inactivity. But God, the *Kairos Document* argues, is not neutral. He takes the side of the oppressed, the downtrodden, and the marginalized. Thus the commitment to a "prophetic theology." Liberation theology calls for active involvement in the struggle against apartheid. The church's services, ceremonies, and rituals should express its new prophecy. It must engage in special campaigns and projects for liberation, not as a "third force" located somewhere between oppressor and oppressed but as an integral part of the liberation struggle.

And so, as the storm of confrontation gathered during the 1980s, the theological civil war became active in the streets of Soweto and other townships. Black clergymen were everywhere in the forefront, organizing, supporting, interceding, and providing advice and relief services. Churches became meeting places and centres of information. Clergymen provided leadership at both national and local levels. They buried the dead, comforted the bereaved, and were among the foremost speakers at the great funeral rallies. Reporters needing a briefing on the situation in a township where new conflicts were erupting learnt to head for the churches and speak to the preachers, who always seemed to know what was happening. They were in touch. Nowhere else in the world except perhaps in Poland is the Christian church so closely identified with a people's struggle for freedom.

THE LITTLE black bishop stabbed a finger toward the five white commissioners sitting before him and declared: "You whites brought us the Bible; now we blacks are taking it seriously. We are involved with God to set us free from all that enslaves us and makes us less than what He intended us to be." Throwing his arms wide in a gesture like a benediction, he boomed at them: "I will demonstrate that apartheid, separate development, or whatever it is called is evil, totally and without remainder, that it is unchristian and unbiblical." Then lowering his voice almost to a whisper he added: "If anyone were to show me otherwise, I would burn my Bible and cease to be a Christian."

Desmond Mpilo Tutu was not yet the Anglican metropolitan of Southern Africa, not yet a Nobel Peace Prize winner, not yet an international figure, yet this was perhaps his finest hour. It was 1981, the year of the heresy declaration, and the government was counterattacking. It had appointed a commission of inquiry into the affairs of the South African Council of Churches, which it rightly saw as the centre of the theological assault on apartheid and the Afrikaner civil religion. Government spokesmen were accusing the council of supporting "left-radical liberation politics," including terrorist attacks in South Africa. They were suggesting that it was part of a "total onslaught" against South Africa being directed from Moscow. Now the commission had been appointed to investigate the council's interpretation of its Christian mission, as well as its foreign connections and financial records, and report to the government on whether it was a subversive organization.

The council's funds, 90 percent of which came from churches in the United States and Europe, had been used to defend political prisoners, sustain their families, provide education for their children, and assist refugees who had fled to neighbouring countries. The financial records were in a state of disarray, partly because of poor management and partly because the council had not recorded the names of some of the people it had helped in order to protect them from security force action. Some $10 million was said not to have been properly accounted for, and the state brought a charge of fraud against the previous general secretary, which then gave it a pretext for ordering the probe. Clearly the authorities hoped to unearth something that could be used to discredit the council and perhaps provide grounds for banning it. For Tutu, the new general secretary, it was a tricky situation, but as he took his seat as the first witness to testify before the all-white commission in a government office building in Pretoria, he was anything but defensive. He used the occasion as a platform, or rather a pulpit, to deliver a major public denunciation of apartheid and an exposition of the theology of liberation.

It made for a curious scene, the black bishop all intensity and animation delivering a theological lecture strewn with Biblical quotations to a stony-faced judge, accountant, retired auditor-general, magistrate, and vice-president of an Afrikaans university. As Tutu said at the outset, he did not recognize their right to sit in judgment on the church council's theological credentials—"only our member churches can do that"—but he let them have it anyway, with a gusto that sometimes had the few blacks in the public benches applauding with delight.

He sat bouncing and twisting in an upright chair, his hands shaping the outline of his ideas with vivid gestures. When he spoke of the resurrection of the body his arms folded around his own body in a hug. His voice was the other instrument in this virtuoso performance, sometimes sonorous, playing with the cadences of his African accent, and sometimes breaking into a high-pitched chuckle as he hit on a pertinent new insight. His delivery was sombre, joyful, impatient, humourous, reflective, switching rapidly through all these registers in response to a quicksilver spirit. And all the while the white commissioners watched expressionlessly.

Tutu's lecture dwelt on precisely those passages of the Bible that form the basis of the theological justification for apartheid: the stories of Genesis and the Tower of Babel, from which the notion of separate nations being part of the "ordinances of creation" is drawn; and Exodus, the paradigm for the sacred saga of the Great Trek and Afrikaner nationalism's "chosen people" mythology. To Tutu they have a diametrically different eschatology, one which proclaims unity and liberation as God's divine intention, not separateness and chauvinism.

From the first eleven chapters of Genesis, Tutu said one learnt that unity and wholeness were God's will for all of his creation. The story of the Garden of Eden was a poetic presentation of God's intention for the universe—a world of peace, prosperity, fellowship, justice, wholeness, compassion, love, and joy, all of which were encapsulated in the almost untranslatable Hebrew word, *shalom*. But this primal unity, Tutu said, was disrupted by sin. Thus Genesis ended with the shattering story of the Tower of Babel, where human community and fellowship became impossible. "This is the ultimate consequence according to the Bible of sin, separation, alienation, apartness," Tutu observed. "It is a perverse exegesis," he added wryly, "that would hold that the story of the Tower of Babel is a justification for racial separation, a divine sanction for the diversity of nations. It is to declare that the divine punishment for sin had become the divine intention for mankind."

The entire story of the Bible thereafter was of God's mission to restore the harmony, the unity, the fellowship, and the spirit of community that were there at the beginning. For that reason God sent his son to affect reconciliation and atonement—"please note that this word is also at-one-ment"—and re-create the *shalom* that was his intention at the beginning. "So Jesus came to restore human community and brotherhood which sin destroyed. He came to say that God had intended us for fellowship, for *koinonia*, for togetherness, without destroying our distinctiveness, our cultural identity. Apartheid quite deliberately denies and repudiates this central act of Jesus and says we are made for separateness, for disunity, for enmity, for alienation, all of which we have shown to be the fruits of sin."

Therefore apartheid itself was clearly a sin. "The only separation the Bible knows is between believers on the one hand and unbelievers on the other. Any other kind of separation, division, disunity is of the devil. It is evil and from sin."

To Tutu and other liberation theologists, the story of Exodus is a paradigm, not for the liberation of a chosen people, but for all who are oppressed. In this sense it is the oppressed and underprivileged everywhere who are chosen, who are the children of Israel. "The God of the Exodus is a liberator God who leads His people out of every kind of bondage, spiritual, political, social and economic," Tutu told the commissioners. "He takes the side of the poor, the weak, the widow, the orphan and the alien. That is the refrain you get in the Book of Deuteronomy—look after these because they represent a class of society which tends to be marginalized, to be pushed to the periphery or to the bottom of the pile."

Because of this, the church council believed Christians were enjoined to take sides in the struggles of the oppressed. It did not accept the notion often expounded in South Africa that religion should be separated from politics.

> If we say that religion cannot be concerned with politics, then we are really saying that there is a substantial part of human life in which God's writ does not run. . . . Religion is not a form of escapism. Our God does not permit us to dwell in a kind of spiritual ghetto, insulated from the real life out there. Our God is not a God who sanctifies the *status quo*. He is a God of surprises, uprooting the powerful and unjust to establish His Kingdom. He cares that children starve in resettlement camps. He cares that people die mysteriously in detention. He is concerned that people are condemned to a twilight existence as non-persons by banning them without giving them the right to reply to charges brought against them.

This was how the members of the church council interpreted their Christian mission. Was it subversive? Was it revolutionary? Yes indeed. "The God of the Exodus is subversive of all situations of injustice," Tutu declared. "And the Bible is the most revolutionary, the most radical book there is. If any book should be banned by those who rule unjustly and as tyrants, then it is the Bible."

Tutu ended with a ringing declaration of determination to continue his Christian mission as he saw it, regardless of what action the government might take against him or the council. "I want the Government to know now and always that I do not fear them," he said. "They are trying to defend the utterly indefensible and they will fail. They will fail because they are ranging themselves on the side of evil and injustice against the Church of God. Like others who have done that in the past, the Neros, the Hitlers, the Amins of this world, they will end up as the flotsam and jetsam of history."

The commissioners stared stonily ahead of them. The blacks in the public benches erupted with delight. Tutu leaned back, closed the old leather-bound Bible he had been brandishing, and mopped his brow. A rearguard battle in the theological civil war had been fought and won. In the end the commission recommended no action against the church council, and it lived to fight another day.

. . .

BUT NOT ALL black South Africans, or all black Christians, subscribe to the theology of liberation. The better educated certainly do, the intellectual elite and the politicized sector in both city and countryside who are the most seriously disaffected and who spearhead the struggle against apartheid. But many from the lower stratum of society, as many as a third of the total black population, belong to a profusion of indigenous African churches that are deeply conservative and quiescent in their politics. These churches call on their members to obey the law and avoid political involvement. They preach that Christians must suffer in silent obedience to God's appointed authorities and that reparation will be granted in the hereafter. Some scholars think they are exerting the same kind of quietistic influence on the urban poor that the Evangelical Revival did on the English working class in the early nineteenth century, sublimating political grievances into religious fervour.[17]

They are in any event the same kind of people, mostly newcomers to the city, middle-aged with little education, and with low-paid, unskilled jobs. They shrink from the radicalism of the resistance movements, find it too modern and strange, feel insecure in the city, and so cling to the old ways of the tribe, to what is familiar and safe. They cling, too, to the old habits of subservience in their relationship with whites, because that is safe also and because they are not yet sure in their own minds that whites are not superior.

There are nearly four thousand of these sects with, at the last official count, more than five million members—and the numbers are multiplying daily. One can see the sect members walking about the streets on Sundays in flowing white robes with blue and green patchwork embroidery, sometimes carrying simple crosses and crosiers. Or hear them singing down by some riverside in richly harmonized voices, an isolated one occasionally rising in shrill, ululating hysteria, as they conduct their baptismal services of total immersion. One can also see them on weekdays wearing the little silver stars or other symbols of their sects pinned to their lapels and bodices.

They first began to appear toward the end of the last century in response, seemingly, to the loss of land and the forces of the industrial revolution. Bengt Sundkler, a Swedish sociologist who did the first detailed study of the movement in 1948, believes it was also a response

17. See Michael Sparks in an honours dissertation, *Has the Role of the African Indigenous Churches Contributed to Stalling or Preventing a Revolution in South Africa?* University of Cape Town, 1986.

to the colour bar then practised in many of the mainline Christian churches, and a need to open up opportunities for black leaders at a time when tribal leadership was collapsing and there were no other such opportunities elsewhere.[18] Since the more churches, the more leaders, from the beginning the sects multiplied rapidly.

Broadly, the denominations can be divided into the Ethiopian and Zionist sects. The Ethiopian churches, the first to appear, are the more politically aware and militant of the two. They had their high point during the Garveyist movement of the 1920s, when they adopted Garvey's slogan of "Africa for the Africans." Symbolically, too, they took their name from a country which for black liberationists at that time personified freedom and independence: Ethiopia and Liberia were then the only independent black-ruled states in Africa.

The Zionist denominations, which have nothing in common with modern Jewish Zionism, have their roots in the American Pentecostal movement, specifically an apocalyptic healing movement founded by John A. Downie in Chicago in 1896 called the Christian Catholic Apostolic Church in Zion. Downie sent missionaries to South Africa, and his energetic revivalist style caught on first among newly urbanized Afrikaners, who founded a church called the Apostolic Faith Mission. From there it spread to the black community, where the many sects that it spawned merged this Christian revivalism in various ways with traditional African religious views and rituals. Today the Zionist sects are by far the more numerous of the two, also the more conservative and schismatic. Splits occur constantly over leadership disputes and doctrinal differences. But what they share is an enveloping warmth, a collective psychology of mutual support and protection.

Some of the sects practice a spiritual, if not political, militancy, downgrading the pale white Christ and at least partially replacing him with a black messiah. One such is the Nazarite Church in Natal, whose founder, Isaiah Shembe, has been deified. The Nazarites have reversed the colour bar in spiritual terms: their black messiah guards the gates of heaven and bars whites from entering. They had their riches and good things during their lifetime on earth, the whites are told, and "nobody can rule twice." Other sects strike a more offbeat note. The expurgating of evil spirits is still important in black social circles where traditionalism remains strong: sometimes they must be flushed out of the body, sometimes they must be washed off. Some sects have thus adopted names reflecting the importance of these rituals, such as the Castor Oil Dead Church and the Sunlight Soap Church.

The biggest and fastest-growing of all the indigenous African

18. Bengt Sundkler, *Bantu Prophets in South Africa*, 2nd ed. (London, 1961), p. 100.

churches is the Zion Christian Church. Every Easter more than a million of its adherents make a pilgrimage to a farm in the northern Transvaal where the church has its headquarters. There for four days they gather on a dusty hillside in the presence of their own black bishop and engage in a great spiritual fiesta—a huge, emotive affair that is half modern Christian revivalism, with faith healing, immersion in water, and speaking in tongues; and half traditional African ancestor worship and the exorcism of spirits.

The sect was started early in this century by a man named Engenas Lekganyane, who attended a Scottish Presbyterian seminary and then fell under the influence of a missionary from Downie's church, which had its headquarters at a place called Zion City, Illinois. Lekganyane proclaimed himself bishop of his new church, and in 1912, months before the Land Act became law, he bought a farm which he called Zion City, Moria, and set up his headquarters there. On his death his son, Bishop Edward Lekganyane, took over; and today Edward's thirty-year-old son, Barnabas, is head of the church. The three form something of a triumvirate deity, being invoked as intercessionists in the manner of traditional African worship. They have also, each in his own time, made a great deal of money from tribute offerings. Members of the sect take vicarious pleasure in seeing their leaders live in conspicuous affluence and so have bestowed expensive gifts on the bishops. Edward used to sport a huge diamond ring and at one stage had forty-five automobiles, including several specially imported Cadillacs and the Daimler in which the British royal family toured South Africa in 1946.

In return, the church offers an extensive, caring support system for its socially vulnerable members, nearly all of whom are elderly or middle-aged, poorly educated, unskilled, and still quite close to their rural roots. The support system helps them adapt to the city, offers them fellowship, a sense of belonging, a new home, and a new loyalty to replace the community spirit of the tribal clan they have left behind. It also offers practical assistance, helping members find food, clothing, and shelter, caring for them when they are sick, and comforting them when they are bereaved.

It offers other forms of comfort and protection, too. "I'll be safe when I get home," an old man whom I met at one of the Moria gatherings told me as he clutched two packets of "Zion tea" that had been blessed by Bishop Barnabas. His hired bus had been sprinkled with water blessed by the bishop so that its passengers would have a safe journey. And when he got home, he said, he would plant two poles outside his front door between which he would string a length of wire that the bishop had also blessed to keep away lightning and cause any intruder to lose his strength on passing it.

It is not surprising that an institution with such priorities—support and survivalism for the weak and insecure—should counsel its members to avoid politics and confrontation with the authorities. Work hard, stay sober, respect authority, obey the law, and keep your head down: those are its injunctions. The justice of even the most onerous apartheid laws is not questioned. As one ZCC evangelist told an interviewer: "We disagree with unjust laws but this is on the political side which the church has nothing to do with. People must not argue with the law, they must pray for the law to be changed. We have been told by the leaders of our church not to try to change the laws."[19]

The caution verges on obsequiousness. When I arrived at Moria to observe the Easter festival, shouting guards ran through the milling crowd clearing a path for the white man's car. I was shown to a reception centre for white visitors which had a small replica of the Voortrekker monument in it and pictures of government ministers and other officials meeting church leaders. When the minister of Bantu Administration visited Moria at the height of the Verwoerd era, Bishop Edward thanked him for leading the black people to an "orderly freedom" and assured him that "in our church there is no room for people who undermine national security and break the law." In 1985 President Botha was invited as a guest of honour to the Easter festival.

The growing influence of the sects presents the government with an opportunity for manipulation and propaganda. Botha's visit to the ZCC was a publicity coup. He was able to claim, with at least statistical accuracy, that he had been welcomed by the biggest black church in the country. In his address, he presented himself to the deferential congregants as a divinely sanctioned ruler. "There is no authority except from God," he told them. "Rulers are not a terror to good conduct, but to bad conduct. Do what is good, and you will receive the approval of the ruler. He is God's servant for your good."

It also offers an opportunity for advancing the strategy of dependency and co-optation with which the government tries to counter its loss of legitimacy in the black community. The sects represent a substantial constituency that can be ingratiated and induced to collaborate in some of the apartheid institutions that the radicals are depriving of legitimacy through boycotts and campaigns of denigration. Thus with the help of Esau Mahlatsi, a ZCC member who held the position of "mayor" of the government-backed community council for the Vaal Triangle townships, Botha was able to make a well-publicized visit to Sharpeville in 1987 and give the impression that the government had achieved a po-

19. Sparks, op. cit., p. 35.

litical breakthrough in this evocative symbol of the black resistance.[20] The government has also cultivated Bishop Isaac Mokoena, head of a group of indigenous churches called the Reformed Independent Church Association and of a putative political organization named the United Christian Conciliation Party, who makes periodic television appearances claiming to be the black religious leader with the largest following in the country and attacking the political standpoint of the South African Council of Churches and Archbishop Tutu in particular.

Beyers Naudé on one side, Isaac Mokoena on the other. The theological civil war, like other aspects of the South African conflict, is not a straightforward black-white affair.

20. Mahlatsi and his council were elected in a 15 percent poll of registered voters in a heavily boycotted election in 1981. When trouble erupted in the Vaal Triangle in September 1984, Mahlatsi's house and a chain of stores he owned were burned by angry residents. He and other councillors fled for their lives, and Mahlatsi lived under police protection until shortly before Botha's visit.

CHAPTER THIRTEEN

The Crisis of Apartheid

In this country we have so many people who want change so long as things remain the same.

ARCHBISHOP DESMOND TUTU

Between separation and integration there is no permanency, only a slippery slope to black domination.

LOUIS STOFBERG

IT WAS MIDNIGHT exactly when the song began, the soft, sad voice of *fado* singer José Alfonso rising tremulously from the jeep radio into the warm Iberian night. "Grandola Vila Morena," he sang, a soulfully spun theme about the people of a poor village in southern Portugal gathering in the village square to show their solidarity. The young lieutenant sitting in the jeep heard it and tensed. That was the signal, dead on time. He checked the magazine of his G-3 rifle, snapped it shut, and waved his arm to the vehicles parked behind. Engines revved and the column swung out on the road to Lisbon Airport.

Fifty miles to the north Captain Maia heard the song, too. He checked his watch. In two hours he would give the order and the Escola Practica de Cavalaria, the most prestigious tank unit in the Portuguese army, would move on the capital. He felt a twinge of nervous excitement. Maia knew that his was the key unit in the whole coup attempt. All the senior officers in the Escola were opposed to the coup, and Maia and the other young lieutenants and captains had arrested them and placed them under guard. It was one hell of a responsibility for men so young. Maia had just turned twenty-five.

All over Portugal the same thing was happening. Young officers, sick of the wasted years of their youth spent in the bush of Angola and Mozambique and the mangrove swamps of Portuguese Guinea, sick of the heat and the flies and the killing and the senselessness of it all, knowing, as only young soldiers who have come face to face with life's ultimate reality can know, that they were trapped in a series of no-win wars that the stubborn old dictatorship would not end, were arresting their commanding officers and preparing their units to march toward Lisbon and Oporto.

Two a.m. and Air Force Major Costa Neves, also in his midtwenties, stepped out of a car parked across the Rua Sampaio E Pina from the long, low, dusky-pink building that houses Radio Club Portugais, Portugal's main private radio station. Other shadowy figures slipped from their cars and fanned out around the building. Moments later Major Neves was standing in a studio handing a slip of paper to an astonished broadcaster. "Read that," he said curtly. But first there was the enactment of a small pantomime, the kind of thing that lends a touch of human levity to even the gravest situations. The instructions on the sheet of paper required that this and all subsequent communiqués by the revolutionary Movement of the Armed Forces be preceded by the playing of patriotic military music. But, said the flustered broadcaster, at this hour we don't have anything like that in the studio. Hardly the stuff for the late-late show. And so the announcement of Western Europe's first postwar revolution was withheld from the nation and the world for half an hour while the rebel officer and the late-night disc jockey scratched through the record stacks looking for an appropriate tune. Eventually they found something that came close. "A Life on the Ocean Wave" had a good martial swing to it, they decided, and perhaps it could be said to have an association with Portugal's maritime history. And so this old English sea shanty, which was once the march of the Royal Marines, became the signature tune of the Portuguese Revolution.

It was nearly 3:00 a.m., and a troubled old man driving home from a late night of drinks and talk with his friends heard the tune on his car radio. Then the announcer's voice. The old man didn't pay attention at first; then he caught the words "a political solution to the conflicts in Africa. . . ." He didn't need to hear more. His grandson would not be going to the war after all. Next day, Thursday, April 25, 1974, he was one of thousands of demonstrators who gathered in the Largo Do Carmo in the heart of Lisbon to see Prime Minister Marcello Caetano, who had taken refuge in the National Guard headquarters there, surrender his regime. Here indeed was a moment of history. The end not just of fifty years of dictatorship for Portugal, but of the age of colonialism itself. Europe's first and last colonial power was pulling out of Africa. Half a millennium of imperialism was over.

In the colonies themselves it was, briefly, a time of joy and redemption before the anguish of internal power struggles and economic collapse overwhelmed them. For the West, the United States particularly, it was a time of shock and dismay. The whole basis of the administration's policy for southern Africa had been thrown into disarray. Five years before, a policy review ordered by Henry Kissinger, then national security adviser to President Nixon, had concluded that there was no prospect of the white regimes of southern Africa being dislodged from power in the foreseeable future. The black insurgent movements were too weak and disorganized, and, the effects of sanctions notwithstanding, the white regimes of Rhodesia, South Africa, and the Portuguese colonies could hold out indefinitely. This National Security Study Memorandum 39 colloquially became known as the "Tar Baby" report—a sticky mess that the United States should not touch, but just accept that the whites were there to stay and work through them.[1] Now just five years later the policy was in a shambles. Not for the first time or the last had a Western power misjudged an African situation by looking at it from an essentially white perspective, dooming themselves, like Giliomee's white South Africans, to be perennially startled—in this case by the depth and permanence of black African resolve and by the effect this would have on the Portuguese will to stick it out in their colonies. It was a political misreading and an intelligence failure with consequences that led the United States into further blunders in Africa and opened an opportunity for Soviet-bloc intervention and propaganda gains.

Though it occurred five thousand miles away among another people in another continent, in South Africa the Portuguese Revolution was an event of catalytic importance that changed the whole directional flow of public affairs. By precipitating the sudden dissolution of the Portuguese empire and the independence of Mozambique and Angola, it gave black South Africans a huge adrenalin shot, changed the geopolitical map of the subcontinent, transformed Pretoria's strategic thinking, and led to a reformulation of apartheid policy. It marked, in fact, a simultaneous turning point, at which the Afrikaner revolution crested and entered a phase of crisis and decline, and at which the black revolution began its rise.

Until then white South Africa had been protected from direct confrontation with the black nations to its north by an arc of white-ruled colonies that spanned the continent from the Atlantic to the Indian Ocean: Angola and Namibia in the west, through Rhodesia to Mozambique in the east. That meant the Umkhonto guerrillas could have no easy access from their exile bases in the north, having to traverse the white buffer first and, if they could do this, had no lines of retreat, communication, or supply. They were desperately vulnerable and as

1. For details of NSSM 39 and an assessment of the American policy misjudgment, see *South Africa: Time Running Out*, report of the Study Commission on U.S. Policy Towards Southern Africa (Berkeley, Cal., 1981), pp. 350–5.

long as that situation obtained there was no prospect of the ANC's guerrilla war becoming a serious threat to the apartheid state.

Now, overnight, the independence of Mozambique and Angola removed two key areas from this buffer and brought South Africa face to face with militant black nationalism for the first time. Isolated in the centre, Rhodesia was soon to fall as well. Black rule in Mozambique opened up a massive second front in Rhodesia's long guerrilla war, stretching stubborn Ian Smith's limited manpower resources between the conflicting demands of army and production in an economy strapped by sanctions. Within five years he had to negotiate a handover to the newly independent black government. Now the protective buffer was not only gone altogether but transformed into a threatening arc of radical black states sympathetic to the ANC. The barrier against guerrillas had become a series of potential springboards for them. The southern part of Mozambique in particular, with Swaziland adjoining it, formed a salient jutting deep into the eastern Transvaal, only a few hours' drive from Johannesburg and the industrial heartland of South Africa. If Namibia were to fall as well under pressure from Angola, South Africa would, like Smith, be vulnerable to attack from all sides and to economic attrition within.

All this white and black South Africans watched and weighed with deep concern on the one side and heady anticipation on the other. The blacks were tremendously encouraged by what they saw as a victory for the underdogs in a situation analogous to their own. Black liberation armies had finally succeeded against a white power establishment that had rivalled South Africa's in its stubborn resistance to the "winds of change." The oldest colonial power in Africa, which had been there even longer than the Afrikaners, had been forced to give way. The effectiveness of guerrilla struggle over superior military forces had been demonstrated in an African situation. Faith in the inevitable triumph of right over might was reinforced. Given this huge morale boost for the black South Africans, it is not surprising that within a year riots erupted in Soweto and set South Africa ablaze for the first time since Sharpeville.

The enforced use of the Afrikaans language in black schools was the detonator that set off the eruption, but the surge of new-found confidence in the black community was what primed the charge. Mozambique's radical president, Samora Machel, became an instant hero in the townships, and scores of Soweto parents named their children after him. A new generation of black students, fired up with Steve Biko's ideas, accused their elders of having been too supine. Why had they tolerated apartheid for so long? Why had they not been more militant? Move over oldies, Machel has shown us the way. *"Viva Samora! Aluta continua!"*—Long live Samora! The struggle continues! The slogans and rhetoric of the Portuguese colonial revolution swept the South African townships and stimulated a nascent rise in revolutionary consciousness.

June 16, 1976. It was a Wednesday morning, sunny and bright. The Reverend David Nkwe was standing at the door of St. Paul's Church on Moroka Street, Soweto, when he saw a column of youngsters come marching by. They looked cheerful enough, he recalls, laughing, singing, and dancing as they went along. One or two recognized him and waved. They were from the Morris Isaacson High School up the road and, as someone in the crowd told Reverend Nkwe, they had walked out of their classrooms that morning to join a protest demonstration against a government edict that half of all classes in black schools be taught in Afrikaans.

For three weeks, in fact, Morris Isaacson students had been travelling from school to school to mobilize others. The plan was for them all to converge on Orlando West, another high school, and then march from there in a single large column to the Orlando Soccer Stadium, where a mass protest meeting would be held.

Reverend Nkwe watched the singing, dancing column make its way down the rutted street toward Orlando West. They turned into Vilakazi Street and were halfway down it, still about a mile from the school, when they were confronted by a small group of armed white policemen. An officer shouted to them to halt. The students jeered and waved their fists. Tear gas was fired, some rocks were thrown, and then the police opened fire with live ammunition. A thirteen-year-old boy, Hector Peterson, was the first to fall, shot in the back. A youth who had been marching next to him scooped the boy up and carried him to a parked car while Hector's sister ran alongside, crying. A photograph of the three of them has become a symbol of the Soweto uprising, reprinted in thousands of books and pamphlets around the world.

The youths first reacted to the police gunfire by scattering into back alleys, recalls Harry Mashabela, a black reporter who was there. Then they regrouped and began to attack anyone and anything that could be identified with the apartheid system. By nightfall Soweto was ablaze. Administration buildings, offices, and beer halls were set on fire. Police vehicles and delivery vans belonging to white businesses were stoned, overturned, and torched. Two white officials from the local administration board were killed.

Before it ended, the violence had spread to 160 different communities. Within a week 176 people were dead, within a year more than 600. The uprising lasted seventeen months before it was finally quelled in another wave of repressive action, with the government banning twenty-two

Black Consciousness organizations. By the end of 1977 Biko was dead, his movement outlawed, thousands of young activists were in prison, and 14,000 people had fled the country for exile abroad.

THE PORTUGUESE REVOLUTION not only boosted black morale and infused it with a new revolutionary consciousness, but prompted changes in white thinking and policy making no less profound.

The collapse of the protective buffer to the north of South Africa was the central strategic concern that led to this reassessment. How could some kind of *Pax Pretoriana* be reestablished over that vital region, at least to neutralize it in the guerrilla conflict? This became the preoccupation of policy planners in their think-tanks. Some thought it might be possible to lure the neighbouring countries into an economic alliance with nonaggression pacts attached. John Vorster, prime minister at the time, spoke of a "good neighbours" policy. He had tried, with conspicuously little success, to establish a détente with some of the more moderate black African countries farther north, and although this "outward-looking" policy had run out of steam he was still thinking in that mode. When Mozambique became independent in 1975 Vorster declared that he had no objection to the Machel government's Marxist orientation, that in fact he didn't mind what sort of governments South Africa's neighbours had, "so long as they are stable." This intended invitation to reciprocal good neighbourliness drew no response. Machel announced that the ANC was welcome in Maputo.

Against this backdrop, events in Angola suddenly presented an opportunity for a dramatic shift in South Africa's geopolitical strategy. Unlike Mozambique, where Machel's Frelimo party was unchallenged in its claim to power at independence, Angola had three rival parties engaged in a bloody struggle for dominance as independence day there approached: the Popular Movement for the Liberation of Angola (MPLA), rooted in the Mbundu people of central Angola and led by Agostinho Neto, a doctor, poet, and intellectual of note; the National Front for the Liberation of Angola (FNLA), rooted in the Bakongo people of the northeast and led by Holden Roberto, who had close ties with President Mobutu Sese Seko of neighbouring Zaire; and the National Union for the Total Independence of Angola (UNITA), rooted in the Ovimbundu people of the south and led by Jonas Savimbi, who had received his guerrilla training in China.

All three had received help from Communist countries at one time or another, but the MPLA had Marxist, anti-imperialist views and had openly criticized the United States for supporting Portugal against the liberation movements. Roberto, on the other hand, had long-standing ties with the United States Central Intelligence Agency, as did his friend Mobutu. As the power struggle among the three intensified, the CIA mounted a covert operation to support the FNLA and to prevent the MPLA, which it regarded as Soviet-backed, from gaining power. According to John Stockwell, who headed the CIA task force, Angola was of little strategic or economic interest to the United States, but Henry Kissinger, frustrated by America's humiliation in Vietnam, was looking for an opportunity to challenge the Soviet Union and so decided to intervene.[2] But the operation had to be covert, which meant working with a limited budget of only $14 million, because Kissinger knew that so soon after the Vietnam withdrawal there was no chance of getting Congress to approve funds for another foreign military intervention. To boost the shoestring operation, secret negotiations were held with South Africa, which was persuaded to intervene in support of Savimbi in the south to increase pressure on the MPLA, which had the advantage of being in control of Luanda, the capital.

For South Africa this was a golden opportunity, both to ingratiate itself with the United States and to establish influence over a key buffer state. Pieter Botha, the innately aggressive minister of defence and General Magnus Malan, the equally hawkish defence force chief, did not hesitate. On Wednesday, September 17, 1975, a task force of fifty light Panhard armoured cars manned by 250 South African soldiers and supported by 750 command artillery struck into Angola. Another two thousand troops provided logistical support from the Namibian border. This action was in direct conflict both with Vorster's "good neighbours" statement of only a few months before and with South Africa's longstanding doctrine of noninterference in another nation's domestic affairs. For years South Africa had stood rigidly by this clause in the United Nations Charter as its main defence against foreign attempts to act against it because of apartheid. It had become the leitmotif of Pretoria's foreign policy. Now suddenly it was being violated with a vengeance, with South Africa involved in a high-risk venture more than a thousand miles beyond its borders in collaboration with the secret service agency of a foreign power. General Hendrik van den Bergh, Vorster's security adviser and chief of intelligence at the time, told me years later that the operation was not discussed in advance with the prime minister; Botha had acted on his own, telling Vorster the task force was going in to protect a jointly owned hydroelectric project at Calueque, just across

2. John Stockwell, *In Search of Enemies* (London, 1979), p 38. Stockwell gives a detailed insider's account of the machinations involved in the CIA operation, code-named Iafeature, and of South Africa's involvement.

the border, while privately authorizing it to strike much deeper into Angola.[3]

In fact it made a blitzkrieg advance up the west coast, capturing the port cities of Mocamedes, Benguela, and Lobito in a matter of days and then knifing through the MPLA defences to take Porto Amboim, only a hundred miles down the coast from Luanda on November 14. With only their light armour and artillery, they had outmanoeuvred Cuban troops who had come to the aid of the MPLA armed with missile-firing helicopters, Russian T-34 tanks, and long-range 122mm cannon. It was a spectacular performance.

More astonishing still was that this entire operation took place under a cloak of deception. As the column plunged five hundred miles into Angola, the South African public was told nothing; like Vorster, it was told the troops were only at the Calueque Dam. Foreign press reports that South African soldiers were deep inside Angola were repeatedly denied, accounts of battles dismissed as untrue. Even when foreign governments began commenting on the South African involvement, Pretoria kept up its denials. In all history there cannot be many instances of a country going into a foreign war without the knowledge of its people.

In the midst of this I received an invitation to attend a briefing of newspaper editors in Botha's office in Cape Town. What took place there was an exercise in media manipulation that can have few parallels. Botha greeted us sternly, seated us around a long table, and told us that in the national interest he had decided to brief us on a matter of great importance, the confidentiality of which was absolutely essential. With that he handed over the meeting to a small, dapper army officer with pale blue eyes, whom he introduced as General Constand Viljoen, chief of operations in Angola.

Viljoen unrolled a wall map of Angola and, using a pointer, talked his way through the military situation there. He showed us the positions of the MPLA, FNLA, and UNITA forces, where the South African column had crossed the border, how far it had advanced, and which towns it had captured. The information was up-to-date to within a few hours, Viljoen told us. A second column was operating further east and a battle was about to be fought that day for the town of Luso, now called Luena,

3. Van den Bergh also alleged that Botha had unilaterally ordered a task force to move into Mozambique on the eve of its independence, but that he, Van den Bergh, had been alerted to this by his intelligence network and had sent agents of the Bureau of State Security to disable the vehicles. However, it must be noted that Van den Bergh had recently been dismissed by Botha and was a bitter man when he made these allegations. He later joined the extreme right-wing Conservative party.

a key point on the vital Benguela railroad, and he expected news of its capture any moment. "Our boys are doing a great job," Viljoen said, his eyes shining. "It proves that our training methods are first-class." Botha was animated, bombastic, as he answered editors' questions. Could South Africa get away with this? Why was it being kept secret? "We're not in it alone," he declared. "You'd be surprised to know who's in it with us." With a knowing smile Botha told us South Africa had been given assurances at the highest level by the other parties involved in the operation, but it was absolutely vital to keep a low profile because they could not afford to be seen associating with South Africa in an operation like this. The real reason, of course, was that the CIA operation was itself clandestine—hence the official denials. As long as Pretoria kept on denying the press reports, nothing could be proved.

The mood of the briefing was euphoric. This was not only a military success, we were told, but a foreign-relations breakthrough, and a breakthrough in Africa as well. Some of those involved with South Africa were African leaders. New relationships were being established. It was a wonderful opportunity.

We filed out of the meeting half impressed, half appalled. We had been given the inside story, but we had been blatantly used and effectively gagged. We knew now that the denials we were publishing daily were a lie, but we had no choice but to continue publishing them as official statements. Knowing the truth on a basis of strict confidentiality, we could not permit our newspapers to probe for it. We had been made instruments of the deception.

It was not for long, however. The venture soon ran into disaster and was exposed. With the FNLA forces poised to launch an attack on Luanda that would carry them into power, Cuban troops in the capital opened up a scorching barrage of 122mm "Stalin Organ" fire. As salvo after salvo of the terrifying rockets rained down on the flat Quifangondo valley twelve miles outside the city, Roberto's poorly disciplined troops panicked and fled. Within days they were a useless, plundering rabble. The CIA chiefs, realizing that only a considerable escalation of their operation could save it, appealed to Congress for funds. Outraged at having been deceived, Congress refused. The operation was scrapped and the South Africans, left out on a limb five hundred miles inside Angola, had no choice but to quit and withdraw in a flurry of embarrassment and diplomatic recriminations while the MPLA took over in Luanda.

On the face of it the venture was a fiasco. Yet it had been a heady experience, similar in its impact on the minds of the defence force chiefs in Pretoria to the Six Day War on Israel. CIA agents had flown in and out of Waterkloof air base at the dead of night; there had been clandestine meetings in Washington and Paris, secret contacts in African capitals.

It was all very exciting and engendered for these international pariahs a sense of belonging in the underworld of *Realpolitik* beneath the public world of anti-apartheid rhetoric and exclusion. Headiest of all was the ease with which the small task force had sliced into Angola. Suddenly there was a realization of South Africa's immense military superiority in the region and what this might mean politically. "Our army can go anywhere in Africa, right up to Cairo," Botha exulted to his cabinet colleagues. It opened up new vistas of opportunity.

Out of this experience a new regional strategy began to take shape. Botha's personal think-tank, the Department of Military Intelligence, began developing the concept of South Africa asserting itself as a Regional Superpower. It was based largely on the model of Israel, whose aggressive strategy for survival in a hostile environment Pretoria's military think-tankers had long admired. The idea was that if South Africa could dominate its region with overwhelming military and economic superiority, then it could call the shots in the area and there would be little anyone else could do about it. The lost buffer would cease to matter. In the language of these securocrats, South Africa could maintain a *dwangpostuur*, or a posture of threat and compulsion, that would intimidate the neighbouring black states and dissuade them from allowing the ANC to use their territory as springboards or even as Ho Chi Minh trails for the insurgents. The formula was simple: keep them destabilized and use their dependence on the South African economy—as a job market for thousands of their citizens, as a source of supply for essential consumer goods, and for access to the outside world via its transportation network—to put the squeeze on them if they did not comply. Conversely, aid and other economic cooperation could be offered if they did.

A whole new foreign policy concept opened up. Stop worrying about political unpopularity: it is respect for your physical power that counts in this hard world of *Realpolitik* to which South Africa believed it now had accreditation. As the brash young men at MI headquarters liked to put it, "If you've got them by the balls, their hearts and minds will follow."

At this point there occurred one of those extraneous fortuitous events that sometimes changes the course of history. The ideas that the military think-tankers were developing were no doubt interesting to them but they were of little relevance to government policy. That was being shaped primarily by Van den Bergh and his Bureau of State Security, Vorster's key advisers and bitter rivals of the military establishment. And, as Van den Bergh made clear to me in later conversations, they were thinking along altogether different lines. Had there not been a sudden and quite unforeseen change of power in Pretoria, the Regional

Superpower strategy and the reformulation of apartheid that flowed from it would probably never have been put into effect.

What happened was the disclosure of a massive political scandal on the scale of Watergate. For two years investigative reporters of the *Rand Daily Mail*, of which I was then editor, and its sister paper, the *Sunday Express*, had been probing the misuse of funds by the government's Department of Information. The cumulative impact of their reports, published in the second half of 1978, brought about the fall of both Vorster and his heir apparent, Cornelius Mulder, who was minister of information and leader of the dominant Transvaal branch of the National party. Pieter Botha, leader of the smaller Cape branch, was able to come from behind and take the premiership.[4] With him came the military establishment that he had built up and nurtured during his twelve years as defence minister. Within months Van den Bergh was out, the Bureau of State Security was dismantled and restructured, and the Department of Military Intelligence became the new prime minister's key advisory body on security matters. Magnus Malan was brought into the cabinet as defence minister, and Constand Viljoen took over as chief of the defence force. The securocrats with their Regional Superpower strategy were in business.

It was the start of a massive militarization of the South African government, indeed of the whole country. Increasingly the concept of security began to supersede ideology as the dominant political theme, the engine of white mobilization. More and more it became the new ideology. More and more the locus of decision making and power shifted from the party to the military-security establishment.

The defence force swelled in size as well as influence. Its budget rocketed from $60 million in 1960 to $3 billion in 1982 and has gone on soaring since. Its fighting strength tripled in that time from 11,500 permanent force members, 56,000 part-timers, and 10,000 national servicemen, to 28,300 permanent force members, 157,000 part-timers, and 53,100 national servicemen.[5]

With this has gone a more subtle militarization of white South African society as a whole. A martial spirit has intruded into the atmosphere, with more and more military parades and fly-pasts and television shows featuring the army's strength and weapons and troops on manoeuvres. The sheer size of the defence force makes its presence per-

4. See Mervyn Ress and Chris Day, *Muldergate* (Johannesburg, 1980).

5. See Kenneth W. Grundy, *The Rise of the South African Security Establishment: An Essay in the Changing Locus of State Power*, South African Institute of International Affairs (August, 1983), p. 6.

vasive, and gives Pretoria the atmosphere of a capital city in wartime, with uniformed men and military staff cars everywhere. At specially signposted lay-bys along the highways motorists can stop to pick up hitchhiking servicemen.

White youth, en masse, have been infused with military doctrine. On leaving school every white male has to do two years' national service, followed by 720 days of annual camps, during which he is constantly exposed to the ideological thinking and worldview of the military establishment. But it begins even before that. The educational process itself has been militarized. Some 200,000 schoolboys are formed into school cadet detachments, where they are drilled and psychologically prepared for national service. Defence force officers regularly visit schools to give lectures on youth preparedness, career guidance, and national service. Even before high school, youngsters are encouraged to attend "veld schools" during vacations, ostensibly to learn about the environment and outdoor survival but also to be given a heavy dose of political and paramilitary indoctrination.

Sometimes the militarization is less than subtle. Not long ago my wife attended a Johannesburg elementary school's fund-raising fete, which was held in the grounds of a prison farm outside the city. The stalls were in brown army tents that had been lent to the school for the occasion, giving the fair the bizarre atmosphere of a military camp decorated for Christmas. Three high-ranking officers were among the guests of honour. And there, in the centre of it all, among the coconut shies, doughnut stands, handicraft stalls, and a beer garden, was an exhibition of "terrorist weapons"—guns, bombs, grenades, and limpet mines—with a security police officer to answer visitors' questions about them. Out front, pinned to the pole of the exhibition tent like a banner, was a bullet-riddled tee-shirt taken from the body of a "terrorist."

The new security ideology that accompanied this militarization changed the tenor of the country's politics. Central to it was the concept that South Africa was the target of a "total onslaught" directed from Moscow. Drawing heavily on the writings of a French antiguerrilla strategist, General André Beaufre, who fought in the Indochinese and Algerian wars, the securocrats concluded that this onslaught was being waged at many different levels—psychological, political, economic, diplomatic, social, and religious, as well as military. What was required, therefore, was a "total strategy" to counter it at all these levels and produce a coordinated response. As Beaufre wrote: "At the top of the pyramid [of different forms of strategy] . . . is total strategy, whose task is to lay down the object for each specialized category and the manner in which all—political, economic, diplomatic, and military—should be woven in together."[6] What this meant was that any and every issue, domestic as well as foreign, local as well as national, was potentially a security issue, which justified the involvement of the military-security establishment in everything.

To achieve the coordinated response Beaufre required, Botha formed an elaborate network of security committees called the National Security Management System, which quickly established itself as a shadow administration. At the top of the system's pyramid structure was a powerful State Security Council headed by Botha himself and including an inner core of cabinet ministers and all the military, police, and intelligence chiefs. Here the major security-related decisions were taken at regular fortnightly meetings, to be conveyed by Botha to the full cabinet next day for ratification. Kenneth Grundy, an American political scientist who spent a year in South Africa studying the influence of the military in government, likened it to the Politburo of the Soviet Communist party—the real decision-making body—with the cabinet, like the Soviet Council of Ministers, a rubber-stamp and policy-coordinating body.[7]

The State Security Council was served by a permanent secretariat, headed by a general from Military Intelligence. Next in the hierarchy was a working committee, where the heads of all government departments were drawn in to coordinate the activities of their departments on security matters. Below that were thirteen interdepartmental committees to ensure coordination down the line, followed by twelve Joint Management Centres roughly coinciding with the country's military command areas and usually headed by a defence force or police brigadier, 60 Sub-Joint Management Centres, and 448 Mini-Joint Management Centres corresponding to local municipal councils where people like civil defence officers, fire chiefs, postmasters, and municipal officials were drawn in to the security network.

The system operated as a two-way process: security information, meaning anything fitting Beaufre's broad definition, was gathered at the local level and passed up the line for evaluation by the secretariat (which had four specialist divisions doing this), whose recommendations would be placed before the security council for decision; directives would then be passed down the line again for implementation at the various levels. In this way the military-security establishment was able to intervene and direct policy making at every level of the civil administration.

Nowhere was this more evident than in foreign policy, where the

6. André Beaufre, *Introduction to Strategy* (New York, 1963), p. 30.

7. Grundy, op. cit., p. 16.

militarists on the council completely eclipsed the foreign ministry in devising a more aggressive regional strategy. Again Beaufre provided the model. The French general presented war as a dialectic struggle between two opposing wills: the one who could strike more forcefully and imaginatively and bring about the psychological disintegration of the other would win.[8] Beaufre had been trained in a hard school against the Viet Minh and he was prepared to use ruthless methods to achieve his psychological results. In Algeria he divided the area under his command into different zones to which he applied contrasting strategies. There were *zones interdites*, sparsely populated areas whose people he resettled elsewhere and then ordered his army to fire on anything that moved; *zones de pacification*, fertile and populous regions where Beaufre concentrated massive forces to ensure total security and then launched a major effort at economic advancement, education, and propaganda indoctrination; and finally *zones d'opérations*, killing grounds where insurgent bands were relentlessly pursued and slaughtered by Beaufre's mobile forces. It was consciously part of his psychological-warfare technique to draw pointed comparisons between conditions there and the security of life in the *zones de pacification*.[9]

The regional strategy devised by Botha's securocrats emulated this soft-hard approach: offer the carrot of economic cooperation to neighbouring states that accept the new *Pax Pretoriana*, use the stick of destabilization on those that do not, then draw pointed comparisons between the conditions of life in the two. Destabilization thus has a dual purpose: it creates a shield of instability around South Africa's borders and at the same time gives point to Pretoria's argument that "black Marxist" rule leads to chaos—the reason that continued white control in South Africa is necessary.

When it comes to destabilizing operations, no holds are barred. Psychological disintegration is the objective. So look and act tough. Terrify them, keep them in a state of nervous anxiety, make them realize they had better do as they are told or they'll be reduced to a state where they can do nothing at all. As one senior official put it: "We want to show that we want peace in the region, we want to contribute and we can help a lot. But we also want to show that if we are refused we can destroy the whole of southern Africa." *Dwangpostuur.*

Sometimes commando forces have been used to strike into neighbouring countries with unrestrained ruthlessness, machine-gunning apartment blocks and killing local civilians, including women and chil-

8. Ibid., p. 24.

9. See Alistair Horne, *A Savage War of Peace* (Hammondsworth, 1985), p. 166.

dren, as well as ANC agents living there. Air attacks, equally indiscriminate, sometimes hit the wrong targets—but no matter, it's the posture of threat and compulsion that counts. Proxy forces have been used, a ragtag army of Renamo renegades in Mozambique and a unit of local dissidents and foreign mercenaries called 32 Battalion in southern Angola, which turned vast tracts of both countries into killing grounds. Apart from the mass starvation resulting from the chaos they caused, a U.S. State Department investigation estimated in 1988 that as many as 100,000 Mozambican civilians may have been murdered in Renamo atrocities.[10]

Indeed the South African army turned the whole of southern Angola into a *zone d'opération*, repeatedly launching massive search-and-destroy operations deep into the territory, erasing whole villages and, in 1978, massacring the inhabitants of a refugee camp at Kassinga which it claimed was a base for Namibian insurgents. The UNITA guerrillas, whom South Africa supported, conducted their own widespread atrocities as they sought to destroy the country's agricultural economy by attacking farming communities and planting land mines in village farmlands, footpaths, and on roads. The result is that Angola today has the highest amputee rate in the world, with thousands of men, women, and children hobbling about on makeshift artificial limbs produced by a Red Cross factory in the provincial capital of Huambo.

Economic muscle was used as well. The chaos in Angola and Mozambique severed the crucial rail arteries through both those countries, rendering the landlocked states between them dependent on South Africa's transportation network for 85 percent of their overseas trade. That made it easy to put the squeeze on them. The dependence was increased by repeatedly blowing up storage tanks at the Mozambique port of Beira containing oil for Zimbabwe and the pipeline from them. When Zimbabwe's anti-apartheid rhetoric reached a point Pretoria considered too sharp, it delayed rail traffic at the border for days on the pretext that Zimbabwe's hostile attitude made microscopic security checks necessary. When tiny Lesotho, completely surrounded by South African territory, insisted on giving sanctuary to black refugees crossing the border, a similar slowdown was ordered at the border posts until the little country started running out of food and other essential supplies.

The strategy produced results. Revolutionary Mozambique, once so

10. *Summary of Mozambique Refugee Accounts of Principally Conflict-Related Experience in Mozambique*, a report compiled by Robert Gersony, consultant to the State Department's Bureau for Refugee Programs and submitted to Ambassador Jonathan Moore, director of the bureau, and Chester A. Crocker, Assistant Secretary of State for Africa. See pp. 41–43.

bold and such a stimulant to black South Africans, was reduced to economic ruin, and in desperation signed a nonaggression treaty in terms of which it expelled all but ten "diplomatic representatives" of the ANC from Maputo. Adjoining Swaziland, which had formed that threatening salient, did likewise and ordered the ANC out. The pressure increased on stubborn Lesotho until it triggered a coup, and a military commander favoured by the securocrats in Pretoria took over.

Only in Angola did the policy fail to achieve its objective. The ambition there, higher than in Mozambique, was to help Savimbi supplant the MPLA so that South Africa would have a client government in Luanda, whereas it had never seen the disjointed Renamo bands as a viable alternative government but only as a tool for maintaining instability. Massive amounts of aid went to Savimbi. Reporters visiting his bush headquarters at Jamba, just across the border from South Africa's supply bases in northern Namibia, saw Pretoria's imprint everywhere, from industrial lathes in the vehicle workshops to drugs and surgical instruments in a well-equipped hospital to soft drinks, cigarettes, and even South African wines. Most important was oil to keep Savimbi's troops mobile.

In the end the effort failed. Once again, as in 1975, South Africa overreached itself. A fit of braggadocio by some of its leaders provoked Cuba into a massive buildup of its military assistance to the MPLA. For the first time Cuban troops were sent south to engage the South Africans in force. A South African column, attempting to deliver a decisive blow for Savimbi by taking the MPLA's main southern stronghold at Cuito Cuanavale, encountered heavy resistance and got bogged down and encircled. As South Africa sought to supply and relieve its men from the air, it discovered to its alarm that it had lost its accustomed air superiority: a sophisticated radar defence network exposed its planes to SAM-8 and SAM-9 missile attacks; worse still, its aging French Mirage fighters, which it had not been able to replace or supplement because of a long-standing United Nations arms embargo, were no match for the Russian MiG-23s and -24s that the Cuban and Angolan pilots were flying. Without air cover, the beleaguered column took a pounding. As the casualty rate soared, the prospect loomed of a political backlash at home, with so many white boys getting killed fighting a black man's war far from home. When the chance of a settlement arose, South Africa was grateful to get out without too much loss of face. It had failed in its major objective but the deal was not unfavourable: independence for Namibia in exchange for Cuban withdrawal and the removal of Umkhonto training bases from Angola.

In its seriously reduced state and without the Cubans or the ANC bases, Angola is no longer a threat to South Africa. Nor is Namibia, isolated and vulnerable, to the south of it. In time, as Angola settles its internal conflicts and gradually recovers from the ravages of war, the Benguela railroad will reopen, a tracheotomy that will bring new breath to the landlocked states. Then South Africa's hold over them will be reduced. So the Pax Pretoriana has not been fully imposed, but for the moment, for all practical purposes, the buffer is still there.

Although it was in this sphere of foreign and regional policy that South Africa's new total strategy was most evident and attracted the most global attention, it was in fact in its domestic political consequences, many of them unforeseen, that it had its most significant effect on the approaching crisis of apartheid.

Fundamental to the new strategy was the need to maximize South Africa's military and economic power—and a whole range of far-reaching political implications flowed from that. For a start it meant forging an alliance between the Afrikaner Nationalist government and the English business sector, badly soured during the Verwoerd years. A tacit working arrangement existed between the two, but it had suited both to keep a certain distance between themselves, the government because it did not wish to taint its ethnic identity, and business because it did not wish to be too closely identified with apartheid. Now the total strategists, thinking in terms of a coordinated national effort, wanted more of a symbiosis. Armscor, a national weapons industry involving both the public and the private sectors, formed after the Security Council imposed a mandatory arms embargo in 1977, provided the model. Both needed to work together like that now to maximize the Regional Superpower's economic strength and produce increasingly sophisticated military hardware. And so in a symbolic gesture Botha convened two large national conferences of business leaders, hoping to lay the basis for a closer relationship.

Allied to this was the need to take the ideological brakes off the economy so that the growth rate could be increased. And so Verwoerd's "poor and white" dictum was literally turned on its head: now, in order to stay white, South Africa had to get rich to be powerful.

Taking off the ideological brakes meant scrapping job reservation and allowing blacks to meet the industrial sector's desperate need for skilled manpower. It meant blacks had to be trained for these skilled jobs, which in turn meant upgrading their education and admitting them to previously whites-only technical institutes and universities. A skilled work force, moreover, must be allowed to unionize in order to regularize labour relations and prevent it from becoming anarchic. A wave of wildcat strikes in Natal in 1973 had driven home this point, when employers found they had no advance warning of worker discontent and no way of negotiating an end to the stoppages. As one put it, they found themselves trying to negotiate "with 1,500 workers on a football field."[11] So the Botha administration decided to permit black trade unionism, which meant giving blacks a basis for organized worker action that would inevitably translate into a form of political power in the years ahead.

Then again, as the businessmen told Botha, if you are going to invest in training staff they must have security of tenure. You can't spend money training migrants who go back to the homelands after a year. That meant accepting the permanence of urban blacks. In any event it was now 1978, and there was no turning of the tide according to Verwoerd's prediction.

Accepting the permanence of urban blacks was to accept another string of implications—from finding some way to accommodate them politically (other than through the homelands) to improving the physical amenities of the townships. The Soweto riots served as a warning that something had better be done to make life more bearable in these drab and featureless ghettos. So reforms were introduced to allow home ownership and commercial development, and the search began for a constitutional formula that could accommodate urban blacks as well as the "coloureds" and Indians for whom there were also no separate homelands.

As Verwoerd had warned, when you start making concessions one thing leads to another. . . .

BUT IT WAS NOT the military strategy alone that brought about this shift of ideological ground. Other, more subtle developments in the Afrikaner community contributed to it. A conjunction of forces had brought apartheid to a point of crisis. For one thing, it had become obvious to even the most faithful believers that the policy's central objective, the reversal of black urbanization in order to achieve at least enough racial separation to legitimize the separate political structures, was simply unattainable. The black tide was flowing more strongly than ever, and the Crossroads squatter camp outside Cape Town was now a monument to the futility of trying to turn it back. Accepting the permanence of the urban blacks was simply coming to terms with a reality that could no longer be denied.

As doubts grew about apartheid's workability, enthusiasm for its messianic purpose flagged too. Afrikaner Nationalism had been in power for thirty years, longer than almost any other political party in the modern world, and, like all chiliastic movements, the original enthu-

11. Steven Friedman, *Building Tomorrow Today* (Johannesburg, 1987), p 55.

siasm was starting to fade. Constant efforts must be made to sustain zeal and revitalize faith in movements like this, but even they lose their effectiveness eventually. You can have only so many cultural revolutions or mass rallies or reenactments of the folk myth before they, too, become a bore, before the quaint rituals and emotional speeches start to seem a little absurd, even embarrassing, to an increasingly mature and travelled following. So the steam starts going out of it. Thermidor sets in.

In the case of Afrikanerdom, something even more important had been happening to hasten this decline. Three decades of power and preferential treatment had wrought its own changes. The poor whites had come in from the cold, been cosseted into middle-class prosperity and were enjoying the warmth. The spread of capitalism was doing its corroding, corrupting work. The ethnic fire in the Afrikaner cracker's belly was going out, to be replaced by the acquisitiveness and consumer culture of an urban bourgeoisie.

He had been lifted into this state by a huge helping hand. Afrikaner nationalism had looked after its own abundantly. It had operated a system of selective socialism, a kind of extended group nepotism. Everywhere the Afrikaner government intervened to help Afrikaners, and the aid became self-generating. Vast amounts went to farmers, and the capital the farmers accumulated flowed through Afrikaner banks to Afrikaner businesses. Other vast amounts were spent on Afrikaner schools, universities, and technical institutions, so that the number of Afrikaners in the professions trebled in those three decades.

The nationalized industries established to absorb the poor whites had developed into a form of Afrikaner state capitalism that operated alongside and in alliance with English private capital. And Afrikaners broke into the private sector too. Some of the old Reddingsdaadbond enterprises had grown into large conglomerates with the benefit of preferential government treatment. One of them, Federale Volksbeleggings, established a mining company called Federale Mynbou which in 1963 took over General Mining and Finance Corporation, with assets of $350 million, from the giant Anglo American Corporation. Thirteen years later General Mining acquired control of Union Corporation, forming Gencor, which is now the third largest of South Africa's mining houses, placing about 30 percent of the gold mines under Afrikaner control.

Out of this a new Afrikaner entrepreneurial and technocratic class was born that made common cause with its English counterparts against the old preindustrial practices. The notion of sending all the blacks back to the homelands, of the townships withering away, not only looked increasingly improbable but was increasingly anachronistic and inimical to their interests. Industry had outgrown the availability of skilled white manpower, and Afrikaner businessmen as well as English were desperate to train and employ skilled blacks. As *Die Vaderland* of Johannesburg editorialized in 1978:

> An unskilled and unmotivated worker is also expensive because he is insufficiently productive. In practice this means that three or four people have to be employed to do the work of one. It also means that the white man is overburdened with the responsibility of providing skilled labour which places too great a demand on him, as well as putting him in an unhealthy bargaining position vis-a-vis his employer. Count up the cost of this and it should be evident that we have for many decades been running our economy with the handbrake on.[12]

And then there was a new intellectual elite. Through the 1960s, a generation of young writers had broken out of the stilted genre of traditional Afrikaans literature, with its sagas of upstanding men and pure maidens bravely facing the hardships of drought on the farm and the inevitable journey to the city. Reacting against the narrowness of their folk culture, these Sestigers, as they called themselves, went to Europe in search of a new universalism. They lived in Paris, studied literature at the Sorbonne, and began writing avant-garde fiction laden with Jungian archetypes and existential philosophy. By the 1970s, the contrived precocity of their early work matured into more searching themes about the mind and values of Afrikanerdom itself. Because these writers were now the deans of Afrikaans culture, with all its interwoven meaning for the Nationalist movement, the impact of their challenging, rebellious literature was very great.

At many levels, then, a new, better educated, more urbane and travelled generation of Afrikaners emerged, aware of the unworkability of apartheid, chafing at its economic restrictiveness, and, not least, embarrassed by its crudity. Pride in their Afrikaner history and heritage was still there, but these modern men and women of the world were pained by the stigma it now bore, of the burden of shame they carried with their South African passports and accents. Apartheid labelled them as racist backwoodsmen, and they hated that, often reacting to the criticisms they encountered abroad with a mixture of aggressive resentment and whining self-justification. They are a warm, gregarious people and they longed to walk tall in the world again.

So it was that the adjustments required of the Regional Superpower

12. It might be considered a perverse analysis that presents the industrial colour bar as a burden on the whites, but the egocentrism is typical of even the most enlightened Afrikaner Nationalist thinking.

strategy coincided with the changing needs and desires of a substantial sector of the Afrikaner community. They took on a political as well as a strategic purpose. "Change" became a vogue word.

Making a virtue of necessity, the Botha administration decided to dump what it called "outdated" and "unnecessary" apartheid statutes at the same time—like the outlawing of mixed marriages and sex across the colour line—and to present a new image of reformism to the world. It almost succeeded. The Western powers, ever eager to read the South African situation optimistically, were deceived for a time into believing that Pretoria really was dismantling apartheid. Had they looked more closely at the nature of the changes and the reasons behind them, they would have seen that it was not so much reform as reformulation. The apartheid system was being changed, not abandoned. It was being adapted to bring it in line with the new needs of the economy and the Regional Superpower strategy, restructured to make provision for its failure to achieve territorial separation of the races, and modernized to make it more acceptable to the Afrikaner modernists. What was not being done was to change any of its bedrock fundamentals which entrench political separation and Afrikaner-dominated white control.

The bottom line remained the same. A black middle class was to be allowed to develop and, with the "coloureds" and Indians, was to be coopted into a new alliance of insiders, rewarded with a greater share of the economic cake and limited political rights over their own ethnic affairs. The outsiders, meanwhile, the mass of poorly educated and unskilled blacks, would be thrust out to the periphery more rigourously than ever with an intensified drive of forced removals and tougher enforcement of antisquatter laws in the cities. It was sometimes called the "Brazilian option," which, by deracializing the insider group, would give the impression that apartheid had been dismantled. But the key to it was that the Afrikaner *volk* was to remain in overall control and South Africa was to remain its nation-state. Abdication of political control, or any reforms that might lead to that, were as far removed from the mind of the National party as ever. Neo-apartheid, *The Economist* called it in a perceptive article by its political editor, Simon Jenkins.[13] In Hermann Giliomee's phrase, it was the search for a formula for sharing power without losing control.

The formula eventually emerged in a new constitution of Byzantine complexity centred on a tricameral Parliament with separate Houses for whites, "coloureds," and Indians in which the white chamber was able

13. *The Economist*, June 21, 1980.

at all times to outvote the other two. Blacks were specifically excluded, Botha saying a solution for them would be worked out later but pledging that it would not take the form of a fourth parliamentary chamber.

Legislative responsibility was elaborately divided into "own affairs," which meant matters relating exclusively to each of the three racial groups, and "general affairs," which were matters relating to the nation as a whole. Black affairs were defined as a general affair. Each of the three houses was given jurisdiction over the own affairs of its race group; general affairs legislation would have to be passed by all three sitting separately. That gave the "coloured" and Indian houses each a veto, but should they use it there was a president's council with a built-in majority of the dominant white party that could exercise a veto override.

Heading the whole system was an executive state-president with authoritarian powers who could bypass the legislature in many instances, select his cabinet from the three houses as he pleased, appoint many members of the president's council, call elections, declare emergencies, and suspend Parliament for up to thirteen months. Because of the white chamber's supremacy, the dominant party in it was assured of always electing the state-president. So it was guaranteed that he would always be an Afrikaner Nationalist as long as the National party kept on winning white elections.

Thus the attempt to co-opt the "coloureds" and Indians while keeping control in white hands. The blacks, being the majority, remained the core of the problem. How could they be given even a token share in the central political system without giving them a toehold that might eventually lead to majority rule? While they pondered that question Botha and his securocrats did no more than indicate the broad direction of their thinking: local municipal councils to run the "own affairs" of the townships, with representatives drawn from them sitting on multiracial Regional Services Councils to coordinate the "general affairs"—such as the allocation of funds for public utilities—of metropolitan areas. Beyond that provision was made for the state-president to invite "community leaders" to form a negotiating council to work out the constitutional future of the blacks at a national level.

Big business, flushed with the novelty of government courtship, gave their backing to this cumbersome contrivance, white voters approved it at a referendum, and South Africa entered a new phase of ideological uncertainty and political flux.

IT IS ONE THING to change a political policy, but if you start reinterpreting theology you invite schism. Botha's revisionism pitched

Afrikanerdom into a schismatic Reformation that has split its followers, broken the monolithic power of its establishment, and weakened the strength of belief in its civil religion.

The immediate issue over which the split occurred was the tricameral constitution. Carefully devised though it was to ensure that power stayed securely in Afrikaner Nationalist hands, the very fact of allowing people of colour into Parliament was apostasy to the fundamentalists of the Deep North. Andries Treurnicht, Transvaal leader of the National party and therefore its most powerful figure after Botha, found the idea unacceptable. He was an orthodox Verwoerdian, a former chairman of the Broederbond, and a Dutch Reformed Church theologian who only a few years before had made a major contribution to civil-religion literature with a book, *Credo of an Afrikaner*, in which he revived all the old Kuyperian themes in a ringing affirmation of the moral justification of apartheid.[14] When he failed to face down Botha on the constitutional issue, he quit the party with fourteen other members of Parliament from the Transvaal and formed the Conservative party in May 1982.

An earlier split had occurred when a small group of hardliners broke away in 1969 in protest against Vorster's permitting some mixed sport—an attempt to counter the growing international boycott of South Africa's whites-only sports teams. Forming what they called the Herstigte (Reconstituted) National party, they hoped to capture some of the aura of Malan's break in the 1930s, but the secessionists were too lightweight, the issue too insubstantial, and the fissures in the party not yet deep enough. It remained a splinter group.

Treurnicht's break was different. He was a heavyweight, a major force in the Afrikaner Nationalist establishment, and the times were different. The rapid growth of class stratification in the Afrikaner community during the 1970s had weakened its solidarity and it was more prone to schism. Afrikaner Nationalism had started out, after all, as a coalition of classes held together by a fierce sense of ethnic purpose. Class stratification had originally been minimal in any event: after the devastation of war and depression Afrikanerdom was close to being a single-class society, with everyone disadvantaged relative to the dominant English bourgeois class. That made solidarity easy. The power of a common ideology and civil religion intensified that solidarity. Now much deeper class differences with conflicting interests were appearing, while at the same time the ideology was declining.

In moving to identify with the new Afrikaner middle class of technocrats, businessmen, and successful young urbanites (the Boer Yuppies, if you will), Botha alienated the original constituency on which Afri-

14. A. P. Treurnicht, *Credo van 'n Afrikaner* (Cape Town, 1975), pp. 1–10.

kaner Nationalism was founded—the farmers and the white workers—who were bitter about the shift of emphasis to the cities and the opening up of skilled opportunities to black workers, which reduced their own scarcity value and the bargaining power of their unions. Nothing illustrates this more sharply than the decline of the white Mine Workers' Union, once the bastion of Afrikaner worker power, which soon found its strikes easily defeated and its strength so reduced that it began recruiting among white industrial workers in the nationalized corporations, while at the same time the black National Union of Mineworkers emerged as the rising force on the labour scene. Suddenly the ghosts of *gelykstelling* were walking again. Not only were blacks now doing equal work in many places, but the lifting of restrictions meant a black bourgeoisie was emerging, with uppity young university graduates speaking in polished accents and driving BMWs. Treurnicht cashed in on the discontent, and within five years his party had supplanted the liberal Progressive Federal party as the main opposition party in Parliament.

Another class, too, of great size and importance, is threatened by the new developments—the army of clerks and officials in the huge state bureaucracy. Nearly half of all economically active Afrikaners work for the government in some capacity. These include the thousands of people who administer apartheid day to day. They are intensely aware of the changes, which affect their work and their relationships with those whom they administer. They are a vulnerable class with limited skills who were accommodated in these jobs during the underdog days of Afrikaner backwardness, and they realize that if the system is dismantled they will go with it. More acutely still, they realize that if there is black-majority rule in South Africa, they will be the first to be squeezed out because any incoming black government will need to place its own underdog people in those state jobs. So the bureaucracy has been another area of ready recruitment for Treurnicht.

Another, more fortuitous factor was Botha's personality. Not only were his policies unpopular among many Afrikaners, so was he himself. His aggressive, bullying manner and explosive temper made him unloved even by those who worked most closely with him, and his abrasiveness alienated many who might otherwise have remained allies. An example is Lourens Muller, a lifelong associate who had been Botha's deputy in the Cape branch of the party for nearly thirty years, minister of transport, and one of the most senior members of the cabinet. Over lunch one day Muller told me the story of the breach between them that resulted in his joining the Conservative party. They had disagreed, Muller said, about his desire to run for the position of figurehead president under the old constitution. He thought Botha had failed to honour a promise to remain neutral in the campaign for the post, and when he went to complain about this Botha lost his temper. "He jumped up from his desk and grabbed hold of me," Muller said. "We went reeling across his office, the office of the prime minister, like wrestlers locked together. His private secretary came running in and separated us. Otherwise I think he would have hit me."

After he became president, Botha shored up his personal authoritarianism with a restructured administration run on increasingly authoritarian lines. This only intensified feelings of frustration and resentment within the party. Until then, for all its overt authoritarianism toward the rest of the South African population, especially the blacks, the National party was a remarkably democratic organism within its own ethnic fold. Through its multifarious component elements, from the Broederbond to the business and cultural bodies, it was able to maintain an almost Athenian sensitivity to the mood of the Afrikaner *volk*. To that extent it functioned much as African one-party states are supposed to function but seldom do, with the responses of the people flowing up from the grass roots to the party hierarchy where the Rousseauistic general will could be determined and political decisions taken accordingly.

It made for a system of intense lobbying within the party, since the party itself was the essential conduit for insider access to the decision-making structure at the top. Not only useful in keeping the party leadership in touch with its voting constituency, it effectively kept different political viewpoints securely within the fold—for to leave the party meant to lose the crucial access to the top without which one could not hope to have one's views prevail. Long after Afrikanerdom's emergent class stratification began to produce discernible left and right political factions (which became known as the *verligtes*, or enlightened ones, and *verkramptes*, literally "the cramped ones"), both stuck determinedly to the party because they knew that only there could they hope to influence decisions. Liberal opposition parties constantly implored *verligtes* to come out into the open and proclaim their true beliefs, but they steadfastly declined because they knew that to do so would be to exchange insider influence for the politics of outsider protest, which the government pointedly ignored. So both they and the *verkramptes* hung in there, waging their battles out of public view within the bowels of the party system and mostly neutralizing each other as the leadership sought to reconcile their views and find a workable consensus. It made for paralysis in government, especially during Vorster's later years, but it kept the party together.

Botha's restructuring changed this. Installed as an executive president with authoritarian powers under the new constitution, he set about centralizing power on himself and the military-security establishment, bypassing more and more cabinet, Parliament, and party. To the State Security Council and the National Security Management System was added a powerful State-President's Office, and together these three bodies became the new decision-making structure. The President's Office, with a hand-picked staff of two hundred, was headed by a shadowy figure named Jannie Roux, a forty-seven-year-old psychiatrist who also held key positions in the other two bodies and quickly became the most powerful man in the government after Botha.

Roux's office was further strengthened by the creation of a Commission for Administration, with a staff of one thousand and powers to intervene in other departments, to examine every memorandum going to the cabinet for consideration and to attach its own comments. The reconstituted Bureau of State Security, now called the National Intelligence Service and run by a thirty-year-old whiz-kid named Neil Barnard, whom Botha plucked out of the University of the Free State, was also plugged in with five thousand employees to be the "eyes and ears" of the President's Office. Not only did this mean large-scale intervention from the top in departmental affairs, but instead of the old system, where the cabinet discussed various policy options and heard dissenting voices on them from ministers and officials, the president and his close security and technocratic advisers now adopted policy positions within the new structure and then used the cabinet to ensure wider government support for them.[15]

This meant that the party became less and less effective as a conduit to the decision-making structure. Decisions were made in a tight closed circle and the party came into the picture only later. Party members found their insider access to this circle closed, with the ubiquitous Jannie Roux—nicknamed "J.R." after the incorrigible baddie in the TV soap opera *Dallas*—blocking the way at every point. The old Athenian responsiveness to grass-roots sentiment was dead and in its place was a top-down system of policy making. As the old lobbying system withered on the vine, there was less and less reason for dissenting elements to stay in the party. If they could no longer work effectively for their causes within the system, it became a viable option to consider leaving it and trying to pressure the government by campaigning publicly for support outside.

The breakaway of the Conservative party was itself both cause and effect in the process of disintegration. The result of weakened solidarity,

15. For an analysis of the workings of the new decision-making structure see Mark Swilling, *The Powers of the Thunderbird: The Nature and Limits of South Africa's Emergency State*, a paper written for publication in the 1989 policy review of the Centre for Policy Studies, University of the Witwatersrand.

it also did a great deal to weaken that solidarity further by legitimizing defection. No longer was it an act of ethnic treason to leave the National party; one could do it in the name of a truer fidelity to Afrikanerdom's sacred history, ideals, and past leaders. You could be a good Afrikaner without being a member of the party.

And so the old disputatious, schismatic tendencies of the frontier individualists reappeared. Not completely, for Afrikaner Nationalism was not dead, but enough to break up its monolithic solidarity and send it into a fractious decline. Splits appeared on the left as well as the right and a ferment of doubt swept the community. Students, scholars, journalists, writers, and professional people, many of them associated with Stellenbosch University, moved radically to the left, outflanking some of the more traditional English liberals in their readiness to negotiate with the ANC and contemplate a future for South Africa under black rule. Others, gripped by a pathological recidivism, moved beyond the Conservative party to form extreme right-wing vigilante groups of the kind that ranged the American South during the civil-rights campaign. There never had been a Ku Klux Klan in South Africa before, and the appearance of several expressed the current sense that one could no longer rely on the state to keep the nigger in his place. The most significant of these groups was the neo-Nazi Afrikaanse Weerstandsbeweging, or Afrikaner Resistance Movement, which uses an imitation swastika emblem and gives stiff-arm salutes.

Nor are the splits confined to the political sphere. They run through all the component parts of the Afrikaner Nationalist movement—through the Broederbond, where a former chairman, Carel Boshoff, who is a theology professor and son-in-law of Verwoerd, broke away to form the Afrikaner Volkswag; through the church, where breakaway ministers have formed the Afrikaanse Calvinistiese Kerk; even through the Voortrekker youth movement that performed at the Voortrekker Monument so spectacularly in 1938.

Two scenes, for me, give visual shape to this sudden diversity within what had been the solid edifice of Afrikaner Nationalism.

It is May 22, 1986, in the northern Transvaal town of Pietersburg. This is the heart of the Deep North, and the foreign minister, Pik Botha, usually a great crowd-pleaser, is due to address a rally. But this night a thousand members of the Afrikaanswe Weerstandsbeweging have broken into the hall two hours ahead of time and taken control of it. All day long they have been arriving in Pietersburg from all parts of the Transvaal. Many are burly farmers in pick-up trucks; in towns along the way they stood at the roadside waving their swastika flags. There are men in stetson hats and high boots, some carrying riding whips, some with revolvers thrust into their belts, and women in Voortrekker costumes of ankle-length dresses and *kappies*. There are posters, some with obscure Biblical quotations, others making racist puns with Pik Botha's nickname, which can be linked to the Afrikaans word for black to make it "pitch-black."

Now, at 7:00 p.m., time for the rally to begin, there is a thunderous commotion inside the hall. At the door I see Pik Botha's private secretary, Awie Marais, looking pale and shaken. "My God, have you been in there?" he asks. "They're barbarians!"

Indeed they are. The hall is jammed with a stamping, cheering mob waving hundreds of the little swastika flags. The tables and chairs up front are smashed, the result of a wild fight with thirty National party heavies who tried to hold the hall for their minister. Eyes are shining with the fever of mob hysteria. "Ah-Vee-Bee! Ah-Vee-Bee!" the crowd chants, giving a pulsating rhythm to the initials of their movement. It is not so much Nuremburg all over again as Munich's Burgerbraükeller, with brown-shirted storm troopers leading the rowdy mob in a political punch-up. The frenzy peaks as the movement's leader, the appropriately named Eugene Terre' Blanche, mounts the stage. Hands shoot up in stiff-arm salutes. He announces that Botha has cancelled his meeting. A great roar. "Tonight," Terre' Blanche bellows above the noise, "was Blood River here in Pietersburg. Tonight the *volk* has won a great victory in the fight to get back our fatherland."

Suddenly a police officer appears. He gives an order for the hall to be cleared. "I give you three minutes," he shouts. The crowd mocks and jeers. There are two dull explosions and tear-gas canisters are launched into the packed hall. Pandemonium. I manage to scramble out in the stampede. A window shatters above me as a man hurls himself through the glass and falls with a thud on the cement walkway. He gets up, blood pouring from his cut face. "The bastards!" he yells. "They're supposed to do this to the kaffirs, not us."

July 13, 1987, a year later and four thousand miles distant in the West African city of Dakar, capital of Senegal. A planeload of sixty Afrikaner reformists have flown here for a week of talks with leaders of the ANC. There has been, as the group leader told a press briefing, "a remarkable meeting of minds." There has also been a remarkable meeting of hearts as black Africans and white Afrikaners found each other and struck up warm relationships.

Now, today being Sunday, the group is taking a break from its talks and making an excursion to Goree Island, a dot in the ocean just offshore from the port city. The island has been turned into a museum of sorts, a monument to the slave trade, for it was the staging post for the shipment of millions of African slaves to the Americas, first by the Dutch, then the Portuguese and finally the French from the seventeenth century onward.

I find myself in the slave house, on an upper-level balcony where the slave traders lived in spacious quarters. Below are the dungeons where the slaves were kept, the dark punishment cell for runaways, and, in the crashing surf in front, the portcullis through which they were taken to the slave ships for their tortuous voyages to death or bondage. The view from the balcony out over the shimmering Atlantic is glorious. A young Afrikaner theology student is standing with me, seemingly transfixed. Then I notice that he seems to be struggling with his breathing. "Are you all right?" I ask, fearing he may be ill. For a moment he does not answer, then he chokes out the words "Robben Island." The analogy with South Africa's prison island and its own spectacular view of the Cape peninsula is obvious, and others in the group have remarked on it already, but the young Afrikaner has not finished: "They'll build a museum like this on Robben Island one day," he says, "and people will come and look at it and wonder how we could have lived with such evil.

"These slave-owners," he went on, gesturing to the spacious quarters around us, "were Christians, too. Yet they lived in all this comfort with all that evil just below them, and they did not see it. How, *how*, can we be so blind?" He turns away, wrestling with his emotions, and I walk with him to join the others. Going down the stairs we pass Thabo Mbeki, leader of the ANC delegation, coming up. His father at that moment is in his twenty-fourth year of imprisonment on Robben Island. Thabo, who is forty-four, has not seen him since he was a teenager. He smiles at us, warm, friendly, unrecriminating.

If the deepening of class divisions is part of the reason for this sudden diversity in Afrikanerdom, at another level the splits reveal different responses to a general loss of faith in the ability of the old ideology to solve the Afrikaners' problem of national survival, and a growing sense that black majority rule is on the way. Those Afrikaners who went to Dakar were responding to this prospect by exploring the possibilities of doing a deal; those who joined the AWB were doing so by preparing for a last-ditch fight.

Part of the configuration on the far right is a small group calling themselves the *Oranjewerkers*, or Orange Workers, who have devised a proposal for a series of separate white "homelands" within the larger South Africa. Headed by Verwoerd's son, Hendrik Jr., another former minister of the Dutch Reformed Church, the group has marked out three small regions of the country where it wants to encourage Afrikaners to settle in concentrated numbers. The aim is for these regions to seek a measure of autonomy and, in the event of black rule, secede from the rest of South Africa.

The Orange Workers take their name from William of Orange, the symbol of the Dutch struggle for national independence from Spanish domination in the sixteenth century. The young Verwoerd believes that Afrikaners face a similar struggle today against a black majority and the fear of losing their identity. By the year 2020, he points out, whites will be only 10 percent of the total South African population, and Afrikaners are only 60 percent of the whites. If they remain thinly scattered among the masses who outnumber them, they will be powerless and in time will disappear. But if they concentrate in particular areas, says Verwoerd, they will be able to retain their identity, like the Basques and the Scots.

Even then, say the Orange Workers, Afrikaners will have to free themselves from dependence on black labour to ensure that they are not outnumbered in their *Boerestaat.* That means they must do their own housework and sweep their own streets—both revolutionary notions among white South Africans. The working day will have to be extended by an hour so that managers can clean their own offices and deliver their own messages. The movement produces a newsletter filled with suggestions like this and articles exhorting Afrikaners to rediscover the spirit of their pioneering days, to live simply and sacrifice luxuries for the sake of national survival. One issue contained a design for an easy-to-clean house with solid cement beds, chairs, and tables that required no polishing and would gather no dust underneath.

This is recidivism with a vengeance, all the way back to Geoff Cronjé and his quest for economic disengagement in order to establish a home for posterity where the Afrikaner could live free of the dangers of mishmash cohabitation and *bloedvermenging.* With all its crack-brained unrealism, this sad plan expresses an awareness of apartheid's failure and the beginning of a desperate search for a fallback position, a last bolthole, perhaps in the end some kind of Afrikaner Quebec, by those who cannot contemplate negotiating a future that would have them living under black rule.

Faced with these schisms and the loss of the old ideological solidarity, Botha tried to substitute an ideology of survival to hold Afrikaner Nationalism together. As Giliomee puts it, if the *volk* can no longer hold together by means of a moral crusade, then at least they can be told their throats will be slit or their homes seized if they lose control. They must stand together in the face of the total onslaught that threatens their national survival. Botha even tried to infuse the survivalist theme with some of the mystique of the old civil religion. In language not unlike Daniel Malan's apologia to the American theologians at Grand Rapids, he presented South Africa as being involved in a life-and-death struggle "between the powers of chaos, Marxism and destruction on the one hand and the powers of order, Christian civilization and the upliftment of the people on the other."

But there are political weaknesses in this strategy. Fostering an ideology of survival may benefit the Conservative party more than the National party, for the Conservatives represent the toughest reaction to the black challenge; and the creation of a war psychosis encourages the growth of right-wing extremism. Nor in its crude utilitarianism is this enough: a true ideology of survival requires a deeper moral dimension. There must be something worth surviving for.

Henry Katzew, a Jewish journalist who was fascinated by the Afrikaner concern with national identity and survival and its many similarities with Judaism and modern Israel, wrote twenty-five years ago about this weakness in the Afrikaner survivalist ethic. Survival is not a fleeting thing, he pointed out, a sentiment to be evoked or conjured up for political exploitation when it is expedient to do so. Survival means continuity, and continuity means a group life persisting and developing from decade to decade, from century to century. "Survival depends on life-carrying *ideas*," Katzew declared. Afrikaner Nationalism, the philosophy of white survival, white mastery, was bereft of those ideas. "It seems to me the Afrikaner is letting all white men down by refusing to formulate a policy of survival that goes beyond the technique of politics."[16]

The decline of the civil religion has left a sterile shell. The government has lost any sense of mission other than simply holding on to power. There is no clear policy goal or direction. It is now a government of crisis management, of ad hoc–ism, dealing with problems as they arise day to day yet still cast in the mould of an ideology that defines its image and restricts its flexibility without any possibility of being implemented. The Afrikaner revolution is over, and all that is left of it is the politics of survivalism. The fortress of the *volk* is to be defended, but there is no faith within its walls.

16. Henry Katzew, *Apartheid and Survival: A Jewish View* (Cape Town, 1965), p. 7.

CHAPTER FOURTEEN

The Revolt of the Eighties

Experience teaches us that, generally speaking, the most perilous moment for a bad government is when it seeks to mend its ways.

ALEXIS DE TOCQUEVILLE

I've often thought, well, our big black underdog, you can't expect to turn him into a spaniel simply by feeding him sugar cubes, even the very best sugar, the most refined.

GUY BUTLER

VERWOERD WAS RIGHT. Concessions don't ease pressure or buy time, and the introduction of piecemeal reforms do introduce illogicalities that make it harder to hold one's ground. The very act of political reform that Botha thought was going to enable him to co-opt the emergent black middle class and win new credibility in the world in fact triggered the most serious black revolt in South Africa's history and plunged its government's credibility to a new low.

It has been the delusion of ruling elites through the ages that they could placate the rising clamour of oppressed masses with a few token concessions and material benefits. "Let them eat cake," said Marie Antoinette. But the hunger for real liberation is increased, not appeased, by nibbles of a better life. As Tocqueville remarked, people may endure a grievance patiently as long as they feel they can do nothing about it, but it becomes intolerable once the possibility of removing it crosses their minds. Granting concessions causes that idea to cross their minds. It is a sign of weakness that encourages the oppressed to clamour for more, and they soon learn that the more they clamour the more they get. The nibbles become a slice, and soon the whole cake begins to look attainable.

It is an enduring fallacy, too, that the downtrodden want only material improvements—better jobs, better housing, better education for their children—and that they are not really interested in the vote. Again and again in South Africa, opinion polls conducted by white market-research companies in black communities show the desire for more pay scoring higher than the desire for political rights. Forgetting that it is human nature to give priority to one's most urgent and personal needs, whites conclude from this that they can offer the one and deny the other. Yet all the great revolutions, from Cromwell's to Lenin's, have occurred at times when new affluence was beginning to flow to the underclass, when they were rising up off the bedrock of absolute deprivation and beginning to achieve something better—and at the same time beginning to compare their lot with those who ruled over them. That is when resentments and revolutionary thoughts begin to stir in people's minds.

It should have come as no surprise in 1984 when only five days after the last votes were cast for the "coloured" and Indian houses in the tricameral system, the great black revolt began. Yet it did come as a surprise. Once again the whites were doomed to be startled by the responses of the subjugated.

Indeed in no other instance have the different worlds and different perceptions within South Africa been so vividly revealed as on the issue of these most recent constitutional reforms. To most whites, the new constitution was a generous concession, a bold, even courageous breaching of the political colour bar, which the government had been prepared to undertake though it meant splitting Afrikaner nationalism. Even many liberals, while critical of the tricameral system's cumbersomeness and the exclusion of blacks, welcomed it as "a step in the right direction."

At a whites-only referendum in November 1983 two-thirds of the white electorate approved the new constitution. Ten months later, when the elections were held, more than four-fifths of the "coloured" and Indian people—ostensibly the beneficiaries—rejected it in a massive election boycott.[1] And the rejection among blacks must have been close to 100 percent.

On one side of the bitter-almond hedge the government scored a landslide victory; on the other side it suffered the most overwhelming defeat in a national poll in South Africa's history. As a black journalist,

1. Thirty percent of registered "coloureds" voted, but since the registration process was also boycotted, and only 60 percent of eligible voters were registered, in real terms the poll was 18 percent. Twenty percent of registered Indians voted, in real terms a poll of 12 percent.

Ameen Akhalwaya, observed wryly: "If you are being oppressed, the view from below is quite different from the one at the top."[2]

The view from below was of a galling piece of political expediency. The new constitution amounted to an admission that apartheid was a failure. The oppressor was casting aside his moralistic cloak, admitting that it was threadbare, but even as he did so he was adding insult to the ancient injury. Not only was he still clinging to power and privilege, but by granting political rights to "coloureds" and Indians and withholding them from blacks he was sharpening the edge of racial discrimination in an especially provocative way. It meant that the Africans, the indigenous people of the country, were singled out for exclusion from the national constitution. Being discriminated against and segregated from the white ruling class was bad enough, but being isolated from the other "nonwhites" was intolerable.

The political threat was equally clear. This was divide-and-rule strategy at its most blatant, not only in the way the new constitution cut "coloureds" and Indians off from blacks but also in the way other, concurrent legislative devices were designed to create new divisions between urban and rural blacks. Three bills, introduced by the euphemistically named Minister of Cooperation and Development, Piet Koornhof, set up black municipal councils to run the "own affairs" of the townships, and at the same time replaced the old influx-control system with a new method of regulation that granted urban status only to those people who had jobs and what was called "approved accommodation," meaning no shanties or leased rooms.

Most whites hailed this legislative package, too, as an important reform initiative following on the recognition of the permanency of urban blacks. Koornhof likened it to Britain's Great Reform Act of 1832 and invoked the name of William Wilberforce to stress its liberatory potential. But to blacks this was meretricious. As Popo Molefe, one of the key figures in the great uprising of the 1980s, said at his subsequent trial: "We saw it as a substitute for political participation in central government. It was a clever way of denying the black people, the African people, the right to participate in the government of the country at a time when the 'coloured' and Indian people were offered a vote in the tricameral system. Our reaction was one of anger."[3]

Viewed from below there were a number of other catches in these "Koornhof Bills." To begin with, the black councils were not represen-

2. *Sunday Express*, August 26, 1984.

3. Testimony, August 3, 1987.

tative. Elections held in the townships in 1983 were heavily boycotted: a 5 percent poll in Soweto, 11 percent in the Port Elizabeth townships, 15 percent in the Vaal Triangle, 19 percent in Durban, 20 percent on the East Rand. Few respected black leaders had offered themselves for election, and for the most part the councils comprised people regarded as quislings.

The councils were not autonomous either. The minister could remove members, appoint others, or dismiss the whole council and nominate a new one. It meant they had to implement government policy rather than be responsive to their own electorates. The black councils, not white officials, had to enforce the new influx system, checking on whether people had proper jobs, probing into their homes to see whether there was an illicit aunt there or a clandestine shack in the backyard, and endorsing people out to the "homeland" dumping grounds. The black councils had to do apartheid's dirty work, policing its oppressive regulations, and if they did not do it satisfactorily they would be replaced by others who would for the pay and the perks that came with the job. The situation was calculated to create strife within the black community.

Worse still, a conjunct government policy held that the townships should become financially self-supporting now that they had their own councils. They should raise their own revenue and no longer be a burden on the national fiscus. Given the low level of commercial development on which taxes could be levied, that could only be done by big rent increases. And it was the black councils that would have to demand these higher rents of the hard-pressed black householders, taking the flak for years of deliberate white neglect.

And so it was that while the whites applauded the reforms, the blacks mobilized opposition to them. In August 1983 more than five hundred community, church, professional, sports, workers', students', women's, and youth organizations formed an alliance called the United Democratic Front to campaign against the new constitution and the "Koornhof Bills."

At a stroke black politics was reactivated. Within a few months seven hundred more organizations joined the UDF, representing more than two million people. Rallies were held everywhere, the old freedom songs rang out again, the old slogans and chants of the 1950s and 1960s, augmented now by the militant spirit of the 1976 uprising and the organizational strength of the rising black trade union movement.

One reason that oppressive rulers find it so perilous to initiate reform is that, though they try to maintain strict control over the process, a chain reaction tends to set off unintended consequences. That is what happened now. A reform package carefully designed to divide the emergent black bourgeoisie from the masses and to co-opt the moderate centre in fact brought a powerful new anti-apartheid mass movement into existence, which in turn identified with the Freedom Charter of 1955 and so, by an association that evaded legal restrictions, brought the ANC back into the centre of the domestic political arena.

For a year the UDF ran its campaign against the reform package, addressing mass rallies and recruiting supporters in every corner of the country: the most vigourous, sustained political campaign that black South Africans had ever been able to run. The level of political consciousness in South Africa rose to unprecedented heights. The boycott was a dramatic success, robbing the new system of legitimacy, and although the government accepted the result on August 28 and installed the new parliamentarians in their seats—one of them on the strength of a paltry 154 votes—a sense of triumph and expectation infused the black community.

Five days later the great revolt began.

IT WAS QUITE fortuitous that it should have begun in Sharpeville. Despite its evocative name, Sharpeville was neither a centre of particular militancy nor the focus of political attention. As in 1960 it was simply a matter of historical accident that events should have occurred there that pitched South Africa into crisis and the name of Sharpeville into world headlines for the second time in its otherwise unremarkable history. It could have happened anywhere, for by then all South Africa was a tinderbox of political tensions waiting for a spark to set it off.

What occurred was a confluence of incidents, each minor in itself, that followed a long buildup of grievances and then flowed together on one particular day into a maelstrom of wrath. To be precise, one might say that the final incident which brought about the greatest revolutionary explosion in South Africa's history was the death of a soccer player. It was a vivid demonstration of how prone South Africa had become to spontaneous combustion.

The buildup of grievances began with the municipal elections in October 1983. Three parties offered themselves for election to the Lekoa Council, which administered Sharpeville and five neighbouring townships of the Vaal Triangle. One of the parties was led by a businessman called Esau Mahlatsi, another by Knox Majila, who had recently been convicted of taking bribes, and a third, calling itself the Baphutsane party, or the party of the poor, campaigned on twin pledges of honest administration and no rent increases.

Two community organizations, the Vaal Civic Association and the Evaton Ratepayers' Association, both of which later affiliated to the UDF, campaigned against participation in the elections. Their campaign was successful, resulting in a poll of only 15 percent of registered voters, or less than 10 percent of those eligible to vote.

So it was an unpopular council that took office. The three participating parties won equal shares of the few votes cast, but Mahlatsi absorbed the party of the poor and became mayor. Eight months later the new council raised rents 10 percent. This was the sixth increase in as many years, and it pushed the Vaal Triangle rents to the highest in the country—a heavy burden for a poor community with a 40 percent unemployment rate. At the same time the council decided to privatize its monopoly of the liquor stores in the six townships, and by a unanimous vote the fourteen councillors agreed to divide the stores equally among themselves and their families. Moreover the deal they worked out for themselves required no down payments: they granted themselves 100 percent loans repayable over twenty years, and at the same time agreed to issue no new liquor retail licences while these council loans were still outstanding—so preserving the monopoly.

It was a nice deal, and while the struggling township dwellers faced their rent increases some of the councillors built themselves two-storey mansions with two-car garages and bathrooms decorated with imported Italian tiles. These new dwellings stood out provocatively among every one else's little matchbox houses and mud-daub shanties, some with sheets of corrugated iron roofing held down with heavy stones.

As anger boiled up over the rents, an Anglican priest in Sharpeville, Father Geoffrey Moselane, decided to call his congregation together to discuss the issue. He called on Nosipho Mieza, part-time secretary of a trade union, to ask her help in printing a notice for a parish meeting. In a casual remark that was to have large consequences, Mieza said to him: "You know, Father, a lot of the workers are coming in here complaining about the rents too. Why don't you make it a general meeting?"

Moselane did just that. Several general meetings of residents were held in a Catholic church at a place called Small Farms, between the townships of Evaton and Sebokeng. At the last of these a proposal was made that residents should protest the increases, due to come into effect on Saturday, September 1, 1984, by staying away from work and boycotting businesses on the following Monday. The meeting was about to agree to this when an elderly man stood up at the back of the church and addressed the gathering. "What's the use of just staying away from work?" he asked. "We have no quarrel with our employers. Let's march to the council offices and tell these councillors and the whites who put them there that we are not prepared to pay this rent." Thunderous applause greeted the suggestion and it was adopted on the spot. So another fortuitous decision linked into the chain.

Meanwhile the residents of Bophalong, another of the six townships, who had not been represented at Moselane's meetings, decided to hold a meeting of their own to which they invited the councillors to come and explain the reasons for the rent increases. The councillors arrived on the evening of August 29 accompanied by a contingent of police who, in an extraordinary display of militarism, marched back to back down the central aisle of the community hall where the crowd had gathered. Residents objected to the police presence and, after some heated exchanges, the councillors asked them to leave. Moments later the lights in the hall were mysteriously switched off. In the darkness and confusion shots rang out. The police fired tear gas into the hall and pandemonium broke out among the choking, gasping crowd stuggling in the darkness. They emerged more furious than ever with the councillors.

After the meeting several councillors accused Moselane of causing discontent in the townships. A security police officer called on him as well and warned him that he would be held responsible if trouble broke out. That night Moselane's house was stoned.

Tensions were rising in the Triangle townships. But they were rising nationally as well. This was the week of the "coloured" and Indian elections, and as the boycott rattled the government, it ordered the detention of nearly the whole UDF national executive. On the last day of voting, August 28, rioting broke out in the Indian township of Lenasia, about fifty miles from the Vaal Triangle.

Sunday night, September 2, the last link dropped into the chain of fateful events. Makeshift barricades were thrown across the road between the still seething township of Bophalong and the white city of Vanderbijlpark. There was anger in the air and the police were jumpy. A police officer spotted a shadowy figure in the darkness and fired a shot. Reuben Twala, captain of the Bophalong soccer team, fell dead. The police claimed he was part of a gang breaking into a liquor store. Twala's friends accused the police of shooting indiscriminately. The facts made little difference. Twala was a local hero and his death was a spark that set off a powder keg. That night enraged youths roamed the streets of Bophalong crying vengeance. "Twala is dead, we are going to get them!" they yelled.

The group swelled to a mob and early next morning it descended on the ornate homes of the councillors, chanting slogans and yelling to them to come out. The first to die was Sam Dlamini, the deputy mayor, who came to his door and was cut down with rough-sharpened *pangas*, homemade weapons similar to machetes. His mutilated body was flung into his car, which was parked in the driveway, and it was set ablaze. Someone filled a tyre with petrol, lit it and rolled it through the open front door down the deputy mayor's hallway. It hit a wall at the end, splashing the blazing petrol into an eruption of fire.

Two more councillors died that morning. Caesar Majeane was cut down in his lime-green palace in Sebokeng, and Dutch Diphoko and a guard were incinerated in Evaton in a blaze that cracked his ceramic floor tiles, scalded his marble staircase, and destroyed two Rovers in his driveway.[4] From there the youths went on a rampage, torching the liquor stores and scores of other buildings belonging to Mahlatsi and his councillors. By midmorning Sharpeville, Sebokeng, and Evaton were ablaze.

Meanwhile, back at Small Farms Father Moselane and his group, unaware of what was happening in the townships, were preparing to start their protest march on the council offices. They set out at nine o'clock, led by a tall man named Ephraim Ramakgula, who had a particular grievance of his own. Ramakgula had fallen behind with his rent and, as it did in such instances, the council had removed his front door in midwinter. To get it back Ramakgula had to pay the arrears as well as a month's rent in advance. He borrowed money from his employer to do this, but when he got the door back the hinges and lock were missing. He was angry.

Slowly the marchers wound their way toward the council offices, picking up supporters as they went until there were fully five thousand of them. They carried a memorandum of protest with them, which the Vaal Civic Association had drafted the previous day and which they planned to hand to the councillors. But they never got there. About halfway to the council offices a large contingent of police in armoured Hippos blocked their way. The townships were on fire, three councillors were dead, the rest had fled for their lives, and now here was a mob marching on the administration offices. The police were convinced they had a major insurrection on their hands. They opened fire on the marchers with shotguns, rubber bullets, and tear-gas launchers.

From then on it was chaos. For two days angry youths stoned the police, burned automobiles, and torched every commercial building in sight, and the police in turn opened fire on anyone moving about in the townships. Thirty people were shot dead, at least two of them young children.

In the inflammable atmosphere of the time riots flared across the country—from the Vaal Triangle to the East Rand to the squatter camps of Cape Town and the townships of the old eastern Cape frontier, to Durban's Umlazi and Inanda and eventually back to Soweto. The disturbances spread wider and deeper than any unrest had done before,

4. The three killings led to the conviction of the so-called Sharpeville Six. Although none of the six was present at the actual killings, the court held that as youth leaders they had incited the mob to commit the murders. All six were sentenced to death, but after an international outcry the sentences were commuted to life imprisonment.

from city to countryside and into small-town South Africa. Outlying *dorps* of the Orange Free State and northern Cape, where blacks had been docile for as long as anyone could remember, suddenly became centres of insurrection. Some of the "homelands" were touched, too, the Ciskei and KwaNdebele, BophuthaTswana and parts of KwaZulu.

A wider range of groups were brought together than ever before. Soweto '76 was a children's revolution, but this time the UDF spanned the generation gap. The generations of the old Defiance Campaign, of Sharpeville, of Soweto '76, and the angry new generation of the day came together with trade unionists and liberation theologists, educators and students as well as politicians—from exiled ANC leaders to former Black Consciousness leaders now incorporated into the UDF. And more than ever before white liberals and radicals were involved, substantial numbers of whom identified with the UDF. Several predominantly white organizations, including the National Union of South African Students, for many years the main students' organization on the English campuses, became affiliates.

The 1984 insurrection was more intense and lasted longer than any previous one. For three years it raged, resulting in more than three thousand deaths, thirty thousand detentions, and untold damage to property and the national economy. The government had to mobilize the army and declare two states of emergency to bring it under control, and even then it was only partially repressed.

It also had more strategic shape and revolutionary thrust than any previous uprising. The participation of politically experienced adults and of a national organization with affiliates deeply rooted in the communities meant that militant young "comrades," the shock troops of the uprising, were subject to some measure of direction and discipline. Although events developed a momentum of their own, impromptu actions taken in one area could be evaluated and, if successful, repeated elsewhere. The result was that a variety of strategies were employed: consumer and rent boycotts, school boycotts, strikes and stayaways, rallies, protest demonstrations, and an intermix of street confrontation and public and private negotiation.

To the extent that there was a central strategic thrust, it was to drive out the township administrations set up under the Black Local Authorities Act and replace them with the UDF's own organizational structures. This would serve the dual purpose of demolishing the neo-apartheid system's co-optive structure at its base and at the same time give the liberation movement control of the townships. The townships would become, if not exactly "liberated zones" in the true revolutionary sense, at least areas where the resistance movement held sway over the people and from which it could then negotiate with the government for national objectives. The call to make the townships "ungovernable" was the battle cry of the uprising.

It is important, though, to stress that this was not a plan worked out by strategists of the ANC in Lusaka or of the UDF in back-street operations rooms, much as the politicians, both black and white for their different reasons, tried to suggest that it was. Rather, the reverse. Things occurred spontaneously, and in the hurricane of events the black leaders did what they could to devise strategies around what was happening. Thus when the wrath of the "comrades" vented itself on the black councillors and they either fled or resigned in scores of townships, street and area committees were set up in the vacuum left behind; these formed a rudimentary alternative government network that effectively took over control of the townships. Residents stopped paying rents to the government agencies, and instead the street and area committees collected fees, conscripted supporters for their campaigns, decided when strikes and boycotts should be called, and organized the funerals of victims of the turmoil, funerals that became giant political rallies. Black police were targetted, too, and as they were driven out of some townships the area committees organized their own crime prevention controls. "People's courts" were set up to try transgressors and punish anyone deemed to be assisting the white administration.

Police still patrolled the streets of these townships in their armoured Hippos, but they dared not venture in on foot. As a Hippo moved down a street all life would disappear in a small radius around it, only to reemerge again as soon as the ungainly vehicle had passed from sight. The range of its control was short and transient.

The alternative structures reached an advanced level in a number of townships. Atteridgeville, a township outside Pretoria, had twelve people's courts, with an appeals court known as the Advice Office. They heard cases ranging from political collaboration to assault, theft, and even civil cases and matrimonial disputes. Some of the trials were reported in the black newspapers. In the Port Elizabeth townships the UDF coalition attained such a degree of control that it was issuing hawkers' licences and fixing the prices for staple commodities in black-owned stores. White businessmen—food wholesalers and bus company owners, for example—despairing of police protection, negotiated safe passage for their vehicles with the front. The key UDF leader in the area, twenty-seven-year-old Mkhuseli Jack, was in such demand among blacks and whites that he carried a beeper so he could be paged.

Its power base in the Port Elizabeth townships established on July 15, 1985, the UDF called a consumer boycott throughout the city to pressure businessmen into supporting its demands for the release of political prisoners and an end to the state of emergency. The strategy worked, up to a point. The boycott drove more than three hundred downtown businesses into bankruptcy. When at the height of it the police detained most of the local UDF leadership, the businessmen pleaded with them to release the leaders so they could negogiate an end to the boycott; the police complied and Jack and his colleagues emerged from jail to talk terms. What failed, though, was the attempt to use the businessmen's plight to lever the government into making national concessions. As part of their deal with the UDF the businessmen agreed to send a deputation to Pretoria, but the government ignored it. The strategy of economic pressure clearly had its limitations.

Confrontation and negotiation, fury and reason. The black shock troops struck and the black leaders offered to talk. Most of the time this was an ad hoc, unstructured, unplanned relationship but it represented a strategy of a kind. As the offers to talk continued to meet with little response at the national level, however, the frustrations increased and the violence intensified. Umkhonto guerrillas slipped into the partially liberated townships and instructed groups of "comrades" at night in the techniques of revolutionary struggle.

By February 1985, for the first time the police found themselves confronted with organized street fighters. In Crossroads the "comrades" made huge shields of corrugated iron which they carried into the streets to protect the stone- and petrol-bomb-throwers from police shotguns. In Alexandra they dug "tank traps"—trenches three feet deep—across the rutted roadways to stop the Hippos driving through the township. And a street riot there was suddenly punctuated by the bark of an AK-47 automatic rifle that sent the police scattering.

In KwaNdebele the trouble swelled to the level of a civil war as "comrades" fought with pro-government vigilantes over the puppet administration's request for the squalid strip of shanty settlements to be granted "homeland" independence. The vigilantes, called the *Mbokodo*—an Ndebele word for the millstone used to grind corn—kidnapped opponents of the independence plan, made them walk barefoot over hot coals, and had them flogged naked in a room flooded with soapy water until they floundered about like stranded fish in the slippery, bloodied grime.

Retribution was swift and violent. Piet Ntuli, the *Mbokodo* leader, was blown to pieces when his car exploded one night in July 1986. In an orgy of celebration, the "comrades" of KwaNdebele rampaged through the shanty settlements setting fire to liquor stores and other business premises which the "homeland" administrators and their *Mbokodo* supporters, emulating the Vaal Triangle councillors, had appropriated for themselves. Before 1986 was out several administrators had quit and the request for independence was withdrawn. For the first time in South

African history, a black resistance campaign had forced the government to back down on a major policy plan.

In BophuthaTswana a black police officer, Brigadier Andrew Molepe, gave the order on March 26, 1986, to open fire when a crowd of 10,000 gathered on a soccer field near the sprawling Winterveld squatter settlement to protest the arbitrary arrest of youths in the area. Eleven people fell dead on the field and scores were wounded. Three months later Molepe was gunned down as he stepped from his car to attend a meeting in Winterveld.

Much as the leaders tried to exercise discipline there was often unrestrained savagery on the part of the "comrades." Every revolution produces its extremists, not only among the leaders engaged in the struggle for power but also among rank-and-filers who get caught up in a fever of idealistic zeal. That is why they produce what Brinton has called the "reign of terror and virtue," the virtue part being a puritanical streak that even led the Jacobins to try to clamp down on brothels and gaming houses in 1794.[5] The drama of revolutionary struggle heightens the passionate desire to eradicate the contaminated past and replace it with a purified future, so the extremists become fanatical in their need to stamp out and cleanse. It is a self-negating slide. Idealists who start out clamouring for liberty and tolerance become increasingly intolerant and authoritarian. And the particular targets of their intolerance are those of their own kind who are seen to be making compromises with the past, who are less than pure in their own commitment to the noble ideal.

What happened in South Africa during the years 1984 to 1987 was less than a full-blown revolution, yet it had many of its characteristics, and the perversion of idealism into the element of terror and virtue was among them. That is when what I have called the Khmer Rouge element made its appearance and the grisly "necklacings" began. Some people who violated the consumer boycotts were "necklaced," or they were forced to eat their purchases—including soap and drain cleaner, which produced severe distress and sometimes death. Young "comrades" would go to the bus stations in the evenings and smell the breath of workers coming home for signs of alcohol. Those who had been drinking were given "Omo treatment," named after a foaming detergent that was forced down their throats until they vomited. Women with permed hair had their heads shaved as a punishment for trying to look bourgeois and Westernized. Attacks on the councillors' luxury homes spread until any large house or car was liable to be attacked as a symbol of affluence and thus of presumed collaborationist behaviour. In Athlone township one

5. Crane Brinton, *The Anatomy of Revolution*, p. 190.

day I saw a mob set fire to a bulldozer, for no apparent reason except that it happened to be there at a moment of conflict and, perhaps, was assumed to be official property.

Yet through it all a spirit of comradeship and purpose in the black community transcended the violence and acts of extremism. The great funeral rallies, for all the grief that attended them, were heart-swelling occasions when the spirit of the people seemed to rise in a crescendo of collective support. They were blatantly political events in which orthodox funeral services featured hardly at all, yet they were as spiritually powerful as any religious ceremony I have ever attended.

The masses at these rallies were the opposite of David Riesman's lonely crowd. Here the anonymous individuals of a humiliated community seemed to draw strength from the crowd, gaining from it the larger identity of the occasion and an affirmation of their human worth. Their daily lives might seem meaningless, but here on these occasions the world turned out, with its reporters and its television cameras, to tell them it was not so, that their lives mattered, that humanity cared, that their cause was just; and when they clenched their fists and chanted their defiant slogans, they could feel that they were proclaiming their equality and that their strength of spirit could overwhelm the guns and armoured vehicles waiting outside.

To pass from the cordon of riot police at the outskirts of the township, with their guns and Hippos and camouflage uniforms, to the township people with their placards and bright colours and noisy chatter was like crossing an international frontier with border guards on both sides: you would go through the police cordon, sometimes presenting your press credentials like a passport to a grim-faced officer, then walk across a stretch of no-man's-land until a young UDF marshal wearing an armband would approach and direct you to where you should sit in the sports stadium where the funeral rally was being held. Inside the stadium you would enter the other South Africa, black South Africa, the one which whites never see but only dread in their dreams—warm, spontaneous, and very different from the uptight, self-indulgent South Africa you had just left.

The funeral might have been scheduled to begin at ten in the morning, but you arrived knowing it would start late and go on all day. Time is not an important factor in this other South Africa. The coffins would be there—five, ten, twenty of them set out in a row on the field in front of a platform where the speakers sat—mostly dark brown wood, but if there were children to be buried, and there always seemed to be children, they would be in little white coffins. There would be banners, too, in the colours of the trade unions and the students' organizations, the yellow and black of the UDF and the green, black, and gold of the

ANC—and, once in a while, in a moment that would send a shiver up the spine, a sheet of red with a hammer and sickle painted on it would be unfurled and held aloft by men wearing face masks.

Slowly the stadium would fill, twenty thousand, fifty thousand, seventy thousand people, and as it did so the singing would begin, thousands of voices coming together in a surging mass harmony that carried your spirit to the heavens, with every now and then a piercing solo voice rising up to ululate or trace its own melodic line above the mass.

The row of coffins, the pained faces of bereaved relatives, the wonderful freedom songs, the preaching, the harsh slogan shouting, the angry speeches, and the aggressive "toi-toi" dancing of the "comrades" as they jogged around the field chanting a call-and-response theme, all merged under the hot African sun into an evocative blend of faith and revolution. It found its ultimate expression in the haunting beauty and terrible words of a hymn of praise to the guerrillas that was sung as the coffins were borne away to the graveyard. *"Hamba kahle Umkhonto,"* the crowd would sing with the lilt almost of a lullaby:

> Go, go well, Umkhonto,
> Umkhonto, Umkhonto we
> Sizwe.
> We, we the people of
> Umkhonto
> Are ready to kill the Boers.

The comrades would carry the coffins on their shoulders, jogging and chanting through the township streets while the police watched from their Hippos and started up the motors. Soon there would be trouble and, sensing it, some of the crowd would begin to slip away.

This is when a bloody drama of sickening inevitability would take place, as the white police and the black "comrades," representing the opposite poles of South Africa's divided society, seemed drawn together by a magnetic force of compulsive confrontation. The young "comrades," after their mass celebration of anger, had an almost irresistible need to act out the heroic passion of the occasion, and the mere presence of the police amounted to an invitation, a provocation, to violence.

For their part, the police were as eager to teach the provocative young blacks a lesson as the "comrades" were to prove their worth. A riot allowed them to vent their frustrations and act out the deep-seated racism that burned in many of them, and the jogging, chanting crowd needed little prompting to provide a pretext for this. So the police would wade in with a viciousness and relish that went far beyond what was required to restore order.

They had been nurtured in a subculture that promoted this kind of response. Many were drawn from that once-poor white element of the Afrikaner community that was racist to begin with, for whom blacks were both a threat and a vulnerable scapegoat. Mix that with the macho code and rugby-playing ethic of the small towns and poorer suburbs where most of them grew up, and you have your average young police recruit—a Southern cracker, a helluva fella with an Afrikaans accent. Put him in a uniform, give him a baton and a gun, and you give him a licence also to go about affirming his manhood and his whiteness by beating up on blacks.

Working in the police force does not temper these impulses. It is brutalizing work anywhere and in South Africa especially it has bred a subculture of violence that feeds upon itself, encouraged by peer-group pressure and, often enough, by superior officers who see the police force as a front line of defence in a war of national survival.

Brigadier Theuns Swanepoel, the officer who ordered his men to open fire in Soweto in 1976, told me some years later that he regretted the police had not been allowed to shoot more protesters at the outset. "I feel the police should have taken sterner action," he said. "When things get to that stage you have no option but to tell your men, 'Open fire on the evil-doers.' Law and order must be restored irrespective of what it's going to cost.

"With blacks when they are out of control they are completely out of control," Swanepoel added. "Then the only way you can get them under control is to use force—more force than they can take."

Swanepoel was one of the most famous interrogators in the Security Police, where he was known as *Rooi Rus,* or the Red Russian, and his reputation among young policemen was enormous. He had retired when I spoke to him and was running for election to parliament as a member of the Conservative party. I asked him how many members of the police force he estimated were supporters of the far-right movement. "At least seventy percent," he replied. I doubt he was exaggerating.

Later in his retirement Swanepoel organized a bodyguard force called Aquila for the leader of the Afrikaanse Weerstandsbeweging, Eugene Terre' Blanche. His own views on race and how to deal with blacks were evident; those among the rest of the police force, who regarded him and other officers like him as reference figures, can be surmised.

And so the two poles of this conflict, the jogging "comrades" and the waiting police, would be drawn irresistibly together. The fact that the police wore no protective gear and carried no plastic shields, as riot squads do elsewhere in the world, was both a statement of their Afrikaner machismo and a further incitement to the "comrades" to throw their stones, so that the police could shoot "in self-defence." They wore camouflage battle dress instead, suggesting that to them this was war. Week after week, in township after township, the bloody clashes took place, each funeral providing the bodies for yet another funeral the following week, a recurring cycle that gave the insurrection a grim momentum. It was as though the bodies fed a furnace of rage; and as the government met the mounting fury with ever more force for fear of seeming weak in the face of it, there seemed no way to break the deadly cycle.

MARCH 21, 1985, and a funeral crowd is gathering on Maduna Square in the centre of Langa township, a run-down jumble of old houses and tin shanties adjoining the industrial town of Uitenhage in the eastern Cape. It is the twenty-fifth anniversary of the Sharpeville massacre, and before this fateful day is over there will be another massacre here, not as big as the first one but as horrifying. A generation has passed, but little has changed in the psyche of repression.

The first step in a sequence of events culminating in this deadly double anniversary was taken six weeks before and seven hundred miles away at police headquarters in Pretoria. The senior officers there were growing exasperated at the increasing boldness of the "comrades" all around the country. They decided it was time to get tougher. Brigadier Bert Wandrag, the head of police counterinsurgency operations, sent a message to all police station commanders authorizing them to switch from light birdshot to heavy buckshot in the shotguns their riot squads took with them into the townships. The message contained another chilling change to the standing instructions as well: station commanders should tell their men they could open fire with their 9mm service revolvers on "selected and properly identified targets."

On March 19, the deputy commissioner of police, General Hendrik de Witt, reinforced Wandrag's message with a second telex authorizing police to use automatic weapons if necessary and to "eliminate" any rioters seen throwing acid or petrol bombs.[6] In their determination to end the township demonstrations, the police were switching from normal riot-control methods to lethal weapons and shoot-to-kill orders.

At all events that was the literal interpretation placed on it in troubled Uitenhage, a depressed industrial town with a 40 percent unemployment rate where there had been a lot of political unrest. Lieutenant Colonel Frederik Pretorius, the station commander there, issued orders that no more tear gas, rubber bullets, or birdshot cartridges were to be

6. General de Witt was later promoted to commissioner of police, the top post in the South African police force.

issued to township patrols in his area. Instead they were given 7.62mm semiautomatic R1 rifles and extraheavy SSG shotgun cartridges. Asked why, a senior officer at the station, Major Daniel Blignaut, told a court of inquiry later it was because the black crowds had become more "aggressive" and the conventional riot-control weapons were useless against them. "People in the townships boast about the number of birdshot wounds they have," Blignaut said. "The more wounds a person has the more esteem he has in the community."

And so it came about that the Hippos that set out from the Uitenhage police station on the morning of March 21 were carrying no riot equipment, only lethal automatic rifles and heavy-gauge shotguns.

The crowd gathering on Maduna Square did not know this, of course. Nor did they know that the funeral they were going to had been banned the night before and that the police would therefore regard the procession they were about to embark on as illegal. The funeral was of four young "comrades" killed in a clash with the police two Sundays before. They were supposed to have been buried the following Sunday, but in an effort to prevent another mass rally and break the cycle of death and demonstration another Uitenhage police officer, Captain Gert Goosen, had ordered the funeral postponed to a weekday—Thursday, March 21.

Like most white policemen, indeed whites generally, Goosen was not in touch with the nuances of township life. Only at the last moment did someone alert him to the fact that Thursday was the Sharpeville anniversary—not only a highly emotional day in the black calendar but also one on which township people would almost certainly stay away from work, treating it as a self-proclaimed public holiday. Goosen hurried around to the local magistrate's home on Wednesday night to ask him to issue a second prohibition order. The magistrate obliged, but in a further blunder this new order was announced only in Uitenhage's second black township, Kwanobuhle, where the funeral was to be held, and not in Langa.

So at about eight o'clock on that brittle-bright autumn morning the people of Langa began arriving in Maduna Square to board buses that would take them to the big sports stadium in Kwanobuhle, on the far side of Uitenhage, where the funeral rally was to be held. It was a slow, leisurely business in the manner of these all-day occasions. It was going to be hot, so people brought hats and sunshades with them and men took off their jackets and slung them over their shoulders as they stood around gossiping and slowly taking their seats in the buses.

Then a Hippo appeared. A young police officer standing in the turret ordered the people out of the buses, telling them they could not ride to the funeral in Kwanobuhle. They spilled out, muttering with annoyance and milled about on the square wondering what the problem was. Four men in long black smocks, local activists who called themselves "Rastafarians," moved among the crowd telling people that if they could not go in buses to the funeral they should walk instead.

So a column of people, perhaps two hundred to begin with but swelling quickly as it moved along, started walking from the square along Maduna Road, a macadamized street that runs southward through a dip and up a rise that overlooks a stretch of open veld and the town of Uitenhage less than a mile away. In the town the road intersects first with Caledon Street and then Cape Road, which bears away to the left through a commercial quarter and over the Swartkops River toward Kwanobuhle six miles away at the foot of a small hill in the distance. That is the way the marching crowd was going.

They sang as they went, one of the "Rastafarians" in the lead, his deep voice booming and his black smock swinging as he strode ahead. People saw that he held a black book in his hand, which some thought was a Bible. A boy on a blue Raleigh bicycle rode out ahead of the column and raised his fist in a Black Power salute. It was hot already and the sunshades were up, making a colourful procession as the marchers moved along behind their Rastafarian Pied Piper and the boy on the bike. They reached the bottom of the dip and began moving up the rise when the Hippo came through again.

Inside the armoured troop carrier Lieutenant John Fouché was on the radio telephone to the police station in Uitenhage. The crowd was marching on the town, he reported, and he asked for reinforcements. The Hippo drove to the top of the rise, made a U-turn, and parked at an angle across the road. As the crowd moved up the rise a white paddy wagon loaded with armed police pulled in beside the Hippo on the rise, and a second Hippo appeared behind the marching column. The crowd slowed but kept on singing—the Umkhonto funeral song. An interpreter in the Hippo, hearing the words of the song, turned to Fouché and told him: "They say they're going to kill the whites." The officer glanced anxiously at the town behind him.

The boy on the bicycle was close now and he moved to pass on the right, but a policeman sitting on top of the paddy wagon waved to him to ride between the two vehicles. He swung back into the centre of the road and was about to pass the paddy wagon when Lieutenant Fouché gave the order to open fire. A shot rang out and with a convulsive jerk the boy catapulted into the air and fell to the ground, blood pouring from his head.

"The guns start shooting from the Hippo and the white truck," recalls Eric Thembani, who joined the column at 15th Street and had been walking in the middle of the crowd.

> A man on top of the Hippo is moving from one side to the other, shooting all the time. I see people falling in front of me and I grab one of them and hold him against me. I stagger backwards holding him against me like a shield. Then I am hit by a shot on top of my head and I let go of this other person and fall down.
>
> I fall face down in the road and lie there dazed. I hear more shots and then a policeman's voice saying in a mixture of Xhosa and Zulu that they should finish off the people lying there because they may bring claims later. I lie there very still, pretending to be dead. Someone near me says, "Here's the leader." There is a shot and I think they have shot the Rastafarian lying behind me because the bullet hits me in the sole of my foot.
>
> I feel someone pricking my ribs with his finger. He grabs hold of my wrist and feels for my pulse, then turns me face upwards and puts his hand on my neck. He opens one of my eyes and shines something like a torch in it, then the other eye. I hear him call out in Afrikaans: "This kaffir is long dead."

Thembani lay there among the corpses in the road, feigning death, until an ambulance arrived and took him to the hospital. At the hospital he threw away his bloodied shirt, borrowed another man's jacket and slipped out of the casualty ward. He says he was still terrified they were going to finish off the wounded and so he ran away.

Another who feigned death was the boy on the bicycle. Witness after witness testified at the inquiry that they had seen him shot through the head, the first victim of the massacre. Equally emphatically the police denied there had ever been a cyclist there. After weeks of contradiction the boy appeared. Moses Bucwa explained that the bullet had grazed his head and stunned him. As he lay on the ground a policeman came up and kicked him and rolled him over to see if he was still alive. "I pretended to be dead. Then he kicked me a second time and I lost consciousness," Bucwa said.

The boy came to in the hospital. He was treated there for a week, then arrested and taken to jail where he remained while the argument went on at the inquiry about whether he existed or not. "The police told me I was arrested for throwing stones," Bucwa told the inquiry when finally he was released.

Twenty people were killed in the Langa shooting and twenty-seven wounded. It was the worst massacre since Sharpeville, but only a small sample of the total violence that shook South Africa during these three terrible years. They buried the victims at a huge funeral rally in Kwanobuhle three weeks later: the sports stadium packed with seventy thousand people reverberated with rage. "This massacre was no accident," thundered Fikile Kobese, a local trade union leader who acted as a kind of master of ceremonies. "It wasn't just a few policemen acting in a panic. They planned to kill our people. That is why they took no rubber bullets or tear gas." To roars from the crowd Kobese added, "They waited intentionally until the people had moved into a position where they could do nothing, then they mowed them down."

In Parliament the minister of law and order, Louis le Grange, said the police opened fire in self-defence. It had been an unruly mob, he said, heavily armed with sticks, stones, and petrol bombs, and it had surrounded the police and attacked them.

The inquiry found otherwise. Judge Donald Kannemeyer, who conducted it, concluded that the police had fabricated the attack on them to justify the shooting and that Le Grange had given a misleading account to Parliament. He criticized the order stopping the issue of riot-control equipment to the police, found it "disquieting" that thirty-five of the forty-seven dead and wounded had been shot in the back, which meant most of the shots must have been fired while the crowd was running away, but in the end concluded that no one was to blame for the massacre.

It was not the kind of verdict to appease the wrath of black South Africa.

AS THAT WRATH ROSE, the government matched it with a step-by-step escalation of repressive violence. Black anger met white fist until the country was in a virtual state of civil war.

The government tried to exercise a measure of restraint at first. Though at ground level the police were going about their business with relish, at the top there was a desire to avoid seeming too ruthless. The government was trying hard to project an image of itself as reformed in character as well as ideology, and it did not want to ruin that. To pull on the jackboots now would be to make life impossible for those "coloured" and Indian politicians who had been lured into its programme, and it would wreck the promising relationship that was developing with the major Western powers and that the government hoped was going to give it international credibility at last.

By a stroke of good fortune Botha's era of neo-apartheid reformism coincided with the advent of a trio of friendly, conservative governments in the three countries that are South Africa's most important emotional reference points and trade links to the outside world. The Thatcher government in Britain, the Reagan administration in the United States, and Helmut Kohl's Christian Democrats in West Germany were all disposed to share in some measure Botha's contention that the black nationalists in his country were violent radicals being manipulated by Moscow and to look favourably on a reform programme that would neutralize them and bring in the "moderates." They accepted this at least to the extent of asserting that Botha should be given a chance, and of resisting moves for sanctions against South Africa. Their benevolent approach found expression in the Reagan administration's policy of "constructive engagement," which eschewed pressure against Botha and relied on quiet encouragement. This suited the embattled Botha down to the ground. As trouble built up he had no wish to take the kind of strong-arm action that he knew would disturb this fortunate relationship.

Through most of 1985 this restraint continued. The reformists in the cabinet, led by Constitutional Affairs Minister Chris Heunis and Foreign Minister Pik Botha, kept hoping the concessions would begin to mollify the discontent, that the "coloured" and Indian MPs would begin to win some recognition and legitimacy and draw support away from the radical movements. But as the trouble mounted the securocrats running Botha's National Security Management System grew increasingly restive.

By mid-July a compromise was reached. Botha declared a state of emergency, albeit only a partial one that initially involved thirty-six of the country's three hundred magisterial districts, with relatively mild terms. Hundreds of activists were detained, but not for long; and in some areas there were local-level negotiations despite the detentions. Most important of all, the UDF remained unbanned.

Then in August there occurred a fortuitous event, neither planned nor anticipated by the strategists on either side, that was to make the deepest and most lasting impact of the whole revolt of the 1980s. In a desperate bid to salvage their position, against the growing pressure of the securocrats, the political reformists in the cabinet persuaded Botha to commit himself to a clear statement of intent that would put the endangered reform programme beyond doubt. Just how bold this statement was to be remains a clouded issue, but what is clear is that the reformists oversold it. The commitment given, Pik Botha flew to Vienna for a meeting with American, British, and West German diplomats, among them the U.S. national security adviser, Robert McFarlane, at which he told them to expect a dramatic statement by President Botha at the Natal Congress of the National party on August 15.

What followed was like one of those whispering games played at children's parties, where the message whispered to the first player gets slightly skewed as it is passed to the next until a hilariously distorted version emerges at the end of the line. Exactly what Pik Botha whispered to McFarlane we do not know, but given his huckstering style and his eagerness to keep the worried Westerners sweet, it seems clear that he embellished President Botha's real intentions. Next in the whispering line was the American press; McFarlane, eager to justify the administration's "constructive engagement" policy, which was coming under heavy fire as American televiewers watched white cops beating up blacks in a nightly replay of their own Southern shame, added his own exaggeration to an already exaggerated intention, as he leaked the good news of apartheid's imminent demise. Finally the press itself, with its natural tendency to dramatize, added its own touch of hype. Startling predictions began hitting the newsstands. President Botha, according to *Time* magazine, was about to make "the most important statement since Dutch settlers arrived at the Cape of Good Hope 300 years ago." *Newsweek* wrote that Botha was going to announce a "giant step" away from apartheid—including power-sharing with blacks, scrapping the black "homelands," granting common citizenship to everyone, and inviting black leaders to a national convention to write a new constitution.

President Botha was furious. He believed he was the victim of a conspiracy to push him beyond where he wanted to go, and that if he complied it would show him to be weak and vulnerable to pressure. So when the great day came, with the Durban City Hall jammed with the largest corps of foreign reporters and television crews South Africa had ever seen, Botha, with a spectacular disregard for the opportunities of the occasion, delivered a king-size damp squib. Worse, he put on a display of finger-wagging belligerence, using the moment to demonstrate to the world that the Iron Man of Afrikanerdom was not going to be pushed into anything by outside pressures, internal unrest, or anything else on God's earth.

The reaction hit South Africa where it hurts most—in the pit of its economy. For some years South Africa had experienced difficulty raising foreign loans, as its image as a politically unstable country had worsened. To get much-needed foreign capital it had resorted to raising high-interest, short-term loans and then getting the banks to roll these over year after year. The result was that in August 1985, a disproportionate 67 percent of South Africa's $16.5 billion foreign debt was made up of short-term loans that could be called up at any time. For a country in political turmoil, this was a financial crisis waiting to happen.

Botha's great-letdown speech was what made it happen.[7] For Chase Manhattan Bank, already under pressure to withdraw from South Africa, it was the last straw. Chase called in its loans. Within days, other American banks followed. As one local banker put it: "Banks are like lemmings. Once Chase made that move, other American banks got the wind

7. It became known as the Rubicon speech, because in the midst of his negative presentation Botha incongruously stated that he had crossed the Rubicon of reform.

up." And once the American banks moved, so did others in Britain, Germany, and Switzerland. It turned into something like a classic bank run and by the month's end South Africa was facing demands for the repayment of $13 billion in short-term loans by December. The shock of it sent the rand currency plunging 35 percent in thirteen days, hitting an all-time low of 34.75 U.S. cents, from which it has still not recovered years later. (Only a few years before, the rand had been trading at between $1.30 and $1.40.)

Unable to meet the demand, South Africa froze the debt and imposed strict foreign-exchange controls, which included the introduction of a two-tier exchange rate for the rand—a "commercial rand" rate for the currency internally, and a lower "financial rand" rate for it externally. Eventually the government engaged a Swiss banker, Fritz Leutwiler, to negotiate a rescheduling of repayments. But the effect of the crisis was to turn South Africa into a siege economy, keep it drained of foreign exchange and development capital, and send white living standards into decline. All of which contributed to the further disintegration of the National party.

Momentarily the financial crisis strengthened the hand of the political reformists. Macho posturing might go down well at home but it could be costly abroad, and so for a time the securocrats went into retreat and the reformists enjoyed something of a Prague spring while they tried to resurrect the image of reform and win back the approval of the benign trio in the West. Botha made a more genuinely reformist speech when he opened Parliament in February. He announced that a national congress of the National party would be held in August—only the third in the federally structured party's seventy-three-year history—to endorse a new constitution. An expensive advertising campaign proclaimed the dawn of a new era. It was a major public-relations operation. The following month the emergency was lifted.

But as the insurrection continued to intensify, tension increased and open rifts began to appear between the securocrats and the political reformers. The crunch came in May 1986 with the arrival in South Africa of a body of people bearing the pretentious appellation of the Commonwealth Eminent Persons Group (EPG). Not to put too fine a point on it, the group had been appointed as the result of a ploy by Mrs. Thatcher to sidestep pressure for sanctions against South Africa at a meeting of Commonwealth heads of government in Nassau, Bahamas, seven months before. Mrs. Thatcher suggested that before a decision was taken a committee of eminent Commonwealth figures should visit South Africa to assess the prospects for change and see whether it could initiate a dialogue between Pretoria and the country's black leaders. This was patently intended as a face-saving compromise to prevent a split in the Commonwealth, but the mission turned out to be the most remarkable attempt at foreign mediation in the South African conflict so far undertaken—largely because of the energy and imagination of its two co-chairmen, former Prime Minister Malcolm Fraser of Australia and General Olusegun Obasanjo of Nigeria.

Obasanjo is an exceptional man. As military ruler of Nigeria, he handed the country back to civilian rule in 1979 and dropped out of the picture to go chicken farming, which in itself stamps him as a rare figure in the power-hungry political world. He is a large, earthy man with an amiable manner and a sharply perceptive mind. In South Africa he also showed himself to have a flair for the unorthodox and no small degree of personal courage, plunging into Alexandra township at the height of some of the worst rioting, spending several days there talking to the people, and seeing for himself the actions of the riot police. There was no bluffing him with political bromides after that.

But Obasanjo made his main contribution to the mission in his personal touch. His easy manner and informality, which would have him kick off his shoes and put up his feet, appealed to the bucolic simplicity inherent in both the white Afrikaners and the black Africans he was dealing with. He struck the common denominator that is there between them if only they would recognise it—people rooted in the soil of this elemental continent. And so a bond was established, and the EPG, as it shuttled back and forth between Lusaka and Pretoria, helped to initiate the first indirect dialogue between the ANC and the National party government.

Its results were surprising. The EPG quickly established that there was both a widespread desire among ordinary people for a negotiated settlement and, on the face of it, enough potential common ground among all major political groups to get negotiations going. While making the cautionary observation that the government's position was difficult to pin down because "it has perfected a specialized political vocabulary which, while saying one thing, means quite another,"[8] the EPG decided to take the government at its word when it said it wanted to scrap apartheid and negotiate a new constitution with the acknowledged leaders of the people, and on that basis it prepared what it called a "possible negotiating concept." This it put to both Pretoria and the ANC.

The concept required the government to make an unambiguous declaration of its reformist intentions and at the same time take a series of "confidence-building steps" to allay suspicions and demonstrate its good faith. These would include releasing Nelson Mandela and other

8. *Mission to South Africa: The Findings of the Commonwealth Eminent Persons Group on Southern Africa* (London, 1986), p. 81.

political prisoners, unbanning the ANC and PAC, withdrawing the army from the townships, and allowing free assembly and political activity. For its part the ANC should announce that it was prepared to suspend its guerrilla struggle and enter into negotiations.

Here was the acid test. For years the government had claimed it was only the ANC's commitment to violent struggle that had led to its banning, and that if it would renounce that Mandela could go free and talks begin. All its actions had indicated otherwise—that in fact the government wanted to eliminate the black Nationalists and do its neo-apartheid deals with more malleable "moderates"—but that was its public position. Now it was being put to the test.

The ANC, sceptical at first, warmed to the idea and indicated it might respond positively but wanted to hear the government's response before making a final decision. Mandela, visited in Pollsmoor Prison, indicated his personal approval but said he would need to communicate with his colleagues in Lusaka before making it official. Pik Botha's foreign affairs department, eager to keep on pleasing the Western trio, made encouraging noises and sent a special envoy to hold further talks with the EPG in London and to invite them to revisit South Africa.

And so it was that the seven-member EPG flew back to South Africa in early May for a week. For the government, the moment of truth had come. The ANC seemed ready to accept the terms of the "possible negotiating concept," and so the government would have to decide: Did it really want to negotiate with them or not? There could be no more ducking and diving, no more doublethink and doublespeak, no more stalling even. The EPG was here and an answer would have to be given. If the answer was yes, neo-apartheid would be down the drain and white rule with it. If it was no, South Africa's relations with the Western powers would be jeopardized and sanctions might follow.

The cabinet met on the morning of Tuesday, May 13, and the decision was taken. The securocrats won: not only was the EPG initiative to be scuttled, but, since one might as well be hung for a sheep as for a lamb, all the stops were now to be pulled out to crush the black revolt. The reaction of Great Britain, the United States, or West Germany was no longer a consideration.

The EPG had an appointment with Pik Botha that morning and they waited in his office while the cabinet meeting overshot its schedule. When he walked in forty-five minutes late he was clearly upset. He and his fellow reformists in the cabinet had not only lost out but been routed, and though he said nothing of this to the Commonwealth group, he harangued them for a half hour on the iniquities of foreign interference and how they were making orderly reform in South Africa impossible.

The *coup de grâce* came the following Monday. The EPG had flown to Lusaka where the ANC had promised them a firm answer within ten days. They returned on Sunday and were due to meet with Heunis and his cabinet constitutional committee in the morning, a meeting they had been told would be vital in determining the government's decision. But as they turned on their radios for the morning news, they heard that South African commandos had launched predawn raids on "ANC bases" in Harare and Gaborone and that the air force had bombed a "base" in Lusaka. As it turned out, the Harare "base" was a house that had been evacuated and the planes hit the wrong target in Lusaka, dropping their bombs on a United Nations camp full of Angolan and Namibian refugees. No matter. It was the EPG that was the real target, and they caught a plane out of South Africa that night, their mission aborted.

The repercussions lived after them, however. With the earlier restraints no longer applying and the securocrats now firmly in command, the reform programme was put aside and the government launched the crackdown that the military hawks had so long been itching for.

When August came the big party congress, its purpose gone, was as much of a fiasco as the EPG mission. There was no new reform constitution to ratify, so Botha used the occasion once again to breathe defiance at the world. "Granting concessions under conditions bordering on blackmail merely encourages the raising of demands," he told the party delegates in a clear reference to the EPG. Begin negotiating with the ANC, he said, and the next threat would be to impose sanctions if the government did not accept the ANC's demands. This was the start of an attempt to force the whites, step by step, to negotiate themselves out of power. Better call a halt and face the threat of sanctions now. Impress the world with the Afrikaners' toughness and determination. "Don't underestimate us," Botha thundered. "We're not a nation of jellyfish."

The crackdown had begun earlier, with the June 12 declaration of another state of emergency, much more stringent and comprehensive than the first one, and which remains in force as this book is written. It placed South Africa under virtual martial law and gave the securocrats a free hand to introduce what they called a "total counter-revolutionary strategy." This was an elaboration of Beaufre's "total strategy." By then the securocrats had discovered another military theorist, an American officer, Lieutenant Colonel John J. McCuen, who supplemented Beaufre's broad concepts with more precise, practical advice on the techniques and tactics to be employed against a revolutionary onslaught. To an astonishing degree, even to the extent of using the same labels and catch phrases, McCuen's ideas (set out in a book published during the Vietnam War) became the operational blueprint for South Africa's drive to crush the rebellion. This reflected the government's view that what they were dealing with was not an internal uprising of a subjugated people against their oppressors but a Communist insurrection manipulated from outside.

The main thrust of McCuen's advice was to analyze the tactics being followed by the insurgents and then apply them in reverse. As he wrote: "A governing power can defeat any revolutionary movement if it adapts the revolutionary strategy and principles and then applies them in reverse to defeat the revolutionaries with their own weapons on their own battlefield."[9]

Since the South African revolt was ostensibly being directed by the multiheaded United Democratic Front, that meant a multifaceted strategy was required which would counter it in all the spheres where its affiliate bodies were operating—the political, social, labour, sports, religious, and so on. Such a concept meshed neatly with Beaufre's notion of the "total onslaught" and the "total strategy" required to counter it.

But McCuen was much more specific in his advice. Since revolutionary strategy was based on mobilizing the masses, he said, it followed that the governing authorities should not only thwart such an effort but mobilize the people themselves. This called for a two-pronged approach: first destroy or neutralize the revolutionary organization and its influence on the people, then replace it with a restructured organization that could win the people over by redressing their grievances and attending to their material needs. "The decisive element in any revolutionary war," McCuen wrote, "is that great majority of the population which is normally neutral and initially uncommitted to either side. . . . The objective must be to mobilize this majority so that it supports the governing power."[10]

Crushing the revolutionary organization presented problems, McCuen warned. It might require heavy-handed action in which the local population might get hurt and alienated and international opinion be outraged. But since it must be done, get it done quickly. With admirable delicacy McCuen quotes Machiavelli's advice that "the conqueror must arrange to commit all his cruelties at once, so as not to have to recur to them every day."

The cruelties accomplished, come the sweeteners. The assault on the hearts and minds of the people, McCuen says, must be undertaken in great depth. It requires fostering all sorts of classes, associations, clubs, groups, and societies. It must be done in sport, agriculture, education,

9. Lieutenant Colonel John J. McCuen, *The Art of Counter-Revolutionary War* (London, 1966), p. 29.

10. Ibid., p. 56.

medicine, religion, in fact everywhere the revolutionaries have been active. The governing authorities must establish person-to-person relationships and in that way detect all the minor complaints and needs of the local people and satisfy them as far as possible. They must build roads, dams, dykes, irrigation systems, schools, and temples. "Actually, the vast majority of the people are far more interested in these practical matters—plus the security of their families and themselves—than the sophisticated questions of the state," McCuen wrote. "The population will be won or lost depending on whether or not the governing power can solve the direct, day-to-day problems of the people."[11]

All of this, McCuen stressed, should be backed up by an all-out propaganda campaign through the newspapers, bulletins, books, pamphlets, theatrical performances, and films. This propaganda campaign should not only aim to sell the reform programme to the population but do everything possible to discredit the revolutionary movement.

This, then, became the pattern of the South African government's "total revolutionary strategy." The emergency regulations furnished the security forces with sweeping powers to launch their crackdown, including press restrictions that helped the propaganda campaign and hindered any international response by keeping away the reporters and television cameras while the "cruelties" were performed. Organizations were banned, open-air gatherings were prohibited, and the police and military swept into the townships to detain thirty thousand people, including eight thousand children and three thousand women—more than in all the twenty-five years since Sharpeville.

McCuen called for the use of locally-recruited militia units, quickly trained special constables, and what he rather delicately described as "counter-revolutionary guerrilla bands" to attack the enemy. South Africa did all this. It recruited *kitskonstabels*, literally "instant constables," from the ranks of local unemployed, and gave them a six-week crash course in political repression; vigilante bands, composed of township residents with cause to resent the excesses of the "comrades" and eager for revenge, were armed and turned loose on the more radicalized townships. There were assassinations and death threats, activists' homes were torched, and the offices of anti-apartheid organizations were bombed.

More subtly, the authorities exploited political rivalries within the black community and through shrewd manipulation turned group against group in recurring sequences of black-on-black violence that left foreign observers baffled. As the repression intensified and black leaders disappeared into detention, discipline deteriorated and direc-

11. Ibid., pp. 59–60.

tionless groups vented their frustrations on one another. Bloody conflicts broke out between the UDF and Azapo in Soweto and the eastern Cape, and between the UDF and Inkatha in Natal, again with the security forces often standing by to observe the spectacle of black self-immolation.

As the street and area committees fled or disappeared into detention, the authorities repeated in reverse what the "comrades" had done to them and filled the vacuum with their own reinstated administrative structures. Thus gradually they regained control of the "ungovernable" townships. Then came the second prong of the strategy, code-named WHAM—Winning Hearts and Minds—aimed, as one of the securocrats put it, at "eliminating the underlying social and economic factors which have caused unhappiness in the population." Roads were paved, sewerage systems laid, and a massive housing programme started. In all, eighteen hundred urban renewal projects were launched in two-hundred townships.

McCuen recommended what he called an "oilspot" strategy, which meant concentrating the operation on specific spots, gaining control of these and then using them as strategic bases from which to operate outwards and pacify the surrounding region.[12] Adopting both his idea and his term, the security managers targetted thirty-four "oilspots"—including the Vaal Triangle, Atteridgeville, the Uitenhage and Port Elizabeth townships, and Crossroads.

Beginning with Sebokeng, troops threw a cordon around each of the Vaal Triangle townships, sealing in the people while police went from door to door searching houses and detaining anyone who smelt of radicalism. At Uitenhage the whole of Langa township was literally erased from the map, its entire population removed to Kwanobuhle, which was then subjected to a series of bloody vigilante attacks in which vengeful bands rampaged through the streets assaulting and killing "comrades" and burning down their homes until the township was purged of them. A year later I met the remnants of the Kwanobuhle Action Committee, who had once controlled the township, living in hiding in Port Elizabeth's Zwide. They told me it was not safe for them to return.

A barbed-wire barricade was thrown around New Brighton township like a Berlin Wall, with a single Checkpoint Charlie through which everyone had to pass. Mkhuseli Jack was detained and held until May 1989. His associate, Henry Fazzie, remained free a little longer by resorting to Scarlet Pimpernel disguises in which he even managed to fly on South African Airways, but in the end he, too, was detained.

McCuen warned about squatter camps particularly. Experience in

12. For a detailed exposition of the "oilspot concept" see ibid., pp. 196–206.

Malaya, he said, had shown that the lack of any administrative structure in these labyrinthine settlements made them ideal havens for revolutionaries.[13] So Crossroads, which had indeed been a focal point of organized resistance, was targetted as an "oilspot." The sprawling complex consisted of a core area, known as Old Crossroads, and a series of satellite settlements in which the "comrades" were known to be most active. Between May 17 and June 12, 1986, in two massive, highly organized raids, bands of vigilantes, known as *witdoeke* because of the white scarves they wore on their heads for identification, razed four of these satellite camps to the ground, driving an estimated seventy-thousand people from their homes and killing hundreds while the security forces stood by and watched. The militant squatter communities and their support groups of political activists from the UDF and its affiliates were routed, and Old Crossroads was placed under the control of a tough local politico favoured by the securocrats.[14]

One year after the state of emergency was declared ninety-seven townships were under military occupation, and by late 1987 the rebellion was pretty well quelled. But though quiet was restored the repression did not succeed in its major objective to crush the resistance and win black majority support for the government's reform programme. The resistance movement might have been disrupted organizationally, but its legitimacy in the black community remained intact. Its work-stoppage calls still drew mass responses and a fresh round of municipal elections in 1988 was again heavily boycotted. Black "moderates" did not come forward to cooperate with the government in negotiating a new constitution that would still stop short of majority rule, because they knew that to do so would be to forfeit what little credibility they had. They laid down the same preconditions as the nationalist movements—release Nelson Mandela and other political prisoners, legalize the ANC and other banned organizations, allow political exiles to return, end the state of emergency, remove troops from the townships, and scrap all discriminatory laws.

Why did the government's strategy fail?

Essentially, the Afrikaner securocrats had read too much foreign military literature and too little of their own history. Their ethnocentric minds were unable to project into the black situation and to recognize that the blacks would respond exactly as they themselves had done when

13. Ibid., pp. 91–6.

14. For a detailed account of the destruction of the Crossroads satellite camps see Josette Cole, *Crossroads: The Politics of Reform, 1976–1986* (Johannesburg, 1987), pp. 131–55.

their own revolution was on the rise. They had never abandoned Afrikaner nationalism for the "moderate" compromisers and dealers. They had never been prepared to settle for less than full power. And the more they had felt themselves persecuted and oppressed, the more politicized they had become and the more committed to their Nationalist cause. Yet somehow they expected the blacks to do all the things they themselves had scorned.

Part of the reason for this failure was that they were so conditioned to thinking of blacks as "different" that they could not imagine them reacting in the same way as themselves. But a more important reason was that they had become victims of their own propaganda, and believed that a black revolution really was being directed from outside and that the uprisings had nothing to do with an oppressed indigenous people yearning to be free. That is why they could follow so literally a strategic blueprint designed to counter a revolutionary war rather than a liberation struggle.

The great majority of the people are "neutral and initially uncommitted to either side," McCuen had written. They are interested more in practical matters like roads and dams and dykes than in sophisticated questions of state. The strategists in Pretoria grasped eagerly at this, for it told them what they most wanted to hear—that the blacks could be satisfied with material rather than political concessions and appeased with something less than majority rule. "The important thing," declared Magnus Malan, "is how many black people are merely interested in satisfying their material demands—housing, education, job opportunities, clothing, bread and butter, etc. There is presently only a limited section that is really interested in political participation. I think for the masses in South Africa democracy is not a relevant factor."[15] Information Minister Stoffel van der Merwe, a political scientist who taught at Rand Afrikaans University before joining the government, gave a more sophisticated gloss to the same idea. The purpose of the crackdown, he said, was to crush the notion that black government was a possibility. Once blacks realized that their ideal was unattainable, they would be prepared to settle for less—"a government which is not white, not black, but is an adequate synthesis of the two."[16] The trick the government needed to pull off was the creation of what Van der Merwe called a "critical mass of moderate support"—20 percent of the black population, according to some securocrats; then the remaining 80 percent (McCuen's

15. Quoted in *Die Suid-Afrikaan*, Winter 1986.

16. Interview in *Leadership*, April 1988, pp. 13–15.

"apolitical majority") would cease to be the support base of the revolutionary movement and would swing over to the government.[17]

It has not worked, nor will it ever, because the masses in South Africa are not apolitical. They are not "uncommitted to either side": they are most emphatically on the side of the blacks, on their own side, however much individuals may conceal this in their day-to-day contacts, in the interest of personal survival. Therefore no critical mass can be swung over to participate in their own oppression.

And so the cruelties of the repression cannot be quickly done and forgotten. They have to be recurred to day after day, year after year, alienating and politicizing more and more people every time.

WHAT, THEN, was the final reckoning? After the longest, most intensive uprising in South Africa's history, the black liberationists failed to overthrow the government. And after the most determined repressive action ever undertaken, the authorities failed to crush the legitimacy of the resistance movement or win legitimacy for its own system. There is a stalemate, or what some analysts call a violent equilibrium.

But things are not as they were. The blacks have grown stronger and the whites weaker, which means the day of transition has been brought closer. The liberation movement knows now that it cannot win by the revolutionary overthrow of the white regime, and it will have to concentrate more on political and diplomatic strategies. It has been knocked back but it has made great gains. Millions of people, even deep in the rural areas where politics are unsophisticated and society shows a traditional black subservience, have been actively aroused and politicized. The labour movement has grown stronger despite the repression, and the focus of the black struggle is shifting there.

The National party fell between stools. Its reform programme was enough to split its ranks, but not enough to win the acceptance of the black community or the acknowledgment of the world. Its ideology dead and its solidarity broken, the monolithic Afrikaner Nationalist movement of Malan, Strijdom, Verwoerd, and Vorster is now in irretrievable decline.

Not only is the apartheid ideology dead, but so is neo-apartheid. The politics of co-optation and collaboration has been seriously discredited. The government will not abandon it because it has no other options within its narrow confines, but its chances of success are greatly reduced. There can no longer be any serious thought of confining black political

17. Quoted by Mark Swilling, *Weekly Mail*, July 22, 1988.

incorporation to powerless local-level bodies and meaningless "own affairs." New strategies will have to go well beyond that, which increases the chances of their developing a dynamic of their own and having unintended consequences outside planned control.

Internationally, the revolt of the 1980s produced the most severe repercussions in South Africa's history, plunging the country into a financial crisis deeper and longer than after either Sharpeville or Soweto. Sanctions and disinvestment campaigns have put its economy under permanent pressure, and the currency crisis exposed a weakness that will surely be attacked again.

As the decade ends, it is evident that South Africa is approaching its time of transition.

CHAPTER FIFTEEN

The Transition

The crisis consists precisely in the fact that the old is dying and the new cannot be born; in this interregnum a great variety of morbid symptoms appear.

ANTONIO GRAMSCI

THE SOUTHERN AFRICA Department of the Soviet Foreign Ministry is housed above a grocery store in a shabby beige building across the street from the ministry's headquarters in a great grey skyscraper of Stalinist Gothic grandiosity that towers over Moscow's Smolenskaya Square. "Gastro-MID," the diplomats who work there call it, with just enough edge to suggest that they feel their accommodation denotes a kind of third-world status in the giant bureaucracy of the Ministervo Inostrammih Del (MID).

Certainly the impression it gives a visitor from South Africa hardly squares with the view that underlies the "total onslaught" theory. That view, as the Stellenbosch Sovietologist Philip Nel testifies, is based on "a fervent belief that when the men in the Kremlin sit down to discuss global strategy, South Africa is consistently the most important issue on the agenda, not Poland, Afghanistan, China, missiles in Europe, or arms control with the Americans."[1] Clearly Moscow has had a longstanding interest in the region through the South African Communist party's early involvement with the black union movement and the ANC, but its priority rating has probably never taken it out of the lower quartile of foreign-policy issues, somewhere after the Middle East and the Horn.

But if the state of the Southern Africa Department's accommodation is enough to cast doubt on the authenticity of the "total onslaught,"

1. Quoted in Kurt Campbell, "Soldiers of Apartheid," *SAIS Review*, Winter 1988, p. 51.

then what is going on there these days destroys it completely. For in the run-down precincts of the Gastro-MID, with its peeling walls and clanking elevators, a major policy revamp is taking place that emphasizes the need to seek political settlements instead of military solutions to Africa's many conflicts—including the race conflict.

It is all part of Mikhail Gorbachev's *perestroika* revolution to restructure and breathe new life into the Soviet system. Gorbachev wants to cut the high cost of Russia's military involvements abroad so that the funds saved can be pumped into the flagging Soviet economy. Settling regional conflicts also means removing points of potential friction with the United States, which the Soviet leader regards as essential if he is to achieve his economic objectives. He needs a stable international environment in order to increase trade with the West, and he must avoid another round of the arms race if he is to channel resources away from defence into the civilian economy.

This is no less a revolution for South Africa than for Russia and for superpower relations. As with the Portuguese revolution, events halfway around the world are having a profound impact on the struggle over apartheid. Moscow's new policy, by leading to peace agreements for Angola and Namibia, is changing the geopolitical map of the subcontinent once again and, with that, the strategic outlook from Pretoria. In a sense it brings to an end the aggressive fourteen-year phase of regional destabilization that began with the collapse of the Portuguese empire, during which South Africa tried to neutralize the threatening arc of radical states around its borders, and it ushers in a new phase in which the strategic focus will be more intensely internal. As this new phase begins, independence for Namibia shows South Africa's first retreat in its struggle with black nationalism, its first hand-over of power.

There are more subtle consequences too. For the new ideologists of Pretoria the Gorbachev revolution poses a crisis no less severe than the death of Satan would for Christianity. How to sustain the yearning for salvation without the fear of its ghastly alternative? *Gogga maak vir baba bang*, goes an old Afrikaans saying—bogey scares baby. But if the *gogga* is no longer scary, if the Russian bear has turned into a teddy, how do you keep baby clinging to mamma? Botha tried to substitute the ideology of survival for the dying ideology of apartheid, the bond of fear for the weakening tribal bond of an obsolescent moral crusade. Now the source of that fear is no more, and the substitute ideology is dying also. All that is left holding Afrikaner nationalism together is the bond of power and the lure of privilege. That may work for a time, but it is an insubstantial thing, which will shift with the changing winds of individual self-interest. This, too, is part of the new phase, with all its morbid variations.

The first indication of a shift in Soviet thinking on South Africa came in June 1986 when Gleb Starushenko, one of two deputy directors of the Africa Institute of the Soviet Academy of Sciences (the institute is headed by Anatoly Gromyko, son of the late Russian president and veteran diplomat Andrei Gromyko), delivered a paper at a conference in Moscow in which he urged the ANC to consider giving white South Africans collective guarantees and group rights in a postapartheid constitution. The proposal caused an outcry, because it would have required the continuation of race classification and representation on a race-group basis, which is anathema to the African Congress. The ANC is committed to establishing a "nonracial democracy" in which all racial classifications will be abolished and everyone will be treated as equals regardless of their race, colour, sex, or creed; within that framework, the ANC is prepared to guarantee the protection of individual rights, as well as language and other cultural rights, by way of an entrenched Bill of Rights. It condemned Starushenko's idea as retaining one of the core features of apartheid.

Moscow quietly distanced itself from the Starushenko paper. At a conference in Zimbabwe a year later the institute's other deputy director, Victor Gontcharov, stressed that Starushenko had expressed a purely personal opinion that reflected the views of neither the institute nor the Soviet government. But he told a South African journalist that while Moscow's basic position on apartheid remained unchanged, it was ready to act "more realistically, more flexibly, with every side participating in the conflict," including South Africa itself. And for the first time Gontcharov raised the possibility of the two superpowers approaching the South African issue bilaterally. The Soviet Union had no vital interests in Southern Africa, he said, and did not regard the Cape sea route as having any strategic importance in the nuclear age and had no desire to infringe on traditional Western interests and trade ties, so perhaps it could be removed from the framework of East-West competition; the United States and the Soviet Union could develop a joint approach to try to settle the conflict.[2]

Then, in 1987, a number of Soviet Africanists involved in the policy review visited the United States and held talks with key American specialists in government and the universities. At one of these meetings Vladimir Tikhomirov, soon to become secretary of the Africa Institute, offered the personal opinion that a future black government in South Africa should go easy on economic reconstruction, not nationalizing any more of the economy than the substantial sector already under state control. Noting that South Africa has the largest amount of nationalized

2. Interview by Howard Barrell, *Work in Progress*, July 1987.

industry of any country outside the Communist bloc, he said he thought that this, coupled with increased taxation, would be sufficient to bring about a redistribution of wealth without disrupting the economy.

When I visited the Soviet Union in July and August 1988, I discovered that the policymakers and diplomats were engaged in what amounted to an across-the-board reappraisal of policies that had been set in concrete for nearly half a century. There are few parts of the world where Communist theories about the inevitability of the proletarian revolution had seemed more certainly applicable than South Africa, so little attempt was made to assess the details of day-to-day political developments. But there has been a new appreciation in Moscow of the Pretoria regime's repressive power and how unlikely it is that it can be overthrown by popular revolution. "In the past it was always assumed that there would be a classical revolutionary overthrow of the white regime. Now we accept that there will have to be a political settlement," said Boris Asoyan, deputy director of the Southern Africa Department. That means completely reassessing the situation in a new, nonideological way. "We are no longer following prescribed policies taken from scripture," said Apollon Davidson, the Soviet Union's leading African historian.

At every level in the administration and its related think-tanks, the Africa Institute and the Afro-Asian Solidarity Committee, I heard the same theme. The policy is being deideologized. As with other aspects of *perestroika*, realism and pragmatism are the new catchwords. Asoyan and others say they want to reach beyond the anti-apartheid rhetoric of the past and more constructively seek a settlement to a conflict they regard as particularly dangerous, given South Africa's regional involvements and admitted capabilities as a nuclear power. I found them undogmatic, too, about the kind of political system that might eventually evolve in South Africa. "I think it will be some kind of African socialism, not scientific socialism," Gontcharov said.

There is in fact a widespread disillusionment in the Soviet Union at the failure of the Marxist-Leninist model to take root in Africa and other parts of the third world, and a consequent reassessment of its appropriateness for underdeveloped societies. Time and again I heard advisers speak about how sobering the economic decline of Moscow's three main African protégés, Angola, Mozambique, and Ethiopia, had been. In an article in the influential *Literaturnaya Gazeta*, Asoyan wrote stingingly of Russia's naive belief during the "euphoric 1960s" and 1970s that radical socialist solutions based on theories "plucked out of a completely different historical context" could be applied to the economic-development problems of the third world.

The official view now, I was told, is that the socialist revolution is not for export and the Soviet Union does not want to incur any more of the prohibitive costs of having to support failed third-world clients. It has decided to put the whole issue of advancing socialism in Africa on the back burner and concentrate on trying to check the continent's slide into poverty. That, too, Soviets say, will require a coordinated approach with the United States and other Western countries. "Africa is in bad shape," one adviser told me, "and we certainly don't want to see the destruction of its largest and most successful economy, which is in South Africa. That is why we don't want to see too much reconstruction take place too soon down there."

Nor is it only the Soviet Union that is making this reassessment. Eighteen months before, in the course of a long interview in Lusaka, the leader of the South African Communist party, Joe Slovo, told me of his belief that the transition in South Africa would come about through negotiation rather than military victory or revolutionary overthrow. "There isn't a single struggle in the postwar period in the colonies which hasn't ended at the negotiating table," he said. "If there were any prospect of settling this thing peacefully tomorrow, we would be the first to say let's do it." It was a remarkable statement given the fact that twelve years before Slovo had written a book entitled *No Middle Road*, in which he warned against the "illusion" that there might be a route to democracy in South Africa other than through the "seizure of power" by the ANC's guerrilla forces.

Cynics will note that Slovo and the South African Communist party have always followed the Moscow line in everything from Stalinism to the invasions of Czechoslovakia and Afghanistan, and that the enthusiasm Slovo expresses today for Gorbachev's "openness" and the new line on South Africa is just one more example of his ideological subservience. That may be so, though my interview with him took place at a time when Moscow's policy reappraisal was still in its formative stage and there was no clear line on it yet. Slovo's own explanation of his new attitude is that circumstances have changed. "When I wrote *No Middle Road*," he said, "there was not even a peripheral chance of negotiation. The other side was completely intransigent and for us there was only one answer to this. Now the other side is in such trouble that with meaningful international intervention they might come forward."

Since then circumstances have changed even more—and Slovo's position with them. The collapse of communist regimes in Eastern Europe is causing much soul-searching by communists everywhere, South Africa included, and in another interview, in January 1990, Slovo told me he now rejected the principle of a one-party state as being incompatible with democracy, and said he was urging the SACP to adopt what he called "democratic socialism" as its official policy.

The ANC's position has changed too, and it did so even earlier. At a congress in Kabwe, Zambia, in June 1985, the ANC was still holding to the position that it would not seek a political settlement through negotiation and would negotiate a "transfer of power" only with a defeated white regime. A year later its president, Oliver Tambo, spelled out in an interview in Lusaka the conditions under which the ANC would be prepared to negotiate—if the government first released Nelson Mandela and all other political prisoners, unbanned the ANC and other political organizations, allowed exiles to return, lifted the state of emergency then in force, and scrapped key apartheid laws to demonstrate its sincerity and create an atmosphere of mutual trust. Another year on and the ANC issued an appeal to whites to join it in forming "a massive democratic coalition" to end apartheid and establish a new nonracial society that would be run as a multiparty democracy with a mixed economy and in which basic freedoms would be guaranteed. Making the announcement, Tambo said the ANC would "seize any opportunity" to negotiate if Pretoria showed that it genuinely accepted the need to create such a society.

In line with this policy shift the ANC has been widening its contacts with different elements in South Africa, from business leaders to Afrikaner dissidents, in an effort to build a broad alliance of support for a negotiated settlement that it hopes will eventually pressure the government into lifting the ban on it and agreeing to talk. It has not abandoned its guerrilla struggle, but this is no longer sustained in any expectation of a military victory. Its purpose is more political, as a bargaining chip and, more important, to maintain a revolutionary image so that radicalized elements continue to be drawn into its disciplinary structures and do not form an extremist movement to the left of it.

So forces are moving away from long-held positions of intransigence and converging on the idea of a negotiated settlement. As the international climate changes and relaxes, as efforts are made to resolve regional conflicts peacefully throughout the world, as the South African army withdraws from southern Angola and Namibia and the Cuban "internationalist forces" fly out of Luanda, as multinational efforts try to bring Eduardo dos Santos and Jonas Savimbi together and negotiate an end to the terrible civil war in Mozambique, the military phase of the conflict draws to an end and a new political phase begins.

OF ALL THE EVENTS pointing to the end of one phase and the beginning of another, none is so symbolic as the departure of President Botha and his replacement by the younger Frederik Willem de Klerk. The rancorous Old Crocodile, as Botha came to be known in his later years, was the instigator of South Africa's militaristic thrust northward; it was he who militarized both the government and white society; and his aggressive, bullying manner became the symbol of the national posture. Now a different kind of man has taken over, not necessarily a more enlightened man, but a different one—different in personality and in style, more polished, more agreeable, more intelligent, and above all more civilian.

De Klerk is a party man and under him the locus of power will shift back to the political establishment. Just as Botha dismantled his predecessor's personal power structure centred on BOSS and the ubiquitous General Hendrik van der Bergh, so is De Klerk now moving against Botha's overweening military establishment: in November 1989 he disbanded the National Security Management System, national service has been halved, a number of Defence Force units are being scrapped, and General Magnus Malan's influence is clearly in decline. The heavily centralized State-President's Office is likely to change, too, and the political apparatus of the National party will come into its own. With that the emphasis will shift away from security concerns to a political solution.

The change of leadership coincides with a change of needs. The security strategy failed to produce the political breakthrough that was expected of it, and the country is locked in a violent equilibrium between a government that cannot be overthrown and a spirit of mass resistance that cannot be crushed. On the surface it may appear stable, but it is not a tenable condition. As Heribert Adam and Kogila Moodley point out, a country like Lebanon with separate service economies can live with an equilibrium of violence, but not an interdependent one like South Africa where blacks and whites have to work together in the same place.[3] A modern economy cannot function if the major sources of production are alienated. For all its military might, it is the peculiar weakness of white South Africa that it is totally dependent on the people it represses. That imposes limitations on the degree of repression that can be exercised. The dependent white rulers cannot keep tens of thousands of leading members of the productive class locked up indefinitely; sooner or later there must be at least the appearance of a return to normality; a minimum level of worker contentment has to be restored. International opinion has to be mollified, too, to relieve an economy under siege from sanctions, divestment, and a drying up of foreign loans. And when the detainees have to be released, the street and area committees in the townships can be quickly resurrected—for this time, unlike the aftermath of the crises of 1960 and 1976, the organizational infrastruc-

3. Heribert Adam and Kogila Moodley, *South Africa Without Apartheid*, p. 256.

ture of the black resistance has not been eradicated. It has only been damaged and it can be repaired.

The government knows, therefore, that the situation can flare up again at any time. In the imagery of Frantz Fanon it is like the smoking ashes of a burnt-down house after the fire has been put out, which still threaten to burst into flames again.[4] And though the black resistance may not be able to overthrow the regime, it can, as it has shown, wreak economic havoc. This a weakened South Africa can no longer afford.

So De Klerk must try to break out of the violent equilibrium. That he can do only through negotiations with authentic representatives of the black majority. He would still like to pursue the co-optive strategy and do a deal with the "moderates," but such is the stigma that attaches to any black leader perceived as being collaborationist that there are no takers, and even if there were, the takers would shed whatever credibility they had and be a worthless gain. So the only option is to talk to the ANC and its internal associates. De Klerk took a critical step toward this when, in October 1989, he released eight high-profile political prisoners, including Walter Sisulu and six other members of the ANC leadership who were arrested in the 1963 Rivonia raid and sentenced to life imprisonment along with Nelson Mandela. This amounted to the de facto unbanning of the ANC because the freed men immediately began speaking and issuing statements in its name: two weeks after their release in a soccer stadium near Soweto they addressed a huge rally that was opening an ANC event with seventy thousand present, and the authorities did nothing to prevent it.

More importantly, the release of these prisoners followed months of behind-the-scenes contacts between government ministers and Mandela—who by then was being held in a prisons-department house outside the western Cape Province town of Paarl—and was clearly part of a tacit agreement that pointed to Mandela's own release early in 1990, provided that the first releases led to no serious public disturbances. As these words are written that seems a likely prospect, to be followed presumably by the formal legalizing of the ANC and a phased lifting of the state of emergency. That will clear the way for negotiations, or at least talks about talks, to begin. It will be the Rubicon that Botha shrank from crossing, for whatever Machiavellian manoeuvers the government may still try to engage in, however many breakdowns and obstructions may yet occur, there can be no turning back. One thing will lead to another.

Looking back, we can now see that the 1970s witnessed the death of apartheid ideology, fatally wounded by the failure of the black tide to turn and make the multistate solution viable, then given the *coup*

4. Frantz Fanon, *The Wretched of the Earth*, p. 75.

de grâce by the Soweto uprising. The 1980s witnessed the failure of its neo-apartheid adaptation, when the massive black revolt against the tricameral system discredited the attempt to incorporate the original separate political structures in a single-state framework. Now, as we stand on the threshold of the 1990s, the decade of transition is about to begin. It is going to be a muddled decade, full of false starts and failures and Gramsci's morbid symptoms. There will be more weird and wonderful constitutions designed to share power without losing control. There will be attempts to manipulate the negotiating process; strategies to try to split or otherwise neutralize the ANC; the search for a "moderate" collaborator of some stature will continue, and South Africa may yet have its equivalent of the Muzorewa phase, in which a hybrid Zimbabwe-Rhodesia installed the hapless Bishop Abel Muzorewa as the token head of a parity government of white and black ministers that gave the white minority veto power to preserve their privileges. But all these will be transient stages in the decade of transition.

Does De Klerk have the will and capacity to lead South Africa through this difficult transition? He is an able man but not a great one—and South Africa needs greatness at this juncture. Perhaps he will grow with the job: challenges of this magnitude can do that to a leader. More likely the greatness will come from the other side, from Mandela, whose public image, and thus his power to act boldly, has grown during his long incarceration to messianic proportions.

De Klerk brings much ideological baggage to the job. He has always been known as a party conservative, which is why he was chosen as Transvaal leader to counter Treurnicht's challenge in that province. He uses the rhetoric of reform but, like his predecessors, it is in the ambiguous vocabulary of Pretoria-speak. He talks of ending apartheid but has made it clear that he is opposed to majority rule. He told an American television interviewer soon after becoming party leader that the idea of South Africa having a black president was something that lay "far in the future." He is eager to negotiate, realizing this is the key to improving South Africa's international image and easing economic pressure, but as he keeps telling foreign diplomats: "Don't expect me to negotiate myself out of power."

What De Klerk has in mind when he talks of creating a new future is a system in which race groups will function as constitutionally defined political blocs with equal voices, regardless of their size. No group must be in a position to dominate the others, he says. He will not consider majority rule. Decisions will have to be reached by consensus among the race groups, failing which an arbiter, which De Klerk says should be a "maximally depoliticized" body like a constitutional court, will have to break the deadlock.

The black political movements are emphatically opposed to any such system, which they see as a device to thwart the majority's democratic right to rule and to preserve the privileged position whites built for themselves under apartheid. They object to an arrangement based on race, a criterion they insist must be eradicated from a post-apartheid society and replaced with a nonracist ethic; and they oppose a system that would give the white minority veto power to stop affirmative action and retain existing inequalities. They point out, too, that given the power of the presidency to appoint the arbitration bodies, and the fact that De Klerk foresees the presidency remaining in white hands, that mechanism too would surely operate in favour of the whites.

Events will force De Klerk beyond these positions, but he will not move there voluntarily. His older brother, Willem de Klerk, a theologian turned journalist who was active in bringing about the amalgamation of white liberal parties into the Democratic party in 1988, warns that he is unlikely to turn sharply to the left. "He is too strongly convinced that racial grouping is the only truth, way and life," says Willem de Klerk. "He is too dismissive of a more radical style." The course his younger brother will follow, Willem predicts, is a careful, centrist one, hoping to "hold the middle ground by means of clever footwork, small compromises, drawn-out studies and planned processes, effective diplomacy and growing authority through balanced leadership and control." That "is his style, his nature, his talent and his conviction." There will be no leap of faith in a liberal direction.[5]

But as Willem de Klerk also says, his brother is an intelligent man who is responsive to pressures, and there will be a massive convergence of pressures upon him. Once the Namibian independence process is completed, the focus of international attention will shift fully onto South Africa. If De Klerk does not move decisively soon after that, the buildup of pressures will be swift and relentless.

There will be pressures on the ANC as well—a pincer squeeze with the Western powers pressurizing Pretoria and Moscow the ANC. This will present as many tactical problems for the black organization as it will for De Klerk. Some in the ANC worry about being pushed into a negotiation prematurely. They know the South African government is not yet at the point of considering relinquishing power and allowing a genuine transition to majority rule, and that when it considers talking to the ANC *now,* it is with a view to damaging the black organization, hoping to exploit differences within the ANC and eventually split the pragmatics from the militant hardliners. "Pretoria's goal remains to

5. *Leadership,* March 1989, pp. 61–66.

crush the ANC rather than incorporate them as partners," Adam and Moodley say.[6]

Until it is ready to include the ANC, the government is likely to offer it only co-optive deals. The danger is that the ANC may then come under heavy international pressure to accept them and continue its struggle within the political framework established by the government, thereby suffering a serious loss of credibility and the likelihood of being replaced by more radical elements. On the other hand, if it were to refuse it would look like the unreasonable party and be in danger of losing international support. Short of this there is the prior danger that the ANC may be pressured into suspending its armed struggle in order to allow negotiations to begin, and then find itself locked into a marathon that Pretoria could drag out for years, as it did in Namibia, while the ANC's revolutionary image fades and its rivals mobilize the disillusioned masses around more potent themes of Africanist extremism and Fanonesque militancy.

Such fears may cause the opposition to hesitate, but there is an inexorability about the tide of events: once the negotiating begins, whatever the initial motivation, the momentum will develop, and unintended consequences will follow.

SO MUCH FOR the pressures of politics and international diplomacy. Let us turn now to something more tangible and more powerful: the pressure of millions of ordinary people, multiplying and migrating and overrunning the barricades that were erected to preserve the illusion that South Africa was a "white" country.

Thirty years ago, when Verwoerd was in his heyday, Laurence Gandar, who was then editor of the *Rand Daily Mail*, and I, who was his political correspondent, wrote editorials and columns pointing out that what we called the "arithmetic of apartheid" did not add up. The theme, repeated over and over again for a decade or more, was that even if the "homeland" builders exceeded their most optimistic expectations, the demographics of population growth and black urbanization were such that there would still be at least four times as many blacks as whites in "white" South Africa by the end of the twentieth century. The whole elaborate, costly, disruptive exercise would have been for nothing. White South Africa would still not be white. The race problem would still not be solved.

We were ignored, of course, and dismissed as Cassandras. Yet as the

6. Adam and Moodley, op. cit., p. 124.

end of the century draws near it is clear that we underestimated both the trend and its implications. When the year 1978 saw the black tide fail to turn as predicted, it offered a glimpse of a future trend that would not only sweep apartheid away but sweep in its alternative. The cities that were supposed to become white are becoming black instead. "White" South Africa is being Africanized. Instead of the townships withering away, they are colonizing the suburbs; the black tide is flowing more strongly every day, washing away the Group Areas Act, the Separate Amenities Act, and all the other sand castles of white delusion. It is washing away the bitter-almond hedge itself, sluicing great gaps in it and throwing people together in a convergence of mutual discovery that is both traumatic and formative and that will change South Africa forever.

Of all the pressures bringing change, this is the most powerful and most inexorable. The politicians will try to resist it yet awhile, but, like Canute, they know in their hearts that they cannot. And the blacks know it too, with a rising confidence that surmounts their pain and humiliation.

> The Boer came at me again and again, his face so red that it seemed to have become the very blood he wanted to draw out of me. He did not look at me any more; he knew where I was. He looked only at the ground, at his feet, beating down the grass around him, to leave a small patch of clearing as a sign of the futility of his battleground. He seemed to grow smaller and smaller the more he came at me. Then I felt totally numb. My mind had shut out all the pain. And, for the third time in about two weeks, I felt in the depths of me, the beginning of a kind of laughter that seemed to explain everything. And when the sound of laughter came out, it filled my ears, shutting out the pain even further. It seemed to fill out the sky like a pounding drum. And that is when the Boer started weeping. And he seemed to weep louder, the fainter the power of his lashing became.
>
> The blows stopped and I knew I had crushed him. I had crushed him with the sheer force of my presence. I was there and would be there to the end of time: a perpetual symbol of his failure to have a world without me.[7]

The power of that imagery of Njabulo Ndebele's was brought home to me when I returned to South Africa recently after a two-year absence. The sheer force of the black presence was everywhere. The blackening of South Africa's cities has been taking place for some time, but the

7. Njabulo S. Ndebele, *Fools and Other Stories* (Johannesburg, 1983), p. 276.

visible impact of it struck me on my return the way one notices growth in a child one has not seen for some time. It was instantly, overwhelmingly apparent that here indeed was the source of the blacks' strength and of their impending triumph. No ideology on earth, no politician, no guns, no army, no regional superpower strategy, can stem this tide, which is carrying South Africa at last out of its capsule of illusion into the continent of which it is part. Anthony Trollope's words came back to me: this is a country of black people; it has been so; it is so; and it will continue to be so. The blacks are "the people" of South Africa, and ultimately the future of the country will be determined by their interests.

Nowhere is this truth more apparent than in Johannesburg. The city I left had pretensions to being a medium-sized American metropolis, all chrome and glass and conspicuous affluence. The city I return to is an African city, black faces thronging its streets, taking over its shops, moving into its apartments, setting up hawkers' stalls of fruit and vegetables along its sidewalks and giving to the whole a less glitzy, more third-world aspect. Black consumers now account for 80 percent of central-city trade. Hillbrow, a high-rise apartment quarter that was once the residential heartland of young white Johannesburg and the centre of the city's night life, is now two-thirds black. From this core blacks are spreading outward into suburbia, to Yeoville and Brixton, to Mayfair and Vrededorp and soon, no doubt, to Triomf as well.

On Saturdays, when downtown Johannesburg becomes blacker than ever, the area around the train station is converted into a vast *shebeen*, or illegal drinking joint. Alfresco barmen set up stalls on the sidewalks and in the station concourse itself, with piles of beer cans and tin baths with ice from which they serve the passing trade. It is all illegal. The Group Areas Act is still there to prohibit nonwhites from living in the "white" city or owning any kind of business there, and the liquor laws strictly control the sale of alcohol. But these and other apartheid laws are being swamped by the demographic tide. The police have backed off from trying to enforce them, and law making has become largely a matter of post-facto legitimizing of what cannot be stopped. New laws have been passed authorizing the government to reclassify "white" neighbourhoods already invaded by irreversible numbers of blacks as "grey areas."

This new laissez-faire approach by a government long noted for its rigidity is partly due to a shortage of police manpower on the ground. Since the uprising of the 1980s political surveillance has taken precedence over crime prevention. Thousands of police are tied up keeping watch on the seething black townships and monitoring the movements of black activists. The result is a burgeoning crime wave. Muggings, car thefts, and burglaries have become endemic. One can see the evidence of it in Johannesburg's affluent white suburbs where the garden walls, whose steadily rising height over the years has been an index of racial tension, have now reached ten feet and more, many of them with coils of razor wire on top. This presents a curious visual inversion of the apartheid system. As the blacks are bursting out of their ghettos and taking over the inner cities, the whites are retreating behind the high walls into private ghettos of their own.

The Africanizing of "white" South Africa has been under way for some time, but a convergence of factors is causing the recent speed-up. The black population is exploding, while that of the whites approaches a zero growth figure, so that the percentage of blacks to whites is expanding rapidly.[8] At the same time black migration to the cities is accelerating. This is part of a universal trend: everywhere the poor are lured to the cities by the opportunities of the informal labour sector and because even if they can't get jobs they can survive better there than in the countryside. But in South Africa they are driven by another factor as well. The "homelands" into which blacks were packed during the years of the separate development drive are bursting at the seams, ecologically devastated, and in economic despair. Half of South Africa's black population has been crammed into areas that collectively produce only about 3 percent of the country's gross national product.[9] The result is that when the government relaxed its influx regulations in the mid-1980s, this dammed-up rural poverty flooded out to the cities. Various projections show that the flood is peaking right now, that it is going through the steep rise of an elongated S-curve which will not flatten out until the year 2020, by which time 80 percent of the black population will be urbanized.[10]

The statistics are awesome. During the 1990s, what I have called the decade of transition, the population of South Africa's eight main metropolitan areas will double. Johannesburg, Pretoria, and their environs will become a single, overwhelmingly black megalopolis of 12 million people, half of whom will be living in some kind of informal housing,

8. Tim Varenkazis, *South Africa: A Society in Transformation* (Johannesburg, 1988), p. 113. Varenkazis calculates that the white percentage is declining by −.9 percent annually, while the black percentage is progressively increasing by 2.8 percent annually.

9. Daryl Glaser, "Regional Development: Towards an Alternative?" In John Suckling and Landeg White, *After Apartheid: Renewal of the South African Economy* (London, 1988), p. 80.

10. See W. P. Mostert, P. C. Kok, J. L. van Tonder, and J. A. van Zyl, *Demografiese Implikasies van Alternatiewe Migrasiescenario's met Betrekking tot die Suid-Afrikaanse Swart Bevolking*, Human Sciences Research Council (Pretoria, 1985), pp. 71–73.

and there will be at least four other metropolitan centres the size this one is today. The blackening of urban "white" South Africa will have reached 70 percent.[11]

The trend is sweeping the social engineers out of business. Crossroads, the vast squatter settlement outside Cape Town that the government tried for a decade to remove, is now accepted as an ineradicable fact and efforts are being made to upgrade it—ineffectual efforts, because as fast as space is created for improved facilities new squatters move in. Khayelitsha, a new township farther out, where the government tried to resettle the Crossroads people, now has a quarter of a million squatters of its own who are streaming in from the Transkei and Ciskei "homelands" at the rate of five thousand a month.

In and up. Rapid urbanization is accompanied by rapid upward mobility, as blacks fill the vacancies in an economy that has outgrown the limited supply of skilled white manpower. They have moved in massive numbers from the old sectors of unskilled mining and agricultural labour into manufacturing, construction, trade, transport, and service. Only 14.1 percent of the labour force is left in mining today; and as mining became more mechanized and skilled, too, the old stab-wages rose 60 percent through the 1980s.

All this is placing a demand on education and skills. In 1988 for the first time more blacks graduated from high school in South Africa than whites. A generation ago there were fewer than two thousand Africans enrolled in universities, now there are 65,000, with another ten thousand in advanced technical colleges. Add the other racial groups and 40 percent of all South African university enrollment is nonwhite. And these numbers are snowballing too. A decade ago Natal University was all-white except for its medical school, which trained black doctors: today 30 percent of the student body is black and Vice-Chancellor Peter Booysens expects it to be 70 percent by the end of the century.

Black graduates from these institutions are pouring into the job market at the rate of 35,000 a year, transforming the appearance of every company and every city. Black executives are driving company cars and living in company houses in "white" suburbia, sending their children to private schools. A quarter of all pupils in private schools around the country are black, though state schools are still segregated.

Seventeen years ago 3 percent of black workers were unionized, now 30 percent are. Some time in the mid-1990s black purchasing power nationwide will overtake that of the whites. Thereafter white living

11. These projections, given by Ann Bernstein, executive director of the Urban Foundation, at a press briefing in Johannesburg in June 1989, are due to be incorporated in a still unpublished study document.

standards will be dependent on black advancement rather than the other way around.

As blacks take over South Africa's cities and gain economic power within them, they create for themselves another power base. The cities are in fact becoming the bridgehead for a new political campaign in which blacks challenge the rights of whites to decide exclusively how the cities should be run; blacks are demanding a greater share of the services and a say in how they should be allocated and who should pay for them. This amounts to a demand to participate in city government.

Typical of the new campaign is a negotiation that began in late 1988 between a delegation representing Soweto community groups and the townships' official local authority. The ostensible purpose was to end a rent boycott that was crippling the township council; but the community representatives, who call themselves the Soweto People's Delegation, are using it for much more than that: to demand that Johannesburg and Soweto become one city with a single tax base. As it is now, Soweto is deprived of services because it gets no share of Johannesburg's tax revenue and has to depend on rents paid by its residents. The only way it can get adequate services is by raising rents to unaffordable levels: hence the boycott. The argument is that Soweto residents contribute to Johannesburg's wealth because they spend large sums in its shops and keep its factories and all its essential services operating. The city could not function for a day without them. They are therefore entitled to a share of the services that this wealth finances but that are now going exclusively to the residents of the "white" city.

But the delegation is not counting on instant success. Drawing on the negotiating experience gained by the black labour movement, it is striving first for the meeting of "interim demands" that will strengthen its power base. One is that money from the sale of government-owned houses to Soweto residents should go into a community-controlled trust for building more houses. Another is that electricity and water tariffs should be negotiated with the township's community groups, the way wages are with trade unions. "We have learned from the unions," says Frank Chikane, the key figure in the delegation. "We are trying to organize around winnable goals and then use those to demand wider ones."

Meanwhile inner-city blacks are campaigning in similar ways. An organization called the Action Committee to Stop Evictions, formed to fight for the interests of blacks who have won the de facto right to stay in Johannesburg but have no legal rights there and are exploited by landlords who charge extortionate rents for run-down accommodations, is demanding that the city council integrate public amenities and provide nonracial state schools in areas where blacks have moved in. Beyond that, it wants to participate in the government of the city, since blacks now live there. Again this points toward the integration of Johannesburg and its black townships in a single municipal council. The white regime resists the idea strongly, but on the other hand it is nervously aware that if it fails to meet the black residents' needs the threat of instability will persist, and conflict in the inner cities will be less manageable, and more politically damaging, than in the sealed-off townships.

The irony is that this is turning Pretoria's McCuen strategy back on itself—reversing the reverser, as it were. The American military strategist's advice was to analyze the tactics used by the insurgents and apply them in reverse. Now here are the insurgents doing precisely that to the white administration: Pretoria's neo-apartheid strategy was to build a pyramid structure resting on a wide base of separate white and black municipal councils running their "own affairs," which would then nominate representatives to regional services councils and, beyond that, to a National Council at the apex of the pyramid. The black urbanites are attacking the government strategy at its starting point, the way the securocrats went for the street committees in the townships during the 1980s uprising. If they succeed in integrating the municipalities the neoapartheid structure will collapse from the bottom up. That may not happen right away, but the very nature of the campaign suggests how demographic changes are going to thrust their way into the transition process. They turn the 1978 prediction on its head and one can make a new prediction now that the year 2000 will see the birth of a new, nonracial South Africa.

SO WE COME finally to the obvious question: How will it happen?

The answer is, piecemeal. There will be no revolutionary transfer of power, as the Soviets and the Nationalist movements now recognize. Nor will it happen through a change of heart on the part of the white regime: no ruling oligarchy gives up power and privilege until it is compelled to do so. And there will be no magic day when the transition occurs, no equivalent of Zimbabwe's Lancaster House agreement or Namibia's Resolution 435, which set out the rules and procedures for moving from white rule to black, with international monitors arriving to see that they are adhered to. No, this will be an internal, incremental process, with the white power establishment yielding ground reluctantly, inch by inch, trench by trench. There will be interim phases as the regime tries to establish new defensive positions with new reform constitutions. And even when it becomes clear that white control has to be forsaken, there will still be attempts to build in barricades for the future to protect the core interests of the white establishment after a new regime takes over.

An extensive study of the dozen or so countries that have moved from right-wing authoritarianism to democracy without revolution since the Second World War offers some insights into the forms such transitions can take.[12] (The study focusses on, among other countries, Greece, Spain, Brazil, Peru, and Venezuela; Mexico, Colombia, Uruguay, and Argentina.) The authors point out that every case has involved a complex range of features peculiar to itself, and they warn that all such transitions are fraught with uncertainty—with much depending on the quality of leadership at critical moments, on crucial decisions taken in a hurry with inadequate information that have often turned out to have unexpected consequences, and just plain accident and fortuitous timing. But they do draw out some tentative conclusions about common denominators.

They distinguish, first of all, between processes of liberalization and democratization, which do not necessarily follow one on the other. An authoritarian regime may liberalize up to a point, and then stop short of full participatory democracy, remaining in control of a somewhat more open but still essentially undemocratic system. Or it may take fright at the consequences of its liberalizing steps and crack down again. The finely balanced tolerance-repression calculus here is a crucial factor in the transition process.

One of the authors, Robert R. Kaufman, identifies several stages in the liberalization process, beginning with the authoritarian coalition disintegrating—a phase already well under way in South Africa.[13] He says a period of calm following social tension can lead to a decline in the sense of crisis, and the regime's attempts to drum up support—"anti-communist" campaigns and "emergency" alerts—lose their credibility. As pressure to liberalize builds up from below, the regime may respond by linking up with more elements outside the power establishment and allowing more opportunities for "contestation." This usually has consequences different from those the regime intended, as lawyers, journalists, academics, and politicians press for greater legislative autonomy, more of a role for political parties, more freedom of the press

12. A study of the Woodrow Wilson Center's Latin American Program: Guillermo O'Donnell, Phillipe C. Schmitter, and Laurence Whitehead (Eds.), *Transitions from Authoritarian Rule*: vol. 1, *Southern Europe*; vol. 2, *Latin America*; vol. 3, *Comparative Perspectives*; vol. 4, *Tentative Conclusions About Uncertain Democracies* (Baltimore, 1986).

13. Robert R. Kaufman, *Liberalization and Democratization in Latin America, Transitions*, vol. 3, pp. 85–107.

and universities, more opportunities to debate in the electoral arena. They may not seek to dismantle the existing system, but cumulatively they add to the momentum for political change. At the same time, new opposition coalitions begin to form. The middle class shifts from positions of support for the regime to neutrality and from neutrality to opposition. Some former supporters of the regime join the opposition coalition.

"Each of these inititatives," says Kaufman, "can be understood primarily as efforts to stabilize the legal-political foundations of the military-technocratic incumbents, not as a planned first step toward a withdrawal from power. But in each instance, such openings unleashed opposition forces that generated new choices for the ruling elites: either to acquiesce in still further liberalizing concessions, or to roll back existing ones through new acts of coercion."[14] So the repression-tolerance calculus begins.

To tilt the balance in favour of tolerance it is critical at this stage, says Kaufman, to swing key figures in the business and ruling establishment toward liberalization. How these figures perceive the political alternatives becomes a vital matter: "If the opposition forces are viewed as too 'radical' to be trusted, the prospects of liberalizing concessions are obviously dim. But . . . such perceptions can change quite dramatically."[15] It is worth noting how dramatically white perceptions of Jomo Kenyatta in Kenya and of Robert Mugabe in Zimbabwe changed once the campaigns to demonize them ceased and these men were allowed to speak for themselves and make their reconciling gestures.

The most crucial factor of all in propelling the transition process beyond liberalization to democratization is what the authors call pacts, negotiated compromises between parties that define the rules under which they will operate, mutually guaranteeing each other's vital interests, with each participating party agreeing to modify its own policy position to accommodate the others' vital interests. Pacts usually emerge when a series of crises have created an "unstable equilibrium" between the authoritarian forces of the state and those thrusting for democracy, when the regime loses legitimacy but the democratic forces still cannot oust it.

Typically there are tradeoffs, with a restriction in one area being balanced by a compensation in another. Thus trade unions might agree to a wage freeze in return for improved social security benefits. Other features protect ethnic, cultural, linguistic, or religious interests by re-

14. Ibid., p. 93.

15. Ibid., p. 99.

quiring all the parties to reach a consensus agreement before anything affecting them is done. Pacts can be made among opposition parties to establish a grand coalition to defeat the authoritarian regime and establish a new democratic order or to force the regime to change. Or they may be between the regime and the opposition. Or they may be a combination of these, with pressure from a united opposition forcing the regime to negotiate a pact that then becomes the basis of a new national system.

Sometimes a pact lasts only as long as the transition period to democracy, with the participating parties going their separate ways after the new system is in place. Sometimes it continues into the new era, with opposition coalitions becoming governing coalitions. Sometimes pacts become the new law of the land; sometimes they are written into the constitution of the new democracy. But always they are an essential catalyst for change, the means by which the society can break out of its "unstable equilibrium." They have another value, too: the negotiation and compromise required to establish them helps to reduce historic antagonisms and promote a spirit of pragmatism and political tolerance.

Just as there are many different kinds of pacts, so are there many different forms that the transition can take: from "continuous" transitions, where the changes were undertaken by the old regime and it was not replaced, as in the case of Brazil; to "discontinuous" transitions, where a new regime takes over and introduces changes negotiated beforehand in an opposition pact, as in Venezuela. In between are mixed situations such as in Spain, where elements of the old power establishment dealt with elements of the democratic opposition to produce a transition within the existing legal framework.

By their nature political transitions of these sorts are turbulent, uncertain, and often violent processes. And it would be foolish to suggest that any one of these cases might provide a model for South Africa to follow, especially since the South African conflict is played out in an ethnically divided society. Yet the experiences of these other societies do suggest the general direction the South African transition may take, a route of negotiation and pact-forming nudged along by recurring confrontation and crisis. The precise form it takes is unpredictable, shaped by events as they occur, decisions taken at crucial junctures, the regime's skill or ineptitude, the nature and extent of foreign intervention, and, most important of all, the ability of the opposition to exert pressure from below.

What *is* predictable is that the process would be hastened if the opposition were to move early to form a broad alliance. At the moment, attention is focussed almost entirely on the possibility of ANC negotiations with the government, but as the Venezuelan, Spanish, and other examples show, pact-making among many opposition groups can be the crucial factor in getting the transition under way. In Venezuela opposition leaders from a wide range of interests—political parties, the Catholic Church, the chambers of commerce and industry, the trade unions—negotiated a joint agreement, the Pact of Punto Fijo, which enabled them to isolate and overthrow Perez Jiménez and institute a democratic system based on the terms of the pact. The Punto Fijo Pact was later incorporated in the Venezuelan constitution.[16] In Spain, a broad alliance of Opposition parties moved quickly in the critical months after Franco's death to compel the new prime minister, Adolfo Suarez, to negotiate with it.[17]

Is such a broad Opposition pact feasible in South Africa? The antagonisms between certain of the parties are no deeper than those in other societies where such pacts of convenience have been successfully negotiated. After all, as in a negotiated agreement between an industrial management and a trade union, the parties do not have to accept one another's policies or even share long-term objectives in order to reach a workable arrangement for attaining a shared, limited objective.

If there are difficulties in the way, there are plusses as well. A political tradition of pact-forming is in fact rapidly establishing itself in South Africa. The United Democratic Front, and its subsequent expansion into the Mass Democratic Movement, is a striking example of a political pact involving more than a thousand community organizations of various kinds, many of them with different interests and objectives. Similarly, the big trade-union federation, Cosatu, itself part of the United Democratic Front, is trying to link up with another union grouping whose ideological leaning is more toward the Black Consciousness movement. The African National Congress itself is a coalition of people with different ideological slants but the same dominant objective, and it has a pact with the Communist party on the same basis. This is why the ANC has always kept its policy positions defined in general rather than specific terms within the broad conceptual framework of the Freedom Charter. And then, of course, the ANC, UDF, and Cosatu are all allied through their mutual adherence to the charter.

On the white side, too, there has been coalition-forming. In the 1970s the liberal Progressive party merged first with the Reform party, then

16. For a detailed analysis of pact-making in Venezuela see Terry Lynn Karl, *Petroleum and Political Pacts: The Transition to Democracy in Venezuela, Transitions*, vol. 2, pp. 196–219.

17. José Maria Maravall and Julian Santamaria, *Political Change in Spain and the Prospects for Democracy, Transitions*, vol. 1, pp. 71–108.

with another Opposition group, to form the Progressive Federal party; now that has merged with two parties made up mostly of Afrikaner dissidents, the National Democratic Movement and the Independent party, to form the Democratic party. Further to the left, a number of extraparliamentary organizations—the Black Sash, the Johannesburg Democratic Action Committee, the National Union of South African Students, the End Conscription Campaign, the Detainees' Parents' Support committee, and Women for Peace—subscribe to an alliance called the Five Freedoms Forum. Some of these organizations are also affiliated with the United Democratic Front, and the forum itself also coordinates some activities with parliamentary bodies.

So an extensive base already exists on which to build a grand Opposition alliance. What is needed is a series of negotiated pacts to link the existing blocs together—the parliamentary and extraparliamentary blocs and, most important and difficult of all, the ANC-MDM-Cosatu alliance with Chief Buthelezi's Inkatha movement and the National Forum, an alliance of Black-Consciousness organizations. The ultimate goal should be a pact negotiated among all these elements of the democratic Opposition and other key interest groups in the business community, the churches, and professional associations.

In other words, instead of waiting for the government to convene an all-race national convention to work out a new postapartheid constitution, the opposition could hold a national convention of its own, involving all those committed to achieving the transition to a democratic nonracial future for South Africa, a pact-making convention at which the various parties and interest groups could negotiate on how the new democratic system should be run. This would mean negotiating the kind of compromises that will eventually have to be reached anyway—between the concern of the haves not to be dispossessed and of the have-nots not to be deprived, between the landowners and the landless, between the majority's demand for sovereignty and the minorities' need for protection, between business and the socialist politicians over how much state intervention in the economy there should be.

A pact embodying these agreements could serve as an interim constitution, defining the rules by which, for a while, power is to be exercised. It would make a major impact on the current political situation, presenting a position agreed to by representatives of more than 90 percent of the total population; secondly, it would do much to reduce the level of anxiety in the white community and make the prospect of change easier to contemplate. Because of the long suppression of black dissent, ordinary whites do not really know with whom they should be negotiating their future or what blacks might be prepared to settle for, and they fear the worst. But a pact setting out such a settlement and endorsed by leaders they know would help to allay those fears.

What are the prospects of agreement being reached between such a range of groups? On the evidence of the 1987 Dakar meeting between Afrikaner dissidents and the ANC, as well as other meetings since then, they are decidedly good. As the organizer of the Dakar meeting, Frederik Van Zyl Slabbert, said at the time, an "extraordinary meeting of minds" occurred there. "We found that we have a great deal in common," he said, "and although there are some differences we found that there is a great deal of flexibility and negotiability." The 1986 Natal-KwaZulu *Indaba*—a Zulu word meaning a tribal powwow or conference—in which white interest groups in Natal agreed with Inkatha that the province and the black "homeland" should be merged in a single regional legislature, revealed the same. Once whites show themselves to be genuinely prepared to abandon apartheid and move toward a nonracial future, the black response is positive and pragmatic. Another positive factor is that black politics is developing its own culture of negotiation. In the ten years since black trade unionism was legalized, thousands of shop stewards have learned the processes and techniques of negotiation; and especially during the crisis of the mid-1980s, when many political leaders were swept into detention, these union men and women were thrust into political roles in their townships. Their understanding of negotiation politics has had a strong influence on the strategic thinking of the black movement.

Ironically, getting agreement among some of the black groups may be more problematical. Antagonisms between Inkatha and the ANC-MDM-Cosatu alliance are intense and highly emotional, as are those between the Charterists and the Black Consciousness movement and between BC and Inkatha. This is in the nature of fratricidal conflicts in oppressed communities. Yet even here there are some hopeful signs. Negotiations between Inkatha and the Charterist alliance to end faction fighting between their supporters in Natal could establish a point of contact and perhaps expand into wider deal making. And despite deep differences, a range of black political organizations—from the ANC and the Charterist alliance to Inkatha, the United Municipalities of South Africa (representing most black mayors who have accepted office in the government system), the Congress of Traditional Leaders of South Africa (representing 670 tribal leaders who reject the apartheid system), and even some "homeland" leaders—have all set the same preconditions for participating in constitutional negotiations with the government: the release of Nelson Mandela and other political prisoners, the unbanning of the ANC and other political organizations, the return of exiles, the lifting of the state of emergency, the removal of troops from the townships, and the repeal of discriminatory laws. Though there has been no negotiation, this amounts to a de facto pact between them from which to expand to a more comprehensive one.

The issues on which agreements will have to be reached in order to form a comprehensive opposition pact are clear enough. Heading the list is group rights. On the one hand this issue goes to the heart of Afrikaner nationalism's survivalist fears, which the opposition groups will have to take account of if their formula for a democratic South Africa is to be viable: the social contract must include everyone and not alienate any potentially disruptive elements, which a disaffected Afrikaner community (even if only its right wing) certainly would be. On the other hand the neo-apartheid formula of "own affairs," or even a constitutional guarantee of group rights, is unacceptable to the ANC and other black Nationalists because it would require continued racial definition and classification and perhaps even racially separated political representation. Finding a compromise between those two positions is the most difficult problem the pact-formers will face. What is really involved?

The ANC, in constitutional guidelines published in 1988, committed itself to a Bill of Rights guaranteeing the fundamental human rights of all citizens, and said the state should recognize the linguistic and cultural diversity of the people and provide facilities for free linguistic and cultural development.[18] A year later the South African Law Commission produced a working paper at the government's request in which it effectively endorsed the ANC position by expressing the view that it is not the group as such that needs legal protection but rather group values and interests, which are manifested mainly in culture, religion, and language.[19] In other words the Afrikaner nationalist demand that group rights be protected does not stem from a realistic fear that without this the survival of Afrikanerdom would be in jeopardy: the constitutional entrenchment of individual rights within a multiparty democracy and with an independent judiciary are the real mechanisms for ensuring its survival as a cultural and linguistic entity. Indeed one might go further and suggest that seeking special "group rights" is the worst thing a potentially vulnerable minority could do. The better security, as minorities have found through the ages, is to blend in with the community at large, to be as inconspicuous as possible and certainly to do nothing

18. See "Constitutional Guidelines for a Democratic South Africa: African National Congress Proposals 1955 and 1988," a document published by the Institute for a Democratic Alternative for South Africa.

19. South African Law Commission, Project 58: Group and Human Rights (Pretoria, 1989).

to draw resentful attention to oneself. By defining themselves as a separate racial category requiring special protection, whites would be setting themselves up as a target for resentful and hostile feelings; bitter memories of racial humiliation and exploitation that might otherwise fade into the background would find a new focus of attention in those special rights and veto powers, which would rightly be seen as mechanisms for safeguarding the advantages built up during the years of unequal opportunity. Every largely black political movement would be bound to make them a target of attack, and there would be no real possibility of racial harmony until they were eliminated. Only when whites stop isolating themselves from the larger national community and start identifying with it, will they in turn be fully accepted and free to live according to their own cultural preferences without stirring up old resentments.

But Afrikaner nationalism has seen its survival in terms of the retention of power too long for it to be easily able to come to terms with such a radical idea. A considerable number of individual Afrikaners are doing so with great moral and intellectual courage, but the National party leadership is still too locked into the old mind-set to make the break. Its insistence on "own affairs" and "group rights" is a reflection of the extent to which it is still a captive of the old obsession with securing the Afrikaner "nation": a more extreme manifestation of the same thing is the call by the far-rightists for a *Boerestaat*, or Boer nation, which would have the right to secede as the rest of South Africa falls under majority rule. It is not really a survivalist fear as such but the residual civil-religion imperative, a way of clinging to the belief that this is still their God-given country even when they no longer have total control of it. And, because blacks know that to be the case, they are passionately opposed to accommodating it.

Yet such attitudes cannot be dismissed simply because they are unpalatable or unwise. The sentiments they reflect are political facts that have to be faced and dealt with. The far-rightists especially are a potentially disruptive element that the nonracial opposition should pay far more serious attention to than it does. Other African countries, when they became independent, were purged of their hard-line racists: they migrated southward, first to Rhodesia, then to South Africa. But there is no place farther south for South Africa; we cannot excrete our racists upon Antarctica. We shall have to digest them, and that means trying to accommodate them in the new democratic social contract. If they were regionally concentrated, one might consider letting them have their *Boerestaat* in a federal South Africa or even in a separate, independent nation, but there is no part of the country, no town, district, or farm even, where whites—let alone right-wing Afrikaner whites—are in the majority. So they could only be given that by disenfranchising blacks, which is unacceptable in any nonracial society.

Nevertheless the pact-formers must recognize the need and declare their willingness to draw Afrikaner right-wingers into the negotiating process. It may be impossible to accommodate their demands, but they must be given the chance to negotiate, perhaps to be offered special cultural councils with the right to administer their own cultural institutions—historical societies, literary associations, youth groups, old-age homes, even private schools and universities—and perhaps a special watchdog body over Afrikaner cultural interests. They must be included in the process, made part of the social contract, just as Adolfo Suarez included Basque and Catalan nationalists in Spain's transition negotiations even though their demands for autonomy could not be fully met.

The next issue on the negotiating list concerns the shape of the South African economy. The ideological conflict is between white free marketeers and a black organizational structure with a strong commitment to socialism superimposed on an older African tradition of communalism. The conflict of interest here involves the English sector of the white community more than the Afrikaners, for it is the English, with their big-business interests and Reaganite ideas, who are most directly at odds with the black socialists. (The Afrikaners, for all their latter-day role as a ruling oligarchy, have elements of socialism in their background that makes them viscerally less hostile to the black economic standpoint.) On this issue, too, there are signs of a new flexibility. The ANC's position, as initially expressed in the Freedom Charter, used to be that all the means of production should be nationalized. More recently the ANC has favoured a mixed economy and said that it would nationalize only what it calls "the commanding heights" of the economy, meaning, presumably, the half-dozen conglomerates that between them control more than 80 percent of South Africa's private industrial sector.[20] At a conference in Paris in December 1989 a Cosatu representative said that the black left was moving away from nationalization altogether and looking at possible alternative methods for giving the people some say in the control and disposal of big-company assets.

A synthesis is necessary for practical reasons, because neither of the two ideological positions offers a solution in itself. The great economic

20. See Robin McGregor, *Who Owns Whom* (Johannesburg, 1989). According to McGregor, Anglo American Corporation (49.6 percent), Sanlam (10.8 percent), SA Mutual (9.8 percent), Rembrandt (7.6 percent), the Liberty Group (2.6 percent), and Anglovaal (2.2 percent) control 82.5 percent of the market capitalization of the Johannesburg Stock Exchange. The first four alone control 77.7 percent.

revelation of the second half of the twentieth century has been the failure of socialism as an energizer of societies and a generator of wealth. It kills initiative and suffocates motivation. The socialist world is in economic crisis everywhere, while the newly industrialized capitalist countries of the Pacific basin have far outperformed their socialist third-world counterparts in Africa and Asia. From China to the Soviet Union to Eastern Europe, the search is on for a neo-socialism that moves away from state ownership and central planning and recognizes the productive power of the market. The evidence of this failure is too overwhelming for the planners of the new South Africa to ignore.

It is clear that the free marketeers do not have the answer either. South Africa has the widest gap between rich and poor of any country in the world for which data are available.[21] Eighty-seven percent of its land and 95 percent of its industrial undertakings are in white hands. That degree of inequality cannot be left to the free market to rectify. As Adam and Moodley warn, with such grossly unequal bargaining units, unchecked market forces could result in even greater inequalities.[22] One cannot hobble people for centuries, give others every possible advantage for generation after generation, then put both in the same starting blocks for a flat race and say piously, "May the best man win." Anyone who doubts that should try joining a Monopoly game late, after the other players have bought nearly all the properties and built houses and hotels on them, and see how he fares.

An emotional factor, too, makes the capitalist ethic politically unattractive in the black community, just as it once was among Afrikaners. White capitalism has been uniquely tainted by a long and close association with racism, from the days when blacks were dispossessed of their land to turn them into a captive labour pool for farmers and mining companies to draw on cheaply. In South Africa it has been so blatantly exploitative, and is today so loudly and dogmatically supportive of the free-market ideology in its most extreme form, so conspicuous in its display of wealth, with ostentatious mansions, luxury cars, and a nouveau-riche lifestyle, that inevitably the blacks have developed a counterculture. They want a redistribution of wealth not only to ease the economic pressure but quite simply to punish the stinking rich. There is a dislike, too, of the tendency of the emerging black middle class to emulate the lifestyle of moneyed whites. Among the politically

21. Francis Wilson and Mamphela Ramphele, *Uprooting Poverty: The South African Challenge* (Cape Town, 1989), p. 18. The measurement system is known as the Gini Coefficient, and South Africa's rating of 0.66 is the highest of the fifty-seven countries for which data are available.

22. Adam and Moodley, op. cit., p. 19.

aware, austerity has become a virtue and any show of wealth or luxury living is frowned on.

Whites will have to recognize these political realities in the black world and come to terms with them. Just as no Afrikaner party in the 1920s could do other than campaign on a socialist ticket and show a special responsibility toward its indigent kith and kin, so with the black political movements today. Capitalism is not a viable political platform in the black community. So any synthesis that emerges will have to contain substantial elements of socialism and will have to be presented with a socialist label. This need not be economically inhibiting. After all, the years of state intervention and affirmative action on behalf of a disadvantaged Afrikanerdom did not prevent a spectacular postwar growth in South Africa's industrial economy.

And so to the shape of South Africa's political system. Blacks want a unitary system of government; whites want government to be decentralized. Again the difference has to do with the desire for redress on the one hand, and for safeguarding established advantages on the other. Any devolution of power weakens a government's ability to bring about changes, so that the whites want more of it and the blacks less of it.

In reaching a compromise the blacks may well be prepared to settle for a territorial federation (not a racial federation, which is what the Pretoria government seems to have in mind). But there is an ambiguity in this. At the height of the 1980s uprising the United Democratic Front issued a policy statement about the kind of constitutional future it envisaged for South Africa. Drawing on the experience of its own modus operandi at the time, it advocated collective decision making and a high degree of consultation with the community; this is the way the community organizations have been operating and a whole black political culture has developed from it—highly democratic, almost Grecian in concept. But it is doubtful whether it would be practical at a national-government level. Certainly it would become less so the more centralized the government was, since centralizing power makes it remote from the grass roots, while a greater devolution of power would get closer to the UDF ideal and the political culture of the townships. So there are compromises to be reached within the black Nationalist bodies as well and they all point to some kind of federal structure.

Another factor causes the Charterist alliance to resist federalism: it is seen as a way of accommodating tribal differences. Whites especially are obsessed with a belief that black majority rule would quickly degenerate into a bitter power struggle among tribes that would destabilize South Africa, ruin the economy, and probably bring about a one-party system run by the dominant tribe. Certainly there is evidence in the rest of Africa to give credence to such fears. The pattern all too often has been of African freedom movements uniting in the struggle for independence, then falling apart after the colonial power has departed and engaging in bitter internecine conflicts rooted in ethnic rivalries.

Will the same happen in South Africa? It is possible, of course, but a number of factors are working against it. One is that the length of white settlement in South Africa, the extent of land dispossession, and the scale of industrialization and urbanization have detribalized the people much more than in any other African country. The tribes lost their land and the authority of the chiefs was effectively broken by the mid–nineteenth century, before the colonization of most other African countries had even begun. A second factor is that apartheid itself has further weakened tribalism by using it as a tool of oppression and making it a justification for the ideology. Blacks have been divided on tribal lines and chiefs have been installed as agents of the system, thus discrediting both. For a black person to proclaim any kind of tribal nationalism today is to label himself a collaborator.

Most important of all, black politics in South Africa is not structured on tribal lines the way it is almost everywhere else in Africa. This is not to say that political parties in other African countries are tribal in a traditional sense. They are modern parties whose leaders are members of the modern intellectual elite. Nevertheless, their power bases are tribal and it is to those power bases that they appeal when they wish to mobilize their political forces. Jomo Kenyatta was not a Kikuyu chief, but his power base was among the Kikuyu. Robert Mugabe is not a traditional leader among the Shona, nor is Joshua Nkomo among the Ndebele, but both have their power bases among those tribes, and when they have to they mobilize their tribal forces to achieve their political objectives.

From the day Pixley Seme formed the ANC more than three-quarters of a century ago, black South African politics has been pan-tribal, and its differences have been ideological rather than ethnic. Seme himself was a Zulu who dreamed of recreating Shaka's kingdom while he was at Oxford, but when he returned to South Africa the Land Act galvanized him into realizing that Africans would have to unite if they were to withstand the assault upon them. That is why he invited black people from all parts of the country and from neighbouring territories to that conference in 1912 at which South Africa's oldest political party was formed. The purpose of the meeting, he told the delegates, was to create their own "national unity" to defend black rights and privileges in the face of the exclusionist white unity that had formed the Union of South Africa and was now dispossessing them. "We are one people," Seme told the gathered assembly of chiefs and commoners from every tribe in the subcontinent. "These divisions, these jealousies, are the cause of all our woes and of all our backwardness and ignorance today."[23]

That was the source of the ANC's pan-tribalism which later broadened into its nonracialism, which is today its most definitive ideology. It was the core political movement: others—the Pan-Africanist Congress and the Black Consciousness movement—have broken away from it but have taken with them its pan-tribalist character. None of the breaks has been for tribal reasons; they have all been ideological, and all of them are as pan-tribal as the ANC itself. In a postapartheid South Africa, whatever power struggles arise in the black community, the competing political leaders will not be appealing to tribal power bases but to ideologically defined political bases. Only one major political organization is tribally based, and that is Inkatha. Though it claims to have non-Zulu members and Buthelezi professes to reject tribalism, Inkatha is in fact a typical ethnic party of the kind found elsewhere in Africa, which is one reason why whites who are still interested in divide-and-rule find it so interesting and why it arouses such strong emotions and intense anxiety among the nonracialist movements.

But if ethnicity is an overrated fear, other black political differences are not. The ANC has pledged itself to a multiparty democracy, but if that is to have any credibility then it and all other black political organizations will have to raise their threshold of tolerance of political opposition. It is no good saying you will have a multiparty democracy and in the same breath denouncing those who differ from you as sellouts and traitors, for if you feel that way about them now you will crack down on them when you are the government and they are the opposition and then there will be a one-party state. A multiparty democracy requires tolerance of opposition, even to the point where the opposition can take over power. Listening to the intolerance expressed between the ANC and PAC, between the UDF and Inkatha, between the Charterists and the Black Consciousness movement, I am sometimes left feeling that this rather than differences with whites is the greatest danger to the future nonracial democracy. But the therapeutic exercise of forming an opposition pact could reduce that danger, too.

CAN OUTSIDERS HELP? The West, the rest of the world?

Yes indeed. If it is axiomatic that no ruling oligarchy gives up power

23. Mary Benson, *The Struggle for a Birthright*, p. 24.

and privilege until it has to, then pressure is the name of the game. The question is, what kind of pressure? It is likely that international pressures could be of greater relative importance in South Africa than elsewhere because the apartheid issue is so uniquely internationalized, a moral issue that arouses strong feelings worldwide with no public allies anywhere (though it certainly has closet supporters).

This brings us to the issue of sanctions. The idea of foreign countries and interests using economic sanctions against South Africa in order to weaken the regime and bring an end to apartheid has become so charged with emotion on all sides that rational consideration of it is almost impossible. To many, one's position on sanctions is a litmus test of one's racial morality: to be critical of sanctions is to be a closet apartheidist. To others, support for sanctions is to be a moralistic carpetbagger who is prepared to raze a viable economy and inflict mass human suffering in order to satisfy one's own sense of self-righteousness.

The claims made on both sides of the argument are equally wild. To the advocates of sanctions, they are a decisive instrument of coercion, a substitute for military conquest or revolutionary overthrow; all that is required is for the world to be persuaded to act decisively and in concert and the apartheid regime will be brought to its knees. To opponents, sanctions have never worked anywhere because countries will always find a way around them; and, in a somewhat contradictory argument, they work against change by preventing economic growth, the one thing that does break down institutionalized racism.

The truth lies obscured by emotional dust between these polemical extremes. A comprehensive study of 103 cases of economic sanctions imposed since 1914 shows that 39 of them were successful in achieving specific goals but only three of those goals were major policy changes; the other 64 cases were ineffective, mostly because they set unrealistically high targets. In other words, economic sanctions can help to achieve foreign policy goals, but only if used judiciously to reach carefully defined objectives.[24] They are a useful but limited instrument of coercion, best used in combination with other initiatives. They seldom induce a target country to undertake major changes in domestic policy, but they can effect modest changes that, if skilfully selected, will create pressures leading to bigger changes. They do not bring countries to their knees, nor do they wreck economies. And they do not do callous harm to the people they are supposed to help: the study found that they

24. Gary Clyde Hufbauer and Jeffrey J. Schott, assisted by Kimberley Ann Elliott, *Economic Sanctions Reconsidered: History and Current Policy* (Washington, 1985), pp. 79–91.

become effective when they inflict a cost above 2 percent of the target country's Gross Domestic Product.[25]

In one thing the opponents of sanctions are correct: there are no sanctons that cannot be circumvented. There are always buyers and sellers somewhere willing to do a deal, always middlemen prepared to facilitate such deals—but at a price. The victim of sanctions trades at a bargaining disadvantage, and the middlemen have to be paid their cut, so he sells cheap and buys expensive; the differential is the price of whatever it is he is being attacked for. In South Africa's case, the price of apartheid, the price the government has to pay to maintain white supremacy. It is always going to be measured against the imagined cost of disinheritance, and since that cost is greatest for those at the top who have the power to coerce, it will go on being paid to a very high level. That is why sanctions seldom threaten the ruling oligarchy's hold on power. But if the price is exacted nonetheless, it can cause disaffection further down the social ladder and so increase the pressure for change from below.

Another popular fallacy needs to be addressed: the notion that economic development in and of itself produces political change. In South Africa, this idea was given currency and a certain intellectual respectability by an article entitled "The Green Bay Tree" written in 1968 by the deputy editor of the *Economist*, Norman Macrae.[26] After a visit to South Africa Macrae was filled with an optimistic belief that the raw entrepreneurial energy he encountered there was going to generate a great industrial upsurge which, like the spreading bay tree, would extend its benefits to all and transform South African society the way it transformed Victorian England and the United States in the age of Andrew Carnegie. This was a wonderfully convenient analysis for a business community that wanted to dissociate itself from the stigma of apartheid while taking no overt action against it, so that the Green Bay Tree thesis was eagerly adopted as conventional wisdom in white establishment circles.

But it is flawed. The 1960s, when Macrae made his visit, was a decade that saw both the most rapid economic growth in South Africa's history and its most severe phase of political repression. It was during those boom years that the main structures of Verwoerdian ideology were put in place, when the "homelands" were established and the forced removals began, and when an avalanche of security laws were enacted and the Rule of Law was demolished with the introduction of detention

25. Ibid., pp. 86–87.

26. *The Economist*, June 29, 1968.

without trial. Only after the 1976 Soweto riots and the 1980s uprising ushered in a period of economic crisis did the government begin to talk seriously about reform and about dismantling the apartheid system.

Certainly industrial revolutions do transform societies and they do bring economic benefits to the disadvantaged as well as the privileged, but they do not automatically translate those economic advantages into political gains. Indeed it is their failure to do that which has caused so many industrial revolutions to be precursors of political revolution, as almost happened in Victorian England. It requires a political crisis to bring about the transition; very often economic setback following a period of rapid development brings this crisis to a head and sets the transition in train. "One may hypothesize," says Luciano Martins in his study of political change in Brazil, "that an economic crisis of great magnitude may play an analogous role (although not equivalent) to that played in other countries by military defeat as the catalyst of the demise of an authoritarian regime."[27]

There can be no doubt, as I have noted, that industrialization and urbanization—the unstoppable black tide—are the forces that rendered South Africa's apartheid ideology unworkable. But economic growth cannot shift South Africa from apartheid to nonracialism. It cannot produce the political transition from authoritarianism to democracy. Only political action can do that.

What, then, would be an effective policy strategy for the Western powers to follow toward South Africa?

A conceptual framework for such a policy must be built on two basic principles: the first is that there can be no knock-out blow, since no country has that kind of power over another and sanctions certainly do not pack that kind of punch; so any policy must be realistic, with attainable targets that add to a sum total of pressures pushing South Africa toward transition. The second is that one must focus less exclusively on the white power structure and give more attention to actions that will strengthen the opposition. For too long Western powers have based their policies on the assumption that the whites are the sole agents of change, and whether the policy has been one of "constructive engagement" or sanctions, it has been aimed at trying either to sweet-talk or to bludgeon the ruling whites into giving up power. "The essential precondition for progress is change in the hearts and minds of white South Africans and in the white political alignments they give rise to," said Chester Crocker, the Reagan administration's assistant secretary of

27. Luciano Martins, *Transitions*, vol. 2, p. 91.

state for Africa.[28] He was wrong. The essential precondition for progress is pressure from opposition forces demanding democracy. An effective foreign-policy strategy should do everything possible to strengthen those forces. There should be a policy of "constructive engagement with the opposition."

Within that broad conceptual framework, a number of guidelines should be observed. The idea of starting small and ratcheting up slowly to more intensive sanctions can be counterproductive.[29] As one saw in Ian Smith's Rhodesia, that not only gives the regime time to adjust, to find alternative suppliers and build new alliances, but helps it to mobilize a nationalism among its followers that increases their determination to carry on as before. To achieve maximum effect, decisions about sanctions should be carefully evaluated beforehand, then applied swiftly and decisively.

There needs to be a balanced and realistic pressure-and-demand formula. It is no good for a foreign government to demand that South Africa introduce one-person-one-vote if the only pressure it is going to apply is to withdraw its military attaché from its Pretoria embassy. On the other hand, threatening to withdraw the attaché and sever all military contacts if South Africa does not sign the Nuclear Nonproliferation Treaty might achieve better results. Conversely, too little pressure enforcing the demand also leads to a sense of achievement in the target regime and an intensified spirit of national pride and determination.

It should be obvious, too, that sanctions will be less effective the more harm they do to the country applying them. "Countries that shoot themselves in the foot may not mortally wound their targets."[30] South Africa's vulnerable black neighbours, the so-called front-line states, should not dream of joining a sanctions campaign that would weaken them to Pretoria's advantage and provide white South Africa with a gratuitous morale boost. Nor should Western powers point fingers at these front-line states, as Britain in particular is wont to do, and use those countries' obvious reluctance to justify their own inaction: such needling might provoke them into taking foolhardy action that would seriously damage the region and the democratic cause in South Africa. If international action is to be meaningful at all, the major pressure has to come from the major powers.

28. Chester A. Crocker, Current Policy No. 688, United States Department of State, Bureau of Public Affairs, April 17, 1985.

29. Hufbauer and Schott, op. cit., p. 86.

30. Ibid., p. 88.

Given the guideline that the least costly sanctions are the most effective, close attention should be given to those that make use of financial leverage. They are easily and quickly applied and do minimal damage to the target nation's economic infrastructure. As the 1985 currency crisis showed, when international banks refused to roll over their short-term loans, the South African economy is particularly vulnerable to this kind of pressure.

But let us return to the matter of pressures aimed at strengthening the opposition, which I have suggested should be the main thrust of any policy on South Africa. The aim should be to raise the opposition's status, boost its morale, help it materially, and apply pressures to create more space in which it can operate. Diplomatic recognition is one way. Western leaders should meet with the president of the ANC and instruct their Pretoria embassies to maintain regular diplomatic contact with the ANC's exile headquarters in Lusaka to show that they recognize it as part of the South African political structure. Gestures like that would do much to offset Pretoria's long campaign to demonize the ANC. Major internal organizations should likewise be accorded some kind of formal recognition and their leaders dealt with and invited to Western capitals as representatives of South Africa's majority population. Visiting diplomats should stop over in Lusaka as a matter of course and, in South Africa, spend at least as much time with representatives of the Opposition as they do with the government.

Pressure to release more political prisoners and lift restrictions on political organizations is also of paramount importance. Helping these people and agencies be active is the single most important step toward achieving change in South Africa. Preemptive threats and retaliatory sanctions can be used to deter the government from taking new restrictive steps—including press restrictions, which effectively silence the Opposition. The detention of an important political leader or the banning of a significant organization should trigger a swift sanctions response. The closing of a newspaper or restriction of an editor, even the expulsion of a major foreign correspondent, should be followed by the expulsion of information attachés from South African embassies in the West. This would cause Pretoria to hesitate before taking the kind of action it now takes with impunity, and create more space for the Opposition to organize and operate.

But there should be incentives as well, and encouragement. When the South African government meets a demand, the pressure to achieve it should be lifted instead of the demands being escalated, as has tended to happen in the past, which produces a backlash of resentment and destroys the credibility of the sanctions strategy. There should be diplomatic rewards for significant reforms, and South Africa should be made aware at all times of the tremendous diplomatic, economic, and personal advantages to be gained from shedding its pariah status and being readmitted to the world community of nations.

Above all the aim should be not to punish South Africa but to help it through a formidably difficult transition. The objective is not to damage the country but to bring it through its transition as intact as possible. It is easy to wax emotional over the South African government and allow a vengeful attitude to take over, but it should be remembered that the nation is enduring a conflict of human relationships that might have occurred anywhere given the same circumstances. White South Africans do not behave the way they do because they are innately evil, but, as I hope this book has shown, because they are caught up in the vortex of their own history. There is nothing about them that is irredeemable, as I believe they will show in due time.

When that time comes, South Africa has within itself the ability to transform both its image and its role. It could become an industrial powerhouse that would transform the African continent, now mired in economic stagnation and mass poverty. It has resources beyond its needs: a well-developed industrial base, a bountiful supply of raw materials including more than forty valuable minerals, and an abundance of cheap coal; it generates more than half of all Africa's electrical power and has an almost infinite capacity to generate more; it has nuclear technology, a sophisticated transport infrastructure and communications network, the continent's largest skilled industrial labour force and, to go with it all, tremendous entrepreneurial energy. It is a hobbled giant, and once its political shackles are removed, it can lend its energy to the huge continental hinterland north of it. When that happens South Africa could become to Africa what Japan has been to the Pacific Basin, the dynamo that energizes and drives those languishing countries to become economically viable.

It has that potential and more. For South Africa also has the ability to transform itself into one of the world's few truly nonracial societies.

Epilogue

A GREAT DEAL has happened in the year since the closing chapters of this book were written for the hardcover edition. Much of it was foreseen in those chapters: that 1990 would be the start of South Africa's decade of transition; that the De Klerk government, realizing the co-optive strategy was as dead as apartheid itself and that the only option left was to negotiate with the ANC, would release Nelson Mandela early in the year, legalize the ANC and begin talks about talks with it.

But I was wrong about one thing: President de Klerk himself. While recognizing that he was more intelligent, polished, agreeable and pragmatic than his belligerent predecessor, I did not anticipate that he would be particularly bold or enlightened. His record was that of a party conservative, and his brother, Willem, portrayed him as a cautious centrist who would use small compromises and clever footwork to hold the middle ground. "There will be no leap of faith," Willem de Klerk had warned.

He, and I, could not have been more mistaken. President de Klerk's blockbuster speech opening the 1990 session of Parliament on February 2, in which he lifted the bans not only on the ANC but on the South African Communist Party, Umkhonto we Sizwe, the PAC, Black Consciousness and all, must rank as one of the great leaps of faith in the annals of political leadership. Even his own Cabinet was taken aback by the sweep of it. In the space of forty-five minutes De Klerk transformed South Africa's political landscape and pitched the country into its transitional phase.

Here was the Rubicon Botha had baulked at crossing. It was obvious from the moment De Klerk had spoken that there could be no turning back, and that before the decade was out apartheid would have given way to majority rule. Indeed the dramatic impact of the statement and the sequence of events it has unleashed are compressing the timespan, which may now be considerably less than the decade I had forecast: 1994 seems a more likely target, not least because the next general election is due then. With his own constituency in tatters and the Conservatives rampant, De Klerk dare not risk another whites-only election.

Coupled with the emergence of De Klerk as a leader of stature has been the appearance on stage of his counterpart, Nelson Mandela. One had always wondered while he was still in prison how Mandela the Man could possibly live up to Mandela the Myth. Yet he has come as close as any flesh-and-blood human could to doing so. His political performance has not been flawless, but given the circumstances in which he has had to operate, it has been remarkable.

Other prisoners, after much shorter spells of incarceration, sometimes need psychiatric help to cope with everyday life on the outside. Mandela stepped out of prison after a mind-blowing 27 years at 4:16 p.m. on February 11, and three hours later he was addressing a crowd of 60,000 on Cape Town's Grand Parade. After being cut off from the world for more than a generation he had to assume the role of instant leader of his people and cope with the hurly-burly of South Africa's transitional politics, meshing with colleagues to many of whom he was a total stranger in all but name.

It has been a nonstop roller-coaster ride ever since, with mass rallies of up to 150,000 people, getting the ANC's organizational structure set up inside South Africa after thirty years in exile, planning strategy, engaging in tough negotiating sessions with the government, coping with crises, dealing with the media (up to nine international television interviews in a day), and travelling to the major capitals of the world to exploit his status as an international celebrity to help the cause of his organization and his people. In between Mandela has had to adjust to regular family life, with a wife he had been married to for thirty-one years but had actually lived with for a total of only a few months, and cope with controversies involving her that in themselves would have destabilized a lesser man.

He has done it all with a stately dignity and an unruffled calm. He is an imposing, if slightly austere, man. His upbringing in the royal household of the Tembu king, David Dalindyebo, has given him an easy personal assurance rare among oppressed people. His years in prison, studying law, debating with colleagues and spending hours in solitary reflection, have sharpened his arguments and produced a long-term perspective. His relationship with warders and other prisoners has given him a directness and intimacy of personal contact. It is an unusual combination that equips him to be both a monarchical figurehead and an effective political negotiator.

So from a situation a year ago when South Africa seemed devoid of quality leadership, it now has two men of stature on whose relationship much will depend. So far it is a good relationship. The two met for the first time in Mandela's prison quarters on December 13, 1989, three months after De Klerk became president, and immediately established a rapport. "My first impression was that he was a man of integrity, a strong personality, and even more a man who knows what he is doing and is determined to defend the new approach he has taken," Mandela told me ten months later. "I still have that impression of him and I think he feels the same way about me. We have developed enormous respect for each other, and we talk very frankly. I can call him at any time, I can get him out of bed or call him out of Cabinet meetings. We have that kind of personal relationship."

It is a unique relationship, of two political opposites, sworn enemies for most of their lives, who have become political partners in a quest to end apartheid and lay the foundations for a new South Africa. It is a quest in which each is totally dependent on the other, for neither has a viable fall-back position. De Klerk cannot outlaw the ANC again, send Mandela back to prison, and revert to apartheid. Having raised internal and international expectations of change, he dare not even stand still; to survive he has to keep moving forward, and he can only move if Mandela moves with him. Likewise, the de facto ANC leader cannot revert to a revolutionary war he now knows he cannot win, especially with the Soviet Union no longer interested in sponsoring it. He, too, must move to survive, and he can only move in tandem with De Klerk.

The process of pact-forming between them has begun, with the Groote Schuur Minute of May 4 and the Pretoria Minute of August 7 setting out the initial agreements for creating a suitable climate for more substantive negotiations, which hopefully will begin early in 1991. The Pretoria pact included the suspension of the ANC's armed struggle, thus effectively completing the implementation of the proposals contained four years before in the Commonwealth EPG's "possible negotiating concept"—which has to be seen in retrospect as a groundbreaking initiative.

More pact-forming will follow as deals are struck, issue-by-issue, on the remaining obstacles in the way of negotiations, then on the fundamental questions of the constitution itself. Only when understandings have been reached in this way on all the basic issues is there likely to be some kind of national convention to collate and ratify what has already been agreed.

That is the positive side to what has happened. There is a negative side as well. It is already evident that agreement on the constitution will not come easily. The government has accepted, at least nominally, the principle of one-person-one vote, but it is still intent on doing everything possible to limit the power of the future black majority and protect the status quo—especially the economic status quo—from radical change. It wants a constitution with complicated arrangements for entrenching "group rights" by providing veto powers for minorities (i.e. whites), a "colleagiate Cabinet" drawn from all parties and groups which must reach agreement by consensus, and a rotating chairman/President of this Cabinet as in Switzerland. It calls this "power-sharing." The object, all too clearly, is to create an illusion of a transfer of power to the black majority while so emasculating that power as to ensure that the established situation remains.

For its part, the ANC will insist on majority rule without too many fetters. While it is prepared to entrench individual rights, even cultural rights, it will be on its guard against any disguised form of perpetuating the notion of racial "rights." Above all the ANC dare not allow the ruling majority to be so paralyzed by constitutional restrictions that it cannot bring about a tangible redressing of South Africa's grotesquely lopsided socio-economic dispensation in a reasonably short time.

Bridging this gap will require another leap of faith by De Klerk, but it should be easier than the one he has already taken. The point the whites have to grasp is that the kind of protectionism they now seek is not really in their interests. On the contrary. A system that paralyzes the new regime and prevents it from meeting the raised expectations of the black majority will quickly be discredited, leading to a renewal of unrest and demands for ever more radical solutions. That is the road to anarchy and ruin. Moreover, it would be difficult to imagine anything more calculated to build anti-white feelings in the new South Africa than a system that has white representatives fighting and obstructing the black regime's reforms every inch of the way. In the end, white security depends on black satisfaction. Only when that penny drops will agreement be reachable.

Nor has the speed-up in the pace of events been all positive in its effect. Just as the dramatic impact of De Klerk's February 2 speech captured world attention, so, too, did it galvanize white right-wing reaction. Only four months earlier the National Party had run an election campaign in which it denounced the liberal Democratic Party as traitors for talking to the ANC: a picture of one of its leaders, Wynand Malan, meeting the Communist leader, Joe Slovo, was widely publicized to smear the opposition. Now here was De Klerk legalizing the ANC and preparing to negotiate with it and meet Slovo himself. It was an invitation to Treurnicht and his Conservatives to charge him with duplicity and betrayal. De Klerk could perhaps have lessened the impact by embarking on a national speaking tour, or giving a series of "fireside chats" on television, to explain his astonishing U-turn to his people, but in what may have been his single most serious mistake he failed to do so. The result has been a haemmorhage of support, especially in the Deep North, where it is difficult today to find an enthusiastic supporter of the National Party and feelings against De Klerk run high.

The National Party has compensated for this loss by gaining large numbers of English-speaking supporters. It has effectively usurped the role and the constituency of the Democratic Party. While this leaves it more or less where it was numerically, it has radically changed the character of the party. It is no longer the embodiment of Afrikaner Nationalism; that role has passed irrevocably to the Conservative Party, the new keeper of the Kuyperian holy grail. Daniel Malan's purified *volksparty* has become just another political party with heterogeneous membership, a change emphasized by its renunciatory decision at the 1990 provincial congresses to open its membership to all races. That puts the National Party in a more flexible position to adapt to the new South Africa, but it also means it has lost its hold on its old white Afrikaner constituency that has been its power base through all its history. Its ability to bring the bulk of that constituency with it into the new social contract it hopes to negotiate with the ANC is accordingly diminished, which poses a threat to the future stability of that deal.

It is a threat made worse by the growth of revolutionary extremism to the right of the Conservatives. A crop of menacing new movements has sprung up beside and beyond the AWB, posing the alarming prospect of a coalition of white racist fanatics with access to arms through the close contacts many of them have with special undercover police and Defence Force units.

Added to this is the fact that the security forces as a whole, resentful of their diminished status under the new administration and time-warped in the Botha era, are not supportive of De Klerk's initiatives and have become an adjunct of the right wing. It has been too much too quickly for many of them. They have been conditioned to regard the ANC as the enemy; now they are required to regard it as a benign political partner and possible future government. A year ago, a young police constable would have been assured of promotion if he had shot Chris Hani, the Umkhonto chief of staff, dead on sight; now he is required to protect him. Instead of being a force for impartial peace-keeping through the rocky transition, the police especially, and to a lesser extent the army, are themselves a destabilizing factor.

There are problems on the black side as well. In a situation where the center needs to be driven forward to keep up the momentum and stop the process fraying at the edges of left and right extremism, the ANC has taken an inordinately long time getting its act together. Nine months after it was legalized, it is still struggling to consolidate.

There are practical reasons: the ANC has had to integrate a scattered leadership, prepare to bring home 20,000 exiles, and build up an internal organizational structure from scratch. There are also less tangible reasons in the psychological adjustment from being a revolutionary movement to being an orthodox one, ready for participation and bargaining in conventional politics. This is a massive switch of political culture and the ANC has not found it easy. For decades its strategies and way of thinking have been of confrontation and combat. To switch to cooperation with yesterday's enemy in building a new center coalition is not only a difficult mental adjustment, it also carries the risk of estranging the ANC's following.

Differences in style between the ANC and its internal allies has also kept them in disarray. The United Democratic Front in particular developed as a grassroots organization whose participatory methods of decision-making produced a bottom-up style in which leaders are mandated by the communities they represent. The ANC is not like that. The exigencies of exile, with members cut off from the leadership and scattered across many countries, and of underground survival within South Africa, made this kind of democratic decision-making impossible. So the ANC became a top-down organization, with the leadership making decisions and issuing directives to its members.

For many years, the Communist Party regarded itself as a "vanguard" party, the decision-makers whose task was to spearhead the working-class struggle. It is a concept that makes for authoritarianism. This vanguardism and top-down style clashed with the bottom-up culture of the UDF, causing friction and making it difficult for the organizations to mesh. Old-style leaders back from exile or emerged from prison had little feel for local communities they had been out of touch with for years, causing resentment and a loss of the responsiveness and control that had been there during the glory days of the 1980s uprising.

Out of this conflict of leadership roles arose Mandela's failure to meet and make common cause with Buthelezi, to get him on-side, as had been his intention while he was in prison and which was almost certainly possible. Other leaders, especially some doctrinaire hardliners in Natal, opposed the idea vehemently and Mandela backed down. His failure to follow his own instincts has probably been his single most serious mistake.

Instead, a campaign to "marginalize" Buthelezi was launched, once again aggravating the worst features of the Inkatha leader's hypersensitive personality. His movement lashed back and a bitter power struggle ensued, escalating the black civil war in Natal and extending it into the Witwatersrand. This presented the burgeoning right-wing, with its allies in the security underworld of hit-squads and dirty-tricks units, with an opportunity to fan the flames and try to destabilize the negotiating process. Once again one saw the technique of aggrieved vigilante bands being used to launch terror raids on whole communities. Hit squads rampaged through commuter trains, hacking people to death and flinging them through the doors. The terrible bloodbath, in which the four-year Natal death toll rose to more than 4,000 and 750 people died in the Transvaal townships in a month, brought the peace process to a point of crisis where the right-wing objective was almost attained.

It is clear now that the low tolerance threshold for political opposition in the black community, and the disruptive potential of the right wing with their connections in the security forces, are the two gravest threats not only to the negotiation process, but, beyond that, to the survival prospects of a future nonracial democracy.

Yet I remain optimistic. No country can hope to move from the kind of past South Africa has had, with its centuries-old accumulation of hate and prejudice, inequality and injustice, into a bright new future without turmoil. France couldn't do it. Nor could Portugal after its fifty-year dictatorship. The Soviet Union and Eastern Europe are currently experiencing the trauma of their transformation. The morbid interregnum is inescapable.

But the future will be born, whatever the birth pains. And when it is, South Africa will cease to be a world symbol of racism and division and become a symbol instead of national reconciliation and racial harmony of coexistence between black and white, a bridge between the haves of the first world and the have-nots of the third.

That is my dream for the new millennium.

Bibliography

Adam, Heribert. *Modernizing Racial Domination: The Dynamics of South African Politics*. Berkeley: University of Califorina Press, 1971.

——— and Hermann Giliomee. *Ethnic Power Mobilized: Can South Africa Change?* New Haven: Yale University Press, 1979.

——— and Kogila Moodley. *South Africa Without Apartheid: Dismantling Racial Domination*. Berkeley: University of Califorina Press, 1986.

Adonis, Johannes Cornelius. *Die Afgebreekte Skeidsmuur weer Opgebou*. Amsterdam: Rodopi, 1982.

Agar-Hamilton, J. A. I. *The Native Policy of the Voortrekkers: An Essay in the History of the Interior of South Africa, 1836–1858*. Cape Town: Maskew Miller, 1928.

Armstrong, H. C. *Grey Steel: J. C. Smuts*. London: Methuen, 1951.

Beaufre, André. *An Introduction to Strategy*. New York: Praeger, 1963.

Becken, H. J. (Ed.). *Relevant Theology for Africa*. Durban: Lutheran Publishing House, 1973.

Becker, Peter. *Hill of Destiny: The Life and Times of Moshesh, Founder of the Basotho*. London: Longman, 1969.

Benson, Mary. *South Africa: The Struggle for a Birthright*. London: International Defence and Aid Fund for Southern Africa, 1985.

———. *Nelson Mandela: The Man and the Movement*. New York: W. W. Norton, 1986.

Beyerhaus, Peter, and Henry Lefever. *The Responsible Church and the Foreign Mission*. London: World Dominion Press, 1964.

Bohannan, Paul, and Philip Curtin. *Africa and Africans*. Prospect Heights, Ill.: Waveland, 1988.

Boesak, Allan. *Farewell to Innocence: A Socio-Ethical Study on Black Theology and Power.* Maryknoll, N.Y.: Orbis, 1977.

______. *If This Is Treason I Am Guilty.* Grand Rapids, Mich.: Eerdmans, 1987.

Botha, Andries Johannes. *Die Evolusie van 'n Volksteologie.* Bellville: Publikasies van die Universiteit van Wes-Kaapland, 1984.

Boxer, C. R. *The Dutch Seaborne Empire, 1600–1800.* London: Hutchinson, 1965.

Boyer, Paul, and Stephen Nissenbaum. *Salem Possessed: The Social Origins of Witchcraft.* Cambridge, Mass: Harvard University Press, 1974.

Bradlow, Frank R., and Margaret Cairns. *The Early Cape Muslims: A Study of Their Mosques, Genealogy and Origins.* Cape Town: A. A. Balkema, 1978.

Breytenbach, Breyten. *'n Seisoen in die Paradys.* Johannesburg: Perskor-Uitgewery, 1976.

______. *The True Confessions of an Albino Terrorist.* Johannesburg: Taurus, 1984.

Brinton, Crane. *The Anatomy of Revolution.* New York: Vintage, 1938.

Brown, Douglas. *Against the World.* New York: Doubleday, 1968.

Bulpin, T. V. *Lost Trails of the Transvaal.* Cape Town: Books of Africa, 1965.

Bundy, Colin. *The Emergence and Decline of a South African Peasantry.* Oxford: Oxford University Press, 1972.

Burton, A. W. *Sparks from the Border Anvil.* King William's Town: Provincial Publishing, 1950.

Butler, Guy. *The 1820 Settlers: An Illustrated Commentary.* Cape Town: Human & Rousseau, 1974.

Butler, J. R. M. *A History of England, 1815–1918* London: Thornton Butterworth, 1914.

______. *The Passing of the Great Reform Bill.* London: Longmans, Green, 1914.

Carlyle, Thomas. *Chartism,* in Carlyle's *Works,* Vol. 3. New York, 1869.

Carter, Gwendolen M. *The Politics of Inequality: South Africa Since 1948.* New York: Praeger, 1958.

Ciskei Commission. *The Quail Report.* Silverton: Conference Associates, 1980.

Clark, G. Kitson. *The Making of Victorian England.* Cambridge, Mass.: Harvard University Press, 1962.

Cole, Josette. *Crossroads: The Politics of Reform and Repression, 1976–1986.* Johannesburg: Ravan Press, 1987.

The Commonwealth Group of Eminent Persons. *Mission to South Africa.* New York: Viking Penguin, 1986.

Cronjé, G. *'n Tuiste vir die Nageslag—Die Blywende Oplossing van Suid-Afrika se Rassevraagstuk.* Johannesburg: Publicite Handelsreklamediens (Edms.) Bpk, 1945.

______, W. Nicol, and E. P. Groenewald. *Regverdige Rasse-Apartheid.* Stellenbosch: Christen Studente Vereeniging Boekhandel, 1947.

Davenport, T. R. H. *South Africa: A Modern History.* Toronto: University of Toronto Press, 1977.

Davids, Achmat. *The Mosques of Bo-Kaap: A Social History of Islam at the Cape.* Athlone: The South African Institute of Arabic and Islamic Research, 1980.

Davidson, Basil. *The African Genius: An Introduction to African Social and Cultural History.* Boston: Little, Brown, 1969.

De Gruchy, John. *Bonhoeffer in South Africa.* Grand Rapids, Mich: Eerdmans, 1984.

______. *Theology and Ministry in Context and Crisis: A South African Perspective.* Grand Rapids, Mich: Eerdmans, 1987.

______, and Charles Villa-Vicencio. *Apartheid Is a Heresy.* Grand Rapids, Mich: Eerdmans, 1983.

De Jong, Constance and Philip Glass. *Satyagraha: M. K. Gandhi in South Africa, 1893–1914.* New York: Tanam Press, 1983.

De Kiewiet, C. W. *A History of South Africa, Social and Economic.* London: Oxford University Press, 1941.

De Klerk, W. A. *The Puritans in Africa: A Story of Afrikanerdom.* Hammondsworth: Penguin, 1976.

De Tocqueville, Alexis. *The Old Regime and the French Revolution.* New York: Doubleday-Anchor, 1955.

Diederichs, N. *Nasionalisme as Lewensbeskouing en sy Verhouding tot Internasionalisme.* Pretoria: Nasionale Pers Beperk, 1936.

Du Toit, André and Hermann Giliomee. *Afrikaner Political Thought: Analysis and Documents.* Vol. 1: *1780–1850.* Cape Town: David Philip, 1983.

Edgar, Robert. *Because They Chose the Plan of God.* Johannesburg: Ravan Press, 1988.

Edwards, Isobel Eirlys. *The 1820 Settlers in South Africa: A Study in British Colonial Policy.* London: Longmans, Green, 1934.

Eisenstadt, S. N. *The Protestant Ethic and Modernization: A Comparative View.* New York: Basic Books, 1968.

Elphick, Richard. *Khoikhoi and the Founding of White South Africa.* Johannesburg: Ravan Press, 1985.

______, and Hermann Giliomee (Eds.). *The Shaping of South African Society, 1652–1820.* Cape Town: Longman, 1979.

Emerson, Rupert. *From Empire to Nation: The Rise to Self-Assertion of Asian and African Peoples.* Boston: Beacon Press, 1960.

Ergang, Robert Reinhold. *Herder and the Foundations of German Nationalism.* New York: Columbia University Press, 1931.

Fanon, Frantz. *The Wretched of the Earth.* New York: Grove Press, 1963.

Fichte, Johann Gottlieb. *Addresses to the German Nation.* London: Open Court Publishing, 1922.

Friedman, Steven. *Building Tomorrow Today: African Workers in Trade Unions, 1970–1984.* Johannesburg: Ravan Press, 1987.

Fromm, Erich. *The Fear of Freedom.* London: Routledge & Kegan Paul, 1961.

Gandhi, M. K. *The Selected Works of Mahatma Gandhi,* Vol. 3. Ahmedabad: Navajivan Publishing, 1968.

Gerdener, G. B. A. *Recent Developments in the South African Mission Field.* London: Marshall, Morgan & Scott, 1958.

Gerhardt, Gail. *Black Power in South Africa: The Evolution of an Ideology.* Berkeley: University of California Press, 1978.

Giliomee, Hermann and Lawrence Schlemmer. *Negotiating South Africa's Future*. Johannesburg: Southern Book Publishing, 1989.

______. *From Apartheid to Nation-Building*. Cape Town: Oxford University Press, 1989.

Halévy, Elie. *England in 1815: A History of the English People in the Nineteenth Century*. New York: Peter Smith, 1949.

Hartz, Louis M. *The Founding of New Societies*. New York: Harcourt, Brace & World, 1964.

Hockly, Harold Edward. *The Story of the British Settlers of 1820 in South Africa*. Cape Town: Juta, 1957.

Horne, Alistair. *A Savage War of Peace: Algeria, 1954–1962*. Hammondsworth: Penguin, 1985.

Huddleston, Trevor. *Naught for Your Comfort*. London: Collins, 1956.

Hunter, Guy. *The New Societies of Tropical Africa*. London: Oxford University Press, 1962.

Johnson, Phyllis, and David Martin (Eds.). *Destructive Engagement: Southern Africa at War*. Harare: Zimbabwe Publishing, 1986.

Johnstone, Frederick. *Class, Race and Gold*. London: Routledge & Kegan Paul, 1976.

The Kairos Document: Challenge to the Church: A Theological Comment on the Political Crisis in South Africa. Johannesburg: 1986.

Karis, Thomas, and Gwendolen Carter (Eds.). *From Protest to Challenge: A Documentary History of African Politics in South Africa, 1882–1964*. Vol. 1: *Protest and Hope, 1882–1934*, by Shedridan Johns III; Vol. 2: *Hope and Challenge, 1935–1952*, by Thomas Karis; Vol. 3: *Challenge and Violence, 1953–1964*, by Thomas Karis and Gail M. Gerhardt; Vol. 4: *Political Profiles*, by Gail M. Gerhardt and Thomas Karis. Stanford, Calif.: Hoover Institute Press, 1987.

Katzew, Henry. *Apartheid and Survival: A Jewish View*. Cape Town: Simondium Publishers, 1965.

Kenney, Henry. *Architect of Apartheid: H. F. Verwoerd, an Appraisal*. Johannesburg: Jonathan Ball, 1980.

Kruger, Rayne. *Goodbye Dolly Gray: A History of the Boer War*. London: The New English Library, 1964.

Kuyper, Abraham. *Calvinism: Six Stone Lectures*. Grand Rapids, Mich: Eerdmans, 1931.

Lacey, Marian. *Working for Boroko: The Origins of a Coercive Labour System in South Africa*. Johannesburg: Ravan Press, 1981.

Lefebvre, Georges. *The Coming of the French Revolution*. Princeton: Princeton University Press, 1947.

Leipoldt, C. Louis. *Jan van Riebeeck*. London: Longmans, 1936.

Lichtenstein, Henry. *Travels in Southern Africa: In the Years 1803, 1804, 1805, and 1806*. 2 vols. Cape Town: Van Riebeeck Society, 1928, 1930.

Lodge, Tom. *Black Politics in South Africa Since 1945*. Johannesburg: Ravan Press, 1983.

Luthuli, Albert. *Let My People Go*. London: Collins, 1962.

Mair, Lucy. *African Societies*. London: Cambridge University Press, 1974.

Malherbe, Ernst G. *Education in South Africa*, Vol. 2. Cape Town: Juta, 1977.
Mandela, Nelson. *The Struggle Is My Life.* London: International Defence and Aid Fund for Southern Africa, 1978.
Marais, J. S. *The Cape Coloured People, 1652–1937.* London: Longmans, Green, 1939.
Marks, Shula, and Stanley Trapido. *The Politics of Race, Class, and Nationalism in Twentieth Century South Africa.* New York: Longmans, 1987.
Martin, C. A. *The Concentration Camps, 1900–1902.* Cape Town: Howard Timmins, 1957.
Mayer, Philip. *Townsmen or Tribesmen.* Cape Town: Oxford University Press, 1961.
McCuen, John J. *The Art of Counter-Revolutionary War.* London: Faber and Faber, 1969.
McGregor, Robert. *Who Owns Whom?* Cape Town: Juta, 1989.
Mermelstein, David (Ed.). *The Anti-Apartheid Reader.* New York: Grove Press, 1987.
Millin, Sarah Gertrude. *The South Africans.* New York: Boni & Liveright, 1927.
Moodie, Donald. *The Record or a Series of Official Papers Relative to the Condition and Treatment of the Native Tribes of South Africa.* Compiled, translated, and edited by Moodie. Amsterdam: A. A. Balkema, 1960.
Moodie, Duncan Campbell Francis. *The History of the Battles and Adventures of the British, the Boers, and the Zulus, etc. in Southern Africa.* Cape Town: Murray and St. Leger, 1888.
Moodie, J. W. D. *Ten Years in South Africa: Including a Particular Description of the Wild Sports of that Country.* 2 Vols. London: Richard Bentley, 1835.
Moodie, T. Dunbar. *The Rise of Afrikanerdom: Power, Apartheid, and the Afrikaner Civil Religion.* Berkeley: University of California Press, 1975.
Morris, Donald R. *The Washing of the Spears.* London: Sphere Books, 1973.
O'Donnell, Guillermo, Philippe C. Schmitter, and Laurence Whitehead. *Transitions from Authoritarian Rule.* Vol. 1: *Southern Europe*; Vol. 2: *Latin America*; Vol. 3: *Comparative Perspectives*; Vol. 4: *Tentative Conclusions About Uncertain Democracies.* Baltimore: Johns Hopkins University Press, 1987.
Pakenham, Thomas. *The Boer War.* New York: Random House, 1979.
Peires, J. B. *The House of Phalo: A History of the Xhosa People in the Days of Their Independence.* Berkeley: University of California Press, 1981.
Pelzer, A. N. (Ed.) *Verwoerd Speaks: Speeches, 1948–1966.* Johannesburg: APB Publishers, 1966.
Pienaar, S., and Anthony Sampson. *Two Views of Separate Development.* London: Oxford University Press, 1960.
Pirow, Oswald. *James Barry Munnik Hertzog.* Cape Town: Howard Timmins, 1957.
Plaatje, Sol T. *Native Life in South Africa: Before and Since the European War and the Boer Republic.* London: London University Press, 1916.
Platzky, Laurine, and Cherryl Walker. *The Surplus People: Forced Removals in South Africa.* Johannesburg: Ravan Press, 1985.

Prall, Stuart E. *The Puritan Revolution: A Documentary History.* New York: Doubleday-Anchor, 1968.

Preller, Gustav S. *Voortrekkermense,* Vol. 2. Cape Town: Nasionale Pers, 1920.

Pringle, Thomas. *Narrative of a Residence in South Africa.* Cape Town: Struik, 1966.

Reader, D. H. *The Black Man's Portion.* Cape Town: Oxford University Press, 1961.

Rees, Mervyn, and Chris Day. *Muldergate.* Johannesburg: Macmillan South Africa, 1980.

Reitz, F. W. *A Century of Wrong.* London: "Review of Reviews" Office, 1900.

Roberts, Brian. *Kimberley: Turbulent City.* Cape Town: David Philip, 1976.

Roberts, Michael, and A. E. G. Trollip. *The South African Opposition, 1939–45.* London: Longmans, Green, 1947.

Ross, Robert. *Cape of Torments.* London: Routledge & Kegan Paul, 1983.

Samkange, Stanlake. *African Saga: A Brief Introduction to African History.* Salisbury: Harare Publishing House, 1971. Published by arrangement with Abingdon Press, Nashville, Tenn.

Saunders, Christopher, Howard Phillips, and Elizabeth Van Heyningen (Eds.). *Studies in the History of Cape Town,* vol. 4. Cape Town: University of Cape Town Press, 1981.

Schama, Simon. *The Embarrassment of Riches: An Interpretation of Dutch Culture in the Golden Age.* New York: Knopf, 1987.

Schapera, Isaac (Ed.). *David Livingstone South African Papers, 1849–1853.* Cape Town: Van Riebeeck Society, 1974.

Schreiner, Olive. *Closer Union.* Cape Town: The Constitutional Reform Association, 1960.

Shinnie, P. L. *Meroë: A Civilization of the Sudan.* New York: Praeger, 1976.

Smith, Preserved. *The Reformation in Europe.* New York: Collier Books, 1962.

———. *The Social Background of the Reformation.* New York: Collier Books, 1962.

Sparrman, Anders. *A Voyage to the Cape of Good Hope Towards the Antarctic Polar Circle Round the World and to the Country of the Hottentots and the Caffres from the Year 1772–1776.* 2 vols. Cape Town: Van Riebeeck Society, 1975.

Stern, Fritz. *The Politics of Cultural Despair: A Study in the Rise of Germanic Ideology.* New York: Doubleday-Anchor, 1965.

Stockwell, John. *In Search of Enemies.* London: Futura Publications, 1979.

Stubbs, Aelred (Ed.). *Steve Biko—I Write What I Like.* San Francisco: Harper & Row, 1978.

The Study Commission on U.S. Policy Towards South Africa. *Time Running Out.* Berkeley: University of California Press, 1981.

Sundkler, Bengt. *Bantu Prophets in South Africa.* London: Oxford University Press, 1961.

Swan, Maureen. *Gandhi: The South African Experience.* Johannesburg: Ravan Press, 1985.

Theal, George McCall. *History of the Boers in South Africa.* Cape Town: Struik, 1973.

Thompson, E. P. *The Making of the English Working Class.* New York: Vintage, 1966.

Thompson, Leonard. *The Political Mythology of Apartheid.* New Haven: Yale University Press, 1985.

Torres, Sergio, and Kofi Appiah. *African Theology en Route.* Maryknoll, N.Y.: Orbis, 1977.

Treurnicht, Andries P. *Credo van 'n Afrikaner.* Cape Town: Tafelberg, 1975.

Trollope, Anthony. *South Africa.* A reprint of the 1878 edition with an introduction and notes by J. H. Davidson. Cape Town: A. A. Balkema, 1973.

Troup, Freda. *South Africa: An Historical Introduction.* London: Eyre Methuen, 1972.

Van Arkel, D., G. C. Quispel, and R. J. Ross. *"De Wijngaard des Heeren?" Een onderzoek naar de wortels van "die blanke baasskap" in Zuid-Afrika.* Leiden: Martinus Nijhoff, 1983.

Van Jaarsveld, F. A. *The Afrikaner's Interpretation of South African History.* Cape Town: Simondium Publishers, 1964.

_____. *The Awakening of Afrikaner Nationalism, 1868–1881.* Cape Town: Human & Rousseau, 1961.

_____. *From Van Riebeeck to Vorster, 1652–1974.* Johannesburg: Perskor Publishers, 1975.

Van Onselen, Charles. *Studies in the Social and Economic History of the Witwatersrand, 1886–1914.* Johannesburg: Ravan Press, 1982.

Varenjkazis, Tim. *South Africa: A Society in Transformation.* Johannesburg: Fedgas, 1988.

Villa-Vicencio, Charles (Ed.). *Theology and Violence: The South African Debate.* Grand Rapids, Mich: Eerdmans, 1988.

Walker, Eric A. *The Great Trek.* London: Adam & Charles Black, 1920.

Walton, James. *Homesteads and Villages of South Africa.* Pretoria: J. L. van Schaik, 1952.

Weber, Max. *The Protestant Ethic and the Spirit of Capitalism.* New York: Scribner's, 1958.

Webster, Eddie (Ed.). *Essays in Southern African Labour History.* Johannesburg: Ravan Press, 1983.

Welsh, David. *The Roots of Segregation: Native Policy in Colonial Natal, 1845–1910.* Cape Town: Oxford University Press, 1971.

West, Martin. *Bishops and Prophets in a Black City.* Cape Town: David Philip, 1975.

Wheatcroft, Geoffrey. *The Randlords: South Africa's Robber Barons and the Mines that Forged a Nation.* New York: Simon & Schuster, 1985.

Wilkins, Ivor, and Hans Strydom. *The Super-Afrikaners: Inside the Afrikaner Broederbond.* Johannesburg: Jonathan Ball, 1978.

Wilson, Francis, and Mamphela Ramphele. *Uprooting Poverty: The South African Challenge.* Cape Town: David Philip, 1989.

Wilson, Monica, and Leonard Thompson (Eds.). *The Oxford History of South Africa,* 2 vols. Oxford: Oxford University Press, 1969.

Index

Abantu-Batho (newspaper), 145, 254
abolitionist movement, 56, 67, 77
Abolition of Passes and Coordination of Documents Act, 36
Action Committee to Stop Evictions, 377
Adam, Heribert, 36, 210, 368, 371, 388
Adonis, Hannes, 159
Africa Institute of Soviet Academy of Sciences, 364–5
African Farmers Association, 145
Africanism, 237, 253–60, 262–3
Africanist, The (journal), 256
African Mine Workers' Union, 237
African National Congress (ANC), 68, 74, 109*n*, 195, 233–4, 236–40, 268–72, 279, 280, 324; Africanism and, 253–9; Afrikaner dissidents and, 250, 325–6; demand for legalization of, 358; EPG and, 252–4; in exile, 263, 264, 268; formation of, 144–5, 236; Freedom Charter and, 146, 239–40, 253, 333; and future of South Africa, 369–72, 381–5, 387, 390, 395–6; Gandhi's influence on, 73, 90, 236; guerrilla war of, 70, 243–4, 246–8, 263, 276–7, 301 (*see also* Umkhonto we Sizwe); and independent black nations, 301, 303, 307, 312, 313; Inkatha and, 274, 275; nonracialism of, 250–3, 256, 277; policy shift of, 366–7; Sharpeville and, 233–4, 242; Soviet support of, 362, 364; UDF and, 333, 337, 338, 342
African People's Organisation, 109*n*
African World, The, 254
Afrikaans language, development of, 79–81
Afrikaans Language and Cultural Union of the South African Railways and Harbours (ATKV), 169
Afrikaanse Calvinistiese Kerk, 324
Afrikaanse Weerstandsbeweging (AWB), 324, 326, 343
Afrikaner party, 173
Afrikaner Resistance movement, 41, 324
Afrikaner Volkswag, 324
Afrikaners, 23, 30–33, 78, 177–8, 191, 223, 228; antipathy to physical toil of, 43–4; Apostolic sect of, 294; and British annexation of Cape Colony, 45–6, 51, 56; Cape, 116–17; class stratification of, 316–17, 320–2, 326; "coloureds" and, 73–4; in competition with blacks for jobs, 131, 133–6; dilemma of, 209–13; dissident, 250, 268, 284, 367, 382, 384; Dutch heritage of, 24, 28–30, 32, 33; economy and, 176–7, 387; English-speaking South Africans and, 47–9, 62, 66, 70, 217; and EPG, 352; and eviction of blacks from land, 138, 139; individualism of,

Afrikaners, (*cont.*)
42–3; and industrial revolution, 121; intelligentsia of, 147–9, 162, 166, 169, 172, 175, 193, 317; justification of apartheid of, 88; in Kenya, 248–9; moral ambivalence of, 34–7; on police force, 343; nationalism of (*see* nationalism, Afrikaner; National party); Nazi Germany and, 160–4, 172; and reconstruction programme, 125–6; reformist, 324–6; religion of (*see* Dutch Reformed Church); schisms among, 324, 327–8; slavery and, 60, 72, 85; symbolic politics of, 169–72; urbanization of, 130–4, 142, 146, 155, 182; Verwoerd and, 192, 193, 197–8; VOC and, 37, 38; during World War II, 171–5, 236; *see also* Boers
Afro-Asian Solidarity Committee, 365
Akhalwaya, Ameen, 331
Alba, Duke of, 25
Albany, *see* Suurveld
Alexander, Neville, 243
Alexandra township, 266, 339, 352
Alfonso, José, 298
Algeria, 244, 245, 270, 309, 311
Alliance of Black Reformed Christians, 285–6
Amanzimtoti, 247
American South, 23, 41, 126, 184, 324
American War of Independence, 54, 270
Amiens, Peace of, 46
Amsterdam, 25, 34
Anderson, Benjamin, 63
Anglican Church, 54, 188, 251, 287, 289, 334
Anglo-American Corporation, 121
Angola, 248, 253, 275, 300, 301, 303–7, 312–14, 363, 365, 367
anti-Semitism, 172, 174, 194
apartheid, 23, 42, 49, 50, 61, 84, 88, 145, 189, 214, 237, 271, 273, 276, 363, 367, 370; black councils and, 332; crisis of, 314, 315, 317; economy and, 78; effect on whites of, 217–18, 222, 223; English-speaking South Africans and, 48; ethnic categories of, 12; euphemisms for, 36; evictions under, 86–7; and fear of bloodbath, 249; "homelands" and, 35–6, 68, 97, 136, 138, 206–7, 212; ideology of, 66, 111, 147–9, 158, 175, 177–82; international pressure against, 304, 391–6; legislation of, 189–91, 235, 238; liberals' view of, 259; nationalism and, 31; Nazi influence on, 160, 163–4, 175; nonviolent struggle against, 238–44; psychological damage resulting from, 223–9; racial categories of, 85, 86; reformulation of, 318–21, 337, 348–50, 353, 360, 369, 378, 385; and Regional Superpower strategy, 308; religion and, 67, 161, 278–9, 281, 283–93; riots against, 302; Romanticism and, 165; roots of, 31–2; Soviet position on, 364, 365; tribalism weakened by, 390; unenforceability of, 374; under Verwoerd, 192–202; violence and, 219–23, 267; white opponents of, 50
Apostolic Faith Mission, 294
Aquila, 343
Arabs, 4
Argentina, 379
Arminians, 27
Arminius, Jacobus, 27
Armscor, 314
Armstrong, James, 76
Asoyan, Boris, 365
Athlone township, 81, 219–20, 266, 340–1
Atlantic Charter, 237
Atteridgeville township, 338, 357
Australia, 48, 71, 352; Aborigines of, 184
Australopithecus africanus, 6
Azanian People's Organization, 263, 267
Azapo, 357

Bagehot, Walter, 71
Bakongo people, 303
Bakwena tribe, 206–8
Ballinger, Margaret, 48–9
banning orders, 230, 239, 243, 285, 302–3
Bantu Administration and Development, Department of, 36, 296
Bantu Authorities, 195
Bantu Education Act, 196
Bantu Education system, 224–5, 263
Bantustans, 193–5, 197–201
Baphutsane party, 333
Baptists, 54
Baraka, Amiri, 260
Baralong tribe, 136*n*
Baring-Gould, S., 278
Barmen Declaration, 282, 284
Barnard, Neil, 323
Barnato, Barney, 120
Basotho, 102, 104, 113
Basutoland, 138, 144, 179
Batavia, 29*n*, 30
Batlokwa, 102, 103

Beaufre, General André, 309–11, 354, 355
Bechuanaland, 144, 179
Becker, Peter, 102
Beit, Alfred, 120
Belgium: Boer War and, 129; in World War II, 171, 186
Bengal, 80
Benson, Mary, 144, 240–1
Bentham, Jeremy, 53
Bergen op Zoom, battle of, 25
Bernstein, Ann, 375*n*
Bethanie squatter camp, 208
Beyers, Christiaan Frederick, 284
Beyleveld, Piet, 240
Bezuidenhout, Freek, 92–4, 105
Bezuidenhout, Hans, 94
Bezuidenhout, Martha, 94
Bible, 25, 35, 67, 119, 124, 143, 160, 169, 284, 286–8; quotations from, 22, 35, 91, 161, 214, 280, 290–2, 325; States, 40, 41
Bidault, Hendrik, 44
Biko, Hlumelo, 231, 232
Biko, Steven, 74, 109, 150, 221–2, 230, 231, 251, 259–60, 262, 263, 284, 301, 303
Bisho, 36, 205
Black Administration, Department of, 138, 207
Blackburn, Molly, 251–2, 264
Black Consciousness movement, 74, 109, 150, 221, 230, 251,259, 260, 262–3, 271, 275, 276, 284, 285, 303, 337, 382–4, 391
Black Local Authorities Act, 337
Black Power, 260, 265, 283
blacks, 91; Africanist, 253–60, 262–3; Afrikaner determination of future of, 212–13; Boer War and, 130, 136; and British annexation of Cape Colony, 45, 46, 51, 56; class conflict and, 92; coalition forming by, 382–4; collaborators, 264–6, 275; "coloureds" and, 74–5, 88; conservative Christian, 294–7; cultural renaissance of, 260–2; decolonization and, 301, 303; dependence of economy on, 368–9; in diamond mines, 122–3; dispossession of, 96; in Dutch Reformed Church, 154, 159, 161; economic views of, 387–9; education of, 68, 179, 195–6, 224–5, 301, 302, 376; English-speaking South Africans and, 48, 50; eviction from land of, 136–41; and expansionism, 65, 105; fear of mixing with, 148; forced removal of, 205–8; and future political system, 389–91; Great Trek and, 106, 107, 109, 111–13; in gold fields, 123, 124; Gandhi and, 73, 90; "homelands" rejected by, 97; and ideology of apartheid, 178–82; and industrial revolution, 121; institutionalized violence against, 219–23; and legislation of apartheid, 189–91; middle class, 318, 321, 329; migration to southern Africa of, 7–8, 10, 13; missionaries and, 66–8; in Natal, 66; nationalism of (*see* Africanism; nationalism, black); nonracialism of, 250–3, 256, 257; percentage of land apportioned to, 211; psychological damage to, 223–9; in resettlement camps, 202–6; resilience of, 229–30; resistance movement of, 68–70, 144–6, 235–44, 246–8, 272–7; revolt of, 329–61; in Rhodesia, 49–50; rioting by, 215–16; segregation of (*see* apartheid; segregation); as serfs, 66, 84; as skilled workers, 314–15, 317, 321; of Sophiatown, 188–9; subjugation of, 107–9; of Suurveld, 57, 58, 60–4; theology of liberation of, 278–93; traditional culture of, 12–21; Trekboers and, 43, 46; tribal reserves for, 193–5, 197–201; in tricameral Parliament, 319, 330–1; in United States, 74; urbanization of, 131, 133–6, 139, 141–3, 146, 147, 151, 315, 372–8; U.S. policy and, 300; violence among, 365–9, 375–6; warfare traditions among, 8–10, 100; white stereotype of, 214–15; in World War II, 236–7; of Zimbabwe, 50; and Zulu eruption, 95–104
Black Sash civil rights movement, 129, 251, 383
Bloemfontein, 144, 145
Blood River, battle of, 110, 112–13, 169, 183, 244
Bloom, Anthony, 71
Blignaut, Major Daniel, 345
Boers, 40–3, 46, 62, 65, 69, 92–3, 96; gold and, 123, 124; Great Trek of, 95, 104–7, 109–12, 119; hunting of San by, 11; Khoikhoi and, 84; missionaries and, 67; slavery and, 78; subdivision of farms of, 121; subjugation of blacks by, 107–9; subsistence farming of, 64; and Suurveld settlement of, 57, 60; uprising against British of, 93–5, 105; *see also* Afrikaners
Boer War, 95*n*, 125–30, 136, 204, 235, 284

Boesak, Allan, 75, 86, 218, 251, 278, 281, 283, 285–6
Bol, Ferdinand, 26
Boland, 40, 85
Bonhoeffer, Dietrich, 281–2, 285
Booy, 92
Booysens, Peter, 376
Bophalong township, 334–5
BophuthaTswana, 138, 206, 212, 337, 340
Boshoff, Carel, 278, 324
Botha, Louis, 134
Botha, P. W., 75, 86, 127, 128, 185, 202, 206, 279, 296, 304–8, 310, 311, 314, 315, 319–23, 327, 329, 348–51, 354, 363, 367–9
Botha, Pik, 324–5, 349, 353
Botshabelo, 138
Botswana, 12
Bowker, John Mitford, 64
Boxer, C. R., 29*n*, 76*n*
Brandfort, 227, 251
Brazil, 379, 381, 394
"Brazilian option," 318
Breugel, Pieter, 34
Breytenbach, Breyten, 129, 211, 218, 220–1
Brink, André, 77*n*
Brinton, Crane, 150, 152, 245, 246, 340
British: blacks as subjects of, 108, 113–14; Boer republics and, 113–15, 117; Boer uprising against, 93–5; and Boer War, 125–30; Cape Afrikaners and, 115–17; and Dutch Reformed Church, 154*n*; economic development and, 91; expansionism of, 64–5; first settlers, 50–2, 55–6; gold and, 123, 125; Great Trek and, 105, 106, 109–11, 119; indirect rule of, 195; labour regulations of, 83, 93; legacy of Afrikaner conflict with, 150, 151; as missionaries, 66–8; Natal annexed by, 73; occupation of Cape by, 32, 45–6; protectorates of, 179; racial attitudes of, 23, 60, 62; slavery and, 77, 84; Suurveld settlement of, 57–64; Zulus and, 97; *see also* England; English-speaking South Africans
Broederbond, 162, 163, 167, 169, 175–8, 181, 186, 284, 320, 322, 324
Brown v. Board of Education (1954), 186
Bucwa, Moses, 347
Bulhoek Massacre, 242
Bundy, Colin, 140
Bunting, S. F., 252
Bureau of State Security (BOSS), 172, 307, 308, 323
Burger, Die (newspaper), 151
Burundi, 248
Bushmen, *see* San
Buthelezi, Chief Mangosuthu Gatsha, 97, 271, 274–5, 383, 391
Buthelezi clan, 100
Butler, Guy, 60, 329
bywoners (squatters), 134, 139, 140

Caetano, Marcello, 299
Calvin, John, 23
Calvinists, 24, 26–7, 116, 158, 219
Campbell-Bannerman, Sir Henry, 130
Cambridge University, 51, 184
Canada, 48
cannibalism, 103
Cape Coloureds, 85
Cape Provincial Council, 251
Cape Times, 198
Cape Town, 22, 34, 38, 40–2, 57, 60, 71; Africanists in, 254; "coloureds" in, 75, 86, 193; growth of, 116; Muslims in, 80–2; shantytowns around, 200; slaves in, 76, 77; squatters camps at, 336; University of, 196, 232
capitalism, 45, 142; Afrikaner, 316; apartheid and, 32; racial, 92, 191, 253, 388–9; rise of, 24; socialist response to, 56
Carlyle, Thomas, 55
Carmichael, Stokeley, 260
Carter, Gwendolen, 132
Catholicism, *see* Roman Catholic Church
Central Intelligence Agency (CIA), 304, 306
Ceylon, 72, 186
Chagga tribe, 159
Chamber of Mines, 237
Charterist movement, 253, 263, 275, 384, 389, 391
Chase Manhattan Bank, 350
Chikane, Frank, 251, 278, 377
China, 303, 387
Chinese, 85, 217
Christian Catholic Apostolic Church, 294
Christian Institute, 284
Christianity, 143; apartheid and, 279; black liberation and, 278–93; conservative black sects, 293–7; nonracialism and, 250–1, 253; slavery and, 326; *see also specific denominations*
Churchill, Winston, 48*n*, 174, 184

Cilliers, Sarel, 112, 169
Ciskei, 202–6, 212, 265, 337, 376
Claassens, Jonathan, 82
Clark, G. Kitson, 51
class conflict, 52, 92, 253
Cleaver, Eldridge, 260
Cobbett, William, 53
Coleridge, Samuel Taylor, 53
Colley, General Sir G. Pommeroy, 114, 115
Colonial Office, 67
Coloured People's Congress, 240
"coloureds," 12, 72–5, 84–8, 93, 178, 179, 193, 200, 217, 220, 315, 318; disenfranchisement of, 181, 190; in Dutch Reformed Church, 154, 155, 159, 161; on Great Trek, 107; Muslim, 81; in resistance struggle, 240, 243; removed from voter rolls, 49; and tricameral system, 318, 330–1, 335, 348, 349
Columbus, Christopher, 24
Commission for Administration, 323
Commonwealth, 49
Commonwealth Eminent Persons Group (EPG), 351–4
Communists, 130, 135, 242, 257, 258, 272, 303, 362, 365; *see also* Marxism; South African Communist party
concentration camps, 128–30, 235
Cone, James, 282–3
Congo, 7, 248, 270, 275
Congress of Democrats, 240
Congress of the People, 239–41
Congress of Traditional Leaders of South Africa, 384
Conservative party, 41, 177, 305, 320, 321, 323, 328, 343
Constantine, Emperor of Rome, 280
Constantinople, 23
"constructive engagement," 349, 350
Cooper, Saths, 267–8
Cooperation and Development, Department of, 36
Corn Laws, 113
Cory, Giles, 18
Cosatu, 382–4
Cottesloe Consultation, 283–4, 286
Cradock, 93
Credo of an Afrikaner (Treurnicht), 320
Criminal Law Amendment Act, 238
Crocker, Chester, 394
Cronjé, Geoff, 147–50, 163–4, 172, 177–82, 188, 192, 193, 211, 212, 214–15, 228
Crossroads squatter camp, 200, 315, 339, 357, 358, 376
Crucible, The (Miller), 19
Cuba, 305, 306, 313, 367

Dart, Raymond, 5–6
Davidson, Apollon, 130*n*, 365
De Beer, Johannes Nicolaas, 120
De Beers Consolidated Mines, 120, 121
Decline of the West (Spengler), 148
Defiance Campaign, 219, 238–9, 241, 251, 337
De Gruchy, John, 281
De Kiewiet, C. W., 42, 105, 107
De Klerk, Bill, 135
De Klerk, Frederik Willem, 248, 367–71
De Klerk, Willem, 371
Democratic party, 371, 382
Descartes, René, 25
destablization, 311, 363
Detainees' Parents' Support committee, 383
De Witt, General Hendrik, 344
diamonds, 46, 56, 62, 113, 119–23, 142
Dias, Bartholomeu, 23
Diederichs, Nico, 163–4, 167–8, 176, 177
Dien Bien Phu, battle of, 270
Difaqane, 102, 106, 113, 137, 139
Dimbaza resettlement camp, 204–5
Dingane, 111–13
Dingiswayo, Chief of the Mtetwa, 93, 95, 96, 99–102
Diop, Cheikh Ante, 260
Diphoko, Dutch, 336
diseases: during Boer War, 128; brought by whites, 12, 84; indigenous to Africa, 4; in resettlement camps, 203
Disenfranchising Bill, 89
District Six, 86–7
Dithakong, 67
Dlamini, Sam, 266, 335
Dlamini clan, 103
Dletsheni clan, 99
Dort, Synod of, 27, 28, 40
Dos Santos, Eduardo, 367
Downie, John A., 294, 295
Drake, Sir Francis, 45
Duduza township, 266
Du Plessis, Daniel, 204
Du Plessis, Johannes, 155–6
Du Plessis, L. J., 177
Durban, 247, 248, 264; townships of, 332, 336
D'Urban, Sir Benjamin, 63
Dutch, 15, 22–9, 56, 117; Boer War and, 129; educational policy of, 156, 158; first settlers, 8, 25, 27–30, 37–8;

Dutch, (*cont.*)
Khoikhoi and, 83; loss of Cape Colony by, 45–6; moral ambivalence of, 33–4, 55; Muslims and, 80, 81; racial attitudes of, 23, 29–30, 32; religious conflicts among, 27; slavery and, 72, 76, 77; Trekboer rebellion against, 104; war with Spain, 24–6, 76, 327; in World War II, 171, 186
Dutch Reformed Church, 32, 35, 74, 75, 81, 114, 116, 117, 149, 152–6, 158–61, 164, 170, 178*n*, 193, 250, 251, 278, 279, 283–4, 286, 320, 326
Du Toit, André, 28, 33
Du Toit, S. J., 117, 118, 147, 155, 166, 278

East London, 239, 249
East Rand, 332, 336
Ebden, Alfred, 120
Economist, The, 318, 393
Edelstein, Melvyn, 249
education: of Afrikaners, 116, 147, 149; of blacks, 68, 179, 195–6, 224–5, 301, 302, 376; Dutch, 156, 158; militarization and, 309; in Nazi Germany, 163
Effendi, Abu Bakr, 81
Egypt, 186; ancient, 3, 4
Eiselen, Werner, 194, 195
El Alamein, battle of, 175
Eliade, Mircea, 398
Elizabeth I, Queen of England, 18
End Conscription Campaign, 383
Engels, Friedrich, 270
England, 353; banks in, 351; Dutch victory over, 26; evangelical movement in, 53–5; Germany and, 149; Great Reform Act in, 331; industrialization of, 51–2, 121, 393; non-white immigrants in, 184, 210; revolutionary movements in, 53, 55; Thatcher government in, 348; witchcraft executions in, 18; in World War II, 152, 162, 171, 174, 184; *see also* British
English-speaking South Africans, 46–7, 56, 66, 176, 193, 209–10; and apartheid legislation, 191; in cities, 130; divisions between Afrikaners and, 217; economy and, 62, 314, 316, 387; gold mining and, 133; Indians and, 90; industrial revolution and, 121; in Johannesburg, 124; in Natal, 73; politics and, 47–51, 70–1; *see also* British

Enlightenment, the, 164
Enslin, Johan Adam, 41
Ergang, Robert, 165
Ethiopia, 365
Ethiopian churches, 294
evangelical movement, 53–5, 62, 67, 250, 293
Evaton, 333, 334, 336
evolution, human, 5–7
expansionism, 64, 105
Extension of University Education Act, 36, 196

Fairbairn, John, 71
Fanon, Frantz, 239, 245–8, 255, 260, 266, 268, 270, 368
fascism, 148, 163
Fazzie, Henry, 357
Federale Mynbou, 177
Federale Volksbeleggings, 176, 177
Federation of Afrikaner Cultural Unions, 176
Ferreira's Camp, 124
Festinger, Leon, 153
Fichte, Johann Gottlieb, 164–7
First, Ruth, 252
Fischer, Bram, 252
Five Freedoms Forum, 383
forced removals, 205–8, 210, 393
foreign debt crisis, 350–1
Fort Hare, University College of, 68, 196, 275
fossils, 5–6
Fouché, Lieutenant John, 346
France, 23, 45–6; Algerian independence from, 245, 270, 309, 311; Boer War and, 129; in Indochina, 270, 309, 311; in World War II, 171, 186
Franco, Generalissimo Francisco, 163, 172, 382
Fraser, Malcolm, 352
Freedom Charter, 239–42, 253, 256, 333, 382, 387; *see also* Charterist movement
Frelimo party, 303
French Equatorial Africa, 231
French Revolution, 53, 55
Fromm, Erich, 27
frontier wars, 60, 62–3, 65, 68–9, 108, 250
Fugard, Athol, 188
funeral rallies, 82, 341–7
Fynn, Henry Francis, 96

Gama, Vasco da, 23, 24
Gander, Laurence, 372

Gandhi, Mohandas Karamchand, 73, 88–90, 186, 236, 237
gangs, 87, 143, 224, 225
Garvey, Marcus, 253–4, 294
gelykstelling (equalization), 67, 105, 106, 131, 148, 154, 181, 321
Gencor, 177
Gendeyana, 98
General Laws Amendment Act, 272
General Mining, 177
Genootskap van Regte Afrikaners, 117
Gerdener, G. E. B., 160
Gerhardt, Gail, 255, 258
Germany, 284; Boer War and, 129; missionaries from, 159–60; Nazi, 148–9, 152, 160–4, 166–8, 173–5, 178, 186, 193–4, 236, 278, 281–2; during Reformation, 281; *see also* West Germany
Geskiedenis van ons Land in die Taal van ons Volk, Die, 117
Gestapo, 281
Gesuiwerde Nasionale party, 151, 153, 172, 190, 257
Ghana, 4, 193, 250, 256
"Ghetto Act," 237
Giap, General Vo Nguyen, 270
Giliomee, Hermann, 31*n*, 218, 300, 318, 327
Goa, 23
Goebbels, Joseph, 172
gold mines, 46, 56, 62, 120, 121, 123, 124, 130, 177, 180; blacks employed in, 139, 142, 145, 191, 204, 237; job protection for whites in, 134
Gomarists, 27
Gontcharov, Victor, 364, 365
Goodwill, Zwelithini, 274
Goosen, Captain Gert, 345
Goosen, Colonel P. J., 222
Gorbachev, Mikhail, 363, 366
Graaff-Reinet, 104
Grahamstown, 61; battle of, 9, 68
Gramsci, Antonio, 362, 370
Great Depression, 132, 147, 151, 236, 254
Great Trek, 95, 104–7, 109–12, 124, 126–8, 154, 291; reenactment of, 169–72, 176
Greece, 379; ancient, 3, 185
Grey, Sir George, 68
Greyshirts, 172, 174
Grey University College, 167
Griquas, 85, 120
Groenwewald, E. P., 178*n*
Gromyko, Anatoly, 364
Grotius, Hugo, 27
Group Areas Act, 373, 374
Grundy, Kenneth, 310
guerrilla warfare, 269–70, 303, 366, 367; *see also* Umkhonto we Sizwe
Guchkov, Alexander, 129–30
Guriqua, 83
Gutenberg, Johann, 24
Gutmann, Bruno, 159–60

Halevy, Élie, 53
Hals, Frans, 25
Hamilton, Charles, 260
Hani, Chris, 247
Hardy, Thomas, 53
Havenga, Klasie, 173
Healdtown school, 68
Hegel, George Wilhelm Friedrich, 218, 220
Herder, Johann Gottfried von, 160, 165, 166
Herstigte (Reconstituted) National party, 320
Hertzog, James Barry Munnik, 128, 134–5, 139, 144, 150–3, 162, 172, 173, 255, 257
Heunis, Chris, 349, 354
Hintsa, King of the Xhosa, 63
Hitler, Adolf, 148, 152, 162, 163, 168, 169, 172, 174, 190, 193, 237, 281, 282
Hlubi clan, 102, 103
Hobhouse, Emily, 129, 130
Holland, *see* Dutch
Holocaust, 186, 281
Home for Posterity, A (Cronjé), 177
"homelands," 68, 136, 211, 212, 230, 232, 273, 315, 316, 332, 372, 375, 384, 393; black administrators in, 227; collaborators in, 275; financing of, 36; resettlement camps in, 202–6; revolt in, 337; Tswana, 138; white, 326–7; Zulu, 97, 264, 274
Hoover, Herbert, 121
Hottentots, *see* Khoikhoi
Houphouet-Boigny, Felix, 270
Huddleston, Trevor, 188, 228
Hughes, Langston, 260
Huguenots, 28, 29, 40, 117, 118
human evolution, 5–7

Ilingelihle township, 266
Immorality Act, 87
Improper Interference Act, 259
Inanda township, 336
Independent party, 382

India, 46, 72, 90, 186
Indian Congress, 73, 89, 186, 240
Indian Opinion, 90
Indians, 73, 75, 85, 87–90, 179, 217, 315, 318; in Dutch Reformed Church, 160; in resistance struggle, 237, 240, 241, 257; and tricameral system, 318, 330–1, 335, 348, 349
Indochina, 72, 186, 270
Indonesia, 4, 72, 80, 186
Industrial and Commercial Workers Union, 146, 236, 253
industrial revolution, 51, 52, 54, 56, 121, 122, 135, 142, 168, 181, 200–1, 393
Information, Department of, 308
Inkatha, 264, 274, 275, 357, 383, 384, 391
Inquisition, 25
interrogation, 220–2
Inyembezi resettlement camp, 204
Iron Age, 5, 7, 21
Isaacs, Barnett, 120
Isandhlwana, battle of, 97*n*
Islam, 3, 29*n*, 80–2, 266
Israel, 306, 307, 328
Israelites, 242
Italy, fascist, 163, 175
Ivory Coast, 270*n*

Jack, Mkhuseli, 338, 339, 357
Jackson, Jesse, 184
Jacob, Daniel, 119
Jacobins, 55
Jakobs, Dominee Danile, 35
James I, King of England, 18
Japan, 186
Java, 80
Jenkins, Simon, 318
Jericho, 7
Jerusalemgangers, 41
Jews, 56, 120, 124, 133, 172, 174, 194, 250, 328; in Nazi Germany, 281, 282
job-reservation laws, 134, 180–1, 191, 201, 314
Johannesburg, 90, 121, 123–4, 132, 142, 144, 145, 162, 194, 215, 248, 253, 301; Africanists in, 254; blacks in, 374, 377; Great Trek centennial in, 170; sabotage in, 244; stock market of, 242; violence in, 247
Johannesburg Democratic Action Committee, 383
Johannesburg *Star*, 194*n*
Johannesburg Stock Exchange, 121
Joint Management Centres, 310
Jonker, Ingrid, 171
Jordan, 186
Joubert, Piet, 115, 129
Jussen, Hubert, 216–17

Kadalie, Clemens, 145–6, 236, 253, 254
Kairos Document, 287–9
Kammaskraal resettlement camp, 205
Kannemeyer, Donald, 348
Karanga, 12
Katzew, Henry, 328
Kaufman, Robert R., 379–80
Kaunda, Kenneth, 260
Keate, Robert, 113
Kennedy, Robert F., 259
Kenney, Henry, 197
Kenya, 4, 248–50, 380
Kenyatta, Jomo, 248, 380, 390
Keysser, Christian, 160
Kgobadi, 137
Khayelitsha township, 376
Khoikhoi, 7, 8, 10, 12, 29–30, 38, 50, 60, 66, 72, 76, 79, 82–5, 91–3, 105, 113, 120
Kimberley, 56, 62, 120–3, 135, 239, 243
King, Martin Luther, Jr., 240, 241
King William's Town, 230
Kikuyu, 390
Kinikini, Benjamin, 266
Kirchenkampf, 282, 284
Kissinger, Henry, 300, 304
Kitchener, Lord, 128
kitskonstabels ("instant constables"), 356
Kivnick, Helen, 223–5, 228
Klopper, Henning, 169, 176, 177
Kobese, Fikile, 348
Kohl, Helmut, 348
Koornhof, Piet, 331
"Koornhof Bills," 331, 332
Koran, 80
Kruger (president of Transvaal), 115, 124
Kruithoring, Die (newspaper), 162, 174
Ku Klux Klan, 324
Kuyper, Abraham, 156–8, 165
KwaNdebele, 337, 339
Kwanobuhle township, 266, 345–8, 357
KwaZulu, 97, 274, 337, 384

Labour party, 135
Land Act, 136, 137, 139, 141, 144, 145, 188, 191, 199, 206, 235, 295, 390
Langa township, 344–8, 357
Langenhoven, C. J., 79, 110*n*, 261
Langeni clan, 98, 100, 101

Latin America, 23; liberation theology of, 282
Laurie, Douglas, 86
League of Nations, 152, 235
Leakey, Louis, 6
Leakey, Mary, 6
Leakey, Richard, 6
Lebanon, 186, 368
Lebowa, 230
Le Grange, Louis, 348
Leiden: seige of, 25; University of, 27
Leipoldt, C. Louis, 28
Lekganyane, Barnabas, 295
Lekganyane, Edward, 295, 296
Lekganyane, Engenas, 295
Lekoa Council, 333
Lembede, Anton, 237, 255–7, 262
Lenasia township, 335
Lenyenye, 230
Lesotho, 312, 313
Leutwiler, Fritz, 351
Levant, the, 46
Liberal party, 240, 259
liberation theology, 278–93
Liberia, 294
Libya, 186
Lichtenstein, Henry, 9, 15–17, 19
Literary and Scientific Society, 71
Literaturnaya Gazeta, 365
Livingstone, David, 67, 251
lobola (bride price), 68
Locke, John, 25
London Corresponding Society, 53
London Missionary Society, 67
London *Times*, 58, 128
Louis, Joe, 143
Louw, Eric, 162, 174
Louw, N. P. van Wyk, 79, 261
Lovedale school, 68
Lugard, Lord, 195
Luther, Martin, 281
Lutheran Church, 159–60, 285
Luthuli, Albert, 240, 242–4, 251, 252, 272, 278, 279
Lydius, Jacobus, 26

Machel, Samora, 301–3
Machiavelli, Nicòlo, 355
Macmillan, Harold, 193
Macrae, Norman, 393
Madakeni resettlement camp, 205
Madagascar, 4, 72
Magmoed, Shaun, 82
Magopa, 206–8
Mahlatsi, Esau, 296, 297*n*, 333, 334, 336
Mahoney, Thomas, 61
Maia, Captain, 298
Majeane, Caesar, 336
Majila, Knox, 333
Majuba Hill, battle of, 115, 183
Makanda, 9, 68–9
Malan, Daniel, 31, 48, 49, 119, 127, 128, 151–3, 173–4, 183, 190, 192, 237, 257, 278–9, 320, 327, 359, 360
Malan, General Magnus, 304, 308, 368
Malan, Group Captain "Sailor," 175
Malaya, 72, 80, 358
Malays, 85
Malherbe, Ernst, 163
Mali, 4
Mamelodi township, 268
Mandela, Nelson, 68, 70, 211, 227, 230, 237, 242–4, 251, 255, 272, 352, 353, 358, 367, 369, 370, 384, 399
Mandela, Winnie, 227, 230, 251
Mangope, Lucas, 212*n*
Manicheanism, 245
Manpower Development Center, 202, 203
Mantatisi, 102
Maoris, 68, 202
Maputo, 252
Marais, Awie, 325
Marais, David, 198
Martins, Luciano, 393–4
Marx, Karl, 54, 56
Marxism, 32, 253, 303, 311; black liberation theology and, 279–80
Mashabela, Harry, 302
Mass Democratic Movement (MDM), 382–4
Master and Servants Act, 66, 191
Matanzima, Kaiser, 212*n*
Mathlo, Duncan, 267
Matiwane, Chief of the Ngwane, 102
Maximov, Eugeny, 129
Mbeki, Thabo, 326, 399
Mbokodo vigilantes, 339
Mbundu people, 303
McCarthyism, 19
McCuen, Lieutenant Colonel John J., 354–6, 359, 378
McFarlane, Robert, 349–50
Mcube, Emily, 205, 212
Mda, Ashley, 256
Mdantsane township, 202
Mehlo, Nowatcha, 204, 212
Methodists, 54, 56, 58, 251, 267
Mexico, 379
Meyer, Piet, 163–4, 168, 172, 177
Mfengu, 102

Mfenyana, Buntu, 14
Mgijima, Enoch, 242
Mhlangana, 111
Mieza, Nosipho, 334
migrant labour system, 66, 202–4, 237; impact on families of, 226–8
militarization, 308–11, 367
Military Intelligence, Department of, 307, 308, 310
Miller, Arthur, 19
Millin, Sarah Gertrude, 71
Milner, Lord, 125, 128, 213
Mines and Works Act, 191
Mine Workers' Union, 135, 321
Ming Dynasty, 4
Miocene era, 6
Miranda, Michael, 82
"mishmash cohabitation," 148, 179, 188
missionaries, 66–8, 83, 159, 193, 196, 236, 250–1
mixed races, *see* "coloureds"
Moffat, Robert, 67, 251
Mokoena, Bishop Isaac, 297
Molefe, Popo, 331
Molepe, Andrew, 340
Montmartin, Graf von Durkheim, 163
Moodie, Dunbar, 110, 126
Moodley, Kogila, 368, 371, 388
Moors, 23
More, Isaac, 205–8, 210, 211
Morgan, J. Pierpont, & Company, 121
Morocco, 186
Moroka, 138
Moroka, James, 238, 240
Morris, Desmond, 6
Morris, Donald, 98
Moselane, Geoffrey, 334–6
Moshoeshoe, 104, 108, 113
Motjuwadi, Stanley, 261
Mozambique, 23, 72, 102, 248, 253, 300, 303, 312, 313, 365, 367
Mszawi, 104
Mtetwa, 93, 95, 99–101
Mtshali, Oswald, 229
Mugabe, Robert, 249, 380, 390
Mulder, Cornelius, 136–7, 183, 308
Mulder, Manie, 218
Muldergate scandal, 216
Muller, Lourens, 321–2
Munchener Illustrierte Zeitung, 172
Muslims, *see* Islam
Mussolini, Benito, 163
Muzorewa, Abel, 370
Mxenge, Griffith, 264–5
Mxenge, Victoria, 264–5
Myers, Cecil, 202, 203, 210
Mzilikazi, 103, 111, 112

Namaqua, 83
Namibia, 12, 300, 301, 304, 312, 313, 363, 367, 371, 372, 378
Nandi, 98
Napoleon, 46, 52, 55, 126, 164, 193, 270
Nasionaal building society, 177
Natal, University of, 196, 376
Natal-KwaZulu *Indaba*, 384
National Action Council, 243
National Committee, 174
National Democratic Movement, 382
National Forum, 263, 383
National Front for the Liberation of Angola (FNLA), 303–6
National Intelligence Service, 323
nationalism, 148; Afrikaner, 28, 31–3, 35, 41–3, 45–9, 66, 72, 79, 85, 95, 110, 111, 114–18, 125–8, 133–5, 146, 147, 150, 153, 158, 161, 164, 171, 173, 176, 186–7, 191, 193, 196, 211–13, 251, 254, 255, 257, 261, 278, 284, 317, 328, 330, 359, 363, 285–7 (*see also* National party); black, 47, 68, 146, 150, 211, 235, 243, 253, 261, 278, 349, 353, 358, 363, 385, 389 (*see also* Africanism); in Europe, 163; of Romanticists, 164–7
National party, 42, 150–3, 189, 192, 197, 200, 308, 315, 318–25, 349, 351, 352, 360, 368; and Broderbond, 177; and "coloureds," 74; comes to power, 48–9, 182, 183, 194; Dutch Reformed Church and, 161; English-speaking South Africans and, 70, 314; formation of, 144, 150; ideology of survival and, 327–8; motto of, 187; Opposition and, 240; political myth makers of, 28, 32; political style of, 168–9; during World War II, 152–3, 162, 173–5
National Security Management System, 310, 323, 349, 368
National Socialism, 148–9, 152, 160–4, 166–9, 171–5, 186, 193–4
National Union for the Total Independence of Angola (UNITA), 303, 305, 312
National Union of Mine Workers, 321
National Union of South African Students (Nusas), 259–60, 337, 383
nationalization of industry, 134, 180, 316, 364–5, 387
Native Affairs, Department of, 36, 195–6

Native Affairs commission, 135, 195
Native Laws Amendment Act (1952), 194, 199
Native Life (Plaatje), 136*n*
Native Representative Council, 195
Naudé, C. F. Beyers, 176, 284–5, 297
Naudé, Johannes, 176
Nazarite Church, 294
Nazism, *see* National Socialism
Ndebele, 103, 106, 108, 111, 138, 390
Ndebele, Njabulo, 373
Ndwandwe, 102
"necklacings," 265–6, 277, 340
Nederduitsch Hervormde Kerk, 35
Nel, Louis, 207–8
Nel, Philip, 362
neo-Nazis, 41, 324
Neto, Agostinho, 303
Neves, Major Costa, 299
New Brighton township, 357
New Order movement, 162, 172–5, 242
New Republic party, 47
Newsweek, 350
New Zealand, 68, 202
Nguni, 7–10, 12–14, 65, 92, 95, 96, 98, 100, 102, 103, 105
Ngwane clan, 102, 103
Nicholas II, Tsar, 130
Nicol, William, 178*n*
Nigeria, 195, 275, 352
Nixon, Richard M., 300
Nkomo, Joshua, 390
"*Nkosi Sikelel' i-Afrika*" ("God Bless Africa"), 144
Nkrumah, Kwame, 250, 256
Nkwe, David, 302
Nobel Peace Prize, 231, 244, 289
Nofomela, Butana Almond, 264*n*
No Middle Road (Slovo), 366
Nonconformists, 54, 56
Nongqause, 108, 250
nonracialism, 250–3, 256, 257, 263, 364, 394
North Africa campaign, 175
Norway, 171
Ntuli, Piet, 339
Nuremberg Laws, 190
Nyasaland, 248
Nylstroom, 41

Obasanjo, General Olusegun, 352
"oilspot" strategy, 357, 358
Ojukwu, Odumegu, 275
Oldenbarnevelt, Johan van, 27
Onselen, Charles van, 142
Oppenheimer, Ernest, 121
Oppenheimer, Harry, 70
Opposition, 197, 223, 240
Orange Workers, 326–7
Organization of African Unity, 258
Ortlepp, Sarah, 120
Ossewa-Brandwag (Ox-Wagon Sentinels), 162, 172–5
Ottoman Empire, 81
Ovimbundu people, 303
Owen, Robert, 53
Owens, Jesse, 143
Oxton resettlement camp, 204

Pachsdraai resettlement camp, 206
Pakistan, 186
Pan-Africanist Congress (PAC), 233, 243, 246, 256–8, 263, 353, 390, 391
Parliament, South African, 174, 193, 197, 240, 243, 272, 321, 323, 348, 351; apartheid legislation in, 189; Land Act passed by, 136; liberals in, 236; Purified party in, 151; tricameral, 318–20, 330
Parris, Samuel, 19
pass-law system, 36, 83, 85, 90, 105, 145, 191, 194, 210; protest against, 233–4, 239, 243, 258
Paton, Alan, 47, 188, 259
Patriot, Die, 118
peasantry, black, 139–40
Pedi, 108
Peires, J. B., 63, 64
Peires, Jeffrey, 13
Pentecostal movement, 294
perestroika, 363, 365
Peru, 379
Peterloo Massacre, 53, 56
Peterson, Hector, 302
Philip II, King of Spain, 25
Philippines, 186
Phillip, John, 67, 251
Phoenicians, 3
Phoenix Farm, 89
Physical Planning Act, 201
Pienaar, Schalk, 209–11, 213
Pietersburg, 324–5
Pirow, Oswald, 162, 172–4, 242
Pityana, 251
Plaatje, Solomon Tshekisho, 136–9, 208
Place, Francis, 53
Pliocene era, 6
Plural Relations, Department of, 36

Poland, 289; Nazi invasion of, 152
political system: Afrikaners and, 134; black resistance and, 145; English-speaking South Africans and, 47–51, 70–1; future, 389–91; tribal, 5, 12, 15–16, 195
Pollsmoor Prison, 353
polygamy, 13, 68
Popular Movement for the Liberation of Angola (MPLA), 303–6, 313
Population Registration Act, 85
Population Registration Board, 189
Poqo, 246
Port Elizabeth, 221, 239, 251–2; sabotage in, 244; townships of, 332, 338–9, 357
Portugal, 8, 23, 298; revolution in, 298–300, 302, 303, 363
Portuguese Guinea, 298
Potgieter, Hendrik, 111, 138, 169–70
predestination, doctrine of, 23, 27
Presbyterian Church, 54, 285, 295
Pretoria, 41, 67, 124; blacks in, 375; Gandhi in, 88–9; Great Trek centennial in, 169–71; Mandela's trial in, 70; militarization in, 309; townships of, 338; violence in, 247; women's march on, 239
Pretoria University, 148
Pretorius, Lieutenant Colonel Frederick, 344
Pretorius, Andries, 112, 169
Pringle, Thomas, 11, 59, 63, 71, 84, 93, 121, 251
Prinsloo, Margrieta, 170
Proconsul, 6
Progressive Federal party, 47, 251, 321, 382
Progressive party, 259, 382
Protestantism: racial attitudes and, 23; work ethic in, 33; *see also specific denominations*
Ptolemy, Claudius, 4, 263*n*
Public Safety Act, 238
Punto Fijo Pact, 382
Purified National party, 151, 153
Puritans, 28, 29, 54

Queenstown, 219

Race Classification Board, 189
racial groups, evolution of, 6
Ramakgula, Ephraim, 336
Ramatoto, John, 208, 211
Ramphele, Mamphela, 230–2
Rampou, George, 208
Rand Daily Mail, 216, 274, 308, 372
Randlords, 124
Rapportryers, 176
Rayi, 263–6, 268
Reagan, Ronald, 253, 348, 349, 394
Realpolitik, 307
Reddingsdaadbond, 176
Reformation, 281
Reformed Churches Beneath the Cross, 156
Reformed Independent Church Association, 297
Regional Services Councils, 319
Regional Superpower strategy, 307–8, 314, 317–18
Rembrandt, 25
Rembrandt Tobacco Corporation, 176
Renamo, 312, 313
"reserves," 136, 137, 140
resettlement camps, 202–6, 273
resistance movement, 68–70, 235–44, 246–8, 272–7; Gandhi and, 90; start of, 144–6; *see also specific organizations*
Retief, Piet, 105, 109, 111, 113, 169
Retz, F. W., 95*n*
revolutionary violence, 245–6, 269–71
Rhodes, Cecil John, 45, 49, 70, 121, 124, 141
Rhodesia, 49–50, 193, 248, 249, 300, 301, 370, 386, 394; *see also* Zimbabwe
Riesman, David, 341
Rive, Richard, 86
Ripon, Lord, 89
Robben Island, 68, 70, 80, 243, 326
Roberto, Holden, 303, 306
Roberts, Michael, 173
Robertson, T. C., 170–1
Robinson, J. B., 120
Roman Catholic Church, 282, 285, 334; Dutch, 26; racial attitudes and, 23; Spanish, 27
Romanticists, 164–7
Rome, ancient, 3, 4, 280
Roos, Tielman, 151
Roosevelt, Franklin D., 174, 184
Ross, Robert, 84
Rousseau, Jean Jacques, 107
Roux, Jannie, 323
Ruanda, 248
Ruiterwag, 176
Russia: Boer War and, 129–30; *see also* Soviet Union

Saambou building society, 177
Salaam, Imam Abdullah Kadi Abdus, 80
Salazar, Antonio, 163, 172
Salem (Cape Colony), 56
Salem (Massachusetts) witch trials, 18, 19
Salisbury, 248
Salt, Elizabeth, 9
Sam, Kleinbooi, 204–5, 211
sanctions, 349, 351, 353, 354, 391–5
sangoma (witch doctor), 19
Sanlam insurance company, 176, 177
San people, 7, 10–12, 84
Sarili, Chief of the Xhosas, 108
Saso Newsletter, 262
satyagraha (power of truth), 73, 90
"Savage Parliament," 53
Savimbi, Jonas, 275, 303, 304, 313, 367
Schama, Simon, 24–6
Schleiermacher, Friedrich Ernst Daniel, 165
Schlemmer, Lawrence, 31*n*
Schopenhauer, Arthur, 92
Schouten, Wouter, 29
Schreiner, Olive, 141, 309
Schweitzer, Albert, 231
Sebe, Chief Lennox, 205
Sebokeng township, 334, 336, 357
security laws, 37, 235
Security Police, 343
security system, 309–10
segregation, 66, 85, 134, 179, 183–6, 190, 191; advancement within framework of, 236; class, 273; Dutch Reformed Church and, 154–5, 160, 161; in Natal, 32, 73; in Rhodesia, 49; *see also* apartheid
Seko, Mobutu Sese, 303
Seme, Pixley, 144–5, 390
Senegal, 23
Senghor, Leopold, 260
Senzangakona, 98, 100
Sepamla, Sipho, 233
Separate Amenities Act, 373
serfdom, 66, 84, 85
Serote, Mongane Wally, 261
Sestigers, 317
Shaka, 10, 93, 95–104, 111, 390
Shakespeare, William, 245
Shangane, 102
sharecroppers, 137, 139–41
Sharpeville, 215–16, 266, 296; 1960 massacre in, 233–5, 242–3, 258, 272, 283, 301, 337, 344, 345, 347, 356, 361; 1983 riots in, 333, 334, 336
Shaw, William, 58
Shembe, Isaiah, 294
Sheptone, Sir Theophilus, 32, 66, 73
Shiite Muslims, 82
Shona, 390
Shoshangane, 102
Siflin, Geoffrey, 398–9
Sigcau, Stella, 212*n*
Sisulu, Albertina, 230
Sisulu, Walter, 237, 242, 255, 272, 369
Skeleton Coast, 3
Skosana, Maki, 266
Slabbert, Frederick van Zyl, 384
Slamath, 78
slavery, 4, 23, 43, 60, 72, 76–81, 91, 185–6; abolition of, 50, 55, 66, 73, 77, 78, 84, 85, 105; Khoikhoi and, 84; monument to, 325–6
Slovo, Joe, 252, 366
Small, Adam, 75
Smith, Colonel Harry, 63
Smith, Ian, 249, 301, 394
Smith, Nico, 268
Smuts, Jan Christiaan, 48–9, 90, 95*n*, 126, 134, 151–3, 163, 174–5, 183–5, 200, 237, 240, 242
Sobhuza, 103
Sobukwe, Robert, 243, 256–8, 262, 275
socialism, 387–8
social systems, tribal, 5, 12–15
Society of True Afrikaners, 117
Sofala, 23
Somerset, Lord Charles, 57, 58, 71
Sophiatown, 143, 188–9
Sotho, 7–8, 12, 96, 102–4, 119, 138, 213, 215
South African Broadcasting Corporation, 172
South African Bureau for Racial Affairs, 176
South African Christian National-Socialistic movement, 172
South African Commercial Advertiser, 71
South African Communist party, 240, 252–3, 362, 366, 382
South African Congress of Trade Unions, 240
South African Council of Churches, 279, 285, 289, 297
South African Defence Force, 212, 271, 308–9
South African Law Commission, 385
South African Native Congress, 145
South African Police Force, 271

South African Security Police, 212
South African Students Organization (Saso), 260
Southey, George, 63
"sovereignty in one's own sphere," doctrine of, 156–8, 161
Soviet Union, 272, 304, 362–6, 378, 387; in World War II, 173
Soweto, 189, 199, 215, 240, 273, 289, 336, 357, 361, 369; black council elections in, 332; 1976 uprising in, 196, 217, 218, 221, 247, 249, 267, 301, 302, 315, 337, 343, 393; proposed merging of Johannesburg and, 377; Students Representative Council of, 263
Spain, 23, 379, 381, 382, 387; Dutch war with, 24–6, 76, 327; fascist takeover of, 163
Sparrman, Anders, 77
Spengler, Oswald, 148
spice trade, 23–4, 46
Spinoza, Baruch, 25
Stalin, Josef, 193
Starushenko, Gleb, 364
State President's Office, 323, 368
State Security Council, 310, 323
status confessionis, 282, 284
Stavenisse (ship), 15, 18
Steen, Jan, 25
Steenkamp, Anna, 105
Stellenbosch University, 155, 160, 193, 194, 324
Stockwell, John, 304
Stoker, H. G., 158–9
Stone Age, 5, 7
Stormjaers (Storm Troopers), 172
Strijdom, Hans, 174, 192
strikes, 145, 203, 237, 314; in mines, 134, 135, 145
Stubbs, John, 61
Studentebond, 176
Suarez, Adolfo, 382, 387
subsistence economy, 20, 21
Sun City, 36
Sunday Express, 308
Sundkler, Bengt, 293–4
Sunni Muslims, 82
Suppression of Communism Act, 239
Surinam, 76*n*
Suurveld, 8, 57–64, 69, 94
Swanepoel, Theuns, 343
Swaziland, 104, 108, 144, 179, 301, 313
Swellendam, 104
Switzerland, 351
Syria, 186
Tambo, Oliver, 237, 242, 243, 247, 251, 255, 256, 271, 277, 366–7
Tanzania, 268; fossil finds in, 6
"Tar Baby" report, 300
tenant farmers, 137, 139–41
Terre' Blanche, Eugene, 325, 343
Thaba Ncho, 138
Thaba N'chu, 36
Thaele, James, 253
Thatcher, Margaret, 348, 351
Thembani, Eric, 346–7
theology of liberation, 278–93
Thohoyandou, 36
Thompson, Leonard, 28
Thornhill resettlement camp, 204
Tikhomirov, Vladimir, 364
Time magazine, 350
Tocqueville, Alexis de, 329
Tolstoy Farm, 89–90
torture, 222–3
"tot" system, 85
Totye, Nokwenwa, 205, 211
townships, 87, 199–200, 202, 226, 316; military occupation of, 358; municipal councils in, 331–2; Portuguese revolution and, 302; revolt in, 337–8; rioting in, 215–16, 218; street crime in, 224, 225; violence in, 265–9, 275–6; *see also names of specific townships*
trade unions, *see* unions
Transkei, 212*n*, 376
Transvaler, Die (newspaper), 194, 255
Trekboers, *see* Boers
Treurnicht, Andries, 41, 128, 177, 278, 320, 321, 370
tribalism, 389–91
tribal society, traditional, 12–21
Trichardt, Louis, 169
Triomf, 187, 189
"Trojan truck massacre," 82
Trollip, A. E. G., 173
Trollope, Anthony, 121–3, 135, 374
tsetse fly, 3, 4, 8, 41
Tshombe, Moise, 275
Tshwete, Steve, 264
Tsonga, 12, 102
tsotsi gangs, 224, 225
Tsotsitaal (ghetto slang), 143
Tswana, 7–8, 12, 67, 96, 104, 108, 138, 206, 215, 274
Tunisia, 186
Turkey, 23, 24
Tutu, Archbishop Desmond, 14, 67, 188, 251, 278, 280, 282–3, 287, 289–92, 297, 298
Twala, Reuben, 335

ubuntu, 14, 19, 21, 42, 103, 143, 224, 249, 285, 399
uitbastering ("bastardization"), 148
Uitenhage, 30, 344–6, 357
Ulundi, 97
umfundisis (church leaders), 143
Umkhonto we Sizwe (Spear of the Nation), 244, 246, 247, 251, 267, 271, 300, 313, 339, 342, 346
Umlazi township, 336
Union Corporation, 177
unions: Afrikaner, 176, 321; black, 146, 203, 236, 237, 276, 314–15, 362, 376–7, 382, 384; in nineteenth-century England, 53
United Christian Conciliation Party, 297
United Congregational Church, 285
United Democratic Front (UDF), 263, 264, 275, 276, 323–3, 335, 337–9, 341, 349, 355, 357, 358, 382, 383, 389, 391
United East India Company, 25
United Municipalities of South Africa, 384
United Nations, 184, 186, 192, 237, 258, 313, 340, 354
United party, 47, 48*n*, 49, 90, 151, 240, 272
United States, 184, 353; African policy of, 299–300, 303–4; back-to-Africa movement in, 254; banks in, 350–1; black theologians in, 282–3; civil rights movement in, 186, 238, 260, 324; Civil War in, 128; and diamond mines, 121; industrial revolution in, 393; opening up of West of, 106; Pentecostal movement in, 294; Reagan administration in, 348–50; Soviet Union and, 363, 364, 366; State Department of, 312; Supreme Court of, 184, 186, 238; in Vietnam War, 270, 304
Universal Declaration of Human Rights, 237
Universal Negro Improvement Association, 254
University Christian Movement, 285
Uruguay, 379
Utilitarianism, 53
Utopian Socialism, 53
Utrecht, University of, 156
Uys, Dirkie, 170

Vaal Civic Association, 333, 336
Vaal Triangle, 215, 296, 332–6, 339, 357
Vaderland, Die (newspaper), 317
Van den Bergh, General Hendrik, 172, 304, 307, 308, 368
Van den Bruck, Moeller, 147
Van Goens, Commissioner, 38
Van Jaarsveld, F. A., 118
Van der Kemp, Jan, 67, 251
Van der Kemp, Johannes, 16
Van der Merwe, Johanna, 170
Van der Merwe, Stoffel, 359
Van Niekerk, Schalk, 119
Van Rensburg, Hans, 172, 174
Van Riebeeck, Jan, 8, 25, 27–30, 34, 38, 44, 56, 60, 72, 82, 83, 117, 169, 189, 215
Van Rooy, J. C., 177
Van Staden, Oom Apie, 34
Van den Vondel, Joost, 26
Varenkazis, Tim, 375*n*
Vegkop, battle of, 138
Venda, 12, 108, 274
Venezuela, 379, 381–2
Vereenigde Oostindische Compagnie (VOC), 25, 27, 29, 30, 37–9, 45, 65, 80, 83, 84, 104, 154*n*
Vereeniging, 216; Peace of, 125
Vermeer, Jan, 25
Verryn, Paul, 267
Versailles Peace Conference, 145, 235
Verwoerd, Hendrik Frensch, 163–5, 174, 177, 180, 192–202, 209, 211, 213, 255, 271–3, 283, 296, 314, 315, 324, 329, 360, 372
Verwoerd, Hendrik Frensch, Jr., 326
Verwoerd, Wilhelm, 193
Vietnam War, 270, 304, 311, 354
Viljeon, General Constand, 305–6, 308
violence, 302; adopted by resistance movement, 243–4, 246–8, 272; black-on-black, 356–7; equilibrium of, 368–9; institutionalized, 219–23, 267; repressive, 344–8; of revolt of the eighties, 339–41; revolutionary, 245–6, 269–71; theology of liberation and, 282, 288; in townships, 265–9, 275–6
Volksgeist (folk-spirit), 160, 166
Volkskas bank, 176–7
Volksraad law, 142
Voltaire, 164
Voortrekkers, 49, 103, 106–7, 109–12, 124, 170, 176, 324, 325
Vorster, John, 172, 272, 303–5, 307, 308, 320, 322, 360
Vow of the Covenant, 110, 112, 169, 244
vryezwarten ("free blacks"), 80

Walker, George, 120
Wandrag, Bert, 344
Warneck, Gustav, 159
Washington, Booker T., 236
Waterberg, 41
Waterboer, Nicholaas, 113
Waterloo, battle of, 52, 56
Weber, Max, 30
Weenen massacre, 170
Wehner, Julius, 120
Weichardt, Louis, 172
Wellington, Duke of, 52
Wesley, John, 53–5
West Germany, 348, 351, 353
WHAM (Winning Hearts and Minds) strategy, 357
Whitefield, George, 53
White Man's Burden, 55
whites, 91; assumption of racial superiority of, 183–5; class conflict and, 92; coalition-forming by, 382–4; "coloureds" and, 74–5, 88; decolonization and, 303; effect of apartheid on, 217–18, 222, 223; and employees as property, 78; and eviction of blacks from land, 136, 137, 139–41; fear of retribution among, 248–9; and future political system, 389; guerrilla warfare and, 271; "homelands" for, 326–7; and ideology of apartheid, 178–82; impact of black urbanization on, 372–8; Indian influence on, 73; and industrial revolution, 121; international pressure on, 394; job preference for, 152; Khoikhoi and, 82–4; nonracialism and, 250–3; militarization and, 308–9; in resistance struggle, 240, 241, 257, 259, 262, 272; slaves and, 76; in Sophiatown, 188; stereotyping of blacks by, 214–15; submissiveness of blacks to, 109; in suburbs, 374–5; and tricameral Parliament, 318–19, 330; townships and, 199; in UDF, 337; U.S. policy and, 300; Zulus and, 97; *see also* Afrikaners; British; Dutch; English-speaking South Africans
Wilberforce, William, 56, 67, 77, 331
Wild Coast, 36
William, Prince of Orange, 24–6, 327
Wilson, Woodrow, 145, 184
Winterveld squatter settlement, 340
witchcraft, 17–20
witdoeke (vigilantes), 358
Witwatersrand, 56, 62, 120, 121, 135, 139, 141, 204; University of, 5, 196, 256
Women for Peace, 383
World Alliance of Reformed Churches, 279, 286
World Council of Churches, 283, 284, 286
World War I, 142, 145, 152, 169, 284
World War II, 152, 162, 163, 171–5, 177, 184, 186, 194, 201, 236–7, 242, 278

Xhosa, 3, 9, 10, 13–16, 18, 61–5, 68, 78, 94, 108, 202, 213, 215, 274

Youth League, 237–8, 255, 256
Yussuf, Sheikh, 80

Zaire, 303
Zanzibari Arabs, 85
Zimbabwe, 50, 103, 249, 273, 312, 364, 370, 378, 380
Zinjanthropus, 6
Zionist Christian Church, 294–6
Zondo, Michael, 233–5
Zulus, 10, 73, 95–104, 106, 108, 110–13, 119, 170, 213, 215, 264, 271, 274, 275, 390
Zwangendaba, 102
Zeledinga resettlement camp, 204
Zwide, 102, 103, 357